AMERICAN EMPIRE

Other titles in the Penguin History of the United States series

American Colonies
Alan Taylor

AMERICAN EMPIRE

——————————★——————————

The Rise of a Global Power,

the Democratic Revolution at Home

1945–2000

——————————★——————————

JOSHUA B. FREEMAN

★

The Penguin History of
the United States

Eric Foner, Series Editor

VIKING

973.92
Fre

VIKING
Published by the Penguin Group
Penguin Group (USA) Inc., 375 Hudson Street, New York, New York 10014, U.S.A.
Penguin Group (Canada), 90 Eglinton Avenue East, Suite 700, Toronto, Ontario,
Canada M4P 2Y3 (a division of Pearson Penguin Canada Inc.)
Penguin Books Ltd, 80 Strand, London WC2R 0RL, England
Penguin Ireland, 25 St. Stephen's Green, Dublin 2, Ireland (a division of Penguin Books Ltd)
Penguin Books Australia Ltd, 250 Camberwell Road, Camberwell, Victoria 3124, Australia
(a division of Pearson Australia Group Pty Ltd)
Penguin Books India Pvt Ltd, 11 Community Centre, Panchsheel Park, New Delhi – 110 017, India
Penguin Group (NZ), 67 Apollo Drive, Rosedale, Auckland 0632, New Zealand
(a division of Pearson New Zealand Ltd)
Penguin Books (South Africa) (Pty) Ltd, 24 Sturdee Avenue,
Rosebank, Johannesburg 2196, South Africa

Penguin Books Ltd, Registered Offices: 80 Strand, London WC2R 0RL, England

First published in 2012 by Viking Penguin, a member of Penguin Group (USA) Inc.

1   3   5   7   9   10   8   6   4   2

Copyright © Joshua B. Freeman, 2012
All rights reserved

LIBRARY OF CONGRESS CATALOGING-IN-PUBLICATION DATA
Freeman, Joshua Benjamin.
American empire, 1945–2000 : the rise of a global power, the democratic revolution at home /
Joshua Freeman.
p. cm. — (Penguin history of the United States ; v. 5)
Includes bibliographical references and index.
ISBN 978-0-670-02378-3
1. United States—History—1945–   2. United States—Politics and government—1945–1989.
3. United States—Politics and government—1989–   4. United States—Economic
conditions—1945–   5. United States—Foreign relations—1945–1989.   6. United States—Foreign
relations—1989–   I. Title.
E741.F69 2012
973.92—dc23   2011049263

Printed in the United States of America

ALWAYS LEARNING   PEARSON

For Debbie, Julia, and Lena

Contents

Introduction   ix

Prologue: E Pluribus Unum   1

PART I
Pax Americana (1945–1953)

1. Power and Politics   27
2. Cold War   49
3. Stalemate in Washington   71
4. National Security State   79

PART II
The High Tide of Liberal Democracy (1954–1974)

5. Suburban Nation   113
6. "We the Union Army"   143
7. "Hour of Maximum Danger"   162
8. The Democratic Revolution   187
9. Apocalypse Now   219
10. Sixties to Seventies, Dreams to Nightmares   255
11. The End of the American Century   287

PART III
The Resurrection of Corporate Capitalism (1975–1989)

12. The Landscape of Decline   301
13. The Politics of Stagnation   318

14. The Corporate Revolution   343

15. The Reagan Revolution   367

16. Cold War Redux   390

PART IV
The New World Order (1990–2000)

17. "I'm Running Out of Demons"   407

18. Triangulation   416

19. Living Large   445

Epilogue: America After 9/11   466

Acknowledgments   481

Bibliography   483

Index   517

Introduction

From the end of World War II to the start of the twenty-first century, the United States was at its peak of power, as dominant in the world, in its own way, as Great Britain and Rome had been at the height of their empires. Economically and militarily it far exceeded all its rivals. Politically and culturally it had enormous influence across the world. Its language and cultural references became as close to a global lingua franca as there was. Its scientific and technological achievements were unmatched.

This book tells the story of the United States during those years. It examines the political and economic structures of the country, daily life, regional and national culture, and the relationship between the United States and the rest of the world. In doing so, it tries to explain why the United States took the particular path of development it did. The extraordinary accomplishments of the United States in the second half of the twentieth century brought bounty and freedom to hundreds of millions of Americans but never fully realized the widespread hopes at the end of World War II for a more peaceful world and more equitable society. The prolonged warfare, fearfulness, and economic troubles of the early twenty-first century owe more than a little to decisions made in the earlier epoch.

In the decades after World War II, Americans rarely spoke of empire or imperialism, especially in relation to their own society. Once common terms, widely used by both supporters and critics of policies meant to achieve control over foreign lands, by the mid-twentieth century they had come to be seen as archaic and irrelevant to a world of decolonization and cold war. Until the turn of the new millennium, only on the political left during the Vietnam era did imperialism get revived as a way of understanding the United States. The notion of the United States as an empire reentered political discussion soon before the terrorist attacks of 9/11 and much more so after them, among those who saw American imperialism as good for the world as well as among those who opposed it.

Empire comes in many forms, not just the annexation of territory, the Roman practice, or the creation of colonies, the operating mode of Spain, Portugal, Britain, and other European powers. At its heart, empire involves asserting influence and control over places, people, resources, and trade outside the original boundaries of a national entity. While empires almost always involve at least some use of military force, or the threat of its use, power can be exerted in many ways. Political, economic, cultural, and ideological influence can be as important to empire as ships, planes, and guns. After World War II, the United States did not seek to conquer territory or establish colonies, one reason its citizens rarely thought of it as an empire. But through treaties and alliances, investment and trade, Coca-Cola and rock and roll, Peace Corps volunteers and CIA agents, as well as bombers and infantry, the United States established itself as the most powerful human force on the planet. The American empire shaped the flow of history far from the borders of the United States, just as empire shaped history within them.

An American watching a World War II–era movie about the United States at the end of the twentieth century would have seen a country that in many respects did not look, sound, or seem radically different from the one she or he inhabited. Political and social continuities between World War II and the end of the century would have made it easy to ignore or minimize how much the contours of the country had changed during those fifty-five years (a quarter of the history of the United States to that point in time). From 132 million people in 1940, the population had more than doubled to 281 million. Places that had been nearly empty when the war ended came to house millions of Americans in communities with physical and cultural configurations unknown a half century earlier. Immigration had brought unprecedented diversity to the population. Technology had changed the way people lived, worked, and entertained themselves.

Within enduring social and legal structures—as a continuous constitutional government, the United States has few peers in longevity—America has always been an extraordinarily dynamic society. France, Germany, Russia, and China underwent multiple revolutions, which brought into being new political regimes and fundamental social changes; the United States experienced only one deep disjuncture, the Civil War, and even the aftermath of that traumatic event was resolved within the existing constitutional framework. But the United States has had a series of moments of rapid change that might be thought of as contained revolutions, transformations of society and daily life that had pervasive effects without leading to rupture. Between World War II and the twenty-first century, the country was shaped and reshaped by the militarization of American life that came with the Cold War; the democratization of society set in motion by the African American freedom struggle; the cultural changes that rippled forward from the 1960s; the redefinition of gender roles; the corporate restructuring of the economy in the 1970s and 1980s; and the rise of political conservatism that began at the same time.

Given the size and diversity of the United States and the relatively long period this book covers compared to the usual temporal units into which American history is divided—"Jacksonian America" or "the Progressive Era"—any effort to find defining patterns of change necessarily involves simplification and selective focus. But within the vast array of events, private and public, that make up the history of the post–World War II era, several large-scale arcs stand out that help map the distance the country traveled between the celebration when World War II ended and the shock and mourning five and a half decades later when it suffered the first major attack on its territory since Pearl Harbor.

One of the great stories of U.S. history, and a framing theme of this book, is the long period of sustained economic growth after World War II. When the war ended, the country, though rich by historical and world measures, had a standard of living far below what it would be a few decades later. Most families had little discretion in how they lived or spent their money, needing all their income and energy to get from one week to the next. Limited resources and parochial cultures meant circumscribed lives, rooted in local social worlds, with minimal interaction with people and places even a modest distance away.

Prolonged economic growth brought qualitative change. Rising national and personal incomes allowed people to live more comfortable, secure, and mobile lives than ever before. Prosperity diminished regional differences and supported an expansive notion of state function, including the ongoing projection of American power abroad. As Americans experienced a quarter century of prosperity, after a decade and a half of depression and war, they developed capacious notions of what was possible for themselves and their country, and in myriad ways tried to realize them.

To the surprise and alarm of most Americans, the robust economy of the postwar years came to a crashing halt during the 1970s, as the national and international arrangements that had brought postwar prosperity began to break down. When growth resumed, it did so unevenly, interrupted by periods of economic difficulty and marked by rising economic inequality. Some industries and regions that had been mainstays of the country for a century or more never revived. Others led the way into a new gilded age, in which astounding fortunes were seemingly conjured out of thin air, while much of the population found itself struggling just to maintain what it had. The changes in the economy that occurred during the 1970s and early 1980s help explain many of the cultural and political developments of the late twentieth century and early twenty-first.

A second defining development during the half century after World War II was a multifaceted struggle to make democracy more meaningful. The United States fought World War II, as it has fought most of its wars, in the name of democracy. But democracy had a very different meaning at that time than it would when the century ended. In the middle of the twentieth century, millions of Americans were denied basic citizenship rights. Formal political power was much less evenly distributed than it later would be, individual rights far less robust, and openly discriminatory rules and practices widespread. Who could vote, how legislatures were constituted, who could use which public facilities, who was allowed to work in which kind of job, and how the criminal justice system operated all were very different in the mid-1940s than they would be a generation later. In businesses, families, schools, and churches, on playing fields and in communities, the hierarchies of power and opportunity were structured by race, sex, religion, and ethnicity. Authority was wielded by fewer hands, with fewer challenges and less consultation, than we now take for granted.

The postwar struggle by African Americans for freedom, rights, and equality catalyzed a democratic revolution that transformed the United States and echoed around the world. Expanded notions of rights and democracy and new modes of political action spread from the struggle for racial justice to ever more arenas of American life, changing ideas and practices in local communities, national institutions, and intimate private relations. But even as this democratic revolution reached its peak, power began moving out of the public realm and into private ones, especially the corporate world. While the democratic revolution and the cultural changes associated with it irrevocably transformed daily practices and public attitudes, their structural impact was ultimately checked by a hollowing out of the political sphere, as society was increasingly shaped by corporations and financiers.

An ascendant conservative political movement provided the ideological basis for the devaluation of government and a celebration of the market and business as the leading forces of social progress. Disagreements over the proper role of government in ensuring equality and in regulating individual behavior proved deeply divisive, fracturing the country into what were dubbed blue and red zones of liberalism and conservatism. Even as the country moved into a new century, battles of the 1960s and 1970s over race, gender, sexuality, and culture were refought again and again.

The relationship between the United States and the rest of the world provides a third major organizing theme for this work. The country's massive military, economic, and political engagement with other parts of the world after World War II makes it impossible to understand its history without considering foreign affairs. In no other period of similar length did external relations play as profound a role in the interior life of the United States as they did during the fifty-five years after World War II. The Cold War, the hot wars within it, the effort to create a world economic system advantageous to the United States, and the post–Cold War effort to maintain American global power influenced virtually every aspect of domestic life, from politics and economics to education and culture. The maintenance of a huge military establishment, in peaceful times as well as during war, and its permanent deployment abroad, marked a fundamental change in the American Republic. Military and foreign policy configurations associated with the Cold War outlasted their original reason for being, as they became deeply embedded in the structure of the society. Militarism, once associated with other lands, became a defining feature of the United States, shaping what kind of society it was, how it acted, and what its future held. The full story of global change during the second half of the twentieth century is outside the scope of this volume, but at least some of it has to be told to understand the history of the United States, given how deeply and inseparably its fortune became intertwined with the larger world.

The surprising turns the United States took in the wake of the 9/11 attacks—the grandiose ambitions for world change, the embrace of preemptive war, the open adoption of torture, the centralization of power in the presidency, the xenophobic-tinged patriotism—while in some ways departures from the recent past, in other ways represented a culmination of developments that had occurred during the years since World War II. This book concludes with a consideration of the ways in which the history of the United States during the first decade of the twenty-first century represented a break with the past and the ways in which it represented an extension of the political and social vectors that this book chronicles.

No book that covers more than a half century of the history of the United States can be comprehensive, and this one makes no such claim. Too much happened. Also, as a study building on the work of other scholars, writers, and journalists, this volume benefits in those areas about which much has been written, though trying as well to address aspects of American life that remain largely uncharted. In concentrating on major developments in politics, economics, foreign relations, social structure, popular culture, and everyday life, it gives far less attention to some facets of the country's history than they deserve, from scientific thinking and the arts to sports and sexuality.

The present always reflects the past, even if in its negation, and informs the future. During the years between World War II and the start of the twenty-first century, Americans profoundly transformed their country and much of the world, for better and for worse. The challenges the United States faces in the twenty-first century are in many ways different than those met before. Though very much a work of history, perhaps this book will be helpful in thinking through where the United States, as a society and a nation, should be going in the future.

E Pluribus Unum

Shortly after World War II, writer and photographer George R. Stewart, documenting the 3,091-mile length of U.S. Highway 40 from New Jersey to California, noted the astonishing ecological diversity of the country and the striking regional variations in the social landscape and built environment. The roadway, Stewart wrote, "rises from sea-level to more than two miles above it, [while] . . . the annual precipitation varies from sixty to five inches. . . . Steamboat Springs, Colorado has a recorded temperature of fifty-four degrees below zero but on the slopes of the Sierra Nevada foothills you see palms and orange trees flourishing." The busiest part of U.S. 40, in Delaware, carried an average of 22,688 cars a day, while at the Kansas-Colorado border on average more than three minutes passed with the road empty after each car went by.

When World War II ended, the United States was much more a conglomeration of regions with distinctive forms of economic activity, politics, and culture than it would be when the twentieth century drew to a close. Differences in physical environment and histories of settlement accounted for some of the variations in way of life that Stewart observed during his trip across the country. The New Englanders and middle southerners who settled Oregon set a far more conservative tone than the gold rushers and Scandinavians who went to neighboring Washington, which in the mid-1940s was perhaps the most liberal state in the Union. As states developed differently, disparate sets of laws, institutions, and structures of power molded and protected particular economic, social, and cultural arrangements.

The great size of the United States, its relative political stability, and its extraordinary social dynamism all contributed to its economic and military might, dramatically demonstrated in World War II. Yet even as economic and technological changes drew together various parts of the country, the Constitution, in preserving the importance of the states, had the effect of retarding homogenization. Differences in state economies, social arrangements, and political cultures in turn shaped the national polity.

Mid-twentieth-century portraits of the United States recognized the importance of state and regional variation. Scholarly studies of physical, economic, and human geography typically took the form of surveys that described particularities of each part of the country and compared them to one another. The massive documentation of U.S. history, culture, and built environment undertaken by the Federal Writers' Project during the 1930s conformed to this model, too. Designed to put unemployed writers to work, the project, reflecting a progressive New Deal nationalism that sought authenticity in regional culture, produced a series of superb guidebooks organized by state, city, and highway. *National Geographic Magazine,* with a 1946 circulation of one and a quarter million, had a more centrist perspective, but it shared the New Deal's celebration of local and regional life, regularly featuring state profiles with titles like "Nevada, Desert Treasure House" and "Arkansas Rolls Up Its Sleeves." For a more literary audience, Erskine Caldwell edited a series of books on regional history and folkways by such accomplished authors as Carey McWilliams, Wallace Stegner, and Meridel Le Sueur. Political studies also often took the form of regional excursions, such as journalist John Gunther's 1947 best seller, *Inside U.S.A.*

Recapturing life in the United States at the end of World War II requires looking first separately at the different regions of the country. While Americans shared many national experiences, from presidential elections to Hollywood movies to world wars, their daily experiences were rooted in and bound by particular places, places that as Stewart discovered varied immensely from one another. Regional commonalities shaped political attitudes and cultural inclinations. Conflicts and relationships among the regions helped set the political and social trajectory of the country. Out of many, one.

The Midwest

The Midwest loomed large in midcentury portraits of the United States. More than any other part of the country, it displayed features of the nation as a whole. In 1940, the U.S. center of population lay in the heart of the Midwest, due south of Chicago, where the 39th parallel intersects the Indiana-Illinois border. (Ten years later it had moved a few dozen miles west and south.) Because the Midwest combined physical and social characteristics of the surrounding regions, it often served as a national bellwether. From the start of the Civil War through the end of World War II, nine of the fifteen presidents came from the region.

The importance of the Midwest lay not only in its centrality but also in the size of its population and its economic prowess. In 1950, the East North Central states—Ohio, Indiana, Illinois, Michigan, and Wisconsin—had the largest population of any of the nation's geographic subdivisions and per capita income well above the national average.

The economic strength of the Midwest came from a combination of high-yield agriculture, large-scale manufacturing, and efficient transportation. In the nation as a whole, by 1920 a majority of the population lived in urban areas, but well after World War II much of the Midwest remained over-whelmingly rural. Until 1950 most Minnesotans lived on farms or ranches or in towns with fewer than twenty-five hundred residents. In South Dakota, it took until 1960 for the urban population to outnumber those living in the countryside.

Midwestern farms formed a vast checkerboard of grain, corn, and soy-bean fields that seemed to go on forever. Rich soil, relatively flat land, and heavy investment in mechanization made them extraordinarily productive. In *North Star Country* (1945), Meridel Le Sueur wrote that "on a warm night when the bright moon is up after a shower has fairly wet the earth and waked up the drowsy corn, I will swear that you can see the stalk stretch and swell in its new sheath. . . . You hear the green cry of growth and the potatoes murmur to each other 'move over.'" One economic geographer character-ized western Ohio, Indiana, Iowa, eastern Nebraska, and southern Minne-sota as supporting "probably the most independent and prosperous farm population of similar extent in all the world."

Farm life before World War II meant long hours of very hard work and few creature comforts, even in the relatively well-off Midwest. Farm produc-tivity did not grow greatly during the first decades of the twentieth century, with human and animal power still providing much of the energy for plant-ing, weeding, harvesting, and domestic chores. When in the early 1970s Studs Terkel—a veteran of the Federal Writers' Project, who popularized oral history—interviewed Katherine Haynes for his book *Working,* she re-called a lifetime of "housework and farmin'," working "eighteen hours out of every twenty-four. . . . Just hard work." As late as 1935, only one of ten farms nationally had electricity. During the Depression, plummeting prices and decreasing output brought a massive drop in farm income.

The New Deal and World War II brought relief. Federal programs limit-ing production and subsidizing prices, followed by rising wartime demand, pushed up commodity prices and farm income. Farmers reduced their debt and invested in greater mechanization and fertilizer use, raising farm productivity nationally by more than 25 percent during World War II. By 1950, in the northern half of the country tractors largely had replaced horses, and harvesting combines were drastically reducing the need for seasonal labor.

Meanwhile, the Rural Electrification Administration (REA), one of the New Deal's most successful programs, rapidly electrified the nation's farms. By 1950, 90 percent had been wired. Political reporter Samuel Lubell, traveling the country in the early 1950s to decipher electoral patterns, reported that in Gutherie County, Iowa, "the 3,200 members of the Gutherie REA Cooperative had among them 3,800 radio sets, 1,200 electric cooking ranges, 600 electric water heaters, 2,700 electric refrigerators and 500 television sets" (making them early adopters of what was still a very new technology). The extension of the power grid, in addition to revolutionizing rural domestic life, especially for women, who had done the backbreaking work of drawing water, cooking, and cleaning without electricity, allowed further improvements in farm productivity. Before World War II, an estimated 90 percent of cows were milked by hand. By the mid-1960s, essentially all commercial dairy operations milked mechanically.

Not all of the rural heartland thrived. The western Plains proved too dry for consistently profitable agriculture. Farmsteads tended to be poorly built and maintained, and separated by great distances, creating social isolation, as captured in the bleak opening minutes of MGM's 1939 film *The Wizard of Oz*. In the book on which it was based, L. Frank Baum described a Kansas vista in which "not a tree nor a house broke the broad sweep of flat country that reached the edge of the sky in all directions." Through World War II, shacks originally thrown up to establish residence for nineteenth-century homestead claims continued to be used. In the summer, wrote Eric Thane in a wartime volume on the Dakotas, it could be "so hot that when you sit on the metal seat of the tractor your sweat-soaked overalls hiss." Not surprisingly, a steady stream of young people left the region.

As important as midwestern agriculture was, manufacturing dwarfed it in the number of workers it employed and the value of its output. American industry had long been concentrated in a band stretching from the Atlantic to the Mississippi, bordered on the north by the Great Lakes and on the South by the Ohio and Potomac rivers. During the 1940s, this belt produced three-quarters of the value created by all U.S. manufacturing. Within it, the greatest concentration of industrial power lay in the Great Lakes states.

Midwestern manufacturing exceeded all its rivals, domestic and foreign, in the scale of its productive facilities and its degree of regimentation. No plant more embodied these traits than the Ford Motor Company's vast River Rouge complex, just outside Detroit. Covering over a thousand acres, it was the largest factory complex in the world. In 1947, sixty-two thousand workers passed through its gates, down from a wartime peak of over ninety thousand. River Rouge produced almost everything that went into an automobile. The complex took in raw materials—iron ore, coal, limestone, crude rubber—and spewed out thousands of finished automobiles a day, utilizing its own coke ovens, blast furnaces, steel mill, tire factory, glass factory, foundry, stamping plant, and machine shop. By standardizing products, building highly specialized machinery for parts production, breaking the manufacturing process into small, discrete tasks, and deploying assembly lines to mechanically transfer components and pace the labor process, the approach to manufacturing that Ford developed in the early twentieth century vastly increased worker productivity while decreasing the need for skilled labor.

Artists, journalists, intellectuals, and politicians, in Europe as well as the United States, seized on "Fordism"—the initial term for the mass production of complex consumer goods—as a symbol of modernity and American prowess, while more broadly equating giant industrial facilities with man's Promethean conquest of the material world. Yet Ford-style modernity contained many seemingly archaic elements. Far from an orderly corporate bureaucracy, the Ford Motor Company until the late 1940s remained a privately held, secretive empire, with no clear lines of authority and bitter rivalries among its leaders. Prior to Ford's signing its first union contract, in 1941, several thousand members of the "Service Department"—in many cases convicts paroled to the company—maintained worker discipline within the Rouge complex and undercut efforts at collective action through spy networks and thuggery. After unionization, the department was renamed "Plant Protection," but the penchant for rule by fist was only partially checked. Henry Ford's personal politics—a notorious anti-Semite, before the war he had displayed fascist sympathies—seemed of a piece with the authoritarianism he used to run his industrial domain.

Mass-production facilities could be found in all parts of the country, but as a technical and social system Fordism had originated in the Midwest and remained centered there well after World War II. No other plant matched the Rouge in size or degree of vertical integration, but giant Fordist factories dotted the region. During World War II, Ford itself built a mile-long factory in Willow Run, on the outskirts of Detroit, to make B-24 bombers using assembly-line techniques. After the war, several companies manufactured cars there. In downtown Detroit, the Packard Motor Car Company built luxury automobiles at a ninety-five-building complex that stretched for a mile along Grand Boulevard. The Chrysler Corporation had a dozen factories in the Detroit area, including the Dodge Main plant in Hamtramck, which in 1953 employed thirty-two thousand workers. General Motors, the world's largest automaker, had its corporate headquarters and a dozen factories in Detroit and its environs, but its vast production network was centered seventy miles north, in Flint, where it had a host of parts, body, and assembly plants employing sixty thousand workers. Cleveland, Toledo, St. Louis, Cincinnati, Chicago, Akron, and other midwestern cities housed yet more car, truck, tractor, and vehicle parts plants. Furthermore, many manufacturers outside of the vehicle industry employed Fordist methods adapted from the carmakers.

Fordism constituted more than simply a set of production techniques; it was a complex set of social relationships, business strategies, and existential values. Mass production required and helped create a mass market. Fordist enterprises used standardized product design and production efficiency to keep prices down, while paying by national and international standards high wages. Only by doing so could they retain their workers, given the grueling physical demands and demeaning autocracy of their production regimes, which the arrival of industrial unionism during the 1930s and 1940s had just begun to temper ("reachunder, adjustwasher, screwdown bolt, shove in cotterpin, reachunder, adjustwasher, screwdown bolt, reachunderadjustscrewdownreachunderadjust, until every ounce of life was sucked off into production," was the way John Dos Passos described Fordism in his 1936 novel *The Big Money*). Together high productivity, high wages, and low prices created the basis for the mass consumerism that would be a hallmark of the post–World War II decades.

Though the population makeup varied from city to city, overall European immigrants and their children made up a large part of the midwestern industrial labor force. But Detroit had a significant Middle Eastern population, mostly Palestinians and Lebanese; Chicago and other steelmaking centers were home to many Mexican Americans; and Canadians could be found throughout the upper Midwest. The draw of industrial jobs, especially during the world wars, brought hundreds of thousands of African Americans to the area from the South. The black population of Detroit doubled from 1940 to 1950, reaching 300,506 the latter year, 16 percent of the total population. In Chicago it went from 277,731 to 492,265. Racial and religious tension, exacerbated by insufficient housing and job discrimination, made many midwestern cities tinderboxes, with racial clashes not uncommon.

Midwestern agriculture and manufacturing complemented one another. Farmers provided a significant market for regionally produced manufactured goods. Also, as agriculture grew less labor-intensive, it provided a source of workers for manufacturing. GM populated its Flint plants with recruits from the rural Midwest. It also drew workers from the upper South. During and after the war, a massive flow of migrants left depressed farming and mining regions of that area for midwestern towns and cities and the factories they housed. At the Bal-Band auto parts plant in South Bend, Indiana, during the 1950s half of the six thousand workers had moved up from the South. Many midwesterners did some farming while working part- or full-time in industry, a pattern facilitated by the trend among manufacturers to site new plants in rural or outer suburban locales. Other midwestern factory workers viewed their jobs as temporary, hoping to accumulate capital to go into or back to farming in the areas from where they came.

Midwestern cities, in addition to being manufacturing centers, served as financial, marketing, and transportation hubs for their hinterlands. The Chicago Board of Trade, though hurt by the Depression and government controls during World War II, rebounded after the war to become one of the world's leading agricultural commodity markets. Kansas City, which in 1946 had 350 passenger trains a day passing through (compared to six in 2010), dominated trade for large parts of Kansas, Oklahoma, and Texas. The city housed steel, auto, airplane, and garment factories, yet it also served as one of the country's major markets for cattle, horses, mules, grain, butter, eggs, and poultry. Towering concrete grain elevators—a distinctive feature of the mid-twentieth-century American landscape—lined the Missouri River, while huge stockyards imparted a pungent odor to the city, a daily reminder of the close links between the urban Midwest and the great surrounding agricultural cornucopia.

The Northeast

In the Northeast, manufacturing loomed even larger than in the Midwest but was organized differently. Manufacturing districts dating back to the nineteenth or even eighteenth century, teeming with small factories, workshops, supply houses, diners, and bars, defined the industrial landscape of many northeastern cities, not giant twentieth-century factories, as in Detroit, Flint, and Toledo. At the end of World War II, New York City was by far the nation's largest manufacturing center, with nearly a million manufacturing workers, yet on average its manufacturing establishments had only twenty-five employees. In the garment and printing industries, the city's largest, firms tended to be small, family owned, and manufactured custom items or relatively short runs of ever-varying products. Versatility and fast delivery times mattered more than minimizing unit costs through mechanization and intensive industrial engineering.

A similar pattern could be found in Rhode Island, the most industrialized state in the nation. Half its manufacturing employees worked in the textile industry, which had large plants, heavy capital investment, and long production runs. But the rest worked in industries like costume jewelry and machine tool manufacturing that fashioned a vast array of products, with new designs introduced frequently.

Even many outsize industrial facilities in the Northeast produced goods in small batches or to custom order. The sprawling Philadelphia factories of the Baldwin Locomotive Works, E. G. Budd, and J. G. Brill turned out locomotives, trolleys, and railroad cars whose size, complexity, and low production volume made assembly-line techniques largely irrelevant. The electrical equipment industry was heavily concentrated in the Northeast, in Pittsburgh, Erie, Schenectady, Bridgeport, Lynn, Pittsfield, Camden, and other urban locales. Highly skilled male workers virtually handcrafted heavy equipment, like turbines, large motors, and locomotives, though some plants employed assembly-line workers—many female—to produce consumer goods like radios and refrigerators.

While manufacturing played a leading role in both the Midwest and Northeast, in the Northeast the financial industry rivaled it in economic and political importance. From the earliest days of European settlement, Atlantic coast cities, especially Boston, Philadelphia, and New York, had served as trade and finance centers for the North American, transatlantic, and even transpacific economies. Substantial regional finance centers eventually sprung up farther west, in Chicago, San Francisco, and elsewhere, but the Northeast, and above all New York City, remained the financial capital of the country. In the mental maps of midcentury Americans, Main Street lay someplace in the middle of the country, as an abstraction, without defined coordinates, but Wall Street could be found someplace very specific, on Wall Street.

Part of the economic power of the Northeast came from its control of money itself. The region housed most of the nation's largest banks, especially the commercial giants, like Chase National Bank, with 1945 assets exceeding $6 billion ($75 billion in 2011 dollars). During the decade after World War II, banks in metropolitan New York accounted for roughly a third of the value of all commercial bank loans issued in the country. Chase and its rivals made the bulk of their money by lending to large domestic corporations, with which they had long-standing relationships. They also lent to corresponding banks elsewhere in the country and abroad and financed much of the nation's foreign trade. The Federal Reserve System recognized the unique role of the New York banks by running its open market operations—which determined interest rates and the supply of money—out of its New York branch.

The nation's two largest stock exchanges lay cheek by jowl with the large commercial banks. In the immediate postwar decades, they handled nearly 90 percent of all exchange-traded securities. The Depression and the New Deal greatly diminished the economic centrality and national visibility of the stock market. During the two decades after World War II, corporate use of equity financing fell to a historic low, with just 2 percent of corporate funds raised through stock. Still, the stock exchanges, the brokerage houses that ran them, a half-dozen commodity exchanges, the commercial banks, and various clearinghouses and foreign currency exchanges formed a financial complex in lower Manhattan unrivaled in the country or the world in assets, reach, and power.

The capital and specialized financial and business services available in New York (and to a lesser extent Philadelphia and Boston) attracted a disproportionate number of corporate headquarters to the Northeast. In 1955, of the nation's five hundred largest industrial firms, two hundred eighteen had their headquarters in the Middle Atlantic states and another twenty-two in New England, including many companies whose production facilities lay almost entirely outside the region. The men who ran the investment and commercial banks of the region, the corporations they served and sometimes controlled, and the associated corporate and Wall Street law firms formed as close to a ruling class as the nation had.

During the first half of the twentieth century, the business and financial leaders of the Northeast displayed greater social unity than would be the case in later decades among what would become a farther-flung economic elite. Exclusively white and male, most came from comfortable Protestant families, were educated at private schools and top universities, lived near each other in a handful of city neighborhoods and suburbs, and belonged to the same clubs and organizations. In a 1967 memoir, writer Norman Podhoretz recalled, "When I was in college, the term WASP had not yet come into currency—which is to say that the realization had not yet become widespread that white Americans of Anglo-Saxon Protestant background are an ethnic group like any other, that their characteristic qualities are by no means self-evidently superior to those of other groups, and that neither their earlier arrival nor their majority status entitles them to exclusive possession of the national identity."

Protestants made up a majority of the population in every region of the country except the Northeast, where roughly a quarter of Americans lived. A 1957 survey found 45 percent of northeasterners to be Catholic and over 8 percent Jewish. (Nationally, Catholics made up just over a quarter of the population, Jews 3 percent.) But large parts of the Northeast's economy and many of its social institutions remained closed or restricted to non-Protestants (and nonwhites), from suburban neighborhoods and Park Avenue co-ops to elite universities and white-shoe law firms (which John Gunther called the "last frigid citadel of Anglo-Saxon Protestantism"). There were exceptions to the Protestant domination of big business—Jewish-run investment banks, like Lehman Brothers and Goldman Sachs, and Catholic financiers and businessmen, like Joseph P. Kennedy and J. Peter Grace—but even the wealthiest non-Protestants faced bars of one sort or another. During the middle of World War II, the federal Fair Employment Practices Committee received many more complaints from New Yorkers about religious discrimination (mostly anti-Semitism) than racial discrimination. Many of the Catholics and Jews who swelled the cities of the Northeast, especially the young, were determined to break down the barriers they faced and escape their parochial worlds, an impulse quickened by the experience of serving in the armed services or working in war industry. For critic Alfred Kazin, who like Podhoretz grew up in Brownsville, a poor Brooklyn Jewish neighborhood, the great yearning was to go "Beyond! Beyond! *Beyond.*"

The Northeast's population density and long history of trade, industrialization, and urbanization left it with a more fully developed infrastructure than the rest of the country. Its ports handled over a third of the country's foreign trade, far more than any other region. Passenger and freight railroad lines threaded throughout. Subways and trolleys ran beneath the streets of Boston, New York, Newark, and Philadelphia. Most of the nation's leading private universities lay in the region.

Compared to the rest of the country, the Northeast seemed completed. Pulitzer Prize–winning historian Bernard DeVoto declared New England "the first American section . . . to achieve stability in its conditions of life." The Middle Atlantic states, too, had an aggregation of social and physical development that made drastic change hard to imagine and denied them the aura of mutability and infinite possibility so often associated with America.

By national standards, the Northeast was crowded. In 1950, Rhode Island topped the country with 749 residents per square mile, compared to the emptiest state, Nevada, with but one and a half. The Northeast as a whole had 241 people per square mile, compared to 43 nationally. Only the eastern half of the Midwest came anywhere near its population density. Yet it was a measure of the country's enormous size and relatively thin settlement that, compared to parts of Europe, Asia, and the Caribbean, the Northeast was downright empty.

The concentration of northeastern population in metropolitan centers left much of the region free for agriculture or to revert back to forest after farmers moved on to more fertile land. Pennsylvania, with its coal, steel, textile, and electrical manufacturing industries, constituted an industrial powerhouse, but forests covered half the state. The abandonment of not only farmland but of worked-out mines and depleted oil fields (and not just in the Northeast) reflected the natural and social wealth of the nation. As George Stewart noted after finishing his drive along U.S. 40, "Only a supremely prosperous people could afford to waste so much—to let land revert to unproductiveness, to be careless of erosion, not even to practice forestry."

Moving on, rather than renewing, characterized American culture. By the end of World War II, much of the Northeast's infrastructure, industry, and residential stock showed its age. Half of Philadelphia's housing had been built in the nineteenth century. John Gunther noted the decay of large sections of the city, which he attributed in part to the suburbanization of the upper class. The shabbiness observers noted in Philadelphia could be found in many other cities in the region, too, and in the countryside. Gunther thought half the farmhouses in New York State badly needed painting.

Wealthy and powerful beyond compare, the Northeast nonetheless faced uncertainty about its future position in the nation when World War II came to an end, as other regions underwent more rapid growth and development. Some scions of its ruling elite saw brighter futures elsewhere. Peter H. Dominick, the son of a partner at a Wall Street brokerage firm and nephew of a senator from New Jersey, began his career as a New York lawyer, after graduating from St. Mark's School and Yale. But following wartime service as an Army pilot, he moved to Denver, starting a legal practice and entering politics, eventually becoming one of the most conservative Republicans in the Senate. George H. W. Bush came from a similar background. His father, Prescott, was a New York investment banker and businessman before becoming a senator from Connecticut. Upon graduating Phillips Academy, Bush too served as a military pilot. After the war, he followed his father's footsteps, attending Yale and joining the elite Skull and Bones secret society (a path his son George W. Bush also would follow). But then, like Dominick, he did the unexpected, moving to West Texas to enter the oil business. Though by no means typical, Dominick and Bush were not alone in seeing greater opportunities outside the Northeast, as the growth and success of the rest of the nation challenged its dominance.

The South

In many respects, the South constituted the polar opposite of the Northeast. Though more populous, it had far less wealth and power. With just two cities of more than a half million people, Houston and New Orleans, southern society remained rooted in the countryside. The South's main product, cotton, traded on international markets, generating great wealth for the nation, but the region itself remained far poorer and less cosmopolitan than the North.

Many soldiers sent to the South for basic training during World War II were shocked by the sheer poverty of the region. One New York recruit, traveling by train to Mississippi, noted the "primitive farmhouses" in backwoods Kentucky, including a "ramshackle clapboard hut with a series of additions, each one about a generation older than the previous." Small, uninsulated wooden shacks housed much of the southern population, whether in the countryside, mining camps, mill villages, or beside unpaved city streets. On the eve of the war, just a quarter of the farms in Kentucky had electricity, and only three out of a hundred had indoor toilets. In 1950, the per capita income in the southeastern states equaled only 70 percent of the national average. Mississippi had the lowest per capita annual income of any state, $775, compared to $2,132 in Delaware, which topped the nation.

The reasons for the chronic poverty of the South, which Franklin Delano Roosevelt called "the Nation's No.1 economic problem," lay deep in the history of the region and the nation. The Roosevelt administration and many southerners put the main blame on the region's disadvantageous economic relationship to the rest of the country. They argued that the South had a quasi-colonial relationship to the North, supplying raw materials while importing manufactured goods, with little control over its transportation or credit systems. Others highlighted the legacy of slavery and the failure of Reconstruction, which left the South dominated by rural merchants and planters, crop lien credit, and a system of racial caste, which enriched some individuals but retarded overall economic development.

The prosperity of the Midwest and Northeast stemmed in part from their balanced economies, strong in agriculture, manufacturing, trade, and finance. The South, by contrast, depended heavily on extractive industries: mining, lumbering, oil production, and above all farming. Over a third of the southern workforce, on the eve of World War II, tilled the land.

From the early nineteenth century on, cotton dominated the economy of the South, and it continued to do so into the early post–World War II years.

For a century, cotton ranked first among the nation's exports. On the eve of the Second World War, it remained king in a ten-state area from North Carolina to Texas, accounting for roughly a third of the farm income of the South (down from a half before the Great Depression). Both on small farms and huge plantations, southerners grew cotton much as they had a century earlier, in a highly labor-intensive round of planting, cultivating, and harvesting using mule and horse power as the main supplement to human energy.

The ravages of the boll weevil had led some farmers to abandon cotton even before the disastrous drop in commodity prices during the Depression. New Deal agricultural policy hastened the movement away from cotton; the crop allotment system diminished the acreage put under cotton, while cash payments from various federal programs enabled farmers to invest in tractors and fertilizer, which they deployed to grow a broader range of crops. Some turned to raising livestock. Labor shortages during World War II further eroded the cotton economy. Still, when the war ended, these changes had made only modest inroads toward transforming the way of life that had arisen around cotton cultivation. On the rich flatlands that flanked the Mississippi River between Memphis and Vicksburg, vast plantations, some approaching ten thousand acres and employing over a thousand sharecroppers and tenant farmers, provided their owners with wealth and power nearly feudal in character.

Pervasive authority over the lives of workers and their families, on and off the job, characterized southern agriculture, except in the upland regions. Tenants and sharecroppers lived in homes owned by their employers, and depended on them and local merchants for advances of money, domestic goods, and agricultural supplies to plant their crops and survive until harvesttime. At any time, for cause or whim, they could suffer eviction or withdrawal of credit.

The Southeast had a substantial manufacturing sector, employing one out of five workers in 1950. Southern industry, though, tended to be technically unsophisticated and tightly integrated into rural life. The South's largest industry, textile manufacturing, had close links to the cotton economy. Many southern factories sat in the countryside or in small cities. Their owners and managers intermingled socially with large landowners and often shared their views. Many adopted paternal strategies of social control, much like those in agriculture. In both coal mining towns and textile mill villages, employers generally owned the housing and exerted extensive control over community life. During the mid-1940s, some 60 percent of the workers in southern cotton mills lived in company-owned houses.

Deficient physical and social infrastructure and a paucity of trained workers inhibited industrial development. Poor roads plagued the region. Mississippi had just 36 telephones for every thousand residents, compared to 253 per thousand in California. Low spending on public health facilities contributed to higher levels of infant mortality and maternal death in child-birth than elsewhere in the country. Spending on education lagged way behind other regions. In 1942, Alabama had the lowest value of school property per pupil in the country, less than a sixth the value in New York, the national leader. Georgia did not drop textbook fees and tuition charges for public high schools until the 1930s, and only during World War II did high school attendance for children of white millworkers become the state norm. Rural schools for black children sometimes stayed open only three months a year. The South also trailed the rest of the nation in spending on and use of public libraries.

A pervasive system of racial oppression interwove southern society and contributed to its low level of economic advancement. Slavery in the South—more central and longer-lasting than elsewhere in the country—had ended but a long lifetime before World War II. The economic exploitation of descendants of slaves through a system of racial domination remained fundamental to southern life well into the atomic age.

In the South, more than elsewhere in the country, the past lived on in the present. During the 1940s, elderly African Americans, born into slavery, resided throughout the region, while Virginia still paid pensions to widows of Confederate soldiers. In 1948, Charles S. Reid, a Georgia businessman and writer, in discussing a campaign then under way to allow African Americans to vote, recounted his memories of the Red Shirts bringing Reconstruction to an end in South Carolina. In black families and white, literate and illiterate, stories of slave days and their aftermath were passed on from generation to generation. In Granville County, North Carolina, Novella Allen grew up hearing from her slave-born grandfather about how her great-grandfather had chopped off his hand to keep from being sold away from his family.

The southern system of racial caste survived not as a relic but because it provided a way for landowners and industrialists to maintain tight control over their workers while limiting the impact of the national labor market on wages and working conditions. Allowing only whites to hold many categories of jobs—including most skilled industrial work, virtually all textile jobs, all work involving authority over whites, most clerical and sales jobs, and all but the most menial government positions—forced African Americans to take low-wage jobs in the limited areas open to them. (Vagrancy laws made sure they did not shun work altogether.) For most black men, this meant raising cotton and other crops, generally on land they did not own, or un-skilled manual labor and service jobs in the cities. For black women, domestic and farm labor provided virtually the only earning opportunities. The racial caste system put downward pressure on the wages of white workers, too, by holding out the threat of replacing them with blacks if they got too expensive and making interracial organizing extraordinarily difficult.

Of course, racism was by no means strictly an economic system, nor was it strictly a southern one. In the mid-twentieth-century United States, wherever people of non-European background lived they suffered some degree of discrimination, from the full-blown system of racial domination in the South to informal systems of racial inequality in the most liberal sections of the North. Racism existed as a national way of life, sustained by national as well as local laws and practices.

In most of the country, whites enforced, by law or custom, some degree of racial segregation in public spaces and institutions. The rules tended to be complex and often seemingly arbitrary. Colleges in the North (though not in the South) generally allowed blacks and whites to play football together, but the Big Ten had an unwritten rule barring African Americans from their basketball teams. In Chicago, movies and theaters generally were not segregated, but most hotels, bowling alleys, and taverns were, and neighborhoods tended to be strictly divided along racial lines. Most first-class hotels in Los Angeles and some in San Francisco refused to accommodate African Americans. Missouri segregated schools, theaters, hotels, and restaurants but not public transportation.

The federal government joined state and local governments in enforcing racial separation and inequality. New Mexico and Arizona refused to pay benefits under the Social Security program to Indians who were blind, aged, or dependent children, with no federal repercussions. Federal housing programs permitted and in some cases encouraged segregation. In the District of Columbia, Washington National Airport and swimming pools were segregated. When in 1952 the district government proposed integrating sixteen black firemen into previously all-white firefighting brigades, Congress blocked the move.

Most notoriously, the U.S. armed services remained almost completely segregated through the end of World War II. No racially mixed Army units fought in the war, though late in the conflict some African American infantry platoons were assigned to white companies. The Navy, which traditionally had allowed African Americans to serve only as mess men, placed a small number of black seamen in integrated crews, but by and large its fighting force remained all white. No African Americans served in the Marine

Corps between 1798 and 1942, when they began entering the service in large numbers but were kept in segregated units. Racist thinking so permeated the military that the Army even segregated blood plasma according to the race of the donor.

Racism respected no boundary between the public and the private. At the end of World War II, thirty of the forty-eight states had laws outlawing interracial marriage. Only in the Northeast, Midwest, Washington State, and New Mexico could such unions occur. Antimiscegenation laws targeted black-white marriages, but many states, especially in the West, banned marriages between Europeans and Asians too. A 1935 Maryland law established three population groups, "Malays," whites, and blacks, and allowed persons only to marry within their group. Virginia entitled its 1924 antimiscegenation measure the "Racial Purity Act." During the 1940s, federal courts repeatedly upheld such laws. Not until the 1960s did the Supreme Court deem antimiscegenation laws constitutionally impermissible.

Though national in scope, racism played a far more determining role in the South than elsewhere, for reasons of history and social structure. African Americans constituted a far larger component of the workforce in the South than non–European Americans did anywhere else in the country. They were especially important in the agricultural sector, so central to southern society. The economic advantages for southern employers in maintaining a racial caste system far exceeded the gains to be had elsewhere. The sheer size of the southern African American population—just under half the population in Mississippi, over a third in South Carolina, Louisiana, Alabama, and Georgia, and over a quarter in four more states—meant that under a system of equal rights African Americans would inevitably command more influence on political and social life in the region than in other parts of the nation, a situation the white elite, and most other whites too, worked hard to prevent.

To maintain their system of racial domination, southern whites deployed law, custom, and physical terror. In most of the South, state or local laws explicitly required segregation in workplaces, which made it economically difficult or impossible for employers to maintain biracial workforces. South Carolina forbade black and white textile workers from working in the same room, using the same toilets or washrooms, or utilizing stairways, entrances, exits, or pay windows at the same time. Though employers and state regulations played the leading parts in employment discrimination, some unions in the South (and elsewhere) joined the effort by refusing to admit African Americans and pressing employers to refuse to hire them.

Every detail of daily life had its racial rules. Mississippi law required separate accommodations for blacks and whites in railroad sleeping cars and waiting rooms, trolleys, hospitals, jails, and penitentiaries. Barbershops, beauty parlors, hotels, theaters, restaurants, bars, and billiard halls were strictly segregated by race in most of the South. John Gunther found purdah in India the only analogy that came to mind for the Mississippi practice of using a curtain to separate black and white sections of buses. Atlanta, he wrote, though considered one of the most racially liberal southern cities, "outghettoes anything I ever saw in a European ghetto, even in Warsaw."

In 1896 the U.S. Supreme Court ruled that state laws requiring separate accommodations for blacks and whites did not violate the equal protection clause of the Fourteenth Amendment if those accommodations were equal. In practice, though, separate accommodations in the South almost never were equal. Parks for whites had swimming pools, parks for blacks did not. Streets in white neighborhoods were paved, in black neighborhoods they were not. During the 1949–50 school year, Mississippi spent $123 per pupil on white schools but just $33 per pupil on black schools. In Atlanta, the over 100,000 black residents had the services of only one public high school.

To back up law and custom, southern whites used terror to keep blacks economically and politically subordinate and socially deferential. During World War II, racial violence flared up all around the country, including a horrendous clash between whites and blacks in Detroit that left thirty-four dead, a wave of attacks by white sailors against Mexican Americans in Los Angeles (the so-called Zoot Suit Riots), and clashes between white and black soldiers at domestic training bases. But racial violence occurred in the South with a frequency, sadism, and social legitimacy unmatched elsewhere.

Only in the South did lynching remain a routine practice in the first half of the twentieth century. It became less common in the 1930s and 1940s, perhaps because of the decline of cotton cultivation and the political economy around it, which used extralegal violence to maintain a docile workforce. But the immediate post–World War II years saw a new wave of southern racial violence, mostly directed against black veterans, whose wartime experiences made them less willing to accept established norms and daily indignities. Some of these incidents received national attention, like the blinding of Isaac Woodward, a recently discharged soldier being held in a South Carolina jail after a dispute with a white bus driver, and the murder by a Georgia mob of two black men and two black women.

Most southern racist violence, though, received no publicity, nor resulted in any investigations or repercussions. To maintain or demonstrate their control over blacks, whites committed rapes, beatings, and arson, knowing that authorities would look the other way (or join in), and that in the very unlikely event that criminal charges would be brought, no jury would convict. Black parents schooled their children in behavior they hoped would insulate them from harm. Charles Gratton remembered that as a child in Birmingham, when his mother sent him to the store she would instruct him, "If you pass any white people on your way, you get off the sidewalk. Give them the sidewalk. . . . Don't challenge white people." But the capriciousness and unpredictability of white behavior toward blacks—one moment patronizing or friendly, the next brutal or vicious—made fear a constant presence.

Some observers, at the time and afterward, saw World War II as a turning point for the South. Military service and war industry jobs drew millions of white and black southerners out of the region, disrupting social and economic arrangements, especially in the countryside. Many black veterans returned with a broader sense of possibility and a deeper determination to fight discrimination. As a result of his wartime experiences, which included a stint in Calcutta, Amzie Moore, a key postwar Mississippi black activist, became disabused of his belief that there must be something special about whites that gave them such privileged status, joining the National Association for the Advancement of Colored People (NAACP) even before his discharge. National moves against discrimination, such as the 1944 Supreme Court decision in *Smith v. Allwright,* which declared it unconstitutional to categorically exclude nonwhites from voting in party primaries, convinced some that racism soon would lessen. Meanwhile, government investment in southern military facilities and war industry promoted urbanization and tighter integration of the region into the national economy. But while the war accelerated some long-term trends already at work—most importantly the diminishing importance of the cotton economy as the core of southern life—daily existence at the end of the conflict did not seem much different than before it. Southern society remained rural, poor, and segregated.

The Southwest

On its western side, the South melded into the West in a region that combined elements of both with its own distinct identity. Socially and politically, Oklahoma and Texas shared much with the other states of the South. But environmentally, they more resembled those Mountain states—Colorado, New Mexico, Arizona, Utah, and Nevada—with which they were often lumped together as the "Southwest," sharing a rich mineral endowment and large areas of arid climate. Like the Southeast, the Southwest was more rural and less industrialized than the rest of the country, with a per capita income that exceeded the Southeast but lagged significantly behind other regions of the country.

Extractive industries provided the main source of wealth in large sections of the Southwest. Copper mining dominated the economy in Arizona and loomed large in Montana and New Mexico. Colorado had significant metal and coal mining. Two-thirds of the uranium in the United States lay near the Four Corners where New Mexico, Arizona, Utah, and Colorado meet. In Texas, oil provided much of the wealth, power, and regional cultural identity.

Coal remained the single most important source of energy in the United States through the 1940s, but petroleum surpassed it in 1950 and by the end of the next decade provided more than twice as much energy as coal. In the immediate post–World War II years, the vast majority of petroleum products consumed in the United States came from domestic output, with the country producing nearly two-thirds of the world's oil (as well as a quarter of its coal). Roughly half the domestic production came from the Southwest, where immense petroleum fields had been discovered in the early twentieth century. Texas alone accounted for 37 percent of the total, and Oklahoma another 11 percent. Only California joined them in producing more than 10 percent of the national output. The oil companies and their owners, rich, powerful, and very conservative, gave a politically reactionary flavor to the areas they dominated, like Houston and Tulsa, and exerted great national influence on issues they deemed important to their well-being, such as federal regulation of the price of natural gas.

Dry weather limited the agricultural possibilities in the Southwest. Much of the area could sustain, on an extended basis, at most the grazing of livestock. When, in the early twentieth century, high commodity prices and unusually wet weather led farmers to plow up the southern Plains to plant crops, they harvested disaster. In the early 1930s, a series of dry years resulted in dust storms, severe soil erosion, and economic collapse in what came to be called the Dust Bowl. This in turn led to a massive out-migration that continued through the war years. "From the south land and the drought land, / Come the wife and kids and me, / And this old world is a hard world, / For a dust bowl refugee," sang Oklahoman Woody Guthrie in 1940, on his first commercial recording. By 1950, 23 percent of the people who had been born in Oklahoma, Texas, Arkansas, or Missouri—nearly four million people—lived outside the region, with over a third settled in California.

Irrigation held the promise to transform the region. Even before World War II, pumps provided some water for irrigation, with the windmills that drove them dotting the horizon. Irrigation allowed the value of the agricultural output of Arizona to surpass that of mining for the first time in 1944. After the war, the introduction of diesel-driven centrifugal pumps made irrigation possible on a far vaster scale. As cotton production in the Southeast declined, it rose in the Southwest and Far West. By 1949, more than half of the nation's cotton crop was being grown in Texas, Oklahoma, New Mexico, Arizona, and California, using irrigated land, mechanized equipment, and itinerant labor.

During the 1940s, the Southwest also saw significant industrialization, much of it related to the war. Along the Gulf Coast, in Texas and Louisiana, the petrochemical industry rapidly expanded, in part to produce synthetic rubber once the Japanese cut off the supply of natural rubber from Southeast Asia. In contrast to the German chemical industry, which used coal-based products as its primary feedstock, the U.S. industry depended primarily on petroleum products. Texas saw the expansion of steel mills, shipyards, and ammunition plants as well. Huge factories in Tulsa and Dallas–Fort Worth poured out military aircraft. Phoenix, too, emerged as an aircraft center, as a host of military air bases built during the war drew aircraft manufacturers and parts suppliers to the area.

By the end of World War II, the worst days of the Dust Bowl were behind the Southwest. But most of the region remained sparsely populated and undeveloped. Few envisioned that a half century later it would contain some of the fastest-growing areas of the United States.

The West

In the West, World War II had transformative effects so pervasive that both westerners and outside observers immediately perceived the conflict as a turning point in the history of the region. Some of the oldest continuous European settlements in the United States were in the West (predated only by St. Augustine, Florida, founded by the Spanish in 1565). But population and industry grew more slowly in the region than elsewhere in the country. In 1940, only 13.9 million people lived in the eleven western states, just over 10 percent of the national population and barely more residents than in New York State.

In 1942 and 1943, the United States did the bulk of its fighting in the Pacific. Money flowed to the West on an epic scale to train and equip a fighting force for the war with Japan and for combat elsewhere. The military favored the region because of its proximity to the Pacific theater; its favorable climate, which made year-round outdoor activity possible; its abundant, cheap electricity, needed for the production of aluminum, plutonium, and other war materials; and the availability of huge, remote, thinly settled tracts, which made it possible to build and operate facilities, like the atomic research installations at Los Alamos, New Mexico, and Hanford, Washington, in relative secrecy.

California, along with Texas, served as the most important troop training and staging area in the country. Bases popped up all over the state, some of staggering size. The Army, to prepare for the invasion of North Africa, set up a Desert Training Center in Southern California 180 miles long and ninety miles wide, roughly the size of Denmark. North of San Diego, the Marines took over a 122,798-acre ranch to establish Camp Pendleton. In San Francisco Bay, the Navy built the largest naval repair facility in the country, on Mare Island, and one of the largest airfields in the world, the Alameda Naval Air Station.

Farther north, in the territory of Alaska, the military constructed bases at a furious rate after the attack on Pearl Harbor and the Japanese occupation, six months later, of the Aleutian island of Attu. By the end of the war, the Army and Navy had built some three hundred Alaskan facilities at a cost of $3 billion. The Alaska Highway, one of the largest and most expensive military construction projects of the war, provided the first overland connection between Alaska and the forty-eight states by cutting across northwestern Canada. Once upgraded by civilian contractors, it provided an important postwar link for commerce and tourism.

Up and down the West Coast, the government made massive investments in industry and infrastructure to support the war effort. California alone got 10 percent of all wartime federal spending. Existing aircraft firms in Southern California and Seattle served as seed crystals for what became huge centers of warplane production. At its height, the Southern California aircraft industry employed 243,000 workers. By the end of the war, its value exceeded the prewar dollar value of all industry in Detroit. In the Seattle area, Boeing went from seventy-five hundred workers in 1940 to fifty thousand (nearly half women) in 1944. Shipbuilding similarly boomed. California shipyards, many thrown up almost overnight, employed well over a quarter of a million workers. Portland shipyards employed another 125,000. To support his huge West Coast shipbuilding operations, industrialist Henry J. Kaiser built the West Coast's first integrated steel plant in Fontana, sixty miles east of Los Angeles; threw up new cities to house his workers, like Vanport City in Portland, with homes for nearly ten thousand families; and expanded the prepaid comprehensive medical program he had established for his employees before the war, renaming it Kaiser Permanente.

The end of the war brought a temporary decline of western industry.

Shipyards closed or consolidated. The airplane industry shrank radically. Women (not only in the West) left the industrial jobs that had opened up to them during the war to return to traditional, lower-paid women's work or home life. In much of the region, extractive industries—mining, timber, agriculture—remained dominant. But the manufacturing decline proved short-lived, as the accelerated development of the West continued into the postwar years.

The war opened the eyes of businessmen to the possibilities out west. While after the war the Portland defense industry rapidly diminished, many small factories making civilian goods opened up, taking advantage of the raw materials, cheap power, and good transportation that had made the city an attractive center for military production. The war left the West Coast with much-improved physical infrastructure, a more skilled workforce than in the prewar years, and a scientific community with greatly expanded capacity and international connections as a result of government spending. Technically sophisticated defense contractors, like the airplane companies in California and Seattle, applied expertise developed during the war to making civilian products, which helped tide them over until the Korean and Cold wars brought new waves of military spending.

Many GIs who had trained in the West or traveled through it on their way to the war found it to their liking and returned to settle after demobilizing. Many civilians who had gone west for defense jobs ended up staying. The civilian population of Alaska went from 73,000 in 1940 to 129,000 in 1950. California's grew by some two million residents during the war. When the war ended, people continued to flock into the state, helping boost its population from 6.9 million in 1940 to 10.6 million in 1950 (still small compared to the 33.9 million people it housed in 2000).

By 1949, Los Angeles had grown into the third-largest metropolitan region in the country, with a third of the population having arrived in the previous decade. As the center of the motion picture industry (and later the television industry, which largely relocated there from New York), it played an outsize part in establishing the yearnings, fears, role models, and self-understandings of Americans and in projecting images and values of the country across the globe (counterbalancing radio and newspapers, more decentralized media that reinforced local identities). Stars like Bing Crosby, Gary Cooper, Humphrey Bogart, Betty Grable, and Bette Davis were the face of the U.S.A.

Even with the flood of mostly white or African American newcomers, the West still had a much higher proportion of Asian Americans and Native Americans than the rest of the country. In 1950, nearly 69 percent of the country's 259,397 Asian Americans and Pacific Islanders lived in the West (including Alaska and Hawaii), down from 81 percent ten years earlier, in part reflecting the decision of some Japanese Americans not to return to the West following their wartime internment. The West also housed a majority of the nation's 343,410 Indians, Eskimos, and Aleuts, with the largest Indian settlements in Arizona, New Mexico, and Oklahoma. Large Mexican American populations lived in the Southwest and California, contributing to the polyglot quality that had long characterized the western part of the country.

Ethnic and racial discrimination was as constitutive of the West as the South, at least politically and culturally if not economically. Since the mid-nineteenth century, anti-Asian sentiment had been a binding force among West Coast whites, leading to numerous restrictions on Chinese, Japanese, and Filipino residents and pushing the country to impose extreme limits on immigration from Asia. Discrimination against Mexican Americans was widespread, if not as severe, including, in some areas, segregated schools and public facilities. Native Americans faced a web of discrimination, legal and social, that severely restricted their political participation and contributed to extreme poverty. African Americans found discrimination and segregation increasing during World War II, as their numbers swelled and in defense centers contractors threw up suburban subdivisions for white—and only white—newcomers.

The war enlarged the already massive federal presence in the West. Economic growth in the region, more than elsewhere in the country, depended on government spending. In 1950, 12 percent of employed workers (including military personnel) in the Far West worked for a government agency, compared to 6 percent nationally. The federal government owned huge swaths of western land, including nearly half the land in the Mountain states and nearly three-quarters of Alaska. In Nevada, government agencies owned roughly seven-eighths of the land, just about everything except well-watered pasture or agricultural land.

In the Northwest, cheap power from the federally built Bonneville and Grand Coulee dams (the latter, when completed, the largest structure ever built by man) accelerated industrialization, while associated irrigation projects vastly expanded regional agriculture. In Colorado, California, and Nevada, federal dams and irrigation projects transformed deserts into some of the most productive agricultural land in the world. California's Imperial Valley, irrigated with water diverted from the Colorado River by the Hoover Dam, thrived because its climate made it possible to get fresh produce to eastern markets even in the winter. In California's larger Central Valley, during the mid-1930s the federal government took over a water control and irrigation project planned by the state that eventually involved decades of massive investment in dams, pumping stations, levees, and irrigation canals. The water and electricity that flowed from the project turned the Central Valley into a highly mechanized, highly efficient, capital-intensive farmland, where, unlike in the South and some other parts of the country, by the mid-1940s horses and mules had been nearly totally replaced by mechanical equipment, and electricity had been made available nearly everywhere, so that, as a *National Geographic Magazine* article put it, "Nightfall sees . . . endless farm homes all atwinkle like stars along a man-made Milky Way."

Katherine Archibald, a young anthropologist who worked in an Oakland shipyard during World War II, wrote that the work done in the shipyards and their workforces drawn from across the country were "a continual reminder of the wartime demand for subordination of cherished localisms to larger social unities." Regional differences remained substantial after World War II, continuing to shape the political, social, and economic dynamics of the country. But the war diminished them. Military service and the mass migration of workers seeking war jobs opened up horizons for tens of millions of Americans, while breaking down at least some parochial boundaries and assumptions. Exceptional among American wars in having little organized domestic opposition, World War II brought a sense of common purpose that, though far from complete, provided a renewed feeling of confidence and possibility after the long Depression years. Americans could not help but feel, as the war drew to a close, the enormous power that their nation had: military power, economic power, intellectual power, cultural power. As the postwar era began, the United States, as a society and a nation, confronted the question of how it should use its incredible wealth and power to shape the world and reshape itself, and who would make such decisions.

PART I

Pax Americana

(1945–1953)

CHAPTER 1

Power and Politics

Three related issues, each with deep historical roots, structured domestic politics during the years immediately after World War II. First was the proper role of government in ordering society. Second was what rights individuals should have, both in controlling government and more broadly as citizens. Third was how much power, relative to one another, business, labor, and consumers should have over the economy.

World War II brought the Great Depression to an end, but the questions raised by the economic collapse and the New Deal to which it gave birth remained unresolved. Could the country's system of political economy prevent a return of economic stagnation? How far should the government go in regulating the economy and providing social benefits? Should the redistribution of power and resources that began during the 1930s be continued or rolled back? These questions long remained central to national politics. But within just a few years they began to be answered.

Government

Harry S. Truman discovered upon assuming the presidency, following the death of Franklin D. Roosevelt on April 12, 1945, that the head of the most powerful nation on earth operated with a tiny staff. Only a handful of administrative assistants; a few military aides; appointment, press, and correspondence secretaries; a special counsel; some staff borrowed from executive departments; and the heads of the Office of War Mobilization and Reconversion and the Bureau of the Budget directly aided the president. In spite of its tremendous expansion during the New Deal and World War II, the federal government remained decentralized and ad hoc.

Until the twentieth century, Americans had had very limited contact with the federal government, especially in peacetime. Most rarely, if ever, interacted with federal agencies, except for the post office. Early in the century, that began to change. Rapid industrialization, disruptive labor conflict, urbanization, and the growth of radical political movements led progressive reformers and even some more conservative politicians to broaden their notion of the responsibility of the state in regulating the economy, mediating social conflict, and promoting minimal standards of well-being. Still, until the 1930s, the federal government stayed modest in size, administrative capacity, and penetration into the daily routines of American life.

The New Deal changed that, and did so quickly. In 1930, the federal government had 860,000 employees and a budget of $3.3 billion. Ten years later it had 1.5 million employees and spent $9.6 billion. By then, it had become intricately involved in everything from collective bargaining and old-age pensions to housing construction, the arts, and fighting crime. Almost every county in the country had a new public works project—a school, hospital, courthouse, post office, park, road, or dam—funded by Washington.

The swelling size and scope of government came, in large part, in response to the Great Depression. During Roosevelt's presidency, the federal government hired millions of unemployed; propped up prices and incomes; lent money to keep businesses afloat and homeowners from defaulting on mortgages; and rescued and reformed the banking system. With conservative political and business elites discredited by the economic debacle, reformers had the opportunity to carry out previously blocked plans, including offering subsidies to farmers, creating the Tennessee Valley Authority (TVA), and more actively regulating Wall Street. Under pressure from popular movements of the left and right, Washington established a limited welfare state. The Social Security Act created a national pension system, unemployment insurance, and welfare programs for the dependent poor. The National Labor Relations Act (commonly known as the Wagner Act) protected the right of workers to join a union and engage in collective bargaining. The Fair Labor Standards Act established a national minimum wage and limited working hours.

An electoral realignment accompanied the expansion of the state. By the mid-1930s, a new coalition had emerged in support of Roosevelt. It included immigrants and their children; African Americans; organized labor; big-city Democratic machines; farmers; small businessmen; some corporate leaders; and, at least tacitly, elements of the socialist and communist left (whose influence exceeded their small size). The Roosevelt administration also benefited from solid Democratic control of the South.

Powerful though it was, the New Deal coalition stopped winning major reforms well before the Depression ended. Southern Democrats grew fearful that the extension of federal power into localities would threaten the racial order, while urban politicians fretted that New Deal networks outside their control would undermine local party organizations. As many voters grew disenchanted with the growing size of the government and Roosevelt's failure to bring about sustained economic recovery, anti–New Deal business leaders mobilized through trade associations and the Republican Party. From 1938 on, a stalemate developed in Congress between two blocs, one of pro–New Deal liberals, largely in the Democratic Party, and the other of anti–New Deal conservatives, which joined Republicans with southern Democrats.

Just as the New Deal reached its seeming limits, war brought a further expansion of the state. In 1945, the federal government spent ten times what it had in 1939. While fighting raged across the globe, federal presence deepened in everyday life, as Washington regulated prices and wages; rationed consumer goods; controlled transportation; allocated raw materials; built factories, pipelines, and military bases; carried out a military draft; and held, without trial, thousands of citizens in internment camps.

To finance the swollen state sector, Washington undertook massive borrowing and revamped the tax system. Prior to the war, only the wealthy paid income taxes. During it, Congress drastically lowered the cutoff for income tax exemption, so that middle- and working-class families had to pay federal taxes as well. Filing income tax returns became a yearly national ritual, reminding income earners of the extent and cost of federal power.

Federal growth evoked less controversy during World War II than during the New Deal, since the state expanded to wage a war that most Americans supported. Still, the backlash against the New Deal continued. Business leaders, widely blamed for the economic ills of the 1930s, found their social standing and political influence reelevated, as the Roosevelt administration turned to them to lead the defense mobilization. By contrast, reformers found their influence diminished by the priority given to war needs and an increasingly conservative Congress. The union movement provided something of a countervailing force, growing during the war to 14.7 million members, from 10.5 million before its start, but, committed to military victory, it generally cooperated with government efforts to maximize production and avoid disruptive disputes.

Successful though it was, the wartime mobilization led intellectuals, political activists, and government insiders to rethink the role of government. Many felt that the wartime federal bureaucracy had proved to be an inefficient mechanism for controlling the economy, riven as it was by battles over turf and policy, and generating as it did widespread grumbling about regulations and restrictions. But the expansion of the federal spending had had a miraculous effect on the economy. During the war, the GNP soared from $91 billion to $166 billion. Personal savings reached $37 billion in 1944, a national nest egg that financed a postwar spending spree. With vast investment in capital equipment and the creation of fifteen million new jobs, the United States simultaneously supplied its twelve million soldiers and sailors with arms and equipment; sent shipload after shipload of goods to its allies; and still produced enough consumer items to allow a substantial improvement in the standard of living.

Many New Deal reformers concluded from this experience that fiscal policy, rather than a further expansion of government institutions or a redistribution of wealth, provided the best means of promoting social well-being. Stimulating economic growth through government spending held the promise of keeping employment high and downturns shallow without a large, intrusive federal bureaucracy, avoiding the managerial and political problems evident during the New Deal and the war. Demand stimulation might produce budget deficits, but the wartime experience led many economists and politicians to shed their fears of unbalanced budgets, recognizing that deficit spending, on a scale far beyond what the New Deal engaged in, had led to unprecedented economic growth.

Liberals, leftists, and labor leaders by no means entirely abandoned ideas for extending the New Deal. As the war drew to an end, they promoted sweeping political programs that in various ways combined fiscal management of the economy, expanded social welfare benefits, and direct state spending. Many borrowed language from President Roosevelt's 1944 State of the Union address, in which he argued that since "individual freedom cannot exist without economic security and independence," the country needed "a second Bill of Rights" that would guarantee all Americans a right to "a useful and remunerative job," "a decent home," "adequate medical care," and "a good education." Typical was the "People's Program" put forth in 1944 by the Political Action Committee of the Congress of Industrial Organizations (CIO-PAC), the political arm of one of the two major union federations. It called for full employment at fair wages, federal aid to education, large-scale public housing construction, federally sponsored health insurance, continued rent and price controls, continued agricultural price supports, and compensatory public works spending when the economy softened.

Some of the liberal proposals took specific legislative form. In 1943,

Congressman John Dingell and Senators Robert F. Wagner and James E. Murray introduced a bill to expand the Social Security system to include medical, hospitalization, and disability insurance; improve existing benefits; and create a national network of government-run employment offices. Murray also sponsored a bill to set up a Missouri Valley Authority, the first of what some New Dealers hoped would be a series of new Tennessee Valley Authorities, which would tame rivers, create jobs and electricity, and bring economic and social planning to large sections of the country. To address a severe housing shortage, Wagner joined with Democratic senator Allen J. Ellender and Republican senator Robert Taft to propose a massive expansion of federal funding for public housing and slum clearance.

Some state and local leaders proposed New Deal–type programs of their own. In California, liberal Republican governor Earl Warren unsuccessfully pressed for a state-sponsored compulsory health insurance system. New York City mayor Fiorello LaGuardia, also a Republican, helped set up the nonprofit Health Insurance Plan of Greater New York (HIP). Several states developed plans for public housing.

These liberal proposals received extensive publicity and sparked widespread debate, but, at least in Washington, their backers had little success in getting legislation passed. The necessities of war and the revival of business pushed the political pendulum to the right. The war years hardened an antistatism among conservatives that already had crystallized in their opposition to the New Deal. Looking beyond the borders, conservative intellectuals—and some liberals, too—concluded that fascist and communist dictatorships revealed the threat to individual liberty from any expansion of state power. Some, like Friedrich von Hayek, in *The Road to Serfdom,* published in 1944, argued that only by abandoning state planning and economic regulation for a strictly free-market economy could liberty be preserved, a view that grew increasingly influential in the decades to come.

Conservative critics of the New Deal found allies, at least on some issues, among southern Democrats, who did not necessarily object to expanding government but opposed federal programs that by providing jobs or benefits to African Americans might undermine the southern system of racial rule. During the war, Congress terminated the Civilian Conservation Corps, the Works Progress Administration, the National Youth Administration, and the National Resources Planning Board. The 1944 Democratic Party decision to jettison from its ticket incumbent vice president Henry A. Wallace, a forceful advocate of extending the New Deal at home and abroad, replacing him with Truman, an undistinguished border-state moderate, reflected the changing political balance.

Pro-business forces generally bested liberal and pro-labor elements in battles over economic reconversion. As was the case after World War I, business wanted Washington to dismantle its wartime economic apparatus as quickly as possible, rejecting liberal hopes for a gradual reconversion aimed at maximizing employment and spending power. Even before the war ended, the government began abruptly terminating contracts for war supplies, leading to sudden factory shutdowns and layoffs, while handing over government-built war facilities to private business.

The shifting political tide could be seen in the fate of the Full Employment Bill, introduced to Congress in January 1945. During the war, liberals increasingly focused on full employment as the centerpiece for a postwar economic and social program. More optimistic than in the prewar years, when many New Dealers feared permanent economic stagnation, full-employment advocates believed that government policies could ensure a job for every person who wanted one, which in turn would stimulate consumption and economic growth. In its original form, the Full Employment Bill would have required the president to make an annual assessment of the number of jobs needed for full employment and the level of economic activity required to generate them. If he determined that the private sector would not provide sufficient openings, the government would be mandated to intervene through direct spending, loans, and investments to fill the employment shortfall.

Truman actively backed the Full Employment Bill, as did the CIO and the National Farmers Union. But it faced fierce opposition from business groups and large-scale farmers, who feared that full employment would drive up labor costs. As the employment bill slowly wended its way through the legislative process, one provision after another was stripped from it. Once the war ended and a feared postwar recession failed to materialize, what little enthusiasm there was for a potentially costly new government program drained away. As finally passed in early 1946, the bill retained a rhetorical commitment to government action to ensure a growth-oriented, full-employment society, but it had few mechanisms to achieve it, other than a new Council of Economic Advisers to assist the president.

The one major piece of social legislation that did get passed during the war adopted the language and some of the programmatic ideas of those seeking to expand the New Deal, while moving fundamentally in a different direction. No law from the 1940s had greater impact on the social and physical landscape than the Servicemen's Readjustment Act of 1944, better known as the GI Bill. The law grew out of a modest American Legion proposal for mustering-out pay. When a congressional committee tried to reduce the proposed pay level, the Legion vastly expanded its proposal into what it initially called "The Bill of Rights for GI Joe and Jane."

The GI Bill built on a precedent established early in the war. In 1942, the Roosevelt administration proposed a Federal Rehabilitation Service to help both civilian and military disabled. Veterans' groups, with the support of some New Deal opponents, rejected the measure, arguing that veterans deserved special treatment because of their service, not wanting them to be used to promote a broad new federal program. In its stead, Congress passed a rehabilitation bill covering only veterans, reiterating the idea that men and women who served in the armed services deserved separate, better benefits than the general population.

The GI Bill gave returning veterans $500 mustering-out pay and a comprehensive package of benefits, including health care, up to four years' tuition and living expenses for college or training school, employment counseling, unemployment benefits for up to a full year, and loans on favorable terms to purchase a home, farm stock or equipment, or to start a business (like the many diners onetime Army and Navy cooks put up across industrial America). Although the Roosevelt administration had its own veterans' bill, the president prudently accepted the American Legion proposal, which went through Congress with little opposition in spite of its expansiveness and expense. (In 1948, the GI Bill accounted for 15 percent of the federal budget; the education provisions for World War II veterans alone ended up costing $14.5 billion.)

In its language of expanded rights, and its provision of what in other contexts might have been called social democratic benefits, the GI Bill resembled the proposals of the unreconstructed New Dealers. But its authors rejected some of their key premises. Most obviously, the GI Bill benefited only a particular segment of society. Many New Deal measures had not been universal, including the Social Security Act, National Labor Relations Act, and the Fair Labor Standards Act, which excluded large parts of the workforce and privileged wage earners over homemakers. But New Dealers saw the exclusions as necessary and hopefully temporary concessions to powerful lobbies like farm groups, which succeeded at blocking coverage for agricultural labor, and southern Democrats, who got domestic workers (mostly African Americans in their region) shut out. The GI Bill, by contrast, had categorical distinctions at its very heart.

In some respects, the GI Bill did represent a move toward equal rights. In contrast to New Deal programs that either explicitly provided inferior benefits to blacks or treated disproportionately African American groups, like sharecroppers and domestic workers, more poorly than heavily white ones, the GI Bill treated black and white veterans equally. For this reason, Mississippi congressman John Rankin led a last-minute effort to kill it. But in practice the GI Bill also reinforced or created inequities. For one thing, in a segregated world, many African Americans found themselves less able than their white peers to actually use their GI benefits because colleges would not admit them, businesses would not sell to them, and public laws and private practices limited where they could buy homes. For another thing, though female veterans could take advantage of the GI Bill—getting somewhat less generous benefits than men—there were far fewer GI Janes than GI Joes, since women had not been subject to the draft and caps had been placed on the number allowed to enlist. With women making up only 2 percent of the armed services, the effect of the GI Bill was to further the economic and social distance between the sexes. The GI Bill also became the first federal benefit program to explicitly discriminate against gays and lesbians, when the Veterans Administration decided to deny benefits to veterans given "undesirable" discharges for homosexuality.

Beyond its rejection of universalism, the GI bill departed from the New Deal in its stress on individual benefits and individual mobility. The New Deal provided many of its benefits through government institutions that directly hired people, housed them, educated and entertained them. The GI Bill took a different tack, giving funds to individuals to shop for education, housing, employment, and business opportunities in the private market. (Health care came directly from the government through Veterans Administration hospitals and clinics.) In promoting its bill, the American Legion used the language of individual freedom, not social provision. Some of the strongest congressional support for the measure came from conservative critics of the New Deal.

The GI Bill proved one of the most successful pieces of legislation in the nation's history. By providing veterans with generous unemployment and education benefits, it prevented a postwar flooding of the labor market that might have led to soaring joblessness and discontent. The bill funded a massive expansion of higher education and enabled veterans to equip themselves for upward mobility as wage earners or businessmen. GI Bill mortgages financed one-fifth of all single-family homes built between the end of World War II and 1966. Yet in easing the economic and social transition from war to peace and helping a generation of young men and women reach a level of comfort unknown to most Americans before the war, the bill launched postwar social policy on a trajectory that favored aid to particular groups over universal benefits, promotion of individual mobility over the creation of new social institutions, and pumping money into the private marketplace over the direct provision of government benefits.

Rights

The idea of an economic bill of rights or a "Bill of Rights for GI Joe and Jane" to provide economic and social benefits built on the presumption that political rights already received adequate protection. In practice that was far from the case. By standards that came to be broadly accepted in the late twentieth century, the United States had serious deficiencies as a democratic polity at the end of World War II.

The United States had never been a universal democracy. Over its history, political rights had expanded and contracted, with some groups gaining rights even as others lost them. The New Deal had not made the extension or protection of political rights a high priority. Roosevelt refused to endanger his southern white support by backing measures to protect African Americans from discrimination or violence or to ensure their right to vote. The rhetoric of World War II, however, with its stress on freedom as the defining characteristic of the United States and its allies, along with the need to mobilize millions of African Americans into military and industrial service, made it more difficult for the government to ignore glaring examples of undemocratic ways. During the war, Congress guaranteed the right of all soldiers, regardless of race, to vote without paying a poll tax, while the Supreme Court issued its ruling against whites-only primaries. Congress also eliminated long-existing bars that effectively prevented Asian immigrants from ever achieving citizenship. African Americans and their allies took advantage of wartime conditions to push harder for equal rights, with the percentage of southern blacks registered to vote increasing fourfold between 1940 and 1947, from 3 to 12 percent.

Wartime advances still left a huge gap between democratic verbiage and political practice. Across the South, poll taxes, literacy tests, threats of violence, and the simple refusal by local registrars to enroll them kept the vast majority of blacks away from the polls. Indians, too, faced obstacles to voting. An Arizona law banning Indian voting—one of several such state laws—kept Ira Hayes, a Pima Indian who achieved fame as one of the flag raisers at Iwo Jima, from casting a ballot. In many localities, whites also faced high hurdles when they sought to vote. The poll tax, in place in five southern states through the 1950s, kept more whites than blacks away from the polls. South Carolina and Alabama had property requirements for voting. In one postwar election, out of one and a quarter million Mississippians of voting age, only 180,000 actually cast a ballot. Residents of the territories of Alaska, Hawaii (which in 1950 exceeded three states in population), Puerto Rico (which exceeded twenty-three), and the District of Columbia (which exceeded thirteen) had no representation in Congress and could not vote for the president.

Even when a citizen did get to vote, that vote might count for very little. At the end of World War II, seven western states had fourteen senators to represent their 3.6 million people, the same number as represented 51.9 million residents of seven eastern states. Failure to reapportion as population urbanized introduced further inequities into congressional representation. In Illinois, which at the end of World War II still used congressional district lines drawn in 1901, Cook County had over half the state population but only ten of twenty-six House seats.

Many states had similar skews in the makeup of their state legislatures, with generally more conservative rural areas having disproportionate representation. In California, half the population lived in San Francisco or Los Angeles but elected only two out of forty state senators. Georgia picked its governor and congressmen not by popular vote but by a system that gave the winning candidate in each county a certain number of "units" weighted to heavily favor rural and small counties. In 1946, the governor and a congressman were elected by the unit count even though they lost the popular vote.

In addition to their geographic disproportionality, legislative bodies failed to mirror the population in their sexual and racial composition. In 1949, fewer than 3 percent of state legislators were female. Congress had but eight female House members and one female senator. (Three had taken over their husbands' seats when they died, including Maine senator Margaret Chase Smith, the best-known woman on Capitol Hill.) Only two African Americans sat in the House—William Dawson representing the South Side of Chicago and Harlem's Adam Clayton Powell Jr.—and none in the Senate.

The structure of representation gave a conservative tilt to national and state politics. Working-class men and women tended to be more liberal than their middle- and upper-class peers, but millions of them, particularly non-whites, could not vote, while millions more, living in cities or big eastern and midwestern states, had their political weight diminished by unequal apportionment. Liberals in effect needed a supermajority to achieve power. Only at moments of massive support for change, like the early and mid-1930s, could liberal reformers translate popular backing into legislative action. Had the makeup of Congress and the state legislatures mirrored popular political views, the chances for an expanded New Deal would have been far greater.

Congress's own rules further devalued the political influence of some Americans while elevating that of others. The use of seniority to choose committee chairs favored the southern states, where a one-party system meant that incumbents rarely faced serious challenge. In the Senate, the rule requiring a two-thirds vote to cut off debate ("cloture") gave the South an effective veto over legislation. While these rules were defended in terms of abstract political principles, southern congressmen used the institutional arrangements that favored them primarily to funnel federal appropriations to their region and to block any move toward advancing the civil rights of African Americans. Repeatedly during the 1940s, southern senators used the two-thirds rule to kill anti-lynching and anti–poll tax legislation and bills to make permanent the wartime Fair Employment Practices Committee.

Various state constitutional provisions also limited popular democracy. All but five state legislatures met only every other year, and in many cases for just brief sessions. Many states forbade governors from succeeding themselves, with two-year terms of office common. With most elected state officials rarely present, lacking experience, or both, lobbyists and political insiders wielded inordinate power.

The right to a fair trial, like the right to vote, often proved illusory, in spite of seemingly clear constitutional guarantees. In the South, African Americans facing serious charges routinely suffered beatings in efforts to force confessions, and received only token and often utterly incompetent representation by court-appointed lawyers, in spite of a series of prewar Supreme Court rulings that theoretically gave black defendants greater rights. In places where African Americans or Native Americans were denied the right to vote, they generally could not sit on juries either. Furthermore, in most of the country, women were either barred or discouraged from jury service. In 1946, the Supreme Court forbade the exclusion of women from federal juries in states where they could serve on state juries, but the states themselves could and did continue to discriminate (as did federal courts in states that limited women's jury rights). While many states loosened jury restrictions after the war, three states continued to forbid women from serving on juries into the 1960s, with the last, Mississippi, dropping its bar in 1968. Even then, in twenty-two states women could be excused from jury service on grounds not available to men. Economic conditions also shaped jury composition; in many parts of the country, both state and federal courts systematically favored wealthier individuals in picking petit and grand juries, while weeding out workers and the unemployed.

The democratic rhetoric of the New Deal and the fight against fascism, along with wartime demographic shifts that pulled hundreds of thousands of African Americans out of the rural South, brought increased scrutiny to the limitations on the basic rights of Americans. For the first time since the mass disenfranchisement of black voters at the end of the nineteenth century, equal rights for African Americans got placed on the national agenda— debated in Congress, supported by various black, liberal, and labor groups, and discussed in books by African Americans and white social scientists, most famously Gunnar Myrdal's 1944 study of racial inequality, *An American Dilemma*. But actual progress toward guaranteeing basic political rights proved extremely limited.

Labor

Elections and legislation helped determine the trajectory of postwar society, but so did popular mobilizations, especially by union members and, to a lesser extent, consumers. The union movement loomed large in the immediate postwar years, not only because of its ability to shut down much of the nation's economy. Compared to other non-elite organizations, unions had unusually rich financial and ideological resources and greater capacity to mobilize mass action. In the mid- and late 1940s, they played a larger part in shaping the political economy than would be the case in later years.

Even before World War II ended, tens of thousands of workers began walking off their jobs. Tens of thousands soon became hundreds of thousands, and hundreds of thousands became millions, in the largest strike wave in U.S. history. At its height, in January 1946, nearly two million workers were off the job. All told, some five million workers struck in the year following VJ Day.

The postwar strikes stemmed from specific employer-union disputes over contracts and grievances, but they had broad implications, as labor and management battled to establish the parameters of postwar union power and the relationships among wages, prices, and profits. Given the nature of the issues involved and the repeated efforts by the Truman administration to prevent or end strikes through fact-finding boards, administrative rulings, and threats of repression, the industrial conflict took on a highly political cast.

During World War II, government controls had limited increases in wage rates, but steady work, promotional opportunities, and extensive overtime significantly boosted average weekly earnings. As the war drew to a close, workers wanted to push up hourly rates in the face of diminished workweeks and fears of postwar inflation. Union leaders worried that a drop in national income would lead to falling consumer demand and a downward economic spiral. As one CIO memorandum put it, "Nothing short of big and substantial wage and salary raises will bring earnings up to a level where America at least will have a fighting chance of beating depressions and licking unemployment."

Many rank-and-file workers thought less about the national economy and more about their own hopes for a better life. Wartime prosperity had begun transforming the lives of working-class families. A 50 percent wartime increase in real wages in the southern textile industry allowed workers to begin buying cars and in some cases their mill village houses, which many companies started to sell off. Still, workers generally lived very modestly, at best. In the heavily unionized steel industry, as late as 1942, 15 percent of workers lived in homes without running water and 30 percent lacked an indoor bathroom. The average steelworker family did not move above the federally defined poverty line until 1953. When in 1948 thirteen-year-old Elvis Presley's family moved from Tupelo, Mississippi, to Memphis, they could afford to rent only a single room in a boardinghouse, cooking meals on a hot plate and sharing a bathroom with other families, even though Elvis's father found work at a munitions factory and his mother as a sewing machine operator. Heavy borrowing gave working-class families increasing access to consumer goods but left them susceptible to the effects of unsteady work and the frequent layoffs that characterized many industries.

Leaders of the CIO—the bulk of whose members worked in mass production industry—hoped that at the end of the war the federal government would shepherd through industry-wide agreements boosting wages while keeping price controls in place. At a November 1945 conference, the Truman administration tried to bring labor and management together, but no consensus could be reached on either a wage policy or the role government should play in industrial relations. Leaders of the American Federation of Labor (AFL)—many of whose members were skilled workers organized along craft lines—wanted minimal federal interference. So did business leaders, who sought to keep labor from using the power of the state to advance its cause.

With the government, at least initially, on the sidelines and the rank and file in a militant mood, labor leaders turned to mass demonstrations of worker power to preserve the improved living standards their members were beginning to enjoy and to check management efforts to roll back the institutional position unions had achieved. Many postwar strikes were notable not only for their size and duration—General Motors workers struck for 113 days, textile workers for 133 days, glassworkers for 102 days—but also for the solidarity and feistiness workers displayed. Most struck companies did not use scabs or violence, recognizing that the legal, political, and social climate had so changed during the New Deal and war years that crude strikebreaking efforts most likely would rebound against them. Companies that did try to maintain production at struck plants or terminate collective bargaining unilaterally met fierce resistance. In Stamford, Connecticut; Lancaster, Pennsylvania; Rochester, New York; and Oakland, California, union-busting efforts led to general strikes, rarities in American history.

The militancy of postwar strikers flowed from their fears that peace would bring joblessness, lower income, and weakened unions, but also from their confidence about their social centrality. The years immediately after the war marked the zenith of blue-collar America. In 1950, craft workers, operatives, laborers (not even counting those on farms and in mines), and their supervisors made up 41 percent of the workforce, a twentieth-century high. Manual workers, once treated by those in power as virtual outcasts, had been celebrated in New Deal iconography and rhetoric. During the war, billboards, newsreels, and other propaganda hailed industrial workers, including the two and half million women who took factory jobs, as fighters on the war's home front, whose efforts and sacrifices would be key to victory. (Total female employment during the war jumped from twelve to eighteen million.) Such social validation, along with higher income, steady employment, and, for many, union protection, brought a jauntiness to the working class that carried over into the postwar years, evident in the Oakland general strike, when strikers ordered bars to put their jukeboxes on the sidewalk to provide music for couples dancing in the streets.

Unions gave institutional expression to the workers' power and esprit. During the war, unionists often gained say over production methods, work pace, job assignments, and discipline far beyond what their contracts called for. And with mass memberships, financial resources, and experienced organizers, unions provided much of the clout for liberal coalitions and did nuts-and-bolts political work for Democratic candidates in areas where the Democratic Party itself was institutionally weak.

Organized labor was largely a regional phenomenon; at the war's end, two-thirds of all union members lived in just ten states. But where unions were strong, in the Northeast-Midwest manufacturing belt and parts of the West Coast, they used their workplace strength to win political influence and used their political influence to win government benefits and protection for workers. Michigan provided a dramatic example. In the years after World War II, the United Automobile Workers (UAW), United Steelworkers, and their allies succeeded in taking over and vitalizing the state Democratic

Party, culminating in the 1948 election of liberal Democratic governor G. Mennen Williams, who held office for twelve years. Labor went on to help elect two liberal, pro-union Democrats to the Senate, the first time since the Civil War that at least one Michigan seat was not held by a Republican. Under Williams's leadership, Michigan became a pioneer in promoting civil rights, health insurance, recreation, education, and manpower training.

The postwar strike wave revealed the support labor had amassed inside and outside company gates. During the 1946 steel strike, in town after town where local officials and newspapers had once backed companies in fighting unionism, they now remained neutral or sided with labor. In Chicago, grocery stores and pharmacies extended credit to striking packinghouse workers, and priests joined their picket lines.

With few exceptions, businessmen loathed the position labor had achieved, for what it meant for their own enterprises and for the balance of power in society. Most believed, as an ideological and a practical matter, that their enterprises should be run by themselves and themselves alone. Unions compromised their ability to do so. The increased political activism of unions particularly frightened businessmen, many of whom saw any step toward fulfilling labor and liberal plans for greater economic regulation and enhanced state benefits as a threat to their firms' profitability and their personal liberty.

Businesses fought back in a variety of ways. Many companies that did not already have unions used all the resources they could, legal or not, to resist them. Others accepted collective bargaining as a practical necessity but fought to minimize its scope. Many firms won contractual limits on the number of union shop stewards, severe penalties for unauthorized strikes, and clauses that explicitly spelled out management prerogatives over production methods, job assignments, and worker discipline. By showing their willingness to take long strikes, employers made workers painfully aware of the price of militancy.

Many business leaders and trade associations also came to believe in the necessity of a long-term effort to win public opinion to their side. Companies began mounting large-scale education and advertising campaigns, aimed at schoolchildren, the general public, and their own workers, which stressed the virtues of capitalism and the social good created by business. Some business-backed propaganda amounted to little more than thinly disguised efforts to elect Republicans or to win public support for company positions in collective bargaining. Other campaigns more broadly sought to change public attitudes by equating freedom with the free market and labeling any attempt to interfere with the market, by unions or government, as a step toward tyranny. To promote such ideas, companies and wealthy individuals funded policy centers and networks of conservative academics and intellectuals that slowly but effectively made anti–New Deal thinking more respectable and widespread.

In broad terms, the postwar clash between labor and management ended in a draw. For unions, their ability to survive long massive strikes intact represented a historic achievement in itself, a marked contrast to the strike wave after World War I, when unions suffered numerous defeats that contributed to a sharp decline in their membership and power. With the tacit support of the Truman administration, workers won significant wage hikes in the first rounds of postwar bargaining, with gains of 15 percent and more by the large industrial unions. Many smaller unionized companies and even nonunion firms matched these advances, so that for a brief while unions like the Auto Workers and Steelworkers effectively bargained for much larger constituencies than their own members. In subsequent rounds of bargaining, in addition to further wage increases, unions won a variety of new benefits, including health insurance and pension plans to supplement Social Security. For their part, companies won stricter limits on the parameters of bargaining, clear statements of their "right to manage," and greater stability, as one-year contracts were replaced by agreements lasting two, three, or even five years.

Prices

Workers saw some of their wage gains eaten away by inflation. During World War II, the Office of Price Administration (OPA) set prices. To help enforce its regulations, it recruited a mostly female army of volunteer price checkers, giving consumers an unprecedented position in managing the economy. When the war ended, Truman kept price controls in place, hoping to smooth economic reconversion and check postwar inflation.

Businesses hated price controls and public debates over pricing. Setting prices for the goods and services they sold, they believed, was their prerogative alone. Once the war ended, business groups moved into open, vociferous opposition to price regulation. If companies could not set prices at profitable levels, they argued, they would have no incentive for reconverting to peacetime production, creating shortages that would generate inflationary pressure.

Labor saw prices and wages as deeply intertwined. Both determined the working-class standard of living, with any rise in prices diminishing or wiping out gains won through wage increases. Just two days after the Japanese surrender, UAW leader Walter Reuther (soon to be the union's president) explicitly linked wages and prices when he demanded that General Motors grant its workers a 30 percent wage increase without raising car prices, arguing that large wartime profits made this possible. When the company refused, Reuther announced that he would drop the price demand if GM opened its books to prove that it needed higher prices to pay higher wages. The company ignored Reuther's challenge, leading 175,000 autoworkers to walk off their jobs on November 21, 1945.

Reuther's effort to make unions the agents of price stability won little support. Other unions and many federal officials agreed that companies had the capacity to raise wages without raising prices, but they felt it was the government's job, not labor's, to check inflation. The Truman administration ended up establishing the wage/price relationship when it intervened in steel industry negotiations.

In November 1945, U.S. Steel said that it could not meet the United Steelworkers' demand for a wage increase of twenty-five cents an hour without the OPA raising the ceiling on steel prices. Hoping to prevent a strike, Truman appointed a fact-finding board that recommended workers get an increase of eighteen and a half cents an hour (nearly a 20 percent raise). The union accepted the proposed settlement, but U.S. Steel rejected it. On January 21, 1946, three-quarters of a million steelworkers walked off their jobs. Fearful that an interruption of steel production would sabotage the economy, the Truman administration upped the size of the price increase it would permit if the steel companies settled, until U.S. Steel accepted the proposed wage increase, ending the strike. With this settlement, the pattern was set: across the economy, companies and unions signed contracts with wage increases patterned after the steel agreement, while the Truman administration allowed offsetting price hikes. When Reuther finally ended the GM strike, he did so on essentially the same terms.

Truman's back-and-forth on industrial prices, and the general disarray in his administration over reconversion issues, undercut his effort to get Congress to reauthorize price controls, which were set to expire in June 1946. Just before the deadline, Congress sent the president a bill that kept OPA alive but gutted it of much of its power. In a politically costly miscalculation, Truman vetoed the bill, hoping that Congress would come up with a stronger measure. With no controls in effect, prices shot up, led by food costs, which increased 14 percent in a single month.

Consumers, infuriated by rising prices and the turn of events in Washington, began mobilizing, with a heightened sense of being a distinct social constituency as a result of the wartime OPA experience. Coalitions of unions and their female auxiliaries, middle-class consumer groups, and cooperative organizations demonstrated against price increases and sent delegations to

Washington to lobby for reinstating price controls. In Washington and several other cities, they organized boycotts of high-priced meat and milk.

Faced with consumer uproar, Congress passed a new bill extending OPA, but again giving it very limited power. This time Truman signed. Now producers protested, unhappy with any return of controls. Meatpackers sharply reduced the number of animals they slaughtered, creating widespread shortages of meat. Consumers, who generally had supported OPA, began blaming it for the empty meat counters. Shortly before the November 1946 election, Truman lifted controls on meat prices to get packers to up their output. Soon thereafter, he ended most remaining price controls.

Prices soared. In 1947 the consumer price index jumped 14 percent. The following summer, the left-wing Congress of American Women helped organize a new meat boycott that spread from Texas to much of the nation. Three years later, another wave of meat boycotts took place. But by and large, consumers failed to coalesce as a political force.

With consumer pressure ineffective and price controls gone from the arsenal of government economic regulation (though briefly reinstated during the Korean and Vietnam wars), unions turned to a different device to counter inflation: contractual clauses that automatically raised wages when prices went up, so-called cost-of-living adjustments, or COLAs. The idea had been around for some time but began gaining widespread acceptance only in 1948, when at GM's suggestion a COLA was inserted into its contract with the UAW. By the early 1960s, about half of all union contracts had cost-of-living provisions.

COLAs helped protect union members from inflation, but the linkage between prices and union wages nonetheless hurt labor. Many companies began using contract settlements as an occasion for price increases, justifying them by pointing to rising labor costs. By doing so, they shifted some of the public blame for rising prices away from themselves toward labor. Meanwhile, COLAs created a growing distance between those wage earners at least partially protected from rising prices and those who were not, undermining the ability of the labor movement to present itself as a representative of a broad working class, as opposed to simply its own membership. Over time, the gap contributed to the lessening of labor's social and political clout.

"Had Enough?"

Truman's inept handling of reconversion and wage and price determination had a heavy political cost. Not only were prices shooting up, but many civilian goods were unavailable at any cost. A very slow restart of housing construction left millions without decent dwellings. (In Chicago, things were so bad that the city sold off old streetcars, to be converted into houses.) In the November 1946 congressional elections, the Republicans gained control of both houses of Congress for the first time since 1930.

By the time of the 1946 election, many liberals had come to compare Truman unfavorably to Roosevelt, in whose shadow he had the misfortune to labor. His frequent blunders and reversals left him open to ridicule. "To err is Truman," went one popular joke. His replacement of many Roosevelt appointees (including almost the entire cabinet) with figures of less stature and little commitment to reform, in some cases men whose main qualification was political loyalty, dampened the enthusiasm of many of the liberals who had worked hard to keep the Democrats in power.

Truman's failure to control prices and his episodic attacks on labor diminished support for the Democratic Party among working-class voters and their organizations. The president's May 1946 threat to draft striking railway workers led some labor and liberal activists to begin exploring the possibility of building a liberal, labor-based third party. Although in the end, most unions did support the Democrats, many working-class voters stayed home on election day, contributing to an extraordinary low turnout, with less than a third of the electorate voting.

The Republicans proved more successful than the Democrats at getting their core supporters to the polls, while winning new backers. Their campaign slogan—"Had Enough?"—meant had enough of strikes, shortages, inflation, and administration blundering. But it also meant had enough of the New Deal, big government, powerful unions, and Democratic rule. Apparently many people had had enough, for the Republicans made major gains among middle-class voters, especially farmers, professionals, and small businessmen, and significant though smaller gains among Catholics of Eastern European heritage (to a large measure a reaction to Soviet control of their homelands, which some voters blamed on the Democrats).

State contests confirmed the swing away from the New Deal and the widespread fear of the power of labor. The Republicans made major advances in several large states, including New York, where Governor Thomas E. Dewey, considered a likely Republican standard-bearer in 1948, won reelection with a plurality of 680,000 votes. Nebraska, South Dakota, and Arizona passed constitutional amendments outlawing closed shop contracts (agreements that required employers to hire only union members). A tectonic political shift seemed to have occurred.

At least that was what many Republicans and business lobbyists believed. Frustrated by long years of Democratic control, they saw in the new

Congress a long-awaited opportunity to begin dismantling, or at least diminishing, the legal and institutional structures of the New Deal. The changes they managed to effect turned out to be modest, but they did almost entirely impede Truman's own legislative program, which included proposals to expand the federal role in housing, health security, education, and the protection of civil rights and to initiate new large-scale public works programs.

The first step the Republicans took when the 80th Congress convened in January 1947 was largely symbolic, kicking the corpse of their dead tormentor, FDR, by passing a constitutional amendment limiting presidents to two terms in office. (After state ratification, it took effect in 1951 as the Twenty-Second Amendment.) Congress then tried to weaken the Interstate Commerce Act, remove some workers from Social Security coverage, and reduce federal income taxes. The following year it tried to force the sale of Indian lands and exempt some common carriers from antitrust laws.

Truman vetoed thirty-two bills in 1947 and forty-three the following year in an attempt to stymie Congress. In some cases he succeeded in stopping Republican initiatives, while in others, such as the Social Security measure, he only postponed them. In 1947 he twice blocked tax reduction bills, but the following year Congress overrode his veto and succeeded in lowering taxes and requiring married couples to file joint returns.

The latter provision responded to an inequity among states: married couples, with one partner earning substantially more income than the other, could reapportion their income on their separate tax returns to lower their federal taxes if they lived in a community property state, but not if they lived elsewhere. The joint return provision eliminated this interstate disparity, but did so by forcing two-earner couples to pay more taxes than they would if they were unmarried and filed separate returns. The "marriage penalty" created a disincentive for wives to work, in line with a general trend in the immediate postwar years to encourage women to stay at home, reversing the wartime government message.

The most important piece of domestic legislation to come out of the 80th Congress was the 1947 Taft-Hartley Act, a substantial revision of federal labor law, passed over Truman's veto. For many business leaders and some of their political allies, labor law revision had long been a top priority. The 1946 strike wave reinforced their sense that the Wagner Act had given too much power to workers and their unions. Much of the public agreed, disgusted with the disruptions and price hikes associated with strikes; a public opinion poll taken after the 1946 election found that two-thirds of those questioned favored legal changes to control unions.

The National Association of Manufacturers heavily promoted a set of principles that congressional Republicans and southern Democrats drew on in hammering out the new law. In a host of ways, the Taft-Hartley Act moved the balance of power away from unions toward employers. The act outlawed sympathy strikes, mass picketing, secondary boycotts, and closed shops and gave employers the right to sue unions for broken contracts and damages due to strikes. The president could forestall a strike or lockout that he believed would create a national emergency by obtaining an injunction making it illegal during a sixty-day "cooling off" period. Reflecting the growing power of anticommunism, the law took aim at radical labor leaders by requiring union officers to file affidavits swearing that they were not members of the Communist Party. If they refused, their unions would be denied recognition by the National Labor Relations Board (NLRB)—the federal agency set up by the Wagner Act to supervise labor relations—and banned from NLRB-supervised elections to pick collective bargaining agents.

Besides weakening existing unions, Taft-Hartley made it more difficult for the labor movement to grow beyond its established geographic and industrial strongholds. While the Wagner Act gave only workers a say in deciding if an establishment would have a union, Taft-Hartley allowed employers a voice as well, permitting them to express their opinion for or against a union, a right that over time proved effective in retarding union growth. The law also banned the unionization of supervisors and foremen, blocking a movement that had gained momentum during World War II. During the decades after the war, as the number of white-collar and service workers with some supervisory responsibilities swelled, Taft-Hartley effectively placed them off-limits to unionization. Finally, Taft-Hartley gave states the option of outlawing union shop contracts (which required employees to belong to a union to keep their jobs). Eleven states—seven in the South, four in the Midwest—immediately took up the option.

Increasing union organization in the South was a top labor movement priority when World War II ended. Besides boosting overall membership, labor hoped to halt a growing trend among northern manufacturers to relocate production southward, or at least keep such shifts from undermining wage rates and union power in the North. Equally important, unions saw southern organizing as a political strategy, a step toward liberalizing southern politics and weakening the congressional bloc of Republicans and conservative Democrats. In 1946, the CIO launched "Operation Dixie," a well-funded campaign that put 250 organizers in the field. The AFL quickly responded with a southern organizing drive of its own.

Operation Dixie had some early success among workers at branch plants of northern companies and among largely black tobacco, cotton-press, and timber workers. (The AFL also made gains among African Americans, whom, unlike the CIO, it placed in segregated locals.) But the CIO failed badly at its main target, textile manufacturing, the most important southern industry, in the face of fierce opposition from employers, police, and ministers; the rejection by white workers of the group's support of racial equality; and the policy of many textile firms of raising wages to near union rates.

The southern drives already were flagging by the time Taft-Hartley passed. The new law made substantial gains so unlikely that the AFL abandoned its effort. The CIO kept at it at a reduced level until 1953. That year, an estimated 17 percent of nonagricultural workers in the South belonged to a union, roughly half the national percentage and about the same level as when Operation Dixie had begun. With "right-to-work" laws banning union shops in place in a majority of southern states, the uneven regional pattern of union power had become institutionalized.

By the time Congress recessed in June 1948, the large political issues facing the nation when the war ended had been at least partially resolved. The structure of the GI Bill, the end of wartime economic controls, the gutting of the Full Employment Act, the 1946 election returns, and the work of the 80th Congress all seemed to indicate that political and intellectual momentum had shifted away from support for expanded state function toward a more limited notion of the role of government in welfare provision and economic regulation. Wartime rhetoric of rights and freedom and black protest brought new attention to racial inequality, but social and legal practices remained largely unchanged. In the economic arena, the struggle over price controls showed that consumers would not emerge with much power as an organized constituency. Labor proved durable even in clashes with the most powerful corporations, but its structural and moral ascent that began in the mid-1930s came to a halt with the public backlash against strike disruptions, its failure to increase unionization in the South, and the legal restraints of Taft-Hartley. Business, feeling beleaguered by organized labor and liberal government policies, proved effective in containing labor and promoting conservative ideas and politicians. With Truman widely given little chance for winning reelection, a new era of Republican rule, more limited government, and laissez-faire economics seemed likely. But events took a different turn, partly because of the unexpectedly effective reelection campaign undertaken by the president, and partly because of rapidly unfolding international developments that profoundly affected every aspect of American life.

CHAPTER 2

Cold War

World War II radically altered the relationship between the United States and the rest of the world. Prior to the war, international issues had engaged the United States episodically. After it, they loomed large at all times. Politically and psychologically, life within the United States became less isolated from the world beyond its borders. Foreign policy became a driving force in determining both the nature of government and the character of economic development. The contours of that policy, for decades to come, became set during the years immediately after World War II, as American leaders debated the role the country should take abroad and the wartime alliance with the Soviet Union turned to antagonism.

The American Century

In early 1941, *Life* magazine publisher Henry R. Luce, in a highly influential editorial, "The American Century," argued that Americans "have failed to play their part as a world power—a failure which has had disastrous consequences for themselves and all mankind." Long before then, the United States had emerged as the world's leading economy. In 1938, it produced well over a quarter of the world's manufactured goods. But a huge domestic market, a rich endowment of raw materials, and generations of capital accumulation allowed the United States to achieve its great wealth and productive power with only modest engagement outside its borders. On the eve of the Great Depression, the country exported just 8 percent of its manufacturing output. In 1937, Britain and Germany each sold more manufactured goods abroad than did the United States.

American businesses and government leaders had looked abroad for markets, raw materials, and investment opportunities since the late nineteenth century, believing that the country needed to expand internationally to maintain growth, prosperity, and internal harmony. However, as a latecomer with deep ambivalence about colonialism, the United States had obtained only a small overseas empire. The British, French, Portuguese, and Belgian empires dwarfed U.S. holdings, which were more on par with those of the Netherlands, Italy, and prewar Japan. Instead of colonization, investment in areas outside formal U.S. control became the preferred route for the globalization of American capital. By 1930, the United States accounted for over a third of the foreign investment by leading capital-exporting countries, topped only by the United Kingdom.

America's diplomacy and military might lagged behind its economic power. The Senate rejection of the League of Nations and an inward economic and political turn during the Depression reflected isolationist tendencies— or at least skepticism about formal international commitments—among politicians and the general public. So did the very modest size of the country's armed services, which fell after World War I to under a quarter million officers and men. While the East Coast financial community looked abroad for profits, and leaders in the South, a commodity-exporting region, long had been internationalist, much of the country remained protectionist, fearful of overseas entanglements, and culturally hostile to foreign places and people. Even a year after the outbreak of World War II in Europe, isolationist sentiment remained very strong, cutting across the political spectrum and class lines.

The war changed the context for American thinking about its outward relations. By the time it ended, American economic leadership had grown into supremacy without precedent in modern history. To some extent, the gap between the United States and all other countries reflected the pattern of destruction of the conflict itself. The other major powers all suffered from some combination of massive loss of life, extensive physical destruction, economic exhaustion from the demands of military production, and disruption of trade with colonies and hinterlands. By contrast, the United States suffered no significant damage to its industrial infrastructure and comparatively few casualties—405,000 military deaths, versus roughly 400,000 for Britain (with a much smaller population), 4 million for Germany, 2 million for China, 1.5 million for Japan, and 8 million for the Soviet Union (where as many as 16 million civilians died from war-related causes).

During the war, industrial production in the United States soared. When combat ended, it was making half of the world's manufactured goods. In

1947, American workers produced 57 percent of the world's steel, 43 percent of its electricity, 62 percent of its oil, and 80 percent of its automobiles. Three years later, the United States' GNP in absolute terms more than tripled that of the runner-up, the Soviet Union, while per capita it nearly doubled second-ranking Great Britain. Such gaps put the country in an economic class all by itself.

Militarily, too, the United States made a vast leap forward. When the war ended, it had the greatest war-making capacity in human history. With over twelve million men and women in uniform, it lagged behind only the Soviet Union in the size of its ground forces. In every other regard, including naval power, airpower, and a monopoly on atomic weapons, it had clear military superiority. The American military presence stretched around the world, from China, occupied Japan, and islands dotting the Pacific to the Caribbean, where the United States had obtained new bases from Britain to add to its existing ones in Cuba, Puerto Rico, and the Virgin Islands, to Iceland and Europe, where GIs could be found as far east as Austria.

Diplomatic clout grew alongside military power. In the negotiations and international institutions that shaped the postwar world, four and sometimes five "great powers" played the leading roles—the United States, the Soviet Union, Britain, France, and sometimes China. However, France and China had far less say than the "Big Three," and within that group, Britain stood below the Soviet Union and the United States.

The United States rapidly demobilized its armed services after the war. Popular sentiment wanted the troops home quickly, a feeling understandably shared by the GIs themselves. In late 1945 and early 1946, coincident with the height of the strike wave, tens of thousands of soldiers and sailors in Manila, Guam, Honolulu, Paris, Frankfurt, and London held demonstrations and mass meetings demanding repatriation, while families in the states formed hundreds of "Bring Back Daddy" clubs. In the face of political pressure, Truman accelerated demobilization. His desire to move toward a balanced budget kept him shrinking the military until, in June 1947, it had only one and a half million men and women. Defense spending as a percentage of total federal expenditures fell from 83 percent in 1945 to 38 percent in 1947.

But the decision to lower troop strength did not reflect a consensus for a return to prewar levels of international engagement. To the contrary, from the earliest days of the war on, within the military, among key foreign policy makers, and among influential public figures, a determination developed to expand America's diplomatic, economic, and military presence throughout the world, especially in Europe and Asia. This internationalist orientation reflected long-standing concerns as well as shared reactions to recent events.

Many economists, politicians, businessmen, and opinion makers believed that obstacles to international trade had exacerbated the Great Depression. Looking to the end of the war, they worried that the termination of military production and the demobilization of millions of servicemen would bring a return of mass unemployment. Fearing that the United States had saturated its domestic market for goods and capital, they looked abroad for sales and investment opportunities that would prevent a return to prewar economic stagnation. In 1944 congressional testimony, Assistant Secretary of State Dean Acheson bluntly said, "So far as I know, no group which has studied the problem . . . has ever believed that our domestic markets could absorb our entire production under our present system. . . . We cannot have full employment and prosperity in the United States without the foreign markets."

For Acheson and others, World War II presented an opportunity to reshape the international economic order. In "The American Century," Henry Luce argued that the United States now had "to accept wholeheartedly our duty and our opportunity as the most powerful and vital nation in the world and in consequence to exert upon the world the full impact of our influence, for such purposes as we see fit." To preserve its freedom and prosperity, Luce contended, the United States had to shape "the world-environment in which she lives." That meant promoting what he called "a system of free economic enterprise" globally. Luce envisioned a new kind of imperialism that did not seek control of particular territory—"dear old Danzig or dear old Dong Dang"—but the creation of a world economic, political, and moral system centered on the United States.

Luce's bellicose nationalism and equation of unrestrained capitalism with moral rectitude rubbed many New Dealers the wrong way. They too linked future American prosperity to growing trade but envisioned breaking down international economic barriers as part of a campaign for greater social justice. In 1942, Vice President Henry Wallace repudiated Luce in a speech in which he said, "Some have spoken of the 'American Century,' but I say that the century on which we are entering—the century which will come of this war—can and must be the century of the common man." Rather than imposing its might on the world's peoples, the vice president called on the United States to work with forces abroad advocating social change, taking the lead in a people's revolution in which a humanitarian capitalism, acting through multinational development agencies, would uplift the living standards of the world's poor. Deeply critical of Luce, Wallace nonetheless shared his internationalism, seeing the war as a prelude to a new global order, which the United States had an obligation to help shape.

Drawing one set of imperatives from economic fears, policymakers drew another from the war itself. Pearl Harbor ended illusions that the oceanic separation of the United States from Europe and Asia gave it sanctuary from attack. The wartime development of long-range bombers, rockets, and atomic weapons heightened the national sense of vulnerability. Immediately after the bombing of Hiroshima, leading radio commentator H. V. Kaltenborn fretted, "We must assume that with the passage of only a little time, an improved form of the new weapon we use today can be turned against us."

During the war, U.S. military and diplomatic personnel came to believe that the best way to protect the country from future attack would be to meet potential enemies as far from domestic soil as possible. To allow the country to project its power abroad, they began planning an extensive postwar network of overseas bases. In a letter to top Army Air Force generals, Assistant Secretary of War Robert Lovett wrote, "I cannot over-emphasize the importance that I place on this entire base problem." Convinced that letting any power dominate either Europe or Asia would threaten U.S. security, American officials foresaw a need to engage with the geopolitics of those continents for years to come.

A few nationally prominent voices dissented from the emerging consensus in support of a global U.S. role, however defined. Republican senator Robert Taft, whose political base lay among midwestern businesses with little interest in boosting exports, opposed the country's acting as a global policeman or promoting a worldwide New Deal along the lines Wallace envisioned (which Taft saw as another form of imperialism). Taft believed that American benevolence would not necessarily produce a better world nor raise the living standards of its poor. Equally important, he and other conservative Republicans worried about the cost of any grand program of internationalism, which they believed would undermine the domestic economy while making it impossible to eliminate budget deficits or reduce the size of the federal government and the taxes paid to sustain it. As fiscal conservatives and opponents of New Deal state expansion, they feared that the very act of projecting its power would erode the country's values and social structure.

Congressional critics of "globalism"—a word coined in 1943 by German exile Ernest Jackh to characterize Adolf Hitler's ambitions—had some power over foreign policy, with their ability to hold hearings and vote on budgets and treaties. Both Roosevelt and Truman, remembering Woodrow Wilson's failure to win Senate confirmation of the Versailles Treaty, carefully courted Senate Republicans. But by and large, the formulation and execution of foreign policy remained highly centralized in the executive branch, in a cadre of like-minded policymakers from remarkably similar backgrounds, largely insulated from outside pressure.

What would become the postwar foreign policy establishment assembled during the war in the War Department, State Department, and other executive agencies. Secretary of War Henry Stimson recruited a remarkable group of assistants, including Lovett, Robert Patterson, James Forrestal, John Mc-Cloy, Harvey Bundy, and George Harrison, who would play central roles in directing Cold War foreign policy (as would Bundy's sons, McGeorge and William). They came from an extraordinarily thin segment of American life, having gone from Ivy League colleges to Wall Street law firms, a group, Stimson's biographer Godfrey Hodgson noted, "almost as narrowly based, in social and educational terms, as a traditional British Tory Cabinet." Joining them in making foreign policy and national security decisions were elite Foreign Service veterans, like George Kennan; a few top military leaders, like General George Marshall and Admiral William Leahy; and other men like themselves, who moved back and forth between positions in the executive branch (including the intelligence agencies) and major law firms, financial institutions, internationally oriented corporations, and, later on, academic positions. Almost to a man (it was a group almost exclusively of white men), they shared an unquestioned belief in the moral and economic superiority of capitalism and a deep internationalism, formed in reaction to the isolationist sentiment common before the war. Many filtered their view of the world through a kind of country club racialism that took for granted that there was a hierarchy of races and civilizations, with the United States, particularly its Anglo-Saxon population, having a gift and responsibility for leadership. Rarely involved in electoral politics, many foreign policy makers, like Kennan, had little taste for democratic decision making and little belief in the need to engage the public in discussion of foreign affairs. This internationalist elite, serving in administration after administration, gave postwar foreign policy great continuity, even as control of the White House passed from one party to the other.

Some mass organizations tried to influence U.S. foreign policy. Civil rights and African American groups pressed the government to make good on Roosevelt's rhetorical anticolonialism and, in particular, not to prop up the British Empire with financial aid or diplomatic support. Jewish organizations pressed for increasing the number of Jewish refugees allowed into Palestine and, later, for favorable borders and early recognition of Israel. Catholic and Eastern European groups protested the lack of religious freedom in Soviet-occupied areas of Europe. The CIO pushed for maintaining the wartime alliance into the postwar years and for an independent role for labor in international organizations. The AFL wanted government support for international labor but only for noncommunist groups. Such lobbying had only limited success, as foreign affairs, more than other areas of government, remained largely immune to popular pressure.

International Organization

Harry Truman shared the conviction of his key foreign policy advisers that the United States needed to create what Luce called a new "world-environment" in which the country would be both safe and prosperous. In his very first speech as president, he told a joint session of Congress, "In this shrinking world, it is futile to seek safety behind geographical barriers." Truman defined the country's challenge as not defending particular territory or interests but "our American way of life."

Roosevelt had envisioned achieving security and prosperity through new international institutions in which the United States would play a leading role. The United Nations, founded in San Francisco in June 1945, was to be the main vehicle for settling international disputes. Roosevelt hoped that through it the big powers would jointly police world trouble spots and counter threats to their own security. As things turned out, though, the main threats that the big powers perceived came from each other. With each of the Big Five able to block UN action by using their veto power in the Security Council, in the immediate postwar years the most important international issues were largely dealt with outside of the United Nations structure.

The UN did play a role that had not been high on the agenda of its planners: promoting human rights. Roosevelt had suggested the inclusion of a reference to human rights in the proposals for the UN, but at its founding conference it was delegates from smaller nations (the largest bloc of countries attending came from Latin America) who pressed the issue. To the discomfort of U.S. officials, they succeeded in putting in the UN Charter a call for "encouraging respect for human rights and for fundamental freedoms for all without distinction as to race, sex, language, or religion," a slap at, among other things, racial discrimination in the host country. Nonetheless, Secretary of State Edward Stettinius, after being lobbied by liberal groups, including the NAACP, the CIO, and the American Jewish Committee, backed the idea of a UN Commission on Human Rights. It was chaired by Eleanor Roosevelt, and its work led to the UN adoption in December 1948 of a Universal Declaration of Human Rights, a nonbinding, somewhat abstract but sweeping statement of the political, civil, economic, and social rights of individuals and their equality before the law.

While the UN was meant to handle security issues, Allied planners—led
by Harry Dexter White from the U.S. Treasury Department and British
economist John Maynard Keynes—designed another set of institutions to
regulate international economic relations. At a 1944 conference in Bretton
Woods, New Hampshire, forty-four nations founded the International Monetary Fund (IMF) and the International Bank for Reconstruction and Development (World Bank). The IMF aimed to promote trade by setting up a
system to facilitate currency exchange. Member nations agreed to fix the
value of their currency in relation to gold, with gold in turn set at a fixed dollar price. In effect, the dollar became the benchmark for currency exchange.
The agreement allowed rate adjustments only within limited ranges to avoid
destabilizing fluctuations. To help countries with balance of payments problems, the IMF could provide temporary assistance from its reserve fund. The
World Bank aimed to aid the reconstruction of war-torn nations through
loans. Since voting in both institutions was proportional to contributions,
the United States, by far the largest giver, effectively controlled them.

In practice, neither group proved terribly effective, at least in the short
run. In spite of their nominal commitment at Bretton Woods to liberal, nondiscriminatory trade and currency policies, in practice the Western European powers sought to rebuild their devastated economies by retaining
preferential trade arrangements with their colonies and erecting barriers to
cheap American exports that otherwise would undermine home markets for
their own manufacturers. The United States, by contrast, wanted to end
protected trading areas, both to open markets for its own goods (hoping to
forestall a postwar depression) and to prevent economic autarky from leading to new international conflicts.

In part because of such differences, the United States did not send the
bulk of its reconstruction aid to Europe through the World Bank, and until
the late 1950s the IMF remained relatively inactive. Instead, American officials used their country's overwhelming wealth to try to directly counter
the postwar retreat from free-trade principles. In 1945, Britain, desperate for
cash reserves to fund imports, borrowed $3.75 billion from the United States,
agreeing in return to allow the free convertibility of its currency, sterling,
into dollars, to facilitate trade between its huge colonial empire and the
United States. (Assistant Secretary of State for Economic Affairs William
Clayton, who had cofounded the world's largest cotton trading firm, told
financier Bernard Baruch, "We loaded the British loan negotiations with all
the conditions that the traffic would bear.") Similarly, the United States conditioned a large loan to France on that country's agreement to reduce subsidies and currency arrangements that favored its exports in the world market.

A third economic organization, the International Trade Organization (ITO), meant to encourage and regulate trade, never got off the ground. In the process of drafting its charter, European social democrats and developing nations successfully pressed for the inclusion of provisions linking tariff reductions to full employment policies and improved labor standards. American business objected. When Congress failed to even vote on the ITO, it died stillborn. The UN-sponsored General Agreement on Tariffs and Trade, which had been set up as an interim mechanism for tariff reductions, became the substitute for the far more broadly conceived ITO.

The Wartime Alliance Breaks Down

On paper, the World War II victors had created a remarkable set of institutions to order the postwar world, but they failed to help resolve the most important challenges the Allies faced when the war ended. Most immediately, the victorious military powers had to decide what systems of governance would be put in place in those areas where prewar regimes had been obliterated. A political vacuum existed not only in the defeated Axis countries but also in the areas that they had occupied, including virtually all of Eastern Europe, the Balkans, large parts of China, Indochina, Korea, Malaya, and the Dutch East Indies. In some places, rival resistance groups or self-appointed governments claimed authority. In areas that had been French, Dutch, or British possessions, independence forces resisted the idea of the reimposition of colonial rule. With old social hierarchies toppled and ruling ideologies discredited, the future of much of the world seemed up for grabs. The Allied powers also needed to decide what to do about reparations. The Soviet Union and France sought to make Germany pay for the devastation it had wreaked on them, while the many U.S. policymakers feared that overly punitive terms would create economic and political instability. After Hiroshima, the control of atomic weapons became another imperative. Over these issues, the alliance that defeated the Axis powers began to fracture.

By February 1945, when the Big Three leaders met at Yalta in Soviet Crimea to concretize earlier understandings about postwar arrangements, the Red Army stood but forty miles from Berlin, already having fought its way through Eastern and much of Central Europe, greatly reducing Anglo-American leverage. At that meeting, and for four decades thereafter, the United States tried to lessen the Soviet grip on Eastern Europe, but short of all-out war, which it never was willing to engage in, there was little it could do to control events in areas the Soviet army occupied when Germany surrendered. Similarly, the Soviets, as they themselves recognized, had little ability to influence developments in areas occupied by the Americans, most importantly Italy and Japan.

At Yalta, Joseph Stalin, Winston Churchill, and Roosevelt maintained the Big Three alliance by compromising or papering over differences. Germany, they decided, would be divided into U.S., British, French, and Soviet occupation zones, with a joint council, governed by unanimity, addressing the issue of any possible reunification. Britain and the United States, acknowledging the enormous sacrifices that the Soviet Union had made during the war, accepted borders that gave it considerable land from eastern Poland. While not directly challenging Soviet control over Eastern Europe, Churchill and Roosevelt got Stalin to agree to hold free elections in the region and add representatives from the noncommunist London-based government-in-exile to the pro-communist government that the Soviets had installed in Poland. In Asia, the Soviet Union pledged to enter the war against Japan once Germany surrendered and to sign a friendship treaty with the anticommunist Chinese Nationalist government. In return, the United States and Britain agreed to territorial concessions to the Soviets in Manchuria, Sakhalin, and the Kuril Islands.

Almost immediately after Yalta, tensions between the United States and the Soviet Union began to grow, at first largely over Eastern Europe. Unlike Churchill, who had made it clear that he would be happy with a system of mutually recognized spheres of influence, Roosevelt had accepted the idea only reluctantly, at least as applied to Eastern Europe. He worried that in the United States, voters from Eastern European backgrounds, especially Poles, would turn on any politician who failed to resist Soviet efforts to control the region. Furthermore, he did not want to abandon the principle of national self-determination—the notion that nations have the right to self-government—which was a defining feature of the Anglo-American war aims set forth in the 1941 Atlantic Charter. Stalin, in agreeing to hold free elections in Eastern Europe and reorganizing the Polish government, provided Roosevelt with domestic political cover and some expectation that Eastern Europe might be at least partially included in an American-led liberal world system. But there was only so far the Soviet Union would go.

Soviet leaders, above all else, cared about security, making sure that a ring of friendly states protected their country from yet another invasion from the west. At first, without any set design on how to control Eastern Europe or what economic norms should prevail there, they proved flexible about how to guarantee the allegiance of bordering states; in some countries they imposed governments that they tightly controlled, but in others they permitted relatively free elections. Over time, though, the Soviet government showed no hesitation to do whatever it took to prevent hostile regimes from emerging on its borders, including shattering old elites, purging allied communist parties to ensure their loyalty to the Soviet Union, and engaging in wholesale undemocratic acts.

The United States found it hard to accept Soviet control over Eastern Europe. Economic concerns played some role. Before the war, the United States sent only 2 percent of its exports to the region and had only 4 percent of its overseas investments there. However, it saw the exchange of Eastern European foodstuffs for Western European manufactured goods as integral to European prosperity, which in turn figured large in the American vision for its own postwar development. Soviet control made the possibility of such an arrangement uncertain.

Geopolitics and ideology figured more importantly. For one thing, an expanded Soviet-controlled landmass raised fears among American security experts of the possibility that Soviet military pressure might weaken Western European ties to the United States. For another thing, some policymakers, like Truman and Ambassador to the Soviet Union Averell Harriman, found the way the Soviets played loose with the idea of political self-determination offensive. Stalin and his subordinates liked to point out the Anglo-American tolerance for undemocratic practices in zones they influenced, such as their support of a repressive right-wing regime in Greece. But a faith in their own goodness, deep-seated in American culture, allowed leaders and the public in the United States to be largely undisturbed by such contradictions. As the African American press and civil rights groups noted, American officials, like former South Carolina senator James F. Byrnes, who succeeded Stettinius as secretary of state, pressed the Soviets to allow free elections in Eastern Europe while ignoring a blatant lack of democracy in the South.

For American policymakers, Poland emerged as a key test of Soviet intentions. Shortly after Yalta, Roosevelt complained about the very minimal steps the Soviets took to restructure the Polish government. After Roosevelt's death, Truman raised the issue again in a tense meeting at which he scolded Soviet foreign minister Vyacheslav Molotov. What the Americans saw as an emerging Soviet trend to ignore past agreements and act unilaterally undermined their trust in their wartime ally, just as American decisions to shut the Soviets out of such key matters as the control of atomic weapons and the occupation of Japan would confirm Soviet suspicions of Western hostility.

Truman's assumption of power brought a shift in the tone of American diplomacy. Truman had a tactical decisiveness but strategic confusion that reflected his personality and his insecurity about foreign affairs, coming as he did from a near total lack of experience in dealing with them. More bluntly anticommunist than Roosevelt, Truman put more faith in those advisers he inherited from FDR who wanted to take a tough anti-Soviet stance than in those who wanted to be more accommodating. He held some strange ideas about the Soviet Union, speaking favorably of Stalin as resembling his own political mentor, Kansas City Democratic boss Tom Pendergast, and fretting that other Soviet leaders might block Stalin from working out mutually acceptable arrangements with the United States, a profound misreading of Soviet power. Uncertain in his early years in office, Truman veered between confronting the Soviet Union and trying to accommodate it, before settling into a hard-line position.

In July 1945, Truman, Stalin, Churchill, and Clement Attlee (who replaced Churchill as prime minister when a British election brought the Labour Party to power), meeting at Potsdam, just outside of Berlin, worked out what was meant to be a temporary agreement on German reparations. The Soviets, seeking to rebuild their shattered economy, got the right to all reparations from their occupation zone, which they immediately began stripping of industrial equipment. The industrial heartland of Germany, though, lay in the western zones, where the Soviets were to get a quarter of the reparations, to be partially offset by food sent west from the Soviet zone. The conference also agreed to a new border that gave Poland a great deal of German territory.

Truman felt bolstered in his bargaining at Potsdam when he learned of the successful first test of the atomic bomb. He casually mentioned the new weapon to Stalin (who through spies already knew of its development), but the issue of atomic control did not come up. Nonetheless, for both sides the beginning of the atomic age had profound implications. For the United States, it led to a toughening of its bargaining positions, including its determination to keep the Soviet Union from playing any significant role in the occupation of Japan. For the Soviet Union, it led to a crash program to develop its own atomic weapons.

With long-term arrangements for Germany, Eastern Europe, and atomic weapons remaining to be worked out, new conflicts arose between the United States and the Soviets, this time over the Near East, specifically Iran and Turkey. Early in the war, the United States, Britain, and the Soviet Union had agreed to jointly occupy Iran to keep it from coming under German control. After the war, the Soviets tried to win concessions from Iran by stalling on an agreed-to troop withdrawal and encouraging separatist movements in the northern part of the country.

Oil lay at the heart of the dispute. Iran was a major oil producer, with Britain being the greatest beneficiary of its wealth; the Anglo-Iranian Oil Company, in which the British government held a majority interest, enjoyed a monopoly on Iranian oil production. Both the United States and the Soviet Union sought oil concessions of their own, with the Soviets tying their troop withdrawal to such an agreement. Iran also had strategic importance because of its proximity to other oil producers, most notably Saudi Arabia and Kuwait, where major oil discoveries had been made in the late 1930s.

During World War II, the United States had supplied nearly 90 percent of the oil used by the Allies. The highly mechanized war convinced American policymakers like Secretary of the Navy James Forrestal of the strategic importance of petroleum, already critical to the domestic economy. Government leaders, believing, wrongly as it turned out, that domestic oil reserves were running out, looked abroad for new supplies, especially to the Middle East. To this end, Roosevelt authorized Lend-Lease aid (defense-related material the United States sent to allies) for Saudi Arabia and on his way home from Yalta met with King Ibn Saud. Keeping the Middle East in the Anglo-American orbit became an increasingly important American strategic priority in the postwar years.

Partially for this reason, Truman responded to the Soviet actions in Iran with a firm stand, insisting that they leave the country. Equally important, he believed that future good relations with the Soviet Union depended on forcing it to live up to all its agreements. Like many U.S. policymakers, Truman thought that the outbreak of World War II had proven the futility of trying to appease expansionist dictatorships. Believing that the Soviet Union had territorial designs on Iran, Truman felt that standing up to it there would discourage similar pushes elsewhere. After much maneuvering, the Iranian and Soviet governments resolved the crisis by agreeing to a withdrawal of Soviet troops in return for the establishment of a joint oil company (which the Iranian parliament later refused to establish). The Soviet retreat convinced Truman of the efficacy of a hard-line stance.

An overlapping confrontation involving Turkey proved even more volatile. Prior to Potsdam, the Soviet Union had demanded that Turkey lease it bases on the Dardanelles strait, a strategic pathway to its southern flank, and cede it territory once part of Georgia. At Potsdam, Truman agreed in principle to a revision of the 1936 Montreux Treaty that gave Turkey sole control over the strait. However, the Soviets rejected Truman's proposal for an internationalization of the waterway. As U.S. relations with the Soviet Union chilled, and the Soviets put pressure on Turkey by holding periodic army maneuvers in neighboring Bulgaria, Truman came to believe that the

Soviets were planning to use force to take control of the Dardanelles and bordering Turkish territory. As in the case of Iran, he decided to stand firm.

Tensions peaked in August 1946 when the Soviets presented Turkey with a proposal for joint Turkish-Soviet responsibility for defending the strait. The United States, Britain, and Turkey all rejected the proposal. Fearing a Soviet attack on Turkey (though little evidence pointed in that direction), the Truman administration decided to resist any incursion even at the risk of war. To demonstrate its commitment, it sent a carrier-led naval task force to the eastern Mediterranean, beginning a U.S. military presence in the region maintained continuously thereafter. The Soviet Union kept pressing for a role in defending the strait, but less insistently, while withdrawing its forces from Bulgaria. Once again, Truman concluded, standing firm paid off.

The Iron Curtain

In the winter of 1945–46, with tensions high over Eastern Europe, Iran, and Turkey, a series of messages and speeches in the United States and the Soviet Union crystallized the notion that the world was dividing into two great antagonistic blocs, this time not the Allied and Axis powers but communist and capitalist groupings. Very rapidly, ideas and rhetorical tropes that would shape discourse and policy for decades to come became established.

On the American side, the hardening of lines began with a long telegram to the State Department sent by George Kennan, the number two man at the U.S. embassy in Moscow. Kennan wrote in response to an inquiry about what lay behind a Soviet decision not to participate in the IMF and World Bank. Together with a subsequent Soviet rejection of a U.S. loan offer, made only after repeated efforts by the USSR to get reconstruction assistance and then burdened with conditions bound to be found objectionable, the decision not to participate in the new organizations signaled that the Soviet leadership had decided that the benefits of integrating their country's economy with the emerging U.S.-dominated bloc were too small and the risks (including providing the IMF with extensive economic data) too great. Instead, it would go it alone. Kennan, however, all but ignored the specific issue he was asked to address. Instead, he wrote a long analysis of the outlook of the Soviet leadership that dismissed the possibility of working amicably with it. Kennan described Soviet leaders as "committed fanatically to the belief that with the US there can be no permanent modus vivendi, that [for them] it is desirable and necessary that the internal harmony of our society be disrupted, our traditional way of life be destroyed, the international authority of our state be broken, if Soviet power is to be secure." Soviet power,

Kennan continued, was "impervious to logic of reason," being only "sensitive to logic of force."

Kennan's dark view of the Soviet Union won quick favor among Washington policymakers. Forrestal, one of the most militant anticommunists in the administration, widely circulated Kennan's missive within the government. Within a week both Michigan senator Arthur Vandenberg, a key Republican voice on foreign policy, and Secretary of State Byrnes, until then a believer in the efficacy of high-level talks with Soviet leaders, gave speeches laying out a tougher policy toward the Soviet Union. Just a week after that, with Truman at his side, Churchill, speaking in Fulton, Missouri, called for an ongoing Anglo-American alliance to prevent war, while characterizing the Soviet Union as having placed an "iron curtain" across Europe. Like Kennan, Churchill portrayed the Soviet Union as constantly pressing to expand its power. Even before Churchill's speech, public trust of the Soviet Union had been diminishing. His vivid image of a divided world further reduced belief among opinion makers and the public in the possibilities for Soviet-American cooperation.

In the Soviet Union, too, public rhetoric took a turn away from the wartime language of big power cooperation. In a February 1946 speech, Stalin reiterated the Leninist belief that the dynamics of capitalism and imperialist rivalry led to war, calling for a new program of industrial development to ensure Soviet security in the face of any eventuality. After Churchill's Iron Curtain speech, Stalin attacked the former prime minister as a warmonger. The Soviet leader, however, avoided associating the United States with Churchill's views, continuing to believe in the likelihood of future economic and political rivalry between the United States and Britain, which he thought would present favorable opportunities for the Soviet Union.

Over the course of 1946, the emerging sense of rival, even antagonistic blocs manifested itself in the failure to resolve a number of key issues. After a fierce debate within the Truman administration about whether or not to share information about atomic energy with the Soviet Union, in March 1946 the United States presented a plan for the control of atomic weapons. Developed by a state department consulting board headed by Tennessee Valley Authority chairman David E. Lilienthal, under the supervision of Dean Acheson, it called for the creation of an international agency that would have exclusive control over nuclear weapons, material, and development. However, until the new structure took charge, the United States would retain its atomic weapons monopoly while other countries would be subject to international inspections. Unlikely to win Soviet support in any case, the plan became even less so after modified by Bernard Baruch, appointed by

Truman as the U.S. delegate to the United Nations Atomic Energy Commission. Baruch's plan stipulated that no country could use its Security Council veto to block either inspections or sanctions connected to nuclear weapons control. After long, fruitless discussions, the Soviet Union introduced its own plan that called for, first, the destruction of all existing atomic bombs and an international agreement not to develop or use them, and only then discussion of international controls. In the end, no agreement emerged, and both countries proceeded with large-scale atomic weapons programs.

The United States and the Soviet Union came to loggerheads over Germany as well. The Potsdam provisions for Germany began unraveling in mid-1946. In May, General Lucius Clay, the head of military forces in the U.S. occupation zone, worried about deteriorating economic conditions, halted the dismantling of industrial plants to be sent to the French and Soviets as reparations. To spark an economic recovery, Clay proposed an administrative and economic merger of the four occupation zones. Secretary of State Byrnes then suggested a treaty guaranteeing German disarmament for twenty-five years, which he hoped would address Soviet and French security concerns and open the way toward reunifying Germany. The Soviets, however, rejected the proposal. Stalin hoped, in the long run, for a unified, demilitarized Germany friendly to the Soviet Union. In the short run, though, the Soviet Union wanted to retain control over its occupation zone to keep taking reparations from it. Once the USSR rebuffed Byrnes's initiative, the United States began moving toward unifying the western occupation zones without Soviet involvement.

In spite of their confrontational language and multiplying disputes, neither the United States nor the Soviet Union had any serious fear of military conflict with one another in the foreseeable future. Both countries continued to demobilize, with the Soviet army shrinking from over eleven million troops during the last year of the war to less than three million in 1948. Both countries sought to avoid an irrevocable breakdown of relations, while positioning themselves to be in an advantageous position if one occurred.

Within the United States, though, those still holding forth for Soviet-American cooperation became increasingly marginalized. In September 1946, Truman fired the last important advocate within his administration of a conciliatory stance toward the Soviet Union, Henry Wallace, who had become commerce secretary after leaving the vice presidency. Wallace, the only remaining New Dealer in the cabinet, had been privately critical of Byrnes's "get tough" policy toward the Soviet Union and the Baruch Plan for atomic control. Nonetheless, Truman kept on the former vice president, a popular figure among liberals and leftists, in part with an eye toward the upcoming congressional elections. But once Wallace went public with his criticism, a crisis ensued. In a speech that he had cleared with the president, Wallace told a New York political rally that the Soviet Union had legitimate security fears, given its history of invasions from the west. It needed to be reassured, he argued, that "our primary objective is neither saving the British Empire," a dig at Churchill's proposed Anglo-American alliance, "nor purchasing oil in the Near East with the lives of American soldiers." The United States "should recognize that we have no more business in the *political* affairs of Eastern Europe than Russia has in the *political* affairs of Latin America, Western Europe and the United States." Wallace's support for at least a temporary Soviet sphere of influence in Eastern Europe created a public uproar and infuriated Byrnes, who at the very moment was attending a big power foreign ministers meeting in Paris. Arguing that Wallace's statements undercut his position, Byrnes in effect told the president that either he or Wallace had to go, leading Truman to ask Wallace for his resignation.

Creating Two Blocs

When an irrevocable breakdown in Soviet-American relations came, it arose out of economic and political crises in Western and Southern Europe, not in Soviet-controlled territory. Western Europe proved far slower in reviving economically than United States officials had anticipated. In 1947, its industrial output still had not come close to prewar levels and, disconcertingly, was falling rather than rising. Labor strife and a depletion of gold and dollar reserves needed to import raw materials, food, and manufactured goods hampered recovery. So did an exceptionally severe winter in 1946–47. As transportation ground to a halt, shortages of food and coal developed and unemployment soared. The resulting misery, from the American point of view, added to the political danger associated with the strong position of the European left. In country after country, communists had led wartime resistance movements, winning enormous moral credibility. When the war ended, in many nations they emerged as the largest single political force, joining coalition governments, including in Italy and France. Social democrats, agrarian parties, labor unions, and antifascist committees joined with the communists in complex patterns of coalition and contest in pressing for economic democratization, a redistribution of political power, and some socialization of national resources, challenging the American vision of a capitalist world order.

The economic enfeeblement of Europe converged with the left's thrust for power in Greece, with profound consequences. Great Britain had long viewed Greece as a vital link to its colonial interests in the Middle East and the Indian subcontinent. When, after confronting a strong communist-led resistance movement, German occupiers, facing the possibility of being cut off by the advancing Soviet army, retreated, British troops moved in, working with the Greek king to establish a conservative government and contain left-wing influence. A 1944 government order to the resistance movement to disarm led to a bitter armed conflict between left- and right-wing forces that continued on and off for half a decade.

With its wartime losses and postwar difficulties, Britain's imperial posture outstretched its economic capacity. The cost of maintaining troops in Syria, Egypt, India, and Greece; providing financial aid to Greece and Turkey; and paying occupation costs in Germany were draining the nation's economic resources, especially its dollar reserves. In February 1947, Britain informed the State Department that it would have to terminate its aid to Greece and Turkey, asking the United States to take over its role.

The Truman administration immediately agreed to do so. Administration officials believed that the Greek communists, in leading a guerrilla movement in northern Greece against the right-wing government, were acting at the behest of the Soviet Union, part of a broad communist push toward the Middle East and its oil riches. In reality, Stalin was scrupulously sticking to an agreement with Churchill to stay out of Greece. What outside support the Greek guerrillas did get came, over Soviet objections, from Yugoslavian, Bulgarian, and Albanian communists. Not understanding the complex tensions within the communist world, high-ranking officials like Acheson, Clayton, Kennan, and Forrestal, in their fear of what they had come to believe was inherent Soviet expansionism and of the cumulative effect of European countries adopting socialist policies on American trade and prosperity, decided that the United States had a vital strategic interest in making sure that the left did not come to power in Greece.

Truman needed congressional approval for aid to Greece and Turkey, which presented a serious challenge. The 1946 election had bolstered the ranks of conservative Republicans skeptical of international obligations and their cost, while most liberals preferred working through the United Nations to unilateral action. To garner congressional votes and public backing, the president appealed for his aid proposal in sweeping, near-apocalyptic terms. Truman described the particular problems of Greece and Turkey as part of a global struggle between "alternative ways of life," one based on democracy and freedom, the other on terror and oppression. "The policy of the United States," he said in announcing what came to be called the Truman Doctrine, must be "to support free peoples who are resisting attempted subjugation by armed minorities or by outside pressures." "If we falter in our leadership," Truman concluded, "we may endanger the peace of the world—and we shall surely endanger the welfare of our own nation." Truman's creation of a Federal Employee Loyalty Program to ferret out subversives within the government just nine days after his speech on Greek and Turkish aid heightened the sense of threat posed by world communism. Some critics of the president's pronouncements (if not necessarily his aid program itself), like well-known political writer Walter Lippmann, warned of the dangers of an "ideological crusade" that would draw the country into battles all over the world. But the president's expansive rhetoric and dire warnings proved sufficient to win congressional passage of his program by wide margins. At least rhetorically, the United States had committed itself to resisting communism everywhere.

In Greece, American officials, using aid as a club, became deeply involved in shaping almost every aspect of public life, from the composition of the cabinet to the policies of the trade union movement. Not wanting direct military involvement, the United States pressured Britain to keep a reduced military contingent in the country, which it did until 1954. Meanwhile, U.S. officials supported or condoned wholesale violations of civil liberties, including mass executions of political prisoners, as preferable to communist victory. This initial American exercise in orchestrating another country's anticommunist struggle proved successful when, in the fall of 1949, the left-wing guerrilla movement collapsed.

Well before then, the United States had launched a much larger European assistance program, the European Recovery Program (ERP), better known as the Marshall Plan, to jump-start the stagnating European economies. George Marshall, who had replaced Byrnes as secretary of state, proposed the program in June 1947. American leaders had genuine humanitarian concerns, but they also saw European economic recovery as a way to diminish support for the political left. An element of economic self-interest came into play, too. With Europe importing far more goods from the United States than it exported to it, a growing "dollar gap" raised the specter that soon European countries would not have the currency reserves they needed to continue trade with the United States.

American planners believed that European recovery required multinational economic integration, which would expand markets, facilitate the sharing of resources and industrial capacity, and allow the reindustrialization of Germany, which France as much as the Soviet Union would never tolerate on a stand-alone basis. Rather than propose a specific plan, Marshall called on the Europeans themselves to develop a recovery program. To avoid the negative tone of the Greek and Turkish aid effort, which had stressed resisting communism rather than the positive gains of economic growth and cooperation, administration officials invited the Soviet Union to the planning meetings for the program (though they had no desire to actually have it participate). The Soviets came but soon walked out, objecting to the priority the plan gave to using German production to promote European recovery rather than to pay reparations, as well as the requirements that aid recipients share economic data and integrate their recovery efforts. Soviet leaders then forced the Eastern European countries that wanted to join the plan to walk away, too. The sixteen nations that remained developed a complex program for immediate relief, long-term aid, currency stabilization, and increased U.S. investment and trade, all accompanied by joint economic planning.

In late 1947, Truman sent to Congress a bill to fund the ERP with an initial fifteen-month outlay of $6.8 billion, nearly a fifth of the total federal budget. At first, the plan faced considerable opposition. With Taft on the right and Wallace on the left criticizing the proposal, Congress moved slowly. Many members were as concerned with the huge cost of the plan as with its foreign policy implications. Soon, though, developments in Eastern Europe led Congress to act.

Soviet leaders had not expected the United States to maintain a prolonged postwar presence in Europe and assumed that Anglo-American rivalry would preclude a united, anti-Soviet capitalist front. The Marshall Plan proved both these assumptions wrong and raised the specter of a restoration of German power. In response, Soviet leaders moved to consolidate control over their sphere. To redirect their economies eastward, the Soviet Union negotiated a series of bilateral trade agreements with its Eastern European neighbors. To assert political control, it set up the Communist Information Bureau, which joined together the Soviet, Eastern European, French, and Italian communist parties. Across Eastern Europe, combinations of Soviet and local communist initiatives forced noncommunist parties out of government coalitions. The last Eastern European country to have significant noncommunist forces in its leadership, Czechoslovakia, fell in line in early 1948, when its Communist Party used mass demonstrations, violence, and a rigged election to assume control. The only holdout from Soviet domination was Yugoslavia, whose Communist Party, led by Josip Tito, refused to submit to orders from Moscow.

The Soviet crackdown in Eastern Europe, especially the events in Czechoslovakia, ended congressional hesitation about the Marshall Plan, which in early April won approval by very large margins. Over the next four years, the United States spent $13 billion on Marshall Plan aid. American aid helped reduce balance of payments problems, eliminate industrial bottlenecks, and encourage transnational economic cooperation. Western Europe entered a period of unprecedented growth.

At least in the short run, the Marshall Plan went counter to the hope of the American foreign policy elite to create a world of free markets, free trade, and free currency exchange. European integration created the basis for a new regional tariff union that favored trade within its boundaries. But overall, American leaders proved remarkably successful in moving areas outside of Soviet control toward something approaching the liberal, capitalist world economic system that they saw as critical for American prosperity.

The price for this accomplishment proved high, a long era of international tension and the increasing militarization of American society. As both camps hunkered down for prolonged conflict, the United States created structures for carrying out its side of what Walter Lippmann termed "the Cold War." In mid-1947, Congress passed the National Security Act, unifying the armed services under centralized civilian control by creating a cabinet post of secretary of defense with supervisory power over the Army, Navy, and a new, autonomous Air Force and giving statutory authority to the Joint Chiefs of Staff to coordinate military advice and operations. (Two years later Congress created the Department of Defense, with the three armed services placed within it.) The law also established the Central Intelligence Agency (CIA) to coordinate military and diplomatic intelligence and undertake other actions authorized by yet another new creation, the National Security Council (NSC), a top-level interagency group, headed by the president.

In 1948, the NSC authorized the CIA to create a covert operations staff to undertake a broad range of activities, from propaganda and economic warfare to sabotage and aiding underground guerrilla groups. Very quickly, the CIA got deeply involved in Western European politics, using money and persuasion to get noncommunist trade unionists to break with communist labor organizations and promoting and funding noncommunist parties in the April 1948 Italian election. That same spring, Congress reinstituted the military draft and raised authorized troop levels. In the course of a single year, the country embarked on an unprecedented level of peacetime military preparedness and the creation of a large, permanent national security apparatus at the very center of the government.

Meanwhile, a new, frightening conflict developed with the Soviet Union. In spring of 1948, the French succumbed to American and British pressure, agreeing to merge the three countries' occupation zones to create a western

German entity, which would be included in the Marşhall Plan. To assure the French that they would not again face a hostile Germany, the United States pledged to keep its occupation troops in place for a prolonged period. The Soviets responded to these steps toward creating a western Germany integrated into an American-led bloc by harassing travel between western Germany and Berlin, which lay inside the Soviet occupation zone and like Germany itself had been divided into four occupation zones. When the Western powers announced that they would introduce a new currency in their zones, the Soviet Union began blocking train and truck traffic to the old capital, arguing that having effectively abandoned the idea of German reunification, its onetime allies should leave Berlin.

Faced with a very dangerous situation, Truman decided that the United States would refuse to abandon its presence in the city but avoid a direct military confrontation by using an airlift to supply it. A long, tense stalemate ensued. As positions hardened, the United States, Britain, and France moved toward the creation of a self-governing West Germany, all but accomplished by the summer of 1949. Meanwhile, the United States, Canada, and ten European allies negotiated a self-defense alliance, the North Atlantic Treaty Organization (NATO), to assure the Western Europeans that the United States would come to their defense if they were attacked by the Soviet Union or a resurgent Germany.

The Soviet Union, having seen its effort to prevent a division of Germany boomerang, conceded defeat. In May 1949, it called off its blockade, having alienated Germans on both sides of the east-west divide and solidified a western anti-Soviet alliance. But there was no going back. Within just four years after the end of World War II, the United States and the Soviet Union had gone from being allies to being leaders of opposing political-economic-military-ideological blocs, increasingly entrenched in their hostility to one another.

CHAPTER 3

Stalemate in Washington

On November 2, 1948—election day—Harry Truman slipped out the back door of his home in Independence, Missouri, where he had come at the end of a hard campaign, and, accompanied only by Secret Service officers, drove to an all but deserted hotel in the small resort town of Excelsior Springs. He went to bed early. When he awoke briefly at midnight, he later recalled, a radio announcer said that he was "undoubtedly beaten," confirming the predictions of the polls and major newspapers. Four hours later, a Secret Service agent, after hearing a radio report that the tide had turned, woke up the president. Long before dawn and the arrival of the final tallies, Truman declared, "We've got 'em beat," and left his hideaway.

The 1948 election provided the first opportunity after World War II for Americans to clearly indicate what direction they wanted their nation to go. Earlier contests gave some sense of their will, but local dynamics had played a role along with national issues. Only every four years, in presidential elections, did voters across the country get a chance express a verdict on the same candidates, the policies they promoted, and the visions they put forth.

Developments abroad played a role in the 1948 election, but only indirectly. Truman's handling of foreign policy rarely emerged as an electoral issue. Nonetheless, it proved a great asset. For one thing, it gave him a measure of stature that he had failed to achieve in his handling of domestic matters. For another thing, it helped rally to his side anticommunist liberals, who otherwise had little enthusiasm for his presidency. By adroitly winning bipartisan congressional support for his major foreign policy moves, Truman forced the election to be fought in large part as a referendum on the New Deal, terrain that proved hospitable.

Liberalism Divided

By the time of the 1948 election, liberals had split into two antagonistic camps. Both thought of themselves as heirs to Roosevelt and defenders of the New Deal, but they divided over policy toward the Soviet Union and the role of domestic communists. Tensions between them broke into the open after the 1946 election, during which anticommunist attacks had figured in some contests. The Democratic defeats forced liberals to rethink their strategies.

One group, clustered around the Progressive Citizens of America (PCA), formed in early 1947, sought a flexible policy toward the Soviet Union while fighting at home for a broad extension of the New Deal. Disillusioned with Truman and the Democratic Party, they explored the idea of realigning American politics by creating a new liberal party, unrestrained by conservative elements. Recognizing that the communists had important organizational resources, especially within the labor movement, they were willing to work with them. The idea of a third party became a reality when Henry Wallace—who since leaving the cabinet had been barnstorming the country attacking Truman's foreign policy, calling for a revival of the New Deal, and sharply criticizing racial segregation—agreed to be its standard-bearer.

Anticommunist liberals clustered around the Americans for Democratic Action (ADA), formed shortly after the PCA. They viewed both the Soviet Union and domestic communists as antidemocratic and untrustworthy. Working with either, they believed, betrayed liberal principles. Additionally, they recognized that the conservative tide in the country, evident in the 1946 election, meant that any group that accepted communists in its ranks would be opening itself to attack. ADAers concluded from the election that liberals needed to trim their sails, build alliances with centrists, and remain in the Democratic Party. Like Wallace's backers, they saw Truman as an inept hack, squandering the Roosevelt inheritance. They so desperately sought an alternative that they tried to recruit wartime hero General Dwight Eisenhower for the role, knowing almost nothing of his political beliefs. But in the end, swayed by Truman's foreign policy and his veto of the Taft-Hartley bill, and without any other choice, they reluctantly accepted him as their candidate.

As more and more liberals embraced anticommunism as a central ideological belief, subsuming other causes to it, the split in the left-liberal world spread from organization to organization, weakening or destroying many of them. Fighting between pro-communist and anticommunist factions racked the American Veterans Committee, set up as a liberal alternative to the

American Legion. The Southern Conference for Human Welfare, the most important organization in the South supporting New Deal liberalism and racial equality, lost more and more of its anticommunist members as the organization drifted into the Wallace camp, so weakening it that it folded after the 1948 election. The National Student Association, founded in 1947, managed to keep both liberal camps within it by rejecting a proposal to ban individual communists from belonging, instead barring all national organizations from membership and picking its leaders through local student governments, which made it unlikely that Communist Party members would have much power.

The widening chasm on the left particularly impacted the CIO. Immediately after the war, most CIO leaders, whether they allied with the Communist Party or opposed it, promoted an extension of the New Deal and called for maintaining an alliance with the Soviet Union, which they worked alongside within the newly established World Federation of Trade Unions. But in a much more conservative political environment, many CIO activists came to see the communists in their organization as an unacceptable liability and fell in line with the Truman administration's hardening anti-Soviet foreign policy. The CIO took no official position on the Truman Doctrine, which AFL and railroad brotherhood leaders enthusiastically backed. But sharing the view that future national prosperity depended on expanded trade, CIO leaders found the humanitarian and economic thrust of the Marshall Plan more acceptable. After George Marshall came to the 1947 CIO convention to personally promote the ERP, the labor federation endorsed his proposal.

In early 1948, CIO president Philip Murray began using his power to line up opposition to the Wallace third-party effort. Wallace's break with the Democratic Party, along with Truman's veto of Taft-Hartley, led many labor leaders who had admired the former vice president to shift their allegiance to the president. Having built their organization under the shelter of sympathetic federal policy, CIO leaders feared for its future if the Republicans took over the White House. With Murray making opposition to the Wallace campaign a test of loyalty, in the end only a handful of unions supported it.

Even as the Democrats fractured on their left, civil rights led to a breakoff on their right. In 1948, the treatment of African Americans emerged as a national electoral issue for the first time since Reconstruction. In many parts of the country, local black activists and their allies had begun pressing for equal access to the vote, jobs, housing, and schools. As large numbers of southern blacks moved to northern cities, they became a key electoral constituency in closely contested industrial states like New York, Ohio,

Michigan, Illinois, and Pennsylvania, leading the parties to vie for their support. International developments also thrust the issue of racial discrimination forward. The wartime rhetoric of democracy and antifascism heightened sensitivity about racism at home, as did the UN commitment to universal human rights. Flagrant racial injustice within the United States made it difficult to make a convincing case that the Soviet-American rivalry pitted democracy against totalitarianism. Civil rights organizations moved to take advantage of the new circumstances, filing lawsuits, petitioning the UN to investigate racial discrimination in the United States, and threatening black resistance to the draft if the armed services were not desegregated.

Upon becoming president, Truman, both sets of whose grandparents had owned slaves, zigzagged back and forth on civil rights, sensitive to the political pressures to attack discrimination but fearful of losing southern support in Congress and the 1948 election. Unlike Roosevelt, Truman publicly backed a permanent Fair Employment Practices Committee (FEPC), though he failed to win its congressional approval. In 1946, under pressure from black protest groups and their white allies, who organized a fifteen-thousand-person march to the Lincoln Memorial, and personally shocked by the brutal attacks in the South on black war veterans, Truman established a Committee on Civil Rights to come up with recommendations for action and appointed African Americans to a number of high-profile positions.

Pressure on Truman to take a strong civil rights stand grew as the 1948 election neared, since his likely opponents had solid records of opposing discrimination. New York governor Thomas E. Dewey had signed the first state law outlawing racial and religious discrimination in employment. Wallace held speaking tours in the South where he refused to address racially segregated audiences. In June 1947, Truman became the first president to address a meeting of the NAACP. That October, his civil rights committee came out with a sweeping report. Saying that "the National Government . . . must take the lead in safeguarding the civil rights of all Americans," it recommended the passage of a federal anti-lynching law, federal legislation making police brutality a crime, a poll tax ban, comprehensive voting rights legislation, an end to discrimination in the armed services, a federal FEPC, and an upgraded civil rights division in the Justice Department. The committee did not conceive of civil rights as simply an issue of the treatment of African Americans, as it also called for statehood for Alaska and Hawaii, home rule and voting rights in presidential elections for the District of Columbia, and compensation for the property Japanese Americans lost when forcibly evacuated during the war.

Truman accepted the report and in February 1948 asked Congress for legislation implementing many of its recommendations. He also promised to issue executive orders ending discrimination in the federal civil service and segregation in the armed services. But then, with southern Democrats up in arms—Mississippi senator James Eastland said Truman's message to Congress was proof that the government was controlled by "mongrel minorities" out to "Harlemize" the nation, while Texas senator Tom Connally called it a lynching of the Constitution—the president retreated, failing to issue the promised executive orders and allowing Democratic leaders to sit on the proposed legislation.

Five months later, civil rights splintered the Democrats at their convention. Truman backed a vague platform plank calling on Congress to use its authority to protect civil rights, sparking opposition from delegates who found it too weak and those who found it too strong. Southern Democrats saw Truman's calls for national civil rights action as a threat to the racial structure of power that most of them believed in and benefited from. Fearful that an expanding, nationalizing federal government would destroy the ability of their home region to maintain the system of racial oppression that kept wages low and political power in the hands of small cliques, southern white leaders adopted states' rights as the ideological basis for the defense of racial and class privilege. A group of southern delegates demanded that the Democratic convention amend its platform to declare civil rights a state issue.

A second civil rights challenge came from a coalition of black, labor, and liberal delegates, spearheaded by the ADA. It put forth an alternative civil rights plank that essentially consisted of proposals Truman himself had made. They believed in civil rights on principle but also feared that Wallace would win significant black and liberal support if the Democrats failed to take a clear stand on the issue. (The Republicans represented a threat, too, since their convention had called for anti-lynching legislation, an end to the poll tax, and integration of the military.) ADA leaders like Hubert Humphrey, the young mayor of Minneapolis, saw civil rights as a vehicle for transforming the Democratic Party into a more effective vehicle for liberalism and a way for anticommunist liberals to establish their progressive credentials. In a powerful speech, Humphrey declared that "the time has arrived for the Democratic party to get out of the shadow of states' rights and walk forthrightly into the bright sunshine of human rights." His speech helped garner the support of big-city bosses eyeing the black and labor vote, defeat the southern plank, and win the passage of the liberal proposal.

Many southern delegates responded to the liberal civil rights victory by walking out of the Democratic convention. Others voted to nominate Richard B. Russell, the segregationist senator from Georgia, for the presidency, rather than Truman (who easily prevailed). In four states, leaders of the anti–civil rights effort succeeded in listing South Carolina governor Strom Thurmond, rather than Truman, as the Democratic candidate. (In Alabama, Truman did not appear on the ballot at all.) Elsewhere in the South, Thurmond ran as the candidate of a newly formed States' Rights Party, commonly called the Dixiecrats. With the Democrats split three ways, and Truman's popularity low, few observers gave him much chance for victory.

Truman's Revival

The Republicans had fissures of their own in 1948, though not as deep as those in the Democratic Party. During the 1940s, a more isolationist, conservative wing of the party, headed by Ohioans John Bricker and Robert Taft, vied with a more internationalist, liberal wing, fronted by Wendell Willkie and Thomas Dewey. In 1948, Taft and Dewey emerged as the leading contenders for the Republican presidential nomination.

Taft, the son of a president, led the Republican forces in the Senate, where his fierce partisanship earned him the moniker "Mr. Republican." Deeply skeptical of expanding federal power at home or abroad, he nonetheless sometimes backed sweeping social benefit plans, like the housing program he cosponsored with liberal Democrat Robert Wagner and a proposal for federal aid to education, a measure of how much the New Deal had reshaped political thinking, even on the right. Dewey, who had close ties to Wall Street, held a more expansive notion of the role of government than the leading congressional Republicans, though he too wanted to reduce taxes and see more done by the states than Washington. His wing of the party, better funded and organized, with strength on both coasts, repeatedly bested the midwestern- and southern-based conservatives at national conventions, including in 1948, when Dewey captured the presidential nomination, picking liberal California governor Earl Warren as his running mate.

Though Dewey had lost the presidential race in 1944, most observers assumed he was a shoo-in the second time around. But Truman ran a shrewd campaign, moving to the left to attract labor, black, liberal, and urban voters and to mobilize mass organizations, like unions, which in many cases had greater organizational capacity and esprit than the Democratic Party itself. With the southerners having bolted, Truman finally felt free to issue the executive orders on civil rights he had earlier promised. To highlight the differences between the parties on domestic issues, Truman called a special session of Congress, sending it a long list of legislative proposals, some of which the Republicans had endorsed in their platform. When Congress adjourned after two weeks, having passed little significant legislation, Truman attacked it as a "do-nothing" Congress. At the same time, Truman supporters portrayed Wallace as a dupe of the communists. The indictment, during the campaign, of twelve Communist Party leaders for conspiring to advocate the overthrow of the government hurt Wallace's Progressive Party effort.

Expecting an easy victory, Dewey ran a cautious, low-key campaign. Like many eastern businessmen, he did not share the isolationist views of midwestern Republicans like Taft, which had the effect of removing foreign policy as a campaign issue. Truman rarely discussed foreign policy himself. Instead, crisscrossing the country by train, he stressed the benefits the New Deal had brought various constituencies. If the Republicans took control of the White House, he told voters, those gains would be jeopardized, as the country would become "an economic colony of Wall Street." Abandoning formal speeches, which did not serve him well, Truman adopted a feisty, plainspoken, off-the-cuff speaking style that contrasted favorably with Dewey's stiff, bland demeanor.

In spite of an unusually broad range of choices, the public found the 1948 presidential race less than enthralling, voting in exceptionally small numbers, in the lowest turnout for a presidential election between 1928 and 1976. Wallace and Thurmond did more poorly than expected, each getting only 2.5 percent of the vote. Wallace won no electoral votes, while Thurmond carried only the states where he ran as the Democratic candidate; where he ran under the States' Rights banner he received a fifth of the vote or less. In the popular vote, Truman beat Dewey by 5 percent. He won by holding together the Roosevelt coalition, with a strong showing among union members, urban voters, European immigrants, black voters, Jewish voters (helped by his decision to recognize Israel as soon as it declared itself into existence), and farm voters (scared, in the face of falling crop prices, that the Republicans would cut farm subsidies). Truman easily carried the electoral vote, and the Democrats recaptured control of both houses of Congress.

No Fair Deal

Truman's surprise success reinforced the stalemate in national politics that had more or less existed since the New Deal lost its momentum in the late 1930s. His victory proved too narrow to give much impetus to liberalism. Truman and the national Democratic Party welcomed back with no penalty the southern Democrats who had supported Thurmond (they needed them to maintain congressional majorities), which meant that conservative southerners took control of many key congressional committees. Once again, they used their Senate power to block civil rights legislation, as well as home rule for Washington, D.C., which they feared would elect a black mayor.

Truman saw almost his entire second-term program of domestic legislation, what he termed the "Fair Deal," go down to defeat. In his 1949 State of the Union address, he introduced a remarkably comprehensive, liberal program, including proposals to repeal Taft-Hartley, create new TVA-like authorities, and introduce national health insurance and federal aid to education. He also put forth a farm plan that would have moved toward ending price supports, thereby lowering food costs for urban consumers, while aiding farmers through direct subsidies capped at a level that would ensure that family farms, as opposed to large agribusinesses, would be the main beneficiaries. None of these proposals succeeded in the face of the weakness of congressional liberals and opposition from well-organized interest groups, such as the American Medical Association, which attacked the health insurance plan as socialized medicine.

Truman did substantially increase the minimum wage. Also, with a great deal of help from organized labor, he managed to protect Social Security from the corrosive effects of inflation while extending it to ten million additional workers, including those doing domestic and agricultural labor. But he got through only one major initiative, a housing program that benefited from Taft's support, which authorized the construction of additional federally financed public housing for the poor and federally subsidized slum clearance for urban redevelopment. Postwar prosperity had undercut popular support for a general expansion of domestic government activity, and interest-group politics replaced the advocacy of the kind of broad reform programs liberals, labor, and Roosevelt had once embraced.

Truman's victory failed to revive liberalism, but it did convince most Republicans of the folly of threatening, or even appearing to threaten, the fundamental reforms of the New Deal. Only occasionally, over the next quarter century, would mainstream Republicans attempt direct forays against the welfare state, usually with disastrous results. Conservative efforts to undo the New Deal largely had to operate outside the national political arena, in business-funded educational campaigns, think tanks, and marginal right-wing organizations, or through the growing use of anticommunism as an oblique weapon against liberalism. Too many Americans had benefited too greatly from the New Deal system for it to be overthrown. For all his bumbling, Truman managed to defend the political order he had inherited and win a consensus behind a foreign policy that required the kind of expansive and expensive state apparatus his opponents thought they had been on the road to dismantling just a few years earlier.

CHAPTER 4

National Security State

Very early on a rainy Sunday, June 25, 1950, on the Ongjin peninsula in western Korea, troops from the Democratic People's Republic of Korea (DPRK) and the Republic of Korea (ROK) began exchanging artillery fire. In the past, the two armies had repeatedly skirmished along the 38th parallel, which divided the communist-led north, the DPRK, from the conservative-led south, the ROK. This time, it soon became clear that North Korea had launched a full-scale invasion. DPRK infantry, led by Soviet-built tanks, poured across the border, followed by an amphibious landing on South Korea's eastern coast. Within days, the North Koreans had captured the South Korean capital, Seoul, while steadily advancing down the Korean peninsula.

Though surprised by the invasion, U.S. leaders reacted quickly. Almost immediately they got the UN Security Council to pass a resolution calling for North Korea to return to the 38th parallel, a move made possible by the absence of the Soviet Union, which had been boycotting the council since January 1950 to protest its failure to give China's seat to its new communist government. Two days later, a second Security Council resolution called for UN members to assist South Korea in repulsing the attack. On July 5, the first American soldiers ordered to Korea by President Truman, a small unit flown in from Japan, spotted a North Korean infantry column approaching their position in the village of Osan, thirty-four miles south of Seoul. To the GIs' surprise, the North Koreans, rather than being intimidated by U.S. forces, marched right through them, led by tanks with armor too thick to be stopped by American weapons.

By the time the Korean War ended three years later, fifty-four thousand U.S. troops had died in the fighting, and nearly twice that number had been wounded. For Koreans, the war took a staggering toll; nearly three million people—about 10 percent of the population—were killed, wounded, or missing. Another five million became refugees.

The Korean War has not loomed large in American memory or culture, in spite of its heavy cost. Yet the war had a profound impact on the way the United States developed. It locked the country into an unprecedented militarism, which continued after the war and included the long-term deployment of troops in Europe and Asia. It also brought domestic anticommunism, already a growing force, to new heights, marked by the rise of Senator Joseph McCarthy, political repression, and pressure for cultural conformity.

Neither militarism nor anticommunism broke the stalemate in domestic politics. If anything, they reinforced the status quo. When in 1953 a Republican moved into the White House for the first time in two decades, only modest changes occurred in the contours of domestic policy. The basic structures of an enduring postwar order were in place when the Korean War ended soon thereafter, the outcome of the struggles at home and abroad that had occurred since World War II.

Korea

The Korean War grew out of a combination of local and global circumstances related to the process of decolonization and the deepening division between the communist and capitalist camps. When World War II ended, 250 million people lived under colonial rule, but the war had undermined the ideological, economic, and military bases of colonialism. Starting in Asia and then moving to Africa and the Caribbean, independence movements succeeded with remarkable rapidity in freeing their countries from European rule. By 1970, only a few large territories, all in central or southern Africa, remained colonies.

In principle, the United States supported decolonization. In practice, its record was mixed. The United States gave its own colony, the Philippines, independence in 1946; encouraged the British to leave India, Burma (Myanmar), and Ceylon (Sri Lanka); and pressured the Dutch to abandon their military campaign to retain Indonesia. But American leaders gave a higher priority to winning support from Western European countries for U.S. policy toward the Soviet Union than to backing colonial independence movements, especially those that leaned to the left. Accordingly, the United States allowed its European allies to use Lend-Lease supplies to reoccupy their colonial possessions and looked the other way when they forcibly suppressed nationalist movements.

World War II brought Japanese colonial control of Korea to an end but left open how it would be organized as an independent entity. Korean nationalists, across the political spectrum, had long fought Japanese rule but did so through competing independence movements. During the Second World War, the United States, Britain, China, and the Soviet Union concurred that Korea should be given its independence after a transitional trusteeship, but they failed to develop a specific plan. As the war drew to an end, the United States and the Soviet Union hastily agreed to jointly occupy the country, with the Soviets staying north of the 38th parallel and the United States to its south.

Episodic postwar talks between the United States and the Soviet Union failed to come up with a plan for establishing a government for Korea as a whole. In the north, the Soviets backed a provisional government headed by communist Kim Il Sung. In the south, the United States backed a right-wing interim government headed by Syngman Rhee. On both sides of the border, the dominant factions, with the aid of the occupying powers, repressed their opponents and narrowed their ruling coalitions, so that by mid-1948, when the rival governments assumed full sovereignty over the former occupation zones, Korea had two fiercely antagonistic, authoritarian regimes, each cracking down on internal dissent while seeking control over the whole peninsula.

In early 1949, Rhee unsuccessfully sought U.S. backing for an invasion of the North, with the aim of taking it over. Kim had better luck with the Soviets. In early 1950, Stalin, after first rejecting the idea, agreed to support a North Korean invasion of the south, supplying military equipment and advice but not troops, with the expectation that, aided by communist uprisings in the south, the north would win a quick victory and the United States would not intervene.

In deciding to send U.S. ground troops to Korea, Truman sought to check what he and other policymakers saw as a Soviet probe of American will, believing, wrongly, that the Soviet Union had instigated the North Korean move. The United States cared less about the fate of Korea than the implications of the conflict for the larger Cold War. Dean Acheson, then serving as secretary of state, described Korea as a "vital . . . symbol," a place where the United States had to demonstrate to its allies and enemies its determination to halt Soviet aggression or else face similar moves elsewhere. As in the earlier Iranian and Greek crises, a local conflict took on global dimensions because the United States saw it as test of strength between rival world blocs.

In Europe, in spite of the tension between the Soviet- and American-led camps, the border between them remained stable, essentially along the line where the Allied armies had met at the end of World War II. In Asia, by contrast, the demarcation between the communist and capitalist blocs remained ill-defined and shifting, as the political trajectories of decolonizing nations remained uncertain and the epic Chinese Civil War neared its end.

When the Chinese conflict had reignited after World War II, the Truman administration concluded that a communist victory could not be stopped, given the corruption, inefficiency, and unpopularity of Chiang Kai-shek's Nationalist regime. Accordingly, it gave only token aid to the anticommunist forces. When in 1949 the communists won control over all of mainland China, the administration found itself on the defensive. Chinese Nationalist supporters and conservative Republicans charged Truman with "losing" China. Many Americans, bewildered by the limits of their country's power and the failure to fully use it, found seductive the argument made by administration critics that the communist victory had been the result of treachery by communist sympathizers within the Department of State.

The successful test by the Soviet Union of an atomic bomb in August 1949 contributed to the growing sense that the communists were gaining momentum. American leaders had realized that the Soviet Union would eventually develop atomic weapons, but it happened sooner than they anticipated. With any realistic expectation of effective international control of atomic weapons over, both the Truman administration and public opinion reacted to the unsettling news of the Soviet test by supporting a push to make sure that the United States maintained nuclear superiority. After a heated, secret debate among atomic scientists and government officials, in January 1950 Truman approved the development of a "Super" bomb (or hydrogen bomb, as it was later called) that would unleash the enormous power of thermonuclear fusion.

The Korean fighting set off a broad American mobilization. In addition to dispatching troops to the battlefront, Truman positioned the Seventh Fleet to prevent a Communist Chinese attack on Formosa, where the Nationalists had retreated. He also increased military assistance for the French effort to retain its colonies in Indochina and stepped up aid to the Philippine government, which was fighting a peasant insurgency.

Truman militarized American policy in Asia on his own authority. Nominally, U.S. forces in Korea acted under United Nations command, though in practice the UN commander, General Douglas MacArthur, operated as part of the American command structure, with the forces that sixteen countries sent to Korea (in most cases token units) reporting to him. After Congress had ratified the UN Charter, it passed legislation requiring its consent for the large-scale assignment of U.S. forces to UN peacekeeping missions, but the Truman administration ignored that procedure. Nor did Truman seek a declaration of war or a congressional resolution of support before committing U.S. forces to Korea, though no doubt he could have gotten one. Instead, he rested his action on his view of his inherent power as president, a step that, in seeming contradiction to the Constitution, shifted the authority to make war from the legislative branch—more susceptible to popular pressure—to the executive branch.

Senator Robert Taft criticized Truman's failure to get a declaration of war, but in the heated atmosphere of the early days of the Korean fighting, the constitutional issues surrounding the commitment of American military force received scant attention. Months later, when Truman decided to send a large Army force to Europe without congressional approval, a debate did arise in Congress over his power to do so (impelled in part by Republicans who wanted to see a less Eurocentric national security policy). However, the Senate ultimately ratified Truman's move, and the controversy had little lasting effect on the long-term shift in governance that had taken place. Since Korea, presidents have sent U.S. forces into battle many times, but never with a declaration of war, instead seeking weaker forms of congressional approval, or none at all.

The demobilization of the Army after World War II left the United States ill-equipped for a new ground war. To fight in Korea, the Army had to quickly call up reservists as well as deploy draftees. Many arrived with little training. Corporal Merwin Perkins, a nineteen-year-old Army reservist, who had never received basic training, found himself on the front lines in Korea "one month to the day" after leaving "civilian life in Minnesota." "I didn't even know how to dig a foxhole," he later recalled. "A gunnery sergeant told me how. 'Make it like a grave.'"

The sergeant's comments no doubt reflected the grim situation in which the troops found themselves. The dispatching of U.S. forces failed to stop the North Korean advance until it came within thirty miles of the port city of Pusan, at the southern tip of the Korean peninsula. Only there, in very heavy fighting, did the Americans manage to establish a stable defensive perimeter. Then the tide turned. The failure of communist uprisings to take place in the south, a steady flow of American troops and supplies into Pusan, and heavy American bombing denied the North Koreans the quick victory they had expected.

In mid-September 1950, the UN forces launched a counterattack, pushing north from Pusan and carrying out an amphibious landing at Inchon, not far south of the 38th parallel. The North Koreans, faced with the possibility of being cut off in their rear, rapidly retreated. The UN phalanxes linked up on September 26 and two days later recaptured Seoul in street-by-street fighting.

Now the North Koreans faced catastrophic defeat. When the United States sent troops to Korea, its stated goal was to reestablish the preinvasion status. But as the fighting proceeded, high-ranking policymakers, like John Allison and Dean Rusk at the State Department, argued that the United States should use its military power to unify Korea under a noncommunist government. Shortly before the Inchon landing, Truman approved sending U.S. forces north of the 38th parallel, a step that won UN General Assembly approval on October 7, just as the line was being crossed.

The success of the UN offensive led Kim Il Sung to ask Stalin to bail out the failing North Korean effort with Soviet troops. Stalin declined but urged the Chinese to come to the North Koreans' aid. The Chinese signaled several times that if U.S. troops crossed the 38th parallel, they would enter the war, but American military and civilian leaders ignored the warnings. Instead, giddy with success, MacArthur kept moving his forces north toward the Yalu River, which separated North Korea from China, unaware that the Chinese had begun moving large numbers of troops across the border. An American soldier who arrived in Korea in November remembered that "the mood was, we were going to get up to the Yalu and we were all going to be home by Christmas."

In late November the Chinese launched a massive offensive that panicked UN troops, who retreated in disarray. Washington panicked too; Truman told reporters that if necessary the United States would utilize every resource at its disposal in Korea, including atomic weapons, inaccurately stating that field commanders could authorize their use. In response, British prime minister Clement Attlee hastily flew to Washington for urgent discussions aimed at dissuading the United States from a full-scale war with China. (Britain had some fourteen thousand troops in Korea.) Cooler heads soon prevailed; when MacArthur sought permission to blockade the Chinese coast, bomb Chinese industry, and use National Chinese troops in Korea, his superiors turned him down.

By early 1951, Chinese troops had moved south across the 38th parallel and retaken Seoul. Within a month, though, the UN forces managed to stop the offensive, in part through the massive use of airpower. From the start of the war, the United States took advantage of its air supremacy to fly close tactical support and bomb North Korean industry and troop concentrations. Once the Chinese entered the conflict, MacArthur ended almost all restraints on bombing, calling for the destruction of "every installation, factory, city, and village" in North Korea (exempting targets near China and the Soviet Union, to avoid provoking further foreign intervention). Firebomb attacks, modeled after the raids against Japan late in World War II, caused heavy damage. A January 1951 raid on the North Korean capital, Pyongyang, burned down a third of the city. The United States also made extensive use of napalm (jellied gasoline that stuck to buildings and people while burning intensely).

By March 1951, momentum had shifted back to the UN forces, which recaptured Seoul. Sobered by recent events, the State Department now reversed its earlier position, opposing a new push north of the 38th parallel. MacArthur dissented, making known his desire to fight for the complete defeat of the Chinese in Korea, threatening to expand the war to China itself. After he repeatedly ignored orders not to publicly question U.S. policy, Truman relieved him of his command on April 11. When a new Chinese offensive failed to make headway, the war settled into a stalemate along a line not far from where it began.

On July 10, 1951, with all the major parties except the South Koreans reconciled to the restoration of the prewar situation, armistice negotiations began between U.S. military officials, the North Koreans, and the Chinese. After an agreement was reached for an armistice line along the battlefront, the talks stalled over prisoners of war. The Chinese and North Koreans demanded an exchange of all prisoners, while the United States insisted that captured soldiers who did not want to return to their homeland should not be forced to do so. As negotiations fruitlessly continued, so did the fighting. Some 45 percent of all U.S. casualties took place between the start of the talks and their conclusion two years later. To keep up pressure on the communists, the United States intensified its bombing campaign, demolishing dams and hydroelectric plants along the Yalu River and leaving eighteen of twenty-two major North Korean cities at least half destroyed.

Militarization

The outbreak of the Korean War began a long era of what Robert Taft called "semiwar," in which the distinction between peace and war blurred. Military preparedness no longer was a response to particular crises but became an ongoing way of life. Militarizing the Cold War led to a restructuring of the federal government and its relationship to civil society, as the international contest became a formative presence in almost every sphere of American life.

Prior to Korea, the dominant Washington view saw the Soviet threat as primarily ideological, political, and economic, not military. The policy of containment, which George Kennan had popularized within and outside of the government, called for stopping further Soviet expansion with economic and political measures. Some State Department and military officials saw the need for a big military buildup to confront the Soviets, but Truman disagreed. Even after the Berlin blockade and the Chinese communist victory, he sought to restrain defense spending in order to achieve or at least move toward a balanced budget without cutting domestic programs or raising taxes.

Already, defense dominated federal outlays: national security expenses, including military spending, foreign assistance programs, veterans' benefits, and atomic energy, accounted for three-quarters of the federal government's fiscal 1950 budget. Truman proposed a modest cut for 1951, with $13.9 billion devoted directly to defense (less than an eighth of what the country spent at the height of World War II). Some officials within the administration thought that figure way too low. A National Security Council study of American strategy in light of Soviet nuclear capability, principally written by Paul Nitze, Kennan's successor as head of the State Department Policy Planning Staff, depicted U.S. military strength as "dangerously inadequate" to meet the challenge from the Soviet Union, which it described as seeking "to impose its absolute authority over the rest of the world." The document, labeled NSC-68, called for a buildup of conventional U.S. forces, nuclear weapons, and international assistance programs and new civil defense and psychological warfare efforts. Influenced by Leon Keyserling, a veteran New Dealer recently appointed head of the Council of Economic Advisers, the NSC-68 authors argued that increases in military spending "might not result in a real decrease in the standard of living, for the economic effects of the program might be to increase the gross national product by more than the amount being absorbed for additional military and foreign assistance purposes." To support this Keynesian argument, NSC-68 cited the World War II experience.

Not pleased with the budgetary implications of NSC-68, Truman delayed acting on it. But once the Korean War started he approved its recommendations, ordering a massive increase in military spending. Various supplemental appropriations brought defense spending for fiscal 1951 to over three times the amount Truman had originally requested. Within a year, the armed services more than doubled in size.

The Korean War ended any possible American rapprochement with the Chinese communists. Before the war, some policymakers had argued, unsuccessfully, that the United States should accept the inevitable, recognize the new Chinese communist government (as the British had done), and try to woo it away from the Soviet Union. Instead, the war led the United States to build an anticommunist bloc in Asia, directed as much against the Chinese as the Soviets. The most dramatic turnaround came in Japan. During the first years of its occupation, the United States ordered the Japanese to embark on a radical program of disarmament, democratization, and economic restructuring, designed to make sure the country never made war again. But as the Cold War developed, the United States began reversing course. American occupation authorities took steps to weaken the political left and the labor movement and to reorient the Japanese economy away from China. After the start of the Korean War, the United States moved quickly to finalize a peace treaty with Japan and sign a mutual security agreement that gave it the right to maintain military bases there. American officials wanted Japan itself to rearm as part of an anticommunist bloc, but few Japanese leaders, even among the conservatives, desired to do so. Japan kept the ban on creating a military in its American-written constitution but did agree to create a "self-defense" force. Elsewhere in Asia, the United States, to bolster anticommunist forces and reassure its allies that Japan would not again threaten them, signed mutual security pacts with the Philippines, with Australia and New Zealand, and later with South Korea, the Nationalist Chinese, and Southeast Asian countries.

In Europe, too, the Korean War brought a militarization of American policy. Most dramatically, in September 1950 Acheson publicly proposed rearming Germany. To lessen European fears of possible German aggression, Truman sent four Army divisions to Europe—this sparked the congressional debate—beginning what became a permanent, large-scale deployment of U.S. troops on the continent. The United States also began including nondemocratic states in its anticommunist alliances. Truman had refused to recognize the fascist government in Spain, but after the start of the Korean War he reversed that policy and began negotiations that led, the year after he left office, to a treaty that gave it substantial economic and military aid in return for bases. In Libya, Morocco, and Saudi Arabia as well, the United States secured new military bases without regard to the nondemocratic practices of the host governments.

In 1950 the United States began a massive program to accelerate its production of atomic weapons, part of a nuclear arms race that accompanied the Korean fighting. From an estimated two hundred atomic bombs in mid-1949 the United States upped its arsenal to a thousand in mid-1953 and to an astounding stockpile of some eighteen thousand weapons by 1960. The first thermonuclear device (the "H-bomb"), tested by the United States on

November 1, 1952, on the Pacific island of Eniwetok, had a thousand times the force of the atomic bomb dropped on Hiroshima. It left behind a crater two miles wide and a half mile deep. The Soviets exploded their first hydrogen bomb less than a year later.

As national security became an overriding concern and a hegemonic ideology, the military won unprecedented influence within the government and on the broader society. The nuclear buildup provides a case in point. A 1946 law gave control over nuclear research and weaponry to the civilian-led Atomic Energy Commission (AEC). Though the military lost out in its desire to have direct control over atomic energy, in a compromise arrangement it did get a statutory role in running the AEC. Over time, it steadily increased its influence, in part through a series of political attacks, coordinated with congressional allies, on the agency's civilian leaders for supposedly allowing security breaches. (Soviet spies had penetrated the atomic energy program, but had done so when the Army ran it, before the creation of the AEC.)

The AEC operated under a shroud of secrecy and outside of various laws and regulations that normally governed civilian society. Workers at AEC-run facilities could not go on strike, nor would the agency allow unions with left-wing leaders to represent employees at plants operated by its contractors. Denying security clearances to critics of government policy—including J. Robert Oppenheimer, who had led the scientific team that developed the atomic bomb—shut them out of AEC-sponsored research and advisory committees.

To produce nuclear weapons the government built an archipelago of secret nuclear facilities. The Nevada Test Site, set up in 1951, grew to be larger than Rhode Island. More than nine hundred nuclear weapons were detonated there, most in underground shafts but ninety-six above ground, leaving behind a desert expanse contaminated by radiation, pockmarked with craters, and dotted with partially destroyed buildings that had been erected to measure the destructive impact of blasts. A few bombs were so large that officials worried that testing them at the Nevada site would damage buildings in Las Vegas, fifty miles away, so they blew them up on an island off Alaska.

The major nuclear test sites in the continental United States and most uranium mines lay on or near Indian land, so Native Americans disproportionately suffered from the environmental and health problems that came with nuclear armament. Nearby residents were inadvertently exposed to radiation from bomb testing, while thousands of soldiers and sailors were deliberately exposed in order to study the ability of military units to survive atomic attack. Also, in a series of bizarre experiments justified in the name of national security, doctors under government contract secretly exposed hospital patients, prisoners, pregnant women, and mentally retarded boys to various types of radioactivity and then clandestinely tracked their health for decades thereafter.

The AEC was one of a series of new federal agencies that funded and shaped science, engineering, and, more broadly, intellectual life during the Cold War years. During World War II, the federal government vastly increased its spending on research and development. Unlike during the prewar years, when the modest amount of federally funded research had been conducted for the most part directly by government agencies, much of the wartime research was contracted out to universities and corporations. After the war, there was broad support among science administrators and federal officials for continuing this approach, but disagreement over how to implement it. No centralized science agency emerged. Instead, each of the military services embarked on its own large-scale research and development program, contracting out projects to academic institutions and private laboratories. To fund nonmilitary research, Congress established the National Science Foundation and greatly increased appropriations for the National Institutes of Health.

The massive federal investment in research and development, and the decision to funnel much of it through universities and private companies, helped transform the United States from a scientific and technological borrower into the global leader. During the postwar decades, the United States spent far more on research and development than Britain, France, West Germany, and Japan combined. Federal priorities helped determine how science and academic life developed. In 1948, nearly two-thirds of federal research and development money went to military-related projects. Only in a few exceptional years during the decades that followed did spending on nonmilitary projects match or exceed defense work. Academic disciplines with national security relevance, like electrical engineering and Russian studies, flourished, while others, without obvious importance to state interests, lagged behind.

Federal funding and military priorities could take research in odd directions. During the 1950s, for instance, military and civilian agencies funded studies of dolphins by neurophysiologist John Cunningham Lilly, who claimed that they had exceptional intelligence and advanced communication abilities. His work led to the Navy Marine Mammal Program, which trained dolphins for military missions (they were used during the Vietnam War to defend ammunition depots at Cam Ranh Bay and thirty-five years later to sweep for mines during the Iraq War). But it also produced the cultural projection of dolphins as pacific, spiritual, altruistic companions for humans, first in the 1963 movie *Flipper,* inspired by Lilly's research, then in the counterculture of the late 1960s (by which time Lilly had become deeply involved with using psychedelic drugs for research), and finally in dolphin exhibits and encounter opportunities at marine parks across the country.

The military influenced academic life not only by funding research but also by sponsoring hundreds of Reserve Officer Training Corps programs on campuses. At many schools, marching cadets were a common sight. Civilian intelligence officers hovered around universities too, developing clandestine relationships with faculty and administrators, commissioning research, and recruiting students. The government even secretly funded, through the CIA, political and literary journals, like the *New Leader* and *Partisan Review,* whose outlook it found congenial.

All this cost money, and lots of it. During the first two decades of the Cold War, defense-related outlays accounted for nearly two-thirds of all federal spending. During the Cold War as a whole (from 1947 to 1989), military spending averaged 7.4 percent of the GNP, nine times the figure before World War I and five times the rate between the two world wars. Korea ushered in a new phase in American history, when even in peacetime national security laid claim on a significant share of the total productive output of the society, dominated federal spending, and significantly reduced the resources available for private spending or other public investments.

Domestic Anticommunism

Ideological fervor promoted public acceptance of the costs and dangers of the Cold War. The late 1940s and 1950s saw an intensification of patriotic zeal of the sort normally associated with wartime, even during the years when there was no actual fighting. Patriotism, anticommunism, religiosity, and a search for traitors fortified the country in its contest with the Soviet bloc. They limited internal dissent, weakened the political left, and set the tone for daily living.

Antiradicalism and fear of domestic subversion were not new features of American society; they had been woven into the fabric of the nation almost from its founding, episodically dominating political life. Still, the anticommunist crusade that came after World War II, in its scope, intensity, and duration, exceeded even such past moments of internal repression as the late-eighteenth-century anti-Republican campaign under the Alien and Sedition Acts and the post–World War I Red Scare.

Anticommunism began swelling before the Cold War. During the late 1930s, conservatives used anticommunist charges and investigations to attack the New Deal and the labor movement. Even during World War II, when the Soviet Union and the United States were allied, anticommunism continued to bubble up. During the 1944 presidential campaign, John Bricker, the Republican vice presidential candidate, proclaimed that the Democrats had become a "communistic party with Franklin Roosevelt as its front." After the war, anticommunism grew even more prominent, used as an electoral weapon by some Republican candidates, including Richard Nixon in his successful 1946 bid for a House seat from California, and given legitimacy by a new round of congressional investigations.

Postwar anticommunism had multiple sources and purposes, but without the Cold War it is hard to imagine that it would have become so powerful and pervasive. Patriotism and anticommunism came to define one another during the Cold War. Cold War patriotism contrasted the United States as a land of freedom with tyrannical communist states abroad. World War II Manichean imagery, which juxtaposed the "free world" of the Allied powers with the "slave world" of fascism, morphed into a new, polar vision in which the Soviet Union, once part of the "free" Allied powers, became repositioned as the center of a reconstituted unfree world, now defined by communism instead of fascism. The adoption by conservative newspapers and commentators of the term "Red Fascism" to describe communism aimed to tar it with the near universal public rejection of Nazism and posit continuity between the anti-Axis struggle and the Cold War. So did the use by intellectuals and politicians of the category "totalitarian" to encompass both fascism and communism. The phrase "un-American activities" also originally referred to both fascism and communism, but after World War II it became almost exclusively associated with the latter. As opponents repeatedly described communism as, by definition, un-American, anticommunism came to be equated with Americanism.

The Freedom Train, which traveled around the country with an exhibit of national historical documents, including the Declaration of Independence and the Constitution, illustrated the ideological reconfiguration. Conceived of by the Truman administration in 1946 as a way to contrast American freedom with "Hitler tyranny," by the time the train began its tour it had become reconceived as a way of countering what the attorney general termed "foreign ideologies" and "subversive elements" at home. The huge outpouring of visitors to the traveling exhibit revealed an eagerness to take advantage of what for most people was a once-in-a-lifetime opportunity to see the nation's key political documents, but it also suggested a widespread desire to join in a public display of patriotism at a time of growing international tension.

Other new patriotic commemorations also, implicitly or explicitly, contrasted American virtue with communist evil. June 14 had been informally celebrated as Flag Day since the late nineteenth century, but only in 1949 did Congress formally designate it for national observance, furthering the widespread display and veneration of the flag that so many foreign observers were struck by when visiting America. The idea of designating May 1 as "Loyalty Day" to counter the communist celebrations of May Day reportedly came from aging publisher William Randolph Hearst. In the late 1940s, Loyalty Day parades, heavily promoted by the Hearst newspapers, outdrew May Day parades, even in the New York area, a stronghold of the by then shrinking political left.

The Cold War allowed veteran anticommunist crusaders to move from the margins of American politics to its center by focusing on links, real or alleged, between domestic radicalism and the Soviet bloc. The Special House Committee on Un-American Activities (widely called HUAC) helped establish the pattern. Before Pearl Harbor, the committee devoted itself largely to trying to undermine the New Deal by airing charges that communists and their supporters played significant roles in various federal agencies and in labor unions allied with the Roosevelt administration. After the war, HUAC continued to use charges of communist infiltration to attack liberal institutions and policies, but it added a dimension of national security by highlighting connections between domestic and foreign communism. As part of a highly publicized investigation into communist influence in the entertainment business, begun in 1947, HUAC called witnesses like libertarian novelist and screenwriter Ayn Rand to testify about pro-Soviet films, such as *Mission to Moscow* and *Song of Russia,* made in Hollywood during World War II with the support of the Roosevelt administration. The committee presented a picture of communists and fellow travelers working covertly to advance the interests of another nation, soon to be America's enemy, while government officials did nothing or egged them on.

The Truman administration more explicitly portrayed domestic radicalism as a threat to national security when it launched the Federal Employee Loyalty Program in April 1947. Upon taking office, Truman had rejected the idea that subversive activities presented a serious threat to the country and generally refused to allow executive agencies to cooperate with HUAC. Over time, however, pressure grew on him to act. Some came from evidence of security breaches in the government and the uncovering of a Soviet spy ring in Canada, with indications that it might have been active in the United States as well. Equally important were charges made by Republicans during the 1946 elections of inadequate attention to communist penetration of the government.

Under Truman's program, all new federal employees had to undergo a full-scale loyalty check. Current employees were given a more cursory examination but were fully investigated if any "derogatory information" appeared in their files, which meant that a single informer or complaint could set off an inquiry. The Federal Bureau of Investigation (FBI) carried out the investigations, increasing in size from 3,559 agents in 1946 to 7,029 in 1953. Federal law already called for firing government workers who belonged to a political party or organization that advocated the overthrow of the government, but the Truman program went beyond that to make disloyalty, a term it did not clearly define, a basis for dismissal. Membership in or even "sympathetic association" with any group the attorney general judged totalitarian, fascist, communist, subversive, or dedicated to force or violence could be deemed a possible sign of disloyalty.

Though Truman's loyalty program covered only federal workers, the attorney general's list of suspect organizations and a list of purportedly communist-linked groups HUAC issued became used by other employers in loyalty investigations of their own. Membership in a listed group often led to firing. Not surprisingly, groups on these lists saw members drop out, contributions dry up, and their political efficacy greatly diminish. While some extreme right-wing groups did appear on the attorney general's list, most of the listed groups were left-wing organizations or left-liberal coalitions. By creating directories of disapproved organizations, the federal government went a long way toward limiting the freedom of association and defining what was and was not acceptable political behavior for loyal Americans.

The government also moved to define what was and was not acceptable sexual behavior, making deviations from delineated sexual norms, most importantly homosexuality, cause for dismissal too. The growth of a lively gay subculture in Washington, D.C., during the New Deal and World War II, along with a general increased national awareness of homosexuality, led congressional conservatives and federal security officers to call for the firing of homosexuals working for the government at the same time that they pressed for a political cleansing. In 1947, Congress authorized the secretary of state to dismiss any employee he considered a security risk even if they were not judged disloyal, a power soon given to other federal agencies too. Grounds for being considered a security risk included alcoholism, financial irresponsibility, a criminal past, and homosexuality. In 1950 a State Department official testified that his agency had fired ninety-one employees for homosexuality, a revelation that led to a full-scale Senate investigation of government employment of homosexuals and a widespread hunt for gay and lesbian federal workers.

Publicly, officials in the Truman and Eisenhower administrations, including President Eisenhower himself, argued that homosexuality was unacceptable among federal employees because it created opportunities for blackmail that foreign enemies might exploit. No such case, though, ever surfaced. Among themselves, government officials stressed their moral repugnance with homosexuality and their belief that it reflected an individual's poor character. From the late 1940s through the 1960s, the State Department, which remained the center of the drive for sexual conformity, fired far more employees, roughly a thousand (the overwhelming majority male), for homosexuality than for suspected communist ties.

By 1952, some two million federal employees had undergone some level of loyalty or security investigation. Under Truman, about twelve hundred federal workers were dismissed for disloyalty or security risk, and another six thousand resigned in the course of investigations. A slightly higher number were fired or resigned during the first three years of the Eisenhower administration.

Spies

The loyalty and security programs, by making the dangers of communism seem more immediate than events abroad by themselves suggested, helped build support for Truman's foreign policy. Charges of espionage even more vividly drove home the point that the danger of communism was present even at the very heart of the country's government and defense programs. The Alger Hiss case dramatically raised this possibility. Hiss had been a rising star in the New Deal, accompanying Roosevelt to the Yalta conference and having primary responsibility for organizing the founding conference of the UN. A friend of both Dean Acheson and John Foster Dulles, a leading Republican foreign policy expert who became Dwight Eisenhower's secretary of state, Hiss first surfaced as a purported secret communist agent during a 1948 HUAC hearing on communist infiltration of the government.

HUAC's star witness was Elizabeth Bentley. During World War II, Bentley had carried messages and documents from communists and communist sympathizers working for the federal government in Washington to Communist Party leaders and Soviet agents in New York. At the end of the war, fearful that she might be apprehended, she went to the FBI with her story. A second former communist courier, Whittaker Chambers, also testified before the House committee. Between them, Bentley and Chambers named dozens of current and former government employees whom they claimed had passed on classified information to the Communist Party, Soviet agents, or both. They included Harry Dexter White, the second in command at the Treasury Department before Truman appointed him to a post at the International Monetary Fund, and Hiss.

White denied the charges against him, dying of a heart attack just three days later. Hiss too denied the accusations made against him, but after he sued Chambers for libel, Chambers revealed new evidence to support his claims. In December 1948, a grand jury indicted Hiss for perjury for denying that in the late 1930s he had given Chambers State Department documents. His first trial ended in a hung jury, but a retrial resulted in his conviction. Many liberals believed Hiss's continued claims of innocence, but for people who did not, his conviction demonstrated that even the most respectable officials might be communists or spies.

Other espionage cases soon followed. In 1949, the FBI arrested a Justice Department employee, Judith Coplon, as she was about to hand over information about FBI investigations to a Soviet UN employee. Though she was found guilty of espionage, her conviction was overturned because the FBI refused to reveal what had raised suspicions about her. The tip-off had come from encrypted wartime Soviet diplomatic cables that the American government had begun deciphering in a huge effort later known as the Venona Project.

Venona also led to the exposure of Soviet espionage in the wartime atomic bomb program. Decrypted cables revealed that British scientist Klaus Fuchs had given the Soviet Union information on the Anglo-American effort to develop atomic weapons. Arrested in early 1950, Fuchs confessed, leading the FBI to Harry Gold, who had been his liaison to Soviet agents. Gold in turn confessed, leading to the arrest of others charged with conspiring to commit atomic espionage, including a communist couple from New York, Ethel and Julius Rosenberg. The government's case against the Rosenbergs at their 1951 trial had holes, but in the atmosphere of the Korean War it won a conviction. Once again, the FBI did not want to reveal the existence of Venona. Evidence from it would have confirmed that Julius had passed on classified information to the Soviets but suggested that Ethel had at most a very peripheral involvement in his illegal activities. The Rosenbergs continued to assert their innocence until June 19, 1953, when, amid international protests, they were executed.

The most serious cases of Soviet espionage had occurred when the two world powers were not at odds. Nonetheless, spying that had taken place earlier but was uncovered only during the Cold War served to justify U.S. foreign policy and explain its failings, providing an outlet for frustrations over the enormous gap between official rhetoric and the practical limit of American power. Short of all-out war, the Truman administration could not have forced the Soviet Union out of Eastern Europe or prevented the Communist victory in China. Yet communist advances, rather than sparking a rethinking of American policy, led to a search for traitors who "gave away" Eastern Europe and China. For years, congressional conservatives and executive branch security officers launched one loyalty investigation after another of the wartime State Department officials who had correctly predicted the collapse of the Chinese Nationalist regime and advocated trying to reach an accommodation with the Chinese communists to further the fight against the Japanese. Disloyalty also provided a convenient explanation for America's loss of its nuclear monopoly, inevitable given the sophistication of Soviet science and engineering (though information gotten through spying did speed up the effort).

McCarthyism

The career of Senator Joseph McCarthy reflected the close link between the Red Scare at home and events abroad. A Republican senator from Wisconsin, little known outside his home state, McCarthy captured national attention in February 1950 when he claimed to have a list of State Department employees with communist affiliations against whom the secretary of state had failed to act. Though in this instance and others to come, McCarthy largely recycled old charges with little concern about their veracity, his flamboyant manner and ever-shifting, dramatic accusations, replete with specific numbers and details (often later proved wrong), led to extensive press coverage, bitter partisan controversy, and congressional investigations. The term "McCarthyism," coined in a *Washington Post* political cartoon, became widely used to describe the anticommunist drive, particularly its most lurid and sleazy forms.

The political climate ushered in by the Korean War eliminated any chance that concern about the dangers of domestic communism would begin to die down. Though by 1950 the American Communist Party was in steep decline, congressional conservatives, led by Pat McCarran, an anti–New Deal Democratic senator from Nevada, congressional liberals, and the Truman administration all put forth proposals to legally restrict communist activity and bolster national security laws. Elements of the various plans were combined into an omnibus Internal Security Act that Congress passed by huge margins. Truman, who had sought a more modest measure, vetoed the bill, saying that it would "greatly weaken our liberties," but Congress easily overrode him. The new law required communist organizations and their members to register with the federal government; excluded foreigners who ever had been affiliated with groups advocating totalitarianism from visiting or emigrating to the United States; and authorized the detention without trial of suspected subversives in the event of a national emergency. By 1954, the FBI had over twenty-six thousand people on a list of those to be arrested.

Liberal Democrats had fallen over themselves to prove they were as staunchly anticommunist as conservatives. Nevertheless, in the 1950 election, Republicans, with McCarthy in the lead, charged the Democrats with being soft on communism. The tactic already was well worn. But with U.S. troops fighting in Korea, red-baiting—on the part of both parties—became more common and cruder. In a bitter Senate primary fight in Florida, Democratic congressman George Smathers called his opponent, the liberal incumbent Claude Pepper, "an apologist for Stalin" and claimed that "Red Pepper" was an "associate of fellow travelers." In a California Senate primary, a Democratic opponent labeled liberal congresswoman Helen Gahagan Douglas, a former Hollywood actress married to a movie star, part of a "subversive clique," asserting, in a not uncommon linking of political and sexual transgression, that she was "neither truly representative of her sex nor of her party." After Douglas won the nomination, her Republican opponent, Richard Nixon (seeking to move from the House to the Senate), kept her on the defensive by repeatedly pointing out that her voting record on national security issues heavily overlapped that of New York's radical congressman Vito Marcantonio.

Anticommunist politicians received backing from party leaders and economic interests who sought to use them to advance partisan and policy agendas that often had little to do with national security. Mainstream Republican leaders like Taft and Eisenhower either tacitly supported McCarthy or refrained from publicly criticizing him, seeing him as an electoral asset for their party. Anticommunism provided a way to attack the New Deal, the Fair Deal, and liberalism by implying that they were on a continuum with communism, pink if not red, softer versions of the ultimate evil. Conservative newspapers, elements of the Catholic Church, business groups such as the Chamber of Commerce, and conservative civic organizations like the American Legion and the Daughters of the American Revolution clamored about the dangers of communism as part of a broader effort to roll back the New Deal, or at least stop its expansion.

Business found anticommunism a useful weapon against labor, charging that unions, rather than simply trying to help their members, were advancing an anti-American conspiracy. Within the labor movement, longtime anticommunists found their position bolstered by unfolding events. After a group of unions with ties to the Communist Party dissented from the CIO's backing of Truman and the Marshall Plan, CIO leaders expelled them. The federal government, through congressional investigations, deportations, prosecutions, and an ever-growing web of anticommunist laws and regulations, isolated left-wing unionists and forced many out of the labor movement. The combination of internal battling, government action, and employer attacks left unions weakened and all but ended the historic ties between organized labor and political radicalism.

Real estate interests used anticommunism to try to stop the development of public housing. In 1947, as vice chairman of a joint congressional committee studying housing issues, Joe McCarthy, who raised money not only from businesses in his own state but also from the oil and real estate industries nationally, blamed government housing for broken homes and juvenile delinquency and for serving as "a breeding ground for communists." In Los Angeles, a coalition of business groups, real estate agents, home builders, and the *Los Angeles Times* attacked an ambitious plan to build ten thousand units of public housing as "creeping socialism," leading to a 1952 referendum vote that killed off much of the program. (The city then helped entice the Brooklyn Dodgers to move west by selling them a parcel of land in Chavez Ravine, originally taken for public housing, on which to build a stadium.)

In the South, anticommunism developed largely as a way to block the civil rights movement. The Red Scare started late in the region, which, with a one-party system and a high degree of ideological consensus among its ruling powers, had less occasion than elsewhere for anticommunism to be mobilized for partisan purposes. A 1954 poll found the South to be the only region of the country where more people opposed McCarthy than supported him. But as the movement for racial equality grew, particularly after the 1954 Supreme Court ruling in *Brown v. Board of Education,* southern defenders of segregation increasingly made use of anticommunism, portraying the push for civil rights as a conspiracy orchestrated by communists from outside the region. Most southern states passed laws and set up police agencies or legislative committees aimed at repressing civil rights efforts in the name of anticommunism, often with considerable success.

Sometimes it was unclear how much the Communist Party itself was actually a concern to anticommunists, who deemed disloyal a broad range of social, political, and religious views. McCarthyism was a quest for a conservative ideological and cultural consensus that went far beyond the issue of communism. Many anticommunists worried at least as much about atheists, intellectuals, integrationists, trade unionists, left-liberals, and homosexuals as they did about communists.

HUAC's sustained investigation of the entertainment industries reflected this desire to control mass culture and popular values. In repeated probes searching for communist infiltration, committee members concerned themselves with the content of cultural products. They did not worry about open communist appeals; as actor Adolphe Menjou, a devoted anticommunist, said in HUAC testimony, "I have seen no such thing as Communist propaganda, such as waving the hammer and sickle in motion pictures." Rather the issue was what Menjou called "things that I thought were against what I considered good Americanism."

A large number of leftists worked at one time or another in the culture industries, including several hundred Communist Party members in Hollywood alone. Much of their work differed little from that of their more conservative colleagues, but when they had a chance, left-wing writers and directors tried to project their social values into films, be it prewar gangster movies that portrayed crime as an outgrowth of poverty, wartime antifascist movies, or postwar "message movies," like *Gentleman's Agreement* and *The Big Clock,* that attacked racism and anti-Semitism and were critical of big business. Since communists, former communists, and communist sympathizers were particularly active in pursuing such liberal themes, their expulsion from the industry provided a way to reorient mass culture. The movie studios and, to an even greater extent, the emerging television industry soon began shying away from controversial subjects and avoiding the kind of social-problem themes that had been commonly addressed in the mid-1940s. In commercial culture, as in political debate, the range of discourse narrowed.

A few Hollywood figures who refused to answer questions before HUAC went to jail for contempt of Congress, but in the movie industry, and more generally, the sanctions against those linked in one way or another to the Communist Party came largely from civil society. Congressional committees and other government agencies identified current and former leftists, but their punishment came from being fired by private employers and being put on blacklists of unhirables maintained by trade associations and professional red-hunting agencies. By the early 1950s, anyone who refused to sign a form declaring that they were not a communist or refused to testify before a congressional committee could not work in the movie, radio, or television industries, at least under his or her own name.

By one estimate, over thirteen million Americans, about a fifth of the workforce, came within the scope of government and private loyalty programs. Most simply had to fill out a questionnaire or take a loyalty oath. Even that could have a chilling effect. For tens of thousands, the consequences were direr. Nearly three thousand longshoremen and seamen lost their jobs under a federally established port security program, ostensibly aimed at preventing sabotage but in practice more concerned with ridding the maritime industry of left-wing unionists. On college campuses, some one hundred faculty members lost their jobs, mostly for refusing to cooperate with anticommunist investigations or name leftists they knew. Hundreds of state and municipal workers across the country—social workers, teachers, transit workers, and the like—lost their jobs, too, because of their political affiliations or refusal to testify about them.

The job-based loyalty system could exact a high personal cost. Thomas J. Coleman, an African American employee of the Detroit Garbage Department, was the first worker investigated by the loyalty commission city voters authorized in 1949. A high-ranking Mason with a son serving in Korea, and a civil rights and union activist, Coleman denied ever being a communist. Nonetheless, he was fired after a quarter century on the job. Veteran actor Philip Loeb, a star of the long-running television series *The Goldbergs* and a supporter of various left-wing causes, lost his job after the sponsor of the show, General Foods, refused to keep it going as long as he was employed. Four years later, blacklisted from most other work, running out of money, and no longer able to keep his mentally ill son in a private institution, Loeb committed suicide. Vera Shlakman, a pioneering economic historian, fared better. After being fired by Queens College in 1952 for refusing to tell a Senate committee if she had ever been a communist, she eventually built a second career teaching social work. But she never regained a position in economics.

The many purposes anticommunism served helped sustain it even as the domestic Communist Party all but disappeared. But anticommunism also had a noninstrumental side, an expressive side—often irrational, fantastic, carnivalesque—such as McCarthy's attacks on Dean Acheson and George Marshall for being leaders of a pro-Soviet conspiracy or Indiana senator William Jenner's claim that "this country today is in the hands of a secret inner coterie which is directed by agents of the Soviet Union." Charges that defied common sense often had an emotional and partisan logic. Many were expressions of frustration over the lack of sustained peace after World War II, or reflections of populist antielitism, as in the case of charges against Acheson, whose immaculate tailoring and aristocratic pretensions won him wide dislike. McCarthy's draw lay in part in the antiestablishment image he cultivated, as a drinker, racetrack regular, and harasser of the high and mighty. Hearings and trials served as a kind of theater, sometimes of statecraft, sometimes of cruelty, and sometimes of the absurd.

A semisubmerged current of antimodernism fed anticommunism, a discomfort many Americans felt with the changes wrought by the triumph of urban industrialism over rural life, of individualism and the market over communal ties, of abstract bureaucratic institutions over organic relations, of democracy over hierarchy. (However, plenty of modernist urban liberals embraced anticommunism too.) Antistatism often wore anticommunist clothes, as conservatives saw the growth of the national government (and taxes to sustain it) as a threat to republican values and individual freedom, a way station on the road to full-blown tyranny. Communists provided a symbolic target and anticommunism an organizing framework for a range of resentments and dislikes that in many cases had nothing to do with communism itself.

Cold War Religion

Religion complemented anticommunism and patriotism in bolstering support for Cold War foreign policy and the militarization of American society. In the decades after World War II, the United States experienced an increase in churchgoing and public religiosity. On the eve of World War II, half of all Americans belonged to a church or synagogue; by 1960, that had risen to nearly two-thirds, a remarkable change from a hundred years earlier, when only a fifth of the population had a formal religious affiliation. In its increasing religiousness, the United States differed from other industrialized nations, which generally experienced a decline in churchgoing and a general secularization after World War II.

From the earliest days of English colonization, many white Protestant Americans believed that God had given them a mission to create a model society, a living embodiment of the ideal godly community, which would inspire others to live like them. During the Cold War, some policymakers formulated U.S. foreign policy in this light, believing that in opposing communism and promoting its own values the country was engaged in divine work. Three Cold War secretaries of state had grown up in deeply Protestant environments as sons of ministers: Dean Acheson, whose father rose to be an Episcopalian bishop; John Foster Dulles, the son of a Presbyterian minister, who himself considered becoming a minister; and Dean Rusk, who served under Presidents John F. Kennedy and Lyndon Johnson. Each, to at least some extent, imbued U.S. policy with a sense of Christian mission.

In Cold War rhetoric, Americans often described their enemy as "godless communism." Many Protestant anticommunist activists—like Billy Graham, who emerged in the early 1950s as the country's best-known evangelist—were as distressed by the atheism of communism as by its collectivism. In 1952, Democratic presidential candidate Adlai Stevenson described the international battle the United States was engaged in as against "the anti-Christ." His opponent, Dwight Eisenhower, described the contest with the Soviets as "a war of light against darkness, freedom against slavery, Godliness against atheism."

Catholics, too, embraced anticommunism as a religious cause. New York's Francis Cardinal Spellman and Los Angeles's Archbishop James Francis McIntyre emerged as among the most militant and tenacious anticommunists in the country. Among the Catholic laity, a wave of Marian piety developed during the Cold War that had an explicitly anticommunist dimension. Millions devoted themselves to Our Lady of Fatima, who in 1917 had appeared to three Portuguese children, saying that newly communist Russia could be converted to Christianity and world peace guaranteed if her followers undertook a particular set of prayers and religious acts. In 1950, a homegrown apparition occurred when the Virgin Mary appeared before Mary Ann Van Hoof, a Wisconsin housewife living a few miles from the hometown of Joe McCarthy, then in the process of becoming one of the country's most prominent Catholic politicians. At the height of the fervor about Mary's appearance and her warnings to Van Hoof about communism and Satan, some 100,000 pilgrims gathered on the Van Hoof farm hoping to witness a miracle. Church officials condemned the cult that grew up around Van Hoof but encouraged hundreds of thousands of Catholic adults and schoolchildren to regularly participate in prayers and rallies for Catholic prelates imprisoned in Eastern Europe.

In 1954, President Eisenhower, who after an adult lifetime of nonattendance began regularly going to church upon taking office, backed the successful effort to add the phrase "under God" to the Pledge of Allegiance. (The promotion of the idea of a "Judeo-Christian tradition" helped paper over the question of just what god the nation was putting itself under.) Later Eisenhower ordered "In God We Trust"—which Congress had declared the national motto—added to paper money (coins had carried the phrase since the Civil War). The armed services embraced religion too. Military leaders found it a useful tool for improving the behavior, discipline, and morale of their troops and projecting a clean-cut image to the public (rather than the hard-drinking, carousing reputation that the peacetime military had had in the past). In 1947, the Air Force began requiring all of its uniformed personnel to watch a series of religious films. Military chaplains increasingly came from evangelical denominations, which saw chaplaincy as a way to act on anticommunist beliefs while countering the influence of Catholics and liberal Protestants on American youth.

Official rhetoric and popular belief mirrored one another. Countless Americans of all faiths assumed that the struggle of the United States against the Soviet Union represented a battle between good and evil, not simply a contest between competing national interests, with their country acting on God's side. For many, this moral and spiritual dimension justified the heavy cost of battling communism in Korea, at home, and around the world. Religion helped give meaning to the long, frustrating struggle.

Ike

While most Americans, at least at first, accepted the necessity of the fighting in Korea, they did not like the war, especially as it dragged on, with the chance for anything more than a return to the prewar status gone and U.S. soldiers continuing to die in large numbers. The Truman administration's lack of strategy for either outright victory or disengagement contributed to the president's plummeting popularity. So did his seeming indifference to a series of corruption and influence-peddling scandals that plagued his second term. Inflation and high taxes, in part the result of the Korean War and the broader anticommunist effort, further diminished support for the president. Privately, Truman pretty much ruled out seeking another term well before the 1952 election, but he allowed his name to be entered into the New Hampshire Democratic primary, the first in the country. An embarrassing defeat to Tennessee senator Estes Kefauver closed his options, leading him to announce that he would not run again. Adlai Stevenson, the liberal governor of Illinois, won the nomination with Truman's support.

Among Republicans, the ongoing divide between East Coast moderates and midwestern conservatives again defined the contest for the presidential nomination. Robert Taft had the greatest support among party activists, but his more liberal opponents succeeded in recruiting as their standard-bearer Dwight Eisenhower, who was immensely popular thanks to his military record and nonpartisan demeanor. After besting Taft at the Republican convention, Eisenhower picked as his vice presidential running mate Richard Nixon, whose internationalist views on foreign policy generally coincided with the Dewey wing of the party but whose staunch anticommunism made him a conservative favorite.

As the campaign unfolded, Korea emerged as the leading issue. Though

Eisenhower changed his position on the war several times, his pledge to make ending it his number one priority, his promise to personally visit Korea, and his military background gave him an edge over Stevenson, who defended Truman's handling of the war. Boosted by his personal popularity, Eisenhower easily won the popular vote and carried the Electoral College by a landslide, even prevailing in four southern states, the best Republican showing in the region since 1928. Republican congressional candidates, including such leading anticommunists as McCarthy and Jenner, generally ran behind the national ticket, but the party managed to just barely win control of both houses of Congress.

As the first Republican president in twenty years, Eisenhower sought a smaller government, less involved in regulating the economy and everyday life. Like many conservatives, he wanted to transfer some power from Washington back to the states. But he did not reject wholesale the revolutionary expansion in the functions of the federal government that had come with the New Deal, World War II, and the Cold War. His decision at the start of his presidency not to try to undo the basic social welfare measures of the New Deal cemented the outcome of the postwar political and class contests, keeping in place the basic reform measures of the Roosevelt years but not further expanding the limited welfare state they created. Populating his cabinet with corporate executives, Eisenhower's moderate, pro-business policies sparked liberal and labor opposition, but his acceptance of the basic contours of the evolved social order took many of the most contentious domestic issues of the past off the political agenda. Some of Eisenhower's bitterest critics were on his right, conservatives deeply disappointed that the Republican capture of the White House and Congress did not lead to the dismantling of the New Deal.

Eisenhower faced conservative criticism over foreign policy as well. He generally supported the Cold War policies that the Truman administration had put into place and rejected the idea—though not always clearly, in public—that postwar communist gains had been the result of Democratic treachery. Also, he wanted the presidency to retain its dominant role in foreign policy. This put him at odds with conservative congressional Republicans who objected to the priority given to defending and bolstering Europe and who feared that the United Nations and the country's growing web of international alliances would diminish the sovereignty of the American people.

The battle came to a head over the so-called Bricker Amendment. Introduced by Senator John Bricker (John Gunther wrote of him, "Intellectually he is like interstellar space—a vast vacuum occasionally crossed by homeless, wandering clichés"), the proposed constitutional amendment would have limited the enforceability of international agreements within the United States, not allowing them to go beyond the constitutional limits on domestic legislation and requiring acts of Congress to put them into effect. Though what practical consequences the amendment would have remained unclear, symbolically the measure was an attack on internationalism, the power of the presidency, and, after the fact, the Yalta agreement, which many conservatives blamed for the communist control of Eastern Europe. To Eisenhower's dismay, Bricker's amendment quickly won the support of almost every Republican senator, major veterans' and business groups, southern politicians fearful that UN human rights provisions would mandate desegregation, and members of his own cabinet. After a bitter battle that lasted well over a year, the Senate rejected the amendment only because Minority Leader Lyndon B. Johnson decided that it was in the Democratic interest to ally with the president to defeat it.

While the Democrats helped Eisenhower win the battle over the general direction of foreign policy, Stalin helped the president with his greatest immediate challenge, ending the Korean War, by dropping dead. Upon taking office, Eisenhower rejected the military's plan for a new ground offensive in Korea, but he sent various signals that the United States would escalate the war if a settlement did not come soon. Stalin's death in early March 1953 made that unnecessary. The new Soviet leadership immediately launched a "peace initiative" to lessen international tensions, with Premier Georgy Malenkov saying at Stalin's funeral, "There are no contested issues in U.S.-Soviet relations that cannot be resolved by peaceful means."

After the Soviets and Chinese agreed among themselves to try to bring the Korean War to a rapid conclusion, armistice negotiations resumed in late March on the basis of a new Chinese proposal that no longer insisted on the immediate repatriation of all prisoners of war, whether or not they wanted to go home. The United States, still not satisfied with the terms, intensified the air war, bombing irrigation dams in North Korea to flood the rice fields and create food shortages. But growing dismay among its allies over U.S. inflexibility, along with recognition of the costs and difficulties of a new general offensive, led the Eisenhower administration to reverse course and make concessions of its own in late May. At that point Syngman Rhee, who had no desire to end the war with the north outside his control, tried to sabotage the negotiations, which had reached a tentative agreement that POWs who did not want to be repatriated would be handed over to an international commission. To make that impossible, Rhee unilaterally released some twenty-five thousand North Korean and Chinese prisoners. In spite of this provocation, with the major powers now all wanting the war over, an armistice agreement was signed on July 27, 1953, that divided the north and south along the current battle line, giving the south somewhat more territory than before the start of the war. A conference the following year to address long-term Korean political issues failed to make progress toward reunification, leaving the peninsula divided between two hostile states with little contact with each other. Both China and the United States kept troops in Korea through the late 1950s, when the Chinese withdrew and the United States reduced its force but armed it with atomic weapons.

The "New Look"

The end of the Korean War brought to a close the most dangerous, expensive, and ideologically charged phase of the Cold War (though in the early 1960s a series of confrontations once again raised the specter of all-out war between the United States and the Soviet Union). Even though tensions eased, the United States did not militarily demobilize. Instead, it remained in a state of high readiness, with a draft in place and a quantity of social resources allocated to war-making capacity that was unprecedented for peacetime. As a percentage of the gross domestic product (GDP), military spending did not return to the pre–Korean War level until the 1990s, after the end of the Cold War.

Even in peacetime, militarism shaped the pattern of American economic, technological, and geographic development. Military activities blocked off huge tracts of land from public use and polluted the soil, air, and water. (During the Cold War, in the United States, as in the Soviet Union, the military was the biggest single polluter, for the most part exempt from regulation and scrutiny in the name of national security.) In parts of the country with extensive military facilities, the military and military contractors helped set the cultural and political tone. In Washington, military leaders, the defense industries they sustained (and often went to work for upon retiring), and congressmen seeking military spending in their districts formed a political juggernaut (Eisenhower called it the "delta of power") that kept military appropriations high and initiated the development of many costly, unneeded, technically flawed weapons systems.

Yet even as militarism played an unprecedented peacetime role, the country did not become the garrison state that many feared. In the 1950s, a person walking around an American city or driving through the countryside would have been less likely to see soldiers in uniform or military installations than in many other parts of the communist and noncommunist worlds, from China to France. The military almost never directly got involved in electoral politics, and career military men, with the large exception of Eisenhower himself, rarely held top government positions.

A deep-rooted hostility to federal power, high taxes, and centralized planning, lodged primarily within the Republican Party, mitigated the Cold War trend toward a militarized society and command economy. The broad support for the Bricker Amendment, as well as the demand from powerful figures like Robert Taft for steep cuts in defense spending, reflected substantial elite reservations about the national security state. So did the decision to keep control over civil defense preparedness in civilian hands, largely at the state and local level, and not fund a proposed massive fallout shelter program. Many conservatives who earlier in the century had supported the spread of U.S. power through arms in the Philippines and Latin America did not have the stomach for what it took to maintain a global military presence, fearing that high taxes and a powerful state apparatus would undermine the very republican values they held dear.

Over his long Army career, Eisenhower had worked to deepen the ties between the military and business, and as president he opposed efforts to restrict federal power. Nonetheless, he too remained skeptical of the Cold War arms buildup and the militarization of American life. Eisenhower fought hard to reduce military spending from the levels called for by the Truman administration. Motivated in large part by a desire to lower the cost of military power ("more bang for the buck"), the Eisenhower administration introduced a "New Look" military strategy that called for increased dependence on strategic bombing, nuclear weapons, military aid to allies, and covert action, all cheaper alternatives to maintaining a massive ground force.

Eisenhower spoke eloquently about the costs and perils of militarization. In a speech responding to the 1953 Soviet peace initiative, he cataloged the social price of military spending: "The cost of one modern heavy bomber is this: a modern brick school in more than thirty cities. It is two electric power plants. . . . We pay for a single destroyer with new homes that could have housed more than eight thousand people." The Cold War arms race, he concluded was "not a way of life at all, in any true sense. Under the cloud of threatening war, it is humanity hanging from a cross of iron." Eight years later, in his farewell address, Eisenhower warned of the dangers of what he called the military-industrial complex: "This conjunction of an immense military establishment and a large arms industry is new in the American experience. The total influence—economic, political, even spiritual—is felt in every city, every State house, every office of the Federal government."

But Eisenhower succeeded only in modestly checking defense spending and ended up presiding over the elaboration of the very political and social arrangements he warned against. The New Look, with its stress on nuclear weapons and covert action, turned over inordinate power to an elite of scientists, engineers, and military managers whose activities few Americans could understand, let alone judge or control, and to secret operatives, whose activities most Americans did not even know of, far from the return to republican values many conservative critics of Cold War militarism professed to embrace. The United States did not become a garrison state, but in subtler ways militarism permeated society. At its zenith of power, the United States, as sociologist and left-wing critic C. Wright Mills put it, simultaneously had a "permanent-war economy and a private-corporation economy," as the quests for national security, international power, personal autonomy, and unregulated corporate capitalism lived in complex tension with one another.

McCarthy Falls, McCarthyism Continues

Like militarization, anticommunism declined in intensity with the end of the Korean War but remained a pervasive presence. McCarthy himself became a liability to those in power. Once the Republicans controlled the federal government, his charges and investigations began hurting his own party, which no longer needed him as a partisan tool to overcome entrenched Democratic rule. When McCarthy began going after central institutions of state power, threatening an investigation of the CIA and holding hearings on allegations that the Army harbored communists, his downfall came quickly. Eisenhower, who had kept quiet about McCarthy, moved behind the scenes to undercut him, while public critics became emboldened. A March 1953 broadcast by Edward R. Murrow on the CBS television network, dissecting McCarthy's methods, rebutting his charges, and blaming the country as a whole for allowing him to create an atmosphere of fear, reflected the changing political atmosphere and hastened the senator's decline. A televised Senate hearing in 1954, considering charges that McCarthy had pressured the Army to give a member of his staff preferential treatment, further reduced his backing, to the point that in December of that year his colleagues voted by a large margin to censure him for behavior unbecoming of a member of the Senate.

McCarthy's downfall did not end McCarthyism, which remained institutionalized, inside and outside of the government. Loyalty oaths and investigations continued, the State Department restricted the ability of communists and other dissenters to enter or leave the country, and Congress passed its most draconian anticommunist law yet in 1954, the Communist Control Act, which denied the Communist Party all legal rights. As the Communist Party shriveled, the FBI actually escalated its campaign against it with the 1956 creation of the Counterintelligence Program, or COINTELPRO, an effort to weaken the party through the use of agents provocateurs, the spread of false information, leaks to the media, tax audits, and the like. (Later, the FBI would use COINTELPRO to target other movements it disliked, including the civil rights movement.) In Hollywood, the blacklist remained solidly in place through the end of the 1950s. In television, it lasted even longer.

The hot war in Korea, and the Cold War before and after, narrowed political debate and cultural horizons for an entire generation. In 1952, Supreme Court justice William O. Douglas wrote that someone who left the country for several months would return to "be shocked at the arrogance and intolerance of great segments of the American press, at the arrogance and intolerance of many leaders in public office, at the arrogance and intolerance reflected in many of our attitudes toward Asia. He will find that thought is being standardized, that the permissible area of calm discussion is being narrowed, that the range of ideas is being limited, that many minds are closed." Even after the Korean War ended, few voices challenged the fundamental premises of American foreign policy, as the diversity of views about domestic and international politics never matched that in the immediate post–World War II years. With left-wing radicalism all but eliminated from American life, and conservative antistatism contained, a cultural and political consensus reigned, at least for a while.

PART II

The High Tide of
Liberal Democracy
(1954–1974)

CHAPTER 5

Suburban Nation

I n March 1936, Dorothea Lange, while working for the federal Resettle-
ment Administration, photographed a migrant worker and her daughters
in a farmworkers' camp in Nipomo, California. The image—usually
called "Migrant Madonna" or "Migrant Mother"—of the destitute woman,
thin-faced with worried brow, cradling a dirty-faced baby and flanked by
two children turned away from the camera, received wide circulation at the
time and ever since, seeming to capture the hopelessness of the "Okies"
whom John Steinbeck and Woody Guthrie had brought to national attention. Yet in 1979, when another photographer named Bill Ganzel managed
to locate the photo's subject, Florence Thompson (whose name Lange had
not bothered to learn), he discovered that the family, rather than starving to
death, had achieved a measure of comfort. All ten of Thompson's children
had jobs and their own homes, and together they had bought their mother a
house in Modesto (though when she later got sick they had difficulty paying
for her medical care).

The afterstory of the most iconic image of Depression-era America con-
veys the extraordinary economic upward mobility the country experienced
during the decades after World War II. Sustained, robust economic growth
made possible remarkable changes in the norms of living. After a short economic contraction during the reconversion from wartime to civilian production, the total output of goods and services began rising in 1947 and kept
rising every year until 1969, except in 1954 and 1958 during brief recessions.
Between 1950 and 1960, the gross national product, adjusted for inflation,
increased by 37 percent.

The United States was not unique in its economic performance. Western
European growth rates during what has been called the golden age of

capitalism were higher. But because the United States started the post–World War II era with so much greater wealth and productive capacity than any other nation, the gap between its standard of living and that elsewhere remained huge.

The changes brought by economic growth were not subtle. From 1945 to 1960, life expectancy at birth rose from 66.8 to 70.6 years for whites and from 57.7 to 63.6 years for blacks, huge jumps. Annual per capita consumption of meat went from 161 pounds in 1942 to 208 pounds in 1965, not necessarily improving health but boosting a sense of well-being. By 1960, 75 percent of families owned a car, 87 percent a television, and 75 percent a washing machine. For Americans who came of age during the Depression or the war, postwar prosperity meant not only that they lived better than their parents had but that they lived better than they had ever anticipated they would.

People in many circumstances benefited from the economic boom, but the greatest transformation took place in the new suburbs that sprang up across the nation. During the 1950s, a way of life blossomed that came to be seen as the embodiment of what it meant to be American: racially homogeneous, low-density neighborhoods of single-family homes; automobility; tight-knit nuclear families with stay-at-home mothers; and ever-rising levels of consumption. Idealized in the new medium of television in shows like *The Adventures of Ozzie and Harriet, Leave It to Beaver,* and *Father Knows Best*, suburbanization became the dominant model for development for decades to come. Government officials and business leaders presented backyard barbecues, washing machines, and Coca-Cola as proof of the superiority of mass production capitalism to Soviet-style communism. For better or worse, American suburban-style living and its cultural accoutrements came to be a measuring rod for social mores and economic achievement across the globe.

Mass Production

The economic boom of the postwar years rested in part on the extraordinary productivity of American industry, especially the mass production of consumer goods. The basic elements of Fordist production had been developed long before World War II, but the wartime and postwar years saw a significant renewal and expansion of the country's industrial capability. Many of the facilities the government built or improved during World War II for military purposes were later converted to civilian use. Wartime research breakthroughs in chemical engineering, aviation, computing, and electronics became the basis for new civilian products and production methods. Between 1947 and 1968, a long wave of corporate capital investment more than doubled the real net value of the country's manufacturing structures and equipment. Corporations extended Fordist production both geographically, to regions of the country that previously had few mass production facilities, and industrially, to sectors like home building and restaurants that until the war had almost exclusively used nonstandardized approaches to production that required much skilled labor.

Automobiles, and the companies that made and serviced them, lay at the heart of the postwar economy and culture. Looking back, nothing more quickly suggests the ideal of life in the 1950s and 1960s than a picture of a long, low automobile with huge tail fins, parked in front of a drive-in restaurant or a roadside motel. Driving back and forth across the country, for the sake of the journey itself, became a form of existential expression and cultural Americanism, from Jack Kerouac's *On the Road*, published in 1957, to John Steinbeck's more sedate *Travels with Charley*, published five years later, to Robert Frank's 1959 photo documentary, *The Americans.*

In 1949, when automobile manufacturers completed their reconversion from war production, they sold five million cars, surpassing their best prewar year, and sales continued to rise thereafter. By 1960, over sixty-one million cars were registered, one for every three Americans. By contrast, in Great Britain there was one car for every nine people, in Germany one for every twelve, and in Italy one for every twenty-five. From the mid-1950s through the mid-1960s, at least half of the twenty largest companies in the United States—the big car manufacturers, the major oil companies, and the largest tire maker—depended heavily on automobiles for their profits.

Employment in the automobile industry held steady at about three-quarters of a million during the quarter century after World War II, while output roughly doubled. This was typical of the mass production industries. In spite of a vast increase in the output of consumer goods, between 1947 and 1957 the number of factory operatives fell by 4 percent. Some of the increased productivity came from mechanization, some from new, more efficient management techniques, and some from simply forcing employees to work harder and faster.

Given the enormous attention U.S. foreign policy paid to creating opportunities abroad for American business, international activities contributed only modestly to the postwar economy. Home markets were far more important for industry and agriculture. Between 1950 and 1970, U.S. exports fluctuated between 3.5 and 5 percent of GNP. Imports rose from just under 3 percent of GNP to about 4 percent. These levels exceeded the immediate prewar norms but were not especially high by historic standards, failing to match the figures for the early years of the twentieth century.

Trade figures, however, do not tell the whole story. In some industries, imported raw materials were critical. During the 1950s, for example, most or all of the columbium, nickel, chromium, and cobalt used in the United States—necessary for making high-grade metals for aircraft engines and other advanced products—came from abroad. Also, in some sectors, American companies made more money from foreign investments and overseas facilities than from exporting products. U.S. investments abroad soared from less than $14 billion in 1946 to $120 billion in 1970.

The auto industry provides a good example of how, even with moderate levels of trade, companies benefited from the dominant economic position of the United States. Between 1950 and 1960, American companies exported automobiles and auto parts worth twice the value of imports. They also earned substantial profits from overseas operations. American companies, for example, produced 40 percent of the automobiles manufactured in Great Britain. Meanwhile, foreign car companies, far weaker and less efficient than American firms, presented virtually no competition inside the United States, except in the form of the Volkswagen Beetle at the low end of the market and some sports cars at the high end.

Government Spending and the Free Market

Many industries benefited from the militarization of the country, as federal spending on military goods and services pumped money into the economy on a massive scale. The arms industry was the most direct beneficiary, growing huge not only by supplying the American military but also by selling military goods abroad. The line between military and civilian production often blurred. Chrysler, in addition to being one of the country's largest manufacturers of tanks, also worked on atomic weapons development and along with Ford was heavily involved in defense electronics. American Motors—the fourth-largest car manufacturer—sold Jeeps to the Army. The aircraft, electronics, and metalworking industries were even more dependent than auto manufacturers on military production for sales, profits, and technical innovations.

Defense spending represented just one of the ways the federal government helped stimulate the postwar economy and lay the basis for profitable corporate activity. The government directly subsidized agriculture, shipping, and commercial mail rates and indirectly subsidized a host of industries by allowing accelerated amortization of buildings and equipment and depletion allowances (a form of tax deduction) for oil, gas, and mineral investors. Washington also made massive investments in infrastructure that aided business and reshaped the geography of production and distribution.

The 1950s and 1960s were the heyday of federal dam building, in the number of projects if not their individual size. The new projects lacked the links to social planning and democratic reform of the prewar Tennessee Valley Authority. By the end of the 1940s, the changing political climate allayed business and conservative fears that government dams would be a first step toward broader control over the economy. Agricultural and industrial interests pushed for projects that would provide irrigation, cheap power, and improved transportation. It would be hard to imagine Woody Guthrie singing the praises of the postwar dams built along the Colorado River, very expensive investments to serve very particular interests, as he had once memorialized the Grand Coulee Dam as a people's triumph while on the payroll of the Bonneville Power Administration.

Stripped of the aura of social reform, postwar dam and canal building nonetheless remained deeply Promethean, immersed in a cult of giantism that blithely dismissed the dangers of reordering nature. In 1954, after decades of debate and negotiations with Canada, Congress authorized construction of the St. Lawrence Seaway. Just five years (and a billion dollars) later, oceangoing ships could travel to the Great Lakes and the heart of North America. On the other side of the country, the Army Corps of Engineers spent $100 million to shorten by forty miles the trip between New Orleans and the Gulf of Mexico by creating a new outlet from the Mississippi River. Half a century later, it acted as a funnel for water that Hurricane Katrina drove toward New Orleans, contributing to the disastrous flooding of the city.

Federal highway building even more profoundly transformed the landscape and society. The federal government had been helping fund state road construction since the early twentieth century, but the extent of its involvement leaped upward with the 1956 Federal-Aid Highway Act, which called for the creation of a "National System of Interstate and Defense Highways." During the Roosevelt and Truman administrations, there had been some discussion of linking road building to multimodal transportation planning and urban renewal. But the most powerful proponents of federal road building—the trucking industry, the farm lobby (seeking to make it easier to get crops to market), automobile clubs, state highway engineers, construction companies, vehicle and construction equipment manufacturers, and labor unions—wanted to maximize construction through a narrower program that would use public money solely to lay concrete. The 1956 act, justified in part as a civil defense measure to allow the evacuation of populated areas in the event of nuclear war, gave them what they wanted. The law authorized a $25 billion outlay with which the federal government would cover 90 percent of the cost of interstate highways, with the rest to be paid by the states. To finance this massive investment, the act created a Highway Trust Fund, into which went all federal taxes on fuel, tires, and vehicles. Money from the trust could be used only to build roads.

It took nearly forty years to complete the 41,000-mile interstate highway system, at a far greater cost than originally expected, but its impact was, if anything, greater than anticipated. The new roads made car and truck travel economical for long distances as well as short ones, in the process undermining competing modes of transportation, especially the railroads. Interstates opened up large regions of the country for economic development, as transportation time and costs became less of a factor in decisions about where to locate factories and warehouses and where to live. But the new roads also doomed countless towns that they bypassed, and destroyed urban neighborhoods (often low income) that were sliced up by highways.

Dwight Eisenhower pushed through the interstate highway system in part because, like so many Americans, he associated cars with progress; more automobiles, he said, would bring "greater convenience . . . , greater happiness, and greater standards of living." But he also viewed construction of the system as a means of creating jobs and speeding recovery from the recession that began in mid-1953. Eisenhower and most of his political contemporaries had little interest in directly employing large numbers of workers on government projects, the way the New Deal had, or in having the federal government engage in economic activities in competition with the private sector. But they did not forswear the lesson of World War II that massive government spending could boost the economy and overcome tendencies toward stagnation. Appropriations for defense spending and infrastructure development could be used to hire contractors to undertake work that the private sector would not otherwise do, stimulating the economy without threatening corporate interests. A conservative, militarized Keynesianism emerged as the new fiscal orthodoxy; the government would spend freely on arming itself and building infrastructure, which kept up aggregate demand without threatening the power or profits of private enterprise. Bigness and growth were seen as self-evident goods.

Population, Unions, and Consumer Demand

Efficient production and government spending alone could not have sustained postwar economic expansion. Ballooning consumer demand provided a central economic engine. Between World War I and World War II, a fundamental economic challenge for American capitalism had been an inability to sell all the goods that could be produced. The New Deal tried, with only limited success, to use direct government spending and social welfare benefits to create sufficient demand to lift the country out of the Depression. Wartime military spending did the trick but at a government expenditure level beyond what even the most enthusiastic New Dealers imagined for peacetime. Immediately after the war, a shopping spree financed by the massive pool of wartime savings helped prevent a widely feared return to depression. When that one-time stimulus ended, a variety of developments combined to keep up consumer demand, including demographic and cultural changes, dense unionization, and suburbanization.

Rapidly growing population accounted for some of the increase in consumer spending. Between 1950 and 1960, the population leaped from 151 million to 178 million. This 18 percent increase was the largest since the first decade of the century. With immigration low, as a result of restrictions put in place after World War I, a sharp rise in the birth rate, the "baby boom," accounted for most of the increase.

Unexpectedly, major demographic trends of the twentieth century reversed as World War II drew to a close. People began marrying younger, in greater numbers, and with fewer divorces than in the preceding decades. The median age of first marriage for men fell to under twenty-three, while for women it barely topped twenty. And they had children at a younger age, and more of them. In 1950, 3.6 million children were born, a million more than a decade earlier. In 1960, the number reached 4.3 million.

Population growth and the flood of new households formed—over ten million between 1947 and 1957—combined with rising income and a relatively equitable distribution of wealth to create a huge market for mass production goods. Starting in the Depression and accelerating during the 1940s, income inequality fell substantially. The introduction of the minimum wage, the wartime demand for unskilled labor, rising productivity, higher levels of worker education, and widespread unionization all contributed to a compression of the wage structure. Well into the 1960s, an income distribution markedly more equitable than before the New Deal remained in place.

Unions helped push up working-class spending power. Though labor made few major organizational breakthroughs, union membership grew from fourteen million when World War II ended to seventeen million in 1960, so that roughly a third of nonagricultural wage earners carried a union card throughout the period. Almost every round of contract negotiations became an occasion for raising wages.

Unions also won a growing array of what were called "social" or "fringe" benefits. The United Mine Workers paved the way. In 1945 the union proposed that employers finance health and retirement benefits for its members. It took a fierce, five-year struggle, which involved four large strikes, a temporary government takeover of the industry, and massive fines against the union for defying court orders, for the mine workers to achieve their goal. But when Horace Alinscough, a retired miner from a small town in Wyoming, received the first Mine Workers pension check, a revolution in social provision began. Through trust funds financed by royalty payments on every ton of mined coal, the Mine Workers' plan provided generous retirement payments to supplement Social Security, aid to miners' widows and orphaned children, and medical care. The union even built its own chain of hospitals in medically underserved coal mining regions of Virginia, West Virginia, and Kentucky.

Some other unions took an approach similar to that of the Mine Workers, getting employers to contribute to benefit funds, which in turn were used to finance union-run health facilities and other employee benefits. In New York City, by the late 1950s half a million workers and members of their families were receiving medical care at union clinics. Generally, though, large corporations fiercely resisted paying for benefit plans that they themselves would not control.

Unions won a leg up in 1949, when the federal courts confirmed a National Labor Relations Board ruling that employers had a legal obligation to engage in collective bargaining over pension demands and that workers could strike if they refused to do so. In September of that year, Ford agreed to a pension plan for workers with at least thirty years' service in order to avoid a walkout by the Auto Workers. Soon thereafter, 600,000 steelworkers walked off their jobs, returning to work forty-two days later when their employers agreed to provide pensions and half the cost of a rudimentary health insurance plan. Other corporations followed suit, often reluctantly. It took a 104-day strike before Chrysler broke down and agreed to a pension plan. Next came General Motors, which agreed to a pension plan and the auto industry's first medical insurance benefit as part of a five-year contract it negotiated in 1950. In the years that followed, companies in other industries began agreeing to health and pension benefits too, while the terms of such plans steadily improved.

Private and public welfare benefits were intimately linked. The Auto Workers' and Steelworkers' drives for company pensions stemmed from the inadequacies of Social Security. Inflation had eaten away at the spending power of federal retirement payments, which in 1948 averaged only $25 a month, and nearly half the country's workers were not covered by the program at all. Business opposition had blocked repeated efforts to improve benefits by raising taxes. The CIO unions, by demanding that employers provide retirement benefits above and beyond Social Security payments, created an incentive for business to drop its opposition to improving the government system. After a long legislative battle, in June 1950 Congress passed a law more than doubling Social Security benefits and extending coverage to ten million additional workers, including a million domestic servants and a lesser number of agricultural workers. In 1949, a typical retiring autoworker could count on receiving only $32 a month, all from Social Security. Just three years later, improved Social Security and company pensions combined to nearly quadruple that, to $123 a month.

The United Automobile Workers took the lead in winning yet another benefit, supplementary unemployment payments. In many industries, workers continued to suffer from layoffs as a result of seasonal production patterns and cyclical downturns. During the 1958 recession, steel companies laid off 200,000 workers and put another 300,000 on shortened work schedules. In 1955, Ford agreed to create a fund from which laid-off workers would receive payments in addition to whatever government unemployment benefits they were eligible for. By the early 1960s, such plans covered some two and a half million workers in the steel, rubber, garment, electrical equipment, and auto industries. As in the case of private pensions, supplementary unemployment benefits filled a vacuum created by the inadequacy of government welfare provisions and created pressure to improve them, in this instance leading many states to boost the unemployment insurance benefits they provided.

Many conservatives and businesses remained unreconciled to the growing strength of unionism. In the mid-1950s, midsize manufacturing firms, less able than the industrial giants to pass on rising labor costs to customers, took the lead in a new attack on organized labor, beginning with a political and ideological offensive against the union shop. The newly formed National Right-to-Work Committee framed the issue not as one of the balance of power between business and labor but rather of individual worker rights being impinged upon by compulsory unionism.

Widely publicized hearings between 1957 and 1959 by the Senate Committee on Improper Activities in the Labor and Management Field furthered the notion that unions sometimes exploited the very people they claimed to represent. The committee, led by Arkansas Democrat John McClellan but largely driven by its counsel, Robert F. Kennedy, exposed corruption in a number of local and national unions. The giant Teamsters union came in for a drubbing, as mobbed-up local leaders paraded before the committee. Teamsters president Dave Beck was forced to resign and later went to jail for corruption, while his replacement, Jimmy Hoffa, faced relentless grilling and investigations that made him a national symbol of recalcitrant labor. Public opinion of organized labor, extremely positive before the hearings, fell sharply.

Hoping to capitalize, in 1958 conservative business leaders and Republicans put "right-to-work" referenda on the ballot in six states; if passed, they would have outlawed the union shop in major centers of industry, including Ohio, Illinois, and California. For the most part it proved a disaster. Unions mobilized their members to defeat the ballot measures, succeeding everywhere but Kansas. A large turnout of unionists and liberals contributed to major Republican losses. In California and Ohio, Democratic gubernatorial candidates won in landslides against opponents who endorsed the union shop ban. In congressional races, the Democrats made their strongest showing since the height of the New Deal.

But the victory was short-lived. Divisions within the labor movement and the image of labor leaders as corrupt bosses paved the way for the 1959 passage of the Landrum-Griffin Act, which made only a few concessions to labor while putting in place a new level of government oversight most union officials did not want. The law contained a "bill of rights" for union members; required unions to hold regular, secret-ballot elections and file detailed financial reports; forbade picketing to demand union recognition; and tightened restrictions on secondary boycotts.

Parallel to the effort to check union power politically, employers also tried to check it at the bargaining table. The recession that began in 1957 led businesses to push for greater flexibility on the shop floor, increase workloads, resist union efforts for greater job security, and attempt to weaken or eliminate cost-of-living adjustments, resulting in a series of hard-fought strikes, including in the glass, coal, auto, and copper industries.

The most important clash took place in the steel industry. In 1959, the major steel companies, led by U.S. Steel, set out to undermine the power of the United Steelworkers of America, hoping to force the union to give up contract language that made it difficult for managers to reorganize production and reduce the size of the workforce without negotiating with the union. After the companies put forth demands they knew the union would reject, over half a million steelworkers walked off their jobs. In a remarkable display of solidarity, they stayed out for 116 days, the largest loss of workdays from any labor dispute in the country's history, returning to their jobs only after the Eisenhower administration obtained a court injunction forcing them back. As it became clear that even then no settlement was near, Eisenhower and Richard Nixon pressured the steel companies to back down. The end result was a smashing defeat for the companies, who agreed to a decent wage increase and effectively abandoned their effort to win freedom to unilaterally change shop floor arrangements.

The postwar stream of wage increases and social benefits won by unions revolutionized working-class life. Heavily unionized midwestern manufacturing centers had some of the highest levels of homeownership in the country. Jack Metzgar, the son of a Johnstown, Pennsylvania, steelworker, recalled, "In 1946, we did not have a car, a television set, or a refrigerator. By 1952 we had all those things." Union gains, along with improved government welfare programs, meant not only more money each week but the confidence to spend it, as families knew that government and employer benefits would provide security in the event of sickness, layoffs, or old age. When Metzgar's mother suffered a series of heart attacks, medical bills forced the family to sell their house and move into a government project, but the Steelworkers' health insurance plan allowed them to avoid financial ruin. As wage rates went up and security grew, working-class families found themselves able to send children to college, take vacations, and retire while still healthy, while providing an ongoing stimulus to the economy through the greater consumption of goods and services. Metzgar, remembering the increased income, security, and sense of possibility that the Steelworkers' union brought his family, wrote, "If what we lived through in the 1950s was not liberation, then liberation never happens in real human lives."

Not everyone experienced liberation to the same extent. Over the course of the 1950s, the gap between wage rates for union and nonunion workers increased substantially. Even within the unionized sector, gaps grew. In 1947, workers in the heavily unionized but highly competitive apparel industry earned on average 71 percent of what autoworkers made; by 1965 that had fallen to just 45 percent.

Americans liked to believe that hard work paid off morally and financially, but to a much greater extent than they usually acknowledged, their standard of living reflected circumstances largely or entirely out of their control. A worker in a heavily capitalized, unionized, relatively noncompetitive industry, like auto or steel, brought home more money, received more benefits, and had greater security than a worker who happened to work in a more labor-intensive, nonunion, heavily competitive sector, like retail trade. Which type of job a person held rested, to a great extent, on their sex, race, and place of residence, with whites, men, and northerners having a disproportionate hold on the best jobs. Even education, increasingly touted as key to upward mobility, could not overcome the segmentation of the labor market and the discriminatory processes that slotted certain demographic groups into certain types of jobs. In 1959, the median income of white men with only a high school education exceeded that of African American women with a college degree by nearly 20 percent. And while union leaders saw their drive to improve their members' benefits as promoting an upgrading of social welfare for all workers, it often only added to the social distance between those with extensive private protections and those without.

The Mechanics of Consumerism

A powerful array of cultural and commercial forces helped make mass spending possible. For the most part these forces were not new, but they reached greater sophistication and unmatched pervasiveness after World War II. Already, the national culture had largely repudiated the virtue of thrift. Both Keynesian economic thinking and commercial interests stressed the virtues of spending, not saving. Egging on the buyer were mass marketers who emerged from the war with well-established arsenals of selling techniques, including branded products, credit purchase plans, and extensive advertising.

New sources of consumer credit augmented rising income. Before the war, department stores, hotels, and oil companies had issued various kinds of payment cards and charge plates that could be used to make purchases. After the war, many stores introduced revolving credit accounts. In 1949, the Diners Club went the next step when it introduced a credit card that could be used to make purchases from multiple merchants. By the late 1950s, various competing cards had been introduced, including the American Express Card; Bank of America's BankAmericard, which later evolved into the Visa card; and the Hilton Hotels' Carte Blanche. The tax code encouraged consumers to take on debt by allowing them to deduct interest payments in calculating their federal income tax. The percentage of tax returns with claims for such deductions rose from under 3 percent in 1950 to over 30 percent ten years later. At the end of the 1960s, credit cards still were used for only a very small percentage of all purchases, dwarfed in dollar amount by other forms of consumer credit, like car loans and home mortgages, but the infrastructure was in place for what would become an explosion of credit card buying in the last decades of the twentieth century.

The emergence of discount stores also facilitated mass purchasing, making appliances, furniture, and other items previously sold through specialty or department stores affordable to young families setting up new households. E. J. Korvette, founded in 1948 with a single Manhattan store, perfected the model, generating a huge volume of sales through rock-bottom prices. Keeping costs down by providing a minimum of store amenities, Korvette's learned how to make money even with very small markups. Soon it was building ever larger stores within an expanding radius from New York, locating many in rapidly growing suburbs. Other companies followed a similar trajectory. By 1960, the country had over thirteen hundred discount stores. Two years later, two giant variety store companies, Woolworth and Kresge, started discount chains of their own, as did the Dayton's department store company, which launched its first Target store. That same year, in Rogers, Arkansas, Sam Walton opened his first Wal-Mart Discount City store.

Television, first publicly demonstrated at the 1939 New York World's Fair, provided a potent new advertising medium to promote mass consumption. The percentage of households that owned a television set rose from just over 2 percent in 1949 to nearly 56 percent in 1954 and 90 percent in 1962. By the end of the 1950s, over a billion and a half dollars a year was going to television advertising. By choosing particular radio and television shows, advertisers could aim products at particular segments of the market. Superficially, rising working-class income allowed a kind of democracy of consumption, as categories of goods and services once reserved for the rich—appliances, cars, vacations, and the like—became widely accessible. But within each category, different types and grades of goods and services were produced for different economic strata, and often for different generational and cultural groupings as well. A working-class teenager might be able to buy a well-worn Chevy with savings from a summer job, but it took a hefty income to afford a new Buick, let alone a Cadillac or Lincoln, designed for the country club set.

Suburbanization

Suburbanization promoted consumer spending. It entailed not only spending on dwellings themselves but on furniture and household appliances to put in them, and on all kinds of goods associated with suburban living.

At the end of World War II, the United States faced a huge housing shortage. Since the start of the Depression a decade and a half earlier, very few homes had been built. Returned servicemen and new families found it nearly impossible to find decent housing. Millions doubled up with friends or relatives or crowded into structures thrown up during the war as temporary shelters. After the father of future basketball star Kareem Abdul-Jabbar returned home from the Army, his family spent years "rooming" in a large apartment in Harlem, which they shared with six other tenants, before finally moving to a public housing project.

In spite of government incentives, postwar housing construction ramped up slowly, hampered by shortages of materials, a cumbersome system for distributing them, inefficient builders, and economic uncertainty. But by the late 1940s, a construction boom started. With well over a million new housing units—most single-family homes—being built annually, far above the pre-Depression rate, the landscape of the nation became rapidly transformed.

Between 1950 and 1970, over 80 percent of the population growth of the country took place in the suburbs, which went from housing thirty-six million people to seventy-four million. Cities grew at a much slower rate, with fourteen of the largest fifteen cities actually losing population between 1950 and 1960. Only in the South and West did urban populations shoot up, in many cases because cities annexed adjacent land. The proportion of Americans living in a metropolitan area outside of a city proper nearly matched the population within city boundaries by 1960, and well exceeded it by 1970.

Large-scale developers took the lead in creating the new suburbia, a departure from the past, when small outfits operating in localized markets accounted for most residential construction. Metropolitan outskirts provided large, undeveloped tracts of the sort generally no longer available within city limits, on which developers could build many units. Turning farm fields and forests into suburban communities generated exceptionally large, one-time gains from land appreciation and the development process—part of a long national history of finding profitable opportunities on frontiers of one sort or another, where a way of life could be constructed from scratch. Unlike earlier developers who subdivided tracts, put in roads and utilities, and then sold off parcels to individual owners or small builders, the new breed of postwar developers bought large expanses of land, prepared sites, and then built and marketed houses themselves. The scale of the new developments was unprecedented: five thousand homes in Oak Forest, near Houston; eight thousand in Park Forest, outside Chicago; three thousand in Panorama City, California; 17,500 in Lakewood, California; 17,400 in Levittown, New York; 16,000 in Levittown, Pennsylvania; and on and on, all across the country.

Suburban developers took advantage of economies of scale and innovative production techniques. William Levitt gained national fame in the late 1940s by building a new community that ultimately housed eighty-two thousand people on what had been Long Island potato fields, twenty-five miles from Times Square. To keep down prices, he built small houses, just 750 square feet; put them on concrete slabs rather than basements; used non-union labor; set up his own supply companies; and replaced traditional materials with cheaper ones, like plywood and composition board. He rented his first houses at only $60 a month, soon switching to selling them at the extraordinarily low price of $6,990.

Suburbanization and militarization, two of the great social trends of the twentieth century, had links to each other. Many of the techniques used to make suburban homes affordable had been developed during the war on military-related projects. William Levitt and his brother Alfred learned how to build fast and cheap putting up defense worker housing in Virginia and Hawaii, skills William honed as a Navy Seabee constructing airfields in the Pacific. Industrialist Henry J. Kaiser applied lessons he learned during the war turning out ships, steel, and defense worker housing to mass-produce postwar tract homes near Los Angeles. The federal government requirement that defense plants be built away from existing centers of population created a ready market for suburban homes. Lakewood housed workers from the naval station and Douglas Aircraft plant in nearby Long Beach and from other military contractors that clustered in Southern California. In Levittown, New Jersey, members of the armed services and their families occupied 12 percent of the houses. Veterans Administration loans, authorized by the GI Bill, also connected the military and suburbia. Levitt at first sold houses only to veterans, who had both a moral claim and a ready source of financing for new housing at a time when it still constituted a rare commodity. Nationwide, VA loans financed a sixth of all nonfarm homes built between 1945 and 1955.

A desire to escape overcrowded, dirty city neighborhoods fed suburban growth. The protagonist of the title story in Philip Roth's collection *Goodbye, Columbus* (which won the National Book Award in 1960) quips that it was "as though the hundred and eighty feet that the suburbs rose in altitude above Newark brought one closer to heaven, for the sun itself became bigger, lower, and rounder, and soon I was driving past long lawns which seemed to be twirling water on themselves, and past houses where no one sat on stoops, where lights were on but no windows open, for those inside, refusing to share the very texture of life with those of us outside, regulated with a dial the amounts of moisture that were allowed access to their skin."

Some suburban residents were attracted by the very newness of the communities into which they moved. One pioneer suburbanite in Northern California's Santa Clara Valley recalled, "We were thrilled to death. . . . Everyone else was moving in at the same time as us. It was a whole new adventure for us. For everyone!"

Most people, though, moved to the suburbs not in search of a lifestyle but because there they could find the best and sometimes the only opportunity to get more living space at a price they could afford. With urban houses or large apartments difficult or impossible to find and expensive when available, suburban homes represented a cheaper and more obtainable solution to the housing needs of new and growing families. Often mortgage payments, taxes, and other expenses for a modest suburban home were below the cost of renting an equivalent size city apartment. And suburban homes were more adaptable. Many suburban dwellers added second stories to ranch houses, built porches and additions, and tacked on carports, making modest homes more livable. Where there were affordable urban alternatives to suburbanization, like the modestly priced, nonprofit cooperative housing built by unions and veterans' groups in New York and a few other cities, families lined up to get in. But in most of the country, no such alternatives could be found.

Government policy tilted both house builders and house seekers away from the cities toward the suburbs. No law or document announced that it was the policy of the federal government to promote suburban development as the preferred mode of living, but various statutes and administrative decisions worked together with that effect, reflecting a largely assumed rather than argued consensus among politicians and power brokers.

The mortgage guarantee programs of the VA and the Federal Housing Administration (set up in 1934) were critical to suburban development by making it possible for millions of families to buy homes that they otherwise would not have been able to afford. The federal income tax deduction for interest payments on borrowed funds provided a massive subsidy of home-ownership. Government-backed mortgages and mortgage tax deductions were not statutorily restricted to the suburbs, but FHA and VA policies heavily favored single-family homes in white, middle-class suburban settings over multi-unit dwellings, urban locales, or nonwhite or racially mixed communities. From the beginning of the FHA through 1960, the agency guaranteed mortgages worth $730 per capita in Fairfax, Virginia, a suburbanizing community adjacent to Washington, D.C., but only $87 per capita in the capital itself. Similarly, New York's Nassau County, home of Levittown and other suburban developments, got $601 per capita, while the Bronx got but $10.

Federal infrastructure support also aided suburbanization. The interstate highway system made automobile commuting from bedroom communities to city centers more practical. When, in the 1960s, it became clear that suburban septic tanks had created a major water pollution problem, the federal government began funding suburban sewer systems, spending $30 billion during the 1970s alone. Even when it did not directly appropriate money, by allowing tax-free bonds to be used to finance infrastructure projects, the federal government made rapid suburbanization more practical, lowering the cost of government for suburbanites while forgoing public funds that could have been used in other ways.

While federal aid flowed to the suburbs, Washington provided little help to the cities. Millions of urban renters got no direct benefit from the tax code. And as urban housing aged, the massive federal involvement in private home financing did little to renew or replace it. Relatively little public housing got built either. The 1949 Housing Act authorized the construction of 810,000 units of public housing, most put in urban settings, but it took twenty years, not the intended six, to build all the units. In 1955, a peak year for housing construction, 277,000 units got started with FHA loan guarantees, 393,000 with VA guarantees, but construction began on just 20,000 units of public housing. In 1980, public housing accounted for just 1 percent of the national housing stock, compared to 46 percent in England and Wales and 37 percent in France. Federally funded urban renewal often ended up hurting rather than helping poor city residents by financing the replacement of worn but still vibrant neighborhoods with commercial centers or housing for wealthier residents. Transportation policy also put cities at a disadvantage. The federal government provided no funds for urban transportation systems, standing by as subway, commuter rail, and trolley systems deteriorated or were abandoned.

In moving millions out of central cities, the government-supported process of suburbanization reinforced and extended the barriers that maintained racially homogeneous communities. Some African Americans had long lived on urban outskirts, but after World War II blacks were much less likely to relocate to suburbs than were whites. In 1960, African Americans constituted less than 5 percent of the suburban population. Furthermore, they lived almost exclusively in all-black communities, including new subdivisions put up in the South abutting existing African American urban neighborhoods. Very few African Americans moved into the majority-white suburbs springing up across the country.

Suburban developers, real estate agents, banks, government officials, and homeowners deployed an arsenal of weapons to make sure that they didn't. Until 1948, it had been a common practice to exclude undesired groups through legally binding covenants on deeds, which forbade the resale of a house to people in designated categories, usually nonwhites or non-Christians. Following a campaign led by the NAACP, in 1948 the Supreme

Court, in *Shelley v. Kraemer,* ruled public enforcement of racially restrictive covenants to be unconstitutional. But in practice the ruling did little or nothing to open up white neighborhoods to other groups.

Many suburban developers, like William Levitt, openly refused to sell new homes to nonwhites, resisting legal and political pressure to do so. In the early 1950s, Levittown, New York, was the largest community in the United States without a single black resident. In 1960, it still had but fifty-seven African Americans among its 65,276 residents.

Federal policies made it difficult for builders to develop integrated communities even if they wanted to. Federal agencies ranked the risks entailed for mortgage lending in neighborhoods across the country, automatically assigning black neighborhoods the lowest grade and giving the highest ratings only to "homogeneous" areas. Private lenders used the ratings to deny loans to areas deemed high risk, which effectively included almost all integrated neighborhoods. Though federal practices became somewhat less racist over the course of the 1950s, the FHA and VA continued to promote segregated housing and steer a disproportionate amount of loan guarantees to whites.

Local governments and real estate agents more directly enforced racial barriers. Many suburban communities used zoning and building codes and their discriminatory application to keep out low-income and nonwhite residents. Some suburban towns used urban renewal programs to eradicate existing black neighborhoods. White real estate agents, as an accepted national practice, refused to sell African Americans homes in white areas.

If an African American family did manage to buy a home in a white neighborhood, threats, harassment, or violence were often deployed to try to force them to move and discourage others from coming in. When in 1957 Daisy and Bill Myers and their three small children became the first African Americans to move into Levittown, Pennsylvania, relocating from a nearby community to a small pink house on Deepgreen Lane in search of more living space, they had to suffer through demonstrations outside their home, complete with Confederate flags, rock throwing, and cross burning, not an uncommon experience for black "pioneers." In cities like Detroit, Philadelphia, and Chicago, the resistance to racial integration at times was even fiercer, as homeowner and neighborhood associations, often in conjunction with real estate agents, mobilized residents against nonwhite newcomers. The support that government authorities gave to residential segregation served to legitimate resistance to housing integration, which was stronger than resistance to workplace integration and more likely to move beyond legal boundaries.

A Nation on the Move

Suburbanization constituted one part of a series of large-scale postwar population movements. In addition to outward movement within metropolitan regions, overlapping population flows included rural to urban migration, migration from the South to the North and from the East and Midwest to the West, and an influx of Spanish-speaking people to the continental United States. These demographic shifts helped sustain economic growth in an era of low immigration by bringing workers to expanding areas, while contributing to a process of national cultural homogenization.

In 1950, 36 percent of the population still lived in rural areas. By 1970, that had fallen to just 27 percent. Many people left rural areas because of the allure of city life and urban job opportunities in the expanding postwar economy. Movies, radio, mass circulation magazines like *Life* and *Look,* and eventually television brought images of city living into even the most isolated parts of the country. Many young people eagerly exchanged the hardships of rural living for life in the city. But the drastic decline in rural employment opportunities probably played a more important role in the flight from the countryside. Before World War II, agriculture and mining together supported one in four American families. After the war, consolidation and mechanization radically reduced the number of jobs in these industries. By 1970, agriculture engaged less than 4 percent of the workforce (with many of those workers also holding nonfarm jobs). Mining employment likewise dropped sharply, largely as a result of mechanization. Continuous coal mining machines, a rarity in 1950, accounted for half the underground coal mined in 1967.

The greatest rural job loss occurred in the South. The rapid decline in coal mining employment contributed to a massive exodus from southern Appalachia. Between 1940 and 1970 well over three million people left the region. Some counties in Kentucky and West Virginia lost 40 percent of their population during the 1950s alone. Changes in farming had an even greater effect. During the 1950s, some five and a half million families in the South gave up farming, with three and a half million departing the region entirely.

The most dramatic transformation took place in the Mississippi Delta, where a way of life based on the labor-intensive cultivation of cotton by sharecroppers and tenant farmers, which emerged out of the Reconstruction era, began to disappear. During the 1940s, the possibility of mechanized cotton picking became increasingly attractive to planters, who saw many of their male workers leave for jobs in the North or in southern cities or for the armed services. Women and children who remained behind, getting money from men receiving military pay or working elsewhere, were often no longer willing to toil in cotton fields. The first self-propelled cotton-picking machine went into service in 1947, and within just a few years a substantial part of the southern cotton crop was being harvested by machine. The use of sprayed chemicals rather than hand-hoeing to control weeds complemented the picking machines in drastically reducing labor needs. So did crop diversification. Between 1950 and 1960, the farm population of the Delta fell by half. Elsewhere in the South, too, capital-intensive agriculture replaced labor-intensive agriculture, facilitated by federal subsidy and farm extension programs that favored large-scale operations, mechanization, and the use of chemical fertilizers and insecticides. Tractors replaced mules, sharecropping disappeared, and small farm owners, tenants, and sharecroppers moved on in search of work and a new way of life.

White southern migrants tended to move to the Midwest. By 1970, two and a half million southern-born whites lived in the region, where they made up 5 to 10 percent of the populations of Ohio, Indiana, and Michigan. Overwhelmingly blue-collar, they tended to gravitate to factory, transportation, and service jobs that did not require much formal education. At a time when economic expansion and union strength were pushing up wages and benefits, such jobs offered upward mobility. Some migrants clustered together in urban communities like Uptown in Chicago and Over-the-Rhine in Cincinnati. Others chose to live in rural areas, suburbs, or urban neighborhoods without a distinctive southern feel.

White southern migrants brought with them an intense religiosity, a fervent, expressive Protestantism that contributed to the postwar spread of evangelicalism. In the Midwest, fundamentalist and Pentecostal churches became widespread as newcomers, not finding churches of their denominations, began founding new ones. During the 1940s, the Southern Baptist Convention decided to disregard a half-century-old agreement with the Northern Baptists that set territorial limits for each group. By the early 1970s, the midwestern states had hundreds of Southern Baptist churches, with thirty-three in Wayne County, Michigan (which includes Detroit), alone. Southerners also brought to the Midwest and California forms of entertainment, like country music and stock car racing, that gradually won national audiences. Yet even with their distinctive cultural orientation and close links to the regions they came from—traveling back frequently for visits, vacations, and temporary work—white southerners generally blended in with the rest of the population in the communities to which they moved, not appearing as a highly visible subgroup.

African American migrants from the South did not have that luxury. Most moved to the same midwestern cities as white southerners or to East Coast cities like New York, Baltimore, and Philadelphia. The severe discriminatory bars in the housing market meant that once there they generally could find homes only in inner-city black neighborhoods. With whites moving out to suburbs, the African American proportion of the urban population shot up. In Chicago it went from 14 percent in 1950 to 40 percent in 1980; in Dayton, from 14 percent to 37 percent; in St. Louis, from 18 percent to 46 percent; in New York, from 10 percent to 25 percent.

Residential segregation diminished the economic opportunities for African American newcomers because, just as the southern migration peaked in the 1950s and 1960s, good entry-level jobs, especially in manufacturing, were becoming harder to find in northern central cities. Some were lost to automation, others to new factories being built in suburbs where African Americans could not live or in other parts of the country. Many employers systematically set out to reduce their workforces in the major industrial cities, hoping to undermine the power of the union movement and lower their taxes and labor costs. Manufacturers who wanted to stay in urban locations often found it difficult to get enough land to build the kind of sprawling one-story plants that had come to be seen as more efficient than older-style multistory facilities. RCA began shifting production of consumer goods out of Camden, New Jersey, to Bloomington, Indiana, even before World War II. General Electric began building a series of midsize plants in the South to lessen its dependence on its huge production centers in the Northeast and Midwest, hotbeds of union militancy. The big automobile companies similarly decentralized, building parts and assembly plants in suburban Detroit and other parts of the country, contributing to a drop of 147,000 manufacturing jobs in Detroit proper between 1947 and 1963. Nationally, during that period, manufacturing employment in the twenty-five largest cities fell, but in the suburbs that surrounded them it grew by well over 50 percent. Residential discrimination thus contributed to the divergent trajectories of white and black southern migrants, with the latter failing to achieve the same degree of economic mobility and social integration as the former, even though they shared rural backgrounds and low levels of educational achievement.

At the same time that population flowed northward, it also flowed to the West Coast and Southwest. The transplantation of professional sports teams acknowledged the growing wealth and population of the West, as baseball's Dodgers and Giants left New York for California in 1958, followed two years later by the Minneapolis Lakers, which became the West Coast's first National Basketball Association team. Federal spending spurred westward migration. Western politicians often denounced government spending in the abstract, but they courted federal dollars to develop the region. Federal money kept the defense industries humming; helped pay for the huge public works that provided water for agriculture and burgeoning cities; allowed West Coast universities to develop into major centers of scientific research; paid for highways; and, through the Social Security system, made it possible for people from other parts of the country to retire to the warm climates of Southern California and the desert states.

Air-conditioning made the Southwest attractive to newcomers. The technology was developed early in the twentieth century for large commercial and industrial buildings. Small home units only began to be sold in significant numbers after World War II. In 1952, builders began incorporating air-conditioning into tract houses. The FHA encouraged the practice by allowing, from 1957 on, the cost of appliances to be covered by home mortgages. Builders liked air-conditioning because it allowed them to dispense with features traditionally used to promote cooling and ventilation—overhanging eaves, good insulation, attic fans, movable sashes and screens, shady landscaping—which were expensive to provide. By 1960, six and a half million air conditioners were in use; ten years later, twenty-four million, including seventeen million room units.

As in the case of migration to the North, migration to the West often brought economic mobility, as evidenced in the experience of "Migrant Madonna" Florence Thompson and her children. The relocation of millions of poor Americans to more prosperous regions of the country with greater job opportunities contributed to the postwar rise in average national income. For many, the West did not quite live up to the image of middle-class utopia projected by California governor Earl Warren, whose almost ridiculously attractive family seemed to embody the wondrous possibilities of American life. But the promise that moving on would bring some measure of salvation did not prove completely false for those who made the great trek westward.

Immigration played a smaller role in American life during the two decades after World War II than it had during most of U.S. history. The post–World War I quota system all but banned immigration from Asia and Africa while limiting European immigration to a level far below its peak at the turn of the century. Unlike in the past, the number of immigrants who came to the United States from elsewhere in the Americas, primarily Canada and Mexico, which were not covered by the quota system, was about the same as the number of immigrants from Europe.

Canadian immigrants outnumbered those from Mexico. However, largely English-speaking (with a minority of French speakers from Quebec) and culturally close to the white population of the northern United States, they had little social impact except in the northern parts of New England and the Great Lakes states, where most settled. Mexican immigrants had greater social visibility. World War II and the postwar economic expansion brought increased migration, as Mexicans came north to take advantage of job opportunities, especially in agriculture and transportation. In addition, the wartime shortage of labor led the United States to establish the "Bracero" (from the Spanish *brazo* for "arm") program, under which Mexican citizens could enter the United States as contract laborers to do seasonal agricultural work without facing the military draft. Meant to be a temporary program, it remained in place until 1964 because it provided a convenient source of cheap labor for western growers, who had to pay Bracero workers only 75 percent of the prevailing wage.

On the East Coast, Puerto Rican migration added to the Spanish-speaking population. Though Puerto Ricans had been citizens of the United States since 1917, relocation to the mainland had been modest through World War II. After the war, a decline in rural employment, especially in the sugarcane and coffee industries, led to urbanization on the island and, coming at a time when travel costs to the mainland dropped dramatically, migration to the East Coast, especially New York. By 1970, over one-third of all Puerto Ricans were living on the mainland. New York alone had a Puerto Rican population of 800,000, making it the largest Puerto Rican city in the world.

The population movements of the post–World War II decades resulted in a vast resegregation of the country. While the African American population became more evenly distributed among the different regions, within regions a new segregation was effected as whites left cities for suburbs and nonwhites replaced them. Between 1950 and 1960, some 3.6 million whites moved out of the country's twelve largest cities, while 4.5 million blacks moved in. Many African American migrants found themselves living in far more segregated circumstances in the North than they had in the South. With jobs moving out of the cities too, newcomers found their hopes for better lives circumscribed and frustrated. While whites embarked on the great suburban adventure of the 1950s, blacks, Puerto Ricans, Mexicans, and other minority groups were left to inherit cities with decaying infrastructures, declining or stagnant employment opportunities, inadequate housing, and declining tax bases. By the 1960s, the notion became widely accepted that the country faced an "urban crisis," a crisis that contained within it all the accumulated economic, political, racial, and social tensions created by the mass migrations of the postwar era.

Toward a National Suburban Culture

Suburbanization, especially the rapid development of whole communities, necessitated the creation of new structures of everyday life. One early Levittown resident remembered, "There were no telephones, no shops. . . . There was no grass, no trees, just mounds of dirt and snow covering it all." Along the streets and cul-de-sacs of raw housing tracts, a new national suburban culture emerged.

The car lay at its heart. Suburbanization reinforced the centrality of the automobile to American life. Though residents of new suburban communities often initially traveled back to a city for work, shopping, entertainment, and services, over time that became less common, as employers and services moved outward or sprung up anew in forms built around the automobile. Shopping centers, office parks, drive-in restaurants, and new churches became the hubs of suburban life.

Some pre–World War II suburban developers, most notably J. C. Nichols, who built the upper-class Country Club District in Kansas City, had incorporated shopping districts into residential communities, designing them to have an urban feel but with plenty of room for parking. After the war, developers no longer made any effort to integrate shopping areas into their surroundings, instead planting them in the middle of seas of parking lots. To get to shopping, suburbanites had to drive, but once there the larger shopping centers provided a pedestrian experience, with small shops lining walkways between "anchor" department stores. Shopping center managers, to encourage shoppers to come regularly, tried to make them substitutes for village centers or urban downtowns, with professional offices for doctors and lawyers, space for community meetings, post offices and banks, restaurants, movie theaters, even skating rinks.

The expanding suburban market and favorable federal tax treatment—in 1954, as an antirecessionary measure, Congress amended the tax code to permit the accelerated depreciation of building costs—led to the spread of large shopping centers across the country. More and more were fully enclosed, climate-controlled malls, windowless introverted spaces. By 1970, the country had thirteen thousand shopping centers; by 1984, twenty thousand, which accounted for nearly two-thirds of all retail sales.

Shopping centers spurned the unruliness and heterogeneity of city life. With few exceptions, they aimed to attract white middle-class shoppers, choosing locations and designs meant to keep out others. Store employees also tended to be white, in many cases women living nearby who worked part-time, a contrast to the large department stores in northern cities, which in the decades after World War II finally began to hire substantial numbers of African American and Puerto Rican workers. (Southern stores remained racially segregated in their customers and staff well into the 1960s.) Though they served as surrogate downtowns, shopping centers were not truly public spaces, generally restricting demonstrations, picketing, and other activities deemed undesirable in an effort to maintain controlled, union-free, controversy-free shopping environments.

Shopping centers soon began to supplant downtown shopping districts, as suburban customers preferred the convenience of nearby stores and easy parking. With shoppers and investors going elsewhere, in city after city the old downtowns grew shabby and landmark stores began to close. An exodus of employers also hurt established downtowns. Not only did factories move out but so did many offices, which relocated to nondescript buildings strung along suburban roads or, at the high end, to "office parks" on highly landscaped campuses far removed from the public access, unpredictability, and worn-out feel of their old locales.

A new set of car-oriented services popped up on suburban roadways. The drive-in restaurant was the purest expression of car culture. The first opened in Dallas in 1921. Not long after, the White Tower chain combined fast-food service for automobile travelers with franchise ownership, a combination that proved ideally suited to taking advantage of the market opportunities created by postwar suburban development and the expansion of the national highway network. Franchising opened the door for men and women of modest means to get in on the national romance with entrepreneurship, gave companies capital to grow and a managerial cadre with a stake in their brands, and provided travelers with standardized services across the country. The most successful fast-food chains, like McDonald's, which expanded from a single store in San Bernardino, California, to a pervasive national presence, used the techniques of Fordism—a limited array of standardized products, specialized machinery, and an intense division of labor—to keep prices down and volume up. Hotel and motel chains, like Holiday Inn, likewise used franchising to profit from the increasing dominance of the automobile for long trips as well as short ones and the sprawling character of postwar development.

In many parts of the country, a patchwork of new government agencies formed as suburbs grew—school districts, water districts, fire districts, police districts—fragmenting governance into multitudinous geographic and functional units. (Exceptions to this pattern occurred in areas, mostly in the South and Southwest, where state laws made it easy for cities to annex their suburbs.) Suburban politics often revolved around service delivery, but sprawling growth made regional planning and coordination difficult. Political parties found it hard to build infrastructure in this new terrain, increasingly relying on mass media, rather than local clubs and party leaders, to reach voters.

With population dispersed, town centers not always present, and civil authority fragmented, churches and synagogues emerged as key nodes of suburban social organization. In addition to their spiritual role, suburban religious institutions sponsored a host of secular activities and imparted to their members a sense of community. Their rapid growth contributed to the remarkable increase in formal religious affiliation during the postwar decades and helped sustain a normative acceptance of the divine in the new social landscape.

Suburbanization muted class distinctions. In communities like Levittown, blue-collar and white-collar workers, civil servants, even small business owners lived side by side in houses that looked the same and contained very similar furnishings. "There is . . . no wrong side of the tracks," noted *Harper's* in 1953 about the new suburbs. As diners (popular in the eastern half of the country) and bowling alleys spread from city to suburban settings, they shed their male, blue-collar ambience, deliberately seeking a broader, middle-income, family clientele.

Conviviality and informality characterized the new suburban culture. Many young suburban families did not have parents or older relatives living nearby. (The drive back to the city to visit the folks became a cherished—or dreaded—weekend ritual.) For everyday companionship and support, they turned to their neighbors, minding each other's children and gathering for endless rounds of backyard barbecues, Tupperware parties, and television watching (before a set in every home became common). Children were constantly in and out of each other's homes. Steve Wozniak, the son of a Lockheed engineer who would play an outsize role in the creation of personal computers, fondly recalled that in the suburb where he grew up, "there were kids all over, so many kids on our block, and we would just go up and down the block and run into each other and start riding bikes and agree to do something."

Bike riding aside, the suburban way of life depended on cheap, plentiful energy. Single-family homes tend to be less energy efficient than multi-unit buildings, especially postwar tract housing, much of which was single-story and lacked traditional temperature-moderating features, depending instead on air-conditioning and extensive heating systems. Dependence on

automobiles for so many everyday tasks—getting to work, shopping, transporting children, finding entertainment—contributed to a tripling of national oil consumption between 1948 and 1972, with gasoline accounting for
about 40 percent of the use. In 1949, a gallon of gasoline cost only twenty-
seven cents, and in real terms the price kept falling until 1972. With little
incentive to improve fuel consumption, manufacturers let car mileage slip from
an average of fifteen miles per gallon in 1949 to thirteen and a half in 1972.

Architects, planners, and government officials were not oblivious to the
environmental impact of suburbanization. Recognizing the high energy demands of tract housing, in the early postwar years both solar and nuclear
power were given considerable attention as possible alternatives to fossil
fuels for heating and cooling homes and generating electricity. Some architects and the federal government promoted energy-efficient house designs.
But with oil and coal so cheap and plentiful, home builders and home buyers
saw little reason for making higher initial investments to keep energy usage
down. Similarly, the loss of open space to suburban development, the pollution of groundwater by suburban septic tanks, and the destruction of wet-
lands and floodplains to build tract housing all raised concern but resulted
in little concrete action until the mid-1960s.

Family Togetherness and Gender Divides

Suburbanization coincided with and reinforced an increased emphasis on
the importance of family. In the decades after World War II, cultural authorities and ordinary people embraced marriage and family as the central
sources of personal satisfaction to a greater extent than ever before. Millions
of Americans turned to their families for stability and assurance in a dangerous, uncertain world. And they expected from them more than ever before:
emotional support, recreation, sexual pleasure, self-improvement, and an
existential sense of purpose. The families so weighted tended to be nuclear
families, as many young couples started new households distant from the
homes and neighborhoods in which they grew up.

Sex played a more prominent role in marriage than in the past. The postwar years saw increasing social disapproval and punishment for sex outside
of marriage, especially homosexuality and sexual intercourse by unmarried
women. In the mid-1950s, laws in every state in the Union criminalized sod-
omy, deployed primarily against gay men. Unmarried pregnancy brought
shame and hiding, especially for middle-class white women, leading to hundreds of thousands of dangerous, illegal abortions each year and a very large

number of babies put up for adoption. But within marriage, sex and sexual pleasure were held forth as healthy and desirable by marriage guidebooks, psychological and medical authorities, and in commercial culture.

The ideology of family that pervaded postwar society espoused very different roles for men and women. In a reinvigoration of the notion of the family wage, government, cultural, business, and labor organizations promoted the idea that families could and should live solely on the wages of a male breadwinner. For women, in something of a throwback to the nineteenth century, domesticity, specifically motherhood and wifedom, were widely held forth as the appropriate basis of identity and fulfillment.

Women themselves had complex, sometimes contradictory feelings about what writer Betty Friedan later famously called "the feminine mystique." When the war ended, the percentage of adult women who worked for wages fell from a historic wartime high of 37 percent to under 30 percent. Most women who left their jobs did so voluntarily, eager to start families or simply to escape the hardships of manufacturing or service work. But many were forced out of their jobs, particularly in well-paid, traditionally male bastions, like the automobile, iron and steel, machine-making, and transportation industries, where employers, often with the support of male unionists, reestablished the prewar sexual division of labor. Women also dropped out of college to begin families, making up a smaller proportion of college students and getting a smaller proportion of advanced degrees during the 1950s than before the war.

Soon, though, women began returning to wage labor in increasing numbers. Married women, with older children able to take care of themselves or already out of the house, accounted for the bulk of the growth. By 1960, the percentage of adult women who worked outside their home matched the wartime high.

Most women worked for economic reasons. As had always been the case, for large segments of the population the notion of a family wage taunted reality rather than represented it. Women with no breadwinner to depend on or in households in which the primary earner did not make enough to support a family worked because they had to. This burden disproportionately fell on nonwhite women; continuing a long-standing pattern, a far higher percentage of black women worked for wages than did white women, nearly half in the mid-1950s. Other women took jobs not out of sheer necessity but because doing so enabled their families to afford such discretionary items as vacations, college education for their children, and new appliances.

Working women found themselves clustered, by cultural norms and discrimination, into just a few areas of the economy. For African Americans, household cleaning and laundering provided the largest source of employment; for whites, light manufacturing, retail trade, clerical work, health care, and education. Even within these categories, men and women worked in different tracks. In 1960, 85 percent of elementary school teachers were female, while 90 percent of high school principals were male. Such job segregation, which all but excluded women from many well-paid sectors of the economy, contributed to a median wage for women that was less than 60 percent of that for men.

For women who did not work outside their homes—still the large majority—family life could be satisfying, or not, or both at the same time. Many women cherished the opportunity to devote themselves to raising their children and to home life more generally. One survey respondent reported that marriage had given her a "place in life. I feel I am doing exactly as I am fitted. . . . I am happy or content much more of the time than I am not." But many women chafed or grew depressed by their financial dependence on their husbands and long days spent, without adult company, caring for children, doing laundry, cooking, and keeping up homes to standards being pushed ever upward by advertisers and women's magazines. Technological advances—indoor plumbing, electricity, clothes washers and dryers, electric irons, vacuum cleaners, refrigerators, freezers, and garbage disposals—did not reduce the amount of time spent on housework (from the 1910s through the 1950s, housewives consistently spent a little over fifty hours a week on domestic labor), instead contributing to a rise in norms of cleanliness, cooking, childcare, and family activity. In some cases, by replacing commercial services like laundries, they actually created more work. One mother of four told Friedan, who in 1957 surveyed her Smith College classmates about their lives fifteen years after their graduation, "I begin to feel I have no personality. I'm a server of food and putter-on of pants and a bedmaker, somebody who can be called on when you want something. But who am I?"

Friedan's classmate was far from alone in having an existential crisis in the suburban nation. As suburban living spread across the landscape, it faced a fusillade of criticism, largely on cultural and aesthetic grounds. (Environmental and racial issues received less attention.) Lewis Mumford and other cultural critics excoriated the suburbs for perceived sterility and uniformity. Suburban residents, as well as the communities they lived in, came under attack for conformity, blandness, and lack of taste. Novelist John Keats's *The Crack in the Picture Window* (1956) presented suburbia as a dystopia of predatory real estate practices and pervasive discontent, while Sloan Wilson, whose *The Man in the Gray Flannel Suit* (1955) was made into a popular movie starring Gregory Peck and Jennifer Jones, portrayed a spiritual crisis in the commuting class. (Critiques of suburban living more sympathetic to residents, put forth by Friedan and Herbert Gans, pointed out the isolated lives of many housewives, trapped during the day by housework, children, and a lack of transportation.)

While critics of suburbia pointed out many obvious flaws with the emerging dominant mode of American life, their tone often reflected class snobbery more than anything else, contempt for working people with different values and tastes than cosmopolitan intellectuals, and a lack of imagination and information about the actualities of daily life in the suburbs. Rarely did they point out the benefits the suburbs brought, including affordable dwellings and a measure of personal privacy, something the rich always had but that the urban working class and even middle class often could not find. The much-publicized criticism of the suburbs was at one with a general distrust of mass culture and mass politics that characterized liberal thinking during the 1950s. Only very occasionally did critics of suburban life examine the way core liberal policies, especially the New Deal approach to housing, had created the world they so disliked.

CHAPTER 6

"We the Union Army"

D uring the three decades after World War II, a civil rights movement
radically expanded American democracy. The changes it brought to
the lives of Americans and the structures of governance constituted
the most important political development of the entire postwar era. A prolonged campaign for racial equality, fought largely but not exclusively by
African Americans, propelled the movement. But it entailed more than the
struggle for black advancement, as it transformed fundamental ideas about
the rights of individuals in the society, their social roles, the relationship
between government and the citizenry, and the means of achieving political
and social change.

The civil rights movement sometimes was called the "Second Reconstruction." The term pointed to the way that it could be seen as the last act
of the Civil War, a fight for formal, legal racial equality as promised in the
constitutional amendments and laws passed in the aftermath of the War
Between the States. Like the first Reconstruction, the civil rights movement
at times took on a quasi-revolutionary character, especially in the South,
where it set off deep, sometimes violent social conflict.

The postwar civil rights movement unfolded with both continuities and
breaks with the past. It was not a steady movement forward. Though it did
not reach its high tide until the mid-1960s, much happened before then. Immediately after World War II, civil rights efforts swelled across the country
from bases in established black institutions and liberal and labor groups that
had grown during the New Deal and the war. In the South, the movement
soon came to a halt in the face of a white countermobilization. By the mid-
1950s, however, demographic and legal changes created the basis for the
emergence of a new southern-based mass movement. After some gains, it too

was checked by forces defending the existing racial order. But as the 1950s ended and the 1960s began, a larger, more militant phase of the civil rights movement took off, which ultimately brought about not only an extension and redefinition of democracy but also a reconstitution of almost every aspect of American society.

The Impact of World War II and the Cold War

Wars facilitated moments of advance for African Americans, as the need for social mobilization and the rhetoric of democracy created favorable conditions for knocking down discriminatory barriers in the labor market, the law, and the military. Rosa Parks, who later became world-famous for setting off the Montgomery bus boycott, first rode on an integrated vehicle during World War II, when she took a job at an Army Air Force base in Montgomery, Alabama. A federal order desegregating public spaces and transportation on military bases meant that Parks could begin her trip home from work on a trolley sitting with whites, before transferring to a segregated city bus. During the war, Parks became one of a small number of registered black voters in Montgomery, having joined a voter registration drive pushed forward by E. D. Nixon, a Pullman car porter who headed the local branches of the Brotherhood of Sleeping Car Porters and the NAACP.

As hundreds of thousands of African Americans left the rural South during the war for better jobs and lives elsewhere, they escaped the semifeudal system of social control and outright terror that white southerners enforced in the countryside. With greater latitude for action, they built institutions that provided bases for their struggle for rights. Black trade union membership swelled in the North and some urbanized parts of the South. The NAACP's membership grew, and new civil rights groups, like the Congress of Racial Equality (CORE), were founded.

Changes in political thinking and the law complemented demographic and economic shifts in the push for greater rights. The New Deal forwent a direct attack on voting bars in the South, but it did promote the idea of democratic rights by using racially nondiscriminatory election procedures in a variety of contexts other than the selection of officeholders, such as for determining whether workers would be represented by a union. When Congress failed to make the wartime Fair Employment Practices Committee permanent, a growing number of states and cities, starting with New York State in 1945, passed laws making it illegal to discriminate in employment or union membership on the basis of race, religion, or national origin. While these laws lacked effective enforcement procedures, they represented important public statements against discriminatory practices and exerted some degree of pressure on employers and unions to change their ways. For its part, the Supreme Court, dominated by Roosevelt and Truman appointees, issued a series of decisions during the 1940s that outlawed or limited racially discriminatory practices, including its rulings on whites-only primary elections and housing covenants; a decision requiring unions with exclusive representation rights to equally protect all workers covered by their contracts regardless of race; and a ban on discrimination against black passengers in interstate transportation.

In the South, the drive to improve black life focused on voting. As the war ended, African Americans and their white allies broke with the timidity of the Roosevelt administration to directly attack the political basis of white supremacy. Local voter leagues, the NAACP, heavily black or left-wing unions, and black colleges sponsored voter registration drives, often led by returning veterans. By 1952, a million southern African Americans were registered to vote, 20 percent of those eligible, quadrupling the number registered in 1944. Though in the rural Deep South black voters remained very scarce, in some parts of the region they became a significant political force, undermining or checking segregationist thrusts. In Atlanta, blacks made up about a quarter of the voters by 1949 and had begun to force a change in the city's politics, leading, among other things, to the hiring of the first African American policeman. In North Carolina, African Americans were elected to local government positions for the first time since Reconstruction in Winston-Salem (1947), Fayetteville (1949), Greensboro (1951), and Durham (1953).

Steps to democratize the voting system did not only affect African Americans, nor did they occur only in the South. The New Deal, the democratic rhetoric of the war, and the postwar international discussion of human rights broadened notions of democracy. In 1945, Georgia eliminated its poll tax, which greatly increased the white franchise, while several other states eliminated the tax specifically for veterans. Three years later, the last states to bar Indians from voting or serving on juries, New Mexico and Arizona, ended their prohibitions. In 1952, when the territory of Puerto Rico was reorganized as a commonwealth, it eliminated a literacy requirement for voting by women. Meanwhile, court rulings against laws banning naturalized citizens born in designated countries from voting allowed more Asian Americans to vote. By the early 1950s, something close to universal adult suffrage was becoming the norm, with the very large exception of African Americans in the South (and the lesser exception of felons and ex-felons).

In the North, where African Americans did not face voting bars, other issues, particularly the fight against job discrimination and for the desegregation of housing and public facilities, took the fore as civil rights, African American, labor, left-wing, and liberal groups pressed for racial equality and desegregation using tactics ranging from lawsuits to pressure on elected officials to public demonstrations of various kinds. In Newark, New Jersey, African Americans mounted protests against segregated swimming pools, restaurants, theaters, and bars. When in 1947 the state adopted a new constitution, it barred racial segregation in schools and in the state militia. In New York, ongoing campaigns against segregation led to legislation extending the state ban on discrimination to housing and public accommodations.

As notions of biological racial superiority became less acceptable in the light of changed scientific thinking and the wartime fight against racialist regimes, many northern and national organizations began at least token desegregation. New York University hired its first full-time black faculty member in 1946. Three years later, the American Association of University Women, the American Nurses Association, and the House of Delegates of the American Medical Association all admitted African Americans for the first time.

No change in race relations received more attention than the desegregation of major league baseball in 1947 with the promotion of Jackie Robinson to the Brooklyn Dodgers, after a prolonged campaign to integrate the sport by the black press and communist-led groups. The National Football League began allowing black players in 1946; the National Basketball Association in 1950. Participant sports also began desegregating, often only after considerable struggle. UAW members at the Ford River Rouge plant, many of whom were African American, began a campaign to desegregate local bowling alleys in 1941, throwing up huge picket lines when owners resisted. In 1944, their national union launched a drive to desegregate the American Bowling Congress, attracting various allies including the Catholic Youth Organization and the NAACP. After six years, a failed attempt to start a rival group, and several lawsuits, the country's leading bowling organization finally ended its policy of restricting its leagues and tournaments to members of "the white male sex."

The modest but significant postwar steps toward broader political and civil rights did not generate a self-sustaining process of social change. The year 1948 proved a high point of national concern about civil rights. Though the Dixiecrat revolt failed to cost the Democrats the presidential election, party leaders, in an effort to reintegrate southern segregationists into the party, thereafter distanced themselves from their brief, bold rhetorical support for equal rights. Republicans, seeing the possibility of building up their party in the South by attracting white urban and suburban voters, also downplayed their support for federal civil rights action. In the 1952 election, both parties adopted weaker civil rights platforms than they had four years earlier, and Adlai Stevenson picked a southern segregationist, John Sparkman, as his running mate.

The domestic anticommunist drive hurt the civil rights movement. In the South, a wave of liberals elected to Congress and to statehouses during the mid- and late 1940s found themselves under fierce attack, red-baited by opponents for their pro-labor and progressive economic views and challenged for failing to sufficiently defend the region's racial order. Many went down to defeat or retreated on civil rights. The anticommunist crusade decimated civil rights groups with ties to communist-led organizations while weakening some of the unions that most actively fought for racial equality. It also undermined the influence of left-wing black leaders like Paul Robeson and W. E. B. DuBois, who faced investigations, indictments, and the loss of public venues to express their views.

White liberals, especially in the North, generally supported civil rights but, unlike leftists, not as a matter of urgency. Many accepted the outlook of Gunnar Myrdal's influential report *An American Dilemma,* which suggested that a widely shared American belief in fairness and equality was on the way toward ultimately overcoming racial prejudice. In the liberal view, the key to ending racial inequality lay in education and modernization of the South. Seeking to speed up the process would only incite a white backlash. Optimistic that the problem of racial discrimination would in effect solve itself through general social advancement, most liberals gave much greater attention to the fight against communism, labor issues, and economic growth. When they did get involved in civil rights campaigns, it often was as an offshoot of their anticommunism, either to draw support away from civil rights groups with communist links or in response to Soviet-bloc propaganda attacking the United States for its racial practices.

Buses, Schools, and the Southern Black Movement

A little-noted event in 1953 previewed a reconfigured southern movement for black rights. In Baton Rouge, Louisiana, as in many southern cities, the second-class status of black bus riders provoked deep anger. Baton Rouge buses were divided into sections for white riders in the front and for black riders in the rear. If seats in the latter area were filled, black riders had to stand even if there were empty seats in the white section. In 1953, under pressure from African Americans, a city ordinance modified bus segregation so that it would be first come, first served, with blacks filling seats starting in the back of the bus, and whites from the front. White bus drivers, the day-to-day enforcers of segregation, refused to accept the change. To block it, they went on strike, leaving twenty-five thousand daily riders stranded. "The sole issue is racial segregation," said an officer of their union. Within days, the state attorney general stepped in, ruling the new city ordinance illegal. Victorious, the drivers returned to the buses, but 90 percent of the black riders did not, refusing the travel under the old system. Black churches organized the boycott, under the leadership of T. J. Jemison, a minister and NAACP activist, whose father headed the National Baptist Convention, the largest organization of people of African descent in the world. To transport the boycotters, church leaders set up a network of private cars. To raise money and keep up spirits, they held nightly mass meetings. With black riders accounting for two-thirds of the bus system's revenue, the boycott soon led to a compromise proposal to reserve the two front bus seats for whites, the backseat for blacks, allowing the rest to be filled first come, first served. After much debate, the boycott leaders accepted the settlement, ending the protest after ten days.

Baton Rouge revealed the outlines of a new mode of church-based, nonviolent mass action. The urbanization of southern blacks underlay this approach to fighting for rights, which used the growing economic importance of urban blacks as a lever on the white power structure. Black churches, swelling in size with urbanization, had organizational and spiritual resources, able and well-respected leaders not dependent on whites for their livelihood, and deep community ties that made them unmatched bases for social and political mobilization once they decided to push for civil rights. But such efforts blossomed only after two events further altered the political climate in the South, a Supreme Court decision and a terrible murder.

Brown v. Board of Education changed everything, and very little. The decision—perhaps the best-known in the history of American jurisprudence—was the culmination of an NAACP campaign, conceived of in the early 1930s, to advance black education by attacking through litigation the vast inequality in schooling offered to whites and blacks. At first, the civil rights group did not directly challenge the 1896 Supreme Court ruling in *Plessy v. Ferguson* upholding separate but equal accommodations as constitutional. Instead, it argued that, within the context of segregated school systems, public agencies were failing to provide blacks and whites with equal opportunities, which *Plessy* implied was a violation of the Fourteenth Amendment guarantee of equal protection for all citizens. The first NAACP cases demanded equal access to professional and graduate education. After victories in some of those cases, including court orders that blacks be admitted to previously all-white schools when no equivalent segregated facilities existed for them, the NAACP moved on to elementary and secondary education.

The assault on school inequality, though centrally planned and coordinated, rested on local activism by black parents and students fed up with the woefully inadequate schools and second-class treatment they had to deal with. It took extraordinary courage for them to take on the established racial order. One of the five cases consolidated in the *Brown* decision involved the schools in Clarendon County, South Carolina, where in 1949 the NAACP challenged the vast inequity in schooling for whites and blacks. The plaintiffs in the case soon found themselves fired from their jobs, denied credit, and in one instance the victim of house arson. Another of the *Brown* cases began with a two-week strike by 450 black high school students in Prince Edward County, Virginia, protesting the miserable condition of their school. The parents of the strike leader, sixteen-year-old Barbara Johns, so feared for her safety—the Ku Klux Klan burned a cross on their lawn—that they sent her to Montgomery, Alabama, to live with her uncle, Vernon Johns, a Baptist minister and uncompromising critic of segregation.

Authorities in many parts of the South, worried that the federal courts would find unequal facilities unconstitutional, increased spending on black schools. Prince Edward County built a new high school for black students, which opened in 1953. But by then the NAACP had shifted its line of attack, beginning in 1950 to argue that segregated schools were inherently unequal and therefore unconstitutional. The only constitutional remedy would be desegregation.

The case that gave *Brown* its name carried the most weight in the argument that segregation in itself violated the law. After Linda Brown was denied admittance to a white elementary school in Topeka, Kansas, her father, Oliver, whose unionized job as a welder for a railroad offered him some protection from economic reprisal, became a plaintiff for a suit brought by the NAACP seeking to desegregate the city's schools. The suit highlighted that school segregation was not simply a southern practice but a national one; Kansas was one of four states—along with Arizona, New Mexico, and Wyoming—that allowed school districts to practice racial segregation if they chose to, while seventeen other states, in the South and the border region, required it. In Topeka, there were not gross inequities between the schools for whites and blacks. For the Browns, the chief issue was that segregation meant that Linda had a much longer and more dangerous trip to school than if she could attend the one nearest to her home. The NAACP introduced an additional issue by contending, with support from social scientists it recruited to testify, that racial segregation, especially when enforced by government, had a detrimental effect on black children, denoting their inferiority, undermining their motivation to learn, and retarding their educational and emotional development.

The Supreme Court heard the *Brown* case in December 1952. Not eager to make a quick decision, it asked for a rehearing, which took place a year later. By then President Eisenhower had appointed Earl Warren as chief justice, succeeding Fred Vinson, who had died in September. Finally, in May 1954, the Court issued a short, unanimous ruling that in public education, "separate education facilities are inherently unequal" and unconstitutional. Agreeing with the NAACP, it declared that for black children segregation "generates a feeling of inferiority as to their status in their community that may affect their hearts and minds in a way unlikely to ever be undone."

As a statement of law and national policy, *Brown* proved thunderous, stripping segregation of the legitimacy it had long enjoyed through its endorsement by the federal government. The ruling went a long way toward denationalizing and defederalizing the legal structures of white supremacy, and it inspired civil rights advocates to press harder for racial equality and justice. But *Brown* did very little to change its immediate subject, the racial segregation of public schools.

The Supreme Court took a year to issue an order implementing *Brown*. In the interim, some school districts, largely in border states, desegregated on their own. Baltimore dropped all racial bars to school enrollment, and the city's Catholic schools and public housing authority soon desegregated as well. In Topeka, the school board decided to desegregate even before the Supreme Court heard the case that originated there.

Initial reactions farther south varied greatly. Many of the major white southern religious denominations endorsed *Brown,* including the Methodists, Presbyterians, and Baptists, though local church leaders fell on both sides of the issue. (In the same year as *Brown,* Billy Graham began refusing to allow segregated seating at his revival meetings, even in the Deep South.) Some southern elected officials suggested that they would accept the Court decision, while others vowed to resist it.

Over time, the balance swung to the resisters. In the summer following the *Brown* decision, leading white citizens in the Mississippi Delta founded the White Citizens' Council to resist desegregation, using economic reprisals to discourage African Americans from seeking to register to vote, send their children to integrated schools, or in other ways assert their rights. Similar groups soon sprang up in other states, like the North Carolina Patriots and the Southern Gentlemen in Louisiana. Many prominent southern politicians began coming out against *Brown,* culminating in a March 1956 "Southern Manifesto" signed by 101 members of Congress, condemning the decision as a "clear abuse of judicial power" and pledging that the South would use "all lawful means" to resist it. Many southern states began using anticommunist laws and hearings against the civil rights movement, especially the NAACP, setting up agencies to report on the purported involvement of subversives in the struggle for black rights. Mississippi's State Sovereignty Commission, created in 1956, developed into a secret police force that worked closely with the Citizens' Councils to spy on and undermine civil rights groups.

The unequal apportionment of seats in southern state legislatures, giving disproportionate power to heavily black rural areas, where whites were particularly vehement in opposing desegregation and few if any blacks could vote, contributed to the passage of a rash of new segregationist laws. Louisiana amended its constitution to make school integration illegal. Voters in Georgia and Mississippi approved amendments to their constitutions allowing their legislatures to close schools rather than desegregate them. Georgia made it a felony for a state or local official to spend money on an integrated school. South Carolina repealed its compulsory education law. Virginia authorized closing any school that desegregated and giving tuition assistance to white students who wanted to attend a private, all-white school. Prince Edward County did just that, shutting down its school system for four years rather than allow black and white students to attend it together. North Carolina introduced what proved to be one of the most effective means of resisting desegregation, a pupil assignment law that without mentioning race gave school boards wide discretion in deciding which school each student would attend. Like Virginia, North Carolina also authorized tuition grants to whites attending segregated private schools.

The failure of the federal government to firmly back *Brown* encouraged resistance. Though the Eisenhower administration submitted an amicus curiae brief that largely supported the *Brown* plaintiffs, the president, while saying he would uphold the ruling, never publicly endorsed it. Privately, he thought it a mistake, sympathizing with southern whites, eager to make sure, as he told Earl Warren at a White House dinner during the Court's deliberations, "that their sweet little girls are not required to sit in school alongside some big overgrown Negro." Most national Democratic leaders did not differ with Eisenhower's public stand. Adlai Stevenson urged caution in using federal power to enforce *Brown,* saying that you "do not upset habits and traditions that are older than the Republic overnight." Most importantly, the Supreme Court itself failed to issue a forceful implementation order for

Brown. Rejecting a request from the NAACP for immediate desegregation, the Court remanded the *Brown* cases to lower courts for enforcement, instructing them that the defendants needed to make "a prompt and reasonable start toward full compliance at the earliest practicable date," with desegregation to occur "with all deliberate speed."

The combination of determined resistance and a lack of enforcement meant that very little desegregation occurred during the decade after *Brown.* In five southern states, until the fall of 1960 not a single black child attended a racially integrated school, while in others, like North Carolina, Tennessee, and Virginia, only a tiny fraction of the black student body did so. In 1964, a full ten years after *Brown,* Charleston was the only city in South Carolina that had desegregated any schools. That year, across the South, only 1 percent of black public-school children attended racially integrated schools.

African American Mobilization

The southern mobilization in defense of white supremacy, sparked by *Brown,* reversed some black gains. Black voter registration in the region fell, in Mississippi from twenty-two thousand in 1952 to just eight thousand in 1956, in South Carolina from two hundred thousand to sixty thousand in the five years after *Brown.* New southern laws so restricted the NAACP that over two hundred of its southern branches had to shut down and its southern membership dropped by a third. Extralegal racial violence, which had diminished in the years before *Brown,* rose in its wake, especially in rural areas, as the Ku Klux Klan and other extreme white supremacy organizations blossomed and individual acts of terrorism became more common.

The escalating white southern violence did not go unchallenged. Black migration to the North created interregional networks that could be mobilized to protest violence in the South, and the national media increasingly paid attention to developments in the region, as evident following a particularly horrifying 1955 Mississippi murder. Emmett Till, a fourteen-year-old African American from Chicago, went to a small rural settlement in the Mississippi Delta to spend part of his summer vacation with relatives. A week after arriving, apparently in response to a dare, he walked into a small crossroads store to speak to the young wife of the white store owner, by various accounts whistling at her, speaking cheekily to her, or touching her, all transgressions of the white southern racial code (though some close to the case denied that he did any of these things). When the store owner found out about the incident, he and his brother-in-law went to Till's great-uncle's house, took the boy away, beat him savagely, shot him, and threw his weighted body into the Tallahatchie River, where it was found three days later. Though there was no direct connection between Till's murder and the *Brown* decision, it came at a moment of heightened white southern anxiety that the system of racial supremacy might be eroding, focused especially on the often expressed fear that school desegregation would lead to interracial socializing and sex.

Till's mother's insistence that his mutilated body be returned to Chicago shaped subsequent developments. Thousands of mourners viewed Till's corpse, and shocking pictures of it were published in the black press. The national and international media gave extensive coverage to the case, making Till one of the few victims of southern racial violence to have his name enter national consciousness. Back in Mississippi, Till's murderers were almost immediately arrested and put on trial. In an act of extraordinary courage, defying long-established norms, Till's great-uncle, Moses Wright, a sharecropper, identified them in open court, before fleeing the state to save his own life. Till's murder and the acquittal of its perpetrators by an all-white male jury spread terror among southern blacks but also enraged them, as did the failure of *Brown* to lead to meaningful change in schooling.

Heightened impatience with injustice burst the channels of private sentiment into public action just two months after the Till trial with the mass boycott of buses in Montgomery, Alabama. There, as in Baton Rouge, bus segregation grated on the black community, including its leaders, some of whom had suffered personal indignities using public transportation. In 1954 the Women's Political Caucus, a group of black professional women, asked the city to reform the bus segregation system, making a veiled threat of a boycott if it failed to do so. Meanwhile, the local NAACP chapter, with E. D. Nixon as its driving force, began planning to legally challenge bus segregation. On December 1, 1955, NAACP member and civil rights activist Rosa Parks, who worked as an assistant tailor at a downtown department store, was arrested for refusing to give up her bus seat to a white rider in violation of state law. Upon hearing of her arrest, the small circle of Montgomery civil rights advocates swung into action. Nixon, Joanne Robinson, an English professor at Alabama State College who helped lead the Women's Political Caucus, and Clifford and Virginia Durr, white Popular Front liberals, who had returned to Alabama after Clifford held various posts in the Roosevelt and Truman administrations, bailed out Parks, decided to use her case to legally challenge segregation, and distributed a leaflet calling for a one-day bus boycott.

The individuals who initiated the bus protest represented forces long involved in fighting for black rights in the South: the NAACP, black trade unionists, black academics, and a smattering of white liberals. But Nixon, understanding the limitations of the movement he himself came out of, decided from the start that a mass boycott would succeed only if it had a stronger institutional base, and the only place that existed was the church. Nixon pulled together a meeting of local black leaders to organize the protest, at which ministers played the dominant role. In short order the group constituted itself as the Montgomery Improvement Association (MIA) and picked as its president the twenty-six-year-old Martin Luther King Jr., a Baptist minister new to the city, who had few enemies, an impressive speaking style, and gravity beyond his years.

On the day of the boycott, very few African Americans boarded buses. The solidarity displayed and the enormous turnout at a meeting at the Holt Street Baptist Church called by the MIA led the group to decide to make the boycott open-ended. King—not well known at the time to Montgomery blacks, let alone to the nation—told the crowd, which flowed out of the church for blocks around (with loudspeakers set up outside) that "there comes a time when people get tired of being trampled over by the iron feet of oppression. There comes a time . . . when people get tired of being plunged across the abyss of humiliation, where they experience the bleakness of nagging despair. . . . We are here this evening because we are tired now." "The great glory of American democracy," King declared, "is the right to protest for right." "We are determined here in Montgomery to work and fight until justice runs down like water and righteousness like a mighty stream."

Initially, the boycott made modest demands: a first-come, first-served segregation system (like that asked for in Baton Rouge and already used in a number of Alabama cities); courteous treatment of black riders; and the hiring of African American drivers for routes in black parts of the city. Copying the model developed in Baton Rouge, the MIA set up an elaborate transportation system to carry black boycotters using private cars and later station wagons it purchased. Also as in Baton Rouge, frequent mass meetings held in churches disseminated information, raised money, and kept up morale.

The refusal of city authorities and the bus company to make meaningful changes turned what MIA leaders had expected to be a short boycott into a battle of attrition. City officials tried to break the boycott by going after the MIA transportation system and enforcing an antiboycott law, but their efforts failed. Instead, after King was arrested as part of a police campaign harassing carpool drivers, the MIA upped its demand to insist on complete bus desegregation, the private goal of many activists all along. Bombs thrown at King's and Nixon's homes failed to derail the protest.

As months went by, the Montgomery boycott and King received growing national publicity and increasing support in the North from African American churches, unions, liberal groups, and politicians. King, influenced by veteran practitioners of Gandhian nonviolence who came to Montgomery to work with the MIA, increasingly described the bus protest as an application of the idea of confrontational nonviolence to the struggle for racial equality, an idea he saw as deeply Christian. But while prophetic Christianity kept the boycott going, its triumph came through the law. Even after the Montgomery bus company, seeing its losses mount, indicated a willingness to negotiate an end to the boycott, city authorities resisted any change. In November 1956 they ran out of options; almost a full year after the boycott began, the U.S. Supreme Court declared state and local laws in Alabama requiring the segregation of buses to be unconstitutional.

The Montgomery struggle represented a break from the past. While the NAACP focused on using legal action to push for social change, the MIA made mass, direct action the centerpiece of its strategy, using the courts only as an adjunct. Montgomery also brought the church into a far more central position than it had been in past civil rights efforts. In doing so, it threw up a new southern-based civil rights leadership, most notably in the person of King, whose eloquence and charismatic presence brought him national and international fame.

King and the activists he became close to during the Montgomery struggle hoped to use the excitement it created to launch a new push for civil rights. To coordinate it, they founded the Southern Christian Leadership Conference (SCLC), which served as the political agency of those black churches that embraced civil rights activism. Its strength lay in local affiliates, like the MIA and the Alabama Christian Movement for Human Rights, founded by a militant Birmingham minister, Fred Shuttlesworth, which were being organized in part to fill the vacuum created by the repression of the NAACP. But cash poor and lacking strong central leadership, the SCLC got off to a slow start.

In the meantime, the campaign to desegregate schools remained the main arena of civil rights struggle, as white resistance grew increasingly ugly. It took three years of litigation for Autherine Lucy to win admission to the University of Alabama library school in February 1956. By then, many previously all-white southern colleges and universities had begun admitting black students, at least on a token basis. But at Alabama, white students, joined by older, hard-core white supremacists, rioted to protest Lucy's admission. When a mob of a thousand threw eggs and bricks at her as she left a class and threatened to kill her, the university suspended her, saying that it was to protect her and other students and staff. It then expelled her when she challenged its action in court. This was the first use of organized violence aimed at a student to try to stop school desegregation, the beginning of a trend by segregationists to try to physically harm black students attempting to attend once all-white schools.

Washington Slowly Moves

Federal acquiescence in denying African Americans their rights began to diminish as southern resistance to desegregation hardened. The widespread criticism abroad of the oppression of African Americans caused concern in the Eisenhower administration about its impact on support for the country in its contest with the Soviet Union, particularly in Africa and Asia. More importantly, partisan calculations created a small opening for civil rights advocates. The Democratic retreat on civil rights after 1948 drew a sizable minority of African American voters toward the Republican Party, following the lead of Harlem Democratic congressman Adam Clayton Powell Jr., who in 1956 endorsed Eisenhower for reelection. Many Republicans had long supported civil rights on principle. Some, including Attorney General Herbert Brownell and two leading presidential hopefuls, Vice President Richard M. Nixon and California senator William Knowland, saw an opportunity to use civil rights legislation to win over more black voters.

In the past, the southern Democrats who controlled the Senate had blocked all efforts at civil rights legislation. However, when in 1956 Eisenhower asked Congress to give the federal government greater power to ensure that blacks had the right to vote, Senate majority leader Lyndon B. Johnson, a Texas Democrat, decided that to fulfill his ambition to be president he would need northern liberal support, which in turn meant distancing himself from die-hard segregationists. A complex legislative battle ensued in which Johnson worked to weaken the proposed civil rights bill sufficiently to get enough votes to overcome a southern filibuster. The resulting bill was so meager that it had little practical impact. Still, it was a symbolic step away from the presidential and congressional hands-off stance toward African American freedom when on September 9, 1957, Eisenhower signed the first federal civil rights act to be passed since 1875.

Just days later, Eisenhower found himself forced to go further. In response to a federal court order, the Little Rock, Arkansas, school board had come up with a plan for very gradual desegregation. For the first year, nine black students were to be admitted to the previously all-white Central High School. A new high school in a more affluent part of the city was to remain all-white, so that few whites with wealth or power would be personally affected by the change, a pattern that became common in both the North and the South once schools began desegregating. Just prior to the start of the school year, Governor Orval Faubus, a onetime moderate who had decided to use racism to bolster his political position, announced that Little Rock schools could not be peacefully integrated. Faubus sent National Guard troops to Central High, where they blocked black students from entering. He then defied a federal court order that the school integration begin right away, and, when faced with a second court order, withdrew the Guard, leaving scant protection for the nine black students when they finally were allowed to enter Central High. Huge crowds of white segregationists surrounded the school, with local police barely able to maintain control.

Eisenhower had no desire to use federal force to impose school desegregation. But the images reproduced worldwide of mobs threatening children because of the color of their skin and Faubus's open defiance of the federal courts forced him to act. As events in Little Rock seemed on the verge of spinning totally out of control, the president sent in eleven hundred Army troops and took control of the Arkansas National Guard, using them for the rest of the school year to protect the Central High students. (The following year, Faubus closed all the Little Rock high schools, circumventing the desegregation order in another way.)

The slowly changing mood in Washington about civil rights contributed to breaking a deadlock over another issue, the admission of new states to the Union. Since the end of World War II, there had been growing movements for statehood in the territories of Alaska and Hawaii and for allowing residents of the District of Columbia to vote in presidential elections. These were understood, by supporters and opponents, as civil rights issues, including by Harry Truman, who came out in support of all three steps. But Hawaiian statehood was blocked by southern Democrats, led by Lyndon Johnson, uncomfortable with the territory's racially mixed population and the possibility that it might elect an Asian American to Congress, and worried that its representatives might line up against Senate rules that allowed civil rights legislation to be filibustered to death. Further complicating the situation, since the Republicans dominated Hawaiian politics, congressional Democrats insisted on linking Hawaiian statehood with statehood for Alaska, where their party dominated, even though Alaska had a much smaller population.

Eisenhower had come out in principle for statehood for both territories in 1952, but he did not want to grant it to Alaska until the federal government had assurances that it would retain control over large blocks of land that it wanted for military purposes. By the late 1950s, satisfied with land use arrangements, Eisenhower dropped his resistance to Alaskan statehood. Meanwhile, with the passage of the 1957 Civil Rights Act, southern concerns over filibuster rules diminished, and Johnson, having repositioned himself on civil rights issues, abandoned his opposition to Hawaiian statehood. After much maneuvering, Congress passed legislation that gave both territories statehood in 1959, the first new states since 1912. (It would be several more years until Washington, D.C., residents could vote for president.)

Sitting In

On February 1, 1960, four freshmen from North Carolina Agricultural and Technical College (A&T), a black college, went into a Woolworth's variety store in downtown Greensboro, North Carolina, bought a few items, sat down at the lunch counter, which like such food places throughout the South was restricted to white customers, and asked to be served. Refused, they stayed on their stools until the store closed. The next day, twenty-nine neatly dressed students returned to sit at the counter. The day after, sixty-three showed up. The day after that, so many demonstrators came, including three white students from a local women's college, that the "sit-in" spread from Woolworth's to another store down the street. Soon hundreds of students were demonstrating, led by the A&T football team, which pushed through a crowd of white counterdemonstrators waving Confederate flags. When asked who they thought they were, members of the football team replied, "We the Union army."

To most Americans, the sit-in seemed to come out of the blue. Since Little Rock, civil rights issues had largely disappeared from the headlines. Both the legal movement toward school desegregation and the mass mobilization of black protestors had stalled. But small-scale, local civil rights activity had continued, and the infrastructure to support it kept developing.

In Tuskegee, Alabama, the black community boycotted white-owned businesses to protest the state legislature's gerrymandering of the city's boundaries to exclude most black voters. In New York, a network of NAACP members, leftists, academics, and ministers organized protests by black and Puerto Rican parents over the lack of racial integration and the poor quality of education in the public schools. Nationally, the Catholic bishops, pressed by Pope Pius XII, issued a 1958 pastoral letter, "Discrimination and the Christian Conscience," which denounced racial discrimination and embraced interracialism, a step of symbolic importance and some practical impact.

The SCLC, though it failed to spark mass protests, worked with other groups, like the pacifist Fellowship of Reconciliation, to proselytize nonviolent confrontational action. King's book *Stride Toward Freedom* helped spread the idea. Veteran activists like Bayard Rustin, Glenn Smiley, and James Lawson held workshops to teach Gandhian methods. Nonviolent direct action did not have deep roots in the southern black tradition (though it did resonate with widely shared Christian ideas about redemptive suffering and loving one's enemies). Southern African Americans, especially in rural areas, lived in a world where violence was common and gun ownership widespread. Even many advocates of nonviolent protest accepted the need for self-defense. Armed supporters guarded King's home during the Montgomery boycott and the home of Daisy Bates, the head of the Little Rock NAACP, during the school desegregation crisis. Robert Williams, the head of the NAACP chapter in Monroe, North Carolina, who organized a successful armed repulsion of a Ku Klux Klan attack on the home of another NAACP leader, went further in 1959 when he said publicly that the time had come for African Americans to "meet violence with violence." The NAACP suspended Williams, but he won considerable support among civil rights activists. The sit-downs brought nonviolent action again to the fore.

The Greensboro protests built on past actions. Civil rights activists, many associated with NAACP Youth Councils, held over a dozen sit-ins between 1957 and 1960 at segregated public places in Oklahoma, Kansas, North Carolina, and Florida, though they did not receive national notice. Sitting down had earlier roots in the labor movement, which had made wide use of sit-down strikes in the 1930s and some of whose members had adapted the tactic to protest segregated facilities near northern factories during the 1940s.

Nonetheless, Greensboro represented something new, as the escalating protests quickly gained national publicity and set off a wave of sit-ins in other southern cities. Within a week, sit-ins took place in Durham, Winston-Salem, and Charlotte. From there they spread to Virginia, Tennessee, Florida, South Carolina, Texas, Georgia, and Mississippi. Students played a key role in the explosion, as the growth of higher education among southern blacks created a new base for civil rights activism. Within two months, sit-downs had occurred in scores of cities. In some, like Nashville and Atlanta, they took place on a massive scale as part of well-organized campaigns for desegregation and better economic and educational opportunities for African Americans. Altogether, some fifty thousand to seventy thousand African Americans took part in the protest wave as it spread across the South.

Sit-in demonstrators suffered brutal assaults from white segregationists and thousands of arrests, but they remained undeterred and nonviolent. In the upper South, they began winning some victories, as local authorities and business owners, seeing their cities disrupted and profits reduced by black boycotts and frightened whites staying away, began desegregating lunch counters and other public facilities. In the Deep South, segregation remained firmly entrenched.

The sit-ins invigorated the civil rights movement. In the spring of 1960, leaders of the student protests, brought together by veteran civil rights activist Ella Baker, formed the Student Nonviolent Coordinating Committee (SNCC). The young SNCC activists, mostly black and mostly southern, embraced a Christian vision of creating a beloved community in the course of fighting for racial equality. Meanwhile, SCLC and CORE grew rapidly as a result of their support for the student movement, as civil rights again became a national issue.

At the 1960 political party conventions, King, Roy Wilkins from the NAACP, and veteran labor and civil rights leader A. Philip Randolph led large demonstrations in support of civil rights. (The Democratic convention had 250 African American delegates.) Both parties adopted strong civil rights planks in their platforms, with the Republican position, pushed forward by New York governor Nelson Rockefeller, notable for its support for the sit-ins. The embrace of civil rights, after a decade when both national parties—especially the Democrats—tried to distance themselves from the issue, may have partially stemmed from the quickening pace of protest in the South. Probably more important, though, were polls that showed that black voters did not have a strong preference for one party or the other, making them an attractive bloc that could and ultimately did decide the outcome of the race in a number of key states.

The two presidential nominees, Nixon and Massachusetts senator John F. Kennedy, both had records as moderate supporters of civil rights. Though Nixon had done more to promote federal action, Kennedy outmaneuvered him during the campaign with a rapid response to the jailing of King. In mid-October, King was arrested for taking part in a student sit-in at an Atlanta department store lunch counter, refusing bail as part of a new movement tactic. The mayor, eager to avoid more demonstrations, got the protestors released without bail, but a judge then sent King to do four months' hard labor in state prison for violating his probation from a previous citation for driving without a valid license. (King recently had moved to Atlanta but was still using his Alabama license.) Kennedy's aides convinced the candidate to call the jailed minister's distressed, pregnant wife to express his concern. Later, Kennedy's brother and campaign manager, Robert, called the judge who had jailed King and urged him to release him on bail, which he did. The Kennedys' involvement in the case led King's father, a prominent minister in his own right, to switch his endorsement from Nixon to Kennedy and helped win over black voters.

Though in 1960 civil rights played a role in presidential politics for the first time since 1948, other issues loomed much larger in the race. Even among African American voters, the poor state of the economy, which had been in recession for the prior year, probably had more to do with the two-to-one support they gave to Kennedy over Nixon than civil rights did, on which there was little disagreement between the candidates. Still, given the incredibly close margin between the candidates—Kennedy won the popular vote by 112,000 votes, three-tenths of one percent of the total cast—the strong black support for the Democrats created a potential opening for civil rights advocates. But as the 1960s began, it still remained unclear if the momentum toward greater racial equality would continue or, like the push in the late 1940s, peter out in the face of white southern resistance and national political indifference.

CHAPTER 7

"Hour of Maximum Danger"

At his inauguration, John F. Kennedy made two gestures toward recognizing the intensifying struggle for black rights. First, he had Marian Anderson sing "The Star-Spangled Banner." In 1939, the Daughters of the American Revolution had refused to allow the great black singer to hold a concert in the capital's Constitution Hall. In response, the Roosevelt administration had arranged for her to sing from the steps of the Lincoln Memorial, which won much goodwill from African Americans. Now Kennedy reprised the symbolism by having Anderson open his swearing-in ceremony. Second, Kennedy included in his inaugural address a sentence stating opposition to "the slow undoing of those human rights to which this nation has always been committed, and to which we are committed today at home and around the world," which could have been read—if one wanted to—as an endorsement of civil rights.

In the context of Kennedy's whole inaugural address, the human rights reference more strongly resonated with the struggle against communism. Kennedy's speech, one of the best-known political addresses of the twentieth century, almost entirely concerned itself with international affairs. Kennedy shared the widespread belief, among liberals and conservatives, that the greatest challenges the country faced lay not at home but abroad.

Kennedy's priorities did not greatly differ from Eisenhower's. Both men saw national security as their greatest responsibility. But Kennedy thought his predecessor had been asleep at the wheel. Campaigning as much against Eisenhower as Nixon, Kennedy promised to "Get America Moving Again." His inaugural address called for a remobilization of American society to fight the Cold War, even as he pledged openness to joining with the country's adversaries to seek global security and peace.

Early in his speech, Kennedy, the youngest man ever elected president, took a dig at his predecessor, who had been born in 1890, almost three decades before Kennedy's own birth in 1917: "Let the word go forth from this time and place, to friend and foe alike, that the torch has been passed to a new generation of Americans—born in this century, tempered by war, disciplined by a hard and bitter peace." In language reminiscent of NSC-68, Kennedy declared that "we shall pay any price, bear any burden, meet any hardship, support any friend, oppose any foe to assure the survival and success of liberty." While calling for the Cold War to be waged as total war, Kennedy recognized its costs and dangers; neither bloc could "take comfort from our present course—both sides overburdened by the cost of modern weapons, both rightly alarmed by the steady spread of the deadly atom, yet both racing to alter that uncertain balance of terror that stays the hand of mankind's final war."

The new president embraced the challenge of walking on the edge of apocalypse, seeing it in heroic, spiritual terms. "In the long history of the world," he told the crowd, gathered on a frigid day, "only a few generations have been granted the role of defending freedom in its hour of maximum danger. I do not shrink from this responsibility—I welcome it. . . . The energy, the faith, the devotion which we bring to this endeavor will light our country and all who serve it." If there lay danger ahead, there also lay hope for America and the American Century, but triumph would require subsuming the individual to the national purpose: "And so, my fellow Americans: ask not what your country can do for you—ask what you can do for your country."

From a distance, Kennedy's assertion that in 1961 freedom was "in its hour of maximum danger"—greater than during World War II, greater than during Korea—seems strange and self-aggrandizing. As the 1960s began, the world did face the frightening possibility of nuclear war, and the United States confronted serious challenges in its relationship with the Soviet bloc and in the developing world. But Eisenhower had ended the war in Korea and managed to avoid other military engagements even as he pursued a tough stand toward the Soviet Union. Kennedy's hyperbolic rhetoric, much admired at the time, revealed the extent to which he and many other Cold War liberals derived their sense of personal and political purpose from the struggle to create an anticommunist world order.

Ike's Cold War

The death of Stalin and the end of the Korean War had neither halted the Cold War nor diminished the American effort to best the Soviet Union, militarily and diplomatically. Eisenhower cut defense spending, but he did so by shifting resources and national security strategy toward nuclear weapons and systems to deliver them, including long-range bombers, short- and long-range missiles, and virtually unstoppable missile-equipped Polaris submarines, which began going into operation just as he left office. Rhetorically, his administration upped the ante from the Truman administration, calling for not just the containment of communism within its existing boundaries but also its "rollback," to free what the president termed the "enslaved nations" of the Soviet bloc.

The Truman and Eisenhower administrations took some modest actions aimed at prying nations out of the Soviet sphere. In the late 1940s and early 1950s, the CIA infiltrated agents into Eastern Europe who were supposed to stir up anti-Soviet sentiment and lay the basis for popular uprisings. In most cases, they were immediately rounded up and executed. Under Truman, the spy agency also set up Radio Free Europe and Radio Liberty to foment discontent within the Soviet bloc. Unrestrained by the checks and balances of open government, the CIA sometimes drifted toward the bizarre. In addition to its broadcasts, Radio Free Europe sent propaganda leaflets into Eastern Europe by attaching them to balloons. By 1956, it was dropping leaflets over the region at a rate of fourteen million a month.

The CIA efforts indicated that some elements of the government believed in the rhetoric portraying the Soviet bloc as a mass of anticommunist discontent and the possibility of rollback. Reality, however, had a habit of asserting itself, as more sober American leaders understood that trying to pry pieces away from domination by a Soviet Union armed with nuclear weapons risked world war and mutual annihilation. When in 1953 worker protests rocked East Germany, and when three years later a broad revolt against Soviet control broke out in Hungary, the United States encouraged the rebels in radio broadcasts but did nothing to provide them with concrete aid.

Though the United States tacitly accepted the status quo in Europe, its policy, under Eisenhower, of threatening to use nuclear weapons to achieve policy goals ("brinksmanship") kept tensions with the Soviet Union high. So did the bluster of Nikita Khrushchev, who emerged as the dominant figure in the post-Stalin Soviet leadership. Khrushchev used exaggerated claims of nuclear prowess to try to force the Western powers into agreements that would guarantee the USSR security and its hegemony within its sphere even as it reduced the size of its military. On October 7, 1957, the Soviet Union launched the first artificial satellite, Sputnik I ("traveling companion"), into earth orbit, an impressive scientific and engineering achievement that set off a near panic in the United States. Unlike the United States, the Soviet Union had not developed a large fleet of long-distance bombers, limiting the threat to North America from its atomic arsenal. Sputnik seemingly changed that, as Khrushchev claimed that its launching proved that the Soviet Union had missiles capable of delivering weapons anywhere on earth.

Coming at a time when Soviet diplomatic influence was growing and its rate of economic growth exceeded that in the United States, the launching of Sputnik led many Americans to the disconcerting idea that perhaps their country was beginning to fall behind its foremost adversary. The spectacular failure of the first American effort to send a satellite into orbit, two months after Sputnik—the launch rocket rose just four feet before falling back in flames—did nothing to boost national confidence. Nor did subsequent developments in what turned into a "space race" between the United States and the Soviet Union. When the Army did get the first American satellite, Explorer I, aloft, in January 1958, it weighed only ten pounds. By then the Soviets had launched the 1,121-pound Sputnik II, which carried a dog named Laika into orbit, part of a string of space triumphs that included the first rocket to reach the moon, the first one to circle it and photograph its back side, and the first man into space. For many people in the United States, where it had become common to assume that it was the best in the world at everything, all this came as a rude shock.

Eisenhower tried to resist post-Sputnik pressure from the press, the military, establishment foundations, the scientific community, and politicians to launch a crash space effort, increase defense spending, and create new federal programs to upgrade science and education. Eisenhower had accurate intelligence that in spite of its claims the Soviet Union did not have a single operational intercontinental ballistic missile (ICBM) capable of delivering a nuclear weapon to North America. (It would not until the 1960s.) As Soviet leaders knew, but the American public did not, since 1956 the United States had been flying surveillance flights over the Soviet Union using the U-2 spy plane, a technological marvel that flew at such heights and at such speed that Soviet air defense units could not shoot it down. Reluctantly, Eisenhower made some concessions to those who saw the Soviet space firsts as indicative of a dangerous national complacency, ordering the deployment of medium-range missiles in Turkey and Italy, from where they could reach deep into the Soviet Union, and increasing spending on bombers and missiles. But he succeeded in blocking calls for a large-scale civil defense program and major increases in overall defense spending. A new, civilian agency, the National Aeronautics and Space Administration (NASA), took over much of the space effort (though greater funding went to military space programs, which concentrated on developing spy satellites). Eisenhower also accepted the National Defense Education Act, which increased federal spending on education, especially for science and math. Conservative opposition to state expansion, at least when done in the name of national security, continued to wither.

Khrushchev wanted to take advantage of his seeming (though not actual) position of strength to deescalate the arms race and force the United States into direct negotiations to settle a range of outstanding issues between the two blocs. He had become frustrated by the failure of the United States to respond to what he saw as multiple efforts by the Soviet Union to create a more peaceful relationship. The Soviet Union had withdrawn its troops from Finland and Austria, substantially reduced the size of its army, unilaterally halted its nuclear weapons testing in March 1958, and rejected the idea, held forth by previous Soviet leaders, that war between the communist and capitalist camps was inevitable. Khrushchev tried to use the status of Berlin as his lever. West Berlin had practical and symbolic importance for the communist bloc. The city had become an escape route for thousands of East Germans, who unfavorably compared life in their country to life in the western half of the old German capital, into which the United States and its allies had thrown great amounts of aid. The East German government pressured the Soviet Union to do something about the sore point in its midst. Meanwhile, Soviet leaders grew increasingly fearful about the rearming of West Germany and its military and economic integration with Western Europe. In November 1958 Khrushchev demanded that within six months the Western powers sign a peace treaty with Germany (none had ever been concluded after World War II) and withdraw their troops from West Berlin, making it a "free city," or the Soviet Union would turn control over access to the city to East Germany (which would violate the Potsdam agreement signed by the Allied powers at the end of the war).

Khrushchev's threat failed to have the result he hoped for. The Western powers refused to negotiate over West Berlin and Secretary of State John Foster Dulles said that NATO would use military force if East Germany tried to block access to the city. This tough stand forced the Soviet leader to allow his six-month deadline to come and go without action. But his Berlin move did make the United States more receptive to Soviet requests for high-level direct talks. In the summer of 1959, Vice President Richard Nixon visited the Soviet Union. In September, Khrushchev toured the United States and met at length with Eisenhower. The trip, which received enormous publicity in both countries, produced no major agreements except for a plan for a future summit conference of Britain, France, the United States, and the USSR.

The summit proved abortive. Shortly before it was set to begin, Eisenhower approved a May 1, 1960, U-2 flight over the Soviet Union. This time, the Soviets succeeded in shooting down the plane. Khrushchev, perhaps having decided that the summit, which he had worked so hard to set up, would not achieve anything, ended it before it took up substantial business, saying that his country could not participate because of the U-2 incident. As Eisenhower's term in office neared its end, relations with the Soviet Union seemed as fraught and intractable as they had been when the Korean War concluded.

The Developing World

Even as the nuclear stalemate tensely maintained the status quo in Europe, in the nonindustrialized world, movements for decolonization, democracy, and economic equality led to intense political struggles and armed conflict. Contests over the political and social direction of developing countries were often subsumed into the Cold War. Nixon later recalled that during the 1950s, "For better or worse, the colonial empires were disintegrating. The great question . . . was who would fill the vacuum. . . . If the United States did not move, the Chinese or the Soviets . . . certainly would." Stalin had had little interest in the nonindustrialized world, but his successors saw in decolonization an opportunity to bolster Soviet power and pursue semi-submerged dreams of world revolution left over from their youth. Stalin had traveled outside of the Soviet Union only for meetings with wartime allies; Khrushchev, within a few years of taking power, visited China, Yugoslavia, India, Burma, and Indonesia. But the Cold War was not the whole story. While the United States used the language of Cold War competition to explain its policy in the developing world, it had aims and interests besides competition with the communist bloc.

In the Middle East, oil, along with the desire for geostrategic influence, shaped American policy. The first major move came in Iran. After pressuring the Soviet Union to withdraw its troops from northern Iran after World War II, the United States had deferred to Britain, the major colonial power in the region, whose government controlled Iran's oil industry through the Anglo-Iranian Oil Company. Venezuela and Saudi Arabia pressured foreign oil companies—predominantly American—into agreeing to fifty-fifty splits of profits. When Iranian nationalists demanded a similar arrangement with Anglo-Iranian, the cash-starved British government refused. Internal Iranian politics crosscut the oil dispute, as reformist prime minister Mohammad Mossaddegh, who led the anti-British effort, also tried to limit the power of the hereditary shah, Mohammad Reza Pahlavi, and later the parliament as well.

American policymakers feared that a combination of British intransigence and internal politics would drive Iran toward the Soviet Union. After Mossaddegh nationalized the oil industry and Britain blockaded Iran's oil exports, the United States refused to back a British plan to use its military to restore prior arrangements. Instead, Washington decided to help the shah to depose the prime minister. The CIA, working with British intelligence, plotted a coup and supplied equipment to the shah's backers. After a first effort by the shah to oust the prime minister failed, leading him to flee the country, American agents mobilized crowds in Tehran opposing Mossaddegh and supporting Pahlavi. A mob attack on Mossaddegh's home led to his arrest, allowing the shah to return, greatly strengthened by the American intervention. In negotiations that followed, the U.S. government took the lead in setting up a new consortium of oil companies, in which American firms had an equal stake with the British, which took over oil production in Iran, evenly splitting profits with the Iranians.

Any doubt that the United States had displaced Britain as the dominant Western power in the Middle East was erased during the 1956 Suez crisis. The United States helped provoke the crisis through its wavering policy toward Gamal Abdel Nasser, the charismatic nationalist who had taken power in Egypt in 1954. Nasser helped lead the movement among developing nations for "nonalignment" with either Cold War camp, seeking arms and assistance from both. Initially, the Eisenhower administration agreed to help fund Nasser's plan for a huge dam on the Nile River at Aswan. But opposition to the aid grew in the United States from hard-line anticommunists, disturbed by Egypt's arms deal with Czechoslovakia and recognition of Communist China; supporters of Israel, which was engaged in skirmishing with Egypt and looking to expand its territory; cotton growers, not eager to help an international rival; and fiscal conservatives, worried about the cost of the project. Nasser responded to Dulles's July 1956 announcement that the United States would not fund Aswan after all by nationalizing the French- and British-owned company that ran the Suez Canal, seeking to reassert his position in relation to the Western powers and get a source of income for the Nile dam.

Eisenhower tried to work out a compromise arrangement for running the canal, but the British and French insisted on retaining control. Without informing the United States, they hatched a plot with Israel to capture the waterway. On October 28, Israel invaded Egypt. Using this as an excuse, the French and British sent in their own forces to seize the canal. Eisenhower, furious that France and Britain had moved behind his back in what he viewed as a ridiculously out-of-date effort at using force to reimpose colonial arrangements, decided to block them. A threat by the Soviet Union, which just had crushed the Hungarian uprising, to militarily support the Egyptians, added to his determination to resolve the crisis. The United States got the UN General Assembly to pass a resolution calling for a truce, mobilized its military forces to send a message to the Soviets to stay out, and pressured Britain and France to agree to a cease-fire just hours before they would have taken the canal. Eventually, the UN sent a peacekeeping mission to the region, Israel retreated, and the Egyptians retained control over the waterway.

The resolution of the Suez crisis ended one set of problems for the United States in a region Eisenhower considered vital to the nation's interests because of its oil, but exacerbated others. Nasser emerged from the crisis with enormous influence in the Arab world. The left-leaning Pan-Arabism he promoted gained strength throughout the region. Unreconciled to the United States, Egypt moved closer to the Soviet Union, which agreed to fund the Aswan Dam. To try to restrain Nasser, Eisenhower cultivated a conservative, pro-American alternative to the Egyptian leader in King Saud of Saudi Arabia. To convince the king that if necessary the United States would use force to protect its allies, in 1958 the president sent fourteen thousand Marines into Lebanon at the request of its pro-Western leader, who was beleaguered by opponents at home and worried about the overthrow of the pro-Western monarchy in neighboring Iraq. Khrushchev turned down Nasser's plea for some response, a tacit acknowledgment of an American sphere of influence in the Middle East.

Eisenhower preferred covert action, of the sort that proved successful in Iran, over direct military intervention. It cost less money and had less risk of leading to escalating warfare or lost prestige in the event of failure. American policymakers justified the antidemocratic character of secretly interfering in other nations' affairs by the exigencies of the Cold War. A 1954 report on CIA covert operations by Lieutenant General James Doolittle, which Eisenhower commissioned, set out a moral and political rationale for the kinds of activities the agency already had been undertaking: "It is now clear that we are facing an implacable enemy whose avowed objective is world domination by whatever means and at whatever cost. There are no rules in such a game. Hitherto acceptable norms of human conduct do not apply. If the United States is to survive . . . [we] must learn to subvert, sabotage and destroy our enemies by more clever, more sophisticated and more effective methods than those used against us."

The United States did just that in Guatemala the same year as the

Doolittle report, beginning an ongoing program of covert action in Latin America. A democratic wave that swept across Central and South America in the mid-1940s, forcing out one dictator after another, worried American policymakers. The regimes that came to power generally had a social democratic outlook and in some cases included communists. American interests threatened by land and labor reform, like the huge United Fruit Company, lobbied the government to push back the movement for more equitable economic and social arrangements that challenged the near-feudal power of large landholders and investors. In 1950, George Kennan told a group of American ambassadors to South American countries that the United States "should not hesitate before police repression by the local government. This is not shameful, since the communists are essentially traitors. . . . It is better to have a strong regime in power than a liberal government if it is indulgent and relaxed and penetrated by communists."

Effective American intervention depended on finding or creating local allies. In Guatemala, the landed oligarchy bitterly opposed Jacobo Arbenz, an army officer who had helped lead a 1944 revolution and had been elected president in 1950, but it lacked the social legitimacy or dynamism to rally a broad movement for his removal. When the Eisenhower administration decided to oust Arbenz, who had close ties to members of Guatemala's small Communist Party, the CIA organized anticommunist students, Catholic activists, and dissident army officers to lead the effort. Undertaking a much longer, more comprehensive, and more sophisticated campaign than it used in Iran, the CIA isolated the Guatemalan government from its neighbors, tarred it in the press as communist (which it was not), disrupted the economy, and worked to spread confusion and disarray. When a CIA-equipped force of several hundred exiles based in Honduras invaded Guatemala, with CIA-supplied air cover and a massive propaganda effort that portrayed its victory as inevitable, the army deserted Arbenz, who resigned. In the months that followed, the police, army, and vigilante groups killed thousands of his supporters.

By the time Arbenz fell, the social democratic, nationalist tide in Latin America was already waning, with a new wave of dictatorships coming to power. The Eisenhower administration had not meant to simply back U.S. corporations or local oligarchs. After the overthrow of Arbenz, it brought an antitrust suit against United Fruit and tried to cultivate anticommunist Latin American reformers who would bring greater stability and an improved standard of living through controlled change. But in practice the United States ended up bolstering antidemocratic forces and military leaders who increasingly saw themselves as autonomous agents, entitled to power and wealth in their own right rather than as servants of the old ruling classes. Meanwhile, much of the rapidly growing Latin American population remained impoverished.

Washington policymakers were taken aback by the widespread anti-Americanism on display when Nixon toured Latin America in 1958. The victory of the Cuban Revolution the next year presented the United States with the possibility of a left-wing regime just off its shores, in a country where Americans had very significant economic interests. Initial American government ambivalence toward Cuban leader Fidel Castro soon turned into hostility as he verbally attacked the United States, executed opponents, consolidated power, and postponed promised elections, determined, as revolutionary leaders like Ernesto Che Guevara proclaimed, to avoid the fate of Arbenz.

Cuba's moves toward redistributing wealth, most importantly a sweeping land reform program, and its acceptance of economic assistance from the Soviet Union led the Eisenhower administration to cut off sugar imports from the island and order U.S.-owned refineries in Cuba to refuse to handle Soviet oil. Cuba, in turn, began expropriating American-owned property. In its final months in office, the Eisenhower administration hatched unsuccessful plots to assassinate Castro, broke diplomatic relations with Cuba, banned Americans from visiting the island, and, under the leadership of the same CIA men who had ousted the Guatemalan president, began training a force of exiles to invade it.

Cold War with Vigor

John F. Kennedy shared the basic assumptions about America's place in the world held by his predecessors, but he brought to the presidency new strategies and a heightened combativeness. Kennedy and many of his advisers believed that the Soviet space achievements, the widespread attraction to socialism among leaders of the emerging nations of Africa, the growing strength of communist movements in Southeast Asia, and the drift of the Cuban Revolution toward socialism all indicated that the United States might be losing the Cold War. Kennedy did not share Eisenhower's fear of a society dominated by an ever-expanding militarized state or his longing for a world of individual achievement and decentralized private initiative. Kennedy and the liberals who somewhat belatedly embraced him relished the idea of a potent, centralized state with significant control over the economy. Support for a powerful presidency became a cult belief among intellectuals. The most influential study of the office, Richard Neustadt's 1960 *Presidential*

Power, became required reading for generations of college students and politicians, including John Kennedy, who periodically turned to Neustadt for advice.

Kennedy's desire to lead a bolder, more vigorous Cold War effort stemmed not only from his assessment that the freedom faced "its hour of maximum danger" but also from his extraordinary competitiveness and obsession with manhood and virility, which spilled across his private and public life. The son of a wealthy businessman and chronic womanizer who had served as ambassador to Great Britain under FDR, Kennedy grew up admiring the licentious British aristocracy. Serious, lifelong chronic diseases (largely hidden from the public) seemed to spur on his obsessive need to affirm his vitality and enjoy his prerogatives through sexual conquests, which he relentlessly pursued before and during his marriage and presidency. Especially in conducting foreign policy, Kennedy felt a need to demonstrate his toughness, seeing this as a cardinal virtue for political leaders and manly men.

Kennedy embodied a notion of manhood shared by many middle- and upper-class men of his generation, who feared the stifling embrace of corporate bureaucracy and family togetherness. The astonishing success of *Playboy* magazine, which rejected the pieties of fulfillment through family commitment for the freedom of sexual and material consumerism, reflected the unease many men had with their lives and their longing for something different, even if most never acted on it. As president, Kennedy, a charming, quick-witted man with a beautiful young wife, projected an air of cultural sophistication that won him much admiration among liberal intellectuals, but in private he liked reading James Bond novels, with their middlebrow male fantasies (which, unlike most men, he could act out).

Before becoming president, Kennedy had traveled extensively in the developing world. Sympathetic to the desire of third world nationalists for freedom and the alleviation of poverty, he had repeatedly called for the United States to break with European imperialism and ally itself with emerging nations. But Kennedy did not hesitate to suggest what directions those nations should take. During the 1960 campaign, after criticizing American economic exploitation of Cuba, he declared that "Castro and his gang have betrayed the ideals of the Cuban revolution." A Khrushchev speech promising support for anticolonial "wars of liberation," though standard Kremlin rhetoric, heightened Kennedy's determination to exert U.S. power in the developing world, if need be through military force.

Upon taking office, Kennedy signed on to a CIA plan to overthrow Castro using measures from the Guatemala playbook: training an exile military force and landing it, with U.S. air support, in Cuba, where it would begin a guerrilla war that would spark a popular uprising. The April 1961 invasion at Playa Girón (the Bay of Pigs), an isolated spot on the island's southern coast, proved a complete fiasco. The fourteen hundred invaders failed to get off their beachhead, ultimately surrendering to the larger and better-equipped Cuban force that surrounded them. Meanwhile, the claim by Ambassador Adlai Stevenson at the United Nations that the planes that had bombed Cuban airfields were flown by Cuban defectors was quickly exposed as a lie, as the facts came out about the American government role in organizing the operation and providing airpower.

In the wake of the Bay of Pigs, Kennedy fired the head of the CIA, Allen Dulles (John Foster Dulles's brother), and his deputy, holdovers from the Eisenhower administration. But the Cuban fiasco, rather than deterring Kennedy from covert action, spurred him to develop greater capacity to carry out nontraditional military operations, while convincing him never again to trust formal government channels when dealing with critical national security issues. Kennedy wanted the ability to counter communist moves with something other than threats of nuclear war, a "flexible response" that could be calibrated to particular situations. For the developing world, this meant the creation of counterinsurgency forces beyond what the CIA offered.

Kennedy recognized that anticolonial and anticapitalist movements grew out of discontent with poverty, maldistribution of wealth, lack of democratic freedoms, and foreign economic and political control. Kennedy adviser Walt W. Rostow, an economic historian, argued that the very process of modernization created disaffection in the period when traditional social arrangements were torn asunder and the rewards of capitalist development had not yet reached the masses. Communist insurgents were "scavengers of the modernization process." To stop them, Kennedy sought to speed modernization through economic aid while using diplomatic and military force to check anticapitalist forces until economic growth and political development eliminated the social basis for their popular support. Kennedy set up special forces units within the Army to train and work with third world militaries in fighting guerrilla movements, personally picking the green beret as their emblem. To deal with Cuba, he established "Operation Mongoose" under the supervision of his brother, Attorney General Robert Kennedy, which undertook various covert efforts to get rid of Castro. After John Kennedy's death, his vice president, Lyndon Johnson, characterized his administration as having been "operating a damned Murder Inc. in the Caribbean."

Counterinsurgency formed only part of a military buildup Kennedy embarked on. He also began a large-scale bolstering of nuclear forces, seeking superiority to the Soviets, rather than the sufficiency that Eisenhower accepted. To provide a possible response to a Soviet attack in Europe besides nuclear retaliation, he pressed to increase U.S. and NATO conventional forces.

Kennedy's pursuit of the Cold War also involved nonmilitary measures. He established the Peace Corps as a way to compete with the Soviets for goodwill in the developing world, a program that proved enormously popular at home. For Latin America, he launched what he called the Alliance for Progress, an aid program meant to encourage the governments that the United States supported (often authoritarian regimes) to undertake reforms aimed at promoting economic growth and increasing living standards and opportunities for the poor. (In practice it never had much impact.) The Apollo program, to send a manned craft to the moon, provided another nonmilitary way to compete with the Soviets for prestige.

Even as he built up the military, Kennedy showed caution about using it, especially in direct confrontations with the Soviets. Early in his term, he decided not to increase the American military presence in Laos, where communist forces were making progress in an on-again, off-again civil war. Instead, at a summit conference with Khrushchev in June 1961, he agreed to a cease-fire and negotiations that led to a coalition government. Khrushchev's revival at the same summit of his threat to hand over control of Berlin to East Germany, backed, if need be, by Soviet force, led Kennedy to announce in a nationally televised speech a major military mobilization, including an increase in the draft, the call-up of reserves, the sending of additional troops to Europe, and a request to Congress for increased defense spending and money for the construction of fallout shelters for defense against nuclear war. But when several weeks later Khrushchev unilaterally acted to stanch the flow of East Germans to the West by having a wall constructed severing connections between the two halves of Berlin, Kennedy acquiesced.

The Berlin crisis was a scary moment for all involved, but the true "hour of maximum danger" came the following year, when the Soviet Union took a huge strategic gamble by sending nuclear-armed missiles to Cuba. Khrushchev came up with the plan in response to a number of concerns. In spite of Kennedy's claims during the 1960 campaign that there was a "missile gap" that had the Soviets ahead of the Americans, the reality was just the opposite. With only a few Soviet missiles capable of reaching the United States, the imbalance in nuclear capacity nagged at Khrushchev, who believed that the Kennedy administration, in failing to negotiate a resolution to the Berlin crisis and building up its military presence in South Vietnam, displayed a growing arrogance toward the Soviet Union. At least as important, the Soviets, like the Cubans, feared that the United States might soon launch a new military attack on Cuba, this time using its own troops. In a bold effort to achieve nuclear parity with the United States, force it into negotiations over a range of issues, protect Cuba, and cement the Soviet relationship with Castro, Khrushchev won approval from Soviet leaders for a massive, secret deployment of Soviet arms to Cuba, including bombers, missiles, atomic warheads, and over forty thousand military personnel.

Khrushchev hoped to keep the Cuban operation secret until Soviet missiles had been deployed, but the very size of the operation made its discovery almost inevitable. In October 1962, a U-2 flight over Cuba confirmed that, contrary to explicit assurances from Khrushchev, the Soviets were setting up nuclear missiles capable of reaching the United States. Kennedy immediately decided that the missiles would have to be removed. In secret deliberations, administration officials debated a range of military options, from a full-scale invasion of Cuba to bombing the missile sites to a blockade of the island. Kennedy chose the most moderate course. In a televised address on October 22, he announced a naval "quarantine" of shipments of offensive weapons to the island—U.S. officials thought "quarantine" sounded less warlike than "blockade"—that would be kept in place until the missiles already on the island were removed. With U.S. military preparedness brought up to one level below general war, Soviet ships carrying military equipment to Cuba stopped or turned back just before the quarantine went into effect.

Khrushchev, worried about the possibility of an imminent nuclear war that the Soviet Union could not win, now sought to defuse the crisis. Privately he wrote to Kennedy offering to remove the missiles in Cuba if the United States pledged not to invade the island. While the two sides jockeyed, war fears remained high, especially after the Soviets shot down a U-2 flying over Cuba, killing its pilot. But within two weeks of the start of the crisis the two powers reached an agreement based on Khrushchev's proposal, compromising on an additional demand that he later raised that the United States remove its missiles from Turkey, which Kennedy verbally agreed to do without public notice sometime after the Soviet missiles left Cuba.

During the year that followed the Cuban Missile Crisis, Kennedy took some steps to lessen tensions with the Soviet Union. Eager to move forward with a ban on testing nuclear weapons, in a speech at American University in June 1963, aimed at both the American public (which paid little attention) and the Soviet leadership, the president set out a markedly different view of international relations than he had presented in the past. Kennedy declared that he sought world peace but "not a Pax Americana enforced on the world by American weapons of war." Acknowledging that in a world of nuclear arsenals "total war makes no sense," he called on Americans to reexamine their own attitudes toward peace, the Soviet Union, and "the course of the cold war." Adopting a formulation much like Khrushchev's notion of "peaceful coexistence," Kennedy said that world peace did not require countries to like one another or always agree with one another but "only that they live together in mutual tolerance." In a remarkable rhetorical break from the Manichean language in which America had waged the Cold War, Kennedy said, referring to the Soviet Union, that "if we cannot end now our differences, at least we can help make the world safe for diversity." (How deeply Kennedy was committed to fundamental rethinking remained unclear; just two weeks later, standing at the Berlin Wall, he said that "there are some who say . . . we can work with the Communists. Let them come to Berlin.")

Following Kennedy's American University speech, the Soviet Union and the United States set up a "hot line" for direct communication between their leaders to prevent misunderstandings in crisis situations and resumed negotiations about banning nuclear testing. They could not overcome their differences about inspections to guarantee a total halt, but they did agree to a ban on atmospheric and underwater tests, which unlike below ground explosions could be detected without on-site visits. The two countries also began preliminary discussions about broader arms control talks.

But if Kennedy seemed to be moving toward a détente of sorts with the Soviet Union, he did not seem to take too seriously his injunction at American University that "if all nations could refrain from interfering in the self-determination of others, the peace would be much more assured." Through covert and overt action, the United States continued to try to influence the direction of developing countries across the globe. In South Vietnam, Kennedy had increased the number of U.S. military advisers from eight hundred to sixteen thousand in support of the unpopular, autocratic anticommunist regime of Ngo Dinh Diem. Kennedy privately expressed reservations about a prolonged or enlarged American commitment in Vietnam. But when Diem refused to go along with American demands that he reform his government and end his crackdown on Buddhist protestors, American officials, with Kennedy's approval, encouraged South Vietnamese military leaders to overthrow him. In October 1963 they murdered Diem and his brother. The "hour of maximum danger" (actual, not rhetorical) had led Kennedy to reassess relations with the Soviet Union but not to fundamentally rethink American assumptions about the need to oppose communism everywhere and to achieve political and economic hegemony in the developing world.

The New Frontier at Home

Though he gave much higher priority to foreign affairs than domestic matters, Kennedy did have a domestic legislative agenda as part of what he called the New Frontier. Much of it consisted of ideas that had been floating around the liberal wing of the Democratic Party since the Fair Deal. Kennedy hoped to create new cabinet-level departments to improve transportation, address urban problems, and create affordable housing; establish a medical insurance program for the elderly; provide federal aid to education; and attack poverty. But he got very little domestic legislation passed. His narrow election victory and the continuing dominance of Congress by a Republican–southern Democratic alliance presented formidable problems for the president, who as a congressman and senator had spent little energy mastering legislative craftsmanship and did not want to squander political capital on bills he thought likely to fail. Though most of his major initiatives went nowhere, Kennedy did win a modest expansion of Social Security, a raise in the minimum wage, some new money for housing, and a very modestly funded Area Redevelopment Act, aimed at reducing privation in the Appalachian states.

The one domestic issue Kennedy kept plugging at was economic growth. He shared the consensus outlook of 1950s liberals and centrists that the United States was basically sound, economically and socially. He recognized that there were some groups plagued by poverty, like the elderly and residents of Appalachia, for whom he proposed targeted programs. But he believed that economic growth in itself would go a long way toward solving social ills, without the need for redistributive measures or major structural changes. The demands of the Cold War, he argued, also made economic growth a necessity, claiming, in a bit of 1962 hyperbole, that "the hope of all free nations" rested on congressional passage of an economic stimulus measure, an example of the way national security talk had come to pervade American life.

In the run-up to the 1960 election, the Eisenhower administration's tight money policy and push for a budget surplus had slowed the economy, giving Kennedy an opening to run on a promise of accelerated growth. Once in office he sought a cut in corporate taxes and other tax reforms that he believed would stimulate demand and promote economic expansion. Kennedy rejected the advice of economist John Kenneth Galbraith, a longtime supporter whom he appointed ambassador to India, for economic stimulation through increased government spending on public goods. Kennedy did not share the concern of some liberals, including Galbraith and White House aide Arthur Schlesinger Jr., that increased production in itself would not address the challenges of improving the quality of life at a time when society had achieved aggregate material abundance.

Congress, in the absence of a recession and worried about budget deficits, spurned Kennedy's repeated calls for tax cuts. Kennedy did manage to promote business investment with liberalized depreciation allowances and tax credits for capital spending on machinery and equipment. To make sure that inflation did not accompany accelerated growth, his administration established wage and price guidelines and used public and private pressure on union and business leaders to lessen boosts in wages and prices.

Civil Rights

The thinness of Kennedy's domestic achievements reflected the continued stalemate in Congress, the brevity of his presidency, and the shrinking ambitions of liberalism. It also gave the lie to the centrality that political scientists and many politicians ascribed to the presidency. In the early 1960s, the sources of political innovation and change lay elsewhere, in the civil rights movement and in the courts.

Four months after Kennedy took office, the Congress of Racial Equality launched a new challenge to southern segregation with its "Freedom Ride." In 1947, after the Supreme Court's declaration that laws enforcing segregation on interstate buses were unconstitutional, the Fellowship of Reconciliation and CORE sent a racially integrated group of bus riders through the upper South. The riders desegregated some buses, suffered a dozen arrests, but received little national attention. Fourteen years later, CORE decided to repeat the undertaking, this time going into the Deep South. Though in December 1960 the Supreme Court had extended its earlier ruling to invalidate laws segregating waiting rooms, lunch counters, and bathrooms serving interstate passengers, in practice segregation remained the norm on interstate buses and in their terminals.

The Freedom Ride at least implicitly challenged the federal government, since it aimed to have federal court decisions implemented. The new president disapproved of the effort, seeing civil rights as a low priority, best dealt with through incremental change rather than dramatic confrontation. In the upper South, the travelers were able to use some previously segregated facilities without regard to race. But when they entered Alabama, Ku Klux Klan members, working in collusion with local and state police, unleashed a torrent of violence upon them. Outside of Anniston, they set one bus on fire. When the riders arrived in Birmingham, a mob assaulted them while the police arranged to be absent. The extraordinary brutality directed against the nonresisting Freedom Riders, several of whom were beaten near to death, received extensive national and international publicity. Through an informer, the FBI had detailed foreknowledge of the plans for violence but never warned the riders. For their part, John and Robert Kennedy tried to avoid getting publicly involved, privately urging southern officials to defuse the situation, with no success.

The CORE group, beaten, threatened, and with bus companies refusing to carry it farther, reluctantly terminated its ride in Birmingham. But from Nashville, SNCC activists led by John Lewis and Diane Nash stepped into the fray, organizing an interracial group to ride from Birmingham to Montgomery. When the replacement riders arrived in Montgomery, they found themselves in an ambush plotted by white supremacists and police. With the police nowhere to be seen, a mob viciously beat the debarking riders. John Kennedy's emissary on the scene, John Seigenthaler, was knocked unconscious while trying to rescue a woman under attack.

With violence unabated, the Kennedys decided to intervene. Federal marshals sent to Montgomery barely held off a white mob attacking a church where Martin Luther King Jr. and twelve hundred civil rights supporters had gathered. As the Freedom Riders got ready to go on to Mississippi, Robert Kennedy privately made a deal with Senator James Eastland that if no violence occurred, Washington would look the other way if protestors were arrested for violating segregation laws that the Supreme Court already had invalidated.

During the months that followed, hundreds of Freedom Riders traveled to Mississippi bus and train terminals, where they were arrested. Most refused bail, crowding local prisons until the state began shipping them off to the notorious Parchman Prison Farm, where they suffered beatings, indignities, and solitary confinement. Meanwhile, the Kennedy administration asked the Interstate Commerce Commission, which regulated buses and trains, to enforce the Supreme Court decisions. On September 21, it ordered interstate carriers to post signs in buses saying that seating was without regard to race, color, creed, or national origin and forbade them from using segregated terminals. Over the next few months, continued Freedom Rides, more aggressive federal legal action, and a series of court orders ended the segregation of most interstate travel facilities.

Even before the Freedom Rides ended, Robert Kennedy sought to forestall further violent confrontations by urging civil rights leaders to move from direct action protests to registering southern black voters, implying that the federal government would protect them if they chose the latter path. Activists in SNCC and other southern civil rights groups divided over which strategy to embrace, in the end pursuing both. They centered their efforts in some of the most staunchly racist sections of the South, including the Mississippi Delta. Young organizers, mostly southern-born blacks, moved into rural communities, where they began forging ties to veteran black activists and mobilizing African American communities to try to register to vote and protest against discrimination in employment and public accommodations. But determined resistance by state and local authorities and a continuation of the white terrorism that so boldly surfaced during the Freedom Rides— church burnings, the shooting up of homes, arrests, beatings, and murders— kept advances to a minimum, with the federal government failing to provide civil rights workers with protection.

As the civil rights push in the South stalled, in Washington Congress and the Supreme Court took several steps toward democratizing governance. In 1960, Congress passed the Twenty-Third Amendment (ratified by the states a year later), which gave the District of Columbia electoral votes in presidential elections. In 1962, it passed the Twenty-Fourth Amendment (ratified two years later) that outlawed the poll tax in federal elections (five states still had it). That same year, the Supreme Court took a major step toward greater electoral democracy in its ruling in *Baker v. Carr*, a suit that sought to equalize the representation of voters in the Tennessee state legislature.

Post–World War II population shifts, unaccompanied by reapportionment, resulted in increased inequalities in the number of people in state legislative districts. In Minnesota in 1958, one Senate district contained 16,878 people while another had 153,455. In rapidly growing states, malapportionment was even more extreme. In California, a Los Angeles state senator represented 4.1 million people, while another senator represented three counties with a combined population of 14,014. In Florida, senators and representatives from districts representing less than 15 percent of the population, mostly in rural areas in the north of the state, formed the majority in both houses of the legislature and tightly controlled its actions.

Unequal apportionment had concrete consequences. With rural districts dominating state legislatures, cities got shortchanged in the distribution of state funds. Also, because the state legislatures determined congressional district lines, rural areas had overrepresentation in the House as well, skewing its priorities and policies away from urban needs and toward more conservative positions than held by the population as a whole.

In a split decision in the 1946 case of *Colegrove v. Green,* the Supreme

Court had rejected federal court jurisdiction over redistricting. But within a decade, elected officials in underrepresented areas, trade unionists frustrated by the defeat of pro-labor and liberal legislation in malapportioned legislatures, and political activists affronted or negatively impacted by inequities in representation began filing new legal challenges. At least indirectly, their efforts were linked to the civil rights movement. Both fed off the rhetoric of democracy that came to the forefront during World War II and the Cold War. Also, the civil rights movement brought new attention to using the courts rather than legislative bodies to effect social and political change. The Supreme Court decision to apply the Fourteenth Amendment equal protection clause to voting rights in its wartime decision banning whites-only primaries opened the door to applying the amendment to other voting inequities, an argument successfully made in *Baker v. Carr.*

The plaintiffs in *Baker v. Carr* (Charles Baker, a local government official from Memphis gave his name to the suit) received a boost when the Kennedy administration decided to file an amicus brief supporting them. Solicitor General Archibald Cox played a leading role in arguing the case before the Supreme Court, which held two hearings on what Earl Warren later characterized as "the most important case" he participated in as chief justice. On March 26, 1962, the Court ruled six to two in support of the plaintiffs. *Baker* itself only gave the federal courts jurisdiction to hear legislative apportionment cases, but it opened the floodgates for what became a democratic revolution that swept through the nation's legislative bodies. The next year, the Court, in a decision throwing out Georgia's county unit system of voting, said that constitutionally guaranteed political equality "can only mean one thing—one person, one vote." Subsequent decisions extended that principle from state legislative districts to congressional districts and finally to most local government bodies, including school boards, so that with the major exception of the U.S. Senate, legislative and administrative districts on all levels of government had to be roughly equal in population. It took a few years for the mandated changes to be implemented, but by the mid-1960s they were largely in place on the state and federal level, and by the early 1970s on the city and county level, giving greater representation to cities and suburbs, reducing the rural and small-town hold over lawmaking, and changing the political balance in many legislative bodies.

Federal Intervention

In September 1962, a crisis over the integration of the University of Mississippi led President Kennedy to begin moving gingerly toward greater support for the civil rights movement. After the Supreme Court ordered Ole Miss to admit its first black student, James Meredith, Governor Ross Barnett personally blocked his effort to register, then used state police and county sheriffs to keep him out, and finally, when he did enroll, failed to provide him protection. Kennedy at first tried to safeguard Meredith with federal marshals, but as the danger from segregationist crowds grew, he federalized units of the Mississippi National Guard. By the time the troops reached the university, a huge mob of students and older white supremacists had overwhelmed the marshals in an orgy of violence. Two people were killed and 160 marshals injured. After the fall elections, Kennedy issued an executive order he had promised two years earlier to desegregate federally funded public housing, but still declined to initiate a more comprehensive civil rights initiative.

Frustrated by white southern intransigence and federal passivity, civil rights leaders decided to force federal intervention and create pressure for new legislation by sparking a crisis that Washington leaders simply could not ignore. SCLC chose Birmingham as its battleground. The city—a center of heavy industry and regional services—had a long history of repressing democratic movements, first labor and then civil rights, through legal and extralegal violence, organized or at least tacitly supported by local wealthy interests. City officials, particularly Public Safety Commissioner Eugene "Bull" Connor, used every means at their disposal to keep the city strictly segregated, even if it meant closing parks and other public facilities rather than allowing court-ordered integration.

Martin Luther King Jr., his aide Wyatt Tee Walker, Birmingham minister Fred Shuttlesworth, and other SCLC leaders carefully prepared for an extended nonviolent direct-action campaign, code-named Project C, for "confrontation." Its demands were modest but too much for white Birmingham leaders: desegregation of downtown stores and their adoption of fair hiring practices; equal opportunities for African Americans in city government jobs; the reopening of recreational facilities on an integrated basis; and the creation of a biracial committee to further progress toward desegregation. On April 3, 1963, the campaign began with a boycott of segregated stores and a sit-down at segregated lunch counters. In the days that followed, sit-downs and marches led to the arrest of more and more demonstrators, including King. But after nearly a month of protests, the campaign seemed to be losing momentum.

To escalate the confrontation, SCLC leaders decided to involve black high school students. On the first day they marched, Connor's men arrested more than five hundred students. The next day, Connor used high-pressure water hoses and police dogs to try to stop hundreds more young demonstrators from reaching downtown. The day after, the police grew more violent in their efforts to stop the marches. In response, adult bystanders began stoning the police. In just three days, some fifteen hundred black teenagers and children were arrested.

Civil rights activities during the 1940s had received little coverage in the national press. By contrast, the Freedom Rides and other protests of the early 1960s garnered extensive media attention, including on network television news shows, which were rapidly emerging as a main source of information for the public. Images of police dogs attacking black children and fire hoses ripping off their clothes spread around the world. Their dissemination helped generate growing northern liberal and labor support for the civil rights effort and pushed the president, who had tried to maintain his distance from the Birmingham conflict, to get involved. Kennedy sent in mediators to start negotiations between black leaders and a committee representing the Birmingham white power structure and pressured, with only modest success, national corporations to order their local managers to support desegregation. As the demonstrations grew even larger, the police more brutal, and retaliatory attacks against the police more common, mediators worked out an agreement that provided for the phased implementation of store desegregation and nondiscriminatory employment.

No significant group of southern whites supported desegregation, but their willingness to resist it varied. In Birmingham, as in many other cities, white business owners, when faced with losses as a result of boycotts, demonstrations, and negative images of their city, ultimately abandoned all-out resistance to desegregation, agreeing to gradual change. White supremacist ideologues and some elected officials proved less willing to bend, leading to a fracturing of segregationist forces and the end of restraints on the most extreme elements. Bull Connor and other local and state officials denounced the Birmingham desegregation agreement. Ku Klux Klan members, who for years had undertaken a bombing campaign in Birmingham aimed at terrorizing the black community, rallied in force to protest the agreement and try to intimidate the black community, detonating bombs at the home of King's brother, who was a local minister, and at the motel where SCLC had its headquarters. In response, crowds of African Americans, largely working-class men who had not participated in the earlier protests, began stoning police and firemen. Soon growing mobs attacked police and white passersby and burned down white-owned stores.

Kennedy saw in the violence that came at the end of the Birmingham protests a portent of the spread of civil rights confrontations throughout the country. After tangling with another southern governor over enforcing another court order to desegregate a university—this time Alabama governor George Wallace—Kennedy, eager to find a way to move civil rights issues off of the streets and into the courts, announced that he would seek a new civil rights law.

By then, Birmingham had electrified black America. In its wake, boycotts, marches, sit-downs, and mass arrests took place in hundreds of southern towns and cities, with college and high school students often playing a central role. Some cities began cautiously desegregating. But violent resistance continued, both brutal police action against demonstrators and extra-legal terrorism. Just hours after Kennedy gave a national speech to announce his civil rights legislation, longtime Mississippi NAACP leader Medgar Evers, who had been leading a Birmingham-like campaign in Jackson, Mississippi, was assassinated outside his home.

In the North, African Americans and white allies demonstrated in support of the southern struggle and to protest local discrimination. In New York, a coalition of civil rights groups undertook a summer-long campaign against employment discrimination in the construction industry that included sit-downs, mass picketing, nightly church rallies, and hundreds of arrests. Public officials and construction union leaders proved adept at endorsing the protestors' goals while avoiding meaningful steps toward realizing them.

The August 28, 1963, March on Washington channeled the post-Birmingham explosion of civil rights activity toward pressing Congress to pass a civil rights bill. The idea for a march came from veteran black trade unionists and civil rights leaders, most notably A. Philip Randolph, concerned with the economic plight of African Americans, who had higher levels of unemployment and lower incomes than whites. To improve black living standards, the march organizers hoped to push forward the long-standing labor-liberal agenda of a higher minimum wage, a federal public works program, and a World War II–type Fair Employment Practices Committee. The focus of the march broadened when in the wake of Birmingham and Kennedy's public support for civil rights legislation all the major civil rights groups joined together to cosponsor what became called the "March on Washington for Jobs and Freedom." Bayard Rustin, an African American leftist and pacifist, forced out of a large public role in the civil rights movement by threats to disclose his homosexuality, coordinated the organizing for the ambitious plan. The Kennedy administration first tried to discourage the rally, then endorsed it but worked behind the scenes to soften its radical edges.

The Washington march, with close to a quarter of a million people gathering peacefully in front of the Lincoln Memorial (an estimated two-thirds black and one-third white), had no real precedent for the sheer mass of humanity brought together, the media coverage it received, and the impact it had on the public mood and political consciousness. On a day full of dramatic imagery and rhetorical eloquence, King's speech near the end of the rally captured the most attention. Full of phrases and cadences familiar to black churchgoers and civil rights activists, his painting of his "dream" that one day the country would achieve "the true meaning of its creed" of equality and all people would be "free at last" cemented King's position as one of the country's great orators and moral leaders.

What the march did not do was win rapid passage of civil rights legislation in Congress. Meanwhile, civil rights workers continued to be attacked, arrested, and murdered with no significant federal effort to protect them; schools and public accommodations across much of the country remained segregated; and most southern blacks still could not vote. Within CORE and SNCC, activists questioned the reliability of liberal white allies and the pace of change. Black critics of nonviolence, like Black Muslim leader Malcolm X, who mocked the August demonstration as the "Farce on Washington" and called for black armed self-defense, presented an increasingly influential alternative pole within the black community to civil rights leaders. The September 1963 Ku Klux Klan bombing of the Sixteenth Street Baptist Church in Birmingham, which killed four black girls attending Sunday school, belied the optimism that had infused King's speech just a month before.

Dallas

Violence has always been a feature of American political life. Presidents Lincoln, Garfield, and McKinley were killed in office, and both Theodore and Franklin Roosevelt narrowly escaped death from assassins' bullets. During the Truman administration, two Puerto Rican independence advocates tried to kill the president, shooting three policemen before themselves being shot, and four others opened fire on the House of Representatives from a visitors' gallery, wounding five congressmen. Nonetheless, the assassination of President Kennedy in Dallas on November 22, 1963, shocked the nation. The official, dominant portrait of the country stressed the orderly, democratic nature of its governance, contrasting it to other nations where leaders were put in place or removed through dictatorial measures and violent acts. Southern civil rights workers had an intense sense of violence as a determining and immediate force in American history, but most Americans probably considered events like the killing of Medgar Evers and the Birmingham bombing aberrations. The Kennedy murder, beyond the human tragedy of a father of two dying young, struck at the heart of the understanding most Americans had of their country. Arthur Schlesinger's daughter said to him after he returned home from meeting the plane that carried Kennedy's body back to Washington, "If this is the kind of country we have, I don't want to live here anymore."

Things kept getting weirder after Kennedy died. As was soon revealed, the man arrested for shooting him, twenty-four-year-old Lee Harvey Oswald, a onetime Marine, had defected to the Soviet Union, where he had lived for several years before redefecting with his Russian wife to the United States, where he became active in a group opposing U.S. intervention in Cuba. Before Oswald had a chance to publicly speak about the crime with which he had been charged, he was murdered in front of national television cameras in the basement of a Dallas police station, from which he was being transferred, by a local nightclub owner, Jack Ruby, with a history of connections to the police and organized crime. Both in official and unofficial circles, the belief quickly spread that Oswald and perhaps Ruby could not possibly have acted alone, with the Cuban government, anti-Castro exiles, extreme right-wing groups, organized crime, Teamster leader Jimmy Hoffa (whom the Kennedy brothers had relentlessly pursued on various criminal charges), and the CIA suggested as possible participants in a conspiracy to get rid of the president.

The new president, Lyndon Johnson, moved quickly to reassure the nation that Oswald had acted alone and that no unseen forces had been behind Kennedy's death. He himself doubted that was true, but he told colleagues that unless claims of communist involvement were refuted, war might result. Johnson appointed a commission headed by Earl Warren to investigate the assassination, but the FBI and CIA, with investigatory failings and covert actions to hide, proved unforthcoming in the information they gave the group. The lengthy Warren Commission report, which found "no evidence that anyone assisted Oswald in planning or carrying out the assassination," was quickly ripped apart by critics. But subsequent investigations also failed to provide a convincing explanation of what had happened.

The murkiness of the assassination was in some ways as distressing as the crime itself, suggesting the existence of subterranean layers of American life with power over the government and the fate of the nation. Millions of supporters and opponents grieved for Kennedy, who had increased his popularity during his presidency. His death left the country unsettled, stripped of the civic certainties that the Cold War had made so pervasive.

CHAPTER 8

The Democratic Revolution

On December 2, 1964, Mario Savio, an undergraduate philosophy major, who had grown up in a working-class family in Queens, New York, spoke to a crowd of over a thousand students and their supporters protesting a ban on political activity on the University of California–Berkeley campus. Just before the protestors sat down inside the main campus administration building, Savio told them, "There is a time when the operation of the machine becomes so odious, makes you so sick at heart, that you can't take part; you can't even passively take part, and you've got to put your bodies upon the gears and upon the wheels, upon the levers, upon all the apparatus, and you've got to make it stop."

The next day, on orders from liberal Democratic governor Edmund Brown, police moved into the building and carted off 773 demonstrators, the largest mass arrest in California history. The sit-down and the language Savio used to encourage it reflected a new sensibility that would propel a democratic revolution for years to come.

During the mid-1960s, political change took place with rapidity and on a scale unseen in the United States since the New Deal. Post–New Deal liberalism reached its high-water mark with a flood of federal legislation and a series of Supreme Court decisions that bolstered democratic rights and expanded the role of government in promoting social well-being. Civil rights and student activists energized, criticized, transformed, and undermined liberalism, as politics came to mean more than the sum of discrete issues like civil rights or foreign policy. Increasingly, people began to question the very nature of authority in the institutions that shaped their lives, from local and national government to colleges and universities, churches, and even their own families. A swelling movement for greater democracy pressed liberalism to expand its ambitions, abandon its anticommunist boundaries, and open up hierarchical structures to popular participation.

By the end of 1966, liberalism had reached its apogee. Even as it faced swelling challenges from its left, it came under growing pressure from its right, as conservatives built popular movements and political infrastructure dedicated to ending liberal dominance. As cultural and political divisions within the country grew, to many the nation seemed to be fragmenting. Like most revolutions, the democratic revolution of the 1960s turned out to be a disorderly, exhilarating, frightening affair.

Rebellious Youth

It was far from coincidental that one of the first nationally publicized, militant challenges to a major liberal institution in the name of democracy took place on a college campus. The pressure on liberalism to reinvigorate itself in part stemmed from a generational divide particularly evident in the academy. And what happened on college campuses mattered more during the 1960s than ever before, because higher education played a more significant role in American life than ever before.

After World War II, the federal government fostered the massive expansion of higher education through investment in research and development, the GI Bill, and the National Defense Education Act. A growing demand for trained professionals in science, engineering, and management, and rising family income, which allowed young people to delay entering the workforce, led more and more students to stay in school for longer and longer. In 1946, two million enrolled in higher education programs; in 1960, three and a half million. When the baby boom generation came of age, enrollments exploded, nearing eight million by 1970. In 1946, one out of eight eighteen- to twenty-four-year-olds was attending college or graduate school; in 1960, nearly one out of four; in 1970, nearly one out of three.

The schools they attended varied immensely, from elite private institutions to huge state universities to modest junior colleges. By the mid-1960s, there were twice as many public colleges and universities as private ones. California provided the model. Under its 1960 master plan, the state built an enormous three-tier system to provide free higher education to its residents. The top tier, the research-oriented University of California, took in the highest-achieving high school graduates and offered the most advanced degrees. State colleges provided four-year programs to less qualified students. Community colleges offered two-year degrees.

Standardized tests helped determine which students got admitted to which schools. When California adopted its master plan, it initiated a standardized admission test. The trend spread as more and more colleges required applicants to take the Scholastic Aptitude Test (SAT) or the American College Testing (ACT) exam. The military gave a boost to such testing when it adopted a standardized exam to decide which college students would get draft deferments.

Standardized testing facilitated a push by social and educational leaders to create more opportunities for outsiders to win places in elite institutions. The resiliency of the white, male, Protestant leadership of the country lay in part in its willingness to open its ranks, a bit, to smart young men from families of modest means. Top colleges and universities provided an arena for selecting, socializing, and training such men, who then were recruited for important positions in government and business. The increasing number of students reaching top schools on the basis of grades and test scores rather than social pedigree began changing the culture at many of the nation's most celebrated educational institutions, where students in the past generally had placed little value on academic enterprise, saving their time and energy for social activities, athletics, and dissipation.

As colleges and universities became more linked to the ongoing administration of society, they became poles for cultural and political dissidence. An expanding economy freed college students from fears about their future well-being. Many became drawn to intellectuals and artists who took to task or at least opted out of what looked to them like a hegemonic, corporate, Cold War cultural consensus. Academics like Norman O. Brown, Herbert Marcuse, and Paul Goodman gained followers through their attacks on psychological and sexual repression, which they believed were integral to the dominant culture. European existentialists cut against the grain of Cold War patriotism and demands for social and political conformity with their concern for immediate experience, individual moral commitment, and the need to act against falsehood (themes strongly echoed in Savio's speech).

"Beat" writers—Allen Ginsberg, Jack Kerouac, William Burroughs, Gary Snyder, and Gregory Corso among the best-known—made deviating from conventional mores alluring. Their work burst with Whitmanesque celebrations of America, but of a raucous, down-and-out, drug-using, harddrinking, sexually exuberant, rebellious America. The Beat sensibility soon permeated bohemian neighborhoods like Greenwich Village and the Lower East Side in New York and North Beach in San Francisco. It could be found, too, in the student quarters near large college campuses, in places like Berkeley; Madison, Wisconsin; Austin, Texas; and Minneapolis's Dinkytown. With the middle class deserting cities for suburban living, cheap, run-down apartments were easy to find, providing a material and geographic base for an emerging culture of dissent. But the Beat influence went beyond enclaves of hipness and student life. Ginsberg's 1955 poem *Howl,* initially deemed obscene by government authorities, sold 100,000 copies during its first decade in print, while Kerouac's novel *On the Road* was a 1957 best seller. By the beginning of the 1960s, cultural iconoclasm had begun penetrating some of the mainstream taste-making industries, including advertising, which experimented with selling products by identifying them with authenticity and nonconformity.

Only a minority of students got heavily involved with intellectual and literary dissent, but many identified with a broader youth culture that had been emerging since World War II. At various times in the history of the United States, youth had been prized and celebrated, but generally young people did not think of themselves nor did others think of them as a distinct social formation. In the decade after World War II, that began to change. Adolescents and young adults, coming of age during a period of extended economic growth, chafed under the cultural norms and expectations of an older generation shaped by the Great Depression and World War II. Writer Joan Didion, who attended Berkeley in the early 1950s, recalled that "we were the last generation to identify with adults." During the 1940s, the term "teenager" began to be used, with its underlying assumption of a shared set of experiences among those of a particular age, cutting across other social divisions. In reality, multiple overlapping youth subcultures were emerging, reflecting differences in race, gender, class, and region. Still, a commercial mass culture, aimed at teenagers and young adults, helped create a conscious sense of a distinct generation, with a sensibility different from and in some ways at odds with that of its elders. With young people having more free time (because fewer worked) and more money than in the past, companies designed and marketed clothes, music, and other goods specifically for them.

Comic books set the pattern. Introduced in the 1930s, they were inexpensive enough that children and teenagers could buy them on their own. By the early 1950s, they had grown immensely popular. Estimates of sales ranged from nearly seventy million books a month or higher, with surveys reporting over 90 percent of under-eighteen-year-olds reading them. While some comics upheld adult notions of morality, patriotism, and proper behavior, others provided children and adolescents with an alternative to prevailing pieties and values. Horror and crime comics reveled in the macabre. Scantily clad women, with and without superpowers, exuded dangerous sexuality. Some comic books even disseminated dissenting political views, depicting government authorities as corrupt and the Korean War as a pointless bloodletting.

Parents, cultural arbiters, and government officials fretted about the ir-reverence of comic books and their creation of an imaginative world they neither understood nor liked. Well-publicized charges that comics promoted juvenile delinquency led to a series of government investigations. To protect themselves, in 1954 comic book publishers adopted a system of self-censorship, which led to much more bland content and declining sales, as the medium stopped serving, at least for a while, as a promoter of a youth culture at odds with adult values.

By then, rock and roll had begun taking over that role. Rock and roll defined itself as youth music, engaged with the particular experiences and sentiments of adolescents and celebrating a rejection of the adult world. Mu-sicians like Chuck Berry embodied the amalgam of blues, rhythm and blues, and country music that produced rock and roll. A black man nearing thirty when he had his first hit, Berry appealed to a mostly white teenage audience, carefully crafting his songs to speak to the experience of high school dances, hot rod cars, and teenage infatuation.

Berry achieved modest commercial success, but the best-selling musi-cians of the late 1950s and early 1960s were white. Some made their fortunes doing cover versions of black records, toning them down and desexualizing them. Others, like Elvis Presley, developed styles that drew on black musical genres but did not simply ape them. The racial promiscuousness of rock and roll, along with its general exuberance and open sexuality, gave it a rebel-lious aura. By the mid-1950s, the demand by white southern high school and college students for records by black artists had grown to the point that rec-ord stores serving the white community began to stock them. In the early 1960s, racially integrated rhythm and blues shows toured the South, attract-ing large crowds of blacks and whites and generating considerable tension. Rock and roll was creating a new cultural universe, in which whites imitated blacks and middle-class teenagers made proletarian clothing, especially blue jeans, an international fashion.

Parents and government authorities tried to hold back the tide of youth culture. Schools instituted dress codes. Prosecutors went after radio disc jockeys for taking payoffs from record companies. Southern officials banned interracial concerts, and segregationists physically assaulted black perform-ers. As in the case of comic books, the cultural counterattack had some short-term success. Bland white pop music dominated record sales and the airwaves in the early 1960s. But it was only a temporary reprieve before Brit-ish rock groups, led by the Beatles, and black artists from Detroit's Motown label took over the top of the charts in 1964.

As youthful cultural rebelliousness grew, so did student political activism, most noticeably on the left. Campus leftism fell to a nadir in the early and mid-1950s, as the adult left lost its allure and anticommunist crusading made students fearful of speaking up. It began to revive in the late 1950s, as anticommunist repression diminished. At Berkeley, the country's most politically active campus, left-leaning students and their more moderate allies captured the student government (only to be maneuvered out of office by the college administration); protested compulsory participation in ROTC (a common requirement at state universities); and demonstrated against the House Committee on Un-American Activities when it held hearings in San Francisco in 1960 (marking an end to the fear and deference the committee long had commanded). In February 1962, several thousand students picketed the White House to protest nuclear testing and the civil defense program, the largest demonstration held there in nearly a decade.

In many ways, the campus activists were not that different from a new breed of adult activists who began popping up in the late 1950s and early 1960s. In New York City, "reform Democrats" opposed the backroom dealmaking of established party leaders. The National Committee for a Sane Nuclear Policy and Women Strike for Peace opposed nuclear testing and the arms race. The Fair Play for Cuba Committee tried to stop American intervention in Cuba. The 1962 publication of Rachel Carson's *Silent Spring,* documenting the effects of pesticides on the environment, sparked protests against industrial pollution and the loss of open space and wilderness.

Though they addressed different issues, these groups had common traits. With the exception of the Fair Play for Cuba Committee, which had a number of prominent black members, all were primarily white and middle class. Women played a major role in many of them, especially those concerned with peace and the environment. Their members, like their student equivalents, had great faith in reason and discussion and optimism about the ability of the country to right moral and political wrongs. Confident about their own abilities and standing, they believed it their right and duty to intervene with the government and challenge established powers and policies. Though some of the activists had or once had ties to left-wing groups, they generally played down ideology, focusing on specific issues. Reminiscent in some ways of Progressive Era reform, the new liberal activism was a decidedly polite affair, with the young and old alike generally careful to wear suits and ties and skirts or dresses to picket lines and demonstrations.

Liberal activism soon became more militant, though, especially on campuses, as a result of the civil rights movement. The sight of young southern blacks placing their lives on the line in sit-ins, Freedom Rides, and voter registration drives electrified many northern students. In 1960, thousands of them picketed chain stores that refused to desegregate their southern branches. Some headed south to report on or join the civil rights effort, returning to their campuses transformed by the experience.

In 1964, Mississippi civil rights groups decided to bring northern white students to spend the summer working on a voter registration drive and help run "Freedom Schools," calculating that their presence would bring national publicity and perhaps federal protection to the effort, knowing from bitter experience how little ripple occurred when local blacks were the victims of violence. Before the bulk of the nearly nine hundred "Freedom Summer" volunteers even got to Mississippi, segregationist terror took a heavy toll. Fires and bombs damaged or destroyed churches and civil rights headquarters associated with the project, while unprovoked violence against blacks increased. On June 21, three project members, James Chaney, an African American from Meridian, Mississippi, Andrew Goodman, a white student from New York City, and Michael Schwerner, another white New Yorker and the oldest of the group at twenty-four, on their way back from investigating a church burning, were arrested by a deputy sheriff in Philadelphia, Mississippi, and then released on a deserted road into a Ku Klux Klan ambush. Klan members killed all three and hid their bodies. The disappearance of the civil rights workers, two of them northern whites, brought massive national attention to the Mississippi struggle and increased federal involvement. Still, it took the FBI six weeks to find the bodies, while the reign of terror continued.

The sensibility and political approach of the civil rights movement, especially SNCC, profoundly influenced the emerging student movement. Students absorbed from it the notion of direct action as a form of political pressure and moral witness against perceived wrongs. They also adopted from SNCC a belief in participatory democracy as a social goal and a way of running their own organizations, seeking to develop modes for meaningful involvement of ordinary people in self-governance.

Well into the mid-1960s, programmatically the student movement remained within the parameters of liberalism. The 1962 "Port Huron Statement," issued by one of the new campus groups, Students for a Democratic Society (SDS), put forth a sweeping indictment of American society for racism, inequality, complacency, and bureaucracy. But its suggested remedies—federal initiatives in the areas of civil rights, poverty, housing, and economic development and a realignment of the Democratic Party into a national party of liberalism—went only a bit beyond Fair Deal–New Frontier liberalism.

In its sensibility, though, the emerging student movement represented a challenge to liberalism and even a break with it. The impatience of student activists, black and white, with the gap between the official rhetoric and lived reality gave an urgency to their politics at odds with the unhurried confidence of early 1960s liberalism that America was fundamentally good and was on the inevitable and irreversible road to fulfilling its promises. The desire to breathe mass participation into the idea of democracy and to apply it to every-day situations in schools, workplaces, and communities cut against the faith in expertise, democracy through pluralist representation, and distrust of popular mobilization that characterized post–New Deal liberalism. Also, consistent with taking democracy at face value, the student movement re-jected the anticommunism that had become central to postwar liberalism, refusing to exclude groups or individuals on the basis of their political as-sociations. Early SDS leader Al Haber's comment that he hoped his group would be a "radical liberal force" captured the ideological tension that gave energy to what was becoming known as the New Left.

The Free Speech Movement (FSM) at Berkeley brought the New Left to national attention. More students from the San Francisco Bay Area partici-pated in the Freedom Summer than from any other part of the country except New York, including Mario Savio. But Berkeley administrators seemed indif-ferent to the changing student mood. Most colleges tightly controlled all stu-dent activities and enforced rules that many students found antiquated and ridiculous. At Harvard (then still all male), undergraduates had to wear ties to all meals, a requirement some breakfasters met by wearing their cravats over undershirts. At Radcliffe, its sister school, students could not wear pants to class and could leave their dorms in the evening only by signing out to a specific destination. Almost every college had strict "parietal" rules regulat-ing visits by members of the opposite sex to dorm rooms. At Berkeley, the administration clamped down on political as well as personal behavior, block-ing appearances by controversial speakers and allowing student groups to raise funds and distribute literature concerning off-campus issues only at tables in a small area on the edge of the campus. When in the fall of 1964 the university closed down that area too, students began pressing for greater political rights.

On October 1, university police arrested a former student for soliciting funds for CORE on campus. When they tried to take him away, hundreds of students sat down, surrounding the police car in which he had been placed. The standoff lasted thirty-two hours and led to the formation of FSM. The new organization tapped a well of student discontent. Berkeley was the pro-totypical large liberal university—bureaucratic, closely linked to the busi-ness, government, and military establishments (the first H-bomb had been built at a Berkeley-run weapons lab), and generally more concerned with research than with teaching. Students complained about large classes, a lack of contact with faculty, and a new computerized registration system that for many symbolized the impersonality of the university. And they resented being treated like children.

The failure to resolve issues between FSM and the university administration culminated in the December 2 sit-down. Many of the protestors shared Savio's view that the university and the larger society were impersonal and unjust; that it was a moral obligation as well as an existential act to oppose such a society; and that by nonviolent direct action, social change could be effected. And it was. Within three weeks of the arrests of the protestors, after a student strike and much turmoil, the university board of regents adopted new rules regulating on-campus political activity similar to those proposed by FSM. The national student movement remained small—in December 1964, SDS had only forty-one chapters and twenty-five hundred members— but it had made a dramatic entrance onto the national political stage.

The New Right

At the same time that civil rights and student activists were taking liberal leaders and institutions to task for not living up to their professed beliefs, liberalism also came under attack from the right, from a conservative movement that mushroomed in the early 1960s. Though small in itself, the "New Right," like the New Left, had growing intellectual and political influence. At its forefront stood a charismatic senator from Arizona, Barry Goldwater.

The 1950s had been a difficult time for conservatives. The success of anticommunism as an ideology meant that it provided them with only a limited boost, since liberals and centrists embraced it with equal fervor. The fall of Joe McCarthy tainted conservatism with an image of recklessness and indecency. The death of Robert Taft in 1953 and the control of the national Republican Party by moderates like Thomas Dewey and Dwight Eisenhower thwarted any full-scale effort to reverse the New Deal. The attack on union rights proved a dud, resulting in big defeats for the Republicans in 1958.

Goldwater was the exception to the rule. A member of the Senate committee investigating labor racketeering, he had launched an investigation of the UAW (which turned up no corruption), then won reelection after portraying an effort by the union to defeat him as undue interference in his state's affairs by an outside force. Emerging as a bright star on the conservative horizon, he helped revive the movement by repackaging old themes in attractive new ways.

The breakthrough came with *The Conscience of a Conservative,* a short book prepared as part of Goldwater's unsuccessful bid for the 1960 Republican presidential nomination. Ghostwritten by former McCarthy speech-writer L. Brent Bozell, it portrayed the central political issue of the day as the threat to individual freedom from an unrestrained federal government that unduly interfered in the daily lives of its citizens, hampered business through excessive regulation, and stepped on states' rights. Goldwater had a different notion of freedom than the civil rights movement, which also was making freedom its central demand. For Goldwater, freedom meant not interfering with free-market capitalism, maximizing the social and economic liberty of individuals, and restraining government, including federal interference in southern racial practices. In *The Conscience of a Conservative,* Goldwater said almost nothing about communist subversion at home—a break with a long-standing right-wing obsession. He did take a hard line toward the Soviet bloc; American policy, he argued, should be built around the idea "that we would rather die than lose our freedom." But most of his book focused on proposals for radically reducing federal spending, limiting union power, and leaving economic and social regulation to the marketplace. By November 1960, half a million copies of *The Conscience of a Conservative* had been sold, with sales especially strong at college bookstores. Eventually sales exceeded three million.

Goldwater failed to gain the nomination in 1960, but the election established conditions for a conservative revival. With Eisenhower leaving office, Republicans no longer felt constrained about attacking entrenched programs of the New Deal that the president had supported. Conservative activists who felt betrayed by an agreement Nixon worked out with Nelson Rockefeller that gave the party's 1960 platform some decidedly liberal planks began working, with backing from conservative business interests, to make sure that next time around there would be a conservative presidential candidate running on a conservative platform. Meanwhile, the hyperbolic Cold War rhetoric of the incoming Kennedy administration helped legitimate far-right anticommunism. In 1958, Robert Welch, a right-wing businessman who had been chair of the National Association of Manufacturers' education committee, founded the John Birch Society in reaction to the internationalism and domestic moderation of the Eisenhower administration. Though liberals and moderates derided Welch's charges of communist conspiracies penetrating the government and American society, his emotional tenor and dire warnings did not lie all that far from Kennedy's portrayal of the "hour of maximum danger." By the early 1960s, the Birch Society claimed sixty thousand members, with considerable influence beyond its ranks through its publications and connections within the Republican Party.

The activists drawn to the emerging New Right in some respects resembled their liberal and left-wing counterparts. The young conservatives who in 1960 founded the Young Americans for Freedom (YAF) had a similar combination of earnest engagement with politics, rebelliousness against established positions and institutions, and disdain for compromise. But on many specific issues they took a diametrically opposite position, supporting loyalty oaths for recipients of federal fellowships and student loans; seeking a continuation of nuclear testing; supporting "right-to-work" laws; pressing for the reduction of welfare programs; and promoting a vigorous anticommunist foreign policy. Many YAF supporters had a strong libertarian streak. The novels of Ayn Rand served a similar role for young conservatives as the works of Albert Camus did for New Leftists; both writers laid out notions of freedom and morality that, while differing from one another, demanded individual self-scrutiny and uncompromising action. But among young conservatives, and even more so their elders, there also were "traditionalists" who adhered to religious-based social values, sought moral and legal limits on individual behavior, and feared what they saw as the nihilism and spiritual emptiness of Rand's hyperindividualism.

Grassroots conservatism found many adherents among upwardly mobile professionals, small business owners, and their wives living in socially homogeneous, growing suburban areas in the South and West. Like the liberal reformers, this new breed of conservatives refused to defer to established authorities, having great confidence in their own judgment and right to shape society. Like their liberal counterparts, they tended to be highly literate, influenced by books and journals like *National Review,* a conservative magazine founded by William F. Buckley in 1955; FBI director J. Edgar Hoover's anticommunist tract *Masters of Deceit;* and more extreme literature put out by hard-right groups.

Growth in the western part of the country helped propel the right's resurgence. Western conservatives resented the control Washington had over their region as a landholder and regulator of natural resources, while downplaying the benefits they received from its subsidies. In Orange County, California, the epicenter of the New Right, newcomers flooding in from small towns in the Midwest, upper South, and Southwest brought with them conservative social values and conservative forms of Protestantism. The region's military-industrial complex contributed to its prosperity and its deep anticommunism. Many beneficiaries of the booming local economy attributed their success to individual initiative and ability, reinforcing their free-market ideology, overlooking the massive government spending that sustained the area and the West more generally.

Dismay with changes wrought by liberal hegemony fueled the New Right. The 1962 Supreme Court decision in the case of *Engel v. Vitale* sparked as much or more controversy than *Brown*. A decade earlier, at the height of the anticommunist fervor, the New York State Board of Regents had written a nondenominational prayer that some school districts used to start each day. Ruling on a challenge to that practice, the Court, with only one dissenting vote, decided that having the government compose a prayer to be recited as part of a religious program carried out by a government body violated the First Amendment prohibition of government-established religion. The next year the Court extended its ruling by declaring the recitation of the Lord's Prayer or the reading of Bible verses in classrooms to be unconstitutional, even if children were allowed to excuse themselves from the exercise.

Seemingly overnight, a practice that had been part of the routine of public schools in much of the country since their founding—brief prayer to begin the day—had been banished. Many Jewish and mainstream Protestant leaders supported the Court decisions, but the Catholic Church and many southern Protestant ministers vehemently denounced them. Popular opposition to the rulings, though widespread, proved insufficient to push through proposed constitutional amendments to allow school prayer. But outrage at court-ordered secularization brought new adherents to the conservative movement.

The civil rights movement created other openings for conservatives and the Republican Party. As the Kennedy administration began to more actively support civil rights, southern segregationists again questioned their ties to the national Democratic Party. The embrace of states' rights by non-southern conservatives like Goldwater created the potential for a political realignment. To capitalize, the Republican National Committee launched a southern organizing drive, which it called Operation Dixie, the same name the CIO had used for its largely unsuccessful southern organizing effort a decade and a half earlier. The South, once seen by labor liberals as the key to expanding the New Deal and organized labor, now came to be seen by conservatives as the key to undoing them. In the North, too, some white voters moved in a conservative direction in reaction to the civil rights movement, especially the use of government power to enforce nondiscriminatory practices in home sales, hiring, and school placement.

Barry Goldwater became the rallying point for conservatives. Largely behind the scenes, a group of experienced political operatives worked to secure him the 1964 Republican presidential nomination, quietly lining up delegates from nonprimary states (only sixteen states held primaries that year). In the primaries that were held, Goldwater won the bulk of the delegates. His chief liberal opponent for the nomination, Nelson Rockefeller, hurt his chances by divorcing his longtime wife and soon after marrying a considerably younger woman, who allowed her husband custody of their children, behavior seen as morally unacceptable by many voters. Goldwater's success in winning the Republican nomination and his determination not to compromise his principles—in accepting his nomination he proclaimed that "extremism in the defense of liberty is no vice"—set up one of the most ideologically sharp presidential elections in American history, as the Arizona conservative challenged an incumbent president, Lyndon Johnson, who not only accepted Kennedy-style liberalism but vastly expanded it.

LBJ

Lyndon Baines Johnson spent much of his life trying to become president but fearing that his southernness would doom him to failure. Since the Civil War, only one southerner had reached the White House, Woodrow Wilson, and he had built his career in the North, as president of Princeton University and governor of New Jersey. Johnson's roots lay south of the South, in the Texas Hill Country, where he was born in a small town to a poor family. After attending teachers' college he taught impoverished Mexican American students before embarking on his life's work, politics.

Johnson was a large man—in his physical stature, his energy, drive, and ambition, his vision for the country, his insecurities and contradictions. He entered politics as a New Dealer and in 1937 won a seat in the House of Representatives running as an adamant supporter of FDR. Johnson sincerely embraced reform but not at the expense of furthering his personal ambitions. Even while projecting himself as a defender of the little man, he maintained close ties with Texas business interests, particularly in the oil, gas, and construction industries. After World War II, in tune with the times, he moved in a conservative direction, opposing most of Truman's Fair Deal, supporting Taft-Hartley, embracing anticommunism, and voting against civil rights legislation. In 1948 he was elected to the Senate, becoming majority leader in 1955.

In the late 1950s, Johnson tacked back in a liberal direction, especially on civil rights. After falling short in his long-shot bid for the 1960 Democratic nomination for president, he accepted Kennedy's offer of the vice presidential slot. He hated the job, finding himself with little influence in the administration, shunted off on a series of overseas trips largely designed to keep him busy and away from the action. When assassination handed him the presidency, he seized it with manic energy and a sense of entitlement, immediately planning how to get Kennedy's stalled legislation passed and how to get elected to the White House in his own right in 1964. With deeper ties than Kennedy to New Deal liberalism, Johnson believed he had the opportunity to fulfill the unrealized ambitions of Roosevelt and his followers.

Johnson's first success came with Kennedy's tax bill, which Congress passed in February 1964. Over a period of two years it reduced the top nominal tax rate for individuals from 91 percent, a level that still reflected the tax policy adopted during World War II, to 70 percent, while the bottom rate fell from 20 to 14 percent. Corporate taxes were cut even more sharply. This unprecedented reduction had the effect that Keynesian economists predicted: output and employment rose sharply, driven by increased spending by consumers with more disposable income. The increase in economic activity generated enough additional taxes to make up for most of the decline in government revenue resulting from the drop in tax rates. This seemingly ideal situation, in which stimulation through fiscal policy did not lead to major deficits, cemented moderate Keynesianism as the orthodoxy among economists and policymakers.

The civil rights bill, which Kennedy had submitted to Congress in the wake of the Birmingham demonstrations, presented a much greater challenge. The bill limited the use of literacy tests to block voter registration; forbade discrimination by race, color, religion, or national origin in hiring, union membership, and access to public accommodations (including hotels, restaurants, stores, and theaters); established a Commission on Equal Employment Opportunity; empowered the attorney general to bring suit against public officials who maintained segregated schools (relieving civil rights organizations and black parents of the cost of enforcing *Brown v. Board of Education*); and required the federal government to withhold funds to local programs, including schools, that practiced discrimination.

Johnson had reservations about a federal desegregation law, but after Kennedy's death he told a joint session of Congress that "no memorial or oration could more eloquently honor" him than the "earliest possible passage" of his civil rights bill. It ended up taking seven months. The key to its passage was the support it received from Republicans, who, proportionate to their numbers, provided stronger backing than Democrats. In the House, an alliance of northern Democrats and Republicans overcame the effort by the chair of the Rules Committee, Virginian Howard Smith, to bottle up the bill in his committee. Undaunted, in the floor debate Smith tried a maneuver he had used years earlier in fighting the Fair Employment Practices Committee, introducing an amendment to expand the outlawed bases for discrimination in hiring or union membership to include sex.

Smith apparently hoped his amendment would split the backers of the bill, leading to its defeat, but his position was not entirely disingenuous. He had long backed the Equal Rights Amendment (ERA) to the Constitution, first proposed in 1923, which would have declared that "equality of rights under the law shall not be denied or abridged by the United States or by any State on account of sex." The ERA had won backing from the two major political parties but always fell short of passage. In the early 1960s, though, support for granting women greater equality was growing.

The ERA was one of two strategies during the decades after World War II for improving the status of women. Some feminists opposed it, fearing that it would wipe out laws protecting women in the workplace. As an alternative, they sought measures to guarantee women equal job opportunities and equal pay for work of comparable difficulty as men's work; grant working mothers maternity leave and childcare; prevent discrimination against nonwhite women; and provide an expanded package of social insurance. The centerpiece of the "Women's Status Bill" that embodied their ideas, first introduced to Congress in 1947, was the call for a presidential commission on the status of women, modeled on the commission Truman had appointed to report to him about civil rights, which could put women's rights on the national political agenda.

Congressional support for both ERA and the Women's Status Bill ebbed during the 1950s, but supporters of economic rights for women continued to press their case. Many backed Kennedy's presidential bid, only to see him appoint very few women to high positions. Unlike the previous three presidents, he included not a single woman in his cabinet. But when Esther Peterson, whom he appointed to head the Department of Labor's Women's Bureau, revived the idea of a President's Commission on the Status of Women, Kennedy agreed, appointing Eleanor Roosevelt to head the group.

In 1963, Congress passed the Equal Pay Act, which forbade pay differences between men and women doing identical jobs. Practically, the law had little effect, since men and women rarely did the same work and the measure did not cover domestic or farm labor, heavily female occupations. Still, as an ideological statement it represented a major departure, the first federal law to prohibit discrimination on the basis of sex. The publication the same year of Betty Friedan's *The Feminine Mystique* brought increased public discussion of the unhappiness many women felt with their social situation.

Howard Smith's proposal to add a ban on discrimination on the basis of sex to the civil rights bill thus came at a moment of growing debate over women's rights. A group of congresswomen led by Republican Martha Griffiths pulled together a coalition of women's rights backers and southern

Democrats (many of whom opposed the civil rights bill itself) to pass his amendment. Smith won the battle—in the process helping to push forward a momentous shift in the legal and social status of women—but then lost what for him was the war, as the House proceeded to pass the amended bill by more than a two-to-one margin. In the Senate, opponents of the bill launched a filibuster, but its backers lined up seventy-one votes to end debate, finally breaking the hold that Senate rules gave southern leaders over the body. On July 2, 1964, Johnson signed the act into law.

While Johnson had inherited the tax and civil rights bills, Kennedy's idea for an antipoverty program had not yet been fleshed out when he died. During the late 1950s and early 1960s, the problem of poverty received sustained attention from academics, journalists, and policymakers for the first time since the depths of the Depression. In part, this stemmed from a concern with juvenile delinquency in the cities, which some social scientists attributed to the social environment of impoverished neighborhoods, increasingly inhabited by African American migrants from the South and, in New York, newcomers from Puerto Rico. Poverty, once thought of as largely a problem of exploitation at the workplace, increasingly had come to be seen as an issue of economic and social marginalization, of exclusion from work. Though liberals continued to believe that economic growth would solve most social problems, they acknowledged that well over a decade of economic expansion had not eliminated poverty, even if in absolute terms the poor were better off materially than they had been in earlier eras.

Lyndon Johnson believed that the plight of the poor could be and should be ameliorated, without taking anything away from those better off. Expansive in his outlook and his sense of the still-untapped possibilities for the United States, Johnson had no interest in alienating the bulk of the electorate that was not poor or blaming the rich and powerful for the ills of the country (as Roosevelt and Truman occasionally had done). While some labor liberals and civil rights leaders stressed the need for creating new, well-paying jobs in cities like Detroit and Newark, which experienced deindustrialization long before their plight received national attention following outbreaks of violence, most antipoverty experts and Johnson administration officials instead looked for ways to enable the poor to better succeed in the existing labor market.

The social scientists, social workers, foundation officials, and government experts who established the intellectual framework for the Kennedy-Johnson antipoverty program recognized that in some cases structural impediments kept the poor poor, like racial discrimination and underdeveloped social and physical infrastructure, a problem in some rural areas, like

Appalachia, and decaying inner cities. Beyond that, it had become fashion-able to believe that the poor were trapped by a "culture of poverty." Studies by anthropologist Oscar Lewis of poor families in Mexico and other coun-tries popularized the notion that a self-reinforcing and self-reproducing complex of problems, including broken homes, poor health, low educational achievement, minimal job skills, low income, apathy, and fatalism kept gen-eration after generation in poverty. Only by breaking the cycle and attacking the whole complex of problems could conditions be created for the poor to help themselves and escape their fate.

In his 1964 State of the Union address, Johnson declared "unconditional war on poverty in America." But rather than "unconditional war," in practice he launched a much more limited effort. Johnson asked for nearly a billion dollars for the first year of his program, far more than Kennedy envisioned, but at its peak the antipoverty program spent annually the equivalent of only about $50 to $70 for each poor person in the country.

Johnson made the Community Action Program the core of the antipov-erty effort. CAP called for the creation and funding of local antipoverty agencies, with "maximum feasible participation" by residents of impover-ished areas as a first step toward having the poor solve their own problems. Other antipoverty programs included the Job Corps, a revival of sorts of the New Deal Civilian Conservation Corps, with rural camps for young people to work on conservation projects; the Neighborhood Youth Corps, its urban, nonresidential equivalent; other job training and work-study programs; loan programs for poor city residents and farmers; and VISTA, a domestic ver-sion of the Peace Corps. To coordinate the whole effort, Johnson called for a new Office of Economic Opportunity. Congress, under heavy lobbying from the administration (but with little pressure from the poor themselves), passed the program with only a few changes.

With the passage of the tax, civil rights, and antipoverty acts, Johnson had put into place the main elements of Kennedy's program of growth lib-eralism: an increase in private-sector spending power to stimulate the econ-omy and an attack on structural impediments preventing the poor from benefiting from the resulting economic expansion. But by then, Johnson had begun laying out a vision that went beyond the vistas of Kennedy's domestic program, embracing expansive state action not simply to encourage growth but to improve the quality of life. In a May 1964 speech, Johnson sounded much like John Kenneth Galbraith, Arthur Schlesinger Jr., and other liberal critics of growth alone. Speaking at the University of Michigan commence-ment, the president called for a move "upward to the Great Society . . . where men are more concerned with the quality of their goals than the quantity of their goods." Johnson wanted a commitment to urban renewal, investment in housing and transportation, measures to protect the environment, improvements in education, and an end to poverty and racial discrimination. Johnson speechwriter Richard Goodwin later said that one of his influences in writing the Great Society speech had been the SDS's Port Huron Statement, whose principal author, Tom Hayden, had adopted some of the cadences and tone that John Kennedy had used in his inaugural address, a measure of how much mainstream liberalism and movements to its left had penetrated one another by the mid-1960s.

Liberalism Triumphant

To lay the basis for achieving his ambitious goals and assuage the chronic self-doubt that shadowed his massive ego, Johnson wanted an overwhelming victory in the 1964 election. He was acutely aware that the ongoing civil rights revolution was shifting the national political terrain. By the time of the 1964 election, nearly 40 percent of southern African Americans were registered to vote as a result of efforts by the civil rights movement and more aggressive federal law enforcement, potentially a big boost for liberal Democrats. But Johnson feared that many white Democrats would desert the party because of its legislative support of black rights.

In the Democratic primaries, Alabama governor George Wallace, who had gained a national reputation as a die-hard segregationist, demonstrated the danger. In a hastily put together campaign, Wallace hammered away at what he claimed the Civil Rights Act would mean for northerners—a threat to union-negotiated seniority systems, the imposition of racial hiring quotas, the denial of the right of homeowners to sell their property to whom they pleased, "chaos" for local schools—while attacking the Supreme Court for its school prayer decision and the State Department for abandoning Eastern Europe to communism. In Wisconsin, attracting voters across the economic spectrum, he won over a third of the vote; in Indiana, 30 percent; in Maryland, nearly half.

Johnson's concern about losing white voters led to a bitter clash with southern civil rights activists at the Democratic convention, held in Atlantic City in late August. In Mississippi, where African Americans were excluded from the process of selecting Democratic convention delegates, SNCC and other civil rights groups, bolstered by Freedom Summer volunteers, founded the Mississippi Freedom Democratic Party (MFDP). After a grassroots organizing effort, which drew many poor blacks into the political process for the first time, the MFDP went to the Democratic convention demanding that its multiracial (though largely black) delegation be seated instead of the all-white "regulars."

Johnson saw the MFDP as a threat to what he hoped would be an unruffled coronation. Using FBI surveillance of civil rights leaders to plan his strategy, his forces refused to oust the regulars and rejected a compromise that both delegations be seated. Instead, they proposed that two of the sixty-four MFDP delegates be named at-large delegates, while all the regulars be seated if they pledged loyalty to the Democratic ticket. (Many southern Democrats were toying with supporting Goldwater.) In addition, the party would promise to eliminate all racial discrimination in the delegate selection process before its next convention. Many national civil rights leaders saw the proposed deal as a step forward, recommending that it be accepted, but the MFDP delegates rejected it. They and their supporters left the convention embittered. (Ironically, while most of the Mississippi regulars in the end supported Goldwater—who voted against the Civil Rights Act—the MFDP campaigned for Johnson.)

Once the campaign began in earnest, the Johnson forces succeeded in marginalizing Goldwater as outside the national mainstream. On foreign policy, they portrayed the senator, who had publicly mused about allowing NATO field commanders control over tactical nuclear weapons and repeatedly called for giving no quarter in the battle against communism, as trigger-happy and irresponsible. Just four years earlier Kennedy had made statements nearly as bellicose, but the Cold War was losing much of its ideological and emotional power. In contrast to Goldwater's tough military talk, Johnson portrayed himself as the peace candidate, even as his administration was secretly planning a major escalation of the war in Vietnam. On domestic policy, Johnson turned the campaign into a referendum on the welfare state, portraying Goldwater as a man who would undo the work of Roosevelt and his successors. Here, Johnson was on more solid ground, since Goldwater did oppose the expanded functions the state had taken on during the previous three decades, calling for selling the TVA, dismantling the Rural Electrification Administration, ending farm subsidies, and making the Social Security system voluntary. Many moderate Republicans, long accommodated to federal regulatory and welfare functions, defected to the Johnson camp.

Johnson won by a landslide with 61 percent of the popular vote, a higher percentage than FDR ever achieved. Goldwater, in addition to his home state of Arizona, carried only five states, all in the Deep South, where the Republicans also picked up seven House seats. Elsewhere the Democrats swept the board, increasing their majority in the House to 295 to 140 and in

the Senate to 68 to 32. (They also gained hundreds of seats in state legislatures.) For the first time in a generation, Republicans and southern Democrats did not have enough power to hold back the electoral majority. The
political mood of the electorate, combined with the legislative redistricting
occurring as a result of *Baker v. Carr* and the growing registration of black
voters, opened a rare window of liberal opportunity.

Johnson drove a truck through the window. In 1965 and 1966, the 89th
Congress passed a flood of bills, mostly proposed by the president, which,
combined with those passed between Kennedy's death and the 1964 election,
constituted by far the most important legislative accomplishment since
Franklin Roosevelt's first term in office. With the economy thriving and the
Cold War no longer as scary as it had been a few years earlier, a great sense
of national confidence and possibility underlay the extraordinarily ambitious program that Johnson succeeded in marshalling through Congress.

Medicare-Medicaid, which turned out to be one of the landmarks of the
Great Society, grew out of the failure of Congress in the 1940s to pass the
Wagner-Murray-Dingell bill to create a national health insurance program.
The spread of employment-based insurance provided health security for millions but left uncovered people without jobs, employees of businesses that
did not offer insurance, and retirees. Though companies sold individual insurance, many families could not afford it.

By the early 1950s, health reformers and unionists had abandoned the
idea of a universal national health system, instead seeking targeted government programs aimed at those outside the private welfare state. In 1951, a
bill proposed providing hospital insurance for the elderly through the Social
Security system, what came to be dubbed Medicare. By the end of the decade, the idea had gained considerable support. Though Kennedy backed
Medicare, opposition from Republicans, southern Democrats, and the
American Medical Association kept the bill from emerging from the House
Ways and Means Committee.

Johnson initially sought to make a federally coordinated attack on heart
disease, cancer, and stroke the centerpiece of his health program, but after
facing opposition in Congress and from the medical profession, which did
not like a proposed system of government-financed research hospitals, he
shifted his focus to Medicare. During the 1964 election, Goldwater's opposition to the proposal had proved highly unpopular, sending a warning to
other legislators, while the Democratic sweep eliminated many allies of the
AMA. No longer confident that they could block federal health insurance
entirely, AMA backers and Republicans offered several alternatives to
Medicare.

In a surprise move, Ways and Means chairman Wilbur Mills incorporated these proposals into the administration-backed bill, ending up with a three-tiered program, far broader than proponents of any of the plans had envisioned. As finally passed by large majorities, the Medicare bill included hospital insurance for all the elderly covered by Social Security, financed by an increase in the payroll tax that employers and employees already paid; a voluntary insurance program for doctors' fees for the elderly (Medicare Part B), financed by equal payments from subscribers and the federal government but run by insurance concerns; and health insurance for the indigent of any age (Medicaid), financed by federal and state contributions and run by the states. To blunt opposition from doctors, Mills made sure that the federal government would not get involved in direct service provision, would not set the rates for hospital or doctor services, and would not heavily regulate the industry. On July 30, 1965, Lyndon Johnson flew to Independence, Missouri, to ceremoniously sign the Medicare bill standing next to the eighty-one-year-old Harry Truman, handing him Medicare card number 1.

Medicare proved an enormously popular, well-administered program, helping bring many of the elderly out of poverty and improving the health care they received. In its first year, over nineteen million Social Security recipients registered for the program. Medicaid varied in impact and quality from state to state, but at least in some areas it significantly improved medical access for the nonelderly poor. Ironically, given their opposition to its passage, the medical and insurance interests ended up benefiting from Medicare-Medicaid too, as the programs bolstered the income of doctors and increased the power of the insurance industry (while pushing up the cost of medical care).

Johnson hoped to pass other social legislation before again tackling civil rights, but events in the South upended his plan. The 1964 Civil Rights Act led to a rapid collapse of formal segregation in most of the country, as hotels, restaurants, theaters, gas stations, and other public accommodations abandoned Jim Crow. But in a half-dozen states in the Deep South, especially outside the big cities, local businesses, public officials, and judges openly defied the law, maintaining racial segregation while continuing to exclude all but a few African Americans from voting.

After the 1964 election, the SCLC decided to launch a high-profile campaign to break the remaining resistance to black suffrage, centering it on Selma, Alabama, where only a few hundred of the city's fifteen thousand black residents had been able to register to vote. SCLC planned a rerun of Birmingham, a nonviolent confrontation that would bring national attention to the denial of rights in the South and lay the basis for federal action.

Martin Luther King Jr. brought his newly enhanced prestige to the effort, having just become the youngest person ever to win the Nobel Peace Prize.

As SCLC had expected, sheriff's deputies and state police met a series of demonstrations and voter registration efforts with violence, culminating in a brutal attack on marchers leaving Selma on a planned walk to the state capital in Montgomery. With national media increasingly focused on the Alabama campaign, King called for civil rights supporters from across the country to join another attempt to hold the march. Racist thugs killed one volunteer, a white minister from Boston, and a state trooper killed a black civil rights backer in a nearby town.

The violence forced Johnson's hand. As the events in Alabama unfolded, he decided to seize the moment for a final push to guarantee the right to vote. In a speech to Congress he called Selma "a turning point in man's unending search for freedom," like Lexington, Concord, and Appomattox. Presenting a Voting Rights bill, he said of blacks seeking their rights, "Their cause must be our cause too," adding—using the words of the by then universally known civil rights song—"And we shall overcome."

Much of the country joined Johnson in his embrace of the civil rights movement. Marches in support of the Selma demonstrators were held in many northern and western cities. Whites and blacks, well known and obscure, headed to Selma, including celebrities, labor leaders, and clergy. For the Catholic Church, Selma marked the high point of its participation in the southern civil rights movement, with priests from fifty dioceses, nuns, and laypeople converging on Alabama. The march to Montgomery finally took place peacefully, under the protection of the Alabama National Guard, which Johnson federalized, though immediately after it a white protestor from Detroit was murdered by Ku Klux Klan members.

In the wake of Selma, the Voting Rights Act of 1965 passed both houses of Congress by better than four-to-one margins. The law targeted states and counties where fewer than 50 percent of eligible voters were registered or fewer than half had voted in the 1964 election. In those areas, literacy tests and discriminatory poll taxes would be suspended, even in state and local elections, and federal officials could take over the voter registration process. Government bodies that had denied citizens the right to vote could not change their election systems for ten years without federal approval, to prevent the introduction of procedures designed to limit minority rights.

The Civil Rights and Voting Rights acts were the most important domestic achievements of liberalism since World War II. Together they effectively ended racial discrimination through the law and the denial of political rights on the basis of race, giving meaningful life to long-ignored provisions of the

Constitution introduced in the Fourteenth and Fifteenth Amendments. Within months after the passage of the Voting Rights Act, federal officials registered nearly eight thousand African American voters in Selma. Within a year, the number of registered blacks in five states of the Deep South doubled. By 1969, 65 percent of adult southern African Americans were registered, a massive change from a decade earlier.

The civil rights movement, at least indirectly, helped change immigration policy too. Civil rights protest created a national consensus, except in the white South, around the notion of equal individual rights and equal treatment under the law regardless of race, ethnicity, or national origin. Immigration law, as it had developed over the previous century, embodied just the opposite, treating individuals differently and unequally depending on their race and country of origin.

When Truman vetoed the 1952 McCarran-Walter Act, an omnibus effort to revise immigration law and use it as an anticommunist weapon, he did so in part because it continued the national origins quota system, introduced in the 1920s, which rested on discredited ideas of scientific racism. Congress overrode his veto, but in practice the quota system proved increasingly dysfunctional. By 1960, two-thirds of immigrants entered the country under nonquota provisions. Many came from the Western Hemisphere (mainly Mexico and Canada), which was not covered by the quota system. Others came under programs established to admit anticommunist refugees, foreign spouses and children of citizens (mainly military families), and temporary agricultural workers.

In 1964, a coalition of liberal, labor, and religious groups successfully lobbied to end the Bracero program, appalled by the poor treatment of the migrant farmworkers it brought to the United States and concerned about the depressing effect of the influx of exploited workers on national labor standards. A reform coalition, dominated by Catholics and Jews, next pushed to end the quota system. The immigration reform effort never became a mass movement or the subject of much national discussion, but the civil rights movement and the results of the 1964 election opened up the possibility for action.

The proponents of the Immigration and Naturalization Act passed in 1965 neither desired nor anticipated a significant increase in immigration or a change in where it came from. While the new law eliminated the morally odious immigration quotas for individual countries, it imposed an overall annual cap on immigration from outside the Western Hemisphere and, for the first time, capped immigration from within the hemisphere (which ultimately contributed to the growth of illegal immigration from Mexico). The expectation was at most a very modest increase in the relatively low rate of immigration by historical standards that had prevailed since the beginning of the Great Depression. A modified preference system, which favored relatives of citizens and resident aliens and people with needed occupational skills, was expected to keep the distribution of entrants by country of origin roughly what it had been. However, both supporters and opponents of the bill grossly underestimated its impact, which over the coming decades proved to be massive, as the annual number of immigrants shot up and the distribution of where they came from radically altered.

As in the case of immigration reform, lobbying by relatively small advocacy groups, along with the interest of particular legislators, led to the passage during the Johnson years of a series of environmental laws, without a major popular mobilization. The context was a changing environmental consciousness, largely a reaction against efforts to engineer, control, and transform the environment for purposes of economic productivity and war-making capacity. A rising standard of living, the growth of leisure, and the prolongation of life underlay the new attitudes (ironically, all made possible by industrial and agricultural practices deeply damaging to the environment).

Concern about pesticides exemplified the links between war, economic development, and environmentalism. Chemical warfare research during World War II fostered the postwar insecticide industry. DDT—a powerful pesticide—began being sold right after the war. The availability of surplus military aircraft, which could be converted into crop sprayers, facilitated the adoption, with strong government encouragement, of chemical-intensive agricultural methods that made liberal use of herbicides, insecticides, and artificial fertilizers. Though the high cost of inputs for growing food and commodities this way drove out many small farmers, crop yields rose, the need for farm labor fell, and a cornucopia of produce filled tables across the country and abroad.

At first the environmental impact of the heavy use of insecticides and herbicides received little attention. But fears about the effects of radiation from atomic testing on human health, raised by well-respected scientists, led to greater awareness of invisible environmental dangers. In the early 1960s, with the near-simultaneous ban on atmospheric testing of atomic weapons and the publication of Rachel Carson's *Silent Spring,* pesticides replaced radiation at the forefront of public anxiety about environmental poisons. The growing incidence of cancer—in part the result of longer life spans—heightened concern about the possible carcinogenic effects of man-made chemicals.

Carson's book had a big impact on political leaders. John Kennedy appointed a presidential panel to study the use of pesticides; Connecticut senator Abraham Ribicoff held hearings on environmental pollution; and Stewart Udall, who served as secretary of the interior under both Kennedy and Johnson, converted his department from an advocate for western resource users into a broader agency concerned with recreation and environmental pollution as well. But even as the pesticide issue raised environmental awareness, with the well-being of powerful interests and, more broadly, a whole way of life resting on a chemical regime of land use, such expressions of government concern did not easily convert into action. DDT, which deeply damaged wildlife, continued to be used throughout the 1960s.

Other types of environmental degradation, like air pollution, proved more amenable to regulation. Large-scale industry and electrical generating plants dirtied the air, particularly in the Northeast and Midwest, as did vehicle emissions, which had their greatest impact in the West. As air pollution began choking the breath and watering the eyes of middle-class voters, they began pressing for government action. City and state government took the lead, starting with St. Louis, which began a smoke abatement program in 1940. Los Angeles began regulating air emissions in 1947. California established the first controls on motor vehicle emissions in 1960. Industry generally resisted regulation, but even Gary, Indiana, a steel production center where high school football games occasionally had to be halted when the charging of a coke oven or the tapping of a furnace made the air almost unbreathable, passed an air pollution ordinance in 1962.

The federal government began addressing air pollution with the toothless 1963 Clean Air Act. Johnson opposed an effort two years later for much stronger legislation that included mandatory controls on emissions, apparently reluctant to break with the auto industry and other industrial interests pressing for strictly voluntary measures. In the end a compromise was enacted, which gave the secretary of health, education, and welfare the discretionary power to establish emission standards. Secretary John Gardner moved quickly, requiring all new motor vehicles, starting in 1968, to be equipped with emission control devices. Meanwhile, in 1967, Congress authorized the federal government to set standards for air quality for industry in states that failed to do so on their own. Water quality standards and sewage treatment funding laws added to the growing array of environmental legislation.

The spread of automobile ownership, which caused so much air pollution, contributed a growing interest in protecting wilderness areas and preserving land for recreational use. Auto tourism, along with nature photography and television nature shows, created a growing constituency for wilderness preservation. Hunters and fishermen also pressed for preserving natural habitats and keeping them open to the public. With cars making hunting areas readily accessible even to urbanites, hunting—once largely a rural and upper-class activity—developed a huge working-class following. During the 1950s and 1960s, some midwestern factories simply shut down on the opening day of hunting season, knowing that too few workers would show up for production to take place. Rapid suburbanization provided yet another impetus for preserving open land, as homeowners who had left the city to escape perceived overcrowding often found a lack of recreational areas and residential overdevelopment in their new neighborhoods. The success of conservationists, led by the Sierra Club and the Wilderness Society, in stopping the construction of the Echo Park Dam on the Colorado River, reversing decades of largely unopposed dam building, revealed the political potential of the increasingly well-organized environmental activists.

The fate of a bill to create a national wilderness preservation system reflected the changing public attitudes and resulting political calculations. The bill, first introduced in the Senate by Hubert Humphrey in 1956, faced repeated defeats in the face of opposition by the lumber, mining, oil and gas, and livestock industries and the major business associations. But in 1964 a version of the measure passed Congress with few members willing to go on record against it. The Land and Water Conservation Fund Act, the National Wild and Scenic Rivers Act, and the National Trails Act followed.

The environmental movement and legislation of the Johnson years did not represent a fundamental move away from the ideological and political consensus around a growth economy. At most, it was a gingerly step back from a Promethean view of man's relationship to nature. Even many environmentalists did not see an inherent conflict between growth and efforts to protect the environment. Like so much of the Great Society, the environmental bills Johnson signed rested on a belief that reform could be effected without harming established interests or taking away from the haves.

In 1964 and 1965, Congress also passed a series of laws deepening federal involvement with education, culture, and the arts. The Elementary and Secondary Education Act circumvented the disputes over aid to parochial schools that had blocked earlier efforts to provide substantial federal school funding by coming up with an indirect mechanism to send money to both public and private schools. Johnson conceived of the bill as an antipoverty measure, but as enacted and implemented only about half the spending went to poor children, with the rest serving as a general federal subsidy to school systems that in the past had been almost completely funded by state and local government or by private individuals. Some targeted aid for poor students came through Project Head Start, a preschool program that proved highly effective, and Upward Bound, a college preparation program for poor teenagers. The Higher Education Act funded a loan guarantee program, scholarships, work-study programs, college libraries, and academic programs. The Kennedy administration idea for a National Arts Foundation found realization with legislation setting up the National Endowment for the Arts, the most important federal engagement with culture since the New Deal. Congress added on a National Endowment for the Humanities in response to pleas from academics who were not eligible for funding from the National Science Foundation. Yet another Johnson proposal led to the creation of the Corporation for Public Broadcasting, charged with creating national public television and radio systems.

The Limits of Liberalism

Even as postwar liberalism achieved its greatest accomplishments, counter-vailing tendencies were undermining its electoral and ideological viability. The problems first became evident around issues involving labor and race.

Organized labor played a central role in the Great Society. Unions enthu-siastically endorsed Johnson in 1964 and lobbied hard for his legislative pro-gram. Labor officials even helped draft some Great Society proposals and in several instances left their posts to take positions in the Johnson administra-tion. But in a measure of the limits of Great Society liberalism, labor failed to achieve its own top legislative priority, the repeal of section 14(b) of the Taft-Hartley Act, which allowed states to outlaw the union shop.

By 1965, nineteen states had so-called right-to-work laws. That year Johnson agreed to a request from the AFL-CIO to propose the repeal of 14(b), packaging it with improvements in the minimum wage and unemploy-ment insurance. With the president leaving labor to do most of the lobbying on its own, the bill won slim majorities in both houses but fell far short of the votes needed to end a Republican Senate filibuster. While a political consen-sus had emerged for new federally guaranteed rights and new federal func-tions, no similar consensus backed an increase in the power of workers through self-organization. The point was driven home the next year when Congress raised the minimum wage and extended its coverage to over eight million additional workers. For the first time, the Fair Labor Standards Act, passed during the New Deal, covered a majority of female and minority workers. While organized labor supported the effort, it highlighted the ex-panding role of government in protecting exploited groups at a time when union membership seemed to have plateaued.

The fault lines within the coalition that made the flood of Great Society measures possible became even more evident around issues of race and civil rights. The wave of riots that broke out in northern cities in the mid-1960s made it clear that race had become an urgent national problem, not just a southern one. In the short term, the riots gave new impetus to Great Society reforms, but in the longer run they undermined the political basis for liberalism itself.

The first major racial disturbance took place in Harlem in July 1964. As was to be typical in the riots that followed, an incident involving the police set it off, in this case the killing of a black teenager by an off-duty white policeman. Protests led to rioting and looting in Harlem and parts of Brooklyn that lasted for five days.

Though the rioting had no explicit political agenda, it came against a background of frustration with poverty and racial discrimination, pervasive in black communities of the North. Nonviolent efforts to create greater job opportunities for African Americans and to integrate schools had yielded few successes. With expectations, frustrations, and a sense of assertiveness growing in northern black communities as the civil rights movement in the South reached its peak, the anarchic protest of the Harlem riot proved infectious. In the weeks following it, disturbances broke out in Rochester, several northern New Jersey cities, a suburb of Chicago, and Philadelphia.

The following summer, urban disturbances reached a scale unseen since World War II. Just five days after the passage of the Voting Rights Act, an aggressive arrest of a drunk driver in South Central Los Angeles escalated into a confrontation between a gathering crowd and the police, notorious for their racism and lack of respect toward local residents. When the police tried to calm things down by leaving the area, local teens and young men began attacking white newspapermen and passing motorists. Renewed police presence led to new clashes, which soon involved arson and gunfire from both sides. Though dubbed the Watts Riot, the disturbance encompassed an area equivalent to the size of the city of San Francisco. By one estimate, some thirty-five thousand adults participated. To suppress it, sixteen thousand National Guard troops were deployed. By the time the clashes ended after a week of chaos, thirty-four people had been killed, a thousand injured, and four thousand arrested.

The scale, ferocity, and open antiwhite hatred evident in the Los Angeles riot took whites across the nation by surprise. As in New York, long-standing anger about racial inequality, a lack of good jobs, and police conduct set the background for the conflagration. So did recent political events. In 1963, California passed a law forbidding racial discrimination in the sale or rental of private dwellings. Its enforcement would have had a radical effect on California cities, especially Los Angeles, a city of extreme and increasing segregation. To undo the law, the California Real Estate Association put forth Proposition 14, which in 1964 won approval by a two-to-one vote (though the California Supreme Court later declared it unconstitutional). To black Californians, the vote demonstrated widespread racism among whites. Nationally, it illustrated that northern whites could simultaneously support an end to formal segregation of public facilities, mostly a southern issue, and oppose desegregation of housing in their own communities.

Lyndon Johnson immediately understood that the Watts uprising would foster a white backlash against the civil rights movement and his Great Society. He tried to distance himself from the Los Angeles events, delaying the announcement of a planned national urban policy so that it would not be seen as a concession to rioters. But in the months that followed he paid greater attention to the cities. In 1964, Congress had begun funding urban mass transit projects. Now Johnson wanted a more extensive federal urban role. To coordinate the effort, Congress approved the creation of the Department of Housing and Urban Development. Johnson appointed Robert Weaver to head it, making him the first black cabinet officer in the country's history. Johnson also embraced a proposal to demonstrate, using federal funds, the efficacy of integrated urban planning and redevelopment. In a measure of how Watts had changed the political terrain, when Johnson signed the Demonstration Cities and Metropolitan Development Act he insisted on calling it the "Model Cities" act, as opponents had associated the program with demonstrations by African Americans. The complex initiative, with insufficient funds spread thinly among projects sometimes picked for political purposes, ended up having little impact on the lives of city dwellers.

Civil rights efforts suffered defeats on a number of fronts. The rejection of Johnson's proposal to grant home rule to the District of Columbia, which had a majority black population, represented a rare loss for the administration during the 89th Congress. Meanwhile, the passage of California's Proposition 14 marked the beginning of a new phase of northern white resistance to residential integration. In 1966, Martin Luther King Jr. and the SCLC joined forces with a coalition of civil rights groups in Chicago to press for school and housing desegregation, a major foray for the southern-based black movement out of its home territory. The effort failed miserably. The Chicago black community did not rally to the effort to the extent that the SCLC had anticipated. Mayor Richard J. Daley adeptly made some concessions while resisting any wholesale policy changes. When King led marches against housing discrimination through several Chicago neighborhoods, white crowds taunted, stoned, threatened, insulted, and assaulted the demonstrators in as terrifying a demonstration of racial hatred as anything seen in the South. Unlike in past southern struggles, the ugly display of white racism brought neither a national mobilization nor federal action. Daley, not King, proved to have greater influence in Washington when he succeeded in stopping Johnson administration pressure to desegregate his city's schools.

The press for residential and school desegregation fractured the institutions of the urban North. Local Democrats in various parts of the country split over so-called open housing laws. The Catholic Church found itself deeply divided. Much of its top leadership and many activist clergy and nuns embraced the civil rights struggle, while many urban parishioners and their priests fought against neighborhood change, racial integration, and social activism. When in 1965 Baltimore's Cardinal Lawrence Shehan testified in favor of a proposed municipal law banning housing discrimination by race, hundreds of people attending the hearing booed him, a startling act of disrespect for a leader of the church. A new round of urban riots in 1966 and the shifting rhetoric of black leaders, especially the adoption of the slogan "Black Power" by members of SNCC and other groups, further eroded white support for government action against discrimination. In Congress, the Republican leadership, which had collaborated with the Johnson administration on civil rights legislation in 1964 and 1965, refused to back a new civil rights proposal that included a ban on racial discrimination in the sale or rental of housing, leading to its failure.

Johnson administration policies contributed to growing urban political conflict. With southern whites leaving the Democratic Party as a result of the civil rights thrust, the national party found itself more dependent on winning the key northern states, which in turn meant carrying their major cities, where the African American population had swollen with migration from the South. But most governments in those cities still acted primarily as the representatives of longer-established white groups. To circumvent them in trying to benefit the urban black population and more solidly incorporate it into the Democratic Party, many Great Society programs did not operate through existing government entities but rather through private agencies or newly formed groups, like those running the Community Action Programs. The federal government even provided resources for aggrieved urban residents to challenge municipal and state authorities over housing, welfare, and other local issues through the creation of Legal Services, which provided legal counsel to poor people unable to afford representation.

Mayors and other local officials, many of them Democratic loyalists, jostled with community activists to win control over the antipoverty agencies and new federal programs. They complained bitterly to the Johnson administration when protestors, aided and encouraged by federally funded programs, picketed city offices, sat down in them, or sued local agencies. The administration soon began giving more control over federally funded programs to local elected officials, but by then many of the urban Democratic parties, already weakened by their failure to respond to shifting demography, lay in shambles.

Approval for key Johnson administration policies plummeted. In September 1966, a public opinion poll found 52 percent of respondents saying that the administration was "pushing racial integration too fast." That same month, only 41 percent of those polled approved of the War on Poverty, down from 60 percent the prior October. While domestic issues had the most immediate political impact, the administration also faced growing opposition to its escalation of the war in Vietnam.

Liberal Democrats got routed in the 1966 elections. The Democrats lost three Senate seats and forty-seven House seats, more than they had gained two years earlier. Once again, an alliance of Republicans and conservative (mostly southern) Democrats would have enough votes to block liberal legislation. But the liberal Democratic defeat extended far beyond Congress. Nationwide, the Democrats lost 677 seats in state legislatures and eight governorships. In Georgia, Arkansas, and Maryland, segregationists captured the Democratic gubernatorial nominations, in the latter two states then to be beaten by Republicans with more liberal stands on civil rights.

Perhaps the greatest upset took place in California, where Pat Brown, a genial, liberal political pro, was running for a third term as governor. He first won the job in 1958, defeating right-wing antilabor senator William Knowland. Four years later he kept it by defeating Richard Nixon, who was attempting a comeback after his loss to Kennedy. In 1966 he faced actor Ronald Reagan, running for public office for the first time. Reagan, a onetime New Deal Democrat who over the years had moved to the right, came to national attention as a political figure in 1964 with a speech supporting Barry Goldwater, which used populist language to counterpoise individual freedom to government action. Running for governor two years later, he benefited from a widespread white conservative response to the Berkeley protests and the Watts Riot, winning many white working-class voters away from the Democratic Party, especially in Los Angeles. He beat Brown by a million votes.

Organized labor suffered particularly harsh defeats in the 1966 election. The AFL-CIO had decided to make a major push that year in the hopes of winning enough new liberal seats to be able to get the repeal of 14(b) through the next Congress. Instead, they found their longtime political allies going down to defeat. In Michigan, G. Mennen Williams, the former governor and close ally of the UAW, lost his bid for a Senate seat. In Illinois, another labor favorite, longtime liberal senator Paul Douglas, lost to a liberal Republican, not even garnering support of a majority of UAW voters. In California, Reagan won the votes of a substantial number of union members.

Postmortems revealed how out of touch labor leaders had become with elements of their base. Many white unionists had grown increasingly opposed to civil rights efforts, especially any moves against housing discrimination. These voters tended to be scared and repelled by urban riots, with the drop-off in the blue-collar Democratic vote particularly sharp in areas near where disturbances had taken place. Many union voters, especially those under forty, had little interest in the issues their leaders concentrated on, like 14(b) repeal and improvements in the minimum wage and workmen's compensation. Instead they cared the most about taxes, crime, zoning, and stopping residential integration, which they feared, usually correctly, would drive down the value of their property, issues of particular concern to the growing number of unionists living in the suburbs.

By 1966, an intensification of politics of all kinds, right, left, and center, had taken place. Liberal legislation would continue to be passed for another decade, liberal Court decisions would continue to come out, and liberal politicians would continue to wield power. But the zenith of postwar liberalism already had been passed, as challenges from its left and right took their toll. The Vietnam War, which soon came to dominate American life, would shatter liberalism altogether.

CHAPTER 9

Apocalypse Now

T hey began reading the names shortly after 10 a.m. on November 10, 1982, in the Washington Cathedral. First came Gerald L. Aadland, from Sisseton, South Dakota. Next James Downing Aalund, of Houston. Then Daniel Lawrence Aamold, of Moorhead, Minnesota. It took more than two days to read the names of all 57,939 Americans killed or missing in the Vietnam War.

The candlelight ceremony was part of four days of events saluting the 2.7 million Americans who had served in Vietnam, held in conjunction with the dedication of the Vietnam Veterans Memorial on the Washington Mall. Thousands of veterans converged on the capital, many wearing field jackets or camouflage hats but few in full uniform, in keeping with the decidedly unofficial nature of the commemorations. The memorial, though on federal land, had been paid for by private contributions, many from the veterans themselves. A parade of vets down Constitution Avenue attracted a crowd of 150,000, a large gathering but smaller than the huge antiwar demonstrations that had been held during the 1960s. One columnist noted that the marchers, with beards and ponytails and ragtag outfits, looked much like the demonstrators of a decade and a half earlier. Even retired general William C. Westmoreland, who had commanded the military effort in Vietnam at its height, avoided the spit and polish of a dress uniform, wearing civilian clothes as he led the delegation from Alabama.

The opening of the Vietnam Veterans Memorial transformed the place of the Vietnam War in national memory and political discourse. When the last American troops left Vietnam in early 1973, silence settled in. After years of bitter debate over the war, few people seemed to have much interest in coming to a reckoning with what had occurred. An unglamorous war that ended, shockingly, in a defeat of the United States seemed best forgotten.

Soon, though, the war began reentering national consciousness, in part through films that captured its horror through the eyes of soldiers, like *The Deer Hunter* (1978) and *Apocalypse Now* (1979). The Veterans Memorial opened the floodgates of discussion, recognition, and reconciliation. It did so by narrowing the focus of hindsight around the experience of American troops. A largely unstated consensus emerged that the war had been a mistake. Avoiding discussion of just what the mistake had been allowed a superficial unity in the recognition of the sacrifices and suffering of the troops who had fought the war. In the process, many things got elided: the Vietnamese experience of the conflict; the horrors inflicted by American warriors, as opposed to those they suffered; why the country fought the war; and what it said about American history and society. Even a decade after it ended, the Vietnam War remained too divisive, too painful, and too central to the course of U.S. history to look at it full-faced.

The war in Vietnam ended the post–World War II epoch of seemingly unlimited American power and wealth. The defeat of the United States, militarily and politically, by a communist-led nationalist movement in a small, undeveloped country brought into question the solidity and future of American society. The war occurred at a moment of heightened political mobilization and social conflict over other issues, which amplified its impact. Though other wars had been bloodier, few had greater long-term effect on the trajectory of the country, on the way it looked, felt, and acted, on who had power and how they used it. Vietnam sapped the country's economic and ideological power, shattered the hegemony of liberalism, and undermined national belief in ideas and institutions ascendant since the Second World War.

The war quickened the process by which an ever-growing number of constituencies and interest groups became self-conscious, pressing for recognition and social change and challenging authority. Conflicts of all kinds became sharper and more heated. Across the country, institutions, communities, and intimate relationships fractured. Growing violence within the United States seemed to echo the violence in Vietnam. An air of approaching apocalypse settled over the country, which encouraged extremes of political and personal behavior. To many, the country seemed to be coming apart at its seams. As the war ground on toward the ultimate American defeat, the economic, cultural, and constitutional bases of postwar life seemed in dire danger.

Going to War

American leaders conceived of the Vietnam struggle as a limited war, a test of the ability of the United States to win wars very different from the all-out, industrialized, global conflicts of the first half of the twentieth century. To their surprise, it turned out to be an epic contest, one of the great military and political clashes of modern history. The war constituted one phase of the campaign led by the Vietnamese Communist Party to create a united, independent Vietnam, freed from rule by colonial powers and elites allied with them. Initiated during the 1930s and not concluded until 1975, it was the longest, most sustained revolutionary effort since the idea of revolution emerged in its modern form with the English and French revolutions. U.S. troops fought in Indochina for longer than in World War I and World War II combined.

The United States pursued the Vietnam War with extraordinary intensity. At the height of its engagement, it had over half a million troops in South Vietnam, an area less than half the size of California, the equivalent of one soldier for every forty South Vietnamese. Its concentration of armament surpassed anything seen anywhere in the past. On water, the United States used everything from aircraft carriers and recommissioned World War II battleships to small river patrol boats. In the air, it had a fleet that ranged from massive B-52 bombers and advanced jet fighters to helicopters of all kinds and specialized propeller-driven planes, including one nicknamed Puff the Magic Dragon, capable of firing twenty thousand rounds a minute through its open door. The United States dropped over Indochina three times the bomb tonnage it dropped in all theaters during World War II. In South Vietnam, it exploded the equivalent of a thousand pounds of explosives for every person. It also made extensive use of air-dropped chemicals, including napalm and defoliants that killed off forests and crops, destroying hiding places, shelter, and food (and causing long-term health problems to those exposed to them). Though no accurate count exists, upwards of two million people died during the war. U.S. combat deaths exceeded those in all past conflicts except the Civil War and the two world wars.

For the Vietnamese, the war was about specific geography. The communists and their allies fought to win independence and autonomy for a particular territory that they thought of as their nation. In a conflict that had a large component of guerrilla warfare, they often fought near their homes. Vietnamese anticommunists also conceived of the struggle in geographic terms, about the future of South Vietnam as a sovereign territory and control over specific villages, neighborhoods, and properties. For the United States, the war was largely the opposite, a conflict unconnected to a particular territorial imperative, arbitrary in its location. In and of itself, the country of Vietnam had at most modest value to the United States in the eyes of American policymakers. The United States had very few economic or other interests in Vietnam before the war, little knowledge of it, and no particular expectation that a victory would bring deep or profitable engagement. American policymakers acted primarily out of ideology and a strategic outlook that saw any shift of control or power away from the United States, no matter where it occurred, as threatening its interests and security everywhere. A specific chain of historical developments and decisions brought the United States to battle in Vietnam, but the logic and motives behind its actions had little to do with Vietnam per se, having been applied to many other places before and during the Indochinese conflict.

The United States initially involved itself in Vietnam in support of France. During the nineteenth century, the French had established colonial rule over Indochina (the modern countries of Vietnam, Laos, and Cambodia). During World War II, the Japanese captured the area. When the war ended, Vietnamese nationalists hoped to create an independent nation, while the French sought to reassert their control. The United States, though opposed in theory to colonialism, deferred to France, hoping to win its backing for postwar arrangements in Europe. American policymakers also feared that Vietnam might ally with the communist bloc if it became independent, a distinct possibility given the leading role of communists in the Viet Minh independence movement.

The 1949 communist victory in China and the Korean War heightened American concern about Vietnam, where a war had broken out between the Viet Minh and the French. American leaders feared that a Viet Minh victory would threaten adjacent colonies and countries, which supplied food and raw materials to Japan and Western Europe. U.S. officials had envisioned China as the major trading partner for a revived Japan, but with the communists in control they sought an alternative in Southeast Asia, fretting that Japan otherwise might drift into the communist camp. The American worries did not grow out of much knowledge about Southeast Asia but rather out of a general belief that a communist victory in any country would inevitably threaten others, raising the possibility of cascading defeats for anticommunist regimes. This idea, which Truman put forth in his plea for aid to Greece and Turkey, downplayed the importance of indigenous conditions, portraying revolutions as largely externally imposed (a disastrous misreading of the situation in Indochina). With these concerns in mind, in early 1950 the United States began funding the French military effort in Vietnam. By the time Truman left office, it was paying 40 percent of the bill.

Eisenhower subscribed to the basic assumptions about Indochina of his predecessor. Responding to a press conference question, he put forth the "'falling domino' principle": "You knock over the first one, and what will happen to the last one is the certainty that it will go over very quickly. So you could have a beginning of a disintegration that would have the most profound influences." Eisenhower greatly increased aid to the French, eventually covering three-quarters of the cost of their Indochinese campaign. When in 1954 the French faced defeat at the decisive battle of Dien Bien Phu, he considered direct military intervention, possibly using atomic weapons. However, Britain declined to join a united effort and France refused to pledge complete independence for its colonies, leading the United States to back off. With French public support for the war eroded, France accepted defeat.

At a conference in Geneva, France, China, and the Viet Minh, with support from the Soviet Union and Great Britain, hammered out an agreement to end the Indochina War. It called for a cease-fire and the temporary division of Vietnam along the 17th parallel, with the communists in control of the north and an anticommunist regime, installed by the French with American backing, in control of the south. Elections were to be held in 1956 to choose a government to rule over a united, independent Vietnam, with separate arrangements for setting up elected governments in Laos and Cambodia. No foreign troops or arms were to be introduced into the region.

Neither the Vietnamese communists nor the United States liked the Geneva Accords. The Vietnamese, who felt they were conceding too much, went along under pressure from their communist allies. The United States refused to sign.

The 1956 election and reunification never took place. With U.S. backing, the regime in the southern half of Vietnam, led by Ngo Dinh Diem, a one-time administrator under the French, refused to hold the vote, which most observers agreed would have been won by the head of the northern regime, the longtime nationalist and communist leader Ho Chi Minh. Instead, Diem moved to consolidate his power, defeating challenges from armed religious sects and from within his own army.

Diem lacked a broad class or social base for his regime. Instead, he relied on patronage and repression. Though Catholics made up only about 10 percent of the South Vietnamese population, Diem, a devout Catholic, gave them a disproportionately large share of government posts, alienating many non-Christians. He won the loyalty of the military by picking officers on the basis of personal connections rather than competence and allowing them to enrich themselves through corruption. The United States paid two-thirds of the cost of his government and sent hundreds of military advisers and secret operatives to Vietnam. But Diem often refused to follow American advice, spurning significant land reform and building up a large state-owned economic sector.

At the time of the Geneva Accords, the communists controlled most of the countryside in southern Vietnam—a largely agricultural region—and had a big popular following. Once Diem had firm command over his government, he launched a campaign of arrests and executions that decimated them. He was aided by a decision of the Vietnamese Communist Party to refrain from military action in the south in order to concentrate on consolidating its power in the north. In 1959, the northern-headquartered party gave in to pleas from the south to begin guerrilla warfare against Diem. The following year, the communists established the National Liberation Front (NLF) as an umbrella for anti-Diem forces seeking the reunification of the country.

When Kennedy took office, Vietnam was but one of many areas in the developing world of concern to American policymakers. Kennedy shared his predecessors' belief that a communist takeover in South Vietnam would lead to communist domination under Chinese leadership of all of Southeast Asia. Overlaid on this geographically specific fear was a conviction that American actions in every world hot spot impacted the overall position of the country in relation to all of its adversaries and allies. Kennedy did not believe the United States had to take a hard line everywhere. But after the Bay of Pigs, the widely held view that he had been outmatched by Khrushchev at the 1961 Vienna summit, and the construction of the Berlin Wall, he felt it important to make a strong stand somewhere to demonstrate American resolve.

Kennedy had briefly visited Vietnam in 1951, coming away critical of French imperialism and convinced that the United States needed to win support in emerging nations through ideas, not military might. Apparently, even as president, he realized that a war perceived in Vietnam as between nationalism and foreign control could not be won by outsiders. In the fall of 1961, he rejected the advice of most of his top military and civilian officials to send thousands of ground troops to Vietnam to support the Diem regime, whose position was beginning to deteriorate in the face of the new communist campaign. But he still hoped to block a communist victory and avoid criticism at home for failing to act. So he took a middle course, sending in ever more U.S. advisers who in theory were not directly engaged in combat, though in reality some were.

The Kennedy administration, with its technocratic caste and firm belief in its own abilities, saw Vietnam as an opportunity to try out new ways of fighting limited war, from social science theories about managing third world modernization to military counterinsurgency strategies and deployment of the Green Berets. Because it became an arena to demonstrate American resolve and capability, Vietnam took on symbolic importance far beyond any specific U.S. interests in the region. Vietnam would prove that with money, expertise, and good intentions the United States could defeat left-wing third world insurgencies while building democratic, pro-Western states.

It did not work. As more American money and men poured into Vietnam, Diem got weaker, not stronger. The Communist Party—which linked its drive for reunification with a promise of land redistribution and attacks on large landowners—won growing support in the countryside. To counter it, Diem began a program of forced population movement to "strategic hamlets," further alienating the peasantry. American guns and ammunition, given to the South Vietnamese military, ended up arming the communist forces instead, which captured them or bought them from corrupt officials. In the cities, heavy-handed repression brought escalating protests led by Buddhist monks.

Faced with a deteriorating situation, Kennedy, shortly before his death, sent out mixed signals. His approval of the coup against Diem enlarged the American role in trying to create a functioning state and nation in southern Vietnam. At the same time, he had it leaked that he intended to begin reducing the number of U.S. advisers.

Escalation

Lyndon Johnson turned what had been a limited, largely guerrilla conflict into an all-out war. Except in scale, the effort was consistent with the general thrust of American Cold War policy in the developing world. As nationalist and anticapitalist movements became more powerful, sometimes with political and material support from the Soviet Union, China, or Cuba, U.S. policymakers came to see all revolutions as unacceptable—unpredictable and uncontrollable eruptions that might threaten American interests. The United States preferred autocratic governments and brutal military dictatorships to the possibility of another socialist or communist regime in the developing world. Leading American officials, imprisoned by their anticommunism, indifferent to the daily realities in distant lands, and overconfident about their ability to ultimately shape acceptable outcomes, rarely thought much about the long-term consequences.

In Africa, as progress toward independence spread across the continent, the United States worked to counter radical movements and keep the European powers from maintaining closed economic relationships with their former colonies. Mostly it used diplomacy and foreign aid, but sometimes, as in the Congo, it resorted to military force in the form of CIA-led mercenaries. At the same time, it declined to support the anti-apartheid movement in South Africa, valuing the ruling regime as an anticommunist bastion. In the Middle East, the United States accepted the lack of democracy in allies like Saudi Arabia and Jordan, praising them for moderation in their foreign policy and portraying them as sources of regional stability.

In Latin America, the reformist impulses expressed in Kennedy's Alliance for Progress aid program were eclipsed by heavy-handed opposition to political radicalism and to regimes whose development strategies would limit imports of American products. In 1964, the CIA spent millions of dollars to keep left-wing parties from winning elections in British Guiana and Chile. In Guatemala and Brazil, the United States supported military coups that brutally suppressed their opponents, training police and military forces to fight guerrilla groups. In the Dominican Republic, when in 1965 an uprising broke out against a conservative, U.S.-backed regime, which had overthrown the elected government of left-wing president Juan Bosch, Johnson sent in twenty-three thousand American troops, having convinced himself, falsely, that communists and Castroites were leading the revolutionary movement.

Committed to counterrevolution in the name of liberalism, the Kennedy and Johnson administrations decided that the United States would make its stand in Vietnam. Presidential adviser Walt Rostow bluntly proclaimed, "It is on this spot that we have to break the liberation war—Chinese type. If we don't break it here we shall have to face it again in Thailand, Venezuela, elsewhere. Vietnam is a clear testing ground for our policy in the world."

After becoming president, Johnson privately expressed foreboding about the consequences of deeper American involvement in Vietnam, fearing that he would be blamed for an unpopular war. Nonetheless, determined to prevent a communist victory, by mid-1964 his administration began planning for an expanded military role. Johnson waited until after the 1964 election before moving. But months earlier he had won open-ended congressional approval for any military action he might want to take, remembering the criticism Truman faced for sending troops to Korea on his own authority.

The occasion for congressional action was an incident in the Gulf of Tonkin. The U.S. and South Vietnamese militaries had been conducting a clandestine program of raids against North Vietnam in an effort to undermine its support for the war in the south and to test its air and coastal defenses. In August 1964, in response to one such raid, North Vietnamese torpedo boats attacked an American destroyer sitting off its coast. For a while Navy officers believed that a second attack had occurred as well, though evidence soon mounted that they were mistaken. Johnson seized on the incident to launch air raids against North Vietnam and to seek congressional approval for possible future action. Failing to reveal doubts about the second attack and lying about the American role in the raids against the north, Johnson and his top officials won passage of a congressional resolution authorizing the president "to take all necessary steps, including the use of armed force" in response to any request for assistance from South Vietnam. No one in the House voted against the measure, and only two senators, Democrats Wayne Morse and Ernest Gruening, opposed it.

In late 1964 and early 1965, the communist forces in the south grew increasingly bold. In November 1964 and again in February 1965, they attacked American air bases, destroying planes and killing servicemen. The first raid came shortly before the presidential election, and Johnson declined to respond. But after the second attack he ordered retaliatory airstrikes against North Vietnam that soon turned into an ongoing campaign of bombing. That in turn led to the first deployment of U.S. combat troops in Vietnam (in addition to the twenty thousand advisers and support personnel already there), thirty-five hundred Marines sent to defend the Da Nang air base in March 1965. The next month the president authorized the deployment of additional troops and their use in offensive operations, not just base security (a changed role not publicly acknowledged until later). In June he ordered still more combat units to Vietnam, part of what would be a four-year escalation of troop strength, which reached 184,000 at the end of 1965, 385,000 at the end of 1966, and 486,000 at the end of 1967, peaking in 1969 at over 543,000. With the escalation, the U.S. military largely displaced the South Vietnamese army (the Army of the Republic of Viet Nam, or ARVN) as the main force fighting against the communists and their allies.

The United States already had the infrastructure for large-scale overseas combat in place. Its Pacific fleet was the largest naval force in the world. Its army and other military services had been bolstered by a huge buildup undertaken by the Kennedy administration, designed in part so that the president would have military options other than the use of nuclear weapons or airpower alone for situations like Vietnam. For manpower, the Johnson administration could depend on the system of military conscription already woven into the fabric of American life. For logistics, it had major supply bases available in Okinawa, the Philippines, and Japan as an inheritance of World War II and the Cold War. Two decades of militarism and imperial planning made the path to war in Vietnam an easy one to take.

Explaining it was harder. The Johnson administration had difficulty articulating a reason for going to full-scale war to the public and even to itself. It rang hollow to portray the war as a defense of freedom, since after the overthrow of Diem one coup after another had brought a series of military governments to power, none democratic. Johnson sometimes stressed the domino theory, arguing that the fall of South Vietnam would inevitably bring the communists to the shores of Hawaii or even the West Coast, but an aura of implausibility surrounded such claims about a war in a small country so distant from the United States. Occasionally, as in an April 1965 speech justifying the air attacks against North Vietnam, he defended the war in explicitly New Deal terms, as a prerequisite for schools, dams, electrification, economic development, and improved medical care in Southeast Asia, for programs like the TVA and the Rural Electrification Administration that had transformed the countryside in which he himself had been born. But above all, administration leaders stressed to themselves and others the need to check the influence of China, whose foreign policy intentions and role in Vietnam they completely misunderstood (wrongly believing that it effectively controlled the Vietnamese communists), and the need to maintain the credibility of the United States in carrying out its commitments. The latter argument carried ever greater weight the longer the war went on and the higher pledges to win it piled up. Assistant Secretary of Defense John Mc-Naughton captured the thinking of many policymakers in a memo he prepared for Secretary of Defense Robert S. McNamara in March 1965, describing the U.S. aims in Vietnam as "70%—To avoid a humiliating US defeat (to our reputation as a guarantor). 20%—To keep SVN [South Vietnam] (and then adjacent) territory from Chinese hands. 10%—To permit the people of SVN to enjoy a better, freer way of life."

How the United States Fought

As the United States took over the bulk of combat in Vietnam, a strategy of conventional war and victory through attrition displaced an earlier approach of sociopolitical counterinsurgency, which had not proved very effective. American military commanders believed that the war could be won by killing communist troops and their supporters faster than they could be replaced. Rather than trying to capture and hold specific territory, they concentrated on seeking out the enemy forces and engaging them in battles that allowed them to bring to bear the enormous U.S. advantage in firepower, in many cases then retreating from ground gained. The measure of success became the number of enemy soldiers killed, the "body count," rather than the movement of a line of battle, as in earlier wars. In areas that were deemed under NLF control, U.S. forces often did not even bother identifying specific targets, engaging instead in indiscriminate bombing, use of chemical agents, and aerial strafing. In contested rural areas, the United States and the South Vietnamese government, having failed to woo the population to their side through a reform program or by providing effective security, tried to destroy the NLF infrastructure through "Operation Phoenix," a program of arrests, detention without trial, and, in some cases, assassination. The United States also conducted a massive bombing campaign against North Vietnam and parts of neighboring Laos and Cambodia, which American leaders believed would stop the flow of troops and supplies to the south, demoralize the North Vietnamese leadership, and increase the morale of the anticommunist forces. In this strategy of massive force, the Army, Navy, Marines, and Air Force competed with one another to get into action all their newest and most powerful weaponry, as a fantasia of destruction rained down on Indochina.

For the most part, the American strategy failed. Operation Phoenix, ground combat, and bombing took a heavy toll on the communists and their supporters, but through local recruiting and a growing infiltration of replacements from the north, the communist forces proved able to maintain their strength. Rather than gaining control over the countryside, the main effect of the American effort was to depopulate it, as the civilian population fled to the cities to escape the bombing in the most rapid urbanization of a society in human history. (In 1964, only 20 percent of South Vietnamese lived in an urban area; by 1972, 65 percent.) Meanwhile, the communist forces continued to meet their relatively modest logistical needs through sea shipments and, in spite of constant bombing, an overland route through Laos and Cambodia, dubbed by the Americans the Ho Chi Minh Trail.

The communists could hold their own in part because they conducted war very differently from the United States. The American dependence on high technology, the thick bureaucracy of its military, and its desire to keep its soldiers in creature comforts required a huge logistical overhead. American airfields and bases, some gigantic, sprang up across South Vietnam. Troops had air-conditioned barracks, mess halls, movie theaters, bowling alleys, and post exchanges equipped like American department stores. The Army even set up forty small ice-cream-making plants. By contrast, the Vietnamese communist leadership in the south remained lean, headquartered in cave complexes (to survive bombing) or jungle camps. Some communist guerrillas operated near where they lived, while others tried to live off the local peasantry. Only late in the war did the communists begin using heavy equipment like tanks that required complex logistical support.

The bizarre juxtaposition of American consumer culture and gruesome warfare required the United States to send a flood of arms and material into Vietnam, overwhelming its infrastructure. To alleviate the jam at the poorly equipped and corruptly run South Vietnamese ports, the American military undertook a crash construction program and eventually adopted container shipping, giving a boost to a technology that would transform world trade. Keeping the war going also required huge amounts of logistics, engineering, and supply personnel. During World War II, 39 percent of the U.S. military consisted of combat troops; in Vietnam, by 1967, just 14 percent. As a result, the communists could match the United States and the ARVN in combat troops, even though their overall military force in the south was only one-quarter the size.

As the U.S. military effort escalated, its burden increasingly fell on the shoulders of working-class teenagers. Early in the war, the troops tended to be volunteers, who in many cases went off to Vietnam with great esprit. But as the number of soldiers being sent into combat soared, draftees rose to make up roughly a third of the troops, while men who had enlisted because they expected to be drafted and hoped to get better assignments by volunteering made up another third. The increase in draftees led to a drop in the average age of the American deployment in Vietnam to just nineteen, in contrast to World War II, when it was twenty-six.

Outside of the officer corps, very few of the ground troops came from the middle or upper classes. The post–World War II baby boom meant that the cohort of men coming of age during the Vietnam War far exceeded the manpower needs of the military. Between 1964 and 1973, only 40 percent of the men reaching the draft age of eighteen served in the military (in contrast to the mid-1950s, when 70 percent of draft-age men served), and only 10 percent went to Vietnam. The selective service system acted as a mechanism of class filtration. Until 1968, being in college or graduate school provided an exemption from the draft, which disproportionately benefited the middle and upper classes. Medical exemptions favored them too, in spite of the general correlation between wealth and health. Lower-class teenagers rarely had the wherewithal to get letters from doctors about infirmities—often rather minor—that led to medical exemptions. Occupational exemptions—which during World War II covered many blue-collar jobs—were largely restricted to positions filled by middle-class whites, like teaching, social work, and scientific occupations. Finally, joining the National Guard served as a protection policy for those who could get in, since only a small number of Guard or Reserve units were sent to Vietnam. Getting into the Guard or Reserve often required connections through family or college or politics, which in part explains why African Americans made up just 1 percent of the Guard. The cumulative effect of the system was to produce a military force far more working-class and less white than the population as a whole. Throughout American history, farmers, workers, and the poor bore a disproportionate load of the fighting in the nation's wars, but the exceptional experience of World War II, when men of all classes and a broad age range served in the military, resonated in popular culture as a sharp contrast to the unrepresentative nature of the military in Vietnam.

Political leaders worried about sustaining popular support for the war. Both Kennedy and Johnson fretted that if they did not stop the spread of communism in Indochina, they would be subjected to Republican and conservative attacks, much as the Democrats had been in the late 1940s and early 1950s over the communist triumph in China. In a May 1964 telephone conversation with Senator Richard Russell, Johnson mused that "they'd impeach a president . . . that would run out, wouldn't they?" (Russell disagreed.) But Kennedy's and Johnson's actions reflected another, perhaps greater concern, that if the public had a clear understanding of the situation in Indochina, it would reject either the war or domestic reform during it. In the same conversation with Russell about the war, Johnson freely admitted, "I don't think the American people are for it." While occasionally calling for national dedication to shared sacrifice, Kennedy and Johnson avoided imposing any burden on the public, except the young men they sent off to fight. By waging the war with as little disruption of domestic life as possible, they hoped to maintain public support and keep the war from overwhelming their presidencies, a template that future presidents would use for their military actions.

The most obvious effort to downplay the war was Johnson's decision not to seek a declaration of war, avoiding an extended discussion of the implications of sending the military to Indochina. The Tonkin Gulf resolution, which at the time seemed like authorization for an immediate response to a specific incident, became the basis for years of large-scale combat. Both Congress and the Supreme Court proved complicit in Johnson's maneuver, spurning challenges to the legality of the military effort. The decision not to deploy Reserve units in Vietnam was another attempt to avoid debate and opposition. Johnson also sought to avoid a public acknowledgment of the economic cost of the war, which might have led to cutbacks in Great Society spending and diminished public backing for the fighting. Johnson had the

Defense Department present misleading information on Vietnam's cost, and until 1967, when he unsuccessfully asked Congress for an income tax surcharge, he ignored advice from his economic advisers that without a tax increase the war would lead to inflation.

Lying about the war, or at least giving the public misleading information, became routine. Johnson repeatedly hid or gave deceptive accounts of planned increases in troop strength. To justify the American intervention by portraying the Vietnamese conflict as an attack by North Vietnam against South Vietnam rather than as a civil war, his administration went as far as having the CIA create elaborate fake evidence of large-scale shipments of arms from the north to the south. Meanwhile, in Vietnam itself, military officials gave reporters misleading information, withholding anything that might bring into question official optimism.

The government generated false optimism not only for popular consumption but internally as well. The nonterritoriality of the war made it difficult to judge who was winning and who was losing. Under McNamara, the Department of Defense adopted advanced managerial techniques, developed in academia and industry, to administer the war, using masses of data and quantitative analysis to measure success. Rather than leading to clarity, war by numbers often led to self-deception, as each level of officialdom falsely reported information they believed their superiors wanted. South Vietnamese officers told of patrols and firefights with guerrilla units that never took place. American commanders inflated the body counts after engagements, sometimes including civilian casualties. They also exaggerated the number of their soldiers in combat roles, while undercounting the number of communist combatants. The systematic dissemination of false information had many costs: it bred cynicism throughout the military, undercut esprit for actual warfare, led to decisions based on inaccurate perceptions of reality, and created false optimism that set the stage for later disillusionment.

The Antiwar Movement

Until the spring of 1965, the war in Vietnam did not provoke widespread debate within the United States. The 1963 Diem regime attacks on Buddhist protestors did spark criticism of U.S. policy from liberal journals, pacifists, foreign policy experts, and civil rights leaders. But the overthrow of Diem and Johnson's campaign pledge the following year that "we are not about to send American boys nine or ten thousand miles away from home to do what Asian boys ought to be doing for themselves" defused the issue.

The bombing campaign against North Vietnam and the introduction of

American combat troops ended the silence. The first to mobilize were liberal college faculty, many of whom had supported Johnson in the recent election. At the University of Michigan, a group of professors sponsored a "teach-in" on the war. (The term, with its echo of "sit-in," reflected the pervasive influence that the civil rights movement had had on politics.) Three thousand students showed up at the combination information session, debate, and protest. Soon teach-ins were being held at scores of colleges, sometimes with representatives of the Johnson administration present to defend its policies.

As the military campaign escalated, so did protests against it. Antiwar activists gathered signatures on petitions, took out newspaper ads, and put referenda on local ballots. Large-scale demonstrations, held mostly in Washington, New York, and San Francisco, became semiannual affairs. The first major antiwar demonstration, held in April 1965, drew twenty thousand people to Washington, a small gathering compared to some civil rights demonstrations of the recent past but the largest antiwar protest in the country's history. Two years later, a protest march in New York attracted ten times the number of protestors, while a simultaneous gathering in San Francisco brought out over fifty thousand more.

Opponents of the war soon began engaging in civil disobedience. In October 1965, thousands of protestors tried to block access to the Army Terminal in Oakland, California. A small but growing number of draft-eligible men publicly declared that they would refuse to serve in the armed services, in some cases burning the cards that all draft-age men had to carry.

The antiwar movement had no central organization, nor a shared political line. Some groups called for negotiations with the communist forces, while others insisted on an immediate bombing halt or a complete U.S. withdrawal. A few openly supported the NLF. College students played a large role in the movement, but professionals, unionists, women, and the religiously devout formed antiwar groups too. When in 1966 Robert McNamara went to Harvard to participate in meetings with students and faculty, he found himself trapped by antiwar students who blocked his car, forcing him to answer questions posed by a leader of SDS. A year later, his son, a prep school student, became so distressed by his father's role in the pursuit of the war that he hung an NLF flag on his bedroom wall.

Though highly visible, the antiwar movement constituted an activist minority. In the early years of the military buildup, most of the public did not oppose the war, and most who did took no part in protest activity. Antiwar protests did little to change the course of government policy; troop levels, draft calls, and combat deaths continued to move upward. What the protests did do was accelerate a social and cultural transformation of the country.

The war in Vietnam turned what had been a small New Left into something approaching a mass movement, at least on campuses. The war seemed to confirm many of the criticisms dissident students and intellectuals had been making about American life, giving abstract analyses a bloody reality. For idealist critics, images of death and destruction in Vietnam wrenchingly belied their idea of what their country was, or at least what they thought it should be. From there, it was a short step to question leaders and structures of authority, not only in the government but throughout society. SDS, which emerged as the largest (but far from only) campus left-wing group, went from twenty-five thousand members in October 1966 to an estimated eighty thousand to one hundred thousand members in the winter of 1968–69, with chapters on some 350 campuses.

The effort of the government to disguise the extent of its Vietnam engagement and its unfounded optimistic claims fueled questioning of authority. During the Kennedy administration, some reporters in Vietnam, struck by the disparity between official briefings and what they saw in the field, began challenging the veracity of the government's portrayal of the war, providing a more skeptical, darker account. After *New York Times* reporter David Halberstam wrote in August 1963 that in spite of nearly two years of American military buildup, "South Vietnam's military situation in the vital Mekong Delta has deteriorated in the past year," an angry president demanded analyses of his work from the Pentagon and the CIA, while the secretary of state publicly criticized his story, seeing the problem in the messenger, not in the reality he accurately conveyed. Johnson's later repeated failure to give an honest account of how many troops had been sent to Vietnam and how many he planned to send added to what became dubbed a "credibility gap" that slowly eroded public confidence in the war. By the spring of 1966, just half the public supported a continuation of U.S. policy in Vietnam, while 35 percent wanted an immediate withdrawal, up 15 percent over the previous year.

The sapping of respect for authority became generalized, in part because so many institutions and leaders of American life played a role in sustaining the war. Campus critics of the conflict discovered that they did not have to go far to find targets to attack. Faculty scientists, engineers, and social scientists did research for the military. Foreign policy experts assisted the government, sometimes clandestinely. Career offices hosted recruiters from the military, the CIA, and defense contractors, including Dow Chemical Company, which made napalm. ROTC programs trained students for military leadership. All these became objects of student protests, which challenged not only Vietnam policy but also the rules, claims, and character of the academy.

Revelations of secret government funding of student, political, and cultural groups further undercut the credibility of official authority. In 1967, *Ramparts,* a left-wing magazine, revealed that the CIA, which by law was not supposed to engage in domestic operations, had secretly funded the National Student Association, the main umbrella group for college student governments, using its international programs to promote American foreign policy and launder money. It soon came out that the CIA had clandestinely funded political and cultural journals, publishers, and academic research as well.

The revelations did not stop the president from mobilizing the CIA against the antiwar movement. Local police forces and the FBI already had extensive programs targeting antiwar and left-wing groups (and some white supremacist groups too), which often went beyond surveillance to disruption, harassment, and entrapment. In 1967, Johnson, frustrated by growing antiwar protests and convinced that communists were behind them, ordered the CIA to undertake a program of domestic spying against war critics. The agency's "Operation Chaos" mushroomed into a massive effort that collected information on hundreds of thousands of citizens.

Cultural changes added to a sense of national division. During the second half of the 1960s, a "counterculture" blossomed, at first among the young but eventually infiltrating adult culture as well. More a catchphrase than a coherent outlook, the counterculture encompassed an assortment of behaviors, professed values, artistic developments, aesthetic inclinations, and product choices that departed, or at least seemed to depart, from dominant social standards. Youth began dressing differently than adults, listening to different music, using different mind-altering substances, and spurning the common adult association of maturity with early marriage, career, and family. With extraordinary rapidity, a new cultural landscape of drugs, sexual experimentation, "underground" newspapers, rock and roll, niche FM radio stations, brightly colored clothing, and long-haired men blanketed the country, starting in long-established bohemian centers, spreading to college campuses and big cities, and then reaching suburbs and small towns. By the late 1960s, young America looked and felt very different from just a few years before.

The counterculture was both of and opposed to the dominant national culture. Raised on a steady diet of the professed ideals of American society, many young people sought some higher meaning to life than daily necessity, and more fun too. The civil rights movement and the war in Vietnam fertilized an antiauthoritarian inclination already present in aspects of the Beat and teenage cultures of the 1950s. Meanwhile, prosperity diminished young people's anxieties about their future, allowing many of them to spend a prolonged period of limbo between childhood and adulthood, with few responsibilities, free to experiment. Affluence and birth control made many traditional pieties, like self-denial, deferred gratification, and sexuality only within marriage, seem irrelevant.

Yet the counterculture shared much with what it purportedly rejected. The search for individual fulfillment, central to the counterculture, had deep roots in American culture. So did the fixing of cultural and spiritual meanings to products and fashions. Seen from a distance, much of the counterculture looked simply like a series of aesthetic and cultural choices, long hair instead of short hair, the Rolling Stones instead of Frank Sinatra, John Coltrane instead of Louis Armstrong, marijuana and psychedelics instead of alcohol and tranquilizers. Yet these distinctions became freighted with great political and personal significance because they became associated with divisions over other issues that were increasingly polarizing the country, including the war in Vietnam. Long hair was not simply long hair for a young man in 1967, but rather a statement of rejection of the dominant culture, a refusal to accept its notions of comportment and masculinity, and, at least implicitly, a rejection of the policies and priorities of the nation-state. Or at least it was taken as all that by the millions of adults (and many young people too) who were appalled at such behavior and sometimes moved to take a whack at the offending head of hair.

Law and Order

Other developments, besides the war and the counterculture, contributed to a deepening sense of national division and disarray during Johnson's second term. Particularly wrenching were issues of rights, law, and personal security. During the sixteen years Earl Warren served as chief justice of the United States (1953 to 1969), the Supreme Court reinterpreted federal law and the Constitution to a greater extent than during any equivalent period in the past. Forty-five times the Warren Court overturned previous Supreme Court rulings. Until then, in its entire previous history, the Court had overturned its own decisions only eighty-eight times. Between 1963 and 1969 alone, the Court overruled thirty-three prior decisions, undermining a sense of fixity in the law and adding to the disorienting, liberating, and divisive sense of social transformation sweeping the country.

Some Warren Court decisions, though major breaks with past rulings, generated little controversy because they in effect were catching up with social or political values that already had changed, at least in most of the country. Between 1964 and 1967, the Court largely eliminated the system of anticommunist political control erected during the Cold War, such as loyalty oath requirements, laws allowing the firing of public employees for belonging to the Communist Party, and the denial of passports to communists. These decisions provoked little discussion, a measure of how much the political atmosphere of the country had changed since even the early 1960s and how utterly marginal the Old Left had become.

Other rulings imposed national norms and values on the South, which had retained exceptional ideas and legal practices. In 1964 the Court struck down a Florida law that made interracial cohabitation illegal. Three years later, in the delightfully titled case of *Loving v. Virginia,* it went further to declare all antimiscegenation laws unconstitutional, ending the last major area of legally mandated segregation. By then, laws imposing racial criteria for marriage had been eliminated by state courts or legislation everywhere except in the South. *Gideon v. Wainwright,* the celebrated 1963 decision that required states and localities to provide lawyers to criminal defendants who could not afford one, forced a change in criminal procedure only in a few states, all in the South. Everywhere else, this already was the practice. The Warren Court's most important ruling about freedom of the press, *New York Times v. Sullivan,* which made it much more difficult to win libel suits against publications, also had a regional dimension, since it arose out of the southern effort to block the civil rights movement.

Less commonly, the Court forced other parts of the country into alignment with national norms. In jurisprudence related to sexuality, the Warren Court had the greatest effect on heavily Catholic states that had practices at variance with most of the country. Some states thought of as liberal in other matters, like Massachusetts and Rhode Island, had unusually strict censorship of books, magazines, and movies that the state deemed pornographic or contrary to government-imposed standards of decency. Such controls were all but dismantled by a series of Court rulings that kept narrowing the definition of obscenity, until almost any writing or imagery involving consenting adults came to be seen as protected by the First Amendment.

Contraception was another area in which the Court nationalized legal practices. In 1965, in *Griswold v. Connecticut,* the Court ruled unconstitutional an 1879 Connecticut law that criminalized the use of contraceptives and providing advice about them. *Griswold* rested on an expansion of a line of reasoning the Court had occasionally used earlier, which contended that citizens had certain federally protected rights even if they were not explicitly laid out in the Constitution, such as the right to marry, have children, teach them a foreign language or send them to private school, or, in this case, to a "zone of privacy" within the marital relationship. *Griswold* represented one of the most blatant examples of the Warren Court inventing new rights to meet its sensibility. Later, the decision would become highly controversial as an important step toward the Supreme Court's decision protecting the right to abortion in *Roe v. Wade*. At the time, however, *Griswold* provoked little dissent. Though a few other northeastern states had similar laws to Connecticut's, which had kept birth control clinics out of the state, polls showed a strong national consensus in support of allowing the dispensation of birth control advice to married couples.

The Warren Court decisions that provoked the most controversy were the ones that forced changes not just in one deviant region but nationally, most notably in dealing with crime. In 1962 the Court said that a federal rule that prohibited illegally seized evidence from being introduced in a trial applied to state courts as well. This all but eliminated the routine practice by police departments in half of the states of making raids and arrests without a warrant and then using the illegally seized evidence in court. The Court's exclusionary rule made meaningful the constitutional protection from unreasonable search and seizure, but it also meant that some criminals would be freed because of police misconduct. A decision two years later that voluntary confessions could not be admitted in court if a defendant had requested a lawyer but none was present during questioning again meant that some guilty parties would be freed, provoking sharp criticism from conservatives and police officials. Even more fire was directed at the Court for its 1966 *Miranda v. Arizona* decision, which required police to inform arrestees of their right to remain silent, that anything they said might be used against them, and that they had a right to have an attorney present during questioning. The Court completed the revolution in criminal procedure two years later when it applied the due process clause of the Fourteenth Amendment to say that various protections in the Bill of Rights, including protection from self-incrimination, the right to a speedy trial and a trial by jury, the right to confront witnesses, and protection from double jeopardy, applied to state as well as federal courts.

Taken together, the Warren Court decisions brought a remarkable expansion of individual rights. Largely, the Court moved in accord with shifting public sentiment. But when it did not, notably in regard to criminal procedure, it came under fierce criticism for making up new law and imposing the values of unelected justices on the nation.

Rising fear of crime and disorder heated criticism of the Court. The crime rate rose substantially during the 1960s, both crimes of violence and those against property. There had been periods in the past when crime rates had been higher. The murder rate, for instance, had been over 50 percent higher in 1933 than in 1967. But with crime increasing throughout the Johnson years, more and more people felt personally insecure.

Criminologists attributed much of the crime increase to demography. Many types of crime were disproportionately committed by the young, from rape to auto theft. As the bulging generation born right after World War II reached its teens and twenties, crime rates rose significantly simply as a result of the changing age composition of the population. Crime experts argued that ongoing urbanization also contributed to the rise in crime, since historically rural areas and small towns had lower crime rates than more densely settled regions.

During the 1964 presidential campaign, both Goldwater and Wallace had raised the crime issue, with little impact. But in succeeding years, crime became an increasingly effective issue for conservatives. The conservative discourse on law and order lumped together common crime, civil disobedience, urban riots, and the proliferating use of illegal drugs as all manifestations of a breakdown of authority and respect for the law under the liberal aegis. Liberals, conservative politicians charged, were indifferent to issues of personal safety and were undermining the ability of the police to do their job. They lambasted the Supreme Court for its decisions expanding the rights of criminal defendants, which they portrayed as contributing to the growth of crime and demonstrating callous disregard for the plight of the average man and woman who faced a growing likelihood of becoming a victim.

A 1966 referendum in New York City demonstrated the power of the law-and-order issue. New York's liberal Republican mayor, John Lindsay, had added civilians to an advisory police review board in response to repeated charges of police misconduct against people of color. Though a bipartisan coalition backed Lindsay's board, a referendum measure keeping civilians off it passed by nearly two to one. In a city renowned for its liberalism, the weak support, except in nonwhite neighborhoods, for civilian review of police exposed the rapidly shifting political ground.

Riots contributed to the transmutation. New rounds of urban disorder "brought shock, fear and bewilderment to the nation," as a federal commission later wrote, and added to a yearning in many quarters for a reassertion of law and authority. The year 1967 brought even worse disorders than in past summers. Labor conflicts had once been the main occasion for mobilizing the National Guard to assert the authority of the state against civilian groups; now racial disturbances took their place. In June, the Guard was mobilized to deal with riots in Tampa and Cincinnati, as it had been in Chicago a year earlier. In July, in Newark, New Jersey, a report that the police were beating an arrested taxicab driver set off a massive riot that left twenty-three dead and sparked disturbances in a constellation of other northern New Jersey cities. Less than two weeks later, a police raid on an after-hours club in Detroit led to an even bloodier conflagration that left forty-three dead, seventy-two hundred arrested, and ended only after twenty-seven hundred regular Army troops joined five thousand National Guardsmen on the streets of the city.

Most of the urban riots of the mid-1960s, as the federal commission put it, were "not *inter*racial" but rather "involved action within Negro neighborhoods against symbols of white American society—authority and property—rather than against white persons." The vast majority of riot casualties were African Americans. Some were shot while looting, attacking the police, or running away, but many died from indiscriminate fire by police and National Guardsmen. The New Jersey National Guard, with only 303 African Americans among its 17,529 members, like its equivalents in other states, proved utterly unsuited for patrolling inner-city streets, turning them into something like a free-fire zone. In Newark, victims of law enforcement violence included two children and a seventy-three-year-old. In Detroit, Guardsmen firing a tank-mounted machine gun killed a four-year-old girl and a white businesswoman who had the misfortune of opening her motel window at the wrong moment.

In response to the Newark and Detroit events, Johnson appointed the National Advisory Commission on Civil Disorders, headed by Illinois governor Otto Kerner. The Kerner Commission produced an impressive, thoroughly liberal report on the riots, which became a national best seller. It portrayed the nation's long history of racial discrimination and the harsh conditions in urban black America as the underlying causes of urban disorder. A commission survey of areas hit by riots found the leading grievances to be police practices, unemployment and underemployment, and inadequate housing. Deindustrialization had reduced the number of good jobs for the growing urban black population. Whites leaving cities for racially segregated suburbs left behind shrinking tax bases and deteriorating schools and services, even as they hung on to a disproportionate number of public-sector jobs and positions of power. National policies that directed resources to suburbs at the expense of cities contributed to creating the urban crisis and the riots that brought it to national attention.

The Kerner Commission recommended a national commitment, largely along the lines already established by Johnson's Great Society, to fight racial discrimination, create jobs, renew urban areas, and build more public housing outside of ghetto areas. With atypical honesty for an official document, it concluded its report by quoting one of its witnesses, the psychologist Kenneth B. Clark, who had helped prepare the plaintiff's case in *Brown v. Board of Education:* "I read the report of the 1919 riot in Chicago, and it is as if I were reading the report of the investigating committee on the Harlem riot of '35, the report of the investigating committee on the Harlem riot of '43, and the report of the McCone Commission on the Watts riot. . . . It is a kind of Alice in Wonderland—with the same moving picture re-shown over and over again, the same analysis, the same recommendations, and the same inaction."

For Clark, a longtime integrationist, the riots deepened his skepticism about the kind of liberalism embodied in the Kerner Commission report for its lack of meaningful follow-through. Many white Americans questioned the liberalism of the civil rights movement, the Johnson administration, and the Supreme Court for a different reason, because they believed it contributed to the disorders by showing undue deference to lawbreakers and undermining respect for the police and authority. Johnson largely rejected the Kerner Commission recommendations because he saw no political basis for enacting them and, with the ever-mounting costs of the war in Vietnam, no way of funding them. Instead, he pressed Congress to take up again a crime bill he had introduced in 1967, which it ended up passing with provisions authorizing government wiretapping that Johnson himself had not wanted.

Tet

The year 1967 proved to be a bloody one in Vietnam for the United States: 9,353 American soldiers died. That more than doubled the total American death toll since the beginning of the war. Though everything pointed to a stalemate, Johnson remained committed to seeking military victory, continuing the bombing of North Vietnam and letting U.S. forces carry the main burden of the fighting in the south. Public opinion polls showed widespread public disapproval of his handling of the war (though his critics differed over whether to de-escalate the military effort or intensify it). Dogged by protests wherever he went, the president became reluctant to leave the White House.

In late 1967, U.S. military and intelligence agencies received information that a communist offensive was in the works, but they took only limited action in response. Psychologically and politically committed to the idea—repeatedly stated by General Westmoreland and other administration leaders—that the United States was making significant progress in defeating the communists, American officials could not believe that the enemy was capable of mounting a countrywide offensive. Instead, they assumed that their main challenge would be a nasty battle at the U.S. Marine base at Khe Sanh, which was coming under communist siege. Westmoreland became convinced that the communists were trying to replicate their victory over the French at Dien Bien Phu by luring the United States into a prolonged battle on unfavorable terrain.

Khe Sanh, though one of the bloodiest battles of the war, proved to be a diversion. On January 31, 1968, during the Tet Lunar New Year holiday, communist guerrillas, supplemented in some places by regular North Vietnamese army units, launched a massive offensive that included attacks on thirty-six provincial capitals and five of the six largest South Vietnamese cities. In Saigon, NLF forces attacked a series of high-profile targets, including Tan Son Nhut Air Base, the presidential palace, and the U.S. embassy, and occupied a district of the city for several weeks. The communists held Hue, the former imperial capital, for over two weeks, before falling to an American-led counterattack.

The Tet offensive shocked the American public and American leaders. The ability of the communists to launch such a widespread attack, including in the very heart of Saigon, demonstrated that U.S. officials had either lied to the public about the course of the war or, even worse, had been themselves seriously deluded. The Saigon-based press corps, which often could not get to remote battles before they ended, now saw and reported on combat literally down the street from their hotels and offices. Their reportage came just at the moment when the television networks were beginning to use satellite transmission on a regular basis to get pictures from Asia to the United States on the same day they were taken and when broadsheet newspapers were beginning to make greater use of photography. As a result, the public saw the ferocity and brutality of the war with an intimacy and immediacy without precedent.

Within a few weeks, the U.S. and South Vietnamese military regained all the territory the communist forces had captured, inflicting crippling casualties upon them. By the time the offensive ended, the NLF's urban political and military infrastructure, clandestinely built up over years, had been all but destroyed, as had much of its local guerrilla fighting force. After Tet, the communists increasingly had to rely on political and military forces from North Vietnam for the struggle in the south.

Nonetheless, though they paid an extraordinarily high price to do so, the communists partially achieved their political objectives. The popular urban uprisings they hoped would occur never materialized. But the Tet offensive, which over the course of four weeks killed four thousand American and South Vietnamese soldiers, forced a fundamental U.S. reassessment of the war.

Even before Tet, some top policymakers were acknowledging, at least to themselves, that the United States had no realistic prospect for military victory. In November 1967, McNamara broke with Johnson by privately calling for a halt to the bombing of North Vietnam as a step toward a negotiated disengagement. In response, Johnson eased him out of office. When in the wake of Tet General Earle C. Wheeler, chairman of the Joint Chiefs of Staff, asked the president to send 206,000 more soldiers to Vietnam and call up the Reserves, he demurred. Instead, he asked his new defense secretary, veteran Democratic insider Clark Clifford, to undertake an assessment of the war. Economic and political developments, along with the military situation, were leading to a realization in ruling circles that the United States could not keep doing more of the same in Vietnam.

In March 1968, just weeks after the Tet fighting died down, the Johnson administration faced one of the most serious international economic crises since the end of World War II. It stemmed from the country's post–World War II military and economic expansionism and, more immediately, the cost of the Vietnam War. From 1950 on, the United States had a balance of payments deficit; more dollars left the country than came in. The problem lay not in trade—the United States exported more than it imported—but from overseas military deployments, foreign aid, spending abroad by American tourists, and overseas investments. These were the costs of dominating and defending the world capitalist bloc. The growing pool of overseas dollars helped maintain liquidity for trade (as the dollar became a medium of international exchange) but worried American policymakers, since the postwar Bretton Woods agreement called for the convertibility of gold and dollars at a fixed price. Foreign holders of dollars could, whenever they wanted, ask the U.S. government to redeem them in gold. Kennedy and Johnson took a series of modest steps that reduced the balance of payments gap and, along with a strong economy, lessened fears of a run on gold reserves. But the Vietnam War made the chronic problem acute.

Compared to other twentieth-century wars, Vietnam was cheap. During World War II, the country devoted nearly a third of its GNP to the military; during Korea, a tenth; during Vietnam, less than a twelfth. But unlike World War II and Korea, which occurred during periods of economic depression or at least idle capacity, Vietnam came during a period of economic expansion and near full production. Rather than bringing prosperity, as previous wars had, Vietnam threatened it, by placing excessive demands on industrial capacity and the labor market. By early 1968, inflation reached 4.4 percent, low by later standards but high compared to previous years. Furthermore, while Congress hiked taxes early in World War II and Korea to help finance the fighting, Johnson resisted asking for a Vietnam tax increase. As a result, the federal deficit ballooned, creating further inflationary pressure while making it increasingly difficult to sustain the elevated levels of domestic spending that came with the Great Society. In early 1967, Johnson finally asked for an income tax surcharge to fund the war, but Wilbur Mills, head of the House Ways and Means Committee, refused to go along unless the president agreed to a simultaneous deep cut in domestic spending. Johnson balked, hoping to avoid gutting his social programs. The stalemate continued until mid-1968, when the president reluctantly agreed to reduce domestic spending by $6 billion in return for a 10 percent income tax surcharge.

With overseas spending for Vietnam adding to the balance of payments problem, inflation diminishing the purchasing power of the dollar, and federal deficits growing, international confidence in U.S. currency frayed. A devaluation of the British pound in November 1967 set off a rush to buy gold, destabilizing the market. In early March, a new gold run began, this time from overseas holders of dollars seeking to unload them. As the United States and the European central banks struggled to meet the gold demand without changing its dollar price (which would have meant a de facto devaluation of the dollar), an emergency international economic conference convened, which managed to make patchwork changes in the Bretton Woods system that preserved it for a few more years. But the near default on the American obligation to buy gold at a fixed price demonstrated to political and business leaders the strains Vietnam had placed on the economy and how it was undermining, rather than strengthening, the country's international position.

The North Korean capture of a U.S. ship likewise made painfully clear how far Vietnam had drained national resources. The Koreans seized the USS *Pueblo,* a lightly armed spy ship, off their coast in January 1968, with one crew member dying in the incident. Johnson felt constrained from taking military measures against North Korea with so many resources tied up in Vietnam and the use of force there increasingly unpopular. A second armed engagement would have deeply tested the country's military capacity and had severe economic as well as political ramifications. So the United States found itself sitting by for eleven months until North Korea finally released the eighty-two surviving crew members in exchange for an American admission of guilt and an apology.

Political developments added to the military and economic pressure to change course in Vietnam. By 1967, liberal disillusionment with the war had begun to penetrate into the Democratic Party. That fall, a "Dump Johnson" movement searched for a candidate to challenge the president within his own party. After being turned down by several critics of the war, including Robert F. Kennedy, who had left the Johnson administration to win a Senate seat from New York, Minnesota senator Eugene McCarthy agreed to be the standard-bearer. McCarthy ran as a critic of the war and an alternative to radicalism, hoping to alleviate what he called the "discontent and frustration and a disposition to take extralegal if not illegal actions to manifest protest." For many of his supporters, largely white and middle-class, his candidacy promised an opportunity to overcome deepening social divisions and restore legitimacy to the political system. Thus the rash of publicity about young people who decided to "Get Clean for Gene"—shave off mustaches, cut hair, or change clothes to campaign for McCarthy in the New Hampshire primary, the first of the presidential contests. Many college students did work for him, though few were hard-core New Leftists or counter-culturalists, most of whom had already written off the election process. But the myth that such young people were reentering politics, promoted by McCarthy's advertising, provided comfort to Americans distressed by the generation gap and the growing militancy of the disaffected.

Tet changed the McCarthy campaign from a symbolic effort, as it had been conceived of, into a serious challenge at the polls. In the March 12 New Hampshire primary, McCarthy shocked the country and the Democratic Party by nearly matching Johnson's vote total while winning the bulk of the state's convention delegates. Four days later, Robert Kennedy, having seen Johnson's vulnerability, reversed himself, announcing his candidacy for the presidency. Johnson's worst political nightmare, a tough race that he might well lose against a man he loathed, now lay on the horizon. Even without Kennedy on the ballot, a White House poll found only a slim chance that the president would win the majority of votes in the April 2 Wisconsin primary.

In elite quarters, too, Johnson found his war policies being rejected. In March, Clark Clifford reported, "I make it a practice to keep in touch with friends in business and the law across the land. . . . Until a few months ago, they were generally supportive of the war. . . . Now all that has changed. . . . These men now feel we are in a hopeless bog. The idea of going deeper into the bog strikes them as mad. . . . It would be very difficult—I believe it would be impossible—for the President to maintain public support for the war without the support of these men." Johnson was shaken when the nation's leading television newsman, Walter Cronkite, who normally kept his political views to himself, declared the Vietnam War to be a stalemate, with "the only rational way out . . . to negotiate, not as victors, but as an honorable people who lived up to their pledge to defend democracy, and did the best they could."

With many top government leaders, including Johnson, increasingly convinced of the need for a policy change, the administration convened a late March meeting of the Senior Advisory Group of the State Department, the so-called Wise Men, a collection of key Cold War policymakers, chaired by Dean Acheson. They received frank briefings, some quite pessimistic. While in the fall the Wise Men had backed LBJ's course in Vietnam, now they concluded that U.S. victory was impossible without total war and that the administration's policy had lost the support of the American people. The weight of opinion had shifted in the nation's most powerful circles to conclude that victory in Vietnam was not worth the price that would have to be paid to achieve it. The next morning the president told his top military advisers, "Our fiscal situation is abominable. . . . There has been a panic in the last three weeks." The Joint Chiefs' request for more troops, which had been leaked to the *New York Times,* "would cost $15 billion. That would hurt the dollar and gold. . . . The country is demoralized. I will have overwhelming disapproval in the polls and the elections. I will go down the drain. I don't want the whole [U.S.-led international] alliance and military pulled in with it. . . . We have no support for the war."

On March 31, in a televised speech, Johnson announced that only a limited number of additional troops would be sent to Vietnam, rejecting the military's request for a much larger buildup. He also announced a halt to bombing over the northern part of North Vietnam, where most of the population lived. Furthermore, he appealed to North Vietnam to begin negotiations, saying that "the United States is ready to send its representatives to any forum, at any time, to discuss the means of bringing this ugly war to an end." Finally, at the end of his long address, Johnson said that he would not seek or accept the Democratic nomination for the presidency, an unexpected, startling decision. Though he explained it by a desire to devote all his time to the war and domestic problems, he had long considered not running for reelection, worried about his health and his ability to win.

Johnson had not decided to de-escalate the war, only to limit it within certain parameters and avoid a major commitment of additional resources. In preliminary negotiations with the North Vietnamese, which began in Paris in May, both sides took a hard line, with little progress. Meanwhile, on the ground, fierce fighting brought U.S. casualty rates to their highest level of the whole war, in May doubling the rate during Tet. The United States intensified its bombing of the southern part of North Vietnam, South Vietnam, and Laos. What had changed was that after March 1968 there were no illusions left that the United States could or would even try to achieve outright military victory.

1968

The Tet offensive, McCarthy's and Kennedy's challenges, and Johnson's withdrawal started 1968 with an unaccustomed sense of uncertainty about the future. Within days of Johnson's March 31 announcement, uncertainty deepened and darkened with a cascade of violence, protest, and social disarray. On April 4, Martin Luther King Jr. was assassinated, setting off the most extensive urban rioting in the country's history.

After the passage of the Voting Rights Act, King's national political role had diminished while growing more complex, as the movement for black advancement found new foci. In the South, a long, difficult struggle, largely through grassroots activity, unfolded to implement the guarantees of the Civil Rights and Voting Rights acts. The depth of the challenge became evident even to those far from the South in 1966, when James Meredith, who had been the first black student admitted to the University of Mississippi, was shot while undertaking a "walk against fear" across Mississippi. During a continuation of his march, led by top civil rights leaders, the slogan of "Black Power" first received national attention when SNCC leader Stokely Carmichael began using it at rallies along the way.

A multifarious notion, Black Power in part reflected conditions in the rural South, where many African Americans came to believe that their best chance for improving their lives lay in winning an equitable share of political power and economic resources rather than in focusing on racial integration. In the de facto segregated cities of the North, Black Power also became a rallying cry, sometimes as a call for black separatism, sometimes as a demand for community control over schools, police, and other social resources, sometimes as a push to elect African Americans to office, and often above all else as a cultural mood. Malcolm X, who in his lifetime had failed to build a mass political movement, emerged after his assassination in February 1965 as the symbol and inspiration of the movement toward Black Power. The slow pace and limited returns of the push for racial integration (which Malcolm X had opposed) led many African Americans to question the goal and the use of nonviolent action to achieve it. Both SNCC and CORE promoted the idea of Black Power, converting themselves into exclusively African American organizations. The Black Panther Party, founded on the West Coast in 1966, won growing support through its practice of armed self-defense.

King never completely rejected the idea of Black Power, but he remained committed to nonviolence and conceived of the struggle for black advancement as part of a larger struggle for social justice. He found himself increasingly eclipsed, at least in the media and in popularity among young African Americans, by the diffuse, rhetorically flamboyant Black Power movement. Frustrated by the failure of his efforts to fight segregation in northern cities and the continued poverty of so many blacks, King began giving greater emphasis to economic issues, seeking to build a multiracial movement addressing the plight of the poor. Also, in 1967 he followed the lead of other civil rights leaders, like Carmichael, in becoming an outspoken critic of the war in Vietnam. Long a supporter of the labor movement, in March 1968 King agreed to help black sanitation workers in Memphis who were striking for union recognition. While he was visiting Memphis to lead a march in their support, an assassin, James Earl Ray, shot and killed him.

On the night of King's death, riots broke out in well over a hundred cities and towns. Local law enforcement officials and the Army, having anticipated another summer of urban riots, had created special weapons and tactics (SWAT) teams; bought massive quantities of arms, armored vehicles, and tear gas; and held riot training. Seventy-five thousand Army troops, Marines, and National Guardsmen, in addition to local and state police, patrolled city streets after King's murder. Still, violence raged. The worst rioting took place in Washington, D.C., where hundreds of fires burned, some within blocks of the White House, and ten people died. In Baltimore, four nights of rioting left six people dead, a thousand businesses damaged or destroyed, and five thousand people arrested. In Chicago, eleven died as looting and arson engulfed the city's West Side. Altogether, thirty-nine people died in the disorders sparked by King's death. The eruption demonstrated the civil rights leader's immense stature among African Americans, the outrage at his murder, the widespread rejection of nonviolence, and the thinness of the veneer of order that lay on top of a society that seemed close to flying apart.

In late April, Vice President Hubert H. Humphrey announced that he was joining the race for president. Humphrey inherited Johnson's position as the candidate of the Democratic establishment: southern governors, big-city bosses, labor leaders, and corporate contributors. Though coming in too late to enter most of the primaries, he nonetheless emerged as the favorite for the nomination; most states picked their national convention delegates at state conventions, which Democratic insiders dominated, while in a few of the fifteen states that held primaries Humphrey hoped to inherit delegates won by surrogates or favorite sons. Meanwhile, Kennedy and McCarthy battled it out in the primary states, culminating in a June 4

California election. There Kennedy won a narrow victory over McCarthy, with a surrogate for Humphrey very far behind, but even before the ballots were fully counted Kennedy was dead, shot by an assassin on his way out of the hotel where he had celebrated his victory.

Kennedy's murder added to the growing sense of chaos in the country. In a five-year stretch, Medgar Evers, the two Kennedys, Malcolm X, and Martin Luther King all had been killed by assassins' bullets. Political murder seemed to be becoming normalized, eliminating key African American leaders and helping determine who sat in the White House. The fog of uncertainty surrounding the assassinations added to their ominousness. Hints of conspiracy and the involvement of powerful, secret forces intimated that the real exercise of power happened out of sight of most Americans. At the same time, the seeming marginality and bizarreness of the actual shooters suggested a disturbing randomness to life, that the purposeful action of millions of people could be undone by one oddball, hater, or nut. Either way, the country had moved far from the textbook constitutionalism upon which it prided itself.

A new wave of antiwar and campus protest added to the sense that normal channels of politics were becoming eclipsed. Early in 1968, five thousand women picketed the opening session of Congress behind the eighty-seven-year-old Jeanette Rankin, the first woman to serve in Congress, who had voted against the declarations of war for both World War I and World War II. For many young protestors, World War I, with its large antiwar movement, seemed as long ago as the Civil War or the Revolution, yet Rankin provided living proof of how recent it had been. (So did the gender composition of Congress, which had not changed all that much since Rankin entered the House in 1917; in 1968, Congress had only twelve female members.) More antiwar protests came over the course of the spring, including the burning of draft files at a Selective Service office in Catonsville, Maryland, by a group dominated by Catholic priests and nuns and a one-day school boycott in which upwards of 200,000 high school and college students and teachers participated.

As student protests against the war became increasingly common, so did protests over other issues. At Barnard College, students held a sit-down blocking the president's office after she expelled a sophomore for living off campus with her boyfriend in violation of school rules. At Howard University, hundreds of students occupied the administration building to protest the lack of black history courses at the country's preeminent African American university. Students at Maryland's Bowie State College, another predominantly black college, held a boycott and occupied buildings to protest the miserable condition of their school's facilities. When two hundred of them took their protest to the Maryland statehouse, Governor Spiro Agnew had them arrested and sent state troopers to shut down their college.

At Columbia, students led by SDS and the Student Afro-American Society protested the university's involvement in military research and its plan to use part of a park bordering Harlem for a gymnasium. What began as a spontaneous occupation of one building spread to four others, attracting national and international media attention. After a week, the university called in the police to clear the campus. They did so with brutal gusto, arresting 720 people and beating and bloodying not only the building occupiers but also student and faculty bystanders and even some pro-war students.

The Columbia events took place at a moment of unprecedented student and dissident activity around the globe. During 1968, a surge of protest took place in a score of countries seemingly very different from one another: democratic, industrialized capitalist countries, including West Germany, Italy, France, Britain, and Japan; capitalistic dictatorships, like Spain; communist countries, most notably Czechoslovakia, Yugoslavia, Poland, and China; and parts of the developing world, including Mexico, Brazil, Uruguay, Argentina, Pakistan, and Senegal. Much like in 1848 and 1917–19, a spirit of rebellion danced across borders, making possibilities previously unimagined seem close to hand. While the specific demands in various countries differed, everywhere antiauthoritarianism and a demand for more democracy and personal freedom informed the protests. By 1968, a post–World War II generation had come of age impatient with the social and political arrangements established at the end of the war.

The United States helped set the stage for the global '68 protest. The spread of American popular culture helped create distinct youth cultures in many parts of the world, which in turn contributed to the generational character of much of the protest. Mass demonstrations in many countries against the war in Vietnam established networks and inclinations toward protest that activists then mobilized around local issues. In doing so, they frequently adopted the tactics, political style, and cultural accoutrements of the American civil rights, student, and antiwar movements.

The protests in the United States never came anywhere as near to bringing about fundamental political transformation as did protests in countries like France and Czechoslovakia, where major segments of society beyond the academy mobilized. Even together, the antiwar, student, civil rights, Black Power, and developing Mexican American movements remained too small, marginal, and diffuse to threaten the basic social order. But in the confusing sensory overload of the winter, spring, and summer of 1968, that did not seem clear to many Americans witnessing fierce fighting in Vietnam, extraordinary presidential politics, political assassinations, urban riots, countercultural blossoming, campus protest, and antiwar demonstrations. Even mainstream, mass-circulation magazines adopted an apocalyptic tone in covering politics and society, seeing great threats and possibilities all around and portraying as tangible some sort of forthcoming revolutionary change or social explosion. Looking back at this period, Joan Didion recalled feeling, "I was meant to know the plot, but all I knew was what I saw: flashing pictures in variable sequence, images with no 'meaning' beyond their temporary arrangement." Hospitalized for vertigo, nausea, and feeling that she was about to pass out, she later wrote, "By way of comment I offer only that an attack of vertigo and nausea does not now seem to me an inappropriate response to the summer of 1968."

Of all the events of that summer, none had a more surreal quality than the Democratic National Convention. Back when it looked like it would be a triumphal recoronation of Lyndon Johnson, a loose coalition of New Leftists, antiwar organizers, black activists, and political counterculturalists (who had dubbed themselves Yippies) had begun planning demonstrations for the August convention, to be held in Chicago. They persisted even as the presidential race took one unexpected turn after another. Mayor Richard J. Daley, an old-style political boss who almost single-handedly ran Chicago, privately opposed the war in Vietnam and had his doubts about Humphrey. But he hated demonstrators and counterculturalists and did all he could to prevent their presence in his city. His refusal to grant permits for marches and rallies, the reputation of his police department for brutality, and sabotage by undercover Chicago policemen who infiltrated the groups planning the protests kept the number of out-of-town demonstrators modest. Still, chaos ensued. When demonstrators stayed in city parks past an evening curfew, the police assaulted them and the reporters watching. The clashes soon spread to downtown. On the evening of the presidential nomination, the police indulged in a carnival of violence against protestors outside the hotels where the convention delegates were housed. Their brutality itself was not so unusual, but its broadcast over live national television was, exposing millions of Americans for the first time to such conduct, later characterized in an official investigation as a "police riot."

The chaos in the streets echoed inside the convention hall, as delegates fought over an antiwar platform plank (which went down to defeat) and the presidential and vice presidential nominations. Many delegates expressed outrage at the events outside, including Connecticut senator Abraham Ribicoff, who from the podium referred to "the Gestapo tactics on the streets in

Chicago." Though Humphrey easily won the nomination, by the end of the convention the Democratic Party, as broadcaster David Brinkley put it, "could fairly be classified as a disaster area," riven by political and cultural fissures that would weaken it for years to come.

While the Democrats battled it out for the leadership of their party, Richard Nixon sewed up the Republican presidential nomination. It was one of the great comeback stories of American politics. After losing to Kennedy in 1960 and in his bid two years later for the California governorship, Nixon had renounced politics in a fit of anger. But over the next six years he rebuilt his career, going to endless political dinners and giving endless speeches to shore up his ties with a broad spectrum of Republican politicians.

Nixon's election campaign strategy rested on a shrewd reading of the intense but often confused resentments and fears that so many Americans had in 1968. Like McCarthy, Nixon understood the widespread desire for order and social harmony. Unlike McCarthy, he added a hard edge to his promise of social peace, pledging over and over to restore "law and order." In accepting the Republican nomination, Nixon lauded "the great majority of Americans, the forgotten Americans—the non-shouters; the non-demonstrators" as "the real voice of America."

Nixon was a master at sending mixed signals. In the same speech, in an effort to project himself as a leader who could unite the nation, he appropriated phrases and cadences from Martin Luther King Jr., echoing the civil rights leader's very last address, the night before he died: "The time has come for us to leave the valley of despair and climb the mountain so that we may see the glory of the dawn—a new day for America, and a new dawn for peace and freedom in the world." At the same time, his selection of Spiro Agnew as his running mate reinforced the idea that a Nixon presidency would end the coddling of lawbreakers and advocates of change. Agnew was one of the first national political figures to emerge from postwar suburbanization, having long lived in the Baltimore suburbs. A centrist who had won office as a result of splits in the Maryland Democratic Party, he had gained national attention from his condemnation of moderate black leaders, blaming them for the riots in Baltimore after King's death because they had failed to denounce more militant leaders.

Nixon's effort to simultaneously benefit from the divisions in the country and rise above them was complicated by the presence in the race of former Alabama governor George Wallace, running as a third-party candidate. Wallace played on the same themes of resentment as Nixon, but in a cruder, blunter, wittier fashion. Unlike Nixon, he made no effort to appear statesmanlike. His rallies were wild affairs. Wallace would denounce the "Eastern establishment," "pointy-headed intellectuals," "bearded professors," welfare mothers (who he claimed were "breeding children as a cash crop"), hippies, and demonstrators (whom he called "scum"). He was at his best when he had demonstrators or hecklers to play off, pointing them out as representing all that was wrong with America. Lacking a coherent political program or even a political party behind him (he got financial and organizational help from right-wing groups and conservative evangelical ministers), Wallace's campaign had more than a little dose of nihilism. Perhaps for this reason, it seemed to capture the bitter, dark mood of many Americans who thought that the world they had grown up in and believed in was being destroyed by big government, a failed war, spoiled students, hippies, uppity blacks, and liberals who were responsible for all these woes.

Wallace hoped that his segregationist credentials would enable him to capture most of the South (where African Americans still made up only a modest part of the electorate), while making inroads in the North through antiliberal populism. Still, with the Democratic Party in disarray, Nixon looked like a shoo-in, even if Wallace took much of the South. But in late September Humphrey gave a nationally televised speech in which he promised to unilaterally halt the bombing of North Vietnam in pursuit of peace and set a timetable for troop withdrawals. (For his part, Nixon blandly promised "to bring an honorable end to the war in Vietnam," without saying how.) Though Humphrey added provisos that made the practical meaning of his position unclear, for the first time he broke from his public allegiance to Johnson's policy. By doing so, he at least partially shed his image as a bought man. Meanwhile, Wallace hurt himself badly by picking as his running mate former Air Force chief of staff General Curtis LeMay, who immediately reinforced his image as something of a nut by speaking cavalierly about the possible use of nuclear weapons in Vietnam.

Faced with the threat of a Nixon victory and strong Wallace showing, alienated Democratic constituencies began returning to the party. Labor leaders discovered that a large minority of northern white union members planned to vote for Wallace. In response, they undertook a campaign advertising the poor conditions for workers in Alabama, which proved effective in diminishing Wallace's northern blue-collar support. Then, just days before the election, Johnson announced a bombing halt over North Vietnam, citing progress toward getting peace talks started (having gotten indications from North Vietnam that it would accept the participation of the South Vietnamese government in negotiations, a U.S. precondition). Along with a last-minute endorsement by McCarthy, the bombing halt convinced some war critics to vote for Humphrey.

In the end it was almost enough, but not quite. Nixon achieved a very narrow popular plurality, with 43.4 percent of the vote compared to 42.7 percent for Humphrey and 13.5 percent for Wallace. The electoral vote was not as close: Nixon won 301 electoral votes, carrying most of the upper South, Midwest, and Far West; Humphrey won 191 votes, mostly from the Northeast and Texas; and Wallace garnered 46 votes from the five southern states that he carried. While the Republicans picked up some congressional seats, the Democrats retained comfortable majorities in both houses.

Seen one way, the 1968 election demonstrated remarkable continuity from the election eight years earlier. In 1960, Nixon and Kennedy had virtually tied in the popular vote, just like Nixon and Humphrey did this time, suggesting that the country remained divided between the moderate conservatism and the moderate liberalism of the major candidates. But adding together the Wallace and Nixon vote gave a different picture of a clear rejection of the liberal hegemony of the past decade. Furthermore, since the bulk of Wallace's backers in the South said that if he had not been in the race they would have voted Republican, the election also suggested a possible fundamental party realignment, in which white southern voters would bring the region into the Republican fold and give the party a national base from which to dominate presidential contests.

By the end of 1968, the mood of enormous uncertainty—the sense of impending change, possibly on a cataclysmic scale—began to lighten in the mass media. Life in more or less the form the country had known it might go on after all. The election had done nothing to end social divisions, which deepened over the next few years, nor had its outcome meant either the demise of liberalism or the end of radical challenges. But deep institutional and psychological structures of order had begun to assert themselves, even as the storms of political conflict and cultural change continued to rage.

CHAPTER 10

Sixties to Seventies,
Dreams to Nightmares

D uring the first years of Richard Nixon's presidency, liberal legislation continued to be passed and state function expanded. But by
the early 1970s, the tide began to turn, as Nixon and his allies constructed a new, antiliberal coalition. Even then, democratization advanced.
As African Americans kept pushing for economic and social equality and
more political power, other groups, often using the black freedom movement
as a template, mobilized to overcome discrimination and improve their lives,
defining themselves by ethnicity, national origin, gender, sexual orientation,
age, or other characteristics. Animating them all was an expanding notion
of rights and strongly felt group identification, as the politics of identity
came to overlie political organization based on class, party, region, and ideology. With the seemingly endless war in Vietnam amplifying political and
social discord, the rhetoric coming from ruling circles and dissenting movements became extreme. In one of the most tumultuous periods in the nation's
history, the democratic revolution exploded into new arenas of life even as it
approached its limits.

The Continuing Battle for Racial Equality

In the late 1960s, many southern facilities and institutions, and some in the
North, remained racially segregated, or nearly so. In his inaugural address,
Richard Nixon declared, "The laws have caught up with our conscience.
What remains is to give life to the law." It often took militant local action to
do that.

In the towns, small cities, and rural areas of the South, conflicts could be
fierce. In Oxford, North Carolina, segregation and a caste system of racial

power remained largely intact until 1970. Then the acquittal of a white store owner charged with murdering a young black man set off a wave of street violence by black teenagers, the carefully planned burning down of white-owned tobacco warehouses by a group of black Vietnam veterans, and a black boycott of white businesses. With the cost of segregation skyrocketing, white business leaders finally agreed to desegregate the local movie theater, hire black workers for downtown sales jobs, and increase the number of African American police officers.

Elite groups sometimes held out longer. At Harvard University, the Porcellian Club, the most aristocratic of the undergraduate "final clubs," did not admit an African American member until 1983. At the University of Texas, in 1984 only a single black student belonged to the fraternities affiliated with the Interfraternity Council, and some sororities moved off campus to avoid having to sign an antidiscrimination pledge.

Schools remained a key battleground. After a decade of doing little to enforce *Brown,* in the mid-1960s the federal courts began to more aggressively press for school desegregation. In 1968 the Supreme Court declared that segregated school systems had a duty to eliminate racial discrimination "root and branch," not merely to end the use of government power to enforce racial separation. Three years later, it allowed courts to require mandatory busing to integrate school systems that once had been segregated by law, leading to the imposition of busing plans in more than a hundred southern school districts. In 1973 the Court extended the requirement for active desegregation efforts to school systems that never had de jure segregation. In practice, that meant urban school districts in the North, which by then often were more segregated than those in the South.

As a candidate and as president, Richard Nixon vocally opposed federal intervention to end de facto school segregation, especially mandatory busing. In practice, though, his Justice Department made extensive use of litigation to force school districts to desegregate. During the 1972–73 school year, fewer than 10 percent of black students in the South attended all-black schools, as school desegregation proceeded at a much faster pace than it had during the Johnson administration.

Violent southern resistance to school desegregation had largely abated by the late 1960s. When bureaucratic and legal efforts to block desegregation failed (often after delaying it for years), many southern parents simply pulled their children out of newly integrated schools. Some moved to white suburbs where few if any black children attended local schools. Others enrolled their children in all-white private schools, including so-called Christian academies, which proliferated with the legal assault on school segregation. The white academies benefited from tax exemptions and in over a half a dozen states from direct government subsidies, until the courts declared public funding unconstitutional. Although private southern schools created or expanded to evade desegregation generally provided inferior education to that found in the public schools, their estimated enrollment burgeoned from twenty-five thousand in 1966 to 535,000 in 1972.

The Supreme Court push for equality of schooling reached its limits in the early 1970s, as Nixon moved the Court in a conservative direction and desegregation threatened to impinge on the white northern middle class. (Nixon appointed four justices during his first term, including Warren E. Burger, who replaced the retiring Earl Warren as chief justice in 1969.) In 1973, in a case challenging the greater funds given to schools in white parts of San Antonio than to those in heavily Mexican American areas, the Court ruled that the Fourteenth Amendment did not require equivalent funding for school systems with differing racial compositions. The next year, in *Milliken v. Bradley,* it ruled that courts could not force suburban school districts to merge with urban ones to facilitate integration. This gave constitutional sanction to the segregation of schools that resulted from segregated suburbanization, a process that had been greatly abetted by government policy.

The difficulty of trying to desegregate schools without addressing regional residential segregation became obvious in Boston, where an unusually large proportion of the middle and upper classes lived outside the city proper in almost exclusively white suburbs. In 1974 federal district judge W. Arthur Garrity Jr., in reaction to prolonged resistance by the Boston School Committee to ending school segregation, ordered a large-scale program of busing of white and black students into each other's neighborhoods. Whites, particularly from working-class areas like South Boston and Charlestown, fiercely resisted the effort. They boycotted schools, held raucous rallies, and assaulted black students. Many directed their anger as much at the judge, who lived in a white suburb, as at African Americans, perceiving a class bias in an integration plan that left the suburbs almost untouched.

As in the South, many northern white parents pulled their children out of public schools to avoid integration or mandatory busing. Some moved to the suburbs, while others sent children to Catholic schools. Boston public schools went from being 60 percent white in 1973 to 35 percent in 1980.

Many black students and their parents cared as much about the content of their education as where it took place. When Anita Lafrance Allen, class of 1970, entered the recently integrated Baker High School in Columbus, Georgia, she found that "a white southern Protestant Christian ethos permeated the place," with no nonwhite teachers, staff, cheerleaders, or homecoming queens. "In my classes we did not read a single book, essay or poem written by a person who was not a white American or European." A desire for more African American teachers, principals, and course content animated a push in many cities—most explosively in New York—by black activists and parents for greater control over local schools, as they recognized the diminishing prospects for meaningful integration.

A parallel process took place on college campuses, where African American students pushed for the admission of more nonwhites and the creation of black studies programs. During the 1968–69 school year, students at San Francisco State College struck for four months seeking the establishment of black and ethnic studies programs and open admissions for students of color. At the City University of New York, a wave of sometimes violent demonstrations and counterdemonstrations led to the adoption of an open enrollment policy that guaranteed every local high school graduate a place in the city's free higher education system. At Cornell University, black students occupying a building captured national attention by arming themselves with rifles.

Though administrators and public officials often resisted particular protests and demands, the broad goals of black parents and students gradually were realized. At every level of schooling, curricula began paying greater attention to the experiences of African Americans and other minority groups. Black studies became established as an academic discipline. Leading colleges began admitting more nonwhite students.

In the struggle for control of schools, black nationalists played an important role, as they increasingly set the tone of African American activism. Though nationalist ideas had deep historic roots, they achieved new prominence in the late 1960s. The Nation of Islam continued to have a substantial membership, while new nationalist groups, like the US Organization and the Black Panther Party in California and the Committee for a Unified NewArk in New Jersey, attracted many followers. Often lumped together under the label "Black Power," these groups, though differing in their programs and beliefs, commonly had all-black memberships; rejected deference to white authority; asserted the right to armed self-defense; stressed black pride, unity, and internationalism; had acute understandings of the daily problems of ghetto life; and appealed in particular to urban youth, who were in many cases drawn by the discipline and purposefulness they provided.

The radicalism and armed militancy of Black Power groups provoked government repression, often illegal and sometimes murderous. In 1967 the FBI extended its secret COINTELPRO to black nationalist groups in an effort to disrupt and "neutralize" them. Local police forces repeatedly raided the offices of the Black Panther Party, which had expanded across the country, resulting in fierce exchanges of gunfire. In Chicago, the police assassinated the local leader of the Panthers while he lay asleep. Government attacks, infiltration, and internal feuding contributed to the short life span of many Black Power groups. Among poor young blacks, drugs and violence took a growing toll, contributing to depoliticization.

Though organizationally weak, the Black Power movement left its cultural and political mark. In spite of its often hyperbolic rhetoric, it had some of its greatest success through mainstream electoral politics. Changing urban demographics, combined with the political mobilization of African Americans, allowed black politicians to win election as mayors of many of the nation's major cities, starting in 1967 with Carl Stokes in Cleveland and Richard Hatcher in Gary and continuing with Kenneth Gibson in Newark (1970), Coleman Young in Detroit and Tom Bradley in Los Angeles (1973), Walter Washington in Washington, D.C., and Maynard Jackson in Atlanta (1974). Their success came as part of a nationwide increase in black officeholding, including in the South.

Many of the new African American officeholders, especially in the North, had not participated in the civil rights movement but came out of urban machine politics. Nonetheless, their success often rested on ties they developed to Black Power groups and the climate of assertion of the right to self-determination in black communities. In Newark, the poet and black nationalist Amiri Baraka played a key role in Gibson's election to city hall and the ouster of a corrupt white Democratic machine. Baraka helped organize a series of national black conventions that brought together civil rights activists, nationalists, and elected officials around a shared rhetoric of Black Power and pan-Africanism. In Oakland, the Black Panthers helped to orchestrate the election of the city's first black mayor. But as African Americans began winning positions of official power, the grassroots organizations and radical leaders who had helped them succeed became sublimated to the new regimes they constructed, which often had strong ties to local, mostly white business leaders as well. With patronage, contracts, federal grants, and political favors to distribute, African American officials adopted traditional modes of political operation, giving African Americans a greater share of power without any fundamental transformation of social structures or modes of governance.

Hispanics and Native Americans Mobilize

As the African American movement for rights, equality, cultural pride, and social betterment evolved, it became a model for an ever-growing number of other social movements. Each constituency had its own history, concerns, and political dynamics. But the influence of the black struggle could be seen on all of them. Virtually all the social movements of the late 1960s and 1970s involved not only sharpened conflict between particular communities and the larger society but also conflicts within communities about what goals to pursue and how to pursue them, conflicts between the young and old, traditionalists and modernists, militants and moderates, and separatists and assimilationists.

Mexican Americans provide a case in point. Starting in the 1920s, a series of organizations had been founded to fight discrimination against Mexican Americans, project an image of them as patriotic white Americans, and se-cure them government benefits. In the mid-1960s, some Mexican American activists—in many cases impressed by the successes of the civil rights movement—began forming more militant groups. The United Farm Workers revived the once strong tradition of California agricultural unionism, repre-senting Filipino as well as Mexican American workers. Under the charis-matic leadership of César Chávez, it melded contractual unionism, Mexican American culture, Catholic ritual, and civil rights movement tactics. The strike it led of grape workers and the national boycott of grapes it organized in their support trained a whole generation of labor and political activists. A 1967 armed raid on a New Mexico courthouse, led by Reies López Tijer-ina, in pursuit of long-contested land claims, brought to national attention the lingering bitterness over the loss of land titles when the United States took over Mexican territory.

Though the Mexican American mobilization began in the countryside, it soon spread to the cities where most of the four and a half million Mexican Americans lived. Newly formed groups, like the Brown Berets in Los Ange-les, the Crusade for Justice in Denver, and the Mexican American Youth Organization in Texas, embraced a cultural nationalism sometimes fused with political ideas and accoutrements borrowed from Black Power groups. Many new activists adopted the term "Chicano"—a working-class self-description, which had sometimes been used pejoratively by outsiders—to describe themselves and identified themselves as brown, not white. Like many of the social movements of the time, the Chicano groups danced back and forth across the fuzzy line separating radicalism from reform, simulta-neously denouncing the very nature of American society while pressing for new government programs and benefits. At colleges and universities, they fought for the introduction of Chicano studies programs and the admission of more Mexican American students. At high schools in East Los Angeles and Texas, mass walkouts of Mexican American students protested ill-treatment by authorities little interested in their problems or heritage.

The Chicano movement broke with the strong Mexican American tradition of military service when it began organizing protests against the draft and the war in Vietnam. Rapidly gaining momentum, the Mexican American antiwar movement culminated in the Chicano Moratorium March on August 29, 1970. The twenty thousand to thirty thousand people who marched down the main boulevard of East Los Angeles constituted one of the largest gatherings of Mexican Americans in the country's history. The day ended in violence when sheriff's deputies tried to break up a rally and young demonstrators fought back. Three people died, including Rubén Salazar, a leading Mexican American journalist. The Chicano movement soon splintered, with some more radical activists moving away from community organizing and cultural nationalism toward one or another version of Marxism, and increasing isolation.

On the East Coast, Puerto Rican activists followed a similar trajectory. Influenced by the student movement, the Black Panthers, and various left-wing groups, in 1969 a group of young New York Puerto Ricans, mostly born on the mainland and in some cases barely fluent in Spanish, formed the Young Lords, a radical community group, based in East Harlem. Through a series of demonstrations and building takeovers, they won a broad following in their fight for cleaner streets, better health care, and more government services. But the group had a short half-life, losing its community base when it plunged into independence politics in Puerto Rico and worker organizing, with minimal success.

Other groups also developed heightened ethnic consciousness, launching militant struggles against discrimination and winning substantial political and social gains. Perhaps the most dramatic instance was the new wave of Native American activism that developed during the late 1960s, both within traditional tribal and political structures and from the American Indian Movement (AIM), a militant group formed in 1968. A series of protest actions forced the issue of Native American rights onto the national political agenda for the first time in over half a century, including an eighteen-month occupation of Alcatraz Island that began in 1969, a six-day occupation of the Bureau of Indian Affairs in 1972, and finally the 1973 AIM occupation of the village of Wounded Knee, South Dakota—site of an 1890 massacre of Lakota Sioux by the U.S. Army—which resulted in a prolonged armed standoff between the demonstrators and federal forces. While Native American militants were subjected to an intense campaign of government repression, their actions led to substantial reforms in Indian policy and the revival of many tribes.

The Women's Movement

The social movement of the late 1960s and early 1970s that perhaps had the greatest impact on American life was the women's movement. It had roots in earlier periods of feminist activity, all the way back to the mid-nineteenth century. But it developed in ways deeply influenced by the postwar African American freedom struggle.

The passage of the 1964 Civil Rights Act encouraged women to press for equality and greater opportunity at work, at a time when their labor force participation was continuing to rise. In 1966, three hundred largely female activists, frustrated with the inaction of the Equal Employment Opportunity Commission (EEOC) in countering discrimination on the basis of sex, founded the National Organization of Women (NOW) to fight for equal rights for women and improvements in their daily lives, including more equal marriages and better daycare. Over a third of the delegates to NOW's founding convention came from the Midwest, which since World War II had been the center of efforts to improve the work lives of women. NOW elected New Yorker Betty Friedan as its first president, but it did much of its initial organizing out of Detroit office space lent by the United Automobile Workers.

The push for women's equality gathered strength as women's wage work outside the home went from being the exception to the norm. Nearly half of all women worked for wages by 1975 (constituting 40 percent of the workforce), including an increasing number with young children. With the huge demand for labor during the Vietnam War–driven boom in the late 1960s, women had plenty of opportunities to work if they wanted to or needed to. But more women working did not bring greater equality on the job. In 1966, full-time female workers made on average only 60 percent of what male workers did, a drop over the preceding decade largely as a result of the increasing segregation of women into occupations with lower pay than jobs typed as male. Only 7 percent of doctors were female, less than 4 percent of lawyers.

The civil rights movement produced a language of rights and federal legislation to address these inequities, but little seemed to be changing on the ground. NOW's first campaign was to pressure the EEOC to declare separate classified ad listings for male and female jobs—the common practice—to be illegal, which it finally did in 1968. Fighting sexual discrimination in employment often meant challenging gender stereotypes. Some of the first complaints of sexual discrimination filed with the EEOC came from airline stewardesses, who by industry rules had to be female. Most airlines set age, weight, and appearance guidelines. The EEOC eventually ruled that being female was not a bona fide occupational qualification for the job and deemed it illegal for airlines to fire women when they got married or reached a certain age. But it took extended litigation until the airlines changed their practices, transforming the renamed position of flight attendant from a sexualized job for young, unmarried, usually white Christian women to a long-term occupation for a diverse workforce.

In 1967 and 1968, a network of young female political activists began organizing what came to be called the Women's Liberation Movement, which they saw as a radical alternative to the liberal NOW. Writers and activists, meeting in small groups, developed critiques of almost every aspect of American life as it impacted women, from unequal sexual and marriage relationships to the legal status of women, child-raising practices, cultural notions of beauty and worth, and the treatment of women by the medical and psychological establishments. "Women are an oppressed class," declared the radical feminist group Redstockings in its manifesto. "We are exploited as sex objects, breeders, domestic servants, and cheap labor. . . . Our Humanity is denied. . . . We identify the agents of our oppression as men." Many leaders of the new movement had been involved in the civil rights, student, or antiwar movements, absorbing from them a rights consciousness, knowledge of how to organize, and a strategic sophistication, even as they grew frustrated at being kept in subordinate roles.

Most Americans first became aware of Women's Liberation in September 1968, when a group of women protested the Miss America contest in Atlantic City. Their demonstration, which received a great deal of media attention (mostly dismissive or mocking), criticized the beauty contest as degrading, racist (there had never been a black finalist), and for bolstering the war in Vietnam (the winner got sent off to Vietnam to meet with the troops). Radical feminists never found an organizational mode or a political language that enabled them to construct mass organizations. Yet within a few years, the issues they raised were widely debated throughout the country.

Feminist ideas and initiatives won wide acceptance because they spoke to the daily realities of women's lives: unequal pay and job opportunities, lack of daycare, insensitive and sometimes ignorant doctors, repressive abortion laws, limited educational opportunities. At a time when birth control devices, especially oral contraceptives, had gone a long way toward splitting sexuality away from reproduction and women's wage earning had lessened their dependence on men, long-established cultural norms and social and legal practices seemed archaic and oppressive to many Americans. More and more women became convinced that they should control their own lives, bodies, and property. In 1962, two out of three women polled did not consider themselves victims of discrimination. By 1970, half did. The enormous popularity of the feminist health book *Our Bodies, Ourselves,* which attacked the male-dominated medical establishment and instructed women on self-help techniques, was but one measure of the rapidly spreading change in popular consciousness.

A virtual revolution in the status of women unfolded in the early 1970s, with remarkably little opposition. Starting in 1971, Congress passed a series of laws aimed at eliminating discrimination against women, including a prohibition on sexual discrimination in medical training programs, a ban on discrimination by lenders on the basis of sex or marital status, and a requirement, in Title IX of the 1972 Education Act, that to keep receiving federal funds, educational institutions had to eliminate sexual discrimination, including by giving equal resources to female and male athletic programs. (In 1971, girls made up only 7 percent of high school athletes.) The high point of the legislative flood came in 1972 when the Senate joined the House in passing the Equal Rights Amendment (ERA), in both cases by massive majorities. Twenty-eight states ratified the federal amendment within a year of its passage. Support for ERA came from an extraordinarily broad spectrum of national figures, from actress Jane Fonda, who had become a left-wing antiwar activist, to Richard Nixon and Strom Thurmond.

The Supreme Court pushed forward the feminist revolution. It decided in a series of cases argued by Ruth Bader Ginsburg that the equal protection clause of the Fourteenth Amendment applied to sexual as well as racial discrimination. Its 1973 decision in *Roe v. Wade,* which forbade states from banning abortions during the first six months of pregnancy, brought about an enormous change in women's lives. Starting in the late 1950s, medical professionals and population control advocates had been pushing for liberalization of abortion rules, which in most states banned the practice except under very narrow circumstances. Women's groups joined them in 1970, when New York became the first state to fully legalize abortion. Ten other states soon followed. *Roe* legalized abortion nationally, giving women control over their bodies as an extension of the right to privacy that the Court had earlier created. Other legal changes included the liberalization of the grounds for divorce or the introduction of no-fault divorce in many states and, beginning with Nebraska in 1976, the elimination of the marriage exemption to criminal rape laws.

The floodgates of change opened locally, too. When in early 1972 a group of about twenty women and four children occupied a building at Kansas

University demanding the establishment of a daycare center, an affirmative action program, a women's studies department, the provision of comprehensive women's health care at the student health center, an end to gender-based wage inequalities, and the hiring of more female faculty and staff, the university quickly and with little controversy agreed to their demands, in marked contrast to the resistance and tumult in response to earlier protests by black students and antiwar activists.

Gay Liberation and the Diffusion of Rights Consciousness

The movement for gay rights first drew national attention in June 1969, when the police raided a bar in Greenwich Village frequented by homosexual men, the Stonewall Inn. Such raids were routine in many cities, as law enforcement officials sought to enforce morals laws or collect payoffs. This time, several hundred bar patrons fought back, in what soon turned into a full-scale riot.

Stonewall brought to the attention of the general public—and many gays and lesbians—a movement that had been slowly coalescing for decades. World War II had been something of a watershed for homosexual men and women, creating greater group consciousness. The first male homosexual advocacy group, the Mattachine Society, was founded by leftists in Los Angeles in 1950; the lesbian Daughters of Bilitis was set up in San Francisco five years later.

In 1965, a small group of pickets marched in front of the White House to protest the repression of homosexuals in Cuba and the United States, the first of a series of protests against federal antigay discrimination. A few prominent authors, like Allen Ginsberg and James Baldwin, began openly writing about same-sex sexuality in positive terms. In San Francisco and Los Angeles, patrons of gay bars held street demonstrations to protest raids. Still, through the 1960s, homosexuality remained legally proscribed and widely viewed as sinful and unnatural. If revealed, it generally had severe social and economic consequences.

The Stonewall riot, coming at a moment of heightened rights consciousness and social mobilization, catalyzed an explosive growth in gay and lesbian activism and began to shift social attitudes toward homosexuality, and for that matter toward sexuality more generally. Influenced by the Black Power movement, homosexual groups adopted the slogan "gay is good," which soon became "gay pride." In New York and other cities, they fought against legal restrictions and the notion that homosexuality was pathological. As the gay liberation movement grew, it emboldened many men and women to become open about their sexual orientation. In 1973, the American Psychiatric Association stopped classifying homosexuality as a mental disorder. Two years later, the United States Civil Service Commission ceased deeming homosexuality immoral conduct that precluded federal employment.

As rights consciousness spread ever further in the society, categories of people who had not in the past been thought of as bearers of particular rights began to claim them, or have them claimed on their behalf. Take children, a group whose problems generally had been addressed in terms of social environment or developmental psychology. In the 1960s and 1970s, a body of thinking and law about children's rights developed that called for giving them more autonomy and protection, including from their parents. Presidents Johnson and Nixon promoted political programs aimed specifically at children, and in 1973 Marian Wright Edelman founded the Children's Rights Defense Fund as a legal advocacy, following the model of the NAACP Legal Defense and Education Fund. In 1972, the American Hospital Association issued a twelve-point Patient's Bill of Rights, applying the language of rights to another group not previously conceived of in such terms. Soldiers and sailors, conventionally thought of as having surrendered most civilian rights upon entering the military, began asserting "GI Rights," seeking to exercise their constitutional rights while on active duty, including the right to hold protest meetings and openly criticize the war in Vietnam.

Even opponents of racial desegregation, the issue around which the language of rights had become popularized, adopted its terms. Throughout the postwar period, many segregationists thought of what they were doing as defending their right to choose their neighbors and employees, to decide who should go to school with their children, and to be free of interference from the government about how they used their property and conducted their affairs. By the 1970s, some opponents of integration came to draw directly on the language and tactics of the civil rights movement, sometimes describing themselves as fighting for white rights or white power. In 1975, white mothers in the Charlestown section of Boston, opposing the busing of black students to the local high school, consciously adopted Martin Luther King Jr.'s use of civil disobedience and prayer in the face of repressive authority to promote their cause, at one point even singing "We Shall Overcome" when confronted by policemen trying to stop their march.

Richard Nixon and the Institutionalization of Reform

Many of the demands of the social movements of the late 1960s and early 1970s became encoded into law and government practice during the Nixon administration, sometimes over the objection of the president but often with his acquiescence or support. One of the odder figures in American history, Nixon defied simple political characterization. Born in Southern California to a family of modest means, he rose to power as a belligerent anticommunist, but on most domestic issues he adopted centrist positions, bobbing and weaving in an effort to maintain support from both the liberal and conservative wings of the Republican Party. Prone to seeing conspiracies and enemies all around him, Nixon, even as president, thought of himself as an outsider, fighting a hostile East Coast establishment. Enamored with complex schemes and covert action, he adopted strategies so intricate that his actual views and intentions often remained hidden.

Nixon entered the White House without much of a mandate, having been elected with a minority of the popular vote after a campaign in which he largely mouthed generalities. Democratic majorities in Congress limited his freedom of action, as evident when the Senate refused to confirm two of his Supreme Court nominees. Nixon hoped to win over some traditionally Democratic constituencies to ensure his reelection and rebuild the Republicans as a national majority party. To woo them, he supported the core New Deal economic and social programs from which they benefited, even as he took conservative positions on other issues. Sometimes taken with thinking of himself as a Tory reformer, Nixon proved willing to take innovative steps most conservatives would blanch at. But most of the time he paid little attention to domestic matters, seeing foreign policy as more compelling, or made decisions based out of political rather than ideological considerations. The upshot was that in spite of the electorate's rejection of Hubert Humphrey, whose career had been associated with the New Deal order and the Great Society, the federal government remained largely wedded to liberal domestic policies.

During the eight years Nixon was elected to serve as president (including the period when Gerald Ford finished out his second term), federal social spending, adjusted for inflation, rose at an annual rate of nearly 10 percent, compared to just under 8 percent during the Kennedy-Johnson years. Some of the increase reflected rising costs for existing programs, some the cost of new programs and program extensions. Many of the social welfare improvements were not terribly controversial because they aided broad constituencies that were seen as deserving of support. During Nixon's first term, Social Security old-age benefits went up 52 percent, with future benefits indexed to the cost of living, a huge structural change. The federal government also took over from the states supplementary, needs-based income guarantees for the elderly, blind, and disabled. Elder Americans, who once made up a major component of the poor, all but ceased living in poverty. The Medicaid and food stamp programs were improved, too.

Other proposed social benefit reforms proved more controversial, especially those concerning Aid to Families with Dependent Children (AFDC), "welfare" in the common lexicon. Ironically, one effect of the War on Poverty, meant to deploy innovative approaches to eradicate poverty, was to expand the long-established AFDC program, which did not address the causes of deprivation but only sought to alleviate the plight of the poor (and lessen the social threat they might pose). The welfare system was a maze of complex regulations and demeaning practices that discouraged eligible women from enrolling. Inspired by the black freedom movement, welfare recipients began organizing to protest inadequate benefits and indignities they suffered, like home visits by caseworkers looking for nonspousal live-in companions. Aided by government-funded lawyers and community workers, the Welfare Rights movement proved effective in knocking down barriers that kept poor people off welfare. Some state and local governments consciously loosened regulations to try to lessen the volatility of poor communities. So even as a booming economy and Great Society programs were reducing the number of people living in poverty, the number of families receiving AFDC benefits rose from one million in 1965 to two and a half million in 1970.

Nixon considered AFDC a "colossal" failure. He proposed replacing it with a guaranteed minimum annual income. Some conservatives, most notably Milton Friedman, had long advocated what they called a "negative income tax," seeing it as preferable to the extensive government bureaucracy that had grown up around social benefits. Many liberals and welfare recipients saw an income guarantee as recognition of welfare as a fundamental right. Nixon did not fully agree; his proposal—which covered both single-parent, female-headed households that received AFDC and two-parent families of the working poor—required most recipients to be willing to work in order to receive benefits. But he went a long way in that direction.

The House twice passed versions of Nixon's plan, but the Senate killed it. The stereotype of the welfare recipient as an unwed black woman—in reality, a majority of welfare recipients were white—led much of the public to view those on welfare as undeserving (in contrast to the elderly). With southern senators opposing the plan as too generous and welfare mothers opposing it as not generous enough, Nixon soon lost interest, happy to let his proposal die as long as he did not get the blame.

As the welfare fight showed, Nixon did not shy away from the idea of expansive government, evident as well in his environmental actions. He signed one law after another that fundamentally changed the role of the federal government in protecting the environment, partly in reaction to an explosion of support for conservation and environmental groups. Until the late 1960s, these organizations were modest in size and conservative in their tactics. Then, seemingly overnight, a mass environmental movement sprang up. A 1969 oil spill off the coast of Santa Barbara, a plan for an Alaska oil pipeline, and proposed federal funding for a supersonic passenger plane brought new attention to environmental issues. More important, the political sensibility of the protest movements of the 1960s infused environmentalism. Well-established conservation groups found themselves flooded with young members eager to deploy more militant tactics, while the media, relieved to find an issue other than Vietnam or urban problems to focus on, began providing extensive coverage of environmental issues and protests. As environmentalism became a national craze, few economic or political interests initially opposed it, preferring to hop on the bandwagon or maneuver to keep the movement innocuous.

The high point of environmental action came on April 22, 1970, "Earth Day," when twenty million people took part in rallies, tree plantings, and parades on streets shut to automotive traffic. More a self-congratulatory celebration than a political movement, Earth Day won support from the Nixon administration and many major corporations. But significant legal and administrative changes came too. In 1970 alone, Nixon signed the National Environmental Policy Act, which required environmental assessments of proposed federal projects, the Water Pollution Control Act, and amendments strengthening the Clean Air Act, and created the Environmental Protection Agency by merging various federal units into one body.

National transportation policy began changing too, in part as a result of environmental concerns. Early in his presidency, Nixon supported the decision of his interior secretary, Walter Hickel, to cancel a proposed Cross-Florida Barge Canal, citing environmental concerns, an unusual rejection of the Promethean pork barrelism that had come to dominate public works policy. Not long after, Congress killed the supersonic aircraft program. The Nixon administration also agreed to cancel interstate highway extensions in New Orleans and Boston that would have destroyed the neighborhoods they passed through. In 1973 the president supported the congressional decision to allow money in the Highway Trust Fund to be used for mass transportation projects, rather than be restricted to road building. Highway planners found themselves having to hold extensive consultations with impacted communities and take into consideration the effect of proposed projects on the environment and the quality of life, not just traffic flow, as heightened environmental consciousness converged with the democratization of every-day life.

The implication of the early environmental movement that changes in individual behavior could solve problems of pollution and resource exhaustion—cartoonist Walt Kelly's Earth Day poster declared, "We have met the enemy and he is us"—made environmentalism into something of a mom-and-apple-pie issue. Business and organized labor had little trouble with measures that called for federally funded efforts to limit pollution from nonindustrial sources. But once proposals began being offered that required industrial concerns and energy producers to reduce the pollution they created at their own expense, business opposition flared. Unlike many federal regulations, which targeted specific industries or practices, environmental measures affected business broadly, an expansion of government control that many businessmen found deeply disturbing.

Business found an effective counter to demands for environmental measures in arguing that they would limit economic growth and lead to the loss of jobs. Many unions allied with employers, regarding ecology as "economic pornography," in labor journalist John Herling's phrase, an idea that threatened jobs and stable labor/management relations. Some environmentalists did believe in checking growth. For those who already had comfortable lives, it would mean little. But for the less prosperous, with the redistribution of wealth outside mainstream discourse, limited growth would mean limited opportunity.

Once posed as an issue of growth versus pollution reduction, support for environmentalism diminished. Before the end of his first term, Nixon all but abandoned his support for the environmental movement, with the White House no longer portraying it as a benign endeavor for the general good but as an example of liberal protest gone amok. Meanwhile, business lobbyists fought an effective trench war over specific standards and regulations issued by federal environmental agencies. But if slowed, the movement toward greater environmental regulation continued, along with widespread public concern.

A somewhat parallel trajectory occurred in regulating workplace safety. In 1970 the AFL-CIO, a few of its affiliated unions, and reformer Ralph Nader pressed for the passage of legislation protecting worker health and safety. With the Nixon administration supporting the passage of some such law, in part to woo blue-collar voters, business abandoned its outright opposition, working instead to dilute whatever passed. The compromise Occupational Safety and Health Act created the Occupational Safety and

Health Administration (OSHA) to establish workplace health and safety standards and enforce them through worksite inspections.

Like Title VII of the 1964 Civil Rights Act, which banned racial or sexual discrimination in employment, the worker safety act extended the notion of individual rights into the workplace, with the law stating as its purpose "to assure as far as possible every working man and woman in the Nation safe and healthful working conditions." That proved easier said than done. OSHA moved very slowly in issuing standards for safety and health, an immense challenge given the thousands of chemicals and safety hazards in workplaces, made more difficult by weak technical capacity and business lobbying and lawsuits. Enforcement proved even harder. Individual worker complaints often led to reprisals (even though illegal). With literally millions of workplaces, no effective monitoring system could be erected. So OSHA generally acted only after accidents occurred, when violations were exceptionally egregious, or when a union aggressively pursued health and safety issues. Within the nondemocratic sphere of the workplace, a rights-based approach to improving workers' lives functioned effectively only when workers already had organized themselves or when things went terribly bad.

The individual rights approach to eliminating workplace discrimination also proved problematic. The EEOC, soon after being set up by the 1964 Civil Rights Act, found itself swamped by complaints: its first year of operation, nine thousand cases were filed; by 1975, it had seventy-seven thousand. Quickly, it fell far behind in addressing them. Congress undermined the effectiveness of its own creation by cutting EEOC funding. With the resolution of individual cases prolonged and difficult, class action lawsuits emerged as a more effective means to force equal treatment, especially once the federal courts allowed the use of statistical evidence to prove patterns of discrimination. Between 1965 and 1972, more than twelve hundred class action suits alleging illegal employment discrimination were filed.

Such legal action began to weaken systematic discrimination, especially when economic pressures were pushing employers in the same direction. In the South, the textile industry (the region's largest), which traditionally paid low wages to an all-white and heavily female production force, found itself facing a labor shortage as better-paid industries grew, siphoning off workers. A few companies experimented on their own with hiring black workers. But it took lawsuits and sustained federal pressure to force others to desegregate. By the early 1970s, significant hiring of African Americans had occurred. For many black families, a textile job meant the possibility to buy a car or a home, to give a child a better education, and to transform the fabric of everyday life.

The federal government found a second lever to pry open jobs to excluded groups by requiring hiring targets on federally funded projects. During the Eisenhower and Kennedy administrations, a White House committee had tried to force federal contractors and the federal government itself to hire on a nondiscriminatory basis, but it failed to break long-established patterns of racially discriminatory hiring. Under Johnson, government officials began asking companies in the construction industry seeking federally funded contracts to specify how many nonwhite workers they would try to hire in specific crafts. Many companies preferred this to general injunctions to end discrimination, since it gave them a better sense of what would and would not be acceptable to enforcement agencies. Federal officials also pressed to open up apprenticeship programs to African Americans.

The use of targets as part of what came to be called "affirmative action" to overcome past patterns of discrimination raised complex political and legal issues. The federal government had occasionally employed racial targets in hiring before World War II, as had a few private companies being pressured by civil rights groups. But after the war, as some states and cities began passing fair employment laws, race-based remedies were challenged as violations of bans on discrimination in hiring, as the rights of individual white workers were seen as in conflict with the effort to overcome historic discrimination against black workers by giving them preference as a group. As the Johnson administration drew to a close, the comptroller general used this argument to block a proposed plan to desegregate the Philadelphia construction industry by requiring federally funded contractors to submit detailed targets for nonwhite hiring, claiming it violated the 1964 Civil Rights Act.

The Nixon administration included some strong civil rights advocates, like Secretary of Housing and Urban Development George Romney, who wanted to link federal aid for communities to their willingness to racially integrate through the construction of low-income housing. Nixon rejected Romney's plan, which he called "forced integration of suburbs," and made episodic gestures toward racist white southern Republicans. But in the end he supported the continuation and even expansion of federal civil rights efforts. In 1970 he signed an extension of the 1965 Voting Rights Act that applied provisions originally restricted to use in the South to the whole country. (The extension also lowered the voting age to eighteen, reflecting the widely shared view that men who were old enough to fight in Vietnam were old enough to vote.) And Nixon revived the Philadelphia Plan for construction industry desegregation.

Nixon backed the Philadelphia Plan in part because he believed that increased economic opportunities would be a more effective and less disruptive route to black advancement than educational or residential desegregation. (For the same reason, he promoted black entrepreneurship, "Black Capitalism," a conservative form of Black Power.) But he had other motives too. Nixon had become increasingly concerned by rising construction costs, which contributed to overall inflation and had become the subject of a growing pushback by major corporations. By breaking the hold over construction jobs by craft unions, many of which excluded or largely excluded nonwhites, Nixon hoped to check labor costs. In doing so, he relished the opportunity to drive a wedge between civil rights groups, which supported affirmative action, and the elements of the labor movement that opposed it, playing two of his political opponents against one another.

The Philadelphia Plan proved moderately successful in opening up construction jobs to black workers, but Nixon's support for it proved short-lived. In 1970 he began wooing white blue-collar voters and their union leaders, seeing them as a base of support for his unpopular Vietnam policies and a bloc that the Republicans might win over in the 1972 election. His administration moved away from specific hiring goals and timetables in construction contracting to voluntary agreements to increase training opportunities for black workers. But by then, affirmative action had gained legitimacy within the federal government, with various agencies requiring affirmative action plans as part of contracting procedures in industries other than construction.

Affirmative action got a boost in 1971 when the Supreme Court upheld the use of results-oriented targets in employment practices in *Griggs v. Duke Power Co.* The Court agreed with the Nixon administration that civil rights laws did not require all government policies to be race blind. Affirmative action, initially deployed to upgrade economic opportunities for African Americans, began to be used to assist other groups as well, particularly Hispanics, Native Americans, and Asians. It became entrenched in the academic world when Nixon maintained the requirement, begun under Johnson, that colleges and universities receiving federal aid draft affirmative action plans for recruiting female and minority students and employees. By the time Nixon left office, affirmative action had become woven into the everyday practices of myriad public and private institutions, even as it came under attack from those who saw it as an infringement on the rights and opportunities of whites.

Like affirmative action, bilingual education ballooned as a result of a combination of partisan politics, bureaucratic initiative, ethnic mobilization, and court decisions. In 1967, Senator Ralph Yarborough, a Texas

Democrat seeking to curry Mexican American votes, introduced a measure for federal funding of bilingual education programs, which went into law but received scant money from the Johnson administration. Seeking to do something for Hispanic voters, the Nixon administration modestly raised funding for bilingual education. More importantly, it repositioned it as a civil rights issue. In 1970, the Department of Health, Education and Welfare issued a regulation applying to all school districts receiving federal funds that had more than 5 percent "National Origin–Minority Group Children." If inability to speak or understand English excluded these children from "effective participation" in schooling, a district had to take "affirmative steps to rectify the language deficiency." Under pressure from Washington, with backing from Mexican American lobbying groups, this generally meant bilingual programs, in which basic subject matter was taught in languages other than English, even though no research existed to demonstrate their educational efficacy. A 1974 Supreme Court ruling, upholding this regulation, led to a large-scale expansion of bilingual education. In just a few years, a real problem—school districts that dealt with non-English-speaking students by sticking them in classes conducted in a language they did not understand—had been identified and addressed with little public discussion, using what would become a highly controversial solution. Nixon, motivated in part, but only in part, by political considerations, did not hesitate to vastly expand the role of the federal government in shaping local educational practices in the name of civil rights.

War and Détente

Richard Nixon took office at a time when the global power of the United States was in relative decline. During the previous two decades, the extreme economic dominance that the United States held as a result of World War II had greatly diminished, as Europe, Japan, and the Soviet Union recovered from the enormous damage they suffered during the war. Germany and Japan, in particular, rebuilt their industrial capacity, adopted advanced technology, and established social arrangements that made them formidable competitors to the United States. In 1971, West Germany sold more manufactured goods outside its borders than did the United States. That year, for the first time since 1893, the United States imported more goods and services than it exported.

Over time, the overhead costs of maintaining international hegemony and contesting the Soviet Union took their toll. The expense of a large overseas military force, the cost of the war in Vietnam, and the skewing of domestic investment toward defense industries contributed to rising inflation, decreasing competitiveness, and international pressure on the dollar. And no letup was in sight; the Soviet Union, through massive military investments, had all but caught up to the United States in its nuclear arsenal. For the first time since the beginning of the atomic age, the United States no longer had vast superiority in nuclear war-fighting capacity.

Nixon believed that the country's foreign policy needed to be rethought in the light of the changed international distribution of power. Better informed about world politics than most presidents, in some respects he served as his own secretary of state, though his pompous, self-promoting national security adviser, Henry Kissinger (who also served as secretary of state in his second administration), did much of the legwork and received much of the credit for his foreign policy. Nixon and Kissinger recognized that it no longer made sense to structure foreign policy around the assumption of a bipolar world of U.S.- and Soviet-led blocs struggling for supremacy. Within the capitalist world, the Western European countries, as their economic power grew, began asserting greater autonomy from the United States, evident, among other ways, in their refusal to provide military or in many cases even political support for the American effort in Vietnam. Within the communist world, China had long been asserting its independence from the Soviet Union—in 1969 the countries had serious military clashes along their border—but only with the Nixon administration did the United States make the Sino-Soviet split central to its diplomatic conduct. Rather than a bifurcated global polity, the Nixon administration saw a world dominated by a group of big powers: the United States, the Soviet Union, China, Western Europe, and Japan. Nixon and Kissinger, much like George Kennan two decades earlier, believed that the United States could ensure its national security and promote its interests by establishing, through diplomacy, a balance of power among them. That would entail dropping ideological combat to improve relations with the Soviet Union. It also meant taking a much bolder step that Nixon had been contemplating during his years out of office—establishing a relationship with China, which the United States had treated as a pariah since 1949. Improved relations with the two communist giants would allow the United States to play them off against one another and, Kissinger and Nixon believed, provide leverage to pressure them to cooperate with the United States on a whole range of issues.

What in retrospect appeared as a grand strategy did not emerge whole cloth but developed in response to specific challenges the Nixon administration faced, especially the war in Vietnam. Nixon took office determined not to suffer the fate of his predecessor by allowing the war to dominate or destroy his administration. He believed that he could quickly wind it down, in a matter of months or a year.

Nixon's desire to end the war did not mean that he had any intention to unilaterally withdraw from Vietnam or agree to a settlement that did not leave the incumbent South Vietnamese government in place. A communist victory, he believed, would be a domestic political disaster and undermine the credibility of the country with its allies and enemies. Credibility, rather than any geostrategic calculus or claims about democracy and freedom, dominated the justification of the war under Nixon, as the reasons for it became ever more abstract. Nixon thought he could square the circle, win the war, or at least not lose it, while lowering its profile and drain on resources.

To the extent that Nixon had a plan to do this, it had four components. First, believing that the war ultimately would have to be settled through negotiations, in August 1969 he had Kissinger begin secret talks in Paris with the North Vietnamese, hoping that they might be more fruitful than the public negotiations that had begun under Johnson. Second, Nixon and Kissinger assumed that the Vietnamese communists would make concessions only if they faced continuing military pressure and the threat of its escalation. Fighting in Vietnam remained at a high level during Nixon's first year in office, with more than ten thousand Americans killed (as many as had died in 1967). While Nixon continued Johnson's bombing halt over much of North Vietnam, he intensified bombing elsewhere in Indochina, stepping up the bombing of Laos and, not long after taking office, beginning a bombing campaign in Cambodia aimed at disrupting Vietnamese communist supply routes. Nixon kept the Cambodia attacks secret from the public, Congress, and even most of his own military establishment.

Third, as much as Nixon wanted to keep up military pressure, he believed that he could not maintain public support for existing troop levels, draft calls, and casualty rates for very long. To reduce the need for ground forces, Nixon increased the role of the South Vietnamese army in the fighting, a policy that Secretary of Defense Melvin Laird dubbed "Vietnamization." The U.S. presence in Vietnam went from 543,400 troops in the spring of 1969 to just 24,400 at the end of 1972. The South Vietnamese communists proved unable to take immediate advantage of the American withdrawals because of the losses they suffered during the Tet offensive, low morale, and an increased dependence on North Vietnamese soldiers to replenish their strength. To further lower political pressure to end the war, Nixon moved the draft to a lottery system, which eliminated much of its class favoritism, and announced his intention to institute an all-volunteer Army. Draft calls diminished and in September 1971 ended entirely.

The final piece of Nixon's Vietnam strategy was to seek assistance from the communist superpowers in ending the war. While rhetorically Kennedy and Johnson portrayed the war as part of a global struggle against communism, in practice they sought to win it in Vietnam itself through the application of military and political strategies designed to deal with localized conflicts. The Nixon administration, by contrast, saw superpower diplomacy as the solution to the war, at least in part. In private talks, the administration conveyed to the Soviet Union its interest in improving relations but suggested that progress in that direction would be dependent on cooperation in ending the Vietnam War on terms acceptable to the United States. The United States also suggested that if the Soviets were not cooperative, the United States would reach out to China. (China had been the largest supplier of military equipment and assistance to North Vietnam until 1969, when the Soviet Union took over that role.)

By the fall of 1969, it became clear to the Nixon administration that no quick end to the war was in sight. The Soviets rejected linking Vietnam to other issues, and the North Vietnamese remained unbudged in private talks. Nixon considered escalating the air assault on North Vietnam but backed off in the face of internal administration dissent, the largest and broadest-based antiwar demonstrations yet, and doubts that it would bring any major breakthrough. But Nixon felt he had to do something; with U.S. troop levels in Vietnam slowly dropping, he feared that the communists would simply wait the United States out, refusing to compromise in negotiations. So he tried to signal to the North Vietnamese the consequences of not making concessions by military escalations elsewhere in Indochina. In February 1970, the United States launched a bombing campaign in northern Laos using its heaviest bombers, B-52s, designed to disrupt Vietnamese supply lines that ran through the region and support the neutralist Laotian government, which faced pressure from communist forces. Two months later, South Vietnamese and American forces launched a combined attack into a region of Cambodia bordering Vietnam, which ultimately involved thirty-one thousand U.S. troops. Nixon sought to bolster the new Cambodian government of General Lon Nol, disrupt Vietnamese communist sanctuaries and command centers, and again indicate his determination not to yield in any resolution of the war.

Nixon's April 30 announcement of the invasion of Cambodia set off one of the largest and most intense waves of protest in the nation's history. Within days, colleges all over the country were being shut down by strikes and rocked by demonstrations. The murder of four students at Kent State University on May 4 by Ohio National Guardsmen turned the rapidly growing surge of protest into a tsunami.

The Cambodia invasion protests stood out by many measures. Their sheer size stunned the White House, the nation, and the protestors themselves. Protests took place on more than 80 percent of the nation's nearly three thousand colleges and universities, with five hundred crippled by strikes. Some four million students and 350,000 faculty members took part in protest activity of one sort or another. On less than a week's notice, 100,000 people assembled at a rally in Washington, D.C. Most of the protests were organized by local groups, as the largest left-wing national student organization, SDS, had fragmented the previous year (with one segment turning itself into the violent Weathermen).

The Cambodia protests were remarkable not only for their scale but also for their militancy and the fierce battles they entailed. While on many campuses protests remained peaceful, at scores of others running battles took place with police or National Guardsmen (called out at two dozen campuses in sixteen states). During May, over a hundred protestors were shot by law enforcement officers or guardsmen. Meanwhile, an epidemic of bombing and arson broke out on and near campuses. In the first week of May alone, thirty ROTC buildings were burned or bombed, including at Case Western, Ohio State, Tulane, St. Louis University, and Kentucky. Bombings and arson became almost daily occurrences in Lawrence, Kansas, not the sort of place that generally had been associated with student protest or antiwar activity. But in many ways, Lawrence was typical of the sites of protest in May 1970, as the whole social geography of student activism and antiwar sentiment changed. Earlier student protests had tended to take place at elite colleges or flagship state universities. The May 1970 strikes and demonstrations took place at every conceivable type of college (and many high schools too), including community colleges, religious schools, schools with heavily working-class student bodies like Kent State, and historically black colleges, including Mississippi's Jackson State University, where on May 7 police opened fire on a women's dormitory, killing two students.

Off campus, too, protests drew a broader cross section of society than any previous antiwar actions. Vietnam veterans became a very visible presence at demonstrations. Forty-three Nobel Prize winners wrote to the president urging him to immediately end the war. Labor leaders and corporate executives formed antiwar groups. Twelve hundred Wall Street lawyers went to Washington to lobby against the war.

The protests against Nixon constituted a national crisis, but they by no means represented a national consensus. In New York, construction workers went on a rampage, violently attacking student antiwar demonstrators and anyone who seemed to be sympathetic to them, as the police stood by doing little to stop the carnage. Soon "hard hat" demonstrations became an almost daily occurrence in New York and spread to several other cities, as much an explosion of class resentment at what the construction workers saw as privileged protestors as a measure of working-class support for the war. Nationally, polls showed an increase in support for the president, in part a rejection of the protests and chaos that followed the Cambodian invasion.

In Congress, the invasion of Cambodia and the reaction to it bolstered opposition to the war. The introduction of a flurry of measures to check military action in Indochina contributed to Nixon's decision to pull all U.S. troops out of Cambodia by the end of June, without having had decisive military impact. Congressional critics of the war won a symbolic victory at the end of the year with the repeal of the Tonkin Gulf resolution, and a more practical check on the war with a ban on the use of military appropriations for any further U.S. ground operations in Cambodia or Laos. With the consensus that had sustained the Cold War shattered, Nixon faced the real possibility of congressional action to end the war.

Initially, Nixon made some gestures of accommodation toward the massive wave of antiwar protests, which had taken him by surprise. In the wee hours of the morning of May 9, he went to the Lincoln Memorial to meet students gathered for an antiwar demonstration, trying to talk about football and surfing to the dumbfounded protestors. Afterward, he went over to the Executive Office Building to speak to soldiers camped out to protect the White House from feared antiwar assaults. It was, the president's chief of staff wrote in his diary, "the weirdest day so far."

But Nixon quickly abandoned the idea of trying to appease his critics. Once he announced the Cambodia withdrawal, the nation slowly moved toward resuming business as usual. Looking forward, Nixon began aligning himself with the populist right in an effort to cement a new electoral coalition. Some of the more liberal figures in his administration either resigned or were forced out, while Vice President Agnew became the mouthpiece for attacks on student protestors, liberal elites, and the news media in an effort to mobilize an electoral coalition that the president hoped would include white workers, southerners, and Catholics as well as more traditional Republican voters, what Nixon had taken to calling the "Silent Majority."

At least in the short run, it did not work. In spite of a major administration effort, in November 1970 the Democrats lost only two seats in the Senate while picking up nine in the House. Administration supporters failed to oust a single prominent congressional critic of the war.

Vietnam now hung over Nixon's head, just as it hung over Johnson's. To buy time, he continued to simultaneously reduce American troop levels and launch periodic new offensives, including a U.S.-supported South Vietnamese invasion of southern Laos in February 1971, aimed at communist supply bases. (The recently passed congressional spending restriction kept U.S. ground troops from joining in.) Meanwhile, Nixon's effort to reconfigure the architecture of the Cold War began yielding results, which he hoped would lead to an acceptable settlement in Vietnam.

In April 1971, following indirect signals between the United States and China that they might be open to establishing some sort of diplomatic relationship, after being almost entirely cut off from one another for over two decades, China invited a U.S. Ping-Pong team to visit. A secret trip to Beijing by Kissinger followed, laying the groundwork for a presidential visit the following February. Nixon's trip represented a dramatic reversal of the long-established American policy of refusing to accept the legitimacy of the 1949 communist victory of the Chinese Revolution. It began a process that would culminate in formal recognition of the People's Republic of China in 1979 and a growing range of political, economic, and even military ties.

Just three months later, Nixon traveled to Moscow. Soviet leaders, fearful of improved U.S.-China relations and worried by a stagnating economy and an extraordinarily expensive arms race, proved as eager as Nixon to forge an improved relationship, what soon got dubbed "détente." At their summit, Nixon and Soviet leader Leonid Brezhnev signed the Strategic Arms Limitation Treaty (SALT I), the first arms control measure that the United States had agreed to since the start of the Cold War. SALT I had great symbolic importance but only limited practical effect. The treaty froze the number of missiles the two countries could deploy and severely restricted the installation of antiballistic missile systems but did not control the deployment of multiple warheads on a single missile (MIRVs), a technology in which the United States had the lead. With MIRVs, a single U.S. submarine could deliver the equivalent of 160 Hiroshima-strength bombs. The two countries also signed an agreement to facilitate trade and commercial relations, under which the Soviet Union made a massive purchase of U.S. grain, including one-quarter of the entire 1972 crop of wheat.

Nixon's diplomatic breakthroughs with China and the Soviet Union brought a dramatic easing of big power tensions. Many hailed Nixon as a statesman of the highest stature for breaking with his own past anticommunism to seek mutually beneficial agreements with the countries that had long been designated as the main U.S. foes. Nixon made what had been almost unthinkable seem natural. Until him, no U.S. president had set foot in a communist nation, except for Roosevelt's brief trip to Yalta during World War II. Within just a few months, Nixon journeyed to both China and the

Soviet Union in visits full of ceremonial expressions of goodwill and massive coverage by the media, much of it carefully orchestrated by the White House.

Nixon's willingness to reach accords with the communist superpowers did not represent an end to American anticommunism. Rather, it reflected his belief that the basic status of Eastern Europe, the Soviet Union, and China could not be changed. Where social and political conditions remained fluid, the Nixon administration pursued a highly interventionist course. Improved relations with China and the Soviet Union were intended, in part, to provide greater freedom of action in such situations, since any countermoves by the communist powers might be checked by a threat to withdraw trade and other concessions, what Kissinger liked to call "linkage."

The continued U.S. intolerance for left-wing regimes, especially if democratically elected, played out most starkly in Chile. In the fall of 1970, Salvador Allende, a left-wing socialist, won the presidency of Chile with a plurality of the popular vote in a three-way contest. Determined to prevent another Marxist regime from taking root in Latin America, Nixon authorized the CIA to keep Allende from being inaugurated using any means necessary. "No impression," Nixon said at a NSC meeting, "should be permitted in Latin America that they can get away with this, that it's safe to go this way." Kissinger, his deputy, Alexander Haig, and the CIA failed in their attempt to organize a military coup to keep Allende from taking office, but thereafter the United States moved covertly to undermine his government, funding opposition groups, economically isolating the country, promoting disruptions of all kinds, and cultivating the military. When military leaders did launch a coup in 1973, they knew that they would have the support of the United States, which backed the ensuing dictatorship even as it conducted a prolonged campaign of torture and murder against its opponents.

While superpower diplomacy might have bought the United States some freedom of action in patrolling the noncommunist bloc to stamp out any moves toward the left, it did little to help with the war in Vietnam. The Soviet Union and China proved willing to pursue improved relations with the United States even at moments when it escalated the war, but they were not willing to cut off supplies to the Vietnamese communists or make more than token efforts to pressure them to end the war on terms favorable to the United States. Still, with Nixon continuing to reduce U.S. troop levels in Indochina, U.S. casualty rates going down, fighting at a low level compared to the past, and the draft ended, the Vietnam War diminished as a domestic political issue, even as negotiations with the Vietnamese communists failed to make progress.

Then, in the spring of 1972, the communists launched a major offensive in northern South Vietnam, relying heavily on conventional North

Vietnamese forces. After making significant initial gains, the offensive bogged down, in part because of the improved fighting capacity of the South Vietnamese army and in part because of the massive tactical use of American airpower. Nixon also launched a major air campaign against North Vietnam that included mining its harbors, as his rage at the inability of the United States to defeat "those little cocksuckers" exploded. "For once," he told his top aides, "we've got to use the maximum power of this country . . . against this shit-ass little country: to win the war."

But in spite of one B-52 air attack after another, victory, as always, proved elusive. So with the military situation again stalemated and the U.S. presidential election looming, secret negotiations between the United States and North Vietnam intensified, as both sides saw an advantage in achieving a cease-fire and withdrawal of U.S. forces. In late October, the two countries secretly reached an agreement for an immediate cease-fire in place in South Vietnam, an end to U.S. bombing of North Vietnam, a withdrawal of all U.S. troops from Vietnam within sixty days, the release of American prisoners of war, a commitment to the peaceful reunification of Vietnam, the establishment of a new administrative structure that would include communists to organize new elections in South Vietnam, and contributions by the United States to the postwar reconstruction of North Vietnam. But in the face of objections from South Vietnamese president Nguyen Van Thieu, the United States balked at signing the tentative pact without changes to reassure him. (The National Liberation Front also criticized the pact for its failure to provide for a release of its civilian cadre imprisoned in South Vietnam.) At that point, the North Vietnamese and then the United States publicly announced the outline of the near settlement. Putting a positive spin on the situation, with less than two weeks before the presidential election, Kissinger proclaimed, "We believe peace is at hand."

The 1972 Election

Nixon did not need a completed peace treaty to win reelection. His meetings in Beijing and Moscow and the troop withdrawals from Indochina had helped put him in a strong political position. So did his handling of the economy, which largely postponed the detrimental effects of the Vietnam War and the deteriorating international position of the country.

Though by later standards the economy during Nixon's first term remained robust, both inflation and unemployment exceeded the very low levels of the early and mid-1960s, as the country suffered through a recession in 1970 and a slow recovery the next year. Organized labor, still powerful, responded to rising prices by pressing for large wage increases and other gains. A combination of confidence from years of economic growth and uncertainty about the future made workers exceptionally combative. In 1970, the country lost a higher percentage of working time to strikes than in any year since 1952 (not counting 1959, when the massive steel strike pushed the figure off the charts).

Many of the strikes of the period were unusual in their size, targets, and militancy. In March 1970, post office workers in New York City walked off their jobs, demanding a larger wage increase than agreed to by their national leader and the right to strike, which as federal employees they did not have. The illegal walkout quickly spread across the country until 200,000 postal workers had stopped work in the largest public employee strike in the nation's history. Nixon sent twenty-five thousand unarmed National Guardsmen and reservists to New York, the first time since 1894 that federal troops had been deployed to try to break a strike blocking mail delivery. The walkout ended only when the administration agreed to a double-digit pay increase, a formal collective bargaining procedure, and other concessions. The next month, forty thousand coal miners launched a wildcat strike demanding hospital and pension benefits for disabled workers. In the fall, more than 350,000 workers struck General Motors for nine weeks in one of the largest strikes since the post–World War II strike wave.

The spread of rights consciousness and the culture of protest to workers, especially young, female, and African American workers, contributed to the labor upsurge. Public employees began joining unions in large numbers, sometimes in defiance of state or local laws. In many cases, the public-sector organizing drives had strong ties to the civil rights movement. The antiauthoritarian spirit of the New Left infected labor too, as workers, far more frequently than during the previous two decades, rejected contracts, voted out leaders, and struck without official sanction. The National Guardsmen who shot the students at Kent State had just recently finished patrolling the highways of eastern Ohio, where Teamsters conducting a wildcat strike had taken to shooting at trucks driven by scabs.

Nixon tried to avoid a head-on confrontation with organized labor over inflationary wage settlements, valuing the support he found among unionists for his Vietnam policy and hoping to woo blue-collar workers away from the Democrats. But when the continuing deterioration of the balance of payments converged with inflation, Nixon decided he had to act. In August 1971, he announced what he dubbed his "New Economic Policy" (NEP). To stimulate the economy, he proposed a series of tax cuts. To check inflation, which he blamed on Vietnam, he took the startling step of imposing wage and price controls, a move that horrified many conservatives (though not business, which understood that in practice controls would primarily mean a check on organized labor). To deal with the balance of payments problem, Nixon simply ended the "gold window" that allowed foreign-held dollars to be redeemed at a fixed price. This in turn allowed a devaluation of the dollar, aimed at making exports cheaper and imports more expensive. To further address the trade imbalance and woo manufacturing workers, Nixon imposed a 10 percent surcharge on imported goods. In effect, Nixon threw out orthodox free-market/free-trade economics in recognition of diminished American hegemony and, more immediately, his need to position the economy to boost his reelection chances.

It worked. Probably the economy would have improved anyway, but the combination of the NEP measures, an easy credit policy by the Federal Reserve, and a spurt of federal spending in early 1972 revived the economy, lowered unemployment, and pushed down the inflation rate. Though organized labor resented federal restraints on wage boosts, Nixon shrewdly retained considerable union backing by paying attention to other labor issues and stressing the conservative social values that he shared with many workers. One major federal report sympathetically addressed the depth of worker alienation in terms not much different from those employed by the New Left, while another documented the job loss that would result from cuts to military spending advocated by Nixon's liberal critics.

Nixon helped himself in the 1972 campaign but so did discord among the Democrats (though the president had a hand in that too). In the aftermath of its 1968 convention, the party adopted new rules, developed by a committee headed by South Dakota senator George McGovern, that democratized the nomination process, limited the influence of the traditional power brokers, and mandated an increase in young, female, and nonwhite delegates. The reforms deepened the split within the party between liberal activists and the city bosses, labor leaders, and officeholders who had long dominated it. After a hard-fought primary fight, McGovern, who strongly opposed the war and generally positioned himself on the left of the party, emerged as the nominee. The Nixon campaign contributed to McGovern's success by launching a large covert operation that disrupted the campaigns of his rivals, believing that he would be the easiest Democrat to beat. Nixon may have also played a role, through a covert deal, in George Wallace's decision to run for the Democratic nomination rather than as an independent, eliminating Nixon's fear that a three-way race might end up being decided in the House of Representatives, where the Democrats had the advantage.

McGovern proved to be an inept candidate. He picked a vice presidential running mate, Missouri senator Thomas Eagleton, who turned out to have had a history of treatment for mental illness, first defending him and then ditching him. He never found a way to rebut the Nixon campaign portrayal of him as a left-winger out of touch with the country. Some prominent conservative and centrist Democrats deserted him, much as moderate and liberal Republicans had deserted Goldwater in 1964. For the first time in its history, the AFL-CIO did not endorse a presidential candidate, a huge boost for Nixon, while some southern Democratic governors, including Georgia's Jimmy Carter, refused to back their party's nominee. Meanwhile, the Nixon campaign vastly outspent and nimbly outmaneuvered McGovern.

When the 1972 campaign began, it looked like the presidential race might be close. It ended in a blowout. Nixon won over 60 percent of the popular vote and carried every state except Massachusetts. Just as he hoped, Nixon won big chunks of voters who had traditionally backed the Democrats, including white southerners, Catholics (he was the first Republican presidential candidate to win a majority of Catholic votes), and union members. But Nixon had no coattails, as the Republicans lost two seats in the Senate and, with a gain of only a dozen seats in the House, remained a decidedly minority party in both houses of Congress. The mixed election results reflected the uncertainty and instability of national politics in the early 1970s, as both the democratic revolution and the conservative upsurge had broad public support.

Out of Vietnam

With the election over, Nixon returned to a piece of unfinished business, the war in Vietnam. When the United States tried to modify its tentative agreement with North Vietnam, the communists held fast and negotiations broke down. On December 18, 1972, the United States launched a massive bombing campaign against the Hanoi-Haiphong area. Ostensibly designed to force the North Vietnamese back to negotiations, the renewed offensive also was meant to send a message to both the North and South Vietnamese that the United States would not hesitate to resume the air war if the communists violated any agreement they ultimately signed. The eleven-day bombing campaign caused widespread destruction, killed over two thousand civilians, and provoked worldwide protests. To the surprise of American leaders, it also proved costly to their own forces, as concentrated North Vietnamese air defenses proved effective in downing U.S. aircraft, including fifteen massive B-52 bombers. Well over a hundred U.S. airmen were killed or captured in what was widely called the "Christmas bombing."

When the North Vietnamese agreed to resume negotiations, the two sides quickly finalized a settlement similar except in details to the one they had

come to in November, and for that matter not much different from a proposal the communists had put forth in 1969. The agreement was signed in
Paris on January 23, 1973. All parties, the South Vietnamese government
and the NLF as well as the United States and North Vietnam, expected that
many of its painstakingly negotiated provisions would be quickly violated
by one side or the other, as they were. But the communists and the United
States abided by the clauses that required the release of American POWs and
the withdrawal of U.S. military forces from Vietnam, steps accomplished by
the end of March 1973. Nixon did not see the agreement as ending the American military role in Indochina or sealing the fate of the South Vietnamese
government. In early 1973 the United States continued bombing communist
forces in Cambodia and Nixon fully intended to resume bombing Vietnam
using aircraft based on carriers or in other countries in the event of a communist offensive that threatened the survival of the Thieu regime. But even
many members of his administration recognized that with Congress moving
toward cutting off funds for operations in Indochina and the public long
wearied of the conflict, at the least for the United States, the war was essentially over. In 1946, Ho Chi Minh told the French, "You will kill ten of our
men and we will kill one of yours. In the end, it will be you who will tire of
it." Ho turned out to be right about the French, and right about the Americans too.

CHAPTER 11

The End of the American Century

Richard Nixon did not have much time to enjoy his landslide reelection or the Paris Peace Treaty that got U.S. troops and prisoners out of Vietnam. Almost immediately his presidency started to unravel, as the details of illegal political activities directed by the White House began to come out. Soon, Nixon, his aides, and the whole federal government became enveloped in a political and constitutional crisis with little precedent. In delayed fashion, the consequences of using the power of the state in ways that had become routine during the Cold War took their toll. National divisions, stemming from the Vietnam War and the political mobilizations of the 1960s, undermined the elite consensus needed to sustain imperial rule. As the inner workings and moral standards of the state became exposed, only removing its leaders could restore its authority.

Nixon's fall constituted but one piece of a general crisis the United States entered soon after his reelection. After decades of sustained economic growth, the country slipped into a period of deep recession and economic uncertainty. Its diminished capacity to control world events, made evident by its defeat in Vietnam, contributed to the problem, as rising international commodity prices forced unwanted changes in life at home. By the mid-1970s, the economic and political structures that had brought wealth and power to the United States for a quarter century after World War II no longer could sustain economic progress, domestic harmony, or international dominance. One period of the country's history came to an end, with the shape of the next still very unclear.

Watergate

On June 17, 1972, the Washington, D.C., police arrested five men in the act of breaking into the Democratic National Committee headquarters, located in an upscale office, hotel, and apartment complex on the Potomac River, the Watergate. The burglary team had illegally entered the office a few weeks earlier to tap its phones, but their eavesdropping equipment had not worked properly, so they were trying again. The burglars had been hired by the Nixon campaign, part of a large-scale effort to spy on and disrupt the Democratic Party during the 1972 election. The campaign of "dirty tricks" was directed and financed out of the White House, with the knowledge and approval of top leaders of the administration, including the president.

The police quickly discovered that one of the Watergate burglars was the chief of security for the president's reelection committee, that all five had worked for the CIA, and that they received money from E. Howard Hunt, a former CIA operative who worked in the White House. But the refusal of the arrested men to reveal information about their operation, public denials by the president and his aides that they had anything to do with it, and the destruction of evidence and obstruction of investigations by White House and campaign officials kept the break-in from becoming a major election issue.

In early 1973, the White House–orchestrated cover-up of who ordered, directed, and financed the Watergate operation began falling apart. First, Senate Democrats forced the appointment of a bipartisan committee to investigate the case, chaired by conservative North Carolina Democrat Sam Ervin. Then, in March, one of the burglars, James McCord, wrote to federal district judge John J. Sirica, who had presided over the trial in which he had been convicted, claiming that perjury had been committed and that the defendants had been pressured to maintain their silence. In response, Sirica imposed heavy sentences on the seven men who had pled or been found guilty of planning and carrying out the break-in. But he held out the possibility of leniency if they cooperated with the Senate and other investigations. McCord soon began talking to Senate and Justice Department investigators, which caused other vulnerable officials, most importantly the president's counsel, John Dean, who had coordinated the cover-up, to begin trying to cut their own deals. The press, which had largely ignored or downplayed the Watergate story, with the important exception of Carl Bernstein and Bob Woodward at the *Washington Post,* began to barrage the administration with questions. More and more information about Watergate and other covert

White House doings began leaking out, as Nixon's advisers maneuvered to set one another up to take the fall, including the revelation that the acting head of the FBI had personally destroyed potential evidence taken from Hunt's White House safe on orders from a presidential aide.

On April 30, 1973, Nixon announced the resignations of his two closest assistants, John Ehrlichman and H. R. Haldeman, and fired John Dean, all linked to Watergate in one way or another. Attorney General Richard Kleindienst, who had close ties to many of the officials under investigation, including his predecessor, John Mitchell, the head of Nixon's reelection committee, also resigned. Two weeks later, the new attorney general, Elliot Richardson, appointed a special prosecutor to handle the Watergate case, Harvard law professor Archibald Cox. Meanwhile, the Senate Select Committee began holding televised hearings, where a parade of witnesses, including Dean, linked top White House and Nixon campaign officials to the Watergate break-in and Nixon himself to the payment of hush money to the burglars. Testimony also revealed other White House plots involving break-ins, wiretaps, and—though not carried out—arson. In July, a White House aide told the committee about a secret taping system that Nixon had installed in his offices. The committee promptly subpoenaed tape recordings that they hoped would resolve the conflict between charges against Nixon made by Dean and others and his denials, the first time a congressional committee had ever issued a subpoena to the president. Nixon refused to turn the tapes over to the Senate or to Cox, who also subpoenaed them.

While Cox's subpoena worked its way through the courts, a surprise development weakened Nixon's hold on his office. In August 1973, reporters learned that a federal grand jury in Baltimore was investigating charges that Spiro Agnew had taken kickbacks from contractors while governor of Maryland. He continued to accept cash even as vice president. On October 10, he pleaded nolo contendere to a charge of tax evasion in connection to the bribes and resigned. Agnew and Nixon had presented themselves as morally superior to their political enemies, to liberals, intellectuals, disorderly students, critics of the war, and protestors of all kinds. Now, it turned out, Agnew was a common criminal, a corrupt politician taking money in return for favors. It then came out that Nixon had taken large tax deductions for which he was not qualified by backdating transactions and that the government had spent over a million dollars improving his homes in California and Florida. In November 1973, he told a group of newspaper editors that "people have got to know whether their president is a crook. Well, I am not a crook." His need to address the issue in such terms greatly diminished him.

With Nixon and Agnew having achieved power portraying themselves as advocates of law and order and defenders of the nation's moral standing, the revelations of their greed and personal corruption proved devastating.

The Twenty-Fifth Amendment to the Constitution, put into place after John Kennedy's assassination, specified that a vice presidential vacancy be filled by presidential appointment, subject to congressional approval. Nixon chose as Agnew's replacement House minority leader Gerald R. Ford, a loyalist who would face no problem being confirmed. Many of the president's critics had considered Agnew a worse alternative, but with Ford in place the idea of forcing Nixon out became more imaginable.

Just after Agnew resigned, an appeals court upheld the special prosecutor's subpoena. When Cox refused to accept an arrangement Nixon proposed that would have given him only tape summaries and restricted further tape requests, Nixon ordered the attorney general to fire him. Refusing, Elliot Richardson instead resigned. The deputy attorney general would not oust Cox either. Finally, the third in command, the solicitor general, removed the special prosecutor. A massive public outcry ensued. In the heat of the moment, as the television networks broadcast images of FBI agents sealing off Cox's office and keeping out his staff, many people believed that the very structures of constitutional government were crumbling. The House of Representatives launched an inquiry into the possibility of impeachment, and Nixon found himself forced to appoint a new special prosecutor and agree to turn over the subpoenaed tapes to Judge Sirica.

The tapes haunted Nixon, first in his refusal to release them and then by what they revealed. In April 1974, after the House Judiciary Committee, as part of its impeachment inquiry, also demanded recordings, Nixon finally made public a batch of transcripts. They revealed an ugly picture of a mean-spirited president prone to vulgarity and rambling, obsessed with enemies, racist and anti-Semitic, and clearly involved, at least to some extent, in the illegal activities of his administration and efforts to cover them up. The intimate view of Nixon so differed from the public persona he projected that his credibility collapsed.

Not satisfied with what had been released, the special prosecutor asked for more tapes. Nixon refused, leading to a court test of his ability to withhold material on the grounds of "executive privilege." On July 24, 1974, the Supreme Court, while upholding the previously untested notion that the president could unilaterally withhold information about confidential deliberations, ruled unanimously that in this case other considerations outweighed that right. On the very night of the ruling, the Judiciary Committee began a televised debate of impeachment. Two days later, it voted twenty-seven to eleven for an article of impeachment charging the president with obstruction of justice, later adding two more articles.

On August 5, complying with the Supreme Court decision, Nixon released a tape transcript, which he had jealously guarded, of his discussions two years earlier with Haldeman, in which he ordered his aide to have the CIA tell the FBI to call off its investigation of Watergate because it would jeopardize national security. The recorded conversation provided direct proof that the president had used a government agency, under false pretenses, to try to block an investigation of illegal political activities, precisely the obstruction of justice the impeachment articles accused him of. The tape also made clear that Nixon had repeatedly lied in his public statements about his role in Watergate.

Many Republicans, including Vice President Ford, had continued to defend Nixon even as congressional Democrats moved toward trying to remove him. That all but ended with the release of the "smoking gun" transcript. With impeachment a certainty and conviction in the Senate highly likely, on August 8, 1974, Nixon announced his resignation effective the next day, the only time in American history that a president had left office before the end of his term.

Nixon's conduct alone cannot explain this extraordinary outcome. Nixon later claimed, in a typically self-pitying passage, that he only acted within established norms: "I played by the rules of politics as I found them. Not taking the higher road than my predecessors and my adversaries was my central mistake." Too kind to himself, he nonetheless touched on a partial truth. The growth of the national security state during the Cold War had created the apparatus, opportunity, and even to some extent necessity for the kind of abuses that Nixon had engaged in. Prior presidents had paved the way. But Nixon's contempt for the law came at a moment when changed circumstances led to unexpected consequences.

To fight the Cold War, government officials had created and expanded police and intelligence agencies with covert operational capacities, exempt from public oversight, and promulgated an ideology that justified virtually any action by them in the name of anticommunism and national security. For the CIA, violating its charter and the law became routine, from its penetration of domestic political groups under Eisenhower to its massive domestic spying program under Johnson. The FBI, too, had gone from intelligence gathering and law enforcement to covert activity designed to promote particular political outcomes and eliminate political leaders it disapproved of. None of the Watergate escapades approached the seriousness or moral degeneracy of the secret FBI campaign during the Johnson administration to destroy Martin Luther King Jr. The Cold War not only provided the ideological soil for executive power unchecked by law, it also created the raw material for its execution in the operatives, hangers-on, thugs, and fantasists connected to the CIA and other covert government agencies, including the Watergate burglars and their bosses. For a government that for decades engaged in covert, irregular, and illegal activities directed at those defined as enemies abroad, it came to seem natural to use similar tactics against those defined as enemies at home.

As president, Nixon first turned to irregular and illegal methods not for partisan purposes but in his effort to pursue the increasingly unpopular war in Indochina. The 1969 *New York Times* revelation that the United States was conducting a secret bombing campaign in Cambodia led Nixon and Kissinger to launch a program of unauthorized wiretaps on National Security Council staff members, journalists, and even the military aide to the secretary of defense to try to find out who had leaked the information. The 1971 unauthorized publication of the Pentagon Papers, a massive secret government study of how and why the United States got entangled in Vietnam, which included hundreds of pages of classified documents, led Nixon to create the capacity within the White House itself for cloak-and-dagger operations. One of the authors of the Pentagon study, defense consultant Daniel Ellsberg, having grown disillusioned with the war, gave a copy to the *New York Times* (and later to other newspapers), hoping that its publication would undermine support for continued fighting. Though the Pentagon Papers did not deal with the years after Nixon took office, he sought an injunction to suppress their publication. The Supreme Court refused to go along. Furious, Nixon and his aides, in addition to indicting Ellsberg and an associate, set up a crew inside the White House, dubbed the "plumbers," to stop leaks and engage in covert activities. To try to discredit Ellsberg, a team led by Howard Hunt broke into his psychiatrist's office to steal his records. One reason Nixon and his aides paid hush money to Hunt for his role in Watergate was their fear that he would reveal the Ellsberg break-in. Illegality for purposes of state and purposes of partisanship had become completely intertwined.

Past presidents had blurred the line between partisan and governmental activity and used covert methods. But deep social divisions, especially over Vietnam, had ended the consensus within the federal government and institutions of power that kept covert actions covert. After the Paris Peace Treaty, hesitations about undermining a president during wartime became superfluous, and festering grievances bubbled up at an accelerating rate. Democrats pressed the Watergate investigations in part out of anger at the contempt with which Nixon treated Congress, which cost him support among members of his own party too. The acting associate director of the FBI, Mark Felt, resentful of Nixon's treatment of his agency and failure to appoint an insider as director after J. Edgar Hoover died, leaked crucial information about the Watergate scandal to Bob Woodward at the *Washington Post,* which aggressively pursued Nixon, in contrast to its complicity in hiding John Kennedy's covert actions and personal transgressions. The revelation of a list Nixon kept of enemies he sought to punish using the power of government (through tax audits, denial of contracts and licenses, prosecutions, and the like), which included not only radicals and marginal dissenters but also mainstream figures in journalism, politics, labor, and business, mobilized powerful forces against him.

Many people had supported Nixon because they expected him not to be a shrinking violet when it came to reestablishing order and stability. But by 1974, circumstances had changed greatly from his initial election and even his reelection, with the United States out of Vietnam, the wave of urban rioting over, and the radical and countercultural movements of the 1960s in decline. To the extent that there was lawlessness, chaos, and threats to constitutional government, Nixon himself seemed responsible. To a population and national leadership eager to put Vietnam, racial conflict, and youth rebellion behind it, it was the president who appeared as the main obstacle to social and political normality. Leaders in politics, business, and the media perceived the uncertainty and government paralysis that resulted from the prolonged Watergate investigations as detrimental to the country's well-being. Once the alternative to Nixon was neither George McGovern nor Spiro Agnew but Gerald Ford, Nixon seemed expendable, even to many of his onetime supporters. The international and domestic bases for an imperial presidency had collapsed in the face of the overextension of the empire.

The Fall of Saigon

Watergate extinguished whatever dim possibility Nixon and Kissinger might have had for re-escalating the U.S. military effort in Indochina. After the Paris Peace Treaty, the United States continued to send military aid to the South Vietnamese government and bomb communist supply lines in Cambodia. Nixon and Kissinger repeatedly said that if the Vietnamese communists launched an offensive, they would resume bombing Vietnam itself. But strong public distaste for the war and deepening antiwar sentiment in Congress made that unlikely. Watergate made it impossible. In June 1973, Nixon found himself with no choice but to acquiesce to a congressional cutoff of all funds for military action in Indochina, which ended the bombing of Cambodia and the possibility of new attacks on Vietnam. Later that year, Congress passed the War Powers Act, which required the president to give Congress timely notification of any armed action by the United States and get its approval within sixty days, a symbolic step back from the near-unilateral power to make war that presidents had given themselves since the Cold War began. Soon after Nixon resigned, Congress reduced the level of military aid to the South Vietnamese government.

In early 1975, the communists launched a new military offensive. In response, South Vietnamese president Nguyen Van Thieu made an extraordinary blunder, ordering his forces to abandon the entire central highlands in order to concentrate defenses elsewhere. The chaotic retreat led to a rapid collapse in confidence in the Thieu regime, the progressive dissolution of the South Vietnamese army, and a decision by the communists to shift their objective from limited military gain to outright victory. Gerald Ford, still new as president, unsuccessfully tried to get Congress to increase aid to the South Vietnamese. It would not have made a difference. As the South Vietnamese government and army crumbled, all that was left for the United States was to organize a hasty, disorderly evacuation of the Americans still in the country and as many of its Vietnamese allies as possible. The last Americans flew out of Saigon on helicopters on April 30, 1975, as the communist forces began taking over the city.

The reunification of Vietnam under communist control had no direct impact on the United States, in spite of the enormous effort spent in money and lives to prevent it. The United States never had significant material interests in Indochina and its geostrategic concerns turned out to be needless, as the domino theory proved false. Though the murderous communist Khmer Rouge movement captured control of Cambodia during the final communist offensive in Vietnam, it had strained relations with the Vietnamese. (In 1979, Vietnam and Cambodia went to war, leading to the ouster of the Khmer Rouge government.) Otherwise, no further communist advances occurred in Asia. Vietnam itself entered a long period of suffering as it coped with the physical and social devastation of the war, unassisted by the United States, which reneged on its promise of postwar reconstruction aid. A communist leadership that had been brilliant at war proved incompetent at peace, leaving the country one of the poorest in the world.

The Decline of American Power

The communist victory in Vietnam telegraphed the limits of American power to other nations. An incident just after the capture of Saigon displayed just how inept its effort to police the world had become. In mid-May 1975, the crew of an American cargo ship, the *Mayaguez,* en route from Hong Kong to Thailand, was taken prisoner by the new communist government of Cambodia in what the United States considered international waters. President Ford, eager to demonstrate his willingness to use force, ordered a rescue mission and air attacks. But rather than romping to success, the U.S. forces suffered from poor intelligence and heavy resistance. Forty-one Americans died and fifty were wounded in the attempt to free the crew, which the Cambodians had moved before the rescue force arrived and then released unharmed.

The most consequential sign of the diminished ability of the United States to shape the world came out of the Middle East. In October 1973, the Egyptians and Syrians launched a coordinated attack to win back land they had lost to Israel in their 1967 war. The Israelis, caught by surprise, suffered serious setbacks. With the Soviet Union sending military supplies to Egypt and Syria to replace depleted stocks, the United States responded in kind with a massive airlift of equipment to Israel. A successful Israeli counteroffensive ensued. The United States then helped broker a cease-fire and disengagement of forces, but by then the Arab oil-producing states, led by Saudi Arabia, had begun reducing their output, saying they would continue to do so until Israel returned to its 1967 borders. They also sharply raised the price of oil and imposed an embargo of oil shipments to countries supporting Israel, including the United States. Washington did nothing to force them to back down.

The oil boycott accelerated a run-up of energy prices already under way, part of a broad inflationary surge that pushed the economy into a nosedive. Nixon's expansive fiscal and monetary policy in 1971 and 1972 had ended the 1970 recession, while wage and price controls had helped check inflation. But rapid economic growth pushed up consumer demand, creating inflationary pressure, especially once Nixon began loosening price controls. Wages, which peaked in 1972, stopped keeping up with prices.

Mid-1970s inflation proved difficult to control because of its nature. Since World War II, economists and policymakers had believed that they could stabilize prices by manipulating government and consumer demand. But as Nixon's second term began, supply problems played a large role in pushing up prices, defying the usual government tools for retarding inflation.

First came a sharp run-up in food prices. The Nixon administration had deliberately reduced the size of agricultural surpluses in an effort to boost farm income, leaving little slack in markets at a time when the devaluation of the dollar upped agricultural exports. The consequences soon became evident when poor harvests in a number of grain-producing countries combined with the massive sale of grain to the Soviet Union to create unexpected shortages in domestic and international markets, pushing up food prices. The cost of meat rose so sharply in the spring of 1973 that a consumer boycott movement briefly flourished, a rerun of a spurt of protest against high food prices that had taken place in 1966.

An exceptionally large harvest in 1973 decelerated the rise in food prices, but by then a surge in oil prices had started that would prove far more disruptive. Energy costs had begun rising even before the oil boycott, reflecting long-term changes in demand and supply. Cheap energy had been critical to post–World War II growth in the United States and other industrial nations. With little price disincentive, usage ballooned. The total energy consumption of the United States increased nearly two-and-a-half-fold between 1949 and 1973.

By the early 1970s, oil provided as much energy in the United States as the next most important sources—natural gas and coal—combined. But domestic production of crude oil had peaked in 1970, making the country increasingly dependent on oil imports, which rose very quickly in the early 1970s. A bit less than half the imported oil came from countries that belonged to the Organization of Petroleum Exporting Countries (OPEC), a producers' cartel organized in 1960. Fourteen percent came from Persian Gulf nations. The tight world oil market gave these overlapping blocs inordinate power, which they demonstrated during the Middle East war.

The Arab oil embargo led to gasoline shortages in the United States, evident in the long lines that became common at gas stations. Prices shot up, with the cost of crude oil quadrupling in a single year. Inexpensive fuel had come to be seen as such an entitlement that people were outraged, even though in mid-1974 the price of a gallon of gasoline, an irreplaceable resource that had to be extracted from the ground, refined, and transported long distances, remained only about a third the cost of a gallon of Coca-Cola, essentially carbonated sugar water. For a society long used to infinite supplies of cheap gasoline, waiting on line for expensive fuel came as a visceral blow, a sobering demonstration of the limits of American power and a dark message about the future.

Nixon and Congress took some modest measures to reduce oil consumption—lowering the speed limit to 55 miles per hour and extending daylight saving time—and approved the stalled plan for an Alaska oil pipeline. Nonetheless, oil prices helped push up the inflation rate from 8.4 percent in 1973 to 12.1 percent the following year. With so much money going to energy and average take-home pay falling, spending on other items declined. Manufacturers cut back production and laid off workers, leading to a further decline in spending. In early 1974, the stock market tumbled and housing construction slumped. The unemployment rate reached 8.7 percent in May 1975, as the country experienced the worst recession since the 1930s. Economists, policymakers, and the public all found disconcerting the simultaneous climb of prices and unemployment, which historically had moved in opposite directions.

Nixon's pumping up the economy for the 1972 election and the enormous hikes in food and energy costs helped bring on the recession of the mid-1970s. But more fundamental forces also seemed to be at work, as it soon became clear that something more than a normal business cycle was taking place. Though the recession ended by the spring of 1975, the economy remained weak for another seven years. From 1973 to 1982, the GNP grew at an average annual rate of only 1.8 percent, compared to roughly 4 percent from 1960 to 1973. After decades of broadly shared upward mobility, most people found their standard of living going down.

Other countries also suffered from prolonged periods of stagnation, but in many cases not as deeply. The United States, long the top country in gross domestic product per person, by 1980 had slipped to eleventh, behind not just such economic powerhouses as West Germany and France but also Belgium, Denmark, and Iceland. The post–World War II era, so strongly identified in the United States and around the world with rising material abundance and American hegemony, had come to an end.

The Resurrection of Corporate Capitalism

(1975–1989)

PART III

The Resurrection of Corporate Capitalism
(1975–1992)

CHAPTER 12

The Landscape of Decline

At the end of the 1970s, Thomas and Geraldine Vale retraced the trip George Stewart had taken thirty years earlier to document the American landscape as seen from U.S. 40, from Atlantic City to San Francisco. Large stretches of the road had been replaced by Interstates 70 and 80 and much of the old two-lane highway had been widened to four, six, or even eight lanes. But the views from most of the places where Stewart had stopped to take photographs remained remarkably unchanged. In Ellicott City, the county seat of rural Howard County, Maryland, the streetcars were gone, but otherwise things looked much the same. Where U.S. 40 crossed the Mason-Dixon Line, trees had taken over open pastureland and a barn had been taken down, but the Methodist church that Stewart had photographed had a new roof and fresh coat of paint. Blankenship Drugs inhabited the same building it had three decades earlier on a largely unchanged main street in Marshall, Illinois. In Grainfield and Oakley, Kansas, additional grain elevators had gone up and the old Grainfield railroad station had disappeared, having been moved by the Lions Club to a local park, where it had promptly been burned down by vandals, but otherwise these small wheat towns remained much as they had been.

Some places did look different. What had been farm fields a few miles west of Frederick, Maryland, had become a suburban subdivision. One side of a street of row houses in Baltimore had been knocked down, partially replaced by a high-rise public housing project, while some of the remaining homes had been abandoned. The St. Louis and San Francisco skylines had been altered by large residential and office buildings, though in the former case they hid a deep loss of population and vitality. In the West, the Vales noted the growth of settlements built around recreation, towns like Steam-boat Springs, Colorado, and campgrounds for recreational vehicles.

The seeming sameness of so much of the country after thirty years of growth reflected a very particular pattern of development. The population of the country grew from 151 million in 1950 to more than 226 million in 1980, an increase of one-half. It had thickened to an average density of 64.0 people per square mile, from 42.6 thirty years earlier. But population growth had been highly concentrated. Over the course of three decades, the population in urban areas swelled by seventy million, while the rural population grew by only five million. In 1980, 45 percent of the population lived in a suburb, 30 percent in a central city. Over half the population lived on an edge of the country, in a county abutting the Atlantic or Pacific coast, the Gulf of Mexico, or one of the Great Lakes. Away from the coasts and the metro-politan centers, you could still drive for hours without seeing many people or dwellings, as the Vales discovered. The number of acres of forest had barely dropped in the decades after the Second World War, as the reforesta-tion of abandoned agricultural land and the replanting of trees on cut tim-berland almost fully compensated for the woodlands lost to urban growth and suburban sprawl. Compared to the other industrial powers—with the exception of the Soviet Union—the United States remained a little-settled nation, with large swaths of undeveloped land. France had four times as many people per square mile as the United States; the United Kingdom, nine times; Japan, twelve.

Driving across the middle of the country, the Vales did not much note one of the great developments of the postwar era, the interregional and intrare-gional redistribution of population. The center of gravity of the nation had shifted toward the West and South. In 1950, 29 percent of the population had lived in the Midwest; in 1980, only 26 percent. The Northeast fell from 26 percent of the population to 22 percent. Within these regions, people moved outward from the cities to the suburbs. The South, by contrast, after losing population share between 1950 and 1960, experienced a reversal, going from 31 percent in 1950 to 33 percent in 1980. The West jumped from 13 percent of the population to 19 percent. Though the regional gains and losses in themselves were modest, together they meant that by 1980 a majority of Americans lived in the South or West, a development with profound social, cultural, and political implications. In media and popular discourse, it be-came common to portray the nation as divided into an ascending "Sun Belt" or "southern rim," made up of the South and Southwest, and a declining "Snow Belt" or "Rust Belt," the latter term used particularly for the indus-trial parts of the midwestern and Middle Atlantic states.

The Rust Belt

Thirty years after World War II, the Northeast and Midwest still contained the bulk of the nation's wealth and industrial capacity. In 1977, 70 percent of the pig iron produced in the United States and Canada came from Illinois, Indiana, Ohio, Pennsylvania, Michigan, and New York. That year the New England, Middle Atlantic, and North Central states accounted for 58 percent of all value added in manufacturing. In 1975, they housed the headquarters of 379 of the 500 largest industrial corporations. The Far West had the highest per capita income of any region, as had long been the case, but the New England, midwestern, and Great Lakes states also exceeded the national average.

The pattern of wealth and economic dominance, though, was shifting. With companies and people moving out of the cities of the Northeast and Midwest to suburbs and other parts of the country, many of the traditional centers of national power grew shabby. A train trip in the mid-1970s from New York to Washington would have given a sense of their decay.

After World War II, the private companies that owned the nation's railway system concentrated on freight operations. Dirty, aging passenger trains provided feeble competition to burgeoning car and airplane travel, which received government subsidies through road and airport construction and the provision of air traffic control. In 1970, the Penn Central, a merger of the once mighty Pennsylvania and New York Central railroads, went bankrupt. In an effort to keep at least a skeleton system of passenger rail travel intact, Congress created a nonprofit corporation, Amtrak, to take over and operate intercity train lines. Inheriting a hodgepodge of decaying trains and stations, chronically underfunded, and confronted with an unrealistic expectation that it would become self-supporting, Amtrak struggled to survive in a nation that since World War II had developed along physical and cultural lines defined by the automobile.

During World War II, millions of soldiers and civilians had entered and left New York through Pennsylvania Station, the magnificent McKim, Mead & White building from the early twentieth century, with its soaring steel arches and glass ceiling. But in 1963, over the protest of preservationists, the station had been demolished to make way for a new Madison Square Garden. So during the 1970s, train travelers from New York departed through a cramped, airless station beneath the sports arena.

New York had been an aberration among large northeastern and midwestern cities in holding steady in population after World War II, but between 1970 and 1980 it lost more than 800,000 residents, over 10 percent of its population. The recessions of the 1970s hit New York particularly hard, with the local unemployment rate hitting 12 percent in 1975. As jobs and city services disappeared and crime increased, many city residents, particularly whites, found the suburbs or other parts of the country more attractive. Apartment building owners and the financial institutions that backed them stopped investing in poor neighborhoods, seeing little likelihood for future profit, leading to a wave of housing abandonment and arson. During the 1977 World Series games at Yankee Stadium, ABC television repeatedly turned its cameras on burning buildings in the nearby South Bronx, sending out images of the nation's leading city as a circle of hell. Films like *Taxi Driver* (1976) and *Escape from New York* (1981) portrayed New York as dark, decayed, and dangerous. For literary critic Alfred Kazin, who had lovingly written about the New York of his youth, the city had become "a world coming apart. . . . The great big, dissolving center."

Newark, the first Amtrak stop after New York, once had been a thriving industrial city. But after World War II it bled industry, middle-class residents, and retailing to its suburbs, leaving behind a majority black population, much of it poor. The 1967 riot devastated a city already in crisis. Near the train station, a few major employers remained, notably in the insurance industry, but elsewhere one abandoned factory after another lined the tracks through the city.

Trenton, the New Jersey capital, presented another vista of decline and abandonment. A center of iron manufacturing and pottery making, it had stopped growing by the 1920s. After World War II, many leading companies moved, reduced operations, or shut down, including the historic Roebling ironworks, where the cable wire for the Brooklyn Bridge had been drawn. State offices provided some new jobs, but the workers in them generally drove in from suburbs, on highways that sliced up the city and robbed access to its riverfront. At night they left behind a desolate downtown. As Amtrak crossed the Delaware River, the sign on an adjacent bridge, "Trenton Makes, the World Takes," once an expression of civic pride, seemed to mock the down-and-out city.

The Philadelphia suburbs flourished during the postwar years but at the expense of the city proper, which lost 6 percent of its population between 1950 and 1970 before plummeting another 13 percent during the following decade. The city suffered severely from the decline of manufacturing, which in 1951 had provided 46 percent of its jobs but in 1977 only 24 percent. The number of Philadelphians on public assistance jumped from roughly 200,000 in 1970 to nearly 340,000 in 1980. North Philadelphia so decayed that eventually Amtrak all but stopped using the station there. Baltimore presented a similar, if anything sorrier, picture. After slowly bleeding population during the quarter century after the war, between 1970 and 1980 it lost 13 percent of those who remained, falling to tenth in size among the nation's cities, after having been sixth in 1950. So many row houses had been abandoned that the city started a homesteading program, offering, for a dollar, buildings it had taken over for tax arrears to families willing to fix them up and live in them.

Washington, D.C., was visibly deteriorating too, shrinking from a 1950 population peak of 802,178 to 638,333 in 1980. Leaving the train in Washington, passengers did not actually disembark inside Daniel Burnham's gorgeous 1907 Beaux-Arts Union Station, which had been virtually abandoned as passenger rail use declined. The federal government decided to turn the station into a visitors' center for the 1976 bicentennial, relegating travelers to a cramped, makeshift area behind the station proper. In 1974, Washington finally got to elect its own mayor, as Congress, in the wake of the civil rights movement, ceded much control over the federal district to its increasingly black population. However, as so often happened when an African American got to run a major city, Walter Washington inherited a decaying infrastructure and shrinking tax base.

Urban decline in the Midwest, if anything, was more severe than in the Northeast. Between 1950 and 1980, Chicago lost 17 percent of its population, Cincinnati 24 percent, Detroit 35 percent, Cleveland 37 percent, and St. Louis a staggering 47 percent. (Indianapolis, Columbus, and Toledo bucked the trend with significant population gains.) Between 1948 and 1977, Cleveland lost 46 percent of its manufacturing jobs. It lost an even greater percentage of jobs in retail trade, mostly as a result of suburban shopping mall development.

Companies had been relocating production out of Snow Belt cities for decades: New England textiles had moved to the South, New York garment firms to rural Pennsylvania, midwestern aircraft companies to the West Coast. They relocated to be closer to markets, raw materials, and cheap power and to lower labor costs, find more compliant workers, and escape unions. General Electric and General Motors set an example when in reaction to the display of union power after World War II they began dispersing plants away from their northeastern and midwestern strongholds, building many factories in the South. The weak economy of the 1970s, international competition, the sharp run-up in oil prices, and new pollution control requirements accelerated the abandonment of older industrial facilities.

Infrastructure and technological advances made the dispersion of production easier than in the past. The interstate highway system lowered the cost of truck transportation and made it feasible to locate factories and warehouses in areas previously too inaccessible. Container cargo ships cut the cost of international shipping, while jumbo cargo jets made it possible to move even large goods quickly. Long-distance telephone calls became cheap enough for businesses to depend on them to communicate with distant facilities.

Cities deserted by industry often found themselves devastated. High levels of homeownership made it difficult for workers to relocate from declining cities with falling house prices, as did the thick webs of familial and ethnic ties characteristic of many industrial communities. Pollution also plagued the old manufacturing centers, as heavy industry left behind toxic residues that had been overlooked in earlier years when business boomed, environmental consciousness had not yet blossomed, and local industrialists exerted great power. When the Cuyahoga River, which runs through the center of Cleveland, improbably caught fire in June 1969, it became a symbol of the spoilage of the cities of the old manufacturing belt and the dystopia they had come to represent to many Americans.

Many companies moved their headquarters and offices, as well as their factories, out of the cities of the Northeast and Midwest. Frequently they did not travel far, settling in suburban office parks or nearby towns, as companies sought to exchange high central-city expenses for placid settings near the suburban communities in which their executives lived. Some major universities—like Stanford, Princeton, and Duke—drew companies to nearby "research parks" in bucolic suburban settings, where ideas, money, and personnel could move easily between the academic and corporate worlds.

By world and historical standards, the Northeast and Midwest remained astoundingly wealthy during the 1970s, with large middle and upper classes that could afford comfortable homes, two and three cars per family, vacations, college educations, snowmobiles, boats, recreational vehicles, and all the other accoutrements of the good life. Suburban areas in particular continued to grow and prosper. But the region also contained cities that suffered enormously from the combination of national recession, interregional shift, deindustrialization, and suburbanization, shocking repudiations of the notion so common in the post–World War II years that the United States surpassed all other societies in its standard of living and had achieved an ever-upward trajectory of economic and social development.

The Sun Belt

Long after World War II, the South remained considerably poorer than the Northeast or Midwest, with substantial areas of deep urban and rural poverty. But compared to the Northeast and Midwest, its trajectory was ascending. In the mid-1970s, average income, adjusted for inflation, fell in the North but continued to grow in the South. Some of the income convergence between the South and the rest of the country reflected the postwar exodus of poor southerners to other regions. In effect, the South exported some of its poverty through migration. But the region experienced real growth in productive capacity and wealth, too. The greatest economic development took place along the periphery of the region, in northern Virginia; Charlotte and the Durham–Raleigh–Chapel Hill region of North Carolina; southern Florida; and Houston and Dallas–Fort Worth. But Atlanta, in the heart of the old Confederacy, emerged as the economic center of the region.

Rapid urbanization accompanied southern growth (though it remained the most rural region of the country). In 1980, two-thirds of southerners lived in an urban or suburban area, compared to half in 1950. Unlike in the Northeast and Midwest, Sun Belt cities continued to grow or at least hold their own as their suburbs swelled. Metropolitan Houston exploded from 806,701 people in 1950 to 2,905,353 thirty years later, of whom nearly half lived in the city proper. Metropolitan Atlanta mushroomed from a population of 671,797 in 1950 to 2,029,710 in 1980, though almost all the growth took place in the suburbs. Some of the growth of southern cities reflected the continued annexation of outlying areas, a process that had ground to a near halt in the North, but much of it came from burgeoning corporate offices and service industries. In 1975, the South housed the headquarters of sixty-three of the five hundred largest industrial corporations, compared to just thirty-nine companies twenty years earlier.

Start-ups and in-migration of firms to the South and Southwest far more than compensated for plant shutdowns and out-migrating companies. The region continued to attract and generate jobs in low-wage, labor-intensive industries, like textiles, simple garment manufacturing, food processing, and furniture making, as companies took advantage of the low-tax, anti-union, pro-business environment so heavily promoted by government development agencies and business boosters. But the region also experienced growth in technically sophisticated sectors, particularly the defense and aerospace industries.

The Sun Belt benefited from the changed economics of energy. The huge jump in energy prices during the 1970s brought new wealth to oil-producing areas, notably Louisiana, Texas, Oklahoma, and California, at the expense of the rest of the nation. Houston boomed as the oil capital of the country. The city and its surrounding area contained nearly a quarter of the petroleum refining capacity of the country and over half the petrochemical manufacturing capacity. Over two-thirds of the world's oil production tools were manufactured in Houston, which housed the headquarters of hundreds of oil and oil service companies. But the city also developed into a leading medical, legal, electronics, and aerospace center.

Houston embodied in extreme form the traits of the growing urban South. With business leaders dominating local politics, Houston pursued a pro-growth agenda with a vengeance, being almost unique among major American cities in having no zoning regulations at all (in a state with no taxes on either corporate or personal earnings). Though blacks and Hispanics made up nearly half the population, through the 1970s the Houston government effectively locked them out of power by using at-large elections to choose the city council and continuing to annex white suburbs. Downtown Houston was almost entirely commercial (though some very poor black neighborhoods with shotgun shacks were nearby), with a vast suburban expanse surrounding it, speckled with high-rise office buildings and shopping malls. The near total lack of public transportation led to severe highway congestion and air pollution. Low taxes and rapid growth meant insufficient services. Inadequate policing along with extreme income inequality contributed to a very high crime rate. The helter-skelter, explosive growth in Houston provided something of a national Rorschach test, horrifying many northern intellectuals, exemplary to many southern (particularly Texas) boosters, and attractive to thousands of laid-off midwestern industrial workers who migrated to the city in search of work.

Growth in the Southwest outstripped the South. Trailers and mobile homes dotted the region, a cheap way to accommodate a growing population. By 1980, the Los Angeles metropolitan area had seven and a half million people, with nearly three million in the city itself. The San Diego region was approaching two million people, more than tripling its population in thirty years. Greater Phoenix grew from under a third of a million in 1950 to a million and a half in 1980. Albuquerque was approaching an area population of half a million. Utterly dependent on air-conditioning and imported water for their growth, these sprawling desert cities, with their comparatively inexpensive single-family homes in suburban subdivisions, new shopping malls, and seeming ability to slough off their histories, served as prototypes for polycentric, dispersed, low-density living, with industry, research facilities, retailing, and recreation as likely to be on the outskirts of the metropolitan region as in its center. Small outposts at the start of the twentieth century, by the 1970s these southwestern cities were drawing millions of whites from elsewhere in the country and millions of Hispanic immigrants in pursuit of that core American activity, starting out anew.

As the South, once portrayed outside the region as backward, quaint, or undeveloped, grew more populous and wealthier, its cultural influence increased too. Something of a southernization of national culture began to take place. In part it came from the dispersal of southern migrants to other parts of the country. Southerners carried with them evangelical Christianity and regional musical forms that spread and morphed in northern settings. Country music, largely a white phenomenon, traveled with southern migrants to the Midwest and California, especially the Central Valley. By the mid-1970s, a fifth of all AM radio stations specialized in country music, with most major cities in the North as well as the South having at least one outlet. Black southern music, particularly blues, found a following among young northern whites (even as it lost much of its appeal to young northern blacks). Stock car racing, a white southern sport that grew out of running bootleg liquor, slowly became a national obsession.

As it nationalized, southern culture retained a rural—or faux rural—tinge, but the urban South proved influential too. Nothing better embodied this than the buildings of Atlanta architect John Portman. His breakthrough came with his development of the huge Atlanta Merchandise Mart in the early 1960s, the start of the Peachtree Center and the revival of downtown Atlanta. To capitalize on the growing demand for downtown guest rooms, in 1967 Portman built a twenty-two-story hotel with an atrium that extended up the full height of the building and a revolving restaurant on the roof. To get to their rooms, guests took glass-sided elevators that faced inward toward the atrium. In an era of boring, boxlike hotels and office buildings, Portman's hotel proved a sensation. He followed it up nine years later with the seventy-three-story Peachtree Plaza Hotel, a slim cylinder also equipped with atrium, revolving restaurant, and scenic elevators. By then, Portman was building variations of his atrium hotels and cylindrical buildings in San Francisco, Los Angeles, New York, and Detroit. The national centers of power and cultural sophistication warmly greeted Portman's glitzy if ultimately banal bag of architectural tricks as key to their revitalization. By the early 1980s, Portman's firm was building hotels and merchandise marts across Europe and Asia, including in China. The atrium hotel, a product of the Sun Belt resurgence, became a global emblem of modernity.

Dystopia

While population shifts were an important force shaping American society during the 1970s, the economy proved even more important. Very rapidly, the economic downturn of the 1970s, with its deep recessions, weak recoveries, high inflation, and stagnating income, undermined the confidence and optimism that permeated postwar America, bringing unaccustomed uncertainty and pessimism to politics and culture. The obvious decline of U.S. power, seen in its defeat in Vietnam and inability to check oil prices; the success of its economic competitors; the deep political and cultural divisions at home; and the exposure of political corruption in the Watergate scandal and more minor Washington scandals that followed all added to a widely shared sense that something had gone wrong and no one knew what to do about it.

Many of the most impressive and popular artistic works of the era had a decidedly dark tenor. Perhaps no one better documented the shifting national mood than the San Francisco–based rock group Sly and the Family Stone, which burst on the scene in the late 1960s with a series of joyous, optimistic populist anthems. Racially integrated, the group had female instrumentalists backing male singers, reversing the typical pattern. Its 1969 song "Everyday People," which topped the charts, was an R&B updating of the Popular Front classic "The House I Live In." Calling for tolerance— "different strokes for different folks"—its infectious good spirits seemed to provide reassurance that ultimately people of all races, the "long hair" and the "short hair," "the butcher, the banker, the drummer," the "fat one" and the "skinny one," would see the folly of their hatreds and join together as "everyday people." The group had another number one hit three years later, "Family Affair," this time a slower, druggy, agonizing song that portrayed a family of divided fates and immense sadness, with "one child . . . that just loves to learn, / And another child . . . you'd just love to burn." No hope could be found in the web of emotions that left the singer unable to stay and unable to leave, not wanting to cry but "cryin' anyway 'cause you're all broke down."

Movies likewise captured the downbeat sensibility of the 1970s. After initially avoiding films about the Vietnam War, in the late 1970s the major film companies released a series of powerful and commercially successful movies that looked back at the conflict with a critical eye. Many portrayed the war as not only misguided but as a symptom of deep national flaws. The most impressive of the group, Francis Ford Coppola's 1979 Academy Award– winning *Apocalypse Now,* rendered a sprawling vision of an American army that had lost all moral bearings, a drugged, disintegrating arm of a failing empire. Other films, like *Who'll Stop the Rain* (1976) and *Taxi Driver,* portrayed the violence, drugs, and madness of Vietnam coming back home through war veterans living outside the law and outside sanity. In the early 1980s, several movies extended the hellish vision of urban life in *Taxi Driver* into the future, in dystopian dramas like *Blade Runner* (1982), set in a poor, violent, polluted future Los Angeles, and *Escape from New York,* which imagined the future of Manhattan as a penal colony (using decimated parts of St. Louis and East St. Louis for location shots). Roman Polanski's film noir look at Los Angeles history, *Chinatown* (1974), pictured the wealth and power of society as resting on hidden corruption, greed, and horrifying moral transgression. The notion that real power was not wielded by the citizenry through the open channels of democratic governance but rather by powerful cliques through hidden, evil conspiracies animated other films of the era too, like *Network* (1976), a scathing look at the television industry, *The China Syndrome* (1979), about the nuclear power industry, and *Three Days of the Condor* (1975), about the CIA.

The flip side of the grim view of the immediate past, the present, and the future in so many films of the 1970s and early 1980s was the invention of a fanciful 1950s, which music groups, musicals, movies, and television shows counterposed to the troubling aspects of American life in the 1960s and 1970s. The earliest and most self-conscious effort to create an Edenic, prepolitical postwar past took place at Columbia University in 1969, when members of an undergraduate singing group, the Kingsmen, began performing elaborately choreographed songs from the 1950s, trying to appeal to both sides of the political and cultural divide that rent the campus the previous year. Instantly popular with both SDS and fraternity members, they named themselves Sha Na Na and within months were singing at the Woodstock rock festival. Their success inspired the Broadway musical *Grease* and its filmed version, in which Sha Na Na appeared. George Lucas's 1973 movie *American Graffiti,* set in small-town California in 1962, provided another, less cartoonish fabrication of an idealized American society before its loss of innocence. The popular television shows *Happy Days* and *Laverne and Shirley,* set in Milwaukee in the 1950s and early 1960s, played on the same theme of innocent youth coming of age in a society not yet split by war, racial conflict, or political strife. The producer of those shows, Garry Marshall, said he wanted to be the "Norman Rockwell of television." Though these confections had no explicit political message, they implicitly put forth a deeply conservative notion that America before the rights revolution had been a healthier and happier society.

A retreat from present-day social reality took other forms as well. The 1970s saw a growing interest in the cultivation of the self, therapeutic regimens, and personalistic religion. Many observers, at the time and later, contrasted the period unfavorably with what they portrayed as a more collective and idealistic era that proceeded it. Most famously, in the mid-1970s writer Tom Wolfe, in a self-fulfilling prophecy, declared that "the 1970's . . . will come to be known as the Me Decade." The view of the 1970s as a politically demobilized, narcissistic era rests on an exaggerated picture of mass political activity during the 1960s and a discounting of political activism that occurred thereafter. Left-wing political activity declined but did not suddenly die, while right-wing activism, if anything, was on the rise. Yet perhaps more than in earlier decades, collective efforts coexisted and competed with the search for sustenance and salvation through individual effort.

Rather than a repudiation of the democratic revolution, the inward turn of the 1970s represented a mutation of it. The critique of liberal, bureaucratic rationality mounted by the New Left helped pave the way for many forms of antimodernist and "postmodern" thinking in the 1970s and beyond. In a backhanded way, the rights revolution helped legitimate the search for individual fulfillment by spreading the idea of equal entitlement to all rights, including that elusive but fundamental right, the pursuit of happiness. The cultural trajectory could be tracked in the transformed use of the term "empowerment." First employed to denote the accumulation of political power by subordinate groups, in the 1970s it took on a therapeutic meaning, designating personal transformation that could be achieved by overcoming psychological barriers to self-assertion. By the late 1980s, it reappeared as a business buzzword for getting top managers to cede authority to lower-level employees as way to increase corporate flexibility.

Tom Wolfe connected the narcissism of the 1970s with the enormous boost in national wealth that occurred during the thirty years after World War II. The once exclusive ability of the rich to engage in ongoing scrutiny and reinvention of the self spread through the society during the golden age of capitalism. Millions of Americans could now afford the money and time for spiritual retreats, encounter sessions, and therapy of all kinds. Economic growth had allowed the common man and woman to do "something only aristocrats (and intellectuals and artists) were supposed to do—they discovered and started doting on *Me!*"

Paradoxically, it was not just the long-term growth in wealth that underlay what Wolfe called—in a typical exaggeration—"the greatest age of individualism in American history," but also the economic ills that had brought the golden age of capitalism to an end. With the end of decades of growth came a growing fear that the country had become, as economist Lester Thurow put it in the title of his influential 1980 book, a "zero-sum society," in which each person's gain came at the expense of another's loss. Millions of workers continued to embrace solidarity through unionism as they struggled to survive the hard times, but members of the middle class increasingly looked to themselves for economic and spiritual betterment.

The change could be seen dramatically on college campuses. After student protest reached its high point in the early 1970s, it fell off rapidly with the end of the war in Vietnam and the economic downturn. In its place came what Yale University president Kingman Brewster dubbed "grim professionalism." Middle-class students, instead of assuming secure futures as so many of their predecessors had, now feared downward mobility. To ensure the comfortable lives that they grew up taking for granted, many avoided political and civic activities to concentrate on classes in order to pave the way for career success. Business became an increasingly popular subject of study, to the point that by 1981 more students majored in the field than in history, the social sciences, the arts, philosophy, religion, language, and literature combined. In their anxiety about the future, some white students expressed open resentment toward their nonwhite classmates, who they believed were getting unfair advantages in admissions and financial aid, narrowing their own opportunities in educational and labor markets that had fixed numbers of desirable slots.

Campus life did not return to pre-1960s norms. Student activism continued, though at a diminished level, focused more on campus issues than on larger social concerns. College administrators made little effort to reimpose rules regulating student life. Sex, drug use, and, increasingly, heavy drinking pervaded many campuses. A growing number of older students joined the college ranks; more and more students worked at least part-time, making night classes more common; and coeducation became near universal, including at the military academies, which began admitting women in 1976. By the end of the 1970s, the typical college campus was a very different place than it had been at the start of the decade.

The new obsession with the self and self-improvement also could be seen on the nation's roads, in its parks, and in its living rooms, as much of the country was swept up in a fitness craze that gathered momentum in the latter part of the 1970s. Since the end of World War II, public health experts had been bemoaning the poor state of physical fitness among Americans, especially young people, who fell far behind their European peers. Their cries led to occasional federal government exhortations for the population to get it-self into shape, most famously by John Kennedy, who urged men and women to participate in what he called "this phase of national vigor." But the exercisers of the 1970s and 1980s cared little for national vigor, instead focusing on their personal well-being, good looks, and good feelings. Jogging and distance running, once oddball activities, became a national rage. So did aerobics, popularized by actress Jane Fonda through her workout tapes.

The fitness enthusiasm of the recession years was strongest among the middle and upper classes. Overall, national physical fitness actually began to drop around 1980, while rates of overweight and obesity began climbing. In the late nineteenth century, the typical image of the plutocrat had been a plump man smoking a cigar, a fellow able to afford plenty of good food, tobacco, and rest. By the latter part of the twentieth century, the well-off man was likely to be a nonsmoker devoted to staying slim and healthy. Now it was workers and the poor who were more likely to be overweight smokers.

Seeking reassurance and fulfillment through attention to the self took spiritual as well as secular forms. The 1970s was a golden age for nontraditional religious and quasi-religious movements that claimed to bring enlightenment, peace, and self-actualization, including Scientology, EST, the Hare Krishnas, and Transcendental Meditation. Antirational thinking seemed to be on the rise, perhaps a rational response to a moment when technocratic rationality had seemingly brought social failure on both the national and international fronts. Finding that the larger society could not fulfill sometimes inflated expectations of happiness or peace of mind, many Americans experimented in seeking it on their own, as part of what Wolfe called the "Third Great Awakening."

Established religions, most importantly evangelical Protestantism, proved far more important in the intensified spirituality of the period than the flamboyant though largely ephemeral "New Age" purveyors of hope and fulfillment. Overall church and synagogue attendance remained fairly stable during the 1960s and 1970s, below its late 1950s peak but still high, with about four out of ten Americans reporting in 1975 that they had attended a place of worship during the previous seven days. The biggest change in numbers occurred among Catholics, whose church attendance rate significantly declined between the mid-1960s and the mid-1970s (though it stayed above the rate for Protestants and Jews). Protestant church attendance held steady, but where Protestants worshipped significantly changed. The mainstream, liberal denominations—the Episcopalians, Methodists, Congregationalists, and Presbyterians—all suffered sharp membership drops. At the same time, many conservative, fundamentalist, and evangelical denominations, including the Southern Baptist Convention and the Pentecostal Assemblies of God, grew rapidly, especially in the cities and suburbs of the South and Southwest.

The explosion of evangelical and fundamentalist religion came in reaction to the social liberalism of the late 1960s and early 1970s and the economic uncertainty thereafter, but it did not spring up wholly anew. Many evangelical and fundamentalist denominations had been growing since early in the century. Over time, an infrastructure of seminaries and Bible schools, radio and television stations, publishers, bookstores, and record companies had developed that helped spread their reach. So did ministers who used television to build national followings, like Billy Graham, Oral Roberts, Pat Robertson, Jimmy Swaggert, Rex Humbard, Jim Bakker, and Robert Schuller. Though the growing Protestant groups had intensely personal theologies, built around the direct relationship between the individual and God, their churches provided a sense of community, particularly important in burgeoning suburbs full of newcomers. By the end of the 1970s, evangelical megachurches had started to become common, attracting huge memberships with a combination of conservative theology, an informal atmosphere (including rock music hymnody), and rich congregational life. When during the 1976 presidential campaign Jimmy Carter spoke openly about having found Christ, it jarred a country used to more private devotion from their political leaders, with a sizable number of people unfamiliar with the idea of being "born again." By the end of the decade, such declarations had come to seem normal, a cultural revolution, particularly outside the South, where such public professions of piety had been more common.

In the Northeast and Midwest, another reaction to disenchantment with national culture and the seeming loss of national vitality developed in the so-called New Ethnicity. Starting in the late 1960s and accelerating in the 1970s, many descendants of European immigrants, particularly Italians, Jews, Poles, and other Eastern Europeans, began more strongly and openly identifying with their ethnic background, after decades when assimilation had been the largely unquestioned expectation. Many older white ethnics had never stopped thinking of themselves as members of a particular nationality, as Italians or Lithuanians or Jews. In New York City, some labor unions that explicitly identified themselves by ethnicity did not drop those labels until the 1970s, in spite of the illegality of discriminating on the basis of national origin. But for many children and grandchildren of immigrants, ethnic identification was something new. In Maryland, the moribund Sons of Italy revived with an influx of young members, setting up thirty new chapters over the course of the 1970s. Baltimore began hosting huge annual Italian and Polish festivals, with smaller celebrations for Greeks, Estonians, Lithuanians, Ukrainians, Irish, and Hispanics. In other cities, too, ethnic festivals, with a heavy emphasis on ethnic food, became common. So did ethnic cookbooks, though typically they made considerable use of processed foods rather than the basic ingredients in traditional recipes.

The civil rights and Black Power movements helped spark the ethnic revival. For whites feeling increased competition for housing, jobs, government programs, and college admissions in what became a declining economy, ethnic organization served as a strategy to defend territory and command social resources. It also could be a way to try to reclaim moral ground from African Americans, whose suffering during centuries of violent oppression and pervasive discrimination had received near-universal social acknowledgment as a result of the civil rights movement. Immigrant groups, by pointing out their particular histories and the suffering they had experienced, could disassociate themselves—at least in their own minds—from responsibility for the subjugation of black Americans and make a claim for social sympathy through narratives of hard work and discipline overcoming disadvantage. But African American mobilization not only made white ethnics anxious; it inspired them too. Many whites looked admiringly, even jealously, at the expressions of African American cultural pride and solidarity that came in the wake of the civil rights movement. The enormously popular 1977 television miniseries *Roots,* based on Alex Haley's story of tracing his family lineage to Africa, sparked people of all races to become more interested in celebrating their family and ethnic heritage.

The ethnic revival fed off a sense that liberal politicians had ignored the needs of European immigrant communities, particularly those in declining or threatened urban neighborhoods. Republicans saw in the revived ethnicity a way to pry away groups strongly associated with the post–New Deal Democratic Party. But overall, the New Ethnicity flourished mostly as a cultural rather than a political phenomenon. For millions of children and grandchildren of immigrants, a turn toward their ethnic background provided nourishment at a time when the national culture seemed hollow. Many viewers found the loyalty, devotion to family, and warm sensuality of the Italian mobsters in Francis Ford Coppola's 1972 movie *The Godfather* an attractive contrast to the perceived sterility and treacherousness of the white Protestant establishment. Deeply nostalgic, usually for a very selective, romanticized notion of the past, the ethnic revival represented yet another manifestation of the inability of the national present to provide much inspiration or reassurance to a population worn down by the economic downturn, a lost war, and corrupt national politics.

Highway 40 Revisited

The country that the Vales explored in the late 1970s appeared in many ways quite similar to the one George Stewart had traveled soon after World War II. It remained a vast, richly endowed land, only lightly settled by the standards of advanced industrial nations. But in some ways the United States and the circumstances it faced had changed profoundly. In the decades after World War II, the country seemed ascendant, full of national and individual possibility. After the Vietnam War, it seemed on the decline, in its international position and the opportunities it offered its citizenry. It also seemed more divided than in the past. After World War II, there had been sharp social conflicts, evident in the labor and civil rights struggles. But by the end of the Vietnam War, cleavages had so spread that the United States seemed not divided but fragmented. Regional differences had diminished, but place still mattered. So did race, ethnicity, gender, sexual preference, religion, and even aesthetic sensibility, as identity politics crisscrossed class and ideological divisions. A stalled economy infused social conflicts with bitterness and resentment, unalloyed by confidence in the future.

Deeply dissatisfied with the status quo, Americans groped for a way to revive the economy and restore a sense of progress and well-being, with increasingly disparate notions of what those meant. Since the New Deal, the national government had loomed large in setting the direction of the country. But efforts to use the government as an instrument of national renewal would, at least for a while, largely fail. Instead, the key arena of social innovation and decision making moved to the private sector, where a corporate reinvention of the nation began to unfold, largely outside of the control of democratic structures.

CHAPTER 13

The Politics of Stagnation

B y the time Richard Nixon resigned office, the post–World War II democratization of American life had gone far. For the first time in its history, the United States had embraced universal adult suffrage, with only a few exceptions, like felons and noncitizens. And as a result of *Baker v. Carr* and subsequent court decisions, votes counted more or less equally, except in the composition of the U.S. Senate and the Electoral College. Courtrooms became more democratic when in 1975 the Supreme Court declared it unconstitutional to deny women equal access to jury service.

Democratization entailed not only individual rights but also institutional reforms that diffused power away from central authorities and insider cliques. Congress helped set the tone by moving to limit the postwar centralization of federal power in the executive branch. The 1973 War Powers Act at least symbolically reasserted the power of Congress in making war. The 1974 Hughes-Ryan Amendment required the CIA to report covert activities to congressional oversight committees. The Congressional Budget and Impoundment Control Act restricted the ability of the president to refuse to spend congressional appropriations (a favorite Nixon tactic) and established the Congressional Budget Office to provide independent expertise in economic forecasting and budget analysis. The 1976 National Emergencies Act created new procedures and congressional controls for declarations of emergency (which gave the president extraordinary powers).

Within Congress, rank-and-file members moved to restrict the power of their leaders and create greater opportunities to participate in decision making. The seventy-five new Democratic congressmen elected in 1974 in the wake of Watergate—many of them political neophytes lacking the usual deference to party leaders—forced the ouster of several longtime committee chairs and the reform of House rules. By the late 1970s, a handful of power-ful congressional leaders no longer could make major decisions out of public view.

Across the society, government bodies and public institutions were allow-ing greater access to information once kept confidential and creating more opportunities for public input in decision making. Building a structure, changing a government regulation, or administrating a program often re-quired extensive public consultations and hearings, unlike in the past when leaders could act on their own. With the mass mobilizations of the 1960s still part of social memory, people expected to be heard and did not feel hesitant about taking to hearing rooms or to the streets to press their positions. And when that did not suffice, they often used the courts to block or force govern-ment action.

Yet belying the formal democratization of society were many signs of public disenchantment with politics and public processes. Antiauthoritari-anism, inherited from the 1960s, came to pervade society, with an air of sour disgust rather than liberatory glee. A growing part of the population disen-gaged from politics altogether. Many private interests, finding there to be too much democracy for their taste, began finding ways to exert power out-side of formal procedures of government. As antistatist sentiment grew, de-mocracy expanded and became hollowed out at the same time.

The Crisis of Authority

The most obvious measure of public disenchantment with politics came in the declining participation in national elections. In every presidential election during the 1950s and 1960s, at least 60 percent of the electorate voted. In 1972, just 55 percent did; in 1976, 54 percent; in 1980 and 1984, 53 percent; and in 1988, 50 percent. Even fewer people voted in off-year congressional elections. Participation hit a low point in 1978, when less than 38 percent of the eligible voters cast a ballot, the lowest level in over three decades. Some of the drop came from the lowering of the voting age, since young adults were less likely to vote than their elders. But much more it reflected a blanket re-jection of politicians and a growing belief that elections had little to do with daily reality.

Incumbents suffered from the public disgust. In 1976, Gerald Ford barely managed to win the Republican nomination in the face of a challenge from former California governor Ronald Reagan, only to be defeated in the gen-eral election by an obscure governor from Georgia, Jimmy Carter. Carter, in turn, lost to Reagan in 1980, the first back-to-back defeats for incumbent presidents since 1892. In 1980, independent presidential candidate John Anderson won more than 6 percent of the vote—more than Strom Thurmond and Henry Wallace together got in 1948—to a large extent simply because he did not represent one of the major parties.

Some of the public disgust with politics and politicians stemmed from political scandals and revelations of past government misdeeds. Late one night in October 1974, the Washington, D.C., police stopped a car carrying one of the most powerful members of the House of Representatives, Wilbur Mills, in the company of a stripper named Fanne Foxe, who bolted into the nearby Tidal Basin. When months later Mills appeared on the stage of a Boston burlesque house at Foxe's beckoning, his days as a power broker came to an end. Two years later Wayne Hayes, head of the House Administration Committee, fell from power when a member of his staff told the *Washington Post* that she had been put on payroll to serve as his mistress: "I can't type, I can't file, I can't even answer the phone." A murkier, more serious scandal began unfolding in 1976 with allegations that political operatives acting on behalf of the South Korean government had distributed cash to a large number of congressmen.

From 1970 through the late 1980s, the number of local, state, and federal officials indicted and convicted for criminal activity rose sharply. In all likelihood there were not more crooks than in the past but rather closer scrutiny of politicians by the press, prosecutors, and rivals. With the Democrats and Republicans locked in close national elections from 1976 on, charges of personal wrongdoing became a widely used partisan tool, as the conspiracy of mutually self-serving silence that once reigned among Washington politicians collapsed. The press abetted the process, as Watergate placed a new premium on uncovering official wrongdoing. A 1978 law furthered politics by exposé by establishing a procedure for appointing special prosecutors in cases of alleged wrongdoing by federal officials.

For a brief time, it looked like Gerald Ford might succeed in restoring integrity and confidence in government. He came into the presidency with a surge of public goodwill, a sense of relief that the strange, dark days of Richard Nixon were over. Ford's unpretentious manner and the suburban normality of his family seemed reassuring, whatever people thought of his political views, which on many issues were more conservative than Nixon's. Ford's wife, Betty, signaled how much national social views had changed when she compared trying marijuana with having a first beer or cigarette and said that she would accept her teenage daughter having an affair. But Ford destroyed any chance he had of improving public perception of the political class—and any likelihood of getting elected to the presidency in his own right—when just a month into office he gave Nixon a full pardon for any offenses he might have committed as president. Ford's approval rating plunged, as many people believed that he had made a sordid deal with the former president, or at least perpetuated a different set of rules for political insiders than for everyone else.

Disclosures during and after the Ford administration of past governmental wrongdoing furthered public disenchantment with politicians and the state. The foreign and domestic calamities of the late 1960s and early 1970s, especially Vietnam and Watergate, left in their wake resentment and bitterness among government insiders that opened the floodgates for leaks, revelations, and recrimination. Tales of CIA assassination attempts, coups, illegal spying, and use of psychedelic drugs captured headlines and sparked government investigations, which led to further revelations. Former FBI associate director Mark Felt—the *Washington Post*'s "Deep Throat" source during Watergate—was convicted of illegal break-ins during a search for fugitive radicals. The tawdry picture of covert, illegal, often bumbling, and sometime murderous activities by the government undercut its moral authority. In 1964, a public opinion poll found that 76 percent of the public trusted the government; by 1974, the figure had fallen to just 36 percent. Ironically, liberals, who supported an expansive notion of government, ended up contributing to its delegitimization by aggressively investigating Watergate and other government misdeeds.

The distrust of government leaders and politicians was part of a broader crisis of authority during the 1970s. All kinds of traditional figures of authority were seen as dishonest and self-interested. A 1976 poll reported that only 42 percent of the public trusted the medical profession, down from 73 percent in 1966, and only 12 percent trusted the legal profession. The anti-authoritarianism once associated with the New Left had become the common property of broad sectors of society.

Ford

Even more than the loss of confidence in the probity of national leaders and government institutions, their failure to solve major problems confronting the country fed antistatism and disaffection with electoral politics. Presidents Ford and Carter, though quite different in their ideologies and political styles, both proved remarkably unsuccessful in dealing with serious domestic troubles and foreign affairs. To some extent their failures reflected ineptitude. But the very nature of the circumstances they faced made it almost impossible to succeed.

Economics dominated politics for most of the 1970s. As soon as Nixon left office, national attention shifted from Watergate to the rapidly deteriorating economy, as unemployment and inflation shot up, the GDP shrank, take-home pay fell, and the federal deficit ballooned. The coincidence of a downward business cycle with structural changes in international capitalism threw businessmen and policymakers into confusion. In the past, unemployment and inflation had tended to be reciprocal, with one falling when the other rose. Now they began moving up together, as slow growth (or no growth) combined with inflation in what came to be called "stagflation."

The Keynesian solutions that had become normative government policy in the United States and Western Europe no longer fit the circumstances. If the government tried to lower unemployment by stimulating the economy, it faced the danger of exacerbating already high inflation. If it tried to lower inflation through monetary policy, it faced the possibility of slowing or reversing economic growth and throwing more people out of work.

Ford made inflation his priority. He put much of the blame for surging prices on excessive government spending and the federal deficit. A political and economic conservative, he had never liked the expansion of state function that came with the Great Society, as a congressman opposing Medicare, federal aid to education, and housing subsidies. As president, he tried to trim federal expenditures. He wanted the public to cut spending too. Ford ended an October 1974 address to Congress that laid out his economic program by urging his listeners to spend 5 percent less on food and drive 5 percent less. He then pinned on his lapel a button with the letters "WIN" on it, an acronym for "Whip Inflation Now."

The WIN program superficially mimicked the New Deal. During Roosevelt's first stab at an economic recovery program, the National Recovery Administration (NRA) had used a Blue Eagle symbol to rally public support. Its reincarnation—the WIN name and button design—came at the White House's request from the Benton & Bowles advertising agency, whose cofounder, Chester Bowles, had mobilized millions of volunteers to help fight inflation during World War II as head of the Office of Price Administration (OPA). But both the NRA and OPA used the public to help enforce mandatory government regulations that greatly increased the role of the state in managing the economy. Ford wanted to go the other way, to decrease federal regulation of the economy and use public mobilization as a substitute for state intervention, moving away from, not back toward, the New Deal order. Ford's faith that family belt-tightening could "whip" an inflationary spiral rooted in commodity shortages and deep economic structures seemed to belie much understanding of political economy. WIN buttons immediately became the butt of jokes.

Congress rejected almost all of Ford's proposals. The heavily Democratic, liberal-leaning majorities in the House and Senate, with strong ties to organized labor, gave a higher priority to attacking unemployment. The most ambitious Democratic plan was introduced in 1974 in the House by Augustus F. Hawkins and in the Senate by Hubert Humphrey (who was reelected to Congress after leaving the vice presidency). Their bill was a throwback to the New Deal and the original version of the Full Employment Act of 1946. Picking up Roosevelt's 1944 proclamation of employment as a right, it called for the federal government to set a specific goal for full employment and use fiscal and monetary policy to try to achieve it. If those tools proved insufficient, it mandated the provision of a government-funded job for every adult seeking work.

Ford opposed the Humphrey-Hawkins bill, as did many Democratic economists, fearful that it would drive up inflation. In 1974, Ford did agree to fund 100,000 public-sector jobs through grants to local and state governments under the Comprehensive Employment and Training Act (CETA), passed the previous year to bring together various federal manpower programs. The next year he signed a tax reduction and rebate to stimulate the economy. But in early 1976, Ford vetoed a large public works program and other spending bills. Meanwhile, Humphrey-Hawkins failed to win passage, only becoming law in 1978, by which time—like the Full Employment bill on which it had been modeled—it had been gutted of its most meaningful provisions, including an enforceable public right to a job. By the time of the 1976 election, inflation had fallen to 5.7 percent from 11 percent in 1974, but unemployment remained high, approaching 8 percent.

Ford had no more success with his energy program than with his economic program. The solution to rising energy costs and oil shortages, Ford believed, lay in dismantling the complex web of federal regulations governing the oil and gas industries, including the system of price controls and federal allocations that Nixon had imposed on oil and petroleum products in 1971, which kept domestically produced oil below the world market price. The higher prices that would come with deregulation, Ford argued, would stimulate increased domestic oil production. But Congress found the prospect of sharply higher oil and gasoline prices politically unpalatable. A compromise energy law kept price controls in place until at least 1979, created a strategic petroleum reserve, and instituted a series of conservation measures including energy efficiency standards for appliances, legalizing right turns on red lights, and mandatory fuel economy standards for new cars and small trucks.

The End of Détente

The urgency of domestic matters during Ford's presidency eclipsed foreign policy in public discourse. But in Congress, elite policy circles, and within his administration a sharp debate unfolded over the United States' global standing and its relationship with the Soviet Union, as the 1975 communist victory in Vietnam and images of the chaotic evacuation of Saigon contributed to a widespread sense of national decline. In that debate lay the roots of an eventual return to expansive efforts to assert American power all over the world.

On taking office, Ford seemed inclined to continue the Nixon-Kissinger policy of détente. But by then, détente had begun to stall. Negotiating economic and arms control arrangements with the Soviet Union that would provide sufficient benefits to each party proved difficult, given the different situations of the two superpowers and rising opposition to détente within the United States.

In the mid-1970s, some leading conservatives began criticizing what they saw as the implicit assumption behind détente that declining U.S. military and economic power necessitated accommodations with onetime enemies ideologically and morally at odds with core American beliefs. In doing so, they rejected the conclusion of centrist leaders like Kissinger and later Jimmy Carter that in the light of the American defeat in Vietnam, Watergate, and changing global economic relations the United States could not and should not try to play the same dominant world role it once did. Critics of détente expressed skepticism about accords with the Soviet Union, seeking instead to rebuild American military power and assert core moral values in U.S. foreign policy, especially the defense of liberty. Inside the Ford administration, Secretary of Defense James Schlesinger, Chief of Staff Donald Rumsfeld, who in late 1975 replaced Schlesinger at the Pentagon, and Rumsfeld's deputy, Richard Cheney, who succeeded him as chief of staff, ideologically and bureaucratically challenged Kissinger, whose near total control over foreign policy at the start of the Ford administration steadily eroded. Conservatives outside of the administration also pounded Kissinger and détente, most importantly Ronald Reagan, who was preparing to challenge Ford for the Republican nomination.

Republican critics of détente found allies among some liberals who had long been associated with the Democratic Party. In the early 1970s, a cluster of liberal intellectuals, political activists, and labor leaders, many with youthful roots in the socialist movement, began moving to the right, or, as they saw it, standing firm as the Democratic Party moved to the left. Domestic developments pushed some of them in a conservative direction, specifically their rejection of the New Left. Equally important, they opposed any softening toward the Soviet Union. Some of the most influential "neoconservatives" were Jews for whom the 1973 Middle East war and Palestinian terror tactics loomed large. Strongly committed to the defense of Israel, they reacted to criticism of the Jewish state by the Soviet Union and the political left at home by seeking allies on the right. Irving Kristol, Norman Podhoretz, Nathan Glazer, Midge Decter, and other neoconservative writers provided intellectual credibility and polemical ammunition for the attack on détente and skepticism of multilateralism. Daniel Patrick Moynihan, appointed ambassador to the United Nations by Ford in 1975, shook up the usually decorous world of diplomacy with attacks on what he believed to be the anti-Western and antidemocratic tilt of the UN and his unsuccessful fight against a resolution that declared that "Zionism is a form of racism and racial discrimination."

Senator Henry Jackson, a Cold War liberal Democrat from Washington with strong ties to the AFL-CIO leadership, found an effective device to slow down détente in the issue of Jewish emigration from the Soviet Union. As part of the trade agreements Nixon negotiated, the United States promised to grant the Soviet Union most favored nation status, which would have lowered tariffs on imported Soviet goods. Jackson pushed forward a measure to deny such status unless the Soviet Union increased the number of Jews it allowed to emigrate. In response, Kissinger negotiated a compromise with the Soviets, but Jackson, who had presidential ambitions, scuttled it, leading the Soviet Union to tighten emigration restrictions and become more distrustful of American promises. U.S.-Soviet trade declined, and the movement toward a new arms control agreement stalled.

A wave of revolutions in the undeveloped world and the final push against colonial and white minority rule in Africa added to the growing tension between the United States and the Soviet Union. The revolutionary movements of the 1970s generally had only slight resemblance to orthodox communist parties, but by challenging the status quo, using left rhetoric, and in some cases taking aid from the Soviet Union they sparked enmity from American policymakers. Local wars became proxy conflicts between the United States and the Soviet Union. The largest clash took place in Angola, where rival groups fought to establish control after a coup led Portugal to give up its colonial empire. The United States provided covert aid to the factions it favored (which China and South Africa also assisted), while the Soviet Union and Cuba backed a rival group. The bloody civil war left one of the potentially richest nations on the continent in ruins.

By the 1976 election, détente had all but ended. A framework for a new strategic arms limitation agreement, which Ford negotiated on a trip to the Soviet Union, never led to a treaty, largely because of congressional opposition. Ford himself banished the term "détente" from the administration's lexicon, recognizing that it had become toxic within the Republican Party. Even so, he faced a fusillade of criticism of his foreign policy during his primary battle with Reagan, who accused him of tacitly accepting a Soviet sphere of influence in Eastern Europe (which by then had been in place for three decades) and planning to cede control of the Panama Canal to Panama (in talks over the future of the canal that had been going on since 1964). Ford just barely beat back Reagan's effort to oust him but ended up accepting a conservative platform plank that criticized in everything but name his conduct of international relations.

Carter

Foreign policy did not help Ford in the 1976 general election, especially his blunder during one of the presidential debates—the first since 1960—when he said, "There is no Soviet domination of Eastern Europe." His opponent, Jimmy Carter, claimed common cause with the Republican foreign policy plank, asserting, "Our country is not strong anymore; we're not respected anymore." But the election largely revolved around the poor state of the economy and public disgust with the political class.

Carter had the advantage of being almost completely unknown outside of his home state before the election season began. A onetime Navy officer who ran a family peanut business, he had limited political experience and none in Washington to tar him with a public fed up with their national leaders. Ford, by contrast, could not shake the residual political effect of Watergate and his pardon of Nixon nor overcome blame for the ongoing economic troubles and his inability to work with Congress.

The South proved the key to Carter's victory. Eleven years after the 1965 Voting Rights Act, southern black voters had become a major electoral force, heavily aligned with the Democratic Party. Nationally, Carter captured more than 80 percent of the African American vote, with the percentage even higher in the South. Though southern white voters had begun drifting toward the Republican Party, Carter, as a southerner and professed born-again Christian (by far the most devout president of the twentieth century), also won a large part of the southern white vote, enabling him to carry the entire region except for Virginia. That, along with his capture of most of the large states in the Northeast and Midwest, put him in the White House.

Carter carried Ford's effort to deflate the pomposity of the presidency to an extreme. Calling himself Jimmy rather than James, at his inauguration he wore a business suit and walked from the Capitol to the White House, rather than wearing a morning coat and riding in a limousine, the usual practice. Once president, he sold the presidential yacht, let himself be photographed wearing blue jeans and carrying his own luggage, and gave a televised speech in a cardigan, deliberate breaks with past notions of presidential demeanor.

Carter pushed further Ford's effort to overcome the divisiveness of the Nixon years. He appointed more African Americans and women to significant federal posts than any president until that time and greatly expanded Ford's program to pardon Vietnam-era draft resisters and draft evaders. Carter invited to his inaugural gala musicians, actors, dancers, comedians, and athletes who represented the full range of national culture, from Aretha Franklin and Paul Simon to James Dickey and John Wayne, including Muhammad Ali, who only ten years earlier had been stripped of his boxing championship and sentenced to jail for refusing induction into the Army because of his objections to the Vietnam War.

Carter's political symbolism and rhetoric suggested that the days of American imperial ascendancy were over, and that it was probably for the best. In his inaugural address, he adopted a strikingly modest and somber tone, warning that "we cannot dwell upon remembered glory." "We have learned," he said, "that 'more' is not necessarily 'better,' that even our great nation has its recognized limits, and that we can neither answer all questions nor solve all problems."

Carter's presidency seemed to provide proof of the last contention, as so many of the nation's problems appeared intractable. Carter had no better success than Ford in dealing with the stagflation that brought hardship to much of the country. Coming into office, Carter proposed a stimulus package along traditional Keynesian lines. As finally passed, it provided tax credits for job creation and expanded federal funding for public works, job training, and temporary public-sector employment. Carter invoked the New Deal's Civilian Conservation Corps in calling for the expansion of CETA, which at its March 1978 peak provided jobs for three-quarters of a million unemployed or underemployed workers, by far the largest countercyclical government employment effort since the Great Depression.

But CETA proved to be the last gasp of the Democratic commitment to full employment through direct government job creation, an idea associated with the liberal-labor wing of the party to which Carter had only weak ties. More conservative than most Democrats in Congress, Carter soon retreated from making his top priority unemployment, which slowly fell over the course of 1977. Like Ford, he came to see inflation as a more serious threat to the economy. When Congress reauthorized CETA in 1978, job training rather than direct employment became its main focus. Meanwhile, Carter tried to check inflation through voluntary wage and price guidelines and cuts in federal spending.

Carter also moved away from the New Deal in his embrace of economic deregulation. Since the late nineteenth century, the federal government had imposed an expanding web of regulatory structures over business. In the years before Carter took office, a growing number of economists and political leaders—including Gerald Ford—had pushed for deregulating industry, arguing that overregulation contributed to inflation and economic stagnation. Carter agreed. Under the leadership of economist Alfred Kahn, his administration set out to slash regulations that set price floors and limited new entrants in a host of industries.

Deregulation created unusual political configurations. Many conservatives, committed to the idea of unrestrained capitalism, backed the idea, but so did many liberals, including Senator Ted Kennedy and reformer Ralph Nader, who believed that increased competition would benefit consumers. Some deregulators, including Kahn, quite consciously sought to weaken unions and lower labor costs in monopoly industries in the name of helping out less well-off workers and their families, who would benefit from jobs at new competitors and from lower consumer prices. "I'd love the Teamsters to be worse off," said Kahn. "I'd love the automobile workers to be worse off." Business divided. Many goods producers supported the deregulation of transportation, hoping to lower their shipping costs. Businesses and communities in areas with poor airline service hoped that more competition and new carriers would lead to better transportation links. But companies and unions protected by regulatory structures fought their dismantling, fearing a downward spiral of prices, profits, and wages. It was largely a rearguard action, as the Carter administration pushed through varying levels of deregulation in the airline, trucking, railroad, cable television, and savings bank industries.

Carter's trade policy continued the pattern, begun early in the Cold War, of giving priority to national security concerns over domestic economic considerations. To help out allies also suffering from stagnation, as well as to fight inflation, the Carter administration took only modest steps to stop imported manufactured goods from eroding the position of domestic producers, even when, as in the case of the steel industry, foreign-made products were dumped onto U.S. markets at prices below production costs. More efficient, or at least lower-cost, foreign manufacturers started grabbing larger shares of the U.S. market, with steel imports rising 30 percent in the first eight months of 1978.

At least in the short run, deregulation and trade policy had little impact on inflation, since food, energy, and housing costs (including mortgage interest rates) accounted for most of the rise in the consumer price index during the Carter years. Carter's modest anti-inflationary measures came nowhere near to balancing out the massive jump in crude oil prices that came in the wake of the 1979 Iranian Revolution, which helped push the inflation rate to 11.2 percent in 1979, the highest since 1947.

That year, the lead in fighting inflation moved from the White House to the Federal Reserve System. Paul Volcker, whom Carter appointed chairman of the Fed, made stopping inflation his main goal, even if it took inducing a recession to achieve it. Rather than slowing the economy the usual way, by jacking up interest rates, Volcker used a different approach, having the Federal Reserve System tightly control the growth in the money supply, largely through increases in the requirements for bank reserves. In doing so, the Federal Reserve adopted the prescription of Milton Friedman and other monetarist economists who criticized Keynesianism and argued that the government should abandon trying to regulate the economy with fiscal tools and instead restrict its actions to adjustments in the supply of money.

The Fed, exempt as it was from democratic control, could do what no president or Congress could, deliberately set out to crash the economy and in the process create a sea of human misery in the service of creating price stability. But even it needed some fig leaf of protection from public wrath, which monetarism provided. Controlling the money supply seemed more a technical measure than directly pushing up interest rates, something the public more easily understood as a discretionary act.

The central bank restrictions on the money supply quickly impacted the economy. Interest rates shot up to extreme levels, approaching 20 percent. That in turn led to a sharp drop in consumer spending and, in the second quarter of 1980, the steepest fall of the GNP ever recorded. Yet inflation continued to rise. Meanwhile, increased imports and Volcker's monetary policy led to a massive wave of layoffs and plant closings in the automobile and steel industries, the beginning of a decade of intense deindustrialization that would transform and hollow out the American economy. The economy had been redirected not through public discourse or legislative action but in

the secretive boardroom of the Federal Reserve. Carter, who initially acquiesced with the Fed policy, began speaking out against it during the fall 1980
election, but by then it was too late to halt its downward push on the economy and on his own political fate.

Like Ford, Carter did no better with energy than with the economy. Between the end of the 1973 Arab oil boycott and the Iranian Revolution four
years later, oil prices stabilized and the energy issue receded from public
attention. Nonetheless, Carter made it one of his top priorities, recognizing
the danger of dependence on foreign oil and the limits on fossil fuel supplies.
The Carter administration crafted a complex, comprehensive energy program, designed to reduce consumption, encourage conservation, lessen dependence on foreign oil, and promote the development of renewable sources
of energy, to be accomplished through the partial decontrol of oil and gas
prices, subsidies, tax measures, and regulatory action.

The prolonged fight in Congress that followed reflected conflicting ideas
for a national energy policy, Carter's ineptitude in dealing with Congress,
and the difficulty of governance in an era of fragmented power. Energy issues pitted political factions, economic interests, and regions against one
another. Decontrolling oil and gas prices would bring huge profits to energy
companies and the regions where they were located, while hurting energy
consumers and regions that imported oil and gas, especially the Northeast,
where oil heating made homeowners particularly vulnerable to price hikes.
Carter proposed various tax schemes to recycle revenue from higher oil
prices back to consumers and to encourage conservation, but these raised
opposition from those who would bear them.

Powerful oil and gas interests played a large role in the congressional
handling of energy, but a mobilized public, now conditioned to direct action
to promote its views, played a role too, especially in opposing nuclear power.
In May 1977, 1,414 protestors were arrested at the site of a proposed nuclear
plant in Seabrook, New Hampshire. Taking a page from the civil rights
movement, many refused bail, forcing authorities to hold them in armories
around the state. Meanwhile, the proliferation of committees and subcom-
mittees in Congress provided many entry points for lobbyists and interests.
It took a year and a half for Carter to get an energy law, stripped of many of
his proposals, including tax provisions designed to reduce consumption.

Within months, energy emerged as a major issue again, when the revolution in Iran led to a near complete halt of its oil exports and OPEC took advantage of the tight market to drive up the price of crude oil. With gasoline
lines and shortages spreading across the country and tempers flaring, Carter
used existing authority to phase out controls on oil prices, while proposing a

windfall profits tax, which Congress eventually passed. But consumers bore the brunt of the burden of the transition toward higher energy costs, as they watched the pump price of gasoline more than double in three years. By the time Carter left office, the percent of the GDP devoted to energy spending exceeded 13 percent, up from 8 percent at the beginning of the decade.

The gasoline lines and shortages in the summer of 1979 occasioned one of the most notable presidential addresses of the post–World War II epoch. Carter had planned to give a national address on energy policy but at the last minute canceled it, instead traveling to the presidential retreat at Camp David. There he spent six days meeting with a stream of politicians, academics, religious and labor leaders, and businessmen about the economy, energy, the state of the nation, and his own administration. With the nation wondering just what the president could possibly be up to, Carter then delivered his postponed address to a huge radio and television audience.

"The true problems of our Nation," Carter told his listeners, "are much deeper . . . than gasoline lines or energy shortages, deeper even than inflation or recession." Rather, the nation suffered "a crisis of confidence . . . growing doubt about the meaning of our own lives and the loss of a unity of purpose for our nation." "In a nation that was proud of hard work, strong families, close-knit communities, and our faith in God," Carter continued, "too many of us now tend to worship self-indulgence and consumption. Human identity is no longer defined by what one does, but by what one owns. But we've . . . learned that piling up material goods cannot fill the emptiness of lives which have no confidence or purpose."

After deftly analyzing what he called "the crisis of the American spirit," Carter proposed no strategy to overcome it, no broad program to meet the problems he identified. Instead he itemized his new energy proposals. That reinforced what so many people found inadequate in Carter, a technocratic obsession with detail while lacking a political sense of how to institute large-scale change. Carter followed up his speech by firing five cabinet officers, a gesture that seemed irrelevant if, as he argued, America's problems were deeply rooted in its culture of self-interest. Carter proclaimed in his speech that "all the legislation in the world can't fix what's wrong with America," yet he offered nothing that could—and proved pretty poor at getting legislation passed to boot.

From Human Rights to Renewed Cold War

In foreign affairs, Carter pursued many of the same themes as he did domestically. At times he seemed to believe that American power inevitably was declining in an age of proliferating nuclear weapons, third world economic development, and social revolution. Rather than defending the status quo, in some situations Carter supported a controlled liquidation of American dominance, seeking to ally with or at least avoid open conflict with ascending forces for social change.

Early in his administration, Carter pushed hard and successfully for Senate ratification of treaties ceding control over the Panama Canal and the Canal Zone to Panama, culminating a long process of removing a sore point in U.S. relations with Latin America. When the left-wing Sandinista National Liberation Front led a revolution against Nicaraguan dictator Anastasio Somoza Debayle, a longtime American ally, Carter maneuvered unsuccessfully for the installation of a moderate-led government but, in a break from past practice, refrained from open or covert military action to check radical change.

Carter's policies were animated in part by his desire to make a "commitment to human rights . . . a fundamental tenet" in how the United States acted. In moralizing foreign policy, Carter joined the neoconservatives in sharp criticism of the lack of political freedom in the Soviet Union and Eastern Europe. Unlike the conservative moralists, he also attacked the abuses of human rights by anticommunist authoritarian regimes that in the past could count on U.S. backing. Carter reduced or ended aid to countries like Chile, Argentina, and Uruguay that were engaged in murderous campaigns against left-wing dissidents. But he only went so far, continuing to support regimes engaged in human rights abuses when he perceived their opponents as fundamentally threatening U.S. interests and trying, unsuccessfully, to stop the Mariel boatlift from Cuba, in which Castro suddenly allowed the disaffected to leave the island.

Carter's human rights agenda complicated his effort to achieve further arms control agreements with the Soviet Union. His embrace of Soviet dissidents and criticism of human rights violations in the Soviet bloc, along with his desire for deep cuts in strategic weapons, made negotiating a new Strategic Arms Limitation Treaty, SALT II, a long, difficult process. When the Soviet Union sent troops into Afghanistan in 1979 to try to keep in power a pro-Soviet regime facing a tribal and religious rebellion, Carter swiftly adopted what amounted to a renewed hard-line Cold War stance. He imposed an embargo on grain sales to the Soviet Union; forced American athletes to boycott the 1980 Moscow Olympics; withdrew the SALT II treaty from consideration by the Senate; increased covert action against left-wing governments in Asia and Africa; and accelerated the increase in military spending that he had already begun.

The sharpness of Carter's actions reflected a sense of threat that came from events in Iran as much as Afghanistan. In the years after 1953, when the United States had helped restore the shah to power, Iran had become an increasingly important ally. But the close U.S. ties to the shah proved detrimental as opposition to the modernizing but undemocratic and sometimes brutal Iranian regime gathered strength. In early 1979, the shah left Iran in the face of growing strikes and demonstrations, paving the way for exiled Muslim cleric Ayatollah Ruhollah Mussaui Khomeini, who helped inspire the uprising, to return.

The Carter administration, largely operating within the intellectual framework of the Cold War and with a flawed view of Iranian society derived from the shah and his American backers, found itself at a loss as to how to deal with a cataclysmic social shift that did not resemble other post-Enlightenment revolutions. The United States made no effort to again return the shah to power, but Carter gave in to pressure from Henry Kissinger and other powerful friends of the former Iranian leader to allow him into the country for cancer treatment. In reaction, on November 4, 1979, radical Islamist students took over the U.S. embassy in Tehran and seized more than fifty hostages with backing from Khomeini, who used the crisis to consolidate his power at the expense of secular and left-wing rivals.

For the next fourteen months, Carter tried one measure after another to get the hostages released, from freezing Iranian assets in the United States to attempting to begin negotiations to breaking diplomatic relations, without success. In April 1980, he tried to use military force to free them, but that failed too, when helicopters on the mission suffered mechanical problems. Ultimately, the shah's death, the outbreak of war between Iran and Iraq, and the U.S. presidential election set the stage for a resolution of the crisis. The Iranians, eager for funds for their war and perhaps concerned with what might happen if Reagan got elected president, finally negotiated an arrangement with the Carter administration in which the hostages were released— just after Carter left office—in return for unfreezing Iranian assets in the United States.

The Soviet invasion of Afghanistan, the Iranian Revolution, and the hostage crisis vividly demonstrated the changed circumstances the United States faced in the Near East. It no longer could depend on allies and surrogates, like Britain and Iran, to protect its interests in the region, on which it had become increasingly dependent for oil. It would have to act on its own. In his 1980 State of the Union address, Carter declared, "An attempt by any outside force to gain control of the Persian Gulf region will be regarded as an assault on the vital interests of the United States of America, and such an

assault will be repelled by any means necessary, including military force."
Thus began a military buildup in the Gulf region, the declared possibility
and eventual actuality of direct U.S. military intervention, and the recom-
mitment to a path of development dependent on cheap, plentiful oil. Yet in
spite of his bellicose language and military buildup, Carter suffered politically from keeping the hostages at the forefront of his foreign policy while
proving unable to get them home, and from the failed rescue effort that
seemed to confirm the impotence and ineptitude of the American military
in what looked like an increasingly dangerous and hostile world.

Limiting Government

The inability of Washington to solve big problems the nation faced allowed
efforts to limit the size and functions of government to gain momentum.
Some of the push came from business interests that sought to circumvent
democratic channels, where their power had become constrained. Some of
it came from grassroots activists, as upset by the cost of government as by
what it did.

The Ford and Carter regimes took modest steps back from the New
Deal–Great Society conception of state function. But a much more frontal
attack on the idea of the welfare state took place in cities and states hit hard
by the recession of the mid-1970s. Municipalities found themselves facing
greater needs for social services at the very moment when their tax bases
were deteriorating as a result of the economic downturn, deindustrialization,
and suburbanization. Efforts to hold down the costs of municipal employee
wages and benefits led to labor conflict and disruptive strikes, including a
1974 walkout by Baltimore police, the first significant law enforcement strike
since 1919. In New York and Cleveland, bankers and conservative politicians
took advantage of severe fiscal problems to attack social democratic policies
and populist politics.

New York City had provided a national model for an expansive, liberal
notion of government in the decades after World War II. Government services included a large, free university system; a large public hospital system;
a large mass transit system; public housing projects with over a half million
residents; and a large, relatively generous welfare system. In addition, the
city had tens of thousands of apartments in nonprofit cooperative housing
projects and extensive nonprofit health insurance programs. In effect, a kind
of municipal social democracy had been built.

But New York's large public sector, welfare costs, and Medicaid expenses
proved financially unsustainable on a municipal basis. During the late 1960s

and early 1970s, the city ran up massive debt as the cost of the services it provided outstripped its revenues. During the winter of 1974–75, the market for New York City bonds collapsed when investors grew fearful that the city would be unable to repay what it had borrowed.

For some financiers and conservative politicians, including Gerald Ford and his secretary of the treasury, William Simon, a former bond trader who had helped New York build up its debt, the city's fiscal woes provided an opportunity for an attack on the welfare state and public employee unions. New York's plight confirmed their conviction that liberal attitudes and government programs threatened the economic and moral health of the nation. Many conservatives shared Simon's beleaguered sense that capitalism and the market were in imminent danger from growing government regulation, welfare-state measures, transfers of wealth, and an intellectual elite committed to social democracy or socialism.

New York State and the federal government came up with a series of jerry-built plans to refinance New York City's debt, allowing it to remain technically solvent. But as a condition for refunding, federal officials and business leaders appointed by the state's Democratic governor to new oversight and finance agencies demanded that the city lay off tens of thousands of workers, defer wage increases called for by union contracts, start charging tuition at its university system, cut municipal services, raise transit fares, and reform budgeting and fiscal procedures. In doing so, the coalition of financiers and politicians that all but preempted control over New York City from its local elected leaders showed that the unthinkable could be done, or at least partially accomplished: the half-century-long movement toward expanded state function and social entitlements could be reversed. Conservatives did not transform New York as fully as they hoped. They failed in their efforts to eliminate rent control—a holdover from World War II price controls—or radically reduce municipal worker pay and benefits, as the labor movement and community groups mobilized mass resistance. But they succeeded in ratcheting down public expectations of what government would provide and forcing austerity on New York's working class. With public services slashed in the middle of a severe recession, New York became a grim place to live. Streets grew filthy, roads literally crumbled, crime shot up, subways broke down frequently, libraries opened only a few days a week, and schools crammed children into overcrowded classrooms and eliminated art, music, and sports.

In Cleveland, a clash between local business leaders and a liberal city government led to an actual default, though short-lived. Cleveland's mayor, Dennis Kucinich, elected in 1977 as a populist (when only thirty-one years old), made good on his campaign promise to end tax abatements for businesses. He also refused to sell Cleveland's small municipal-owned electric company to a much larger commercial utility seeking to eliminate its rival. Financial claims by the utility against the city deeply strained its budget. Local bankers told Kucinich they would not roll over short-term city debt unless he agreed to sell the city-owned system. When Kucinich stood his ground, Cleveland became the first major city since the Great Depression to default on its debt. Kucinich rallied public support and won a referendum backing the retention of the power company and raising income taxes to enable the city to become solvent. But enough damage had been done to pave the way for Kucinich's ouster in the November 1979 election by Republican George Voinovich.

In California, government cutbacks came as a result of a tax revolt. In 1953, the average American family paid less than 12 percent of its income in federal, state, and local taxes, but by 1977 that had risen to over 22 percent. Much of the rise, especially in the 1970s, stemmed not from explicit legislative decisions but from the impact of inflation. Inflation pushed families into higher tax brackets for their federal income taxes and in some cases for state income taxes too. It also drove up property taxes, especially in places like California, where a booming real estate market combined with the general inflationary climate to balloon the value of houses. As assessments soared, so did the property taxes based on them.

Episodic protests against high property taxes had taken place in various parts of California during the 1950s and 1960s, with limited success. But changed conditions during the 1970s created more fertile ground. With rising taxes, a stagnant economy, and soaring prices pressing family budgets, the antitax sentiment built into the DNA of the nation heated up. The accumulation by the California state government of a $4 billion surplus rubbed salt into wounds, making the growing tax burden seem unnecessary.

In 1978, Howard Jarvis, a veteran antitax campaigner, got a tax reduction referendum measure, Proposition 13, put on the ballot. It called for capping local real estate taxes at 1 percent of assessed value, scaling back assessments to their 1975–76 level, and, except at the time of sales, limiting increases in assessments to 2 percent a year. It also mandated a two-thirds majority in the legislature to raise state taxes and two-thirds voter approval to raise local taxes. Using populist rhetoric, Jarvis, who had close ties to Los Angeles–area apartment building owners, orchestrated a well-funded campaign in support of the measure.

In spite of opposition to Proposition 13 from most of the political establishment (Republican as well as Democratic), the labor movement, civil rights groups, the Chamber of Commerce, and many large corporations (small businesses tended to support it), it passed by a two-to-one margin. The measure won support from liberal and conservative voters up and down the economic ladder. Among major constituencies, only African Americans and public employees cast a majority of their votes against it.

Proposition 13 had a more conservative cast than the language used to promote it suggested. Earlier failed tax limitation efforts in California and Massachusetts had targeted the tax burden on middle- and lower-income families, proposing to shift more of the tax load to businesses and the well-off. By contrast, nearly two-thirds of the tax relief Proposition 13 provided during its first five years went not to homeowners but to landlords, farmers, and owners of commercial and industrial property.

Proposition 13 proved contagious, sparking a round of tax-cutting efforts elsewhere. Idaho and Massachusetts voted in steep property tax cuts, in the latter case with strong backing from high-technology companies, which funded a referendum campaign. Voters in over a dozen other states passed more modest tax limitation proposals. Elsewhere, dozens of state legislatures, hoping to avoid voters taking things into their own hands, preemptively reduced income and property taxes.

The antistate animus reflected in the tax revolt was in part fostered by the bifurcated system of social provision that had developed since World War II, with some people receiving benefits from private entities and others from the government. Homeowners resented paying taxes to support public housing and rent subsidies. Employees who received health insurance and other benefits through their jobs resented paying taxes to finance parallel state benefit systems, which in some cases provided more generous benefits. Southern white parents who put their children in private schools to avoid racial integration resented paying taxes for public schools they did not use and pushed for tax credits or government vouchers for private education, an idea many Catholics supported too. By contrast, government programs that had near-universal coverage, like Social Security and Medicare, remained largely exempt from popular antistate sentiment.

The antitax campaigns of the late 1970s, like the New York fiscal crisis, worked to delegitimize government, or at least an expansive notion of state function. The essential argument of the fiscal regulators in New York and the antitax rebels elsewhere was that the public good would be best served by less government, not more. Both suggested that government had become riddled with inefficiencies, self-serving leaders, and entrenched interest groups. The relatively modest cutbacks in state and local services that occurred in most states after tax limitation measures (California had its huge surplus to spend down and other states raised miscellaneous fees and taxes to make up for property and income tax reductions) seemed to give lie to claims by liberal opponents of tax reductions that they would have disastrous consequences, while suggesting that antistatist outsiders like Jarvis, with common sense rather than technical expertise, knew more about how the world really worked than the established political class and credentialed policy specialists. By merging the interests of large property holders and businesses with middle-class families pressed by hard times and resentful about paying taxes to help the less well-off, the tax revolt helped lay the basis for a broader assault on the New Deal order in the years to come.

Crime and Punishment

At the same time that pressure grew to lessen the presence of government in everyday life through reduced taxes, regulations, and social benefits, calls grew for increased use of state power to deal with criminality. Crime had been an important political issue since the late 1960s, as the rate of violent offenses more than doubled between 1965 and 1975. Liberals sought to limit access to firearms as a way to check crime, winning a federal gun control law in 1968. But efforts at further gun legislation floundered in the face of a reaction from conservatives and gun owners, who saw gun control as an unconstitutional limit on the rights of law-abiding citizens.

More incarceration, rather than gun control, emerged as the main approach to crime control. Conservatives rejected the widespread liberal analysis that stressed social circumstances in explaining criminality and spurned therapeutic approaches to dealing with lawbreakers. Instead, they promoted incarceration as a means of punishment, retribution, and prevention, getting dangerous people off the streets and keeping them off. So did the victims' rights movement—another manifestation of the rights revolution—which pressed for longer prison sentences and harsher prison conditions. Liberal criminologists and public officials inadvertently bolstered the movement when they began to doubt the curative assumption behind the common practice of indeterminate sentencing. State legislatures took up their call for fixed sentencing, but in a political climate in which the population at large, fearful and angry, saw in the application of state power an emotional outlet and a path toward greater personal security, they ended up extending sentencing norms rather than reducing them.

The combination of more crime, more arrests, and longer sentences swelled the prison population. After a half century during which the incarceration rate had fluctuated only moderately, in the mid-1970s it began to rise steeply. It kept rising until the end of the century and beyond, even after crime rates dropped. Mass imprisonment became a distinguishing feature of the United States, as its incarceration rate came to far exceed that in other industrial nations (including the Soviet Union). The bulk of the increase in the prison population consisted of nonviolent offenders. Many were there for violating stiffened drug laws. Black men made up a disproportionate share of the newly incarcerated, in part because they were more likely to be arrested for drug violations than white men (though the two groups had roughly the same rate of drug use) and when convicted were typically given much longer sentences than whites.

The United States became an outlier in its use of capital punishment as well. Executions became much less common during the two decades after World War II, especially outside the South. Then, as a result of a series of Supreme Court decisions that deemed unconstitutional various procedures used in capital cases, no criminals were put to death between 1967 and 1977. For a while it looked like the death penalty might disappear. But once the Supreme Court made it clear that under some circumstances capital punishment would be constitutional, thirty-five states passed new death penalty laws. Proponents and critics of capital punishment heatedly debated its value as a deterrent to crime, but support for the death penalty did not rest strictly or even mainly on instrumental grounds. For many of its supporters, it served as an expressive act, a symbolic counterweight to a perceived breakdown of moral standards and respect for authority.

Capital punishment resumed with the 1977 Utah firing squad execution of murderer Gary Gilmore. That same year, an execution in France became the last use of capital punishment in Western Europe. As abolition became the norm in noncommunist industrial countries (with Japan the other exception), in the United States the annual number of executions grew through the end of the twentieth century. As in the case of incarceration, at a moment of political transition, economic travail, and cultural uncertainty, the United States embarked on a road very different from other industrial nations.

Sex and Sexuality

Some of the most wrenching political debates of the 1970s revolved around gender roles and sexuality. As the revolution in the status of women swept forward and sexual mores continued to change, adjusting the law to new attitudes and norms proved extraordinarily contentious. Many religious leaders and political conservatives began the decade seeking to counter changes in sexual behavior and gender norms by encouraging their followers to maintain families structured around a stay-at-home mother and shun permissive cultural standards. Their pleas proved puny weapons in the face of wage stagnation and inflation that made it increasingly difficult for one-wage-earner families to survive and a commercial mass culture perfectly happy to profit by endorsing greater sexual freedom and the achievement of satisfaction through consumption. Frustrated, activists averse to state power in other realms began looking to government to regulate sexuality, reproduction, and the family.

The fate of the Equal Rights Amendment (ERA) demonstrated how divided the country had become over women's rights and sexuality and how quickly political dynamics changed. After a substantial majority of the states endorsed the ERA, in 1974 the push for ratification stalled. Phyllis Schlafly, a longtime conservative leader, spearheaded opposition to the amendment. At first she was a lonely voice against what was widely seen as inevitable ratification, but established conservative groups and new grassroots anti-ERA organizations (many all-female) joined the effort. Conservative religious denominations, notably the Mormons and Baptists, joined in too.

The claim by opponents of the ERA that it might lead to drafting women into the military, abortion on demand, unisex bathrooms, homosexual marriages, and other unwanted social changes resonated with many women and men disturbed by the rapid transformation of gender roles. Over the course of the 1970s, the number of divorces per capita continued to rise. By the mid-1970s, families consisting of a stay-at-home mother living with a working husband and children constituted less than a quarter of families. ERA opponents feared that the amendment would legitimize the changes in family structure and gender relations that had occurred and further undermine social and moral structures built around the notion of different roles for men and women. Schlafly framed her opposition to the ERA as a defense of women's existing legal protections. She claimed that if the amendment won ratification, it would relieve husbands of the obligation to support their families or to pay alimony after divorce, a worrisome possibility to millions of housewives who depended on men for support and for whom taking a poorly paid job in a labor market stacked against women held little attraction.

ERA opponents did not have to win majority public support or even majority support from the nation's state legislators to block it. All they had to do was keep thirteen legislatures from ratifying it, which in most states meant wooing just a third of the members, since typically a two-thirds vote was required. After 1974 only a trickle of additional states ratified the ERA, leaving it three states short of the needed three-quarters when the prescribed ratification period ended in 1979. Except for Illinois, all the states that did not ratify the ERA were either in the South or Rocky Mountain states with large Mormon populations.

Opponents of the ERA benefited from the backlash to the 1973 *Roe v. Wade* decision, which broadened into a general antifeminist offensive. Catholic housewives—with support from their church—played a leading role in the "Right to Life" movement, which sought to limit and recriminalize abortion. Adopting tactics made popular by the civil rights movement, they picketed abortion clinics and engaged in civil disobedience, joined over time by evangelical Protestants, who took up the issue as well.

The debate over abortion proved contentious and prolonged. Abortion opponents won an important victory in 1976 with congressional passage of the Hyde Amendment, which banned the use of Medicaid funds to pay for abortions, restricting the ability of low-income women to terminate unwanted pregnancies. But both sides dug in for a war of position, in which electoral politics became a central front. At stake were not simply abortion laws but notions about the definition of life, women's rights, their proper role in society, and the extent to which it should be defined by motherhood.

Debate over gay rights similarly provoked intense emotion and sharp divisions because it concerned not only specific legal issues but also broader notions about sexuality, morality, family, and gender roles. Gay activists, adopting the rights revolution model, pressed in the 1970s for policies and statutes to end discrimination on the basis of sexual orientation. Their initial success led conservatives to campaign against such equal rights mandates and, more broadly, against the normalization and moral legitimation of homosexuality.

As with the anti-ERA movement, the anti–gay rights movement gained national attention through its embrace by an effective female leader, in this case pop singer and former beauty pageant contestant Anita Bryant, who was the national spokesperson for the Florida orange juice industry. When in 1977 Dade County, Florida (which included the city of Miami), passed an ordinance prohibiting discrimination on the basis of "affectional or sexual preferences," Bryant launched a campaign for its repeal that received national media coverage. She portrayed homosexuality as sinful and homosexuals as potential child molesters seeking to recruit children to same-sex sexuality. She called her organization "Save Our Children."

Bryant's campaign came at a moment of increased public and government concern about child abuse. Expanding notions of children's rights, liberal and feminist critiques of authoritarian and patriarchal family relations, and the more open display of sexual images of children (part of the general spread of pornography) led to demands for child protection from feminists, lawmakers, journalists, and parents. Bryant's campaign wedded fears that changing moral norms threatened children to more traditional religious opposition to homosexuality. When voters repealed the Dade County ordinance by a more than two-to-one margin, they made opposition to gay rights a national movement and a mobilizing issue for conservatives, while sparking a new wave of political organizing by gay activists. Voters in Wichita, Kansas, St. Paul, Minnesota, and Eugene, Oregon, passed ballot initiatives repealing gay rights laws. In California, a proposition on the 1978 ballot, the Briggs amendment, supported by Bryant, called for firing gay and lesbian public school teachers and banning teachers from speaking favorably about homosexuality in the classroom. A campaign spearheaded by openly gay San Francisco supervisor Harvey Milk led to its defeat. (Just weeks later Milk and San Francisco mayor George Moscone were assassinated by a homophobic former supervisor, Dan White.)

In deploying state power to impose moral norms, conservatives took the notion that "the personal is political" much further than the women's movement, which had originated the slogan. In the process they found a strategy for widening the narrow base for their economic program, which favored the well-off, by winning over voter groups deeply concerned with what came to be called social issues. The coalitions that emerged in the struggles against the ERA, abortion, and gay rights pointed the way toward a reconfiguration of electoral politics at the end of the 1970s, after a decade during which the political system had proved largely incapable of dealing with the most serious problems Americans experienced. Meanwhile, outside the political arena, in the private economy, a profound restructuring was beginning that would transform the country in the decades to come.

CHAPTER 14

The Corporate Revolution

During the 1970s and early 1980s, American businesses faced their greatest challenge since World War II. Recession, inflation, tight credit, and growing international competition combined to push down profits and drive up the rate of business failure to the highest level since the Great Depression. Some of the country's best-known corporations, like Chrysler, tottered on the edge of bankruptcy. Millions of workers lost their jobs in wave after wave of layoffs. The core model of corporate America no longer seemed to work.

Many business owners and executives linked their difficulty making profits to what they perceived as growing limits on their freedom of action. Unionized workers had displayed uncommon militancy in the late 1960s and early 1970s, with strikes reaching a level unseen since the immediate post–World War II years. Governmental rules and regulations grew in number and complexity.

Business leaders worried about what they saw as a general anti-business climate. During and after World War II, businessmen and free-enterprise ideologues had largely succeeded in restoring respect for business, which had plummeted during the Great Depression. But in the 1960s and 1970s, criticism of the corporate world, its values, and even of capitalism itself became commonplace, not just on the left but in mainstream institutions, from churches to colleges to the mass media. William Simon was not alone in his sense that business and free-market values were under siege. Lewis Powell, an influential lawyer who sat on many corporate boards, wrote a memorandum in 1971—shortly before he was nominated by Richard Nixon to the Supreme Court—to the U.S. Chamber of Commerce on "The Attack on the Free Enterprise System." Businessmen, he wrote, needed "to recognize that the ultimate issue may be survival—survival of what we call the free enterprise system, and all that this means for the strength and prosperity of America and the freedom of our people." Simon and Powell greatly exaggerated the existential threat, but clearly business had lost some of its hegemony.

Over the course of the 1970s and 1980s, business launched a remarkably successful campaign to restore its standing. Many businesspeople concerned themselves solely with making money for their companies and themselves. This often entailed extensive reorganizations and fundamental changes in labor relations, production techniques, and business models. But businessmen and their allies also mobilized politically, to shape legislative and regulatory decisions and increase the influence of business on government. To achieve long-term change, a network of conservative activists, business groups, and business-oriented philanthropies worked to bolster the intellectual infrastructure promoting free-market ideology.

The business rehabilitation took time. But by the end of the 1980s, its complementary strands—economic, political, and cultural—had together effected what amounted to a reconfiguration of the corporation and a transformation in the political economy. A corporate revolution—or counterrevolution—had taken place that left the United States a very different place than it had been a decade and a half earlier.

Downsizing

In the mid-1960s, the average rate of profit for business began to fall, after having remained relatively steady since the end of World War II. It continued to drop until the early 1980s. The slide for manufacturing was steeper than for the economy as a whole. After averaging near 25 percent (before taxes) from 1948 to 1969, the manufacturing profit rate slipped below 17 percent from 1969 to 1973 and then fell to 14 percent from 1973 to 1979 and 13 percent from 1979 to 1990.

Various explanations were put forth for the drop. Some people pointed to a slowdown in the growth of labor productivity (though the profit slide preceded the productivity slump that began after 1973). Others pointed to a rise in real wages and the increased costs of doing business, including greater regulatory requirements. High energy and commodity prices and interest rates hurt too. Problematic in themselves, these developments were much harder to deal with than in the past because of growing international competition.

Worldwide, heavy investment and national competition led to overcapacity in many manufacturing sectors. Foreign companies often had lower labor costs, and some more efficient production methods, than U.S. firms. Combined with a lowering of trade barriers, the result was downward pressure on the prices for finished goods. American companies that in the past could pass on higher labor and raw material costs to their customers found themselves constrained by competition.

The rising value of the dollar exacerbated the problems faced by American manufacturers. The very high interest rates that resulted from the Federal Reserve's effort to fight inflation attracted foreign investors, driving up the cost of dollars relative to Asian and European currencies. The strong dollar made it cheaper for Americans to import goods and more expensive for people in other countries to purchase things made in the United States.

As profits fell and stagflation settled in, companies and investors grew reluctant to put capital into expanding or upgrading plant and equipment or into research and development. Investment in manufacturing fell by 8 percent between 1979 and 1982 and another 15 percent in 1983. That left companies in many industries slipping behind their European and Asian competitors in the quality of their products and the efficiency of their production processes. Many companies, faced with escalating difficulties and little prospect of robust future profits, shut down facilities, laid off workers, or went out of business entirely. In some cases, whole industries imploded.

Steel provides a case in point. U.S. steel production remained fairly steady from the mid-1950s through the 1970s. A few giant, integrated companies, which made their own iron and steel and fabricated finished products, dominated the industry. By avoiding price competition, they kept profits strong. Their failure to spend much money on research and development or to move quickly to adopt new technologies had few immediate adverse consequences.

Over time, though, new competition developed. Overseas, steel production grew dramatically, helped in many countries by cartelization and government financing, subsidies, and export promotion. Often foreign producers had cost advantages over U.S. companies as a result of more modern production techniques and lower wages. The boost U.S. producers once got from having rich domestic ore deposits diminished. Domestic mines began to be depleted, while new high-grade foreign mines opened up and shipping costs dropped, so that even countries without iron deposits, like Japan, could get ore cheaply. The United States began importing steel in the late 1950s, at first largely to meet demand that domestic producers could not cover, but soon price competition came into play. The major U.S. companies faced another challenge from mini-mills. These small, efficient domestic producers used scrap metal as raw material and generally employed nonunion workers, enabling them to sell simple products like bars and bolts at signifi-cantly lower prices than the integrated firms.

For the giant steel companies, competition went from being a nuisance to a serious threat once the domestic demand for steel began dropping in the early 1970s. The increasing use of alternative materials in manufacturing and construction—aluminum, plastics, and prestressed concrete—contributed to the decline. So did the growing flow of imported goods containing steel, especially automobiles, which had the effect of reducing the demand for domestically produced metal.

Though long-term trends underlay the problems the steel industry faced, its crisis came suddenly. The industry made money every year from World War II until 1982. Then the recession induced by the Federal Reserve brought disaster. Demand for steel plummeted just when the strong dollar made imports cheaper. Between 1982 and 1986, the industry lost more than $15 billion.

During the course of the 1980s, some two dozen steel mills were shut down and 230,000 jobs eliminated. Between 1979 and 1982 alone, steel com-panies discharged more than 150,000 production and maintenance workers. Employers used threats to shutter mills to win concessions from the United Steelworkers, which over a half century of battling had made steel jobs among the best-paid blue-collar work in the country. Companies also pressed local and state governments to ease pollution standards and give tax breaks as their price for continuing operations. But often they shut mills anyway, seeing the prospects for the industry too bleak to invest more money. U.S. Steel used its capital to buy an oil company and swapped stock to acquire another, changing its name to USX to symbolize its diversification away from its historic role as the world's largest steel producer. By 1981, companies that made steel had nearly 40 percent of their assets in nonsteel operations.

Steelmaking communities in the Northeast and Midwest were devastated by the closures. Bethlehem Steel eliminated ten thousand jobs at its Spar-rows Point complex outside Baltimore, ended steelmaking in Lackawanna, New York, and phased out operations in Johnstown, Pennsylvania, where the unemployment rate shot up to 25 percent. In Youngstown, Ohio, mills that had employed over nine thousand men and women shut down. The Pittsburgh area suffered through one closure after another, including the 1986 shuttering of the U.S. Steel Homestead works, once the center of An-drew Carnegie's empire. On the Southeast Side of Chicago, nearly fifteen thousand millworkers lost their jobs as a result of closures or layoffs, and many nearby steel-related plants shut down or shriveled, including the historic Pullman railcar factory, which ceased production, putting three thousand people out of work.

The automobile industry underwent a similar, if not quite as severe, cataclysm as a result of recession, high interest rates (pushing up the cost of auto loans), and high gas prices. Total car sales fell from over eleven million in 1978 to fewer than eight million in 1982. Sales of domestically produced cars plunged even more steeply, from 9.3 to 5.8 million, as car buyers turned to foreign companies, particularly Japanese automakers, for vehicles that were less expensive and more fuel-efficient than domestic models. Nearly half the capacity of the auto industry lay idle (bad, but not as bad as steel, where two-thirds lay unused). In 1981, General Motors lost money for the first time since the early 1920s. Chrysler, the smallest of the "Big Three" automakers (but still the ninth-largest company in the country), survived only because the federal government, in a deal modeled on its help to New York City, guaranteed loans to the company on the condition that the United Automobile Workers (UAW) agree to cuts in wages and benefits and suppliers and creditors grant concessions.

To reduce overcapacity and restore profits, the auto industry undertook a massive program of plant closings and cost reduction. In Wayne County, Michigan, which includes Detroit, more than three dozen auto-related plants shut down between 1978 and 1981, from the gigantic but technologically outmoded Dodge Main complex to small parts suppliers. Nationally, employment in the industry fell by a third between 1978 and 1982. The unemployment rate in Michigan, the center of the industry, hit 17 percent in 1982. Most autoworkers who kept their jobs took reductions in compensation to do so, as GM, Ford, and smaller companies followed in the wake of the Chrysler bailout by demanding that wage increases be delayed or eliminated and benefits cut. When auto sales picked up after 1982, employment levels did not rise proportionally because companies preferred using extensive overtime to adding to their head counts and invested in automated equipment, like robot welders, to reduce manpower needs.

The plants shut down by steel and auto companies and in related industries, like tire making, tended to be clustered in industrial cities in the Northeast and Midwest. Because neighborhoods and sometimes whole cities had grown up around them, their closure had wrenching impact that rippled far beyond the workers immediately affected. Supply, service, and shipping firms shut down. Businesses that catered to plant workers and their families—from auto dealers to grocery stores to bowling alleys and bars—suffered. Empty stores soon lined commercial streets. With tax bases shriveling, public services diminished and infrastructure eroded. In Gary, Indiana, where U.S. Steel invested heavily in its steelmaking operation but, largely as a result of automation, eliminated twenty thousand jobs, more than a third of the retail stores closed, including all five department stores. Even when new industrial employers set up shop in areas hit by shutdowns, the jobs they provided rarely matched in pay or benefits the ones that had disappeared.

The desperation for work in what had been the industrial heartland of the country was palpable. In early 1983, when a Milwaukee factory announced it had two hundred job openings, nearly twenty thousand people lined up to apply. Many laid-off workers found themselves forced to move to where jobs were more plentiful. Youngstown saw its population shrink by twenty-five thousand after its steel industry evaporated. The Fordist system of production, for seventy years a pillar of prosperity, especially in the Midwest, no longer could carry the weight it once did.

When factories and the jobs they provided disappeared, a whole way of life faced collapse. In industrial centers like Homestead, Flint, South Chicago, and Youngstown, work, family, and church provided moral and cultural poles for communities rich in solidarity and shared values, if inward-looking and still to a great degree structured by patriarchal authority. "Steel workers, especially men," reported the head of a job counseling center at a U.S. Steel plant in South Chicago, "think of work as the most important part of their life. The job provided a structure; once that structure crumbles, people's personality crumbles."

African Americans were particularly hard-hit by the downsizing of heavy industry. The automobile and steel industries had provided black workers with opportunities for better-paid jobs, with more security and benefits, than they could get almost anywhere else. By the 1970s, most racially discriminatory employment practices had been eliminated. The shuttering of older factories—which were more likely to be near substantial black populations than newer plants, many of which were sited in suburbs or semirural locales—took a heavy toll on black workers. The number of African American steelworkers fell from 38,098 in 1974 to just 9,958 in 1988. Majority-black cities dependent on heavy industry, like East St. Louis, Illinois, and Gary, Indiana, tumbled into poverty, dilapidation, and abandonment. In Memphis, where decades of struggle had won African Americans greatly expanded job opportunities, the shutdown of RCA, Firestone, International Harvester, and Memphis Furniture Company factories threw thousands out of work. Nearly half the black community lived in poverty into the 1990s.

The trauma of the disappearance of so many well-paying jobs during a period of deep recession made it easy to forget the downsides of industrial employment and the kind of life it sustained. In a 1977 interview, Edward

Sadlowski, an insurgent candidate for the presidency of the United Steel-workers union, remarked, "Working forty hours a week in a steel mill drains the lifeblood of a man." There were millworkers "who are full of poems," he said, who had the potential to be lawyers or doctors but lacked the opportunity to try. The goal of organized labor, he added, in a comment that hurt his unsuccessful election bid, should be to eliminate jobs as arduous as those in steel. Doris McKinney, laid off from the finishing department of a Buffalo steel mill, was delighted when she found a job as an occupational therapist, which she much preferred to burning metal. A sociological study of workers who accepted a buyout at a New Jersey automobile plant found that they generally later expressed few regrets at doing so, even when it meant, as it usually did, a drop in income. (African Americans, who because of discrimination found it harder to find decent new jobs than did whites, had more regrets.) Many of the former autoworkers were happy to have left behind the physical toll and autocratic atmosphere of life on the assembly line. Still, given the limited alternatives, few workers celebrated the contraction of heavy industry.

The speed and extent of the transformation of the automobile and steel industries disarmed the unions that represented their workforces. Mostly they fought rearguard battles to minimize layoffs and concessions. In the Pittsburgh area, local union activists, ministers, and community groups proposed the public takeover of steel mills facing closure, winning halfhearted support from their national union but failing to stop the shutdown wave. The UAW called for greater union involvement in managerial decisions and a national industrial policy, with government-coordinated planning and public redevelopment banks aimed at preserving and renovating manufacturing, but its proposal won little traction. It won greater attention in calling on the public to "Buy American," a campaign that at the grass roots sometimes took on a racist, anti-Japanese cast. An accompanying bid to require specified levels of domestic content in vehicles sold in the United States failed to make headway in Washington.

Lowering the Cost of Labor

Labor costs were but one factor—and often not the most important one—in declining corporate profits, but, unlike international competition, interest rates, and demand, they were something business executives felt they could address. To save money, companies slashed both production and managerial ranks. The changed economic and political climate of the late 1970s and 1980s allowed many unionized firms to do what they had long wanted to but had not dared: launch a full-blown attack on organized labor to weaken it and, where possible, eliminate it altogether.

Some companies used relocation as an anti-union strategy, moving their production out of the urban Northeast and Midwest to plants in the South and Southwest and in semirural settings, where they believed that workers had a stronger work ethic and unions would have a hard time getting a foothold. In 1967, nearly two-thirds of all manufacturing jobs were in the Northeast and Midwest; by 1992, only half. As unionized companies set up nonunion plants and conglomerates bought up manufacturing firms, executives felt better positioned to take on organized labor, knowing that they could maintain some production and draw on deep corporate pockets if their aggressive stands led to strikes.

Workers recognized that with unemployment high, odds were turning against them. Starting in the mid-1970s, the annual numbers of strikes began to fall. But when pushed hard enough, workers did fight back.

In 1977, coal miners struck in response to employers' demands for union concessions, including restraints on wildcat strikes, which had become epidemic in the industry, and changes in the community health system that the United Mine Workers had established over years of collective bargaining. After the 160,000 strikers twice rejected settlement terms that top union leaders had accepted, Jimmy Carter invoked the Taft-Hartley Act to order them back to work. In an extraordinary defiance of federal power, the miners refused to end their walkout, forcing the Carter administration to effectively back down. After 110 days, the strike ended on terms more favorable to the workers than the initial proposals (but still requiring givebacks).

The coal strike proved exceptional. In the years that followed, there were other large strikes resisting employer demands for union concessions, but most failed. Meanwhile, the percentage of the private workforce that belonged to a union dropped. The weakness of organized labor, combined with bouts of high unemployment, allowed employers to reduce wages. Between 1979 and 1989, average hourly earnings for production and nonsupervisory workers (who made up more than four-fifths of the workforce) fell by an annual average of 0.7 percent (after adjusting for inflation). Their average weekly wages (expressed in 1982 dollars) fell from a 1972 high point of $315 to a 1993 low point of $255, a 19 percent drop. Workers lost benefits too; between 1979 and 1989, the percentage of workers with employer-provided health insurance fell from 69 percent to 62 percent and with employer-provided pensions from 51 percent to 44 percent.

Even as hourly wages dropped, per capita and family income rose. Several factors accounted for this seeming anomaly. For one thing, workers on average worked more hours a year than in the past. Many companies, when business picked up, preferred allowing or requiring employees to work over-time to adding new workers. That made it easier to quickly cut costs if busi-ness slowed and avoided benefit costs for additional employees. (For the same reason, companies increasingly hired temporary workers and ones they could categorize as independent contractors.) For another thing, the number of women who worked continued to grow. By 1985, well over half of married women with children under six held a job or were looking for one, up from fewer than a third in 1970. The need, because of the decline of hourly wages, for a higher percentage of the population to work, and work more hours than before, in order to keep family and per capita income rising was a measure of the success of the antilabor offensive.

Many companies, as they cut hourly labor costs, also sought to increase productivity and improve product quality. Belatedly, they began studying the practices of their foreign competitors. Abandoning a long-standing pa-rochial hauteur that took for granted American superiority, executives, busi-ness consultants, and economics writers adopted a newfound respect for foreign corporate cultures and expertise, particularly Japanese business, around which a cultlike obeisance developed.

The automobile industry took the lead in adopting and publicizing Japanese-style "lean production," a program of mechanical and social engi-neering designed to squeeze waste from the production process and boost productivity and quality. Companies made greater use of robotic devices, trained workers in more than one job, rotated assignments, had production workers also do some maintenance and quality control, and used monitoring systems to keep them working more constantly. "Just in time" inventory, also copied from the Japanese, eliminated the cost of maintaining stockpiles of parts and raw materials by having them delivered only as they were needed, an approach made possible by more efficient shipping methods and computerized tracking.

Companies also took aim at what they saw as bloat in the ranks of white-collar staff and middle management. A hierarchical, adversarial system of labor management had led companies to keep adding supervisors, manag-ers, and administrators, as did the growing importance of marketing and accounting functions. During the years when companies faced little compe-tition from firms in Europe and Japan (where managerial and administrative employees made up a much smaller percentage of the workforce), they could afford ever larger fleets of managers, whose very number made planning, decision making, and new initiatives ponderous. Jack Welch, who became the head of General Electric in 1981, complained that "we were hiring people

[just] to read reports of people who had been hired to write reports." The economic troubles and falling profits of the 1970s and early 1980s led to corporate rethinking. Companies began laying off large numbers of middle managers, something previously unheard of at many firms. Laid-off managers suffered psychological as well as economic trauma, having been raised with the expectation that a job in corporate management meant lifetime employment and upward mobility. Companies also began contracting out functions like data processing and communications that they had formerly performed themselves. Some large firms specialized in providing such services, but the effort by corporations to be leaner and more flexible also created entrepreneurial opportunities for consultants, technical experts, and subcontractors, some of whom had been forced into self-employment by corporate downsizing, a new stratum of small businesspeople tied economically, and often politically, to big business.

The Financialization of Capital

A wave of company takeovers by investors seeking to extract cash and increase shareholder value accelerated corporate downsizing. The late 1960s had seen a flurry of corporate acquisitions, as companies, facing declining profits or limited growth opportunities in their traditional lines of business, sought to diversify. Many of the resulting conglomerates proved inefficient, arbitrary collections of divisions, poorly managed by executives who possessed only dim knowledge of the businesses they had bought. Some investors realized that the separate parts of these assemblages would be worth more if broken apart than if kept together. They also eyed the cash reserves that corporations had built up during the years of high interest rates as protection against unforeseen contingencies. A sharp drop in stock prices during the second half of the 1970s—the Dow Jones Industrial Average fell by over a quarter and did not begin a sustained rise until 1982—created an opportunity for corporate raiders to gain control of companies they believed undervalued, strip them of their cash, cut their costs, and reorganize them or break them up.

The corporate takeovers and reorganizations in the 1980s entailed a revolution in the finance industry and corporate culture. Companies came to be seen as virtual commodities, which could be bought, reorganized, and sold, generating huge profits for those who got in on the action. Investors began moving massive amounts of capital into the financial sector, seeing greater opportunities for making big money there than in the more mundane activities of producing products, transporting goods, or providing personal services. A group of self-styled financial rebels, including Ivan Boesky, Carl Icahn, Saul Steinberg, Ronald Perelman, and Michael Milken, led the charge. Decrying corporate executives for failing to maximize shareholder gains through their ineptitude, passivity, or self-serving priorities, they used borrowed money and alliances with large shareholders to gain control of companies or extract "greenmail" payments for abandoning their efforts.

Structural changes promoted financial maneuvering. The 1975 decision by the Securities and Exchange Commission to end fixed fees for stock transactions led to declining brokerage house profits from trading. Firms began looking to hostile takeovers, leveraged buyouts, and taking companies private to boost their bottom lines. The increasing concentration of stock ownership and the large pools of capital in mutual and pension funds, college endowments, and other large institutional holdings made such maneuvers easier than when stock shares had been largely owned by individuals and money could be borrowed only from banks. (The involvement of these institutions spread the gains of the frantic round of acquisitions, mergers, and divestments to a broader public than the Wall Street insiders of earlier years.)

Once raiders got control of companies, they had to quickly extract cash and cut costs to pay back the loans they used to finance the takeovers. In an often slapdash manner, divisions and factories were sold, workers and managers laid off, and wage rates lowered. New corporate owners and the executives they hired did not hesitate to break long-standing company bonds with communities, workers, managers, and suppliers in the name of increasing shareholder value, while paying themselves vast sums of money.

The new corporate ethos quickly spread. At GE, Jack Welch reduced the workforce from 411,000 in 1980 to 299,000 in 1985, selling units that did not hold a dominant position in their businesses and slashing payrolls in those he retained, winning praise from stockholders who saw the value of the company soar. For their efforts, CEOs like Welch were very well rewarded. Over the course of the 1980s, the annual salaries of CEOs, after taxes and adjusted for inflation, rose by two-thirds, while the real hourly pay for production workers declined. In 1981, the top-paid executive in the country, the vice president of an oil industry service company, received $5.7 million in salary, bonus, and long-term compensation. Six years later, the best-paid executive, the head of the Walt Disney Company, took home $40.1 million. Top executives also received ever more opulent perks, from access to corporate jets to company-paid housing to extraordinarily generous retirement plans. The financiers who engineered corporate takeovers did even better. In 1987, Michael Milken, who sold junk bonds to finance start-up companies, corporate expansions, and takeovers (and who would eventually go to jail for securities law violations), was paid an astounding $550 million by the brokerage house he worked for, surpassing—adjusted for inflation—even the income of John D. Rockefeller during his peak earning years before World War I.

By the end of the 1980s, the corporate world had been thoroughly transformed. Compared to other eras, not much money had been invested in plant, equipment, or research and development. Instead, it had gone into the elaborate and often highly profitable financial maneuvers that characterized the decade. The process of constant reorganization resulted in layoffs and plant closings that cost millions of workers their jobs and decimated whole communities. Some companies failed to survive the turmoil, but others, by shedding noncore businesses, closing inefficient plants, and reducing payrolls, became more efficient producers and more effective competitors in international markets. The stagnation of wages, cuts in corporate taxes, and the fall in the value of the dollar after 1985, which boosted exports, buoyed corporate profits. Shrewd executives, investors, and financiers had found a way out of the deep economic troubles of the 1970s and early 1980s that benefited themselves, if not necessarily the nation as a whole.

Business Politics

The corporate transformation that boosted profits involved political action as much as economic change. The shifts in labor policies and investment strategies that occurred in the late 1970s and 1980s required a congenial legal and political atmosphere. To create it, businesses, their leaders, and their owners mobilized politically to an extent that had few precedents in the recent history of the country, resulting in a major change in the national political trajectory.

Business had long tried to shape federal legislation and policy but generally did so on a parochial basis, promoting the interests of specific companies, industries, and regions. The political and economic challenges of the 1970s led business to organize on something like a class basis, subsuming particular needs to a broad offensive aimed at stopping labor advances, checking regulation, and lowering taxes on companies and their owners.

Long-established national business organizations, like the U.S. Chamber of Commerce and the National Association of Manufacturers (NAM), became far more oriented toward political lobbying than in the past, recruiting more members, building up their budgets, and hiring fleets of Washington operatives. Some openly identified with the political right, with the Chamber taking conservative stands not only on economic issues but on social and foreign policy ones as well. These broad-based groups helped bridge the gap between the major national corporations and smaller, local businesses that could exert pressure on members of Congress in their home districts. New groups formed too, most important, the Business Roundtable, a group of CEOs from the nation's largest companies who committed themselves to personally lobbying Congress and the White House on key issues.

Individual companies and trade associations also ramped up their involvement in politics. Ironically, their increased influence was facilitated by the 1971 Federal Election Campaign Act, which the labor movement had pushed, authorizing political action committees (PACs). By 1978, more than eight hundred corporate PACs had been set up, becoming a significant force in Washington politics. So were lobbyists hired by companies and trade associations. Over the course of the 1970s, the number of businesses with registered Washington lobbyists increased tenfold. Businesses used lobbyists to influence not only Congress and the White House but also the many new regulatory agencies that could have significant impact on their day-to-day operations.

Some companies and wealthy individuals, looking beyond particular measures, sought to shift the national climate of opinion about business in general and about the market, social policy, and the role of government, much as some conservatives had tried to do in the late 1940s and early 1950s. Washington-based think tanks became a favorite vehicle for doing so. Through them, scholars, journalists, and once-and-future government officials could develop policies and promote them with at least a veneer of objectivity. The American Enterprise Institute, a long-established conservative think tank devoted to promoting free-market ideas, expanded with an influx of contributions from corporations and conservative foundations. The Heritage Foundation, founded in 1973 with money from beer magnate Joseph Coors and Mellon family heir Richard Mellon Scaife, flooded the media and Congress with conservative press releases, speakers, and position papers. Businesses and foundations also funded institutes and professorships on college campuses, designed to chip away at what conservatives believed—with some truth, but not as much as they thought—was a liberal hegemony at leading institutions of higher education.

The business lobby first fully mobilized in a series of fights over proposed changes in labor law. Preliminary skirmishes occurred over bargaining rights for state and local government workers. A measure introduced into Congress in 1971 would have established a federal law governing public-sector labor, at a time when many states either did not have a legal framework governing public employee unionism or banned or restricted it. Labor leaders also hoped to repeal the 1939 Hatch Act, which severely restricted the right of federal employees to engage in political activities. A business/ conservative offensive helped kill both measures. (The labor movement proved more successful on issues not directly related to its own organizational power, such as getting Congress to raise the minimum wage in 1974 and, over sharp business opposition, institute federal regulation of private pensions.)

The next fight occurred over so-called common situs picketing. For years, construction unions had sought an exemption from the Taft-Hartley ban on secondary boycotts and strikes, to allow them to use picket lines to keep employees of all contractors out of a construction site, not just those of a contractor with whom they had a dispute. This would have given labor a powerful weapon to fight the increasing use of nonunion construction workers. In 1975, Secretary of Labor John T. Dunlop came out in support of a common situs bill. In spite of opposition from the Business Roundtable and the Chamber of Commerce, Congress passed the measure, but President Ford, under pressure from business groups, vetoed it, leading Dunlop to resign. In a measure of the declining influence of labor, in 1977, after Carter pledged to support the bill, the House of Representatives narrowly failed to pass the reintroduced bill in the face of intensive business lobbying.

The climactic battle came over a bill amending the National Labor Relations Act. Over time, businesses had become increasingly aggressive and effective in fighting unionization efforts. Advised by lawyers and consultants specializing in defeating unions, they delayed representation elections, pressured workers to vote against unionization, fired activists, and threatened to close their plants rather than accept collective bargaining. The penalties for violating labor law were so modest that many companies made the calculation that breaking it made business sense. In 1946, unions won 80 percent of representation elections; in 1967, over 60 percent; by 1977, fewer than half.

A bill introduced to Congress in 1978 would have speeded up the representation election process and the resolution of claims of unfair practices. It also would have given unions a right, already held by managers, to address the workers scheduled to vote for or against having a union; increased penalties for violating the right of workers to freely choose representatives; and in cases of "willful" violators disqualify them from holding federal contracts. Business launched an all-out offensive to defeat the bill, led by the Chamber of Commerce, NAM, construction industry groups, and the Business Roundtable, outspending labor almost three to one. In the end, though the bill won majority support in both houses of Congress, it fell short of the sixty

votes needed to break a Senate filibuster. Even with the Democrats controlling the White House and Congress, business bested labor on the issue both
sides saw as paramount.

The victories over labor convinced business leaders of the efficacy of aggressive political action. After labor, they most worried about federal regulation. Though many of the more radical movements of the late 1960s and
early 1970s had short half-lives, environmental groups and consumer activists remained influential. Common Cause, Public Citizen, the Sierra Club,
Friends of the Earth, and consumer advocate Ralph Nader's organizations
used direct-mail solicitations to raise money from the public, allowing them
to develop substantial research operations and professional staffs. Court
rulings that broadened who had legal standing to challenge regulatory decisions gave these groups the ability to get involved in the nuts and bolts of
federal rulemaking. Their expertise about regulatory rules and procedures
often equaled or surpassed that of affected industries. Partially as a result of
their pressure, new federal regulatory agencies were created, including the
National Highway Safety Commission, the Consumer Product Safety Commission, the Mine Safety and Enforcement Administration, the Occupational Safety and Health Administration, the Commodity Futures Trading
Commission, and the Nuclear Regulatory Commission.

Business had put up little resistance to the initial creation of some of the
new agencies, including OSHA, but by the end of the 1970s they were working to limit their impact. A barrage of business criticism of regulatory agencies dealing with environmental, consumer, and occupational safety issues
for being intrusive, ineffective, and driving up costs undermined their public
and political support. Business opposition killed a proposed Consumer Protection Agency, undercut a Federal Trade Commission effort to restrict advertising aimed at children, and led OSHA to become less aggressive in its
standards and enforcement (abetted by a 1980 Supreme Court decision
blocking a newly promulgated benzene standard, which raised the bar for
imposing regulations).

Decreased regulation of the financial industry facilitated its transformation. In 1978, the Supreme Court ruled that states could not regulate the interest charged on credit cards issued by national banks based in another
state. Big credit-card-issuing banks, like Citibank, moved their credit card
operations to states like South Dakota and Delaware that agreed to repeal or
revise their anti-usury laws. By charging high interest rates, the banks turned
credit cards into a very profitable business. Then, in 1982, Congress allowed
savings and loan banks to offer money market accounts and to loan money

outside their traditional residential mortgage markets. They also were permitted to purchase the risky "junk" bonds that were increasingly being used to finance company takeovers. The easing of government restrictions on multiple branches and operating across state lines led to a wave of bank mergers.

Business did not effect a complete counterrevolution. Basic labor law remained the same (though practically it became less and less useful to unions), and regulatory agencies remained in place (if somewhat defanged). But the balance of power had changed. Corporations and their allies had built institutions to counter and delegitimize unionism, consumerism, environmentalism, and government regulation that proved to be powerful mechanisms to advance the interests of business, the upper class, and the political right for years to come.

New Corporate Models

Three industries—meatpacking, computing, and retailing—illustrate the transformations in business organization that took place after the post–World War II era of prosperity ground to a halt.

People generally do not think much about meatpacking; who wants to know how the animal you are eating was killed, chopped up, and distributed? To the extent that in the post–World War II years Americans knew anything about meatpacking, most probably conceptualized it as a story of progress. Upton Sinclair's 1906 novel *The Jungle,* a staple in classrooms, brought to generations of students stomach-churning images of conditions in turn-of-the-century Chicago meatpacking plants and the miserable lives of packinghouse workers and their families. A combination of federal regulation and unionization subsequently improved the sanitary and safety conditions in the packinghouses and the lives of their workers. But meatpacking was not a story of continual advance, at least from the point of view of the workers who killed livestock and processed it. Rather, from the late 1970s on, a structural transformation of the industry led to a deterioration of their working conditions and a decline in their standard of living.

When Sinclair wrote about meatpacking, a few giant companies dominated the industry. At huge stockyards in big midwestern cities, they bought livestock that farmers shipped by train, slaughtered it, and sent dressed carcasses and processed meats to branch plants and warehouses across the country. From there, meat was delivered to restaurants, hotels, and retail stores, where butchers did the final cutting and packaging. By the 1950s, most of the workers in the main plants were unionized and earned above-average wages for manufacturing workers.

Even before World War II, smaller independent firms began challenging the big companies by building packinghouses near where cattle and pigs were raised and buying them directly from farmers, rather than through stockyard auctions. Soon the big companies built "direct buying" plants of their own. As the industry dispersed, still concentrated in the Midwest but often in small and midsize cities, so did unionization. Most packinghouses continued to pay wages at or near the level set by union negotiations with the major firms.

In the early 1960s, what amounted to a revolution in the industry began when a new wave of independents, led by Iowa Beef Packers, built technologically advanced plants in rural or small-town locations, taking advantage of improved roads and air-conditioning technology to ship their products by truck rather than by train. Instead of distributing dressed carcasses, Iowa Beef and its imitators cut animals into smaller pieces, which they vacuum-sealed in bags, boxed, and shipped directly to retailers and end users. For the buyers, this had the advantage of requiring fewer skilled workers to do the final cutting and packaging.

Unlike the older packing companies, which had become largely resigned to unionization, Iowa Beef took a militantly antilabor stand. When it could, it kept unions out of its plants altogether. When workers did manage to organize, it insisted on paying lower wages than the major firms.

During the economic downturn of the late 1970s and early 1980s, the growth of Iowa Beef and other firms with more efficient methods and lower costs presented a profound threat to the old-line packers. They reacted not by investing in modernization and new technology but by milking their operations for cash, shutting older plants, diversifying, and in some cases allowing themselves to be purchased. Corporate changes became dizzying. The plants once owned by Armour and Company, for instance, were bought in the 1970s by bus company turned conglomerate Greyhound, and then in 1983 sold to the food conglomerate ConAgra. The older companies also moved to break the national pattern of union-bargained wages and benefits, seeking concessions for individual plants and whole chains and threatening to sell or shutter facilities if they did not receive them.

The United Food and Commercial Workers (UFCW) tried to resist the disintegration of pattern bargaining. Packinghouse workers repeatedly struck rather than accept lower wages and benefits, but with limited success. The prolonged walkout by Hormel employees in Austin, Minnesota, in 1984 and 1985 garnered broad community support and national attention but ultimately failed in the face of determined company resistance, the mobilization of the National Guard to protect scabs, and the opposition of national

UFCW leaders, who rather than protecting high wage rates, like those the strikers received, sought to reestablish national wage standards at a somewhat lower level. That did not work either. By the end of the 1980s, national bargaining in the industry had all but ended, leaving workers at individual unionized plants to cut the best deals they could. The percentage of meatpacking workers covered by collective bargaining fell from 83 percent in 1963 to 71 percent in 1984.

The weakening of unions had a dramatic material impact. The annual earnings of midwestern meatpacking workers peaked in 1977 and then fell by nearly one-half over the next two decades. By 1990, wages in the industry had slipped to 20 percent below the average for all manufacturing workers. New technology, including small, handheld circular saws ("whizards"), and the decreased ability of unions to enforce work rules allowed production to speed up. Injuries became more common, including repetitive stress disorders. Problems that unionization had once eliminated—like the inability of workers to leave production lines for bathroom breaks—again came to plague the industry.

The deterioration of working conditions and the deurbanization of meatpacking led to a wholesale change in the makeup of the workforce. The old urban meatpacking plants had employed European immigrants and their children, African Americans, white transplants from the rural Midwest, and a small number of Mexican Americans. The new rural plants tapped a different labor market, former farmers and other hard-up rural residents (including a growing number of single mothers) who had few alternative sources of employment. But rural areas did not have enough workers to staff the new plants, and few native-born workers were willing to move to take such poor jobs. Employers solved their problem by turning to immigrant workers, particularly from Southeast Asia and, in much larger numbers, Mexico and Central and South America, who by the end of the twentieth century made up a majority of the workforce at most midwestern packinghouses. Turnover in the industry soared, as workers often quit after brief tenures, unwilling or unable to stand the pace of work, dangerous conditions, and low pay.

As the twentieth century ended, animals were slaughtered and dismembered under work conditions not very different from the ones most Americans probably believed had disappeared forever in the years following the publication of *The Jungle*. From a source of stable jobs providing decent livings, meatpacking reverted to its past as a low-wage industry that offered little security or upward mobility. In other industries, like automobile, steel, garment, and airline, the deterioration of wages and working conditions in the 1980s was often attributed to either foreign competition or government deregulation.

Neither played a substantial role in meatpacking. Rather, the industry showed how changed corporate attitudes, the rise of new competitors, the introduction of new technology, geographic relocation, and a political and economic climate in which strikes could be taken and defeated could lead to a radical transformation in the lives of working people and the reemergence of a sweatshop America that until then seemed to have become a distant memory.

In the computer industry, the key innovations were neither in production methods nor labor relations but in the products themselves. The first electronic digital computers were built under military sponsorship during World War II to calculate ballistic trajectories. After the war, the military continued to play a large role in the development of computing, sponsoring research, commissioning advanced machines, and creating programming languages. By the mid-1950s, some large corporations had begun using computers for payroll, billing, accounting, inventory control, and other tasks. IBM emerged as the dominant computer maker, winning control of 70 percent of the commercial market. The computers IBM and its competitors produced were massive, expensive devices, requiring air-conditioned facilities. Programs were executed in batches, submitted to specially trained operators (usually on punch cards), with the results available only after what was sometimes a considerable wait.

During the late 1950s and 1960s, defense spending and heavy investment in computing by the burgeoning space program stimulated a series of technological innovations that laid the basis for a radical transformation of the industry. The desire by the Air Force and NASA for smaller, more reliable, and less power-hungry electronics sped the development of integrated circuits. First produced in 1959, these small silicon "chips," which had etched on them transistors, resistors, and other circuitry, made possible a drastic reduction in the size, power needs, and air-conditioning requirements for electronic equipment. Intel Corporation took the lead in producing integrated circuits for computer memory, one of a number of companies that made the Santa Clara Valley south of San Francisco a hub for computer industry innovation. Integrated circuits in turn made possible advances in minicomputers, smaller, cheaper machines than the "mainframe" computers that dominated commercial work.

Minicomputers allowed computers to be used in new ways. Rather than submitting programs to operators and then waiting for results, students and faculty at MIT, Stanford, and other universities began directly controlling minicomputers through interactive terminals. The Pentagon's Advanced Research Projects Agency (ARPA) funded much of their work, as well as the development of "time-sharing" systems that allowed multiple users to simultaneously access machines otherwise far too costly for individual use. With these developments, computer users could write and revise programs on the fly, unleashing a wave of innovation and unanticipated new uses for computers, from games to communications to text manipulation. ARPA also developed the first network that linked together computer centers in various parts of the country.

The development in the early 1970s of microprocessors—chips that contained the basic processing functions of a general-purpose computer—made possible the next step in the miniaturization and personalization of computing, the development of small desktop machines that possessed computing power approaching that of much more expensive minicomputers. In 1975, Ed Roberts, the owner of a model rocket hobby shop in Albuquerque, New Mexico, began selling a small computer, the Altair, in kit form for less than $400. To provide an easy-to-use computer language for his machine, Roberts bought a version of BASIC, a computer language developed at Dartmouth as a teaching tool, from two young programmers, Paul Allen and Bill Gates, who soon set up their own software firm, Microsoft, aimed at the emerging PC market.

The San Francisco Bay Area, including the Santa Clara Valley (by then dubbed Silicon Valley in recognition of its growing concentration of chip producers and computer companies), was a hotbed of engineers, academics, hobbyists, and students fascinated with the possibilities for building their own computers. They met in small groups, infused with the radical and countercultural sentiments then still common in the Bay Area. For many PC pioneers, cheap, individually operated computers and community-based computer networks represented liberation, a way to spread knowledge and power and undercut control by central authorities. In organizations like the Homebrew Computer Club they exchanged utopian visions, practical tips, hardware devices, and newly minted programs. The most successful of the computers being built in kitchens and garages around the area came from a young chip designer, Steve Wozniak. With his neighborhood friend Steve Jobs, a Reed College dropout, Wozniak set up a company to sell his creation, which Jobs dubbed the Apple. Wozniak soon created an improved version, the Apple II, introduced in 1977, which made home computing a possibility even for technically unsophisticated users. Two years later, a start-up software company released a spreadsheet program called VisiCalc for doing accounting calculations on the Apple II, which brought a flood of business customers to computer stores looking to buy what until then still had been largely a hobbyist's machine.

Unlike most of the tinkerers who created the first personal computers, Jobs, just twenty-two when he cofounded Apple, had a strong commercial orientation and the wisdom to hire professional managers to help guide his company as it explosively expanded. In 1980, it became a public corporation with an initial stock offering that made Jobs and Wozniak together worth over $300 million. Within five years of its founding, it grew into a billion-dollar corporation.

In 1981, IBM came out with its own personal computer that had many of the characteristics of the Altair and Apple II. Like them, it used off-the-shelf parts and adopted an open architecture that allowed other developers to sell add-on components and peripheral devices. IBM offered three operating systems, including one licensed from Microsoft, which proved by far the most popular. The IBM PC became a huge commercial success, legitimated personal computers in the commercial as well as home markets, and set standards for future hardware and software. Ironically, companies that copied the IBM design ultimately eclipsed it in the personal computer market. The chips Intel produced and the software Microsoft wrote, rather than finished computers, became the defining force in the industry.

By the end of the 1980s, some twenty million personal computers a year were being sold. The personal computer had become ubiquitous in offices, schools, and homes. Out of an odd brew of militarism, engineering ingenuity, academic and youth culture, post–civil rights movement antiauthoritarianism, questing for personal empowerment, and venture capital had come a technological and social revolution that interwove computer use into daily life.

The companies that mushroomed up with the personal computer revolution prided themselves on creating work environments very different from prevailing buttoned-down, hierarchical corporate norms. At least on the surface, the California computer industry seemed to embody the spirit of 1960s university towns, with casual dress, all-night work sessions, company-sanctioned play breaks, informal corporate structures, and the extensive use of work teams. Below the surface, though, the labor practices of the emerging high-tech companies represented continuity as much as change.

In the post–World War II years, large unionized companies set many of the standards for national employment practices, but an influential alternative could be found in sophisticated, nonunion companies that developed modernized versions of pre–New Deal welfare capitalism. Rejecting collective bargaining, companies like Sears and Roebuck, Kodak, and IBM sought to maintain employee loyalty and high productivity through job security, good benefits, stock purchase plans, extensive use of teamwork, and worker participation in decision making. Many of the high-tech start-up firms of the 1970s and 1980s adopted this model, with an overlay of countercultural trappings. Given the importance of intellectual capital and innovation to their success, they made it a priority to keep top designers and programmers satisfied, tolerating their idiosyncrasies and enriching them through stock grants and options.

Production workers fared nowhere nearly so well. In the factories that made silicon chips, disk drives, circuit boards, and other computer components, conditions could be harsh. Precise, repetitive work exhausted workers, who often were exposed to noxious chemicals. Many computer companies subcontracted production to firms that paid low wages and provided few benefits. While the managerial and professional ranks of the high-tech firms were heavily male and white, women, minorities, and illegal immigrants made up much of the production workforce. Once products and manufacturing techniques became standardized, companies frequently stopped making goods in Silicon Valley or elsewhere in the United States, subcontracting production to overseas firms in low-wage regions or setting up their own offshore factories. Highly efficient, automated production techniques helped to keep the cost of personal computers low, but like many other industries during the 1980s, profits and success in the computer industry rested in part on a downward spiral of wages and benefits for blue-collar jobs, whether within the borders of the country or by moving beyond them.

Low wages played a key role in the transformation of retailing, which began in the 1960s and accelerated in the 1970s and 1980s. The rise of giant discount chains, most notably Wal-Mart Stores, Inc., changed how Americans shopped and the economics of everyday life. Wal-Mart helped set labor standards across the economy, altered patterns of urban and suburban development, and even influenced cultural trends.

Most of the major discount chains founded in the 1960s—including Kmart, Target, and Woolco (a Woolworth's chain that Wal-Mart bought in 1983)—were creations of existing urban-oriented mass merchandise companies. Wal-Mart had different roots. Sam Walton had owned variety stores in small Arkansas towns. He set up his first discount stores on the outskirts of such communities, where they drew customers from the surrounding regions by offering a wide variety of goods at low prices. Determined from the start to keep labor costs down, Walton fought to keep out unions, which in any case had little toehold in Arkansas and the neighboring states where he initially sited his stores. Walton found a ready workforce among local women, almost all white, willing to work for minimum or subminimum wages in the face of the mechanization of local agriculture and the paucity of alternative employment opportunities.

Spreading out systematically from its original base, by 1975 Wal-Mart had 125 stores and seventy-five hundred employees. That year Congress made it illegal for manufacturers to fix retail prices, opening the door for an expansion of discounting chains. During the 1980s, Wal-Mart began adding stores in the suburbs of large cities and introduced "Supercenters" that combined grocery supermarkets and general merchandise discount stores under one roof. Many Supercenters stayed open around the clock, following a retail trend toward twenty-four-hour operation. (In 1963, 7-Eleven began keeping convenience stores open twenty-four hours; the midwestern Meijer grocery stores adopted the practice in 1984.) In 1990, Wal-Mart became the country's largest retailer. The next year it began an international expansion by opening up a store in Mexico City. By the end of the century, it had become the world's largest private employer, with over 1.1 million workers.

Wal-Mart's success rested on a never-ceasing campaign to drive down prices. The company used its growing size to pressure suppliers to lower their wholesale prices, passing on the savings to shoppers. To further cut prices, it increasingly turned to low-wage overseas suppliers to stock its stores. Though the manufacturers were nominally independent, Wal-Mart, with its enormous purchasing power and marketing expertise, often controlled the production process.

Keeping its own labor costs down also was critical to Wal-Mart's low-price strategy. Wal-Mart offered very low wages and meager benefits, understaffed stores, and frequently violated laws regulating worker hours and wages. In an effort to maintain the loyalty and morale of its workers in spite of these practices, Walton and other company executives crafted an internal company culture that portrayed Wal-Mart as a giant family steeped in patriotic, Christian values. To sustain this ethos, the company recruited store managers from small, often religiously affiliated colleges in the South. High employee turnover purged the firm of discontented workers and potential troublemakers. When a threat of unionization did arise, the company sent out a specially trained team of executives from its headquarters to counter the effort, in virtually every case succeeding in blocking organized labor.

While old-fashioned in its low-wage, paternalist labor policies—common in the South when Walton began his chain—Wal-Mart came to be cutting-edge in deploying technology to facilitate expansion and keep down costs. Using its own trucking fleet and taking advantage of transportation and inventory innovations, including cargo containers and bar coding, Wal-Mart developed a remarkably efficient system of logistics for moving and tracking goods, including the growing flood of items it imported from Asia. It also developed state-of-the-art information technology. Unlike the developers of personal computers, who envisioned the decentralization of information and power through the application of advanced technology,

Wal-Mart used computers to centralize information and authority. With data gathered from every cash register in each Wal-Mart store, relayed back to the company headquarters in Bentonville, Arkansas, through a private satellite system, executives could monitor in real time sales trends, inventory needs, and worker deployment. Eventually headquarters-based managers could adjust thermostats and control cash registers in stores thousands of miles away. Wal-Mart also used its satellite system, along with a fleet of corporate planes, to maintain cultural control over its increasingly far-flung empire. Walton and other executives made frequent trips to inspect stores and via satellite gave pep talks to "associates," as employees were dubbed, assembled in stores across the country.

Wal-Mart and other discounters changed the face of retailing. Lower prices for groceries, clothes, and household goods partially compensated for the wage stagnation that workers experienced during the 1980s and beyond. The wide range of goods that Wal-Mart and its competitors offered gave customers outside metropolitan regions greater in-store choices than ever before, providing the modern equivalent of the service once provided by Sears and Roebuck and other mail-order firms. The discount chains generally located their stores on the outskirts of towns and small cities, where they could find cheap land and offer plentiful parking. Their success in driving many small, locally owned sellers out of business sped the demise of old downtowns, as stores shuttered and shoppers saw no reason to visit. At the same time, Wal-Mart helped push down wages for workers nationally, not only through its own low wage scale but by putting pressure on better-paying rivals, especially in the grocery business where unionization had been common, and by pressing suppliers to keep cutting their prices.

Like the new-model meatpacking firms, Wal-Mart found financial success through innovative business practices, relentless cost-cutting, and low-wage labor. By 1985, Sam Walton was the richest person in the United States (to be succeeded, after his death in 1992, by Bill Gates). Combining parsimonious labor practices, high technology, and an aura of down-home paternalism, Wal-Mart found a formula superbly suited to the political, economic, and cultural moment of the 1980s. If GM and U.S. Steel once epitomized the power of corporate America and a social system that accounted for the country's post–World War II success, by the end of the 1980s Iowa Beef, Microsoft, and Wal-Mart had displaced them as models for corporate America, using formulas quite different from the unionized, urban-centered, New Deal system of social relations. Together these firms pointed toward a set of productive and employment arrangements that represented the new face of American business.

CHAPTER 15

The Reagan Revolution

R onald Reagan was an improbable leader of the political revolution to which his name became affixed. The onetime actor lacked many of the traits that had come to be expected of national leaders. Kennedy, Johnson, Nixon, Ford, and Carter all spent long hours reading memoranda and documents, discussing policy, and overseeing the complex operations of a huge government establishment. Reagan made little effort to disguise his lack of interest in the nuts and bolts of government and most areas of public policy. He did not like to work long hours nor think it necessary. Often he skipped reading briefing books to watch movies. Officials who worked with him were startled by how little he knew about crucial issues before him.

Though the most successful conservative politician of the twentieth century, Reagan rejected many of the ideological beliefs and behavioral expectations of the movement he headed. Many conservatives accepted the inherent faults and fallibility of mankind. For the Christians among them, the notion of original sin sobered their sense of the politically possible, oriented them toward using state power to restrain individual behavior, and added a tragic dimension to their view of the world, giving a decidedly antiutopian cast to their thinking.

Reagan accepted almost none of this. Though he occasionally used the language of evil—most famously in his description of the Soviet Union as an "evil empire"—he had an essentially sunny view of mankind that matched his own upbeat temperament. In his view, the "people" were never the problem, only government, which stood independent from its creators and constituents. The child of a Catholic father and Protestant mother, Reagan as a twelve-year-old chose to be baptized in the Christian Church (Disciples of Christ) and later attended Eureka College, run by the denomination.

Throughout his life he described himself as a Christian, believing that God had a plan for each individual. But as an adult he rarely attended church—an irony, given the importance of evangelical Protestants to his political success—and seemed to have not a trace of the tragic, Niebuhrian Protestantism that was so influential in post–World War II political thought. Reagan believed that a more perfect society could be built here and now, and built by Americans, whom he saw as particularly blessed by God. He spurned the conservative Burkean belief in the value of precedent, tradition, and incremental change, embracing instead Edmund Burke's great critic, the transatlantic revolutionary Tom Paine, whose cry, "We have it in our power to begin the world over again," he quoted in his 1980 acceptance of the Republican presidential nomination.

Reagan's belief in the ability to shed the past extended to his personal life. As a candidate and as president, he welcomed support from promoters of what came to be called "family values," who opposed "abortion, pornography, the drug epidemic, the breakdown of the traditional family, the establishment of homosexuality as an accepted alternative life-style, and other moral cancers that are causing our society to rot from within," as Jerry Falwell, a Baptist minister and cofounder of the Moral Majority, put it. Yet Reagan himself had been divorced and remarried (the first divorcé to reach the White House), had a distant relationship with his adult children, opposed the California ballot initiative that would have banned gays and lesbians from teaching in public schools, and, as California governor, signed a law easing restrictions on abortion.

In his acting days, Reagan had been a strong supporter of the New Deal and briefly on the fringe of the Popular Front. But in the early 1950s he began drifting toward the right. Lemuel Boulware, a vice president of General Electric and architect of its highly effective antiunion strategy, helped shepherd Reagan into the conservative camp. In 1954, GE hired Reagan to host its television series, *General Electric Theater,* and visit company factories as part of an effort to build employee loyalty. Reagan's factory speeches, drawing on material from Boulware, promoted free-market ideas and criticized union political initiatives. Boulware soon had him speaking to civic groups in towns with GE facilities. By the time Reagan left GE in 1962, he had perfected a highly effective stump speech that attacked excessive government and promoted free enterprise.

Yet Reagan never completely embraced the antiunion, anti–New Deal politics that animated the business right. He liked to point out that he was the only union president to serve in the White House, having headed the Screen Actors Guild for two stints, including during a five-week strike in

1960. As president, he undermined organized labor but never completely shunned it. He had just finished addressing construction union leaders when, sixty-nine days into his presidency, a deranged would-be assassin shot him outside a Washington hotel. Many conservatives viewed Franklin Roosevelt as a class or even national traitor, but Reagan continued to admire him throughout his life.

The Conservative Ascendency

Conservatives triumphed in the 1980s by weaving together several different political strands into a national electoral coalition based in the Republican Party. Reagan abandoned his declining acting career for full-time politics in 1965, when a group of conservative California businessmen drafted him to run for governor. His ambition and doggedness led him into a prolonged quest for the presidency, which he ultimately achieved by gaining the support of the conservative movement and helping to expand it. Reagan's eclecticism and political skills allowed him to paper over significant differences within the movement, while his expansive, optimistic demeanor attracted millions of voters for whom the pinched, backward-looking, repressive aspects of conservatism and its ties to the wealthy had little appeal.

One strand of support for the conservative movement came out of white opposition to civil rights. By the 1970s, many white southerners, particularly upwardly mobile suburbanites, had come to oppose racial integration using the language of property rights—the freedom to decide whom to sell their property to and whom to live next door to, free from government interference—rather than that of racial superiority. This helped link anti-integrationists to business critics of the New Deal state, who also prioritized the rights of property over government regulation. Reagan proved adept at deploying the language and symbols of rights-based anti-integrationism. While running for governor he opposed a state bar on racial discrimination in selling or renting homes. During the 1980 presidential campaign, he criticized "the forced busing of school children to achieve arbitrary racial quotas" and defended states' rights in Philadelphia, Mississippi, the town where three civil rights workers had been murdered in 1964.

The backlash against racial integration indirectly provided another boost to Reagan and conservatism by politicizing evangelical Protestants. While some evangelical leaders became politically active as a result of the Supreme Court decisions banning prayer in schools and legalizing abortion, the issue with the greatest mobilizing effect was the denial of tax-exempt status to religious schools that practiced racial discrimination. In 1975, the

Internal Revenue Service revoked the tax-exempt status of Bob Jones University, a Christian college in South Carolina that banned interracial dating by its students. Three years later, the agency began requiring private schools, including so-called Christian academies, which had been founded when public schools desegregated and had few minority students, to prove that they did not engage in discrimination in order to maintain their tax-exempt status. In response, southern evangelical leaders launched a wave of protests and organizational efforts aimed at exerting the power of church followers in the political realm. Coming at a time of increasing conservative dominance of evangelical groups, including the Southern Baptist Convention, this politicization provided an enormous boost to the right.

Conservative political operatives like Richard Viguerie (a former leader of Young Americans for Freedom and fund-raiser for George Wallace), Howard Phillips (another former YAF leader), and Paul Weyrich (a founder of the Heritage Foundation) worked closely with ministers and televangelists in setting up conservative religious political groups like the Moral Majority and tightening the ties between conservative churches, politicians, and the anti-ERA, antiabortion, and anti–gay rights movements. Some evangelical ministers supported the political right for its economic as well as its social positions. As entrepreneurial leaders of churches, schools, seminaries, and radio and television stations, they shared the free-market ideology of business conservatives. Reagan reaped the benefits of this alliance in 1980, using symbolic gestures like a speech at Bob Jones University, in which he called for a "spiritual revival" and denounced the IRS guidelines for private schools for establishing "racial quotas," to erase any doubts that as a non-churchgoing divorcé he better represented the interests of the evangelical movement than the pious, born-again incumbent, Jimmy Carter.

Conservative strategists recognized that to win national power they needed to complement their traditional upper-class base and growing southern base with inroads among northern working-class and middle-class voters who supported the Democratic Party and had liberal economic views. The traditional Republican stress on balanced budgets, lower taxes for business and high earners, and opposition to welfare-state programs had little appeal to this constituency. What came to be called supply-side economics had greater potential.

In the late 1970s, a small group of conservative writers and ideologists, including *Wall Street Journal* editorial writer Jude Wanniski, free-market fundamentalist George Gilder, and economist Arthur Laffer, began arguing that instead of the Keynesian focus on managing demand, national prosperity could best be assured by promoting the increased production of goods and services through supply-side policies. Easing or eliminating the restraints and distortions that the government imposed on the market, they argued, including high taxes, regulatory programs, and preferential treatment for particular industries, would boost investment, create a burst of economic growth, lower inflation, and increase savings. Laffer and some others went so far as to claim that the growth that would result from a steep cut in federal tax rates would be so great that government revenues would not diminish. The supply-siders won an important convert in Robert L. Bartley, chief of the *Wall Street Journal*'s editorial page, who gave them a national platform and legitimized them in the business community.

A few congressmen, including New York Republican Jack Kemp, Texas Democrat Phil Gramm, and Michigan Republican David Stockman, picked up the supply-side banner. In 1977, Kemp and Delaware senator William Roth proposed an across-the-board 30 percent cut in federal income taxes. The Kemp-Roth bill provided a political vehicle for conservatives to take advantage of the antitax, antigovernment sentiment revealed by Proposition 13 and other state tax-cutting measures.

Reagan made Kemp-Roth a centerpiece of his economic program during the 1980 campaign. Adopting Laffer's theory that lower taxes would not reduce federal revenue—George H. W. Bush, Reagan's main rival for the Republican nomination and then his vice presidential running mate, called it "voodoo economics"—allowed Reagan to present tax-cutting as a populist program that would unleash economic growth and provide new opportunities for all Americans, "especially the minorities," without requiring the elimination of popular federal programs. While some business leaders had doubts about Reagan and supply-side economics, once the Californian emerged as the likely Republican nominee, support from business, large and small, flowed heavily to him, as well as to Republican congressional candidates, a departure from the mid-1970s, when business groups generally split their contributions between the two parties.

Democratic weaknesses combined with Republican strengths in the outcome of the 1980 election. Poorer Americans, who had been a mainstay of the New Deal–Great Society electoral bloc, registered their alienation from politics and the Democratic Party by voting in diminishing numbers. The decline in their voter participation rate, which exceeded the general decline, hurt the Democratic Party, as did Senator Edward Kennedy's unsuccessful primary challenge against Carter. The hostages in Iran dominated the news during the 1980 campaign, a nightly illustration of Reagan's argument that under Carter the United States had lost its toughness, confidence, and mastery of world events. But the most important factor in the election was the poor state of the economy. Reagan took what Carter had dubbed during the 1976 campaign the "misery index"—the sum of the inflation and unemployment rates—and turned it against him, pointing out that it had risen to over 20 during his term in office. Reagan asked voters, "Are you better off now than you were four years ago?" For most, the answer was no.

Reagan did not win a massive public endorsement in 1980, receiving a bare majority of less than 51 percent of the popular vote. Carter got 41 percent, with nearly 7 percent going to independent John Anderson. Reagan won a majority of the votes cast by men, while women divided their votes almost equally between Reagan and Carter, an electoral "gender gap" that would continue for years to come.

Though shallow, Reagan's victory was unusually broad. He carried forty-four states and made significant inroads among working-class and lower-middle-class voters, winning close to half the votes from union households. Of all the major components of the old New Deal coalition, only African Americans remained massively loyal to the Democratic Party. In addition to capturing the White House, the Republicans picked up an extraordinary twelve seats in the Senate, giving them control for the first time in twenty-six years. In the House, they added nearly three dozen seats, considerably narrowing the Democratic majority. If not necessarily a ringing endorsement of conservatism, the 1980 election represented a broad rejection of the Democratic Party and a mandate for change, which Reagan and his advisers eagerly seized.

Reaganism

Reagan used his inauguration not only to celebrate his victory but also to set a new national tone. The contrast with the austere, populist Carter inauguration could not have been greater. In 1977, most events had been open to the public and free or inexpensive. Reagan's four-day celebration was an invitation-only extravaganza, an unashamed display of wealth and opulence. Rich contributors, lobbyists, and Republican activists flooded Washington, attending the nine inaugural balls in white ties and tails and sequined designer dresses. Reagan and many key backers were self-made millionaires, for whom wealth measured worth. Money meant virtue, to be displayed without apology. While Carter wore a business suit to his swearing in, Reagan decked himself out in a charcoal gray club coat, striped trousers, and dove gray vest and tie. His wife, Nancy, carried a handbag that reportedly cost more than $1,600 (nearly $4,000 in 2011 dollars).

Although during the campaign Reagan had sharply criticized Carter for a weak economy, the economic program he pushed through during his first months in office contained many of the same elements that Carter had tried, but writ larger. Reagan supported the effort by Federal Reserve Board chairman Paul Volcker to drive down inflation through monetary policy, even if it brought higher unemployment. He embraced and expanded the push toward deregulation that had begun under Carter. Carter had done little to protect unionized workers from economic changes and hardening business anti-unionism, while Reagan actively worked to weaken organized labor. Reagan accelerated the military buildup that Carter had begun. While Carter projected many of these measures as grim necessities, Reagan presented them as steps toward a bright, unlimited future of bounty and national revitalization.

Reagan's top economic priority, tax-cutting (a break with Carter), embodied his belief that reducing the burden of government would unleash the wealth-creating capacity of the public. Reagan's tax cut ended up being even larger than he or his supporters anticipated. He insisted that Congress pass the Kemp-Roth income tax cuts, which most benefited wealthy individuals, with only modest modifications. Business leaders had a different priority; the year before Reagan took office, their lobbying groups agreed on pushing accelerated depreciation allowances rather than sharp cuts in individual taxes. Reagan dealt with this potential conflict by including both in his tax bill. Specific industries then lobbied Congress for additional tax breaks and loopholes. In many cases, they proved successful, as Democrats competed with Republicans to woo business backing (and, they hoped, campaign contributions), shedding their populist clothing from the past decade. The so-called Boll Weevils, House Democrats from conservative districts who feared that if they opposed Reagan they might be ousted in the next election, cut a deal with the White House that in return for their support for the president's tax and spending cuts he would not campaign against them. The result of all this jockeying was a massive tax reduction law, which included a 25 percent reduction in income tax rates, including an immediate reduction in the top rate from 70 percent to 50 percent; accelerated depreciation for business; indexing of tax brackets (to prevent "bracket creep" when inflation pushed up nominal income); tax-free savings plans for the middle class; and a Christmas tree of special-interest business tax breaks. The effective federal corporate tax rate fell from 33.3 percent to just 4.7 percent. Altogether, it was the largest tax cut in U.S. history.

The Reaganites' faith in themselves, their dogma, and the infinite greatness of the country allowed bold steps and even bolder claims. Some Reagan administration insiders, most notably David Stockman, who had been appointed director of the budget, understood that the massive size of the tax reduction along with the president's commitment to increased military spending meant there was no way that even sharp cuts in the rest of the budget could come anywhere near to balancing it, which Reagan had promised to do within three years. But the president and many of his advisers seemed unperturbed by the budgetary implications of the orgy of tax-cutting, either believing Laffer's claims that tax cuts would not reduce revenue, or not worrying about the prospect of a deficit, or simply trusting that everything would work out fine. Reagan's sunny optimism, ignorance of the inner workings of government, and lack of diligence enabled him to pursue big goals, like tax-cutting, without feeling a need to think through their implications. But the realities of the federal budget made it impossible to square the circle.

Upon taking office, Reagan began the largest peacetime military buildup in U.S. history, with annual defense spending (in constant dollars) going from $171 billion at the end of the Carter administration to $242 billion in the middle of Reagan's second term. Believing that under Carter the country had become weaker and vulnerable to its enemies, Reagan wanted to reassert American global influence through military strength and have the wherewithal not to shy away from confrontations with the Soviet Union. Also, his core political base, in California and the rest of the Sun Belt, depended heavily on military spending.

Reagan did not ask for public sacrifice to finance his program of militarization. Earlier in the Cold War, armaments had been paid for by reducing private spending through taxation, a route Reagan spurned. As a result, the 1980s became the only period of the Cold War when both military spending and private consumption rose as shares of the GNP. Reagan frequently praised the military and extolled military values as part of an intense public patriotism he promoted, but supporting the military, as he saw it, did not require either actual service (he never called for reinstitution of national service) or financial sacrifice, only emotional solidarity, public rituals, and—as it turned out—a huge public debt.

The political arithmetic of the budget made it impossible for the Reagan administration to reduce nonmilitary spending sufficiently to meet its goal of ending deficits. It could do nothing about debt payments, and Reagan ruled out substantial cuts in the popular Medicare, veterans', school lunch, Head Start, and summer youth programs. Social Security made up a major component of the budget, but Reagan's one effort to reduce its cost backfired, when his proposal to further reduce benefits for people who chose to retire early led to a congressional uproar, forcing him to retreat. (A bipartisan commission he appointed eventually led to modest cost-cutting changes in Social Security, including a gradual increase in the retirement age from sixty-five to sixty-seven.) What remained were discretionary domestic programs that made up only 17 percent of federal spending, which the Reagan administration tried to slash.

True supply-side believers, like Stockman, wanted to eliminate or drastically cut federal subsidies and spending programs that benefited the well-off as well as the poor. They soon ran into the realities of political power. Reagan originally planned to reduce by two-thirds agricultural subsidies, which mainly enriched large growers of a handful of crops, but fierce bipartisan resistance from farm-state members of Congress ultimately led to an increase in payments rather than a reduction. Stockman hoped to eliminate Import-Export Bank subsidies for giant corporations like Boeing and synthetic fuels subsidies that mostly went to oil companies, but the political clout of the corporate recipients quickly scotched those plans. And on it went, as plans to cut tobacco subsidies, the NASA budget, subsidies for nuclear fuel plants, and spending on local bridges and roads largely were defeated as affected groups and local political interests mobilized resistance.

The administration had greater success with cuts that disproportionately impacted the poor and the urban working class, groups with little clout in the White House or the new Congress. Reagan sharply reduced or eliminated child nutrition programs, CETA, food stamps, and mass transit subsidies. Between 1981 and 1987, the budget of the Department of Housing and Urban Development (HUD) fell by 57 percent. Social spending, which had risen under each of the previous five presidents, fell at an average annual rate of 1.5 percent under Reagan.

The disproportionate impact of the cuts he instituted on the poor did not bother Reagan, as he generally seemed oblivious to their plight or contemptuous of them, especially nonwhites. Counter to its liberatory rhetoric, Reagan's supply-side conservatism had a mean-spirited edge. When a billion-dollar cut in federal subsidies for school lunch programs at a time when the White House was spending over $200,000 for new china led the Department of Agriculture to propose reclassifying ketchup as a vegetable to allow schools to meet its nutritional standards, Reagan had to defend himself from the charge that his administration's style was "millionaires on parade."

Economic deregulation complemented Reagan's tax and spending cuts. For Reagan, deregulation constituted an end in itself, part of his longstanding commitment to diminishing the role of government. But it had an instrumental function, too, to promote economic growth by freeing business of costly regulations and government-imposed fetters and inefficiencies.

Reagan administration deregulation built on the growing support for reducing economic regulation that had developed under Ford and Carter, but it deviated from the earlier efforts in significant ways. During the 1970s, deregulation had been largely legislative, aimed at ending government bars to business entry and price competition. Reagan deregulation largely entailed administrative actions and enforcement policies, which reduced oversight of a wide range of business activities and loosened restraints on company practices in such areas as consumer safety, environmental practices, financial activities, and labor relations. Upon taking office, Reagan ordered agencies to reexamine existing rules; delayed or repealed environmental and safety regulations issued by the Carter administration; required cost-benefit analysis of any new federal rules and the adoption of the least costly alternative; and ended the remaining price controls on oil. The administration also began cutting funding for regulatory bodies, which meant less staff and enforcement activity. The workforce at the Office of Surface Mining, part of the Department of the Interior, fell from 1,000 in 1981 to 628 the following year. Rather than seeing their role as policing business, Reagan regulators tended to conceive of their function as making business more profitable.

To head the Environmental Protection Agency, Reagan appointed Anne Gorsuch (later Burford), a conservative legislator from Colorado who opposed many federal environmental regulations. Gorsuch worked hard to not enforce regulations she disagreed with. She repeatedly reorganized her agency and reduced the number of administrative enforcement orders, civil penalties imposed on regulation violators, and referrals to criminal prosecutors. She also loosened restrictions on pesticide use and tried to ease restrictions on toxic waste disposal. To head the Department of the Interior, Reagan appointed another Colorado conservative, James Watt. Like Gorsuch, a protégé of conservative beer maker Joseph Coors, Watt had started a legal foundation "to fight in the courts those bureaucrats and no-growth advocates who create a challenge to individual liberty and economic freedoms." Under his leadership, the Interior Department threw open federal land for greater private use, leasing offshore sites for gas and oil development, allowing more coal mining, and lowering fees for grazing cattle. Even when money was available, he declined to buy new parkland.

Other Reagan appointees reversed regulatory policy too. The Occupational Safety and Health Administration moved toward employer self-policing, reducing the number of inspectors and inspections. The Federal Communications Commission dropped the long-standing "Fairness Doctrine" that required broadcasters to give balanced presentations on controversial issues; ended requirements for minimum hours of broadcast time devoted to news and public service (among other things leading to a sharp drop in children's programming); increased the number of commercials allowed per television hour; and more than doubled the number of television stations a single company could own. The Securities and Exchange Commission allowed the proliferation of new kinds of ever more exotic and risky securities and financial instruments, including index futures, various kinds of options and derivatives, and mortgage-backed securities (pools of home loans repackaged into tradable securities). Its enforcement focus shifted from corporate practices to individual wrongdoing, and it did not increase its staff even as the number of stockbrokers it supervised doubled. The federal government also became much less active in pursuing antitrust matters. The Reagan administration dropped a prolonged antitrust case against IBM and cut the staff of the Federal Trade Commission by more than half.

In both regulatory and administrative action, the Reagan administration targeted organized labor. Once Reagan appointees achieved a solid majority at the National Labor Relations Board, they issued a long series of pro-business rulings dealing with worker efforts to unionize and management rights. Equally important, they allowed a huge backlog of complaints of labor law violations to accumulate, resulting in such long delays in adjudicating cases that the board stopped being an effective agency to protect the right of workers to join unions of their choice without reprisal.

Reagan showed how strikes could be used to devastate unions in his handling of a 1981 walkout by the nation's air traffic controllers. The controllers, employed by the Federal Aviation Authority, had long complained about overwork, job stress, poor labor relations, and management harassment. By the time of the 1980 election, they had grown so disgusted with the Carter administration that their union, the Professional Air Traffic Controllers Organization (PATCO), broke with most of organized labor to back Reagan. Seven months after he took office, 11,300 PATCO members walked off their jobs. When a decade earlier postal workers had broken the prohibition on federal workers striking, Richard Nixon—though he made a show of calling out the National Guard—allowed negotiations that gave the strikers much of what they sought. Reagan took a very different stand, telling the strikers that unless they returned to work within forty-eight hours they would all be fired. He stuck to his pledge, using military and managerial personnel to patch together the air traffic control system until a new generation of workers could be trained.

Reagan's bold action inspired private-sector managers, showing that what had been virtually unthinkable—maintaining operations during a large, multisite strike through the wholesale replacement of the workforce—could be done. In a series of large, dramatic strikes starting in 1983, in which workers displayed remarkable solidarity in resisting demands for givebacks, major corporations, including Greyhound, the Phelps Dodge copper company, Eastern and Continental airlines, International Paper, the George A. Hormel meatpacking firm, and the *Chicago Tribune,* dealt organized labor stunning defeats. High unemployment facilitated the recruitment of strike replacements, as did a decay of working-class traditions that had once made scabbing all but unthinkable in much of the country. (The sanitized phrase "replacement workers" itself reflected changed attitudes, lacking the moral condemnation associated with the older term "scabs.") Judges and governors proved willing to use the power of the state, in the form of injunctions, state police, and National Guard units, to keep strikers from using force and intimidation to block their replacements from going to work.

Failed strikes hastened the decline in union militancy. The number of workdays lost to strikes (as a percentage of all days worked) declined through the late 1980s, when it settled at a historically low figure and remained there. The large, disruptive strike, after more than a century of playing a prominent role in the political economy, all but disappeared as a feature of American life.

The Limits of Reaganism

Reagan's tax cuts, spending limits, and deregulation were meant to reduce the size and influence of the government while stimulating growth. But during his first years in office, the economy, rather than growing, crashed, in part as a result of the final piece of his economic program, unwavering support for the tight money policy of the Federal Reserve. Federal Reserve chairman Paul Volcker stayed true to his determination to end inflation at any cost, winning strong support from the new president. Volcker drove the inflation rate down from 9 percent in 1981 to 3.5 percent at the start of 1985. But he did so by helping trigger the deepest recession since World War II, as his monetary policy pushed interest rates up toward an extraordinary 20 percent. With mortgage costs through the roof, the housing industry ground to a halt, falling to the lowest level of production since 1946. Automobile sales hit a twenty-year low. Though relatively brief, the economic downturn in 1981–82 resulted in one of ten workers being out of work—the highest unemployment rate since the Great Depression. Small businesses, farmers, and workers all suffered from the government-induced credit squeeze, as business and personal bankruptcies soared. Still, Reagan kept backing Volcker's policies, reappointing the Democrat to a second term heading the Federal Reserve in 1983.

The economic downturn cost Reagan considerable political support, particularly among working-class voters hit hard by the devastation of blue-collar industries. Reagan's approval ratings dropped sharply, as many working-class voters who had supported him drifted back to the Democratic Party. Conservative Democratic House members lost much of their fear of what they had seen as a Reagan juggernaut, weakening the president's ability to get legislation through. In the 1982 elections, the Republicans held on to their Senate majority but lost twenty-six seats in the House.

Missteps and misbehavior by some of the most fervent administration conservatives created additional pressure for a moderated political course. The effort to radically change environmental policy ran against public support of environmental protection. Key Reagan environmental officials acted as if their constituency consisted of particular business interests, with whom they often had cozy relationships, rather than the broad public, and lacked probity and basic administrative competence. Environmental groups tied up proposed regulatory shifts in court, while Congress intervened or threatened to intervene to undo administration giveaways to business and regulatory rollbacks. Scandals soon engulfed the EPA, where twenty top officials including the director were forced to resign (one went to jail). Interior Secretary Watt alienated broad swaths of the public with his pro-development policies and seeming contempt for conservation until forced to resign after making a disparaging comment about African Americans, Jews, and the disabled. Reagan appointed much more moderate replacements, while elsewhere in the administration deregulatory efforts slowed. In the wake of the backlash against its initial environmental policies, the Reagan administration declined even to try to revise environmental laws that conservatives and business leaders had hoped to weaken.

The huge strain on the federal budget that resulted from the recession also forced Reagan to retreat. A budget deficit would have resulted from the 1981 tax cuts under any circumstances, but the shortfall ballooned when the economy nosedived within months of their passage. Congress had no taste for further compensatory spending cuts. In mid-1982, Reagan reluctantly agreed to tax code changes, including reduced incentives for capital investment, which restored about a third of the revenue lost as a result of the 1981 cuts. Even with these changes and further fiscal adjustments in his second term, for the remainder of the Reagan administration the deficit remained at two to three times its level during Carter's last year in office.

Reagan decried the deficit, absolved himself of any responsibility (blaming Congress instead), and backed a constitutional amendment requiring a balanced budget. In practice, though, he accepted record-high peacetime deficits, which in some ways served his administration well. The deficit created ongoing pressure to cut spending and avoid new federal initiatives, furthering Reagan's goal of shrinking government (or at least slowing its growth).

Some of the policies that created the deficit also provided a stimulus to the economy. When the Federal Reserve began to loosen the money supply in mid-1982, reduced taxes and massive defense spending, along with falling energy prices, sped an economic recovery that began in 1983 and continued through the end of the Reagan administration. But contrary to what the supply-siders predicted, the tax cuts did not boost the economy by increasing personal savings (which fell) or investment in plant and equipment (which even during the recovery remained below the rate of previous decades) but rather by boosting consumer spending, which along with military outlays acted as a vast Keynesian stimulus program.

High interest rates reshaped the economy as it emerged from recession. The large federal deficit put upward pressure on interest rates, which only slowly came down as the economy rebounded. The bank prime lending rate did not drop below 10 percent until mid-1985. The unusually large gap between the interest and inflation rates redistributed wealth toward those already wealthy. People with money to lend, either through bond purchases or ownership shares of banks and other lending institutions, made out spectacularly well at the expense of borrowers and taxpayers (who had to fund the interest on the federal debt). In 1982, interest constituted 14 percent of national personal income, an all-time high.

High interest rates attracted foreign investors, who helped finance the spending spree on armaments and consumer goods that fueled the recovery and subsequent economic expansion. In just a few years the United States went from being the world's largest lender to being, for the first time since 1914, a debtor nation, and soon the world's largest debtor. The influx of foreign money not only helped fund the national debt, it also provided investment funds for domestic enterprises and, by strengthening the dollar relative to other currencies, made imports cheaper. But the strong dollar hurt exports, which failed to grow even after economic activity picked up. U.S. manufacturers had increasing difficulty maintaining market share at home and abroad, resulting in a growing trade imbalance. By 1988, waste paper destined for recycling constituted the largest export from the West Coast.

The 1984 Election

The more moderate policies Reagan adopted as a result of the 1981–82 recession helped him in the 1984 election. The resignations of Anne Burford and

James Watt kept environmental policy from being a major issue, to Reagan's advantage. He also rebuilt his political strength through a rhetorical turn away from hard-line anticommunism, as he proposed greater cooperation with the Soviet Union and downplayed his support for anticommunist insurgencies, assuaging public fears that he might lead the country into confrontation or war. But most importantly, the economic recovery enabled Reagan to run again as a pro-growth optimist, claiming that he had restored national strength and values.

The Reagan campaign brilliantly put forth a vision of a restored nation in a series of sentimental television advertisements. The most noted proclaimed that it was "Morning Again in America." Suffused with images of family, patriotism, and small-town life, the ads allowed voters to think that by selecting Reagan they were aligning themselves with an image of the country that made them feel good about themselves, even if in their own lives they chose very different directions from those portrayed in the commercials, abandoning the countryside and small towns for cities and suburbs, divorcing in large numbers, and indulging in—or at least yearning for—conspicuous consumption rather than the simple pleasures of bygone days. Reagan thrived on such contradictions, declaring himself against abortion but doing nothing to end it; calling for a constitutional amendment requiring balanced budgets while creating the largest peacetime deficits in history; and extolling family and community while promoting a deregulated free market that eroded both.

Reagan's opponent, Minnesota senator Walter Mondale, had roots in New Deal–Great Society liberalism. His dull if competent campaign gained a certain excitement from his selection of New York congresswoman Geraldine Ferraro as his vice presidential running mate, the first major-party female nominee for president or vice president. But Mondale never found traction against the Reagan imagery. He tried to exploit the deficit by saying that if elected he would raise taxes to begin reducing it, as, he contended, Reagan also would have to do, taking another step in the Democratic move toward what had in the past been the conservative, Republican stress on balanced budgets and fiscal probity. But the public seemed to share little of the newfound Democratic concern over the growing national debt. Most voters saw little to cheer for in Mondale's plan to raise taxes for more than half the population, in contrast to Reagan's pledge to hold the line on taxation.

The most electrifying candidate in the election was civil rights leader Jesse Jackson, whom Mondale defeated for the nomination. His sharp populist rhetoric and church-cadenced language of uplift helped mobilize the Democratic base, especially African American voters, who, along with

Hispanics, Jews, and low-income voters, Mondale succeeded in carrying. Otherwise, Reagan swept the boards, winning 59 percent of the popular vote. His victory in every state except Minnesota (where he barely lost) and the District of Columbia gave him the largest electoral vote margin in history.

Perhaps Reagan's strongest card was his self-assurance, his seeming resolve and willingness to take clear, bold action. His firing of the striking air traffic controllers brought him admiration, even among some voters who did not share antilabor views, for taking a strong stand and sticking with it. His graceful behavior after being shot (in the hospital waiting for surgery he quipped to his wife, "Sorry, honey, I forgot to duck") cemented his image as calm and self-assured, even, literally, under fire. After the indecisiveness and ineffectiveness of Ford and Carter, Reagan's very person seemed a refutation of the widespread perception of a country adrift, a declining empire that had lost the strength of will and boldness associated with its onetime glory. Like his conservative political soul mate, Margaret Thatcher, Reagan looked like he knew what he was doing (though in reality he was one of the least informed presidents the country ever had) and, more importantly, like he knew what he believed, which made him stand out against a tapestry of dull, poll-watching, equivocating leaders. In the end, voters, by a very large margin, liked the vision Reagan projected—expansive, upbeat, and cost-free—better than the Democratic message of problems, probity, and limits.

Revolution at Bay

Reagan's huge victory did not translate into much in the way of policy initiatives. For one thing, the Republicans as a party did not do especially well in 1984, losing two seats in the Senate and gaining only fifteen in the House, leaving Reagan without strong congressional backing. For another, Reagan himself seemed to have little new that he wanted to accomplish, running a campaign almost devoid of programmatic proposals. Rather than further battling, he preferred to bask in the light of public accolade, an increasingly distant figure who rarely had any unscripted contact with the press, the public, or even other politicians.

After the election, both Democrats and Republicans acknowledged the sheer fantasy of the early Reagan administration claims that taxes could be massively cut without creating a large deficit. In an effort to move toward a balanced budget, the 1985 Gramm-Rudman-Hollings Act established a system for automatic spending cuts if the deficit exceeded fixed targets. Both parties supported the bill. The spending caps reduced the budget shortfall but came nowhere near eliminating it.

In 1986, Congress, again on a bipartisan basis, addressed taxes but not with the aim of increasing revenue. Instead, it sought to revise and simplify the tax code, largely in accord with a soft version of supply-side economics. The Tax Reform Act reduced the top individual income tax rate to 28 percent, further institutionalizing the supply-side idea that cutting the tax rate for the rich would benefit the entire society. (Under the law, the tax rate for the income group just below the top actually exceeded what the wealthiest had to pay.) To make up for the lost revenue, the law closed many tax loopholes and reduced the value of various tax shelters. It also eliminated the deduction for interest on consumer loans (including credit cards but not mortgages), a modest step toward checking consumerism and the rise in personal debt. With some companies gaining from the law and others losing, the business community divided over it, part of a reversion to parochial concerns after the big victories of the late 1970s and early 1980s.

The Reagan administration recognized in 1985 that the strong dollar was causing such damage to exports and manufacturing industries that it could not be sustained. After maintaining a hands-off policy toward exchange rates, it began intervening in money markets and in September 1985 negotiated an agreement with the leading industrial powers to lower the value of the dollar. The new policy contributed to a revival of manufacturing. But the weakened dollar also had the effect of making American assets cheap buys for foreign investors, who gobbled up golf courses, trophy buildings, and corporations at a frantic pace. Direct foreign investment in the United States, which had been $83 billion when Reagan was first elected, reached $304 billion in 1988.

Any chance that Reagan might try to launch another transformative political effort during his second term ended when a series of scandals enveloped some of his key constituencies and his own administration, draining away what little remained of its vitality. Following the arrest of a young investment banker in the spring of 1986, investigators led by U.S. Attorney Rudolph Giuliani uncovered the extensive illegal use of insider information by leading Wall Street figures to make fortunes on mergers and acquisitions. Ultimately, prosecutors won convictions against fourteen people for mail fraud and security and tax law violations, including two of the most prominent figures in the market boom of the 1980s, arbitrageur Ivan Boesky, who bought insider information from leading brokerage houses with suitcases of cash, and Michael Milken, the junk bond salesman extraordinaire whose yearly income had exceeded the GNP of some nations. Rather than great democratic equalizers, the stock and bond markets turned out to be rigged games, in which cheating insiders reaped huge gains. Their malfeasance was facilitated by Reagan administration officials whose connections to Wall Street and ideological belief in the greater virtue of private enterprise than government led to lax regulation.

Images of Wall Street big shots being taken off to jail tainted the ideological and moral claims of boosters of unregulated capitalism, but a more severe blow came in October 1987, when the Dow Jones Industrial Average fell 23 percent in a single day, the steepest drop in its history (including during the Great Depression). The loss of money by millions of people trying to get in on the magic of unearned financial gains led to a widespread sense of betrayal, evident in movies like Oliver Stone's *Wall Street,* with its hero-villain loosely based on Boesky; novels like Tom Wolfe's *Bonfire of the Vanities,* with its unflattering look at a bond trader; and a wave of business books documenting the mercenary culture of 1980s finance. The Reagan administration suffered from its association with the cult of the market and money, though it would only take another upswing for Wall Street and free-market ideology to regain their cultural and political footing in the post-Reagan era.

Lax Reagan administration regulation contributed to another financial debacle, the savings and loan scandal, the full cost of which became evident only after the president left office. The removal of limits on how federally regulated savings and loan associations could invest their money prompted a turn to speculative investments in shopping malls, office buildings, condominiums, ski resorts, casinos, and other endeavors with big potential gains but also big risks. Federal regulators failed to closely monitor the banks, which in many cases morphed from sleepy local institutions to big regional operations, even though federal deposit insurance made Washington liable for a large part of any losses they might incur. Some bankers engaged in unethical behavior or outright thievery, using their institutions to provide favorable loans to themselves and their associates and finance high living. A slowdown in the real estate market, especially in Texas and the Southwest where the savings and loan expansion had been greatest, led to a wave of bank failures during Reagan's second term. In 1989, Congress finally acted to clean up the industry and deal with insolvent banks, at a cost to the government of well over $100 billion, making it the most expensive bank crisis to date.

Scandals in the spiritual world also took some shine off Reaganism. In the spring of 1987, television evangelist Jim Bakker admitted to having had an affair with a church volunteer, whom he paid to keep silent. Jimmy Swaggart, another high-profile television preacher, confessed to having had a sexual relationship with a prostitute. Jerry Falwell, the most visible ministerial link between conservative churches and conservative politics, tried to rescue Bakker's operation but soon gave up on it and his own Moral Majority organization. As the televangelist scandals revealed the hypocrisy that sometimes lay behind the public professions of piety that had become common in the Reagan era, the open association of evangelical church leaders with conservative politics turned into a mixed blessing.

The most serious blow to the Reagan administration came from its own doings, its secret, illegal, semiprivatized effort to pursue foreign policy operations banned by Congress and beyond the pale of public acceptability. In late 1986, news began to filter out about a series of interrelated clandestine government operations, including the supply of arms to the antigovernment Contra forces in Nicaragua in violation of an explicit congressional ban; the sale of arms to Iran in exchange for the release of hostages; and the use of profits from the arms trading to fund the Nicaragua operation. Though Reagan personally managed to avoid legal consequences for the violations of law and the Constitution he and his aides engaged in, his popularity dropped sharply, as he lost the high degree of public trust that had been one of his greatest political assets.

The Iran-Contra affair reflected the Reagan administration's loose administrative style that sometimes verged on chaos, poor oversight of spending and operations, porous boundaries between public and private interests, and lax ethical standards. During Reagan's second term and after he left office, several top administration officials, some with close personal ties to the president, were charged with criminal activities, including fraud, larceny, illegal lobbying, and perjury. Secretary of Labor Raymond Donovan became the first sitting cabinet officer ever to be indicted, on charges related to his work in the construction industry, though he ultimately won acquittal. The most extensive corruption took place in HUD, an agency whose very mission Reagan and his allies largely rejected. Young, politically connected officials, often with no housing expertise, steered massive amounts of federal money to developers who paid high fees to prominent Republicans (including James Watt and former Nixon attorney general John Mitchell) to serve as their consultants and lobbyists, furthering political interests and private wealth at the expense of public housing.

How Reagan Changed America

The Reagan revolution failed to achieve many of its goals. Most basic structures and policies of the federal government did not fundamentally change during the years Reagan occupied the White House. While the public was enamored of the president, it never supported many of his specific plans. But

Reagan did lead a revolution in the assumptions and values of the nation, especially concerning the role of government and political economy.

Coming into office, Reagan promised to balance the budget by 1984. Instead, he ran up deficits of over $100 billion in every one of his budgets, raising the national debt from $914 billion in 1980 to $2.7 trillion in 1989. As a percentage of the GNP, Reagan's deficits exceeded the average of the New Deal deficits during the Great Depression.

Reagan spent decades denouncing excessive government and government bureaucrats, but when he left office the federal bureaucracy was bigger than when he came in. Even agencies he specifically targeted for elimination chugged on. Reagan abandoned his campaign pledge to get rid of the Departments of Energy and Education, which turned out to have powerful constituencies he had no interest in taking on. He did make a serious attempt to first eliminate and then reform the Legal Services Corporation, a Great Society descendant that infuriated conservatives by advocating for the poor and minorities not only in individual cases but also by challenging laws and government policies. Resistance in Congress and court suits stymied his effort. Reagan's attempt to roll back regulation of health and safety and the environment also largely failed, cementing a consensus in favor of at least a mild version of environmentalism (though he did push the government further along the path of economic deregulation). The federal government, with its multiple branches and many constituencies, proved remarkably resistant to institutional change.

Reagan left a profound mark on one aspect of the state, the judiciary. By the time he left office, he had appointed more than half of the sitting federal judges, a higher percentage than any president other than FDR. His administration worked systematically to identify conservative appointees, generally selecting well-qualified candidates to ensure their confirmation. To fill the first opening he had on the Supreme Court, he appointed Sandra Day O'Connor, the first female justice, whom some Reagan backers opposed for being insufficiently conservative on social issues. His other Supreme Court appointees were solid conservatives who furthered the rightward push of the Court that had begun under Nixon.

But no judicial counterrevolution occurred. In spite of fierce conservative attacks on *Roe v. Wade*, the decision remained in force long after Reagan died and his Court nominees began to retire. Similarly, school prayer remained illegal long after the end of the Reagan administration. Nor was there a cultural counterrevolution. Though many conservatives had hoped that Reagan's ascendancy might reverse the drift of public attitudes toward

greater tolerance of homosexuality, pornography, sexuality outside of marriage, and expanded roles for women, no such rollback occurred.

Reagan proved more effective in weakening organized labor, arguably
the greatest practical success of the conservative reign. Reagan's encouragement of strikebreaking through his handling of the air traffic controllers'
strike, his appointment of pro-business members to the NLRB, and his general tilt toward employer interests contributed to a sharp decline in union
membership, as did factory closings and other economic shifts that in many
cases were caused or facilitated by his administration's policies. By 1989,
only 16 percent of the workforce carried a union card, down from 25 percent
in 1980. With public employee unions making modest membership gains,
all of the loss was in the private sector. By the start of the 1990s, fewer than
12 percent of privately employed workers belonged to a union.

Reagan's paramount achievement was to shift the values, language, and
assumptions of the country, fostering an ideological break with the New Deal
order, if not an institutional disjuncture. From the most powerful pulpit in the
country, Reagan promoted the message he had been perfecting since his GE
days, that freedom had its natural home in the marketplace and that government undermined freedom rather than extended it. Until a decade before he
took office, the notion of freedom had been strongly associated with the fight
for racial equality and the use of state power to protect individual rights, but
by the time he left the presidency it had become closely linked to free enterprise.

Conservative, Reagan-era ideas about freedom had an underside of indifference, callousness, or outright hostility to the poor and those left behind.
Tax changes shifted more of the burden for financing the federal government
from the wealthy to the less well-off even as government programs aimed at
low-income families were cut. The decline of organized labor and the shift
in the mix of working-class jobs away from manufacturing to service industries contributed to the growth of income inequality and an increased concentration of wealth by exerting downward pressure on wages at a time when
jumps in interest and dividend income, stock prices, finance industry profits,
and pay rates for upper executives boosted income at the top. Between 1980
and 1988, the top 20 percent of wage earners saw their share of national income go from 41.6 to 44.0 percent, while the bottom 60 percent saw their
share drop. The very wealthiest made out the best, with the top 1 percent of
earners seeing their national income share go from 9 percent to 11 percent.
A new group of hyper-rich emerged during the 1980s, including several
dozen billionaires, the economic winners in a new gilded age.

Americans disadvantaged by patterns of discrimination also found themselves a low priority for the Reagan administration, which reduced funding for civil rights agencies, filed fewer suits against segregated school systems, and launched a rhetorical and legal assault on affirmative action. Reagan's civil rights policy in part reflected a desire to reward white constituencies that had supported him out of disenchantment with the Democratic Party's promotion of black advancement. But the shift in civil rights policy, especially the attack on affirmative action, had a strong ideological component. Reagan conservatives rejected the idea that the government had any obligation to groups that historically had suffered from discrimination other than opposing contemporary acts of discrimination against particular individuals. They portrayed their position as a form of egalitarianism, in which every individual would be treated equally and no special favors or advantages, in the form of quotas, set-asides, or affirmative action, would be granted to particular ethnic, religious, or racial groups, a formulation that proved very popular among whites across the economic spectrum. Actually ending affirmative action programs proved difficult because of resistance in the courts and Congress, which had a more expansive conception of civil rights that took into account the disadvantages groups faced in the job market and in access to education because of prior discrimination. But after Reagan left office, the Supreme Court, with the support of his appointees, began to narrow the circumstances in which affirmative action and set-aside programs could be used as remedies.

A similar indifference and callousness could be seen in the Reagan administration's handling of the AIDS epidemic. The first cases of AIDS in the United States were observed in 1980. By 1982, many doctors had become convinced—correctly as it turned out—that an infectious agent which could be sexually transmitted was responsible for the new disease. Yet during his first term, Reagan made neither the study of AIDS nor its prevention a high priority. Cutbacks in funding to federal health agencies slowed research in general, while the close association of AIDS with gay men, who at first made up the majority of its victims, diminished the interest of the administration (and much of the medical, political, and media establishments too) in making it a major public issue. By the end of Reagan's first term, thirty-seven hundred people had died of AIDS, but not until the 1986 death of Rock Hudson, a Hollywood friend of the president's who never publicly admitted his homosexuality, did Reagan begin to pay some attention to the epidemic, and even then it was another year before he gave his first major address on the subject, which avoided frank discussion of how the disease was transmitted and how its spread might be slowed.

During Reagan's second term, the federal government devoted more resources and attention to AIDS. Many conservatives, inside and outside of the administration, opposed sex education and the promotion of condom use, which would have slowed the spread of the infection. But some administration conservatives, including Surgeon General C. Everett Koop, advocated frank discussion of sexual practices, the distribution of condoms, and bolstered federal heath efforts aimed at drug users and the poor, groups disproportionately hit by the epidemic (an approach followed by the State Department in its international AIDS-related activities). Belatedly, public health needs began counterbalancing ideology.

Reaganism represented a kind of cheerful Social Darwinism, a celebration of the possibilities for economic and social mobility and those who achieved it. As much a cultural mood as a set of policies, its animating spirit held, as the Reaganites' favorite Chinese leader, Deng Xiaoping, once put it, "To be rich is glorious." Reagan helped complete the discrediting of liberalism by associating it with special favors for particular groups and the coddling of people unwilling to help themselves at the expense of hardworking taxpayers. Many Americans credited Reagan with restoring national pride, decreasing social instability, and promoting firmer moral codes.

Reagan helped make conservative thought hegemonic, change public attitudes toward government (more than changing government itself), and boost the national standing of the Republican Party to full equality with the Democrats. But perhaps his most important political legacy lay in his blithe disregard for consequences. Reagan often proved unwilling to confront or even acknowledge problematic effects of his policies or his responsibility for misbehavior or failure by his administration. He seemed to believe the country to be blessed, exempt from the need to consider the long-term effects of its policies and way of life. In this, he represented the spirit that had come to animate elite circles, particularly in the corporate world, as probity, foresight, and stewardship were nudged aside in the quest for quick profits and indulgent consumption. When Tom Paine proclaimed, "We have it in our power to begin the world over again," he had been calling on colonial Americans to make a revolutionary break from the old world of hereditary rule and inequality and create a new republic as an act of social responsibility. For Reagan, faith in the ability to continually reshape the world became a road to irresponsibility, a way of evading the consequences of one's actions. It proved to be a troubling bequest for the nation and the world.

CHAPTER 16

Cold War Redux

On February 4, 1980, Jimmy Carter's national security adviser, Zbigniew Brzezinski, looked through the sights of a Chinese-made AK-47 rifle at a Pakistani army observation post high up in the Khyber Pass, just a few miles from the border with Afghanistan. Brzezinski's visit came during a week of meetings with leaders of Pakistan and Saudi Arabia to discuss the recent Soviet occupation of Afghanistan. At a refugee camp near the border, Brzezinski told Afghan fighters, "That land over there is yours and you will go back one day because your cause is right and God is on your side."

The reporters accompanying Brzezinski did not know that six months before Soviet troops entered Afghanistan, on Christmas Eve 1979, the United States had begun a secret program of propaganda, psychological operations, and logistical support for Afghan groups fighting the communist government that had recently taken power. After the Soviet Union sent its military into Afghanistan to bolster its shaky ally, Brzezinski laid out a plan for more extensive clandestine intervention. He proposed channeling money and advice to the anticommunist forces, working with and through the Pakistani dictatorship of President Mohammad Zia ul-Haq. He hoped that with the American aid, the Soviets could be driven out of Afghanistan. "Even if this is not attainable," he wrote to Carter, "we should make Soviet involvement as costly as possible." Brzezinski's plan soon became U.S. policy, first under Carter and then under Ronald Reagan. As he hoped, funneling American resources to the Afghan anticommunists proved very costly to the Soviet Union. Ultimately, it also proved very costly to the United States.

Afghanistan marked a heating up of the Cold War, after years of improved Soviet-American relations. The 1980s brought increasingly tense relations between the two superpowers, an accelerated arms race, and a series of proxy battles in the developing world, before the Cold War dramatically and rather suddenly came to an end. But international conflict and threats to U.S. security continued. Afghanistan ultimately made clear the fragility of the new world order that the United States tried to construct after the Cold War ended and the continuities in the country's conception of its role in the world before and after the collapse of communism.

Hot Cold War

During the Ford and Carter administrations, the defeat of the United States in Vietnam led to a rethinking of American foreign policy, without much questioning of its fundamental postulates. Across the political spectrum, policymakers continued to believe that the security and prosperity of the United States depended on an active, anticommunist, internationalist foreign policy; that the spread of American investment, ideas, and power around the globe benefited both the United States and the countries with which it engaged; that the Soviet Union remained a dangerous ideological, political, and military enemy; and that the United States had to maintain a very large military to protect itself, its allies, and its interests. But the erosion of public support for the military effort in Vietnam and its ultimate failure did make leaders reluctant, for a while, to use armed force in pursuit of foreign policy objectives, the so-called Vietnam syndrome.

As the foreign policy establishment adopted a more measured approach to advancing traditionally defined American interests, it faced criticism from elements inside and outside of the state apparatus seeking a more militant anti-Soviet, anti-left stance and a remilitarization of foreign policy. Neoconservatives and conservative nationalists led the way in arguing for a hard-edged Wilsonianism that pushed American economic and political systems onto the rest of the world. Like Henry Luce in earlier years, they believed that the United States was justified in using its power as it saw fit.

The Iranian Revolution and the growth of left-wing and anti-Western forces around the world strengthened the hand of the foreign policy hardliners. In Africa, the Near East, and Latin America, economic growth all but ended following the downturn of the 1970s. Growing poverty provided fertile soil for movements challenging the status quo. High oil prices enabled the Soviet Union, the world's largest oil producer, to fund groups in Africa (including in Somalia, Sudan, and Ethiopia) and elsewhere with which it felt political kinship. In some cases it worked in alliance with Cuba, which had its own program of political and military support for left-wing groups in

Africa and Latin America. At the same time, wealthy families and state agencies in Saudi Arabia and the Gulf States, awash in petrodollars, began funding Islamic fundamentalist schools, mosques, and movements across the Middle East and Asia.

Jimmy Carter's moves during his last year in office—the acceleration of his defense buildup, his steps against the Soviet Union, and his cutoff of aid to the Sandinista regime in Nicaragua—steered the country toward a set of policies reminiscent of the early years of the Cold War. Ronald Reagan continued Carter's neo–Cold War policies, amplifying the funding, rhetoric, and, in some arenas, action behind them. In one of the greatest peacetime armament programs in history, Reagan revived the B-1 bomber project that Carter had canceled; proceeded with the development of the B-2 (Stealth) bomber, designed to evade radar detection (at a cost of over a half billion dollars a plane); increased the number of Navy ships by a third; and developed new land- and submarine-based nuclear-armed missiles. In speech after speech, Reagan harshly criticized the Soviet Union, portraying the Cold War as a clash of ideas and values, a Manichean battle between freedom and oppression, a sharply different tone than that used by American policymakers during the 1970s. "So far détente's been a one-way street that the Soviet Union has used to pursue its own aims," Reagan said at his very first presidential press conference. The Soviets "have openly and publicly declared that the only morality they recognize is what will further their cause, meaning they reserve unto themselves the right to commit any crime, to lie, to cheat, in order to attain that."

Even while cranking up the war-making power of the country and throwing rhetorical bombs, Reagan made occasional gestures toward the Soviet Union that he hoped might open the door for fruitful discussions and arms limitation. Early in his administration, he ended the embargo on grain sales that Carter had imposed after the occupation of Afghanistan and began writing a series of private letters to Soviet leaders suggesting that they work together to find "lasting peace." But his episodic efforts failed to engage the Soviet leadership. The declining health of Communist Party head Leonid Brezhnev and the rapid succession of aged leaders after his death contributed to a freeze in Soviet policy toward the United States. Soviet military and civilian leaders lacked the trust in Reagan to join in serious talks, as they came to fear that the United States might initiate a nuclear attack on their country. Reagan's blunt language, including his description of the Soviet Union, in a March 1983 speech to the National Association of Evangelicals, as "the focus of evil in the modern world" and "an evil empire," led them to see him as a very hard-line Cold Warrior.

Especially frightening to Soviet officials was Reagan's Strategic Defense Initiative (SDI), a plan to develop a system to defend against ballistic missiles, which he announced in a nationally televised address two weeks after the "evil empire" speech. Appalled by the idea of mutually assured destruction as the main check on nuclear war, Reagan had long been intrigued by the idea of an antiballistic missile defense system. He had faith (not shared by many scientists) that the formidable technical challenges to stopping incoming missiles could be overcome. The Soviets saw SDI not as a defensive measure but as a prelude to an attack. The sheer number of Soviet missiles, they believed, would overcome a defensive shield if they themselves launched a first strike, so the only purpose of SDI, in their analysis, would be to stop the smaller number of missiles they could launch in retaliation after an attack from the United States.

The beleaguered mind-set of Soviet leaders might have contributed to their decision to shoot down a South Korean passenger jet, KAL flight 007, that in September 1983 strayed over Soviet territory, killing all 269 people aboard, including sixty-one Americans. Their action—based on the false assumption that the airliner was engaged in spying—horrified much of the world and brought new denunciations from the United States, with Reagan calling it "an act of barbarism." The successful U.S. effort to convince its European allies to accept intermediate-range Pershing nuclear missiles aimed at the Soviet Union further increased tensions between the two countries. The United States presented the Pershings as a defensive response to the Soviet deployment of hundreds of SS-20 intermediate-range nuclear missiles targeted at Western Europe. The Soviets had a very different view, seeing the SS-20s as a routine modernization of their defenses while fearing the offensive possibilities of the new NATO missiles, which could reach Soviet territory in just seven minutes.

Reagan had no desire for a direct confrontation with the Soviet Union. When Poland declared martial law in an effort to suppress the Solidarity movement and it looked as if the Soviet Union and its allies might militarily intervene, Reagan did not move to directly involve the United States. Like all presidents since Eisenhower, he tacitly acknowledged Eastern Europe as a Soviet sphere of influence. But in other parts of the world, Reagan aggressively confronted leftists and Soviet allies in a series of proxy wars and clandestine operations.

Central America, where left-wing movements were challenging the oligarchies that, except during brief populist interludes, had controlled the governments and wealth of the region since World War II, became a testing ground for Reagan's policies. In Nicaragua, the Sandinistas were trying to consolidate their power. In El Salvador, the Farabundo Martí National Liberation Front (FMLN) guerrilla movement, with aid from the Sandinistas, had launched an offensive against the military/landowner-dominated state.

Conservatives saw Central America as an ideal place to establish a new tenor to U.S. foreign policy, an arena in which to reintroduce the use of force to achieve American goals and to send a message to the Soviet Union, Cuba, and left-wing movements that they would face sharp opposition if they attempted to extend their reach. The very strategic and economic insignificance of the region to the United States (with the exception of the Panama Canal) made it a well-suited battleground, for it really mattered little to American policymakers or business interests what type of societies emerged there or what price would have to be paid by the local populations in a war against the left. The United States had a long tradition of intervening in Central America, while the Soviet Union never had displayed much interest in the region, making it unlikely that American action would lead to a dangerous superpower conflict. Reagan could indulge the desire for aggressive anti-left action among Christian rightists, neoconservative intellectuals, mainstream conservatives, and intelligence and paramilitary veterans without risking a confrontation that could threaten the United States itself.

At first, the Reagan administration concentrated on El Salvador, increasing military aid, sending more military advisers, and training Salvadoran soldiers in an effort to hold off the FMLN. The United States promoted the Christian Democratic Party of José Napoleón Duarte, a Notre Dame graduate who came to power following a 1979 coup. Duarte presented a much more attractive image than the far-right ARENA party, which had close links to death squads and ultimately proved dominant.

The Reagan administration portrayed itself as a promoter of democracy, but it simultaneously adopted the view that sometimes the road to democracy—or at least the best interests of the United States—lay in supporting anticommunist dictatorships. This was far from a new position for the United States, which over the years had allied with dictatorial regimes in Spain, South Vietnam, Indonesia, and other places in the name of fighting communism and keeping the door open for the eventual emergence of democratic governance. An astringent critique of Carter administration foreign policy by political scientist Jeane Kirkpatrick, "Dictatorships and Double Standards," which restated this view, greatly impressed Reagan and won her appointment as ambassador to the United Nations, the first woman to hold the position and the only woman and only Democrat in Reagan's initial cabinet. Kirkpatrick took to task the Carter administration for naïveté and hypocrisy in abandoning pro-American autocratic leaders like Somoza and the shah of Iran while remaining passive toward left-wing regimes and movements. Ousting "traditional autocracies," she argued, rather than leading to democracy, often led to left-wing totalitarian governments that made the lives of ordinary people more miserable and were less likely to evolve into democratic regimes than the dictatorships they replaced. Kirkpatrick's disdain for what she saw as the simple-minded belief that "it is possible to democratize governments, any time, anywhere, under any circumstances" ran counter to the rhetoric Reagan routinely employed but informed the policies that in practice he pursued.

In Nicaragua, the Reagan administration supported a decidedly undemocratic group, exiled former members of Somoza's National Guard, who came together in 1981 to fight the Sandinista regime. Hoping to use the Contras—short for "counterrevolutionaries"—to disrupt Nicaraguan support for the FMLN and oust the Sandinista government or at least force it to make concessions, in late 1981 Reagan approved $19 million of covert aid to the group, the beginning of what ultimately grew to over $300 million of funding. Unlike in El Salvador, where the Reagan administration was attempting to keep an established government in power, in Nicaragua it was backing an armed group seeking to overthrow a government that had wide international recognition, including from the United States itself. The Reagan administration tried to keep the funding secret, but word of it soon leaked out. At first the United States paid the Argentine military, which in its own country had installed itself in power and fought a brutal "dirty war" against the left, to train and advise the Contras at bases in Honduras. The CIA took over the effort after the Argentine defeat in the 1982 Falklands War led to the collapse of the military regime.

Reagan's anti-Sandinista program never gained much support either on Capitol Hill (though Congress initially voted limited aid for the Contras) or with the public. Two events in 1984 eroded what backing it had. First, the *Wall Street Journal* revealed that sabotage operations in Nicaragua that the United States claimed had been done by the Contras actually had been the work of the CIA. Journalists uncovered a CIA training manual distributed to the Contras that encouraged assassinations, a violation of an executive order Reagan had signed early in his presidency. Second, under pressure from the United States, Nicaragua held its first national election since the overthrow of Somoza, in which Sandinista Daniel Ortega easily won the presidency. Rather than fighting to spread democracy, the United States seemed to be trying to subvert it through covert military force. Perhaps in compensation, Reagan's rhetorical support for the Contras became increasingly extravagant, as he called them "freedom fighters" and "the moral equal

of our Founding Fathers and the brave men and women of the French Resistance."

Congress, unswayed by Reagan, in October 1984 placed tight restrictions
on aid to the anti-Sandinista forces. Anticipating that step, the Reagan administration already had moved to circumvent it, secretly soliciting aid to
the Contras from allied governments. Saudi Arabia began contributing a
million dollars a month (later upped to two million), while other countries
and private contributors chipped in lesser amounts. To funnel the money to
the Contras and buy them arms and equipment, CIA director William Casey
had Marine lieutenant colonel Oliver North, a midlevel NSC staffer, set up
a network of former military and intelligence officers, arms dealers, and private businessmen. White House officials repeatedly lied to Congress and the
public when they denied that the administration was still involved in supporting the Contras.

Elsewhere, too, the Reagan administration worked to reintroduce the use
of force in pursuit of foreign policy goals. In Afghanistan, it increased the
Carter administration funding of the anticommunist insurgents, working
out an arrangement with Saudi Arabia for it to match, dollar for dollar, CIA
spending. American policymakers saw their primary interest in Afghanistan
as making the Soviets suffer militarily, politically, and financially, with little
concern about who would take over if the communists were forced out. That
left the field open for Pakistani-backed Islamic militants and warlords, many
of whom had deep contempt for American society. In 1986, the United States
began giving the Afghan mujahideen fighters ground-to-air Stinger missiles,
which proved highly effective against Soviet airpower.

In Lebanon, the United States introduced its own forces in what initially
was meant to be a peacekeeping role but which morphed into combat. In
1978, Jimmy Carter had brokered the Camp David Accords between Egypt
and Israel, which led to the withdrawal of Israeli forces from the Sinai Peninsula and Egyptian diplomatic recognition of Israel, greased by the promise
of massive U.S aid to both countries. But Israel and Syria remained in a
tense standoff, with Israel refusing to give back the Golan Heights (which
like the Sinai it had captured in the 1973 war) and Syrian forces threatening
Israel from bases in Lebanon. In 1982, Israel invaded Lebanon, attacking
Syrian positions in the Bekaa Valley and moving to the outskirts of Beirut,
hoping to destroy the exile forces of the Palestinian Liberation Organization
(PLO). With Israel bombarding Beirut, causing high civilian casualties, and
threatening a full-scale battle to seize the city, the United States, France, and
Italy sent in troops to separate the parties and supervise the removal of the
PLO, the Syrians, and the Israelis. After the multinational force successfully

oversaw the evacuation of PLO leaders and their supporters to Tunisia, U.S. troops withdrew. But then everything started to go wrong. The Israelis and the Syrians refused to leave Lebanon, and someone assassinated its conservative Christian president, Bashir Gemayel. In retaliation, his supporters, operating under the protection of the Israeli army, massacred hundreds of civilians in Palestinian refugee camps. The Reagan administration sent a reorganized multinational force back into Beirut, but the American Marine contingent soon came under attack from Muslim forces, which saw it as bolstering the Christian-led government, now headed by Gemayel's brother Amin. Skirmishing escalated, with an American battleship stationed offshore firing massive sixteen-inch shells at Druze militia positions and American aircraft joining the fighting.

Hezbollah, a newly formed Shiite group with Syrian and Iranian backing, found a devastating, low-tech way to respond to the high-tech American forces. On April 18, 1983, a pickup truck with two thousand pounds of explosives crashed into the lobby of the American embassy in Beirut, killing sixty-three people, including all six members of the CIA's Beirut station and a high-ranking agency official who happened to be visiting. Six months later, on October 23, a Hezbollah fighter drove a dump truck filled with twelve thousand pounds of explosives into the Marine barracks near the Beirut airport. The massive explosion destroyed the building and killed 241 Americans, including 220 Marines, the highest single-day death toll for the Corps since Iwo Jima. Reagan declared after the bombing that keeping U.S. troops in Lebanon was "central to our credibility on a global scale." But within months, recognizing that there was little popular support for the Lebanon mission, he pulled out the Marines.

The president managed to avoid paying a political price for the Lebanon fiasco because of another military action two days after the bombing of the Marine barracks, the invasion of Grenada. A small island in the eastern Caribbean, Grenada had been a British colony until 1974. In 1979, a bloodless coup led by the leftist New Jewel Movement overthrew the increasingly autocratic prime minister, installing in his place Maurice Bishop. The new regime failed to capitalize on its initial popularity by holding elections, instead suppressing opponents as it allied with Cuba and the Soviet bloc. The Reagan administration charged that a new airport, being built with Cuban help, was designed to accommodate Soviet aircraft, not large tourist jets as Grenada's government claimed.

In October 1983, a hard-line group within the New Jewel Movement ousted Bishop, who seemed to be considering easing relations with the United States. On October 19, Bishop's opponents executed him and members of his cabinet, leading to chaotic conditions. Eight hundred Americans attended medical school on the island. In the name of protecting them, and with a formal request from the Organization of Eastern Caribbean States, the United States invaded Grenada using thousands of Marines and Army troops. The American force met stiffer resistance than expected, particularly from armed Cuban construction workers, but it soon prevailed. Nineteen Americans died in the invasion, as did forty-five Grenadians and twenty-four Cubans.

Though the invasion did not go completely smoothly, it received strong support back home. The military kept reporters away from the fighting, so television coverage of medical students returning home dominated the imagery of the Grenada events, rather than pictures of combat or casualties. Though absurdly lopsided in the size and strength of the adversaries, the Grenada invasion, coming just after the Beirut Marine disaster, bolstered the image of the military and the Reagan administration and served as an argument for the efficacy of the use of force. The military, in an extreme exercise of patting itself on the back, gave out 8,612 medals to officers and service members involved in the invasion, including some who never left the Pentagon.

Early in his second term, Reagan's failed Middle East policy converged with his Central American policy through an off-books NSC operation that constituted one of the gravest breaches of constitutional government since World War II. The U.S. role in propping up the Christian-led government in Lebanon and its support for Israel incited Iranian-backed terrorists to kidnap seven Americans in Lebanon, including the CIA man sent to rebuild the Beirut station. Although as a candidate Reagan had been highly critical of Carter's handling of the Iran hostage crisis, his administration had no clear policy of its own to deal with the problem of hostages. Repeatedly, its spokesmen proclaimed that the United States would not bargain or make deals to release hostages, but privately Reagan encouraged or at least acceded to efforts to bargain for their release. When in 1985 terrorists hijacked an airplane, flew it to Beirut, murdered an American sailor on board, and threatened to kill the other thirty-nine American passengers, the Reagan administration did not object when Israel freed hundreds of prisoners in response to the hijackers' demands in a tacit deal that brought the release of the hostages.

During the summer of 1985, an arms dealer with ties to Iran approached the Reagan administration with a plan for it to sell weapons to Iran, then locked in a long, devastating war with Iraq. In return, he claimed, Iran would arrange for the release of the seven hostages held in Lebanon. With support from the president, the NSC approved Israel's sale of U.S.-made antitank missiles to Iran, with the understanding that the United States would replenish the Israeli stockpile. Once the missiles arrived, one

hostage—not the promised seven—was released, with the Reagan administration falsely claiming that it had made no deal in exchange. In November
1985, the administration engineered a second Israeli sale of U.S.-made missiles, but the Iranians did not arrange the release of any hostages in return,
claiming that the wrong model had been sent. In spite of having been taken
twice, administration officials plunged ahead with a third arms sale to Iran.
This time, instead of working through Israel, NSC staffer Oliver North took
direct charge, running the operation through the network he and William
Casey had put together to supply arms to the Contras.

By mid-1985, the Contra support operation had grown into a major endeavor. To run it, Casey and North had tapped retired Air Force major
general Richard Secord, who set up dummy corporations, opened secret
Swiss bank accounts, and contracted with arms dealers and paramilitary air
transport firms. Secord, who paid himself well for his efforts, called his operation "the Enterprise," while North referred to it as "Project Democracy."
At the beginning of 1986, North shifted the Iran operation to the Enterprise
as well. He added a twist, using some of the money Iran paid for weapons to
support the Contras, a clear violation of the congressional ban.

In May 1986, North and former national security adviser Robert McFarlane secretly traveled to Tehran to again try to arrange for the remaining
hostages in Lebanon to be released in return for arms. McFarlane also
hoped he could initiate a broader rapprochement with Iran. No agreement
could be worked out, but two months later the Iranians engineered the release of another hostage, leading Reagan to approve a shipment of missile
parts in return.

It took one lucky missile shot and a news leak to halt Reagan's covert Central America–Middle East policy. In October 1986, a nineteen-year-old Sandinista soldier on patrol in Nicaragua shot down a Contra resupply plane with
a shoulder-fired missile. Nicaraguan troops captured American crewman Eugene Hasenfus, who told his captors that the CIA had coordinated the resupply operation. Reagan and other top U.S. officials denied government
involvement, but journalists soon uncovered information that corroborated
Hasenfus's story. Even as Casey and North began destroying files to cover
their tracks, the Reagan administration tried to keep trading arms for hostages with Iran, pressuring Kuwait to release prisoners Iran wanted free and
securing the release of one more hostage in Lebanon. But in November, a
Middle Eastern newspaper published an account of McFarlane's trip to Tehran. Soon more details of the arms-for-hostages operation leaked out. Top
Reagan administration officials began intertwined processes of investigation
and cover-up. When an assistant attorney general discovered a memo in

North's files—overlooked in his massive shredding of documents—that described the diversion of Iranian arms sales money to the Contras, the Enterprise reached its end. In short order, Attorney General Edwin Meese revealed the Iran-Contra connection, and Reagan fired North and his boss, National Security Adviser John Poindexter (though he kept on praising them). Administration and congressional investigations began that revealed the operations Reagan had approved, his administration's blatant disregard for the law, its repeated lying to Congress and the public, and its secret pursuit of policies—like making deals with terrorists—that it denounced in public.

Iran-Contra, as the Reagan administration operations became known after their revelation, accorded in methods and morality with the general character of American foreign policy during the Cold War. But Vietnam, Watergate, and the congressional effort during the 1970s to assert control over the intelligence community had at least temporarily delegitimized off-the-books, shadow-government operations. The Iran-Contra revelations led to a sharp drop in public support for the president. The failure of the covert program to achieve its goals—when it became public, the Sandinistas were still in power, the Contras had made little military progress, and more Americans were being held hostage in Lebanon than before the arms sales to Iran began—added to the widespread sense that something very wrong had been done.

Yet the reaction to the Iran-Contra revelations in the end proved remarkably muted. Secord, North, and other key players in "Project Democracy" proved adept in defending themselves during televised congressional hearings, portraying themselves as patriots who had risked their careers in pursuit of worthy goals, bolstered by support from Republican members of Congress who began to realize that they could salvage some partisan advantage from the disaster. (Casey, the central figure in the affair along with Reagan, developed a brain tumor and died before being called to account for his actions.) For his part, Reagan proved almost pathetic as he repeatedly denied established facts, resisted taking responsibility, and finally confessed to investigators, after changing his story several times, that he could not remember what he did or did not approve.

Few members of Congress displayed much interest in pursuing impeachment charges against the president, who had only a year left in office, even though arguably his knowing defiance of Congress and the law in the execution of foreign policy represented a more serious threat to constitutional government than Nixon's illegal political skullduggery and inept cover-ups. Leaders of both parties had no stomach for another prolonged period of uncertainty and national humiliation like that which preceded Nixon's resignation. The Democrats, having captured control of both houses of Congress in the 1986 election, already had the power to block whatever remained of the Reagan revolution. In 1987, the Senate rejected Reagan's nomination of the extremely conservative Robert Bork to the Supreme Court, the first such turndown in seventeen years, and the next year the House again refused further aid to the Contras. Reagan never regained the huge public support he had before Iran-Contra, but he remained a popular president to the end, a measure of how little the citizenry seemed to care about strict adherence to the Constitution by its leaders or the use of irregular methods in the defense of empire.

The Cold War Ends

As Reagan stumbled through the last years of his presidency, he made significant advances in one immensely important area, the relationship of the United States with the Soviet Union. The dramatic improvement in Soviet-American relations occurred largely as a result of changes within the Soviet Union, particularly the coming to power of a new generation of communist officials, led by Mikhail Gorbachev. But Reagan's openness to serious talks with Soviet leaders and his inclination for bold gestures, shared with Gorbachev, contributed to what turned out to be the beginning of the end of the Cold War.

Gorbachev, who in March 1985 became the general secretary of the Soviet Communist Party at the age of fifty-four, brought much more dynamic leadership and a different set of assumptions to the post than the aged leaders he succeeded. Gorbachev's experience as a regional and then national leader convinced him that the Soviet Union had to undertake major reforms to stop its internal decay, propel its economy, and improve the daily lives of its citizens. That, in turn, he believed, required improving its international relations and checking the arms race, which absorbed enormous resources that otherwise could be devoted to the civilian economy. Gorbachev did not fear the United States, confident that the huge arsenal of atomic weapons and missiles that the Soviet Union had built up ensured that no nation would attack it. Over time he even moved away from the axiomatic Soviet belief that the security of the nation required a buffer of allied communist countries.

Soon after taking office, Gorbachev announced a unilateral Soviet moratorium on testing nuclear weapons and sought out a summit with Reagan. At their first meeting, in November 1985 in Geneva, the two leaders failed to come up with an arms control pact but agreed to further summits. The April 1986 nuclear reactor explosion at Chernobyl made painfully obvious the weaknesses in Soviet technology and, along with a drop in world oil prices, led Gorbachev to more urgently seek reforms in domestic life and foreign relations. At a second summit, in Reykjavík, Iceland, in October 1986, Gorbachev and Reagan came very close to an agreement to cut their countries' strategic nuclear arsenals in half and eliminate all intermediate-range missiles in Europe, only to see their effort break down over their disagreement about Reagan's SDI plan.

Gorbachev kept pushing to wind down the arms race, convincing the Warsaw Pact of Eastern European nations to declare that it would never start a war nor make first use of nuclear weapons and dropping his insistence that any agreement on intermediate-range missiles include restrictions on SDI research. The Reagan administration continued to maintain military and ideological pressure on the Soviet Union. It kept funding the mujahideen forces in Afghanistan, even after the Soviets privately indicated their intention to withdraw. And the president bluntly challenged Gorbachev to tear down the Berlin Wall. But Reagan remained eager to find a way to reduce the nuclear arms race and, increasingly, to improve relations with the Soviet Union more broadly. As a result, he found himself publicly attacked by veteran Republican foreign policy experts like Henry Kissinger and Richard Nixon, who had generally been considered more moderate and "realist" than Reagan but who opposed the elimination of nuclear weapons in Europe and remained skeptical that the Soviet Union was undergoing fundamental change.

In December 1987, Gorbachev and Reagan signed a treaty calling for the elimination of all intermediate-range nuclear weapons. Though the countries remained armed to the gills with atomic bombs, for the first time they agreed to get rid of an entire class of weapons. Political conservatives initially tried to prevent ratification of the agreement but failed to gain much support in opposing the leader of their own movement. Ultimately the Senate ratified the pact with only five no votes.

The next moves toward the ending of the Cold War almost all occurred at the Soviet initiative. In February 1988, Gorbachev publicly declared that the Soviet Union would be withdrawing from Afghanistan. The following fall, in a speech at the United Nations, he announced a large-scale reduction in the size of the Soviet armed forces and a major withdrawal of troops from Eastern Europe and repudiated the doctrine, put forth by Brezhnev, that the Soviet Union had the right to interfere in the affairs of other socialist countries. Reagan acknowledged the transformation taking place in the Soviet Union when, during a visit to Moscow, he said he no longer considered it an evil empire.

During the last months of the Reagan presidency and the first months after George H. W. Bush took office, the United States essentially stood on the sidelines as the Soviet bloc underwent cataclysmic changes. Gorbachev's economic reforms had failed to improve the lives of Soviet citizens, while his political reforms allowed his opponents to organize. His rejection of inter-ference in the affairs of other countries opened the door for revolutionary change in Eastern Europe. In Poland, ongoing economic and political prob-lems led the communist government to open talks with leaders of the op-position Solidarity movement. In May 1989, the government held partially free elections in which Solidarity defeated the Communist Party. Gorbachev supported the formation of a power-sharing government, a signal to oppo-sitionalists in other Eastern European countries that it would be possible to peacefully overturn communist regimes. In Hungary, members of the Com-munist Party took the lead in transforming the government into a multiparty democracy. In East Germany, authorities did not use force, as they had in the past, to suppress mass demonstrations. Starting with protest marches in Leipzig in October 1989, in only a matter of weeks popular pressure led to the ouster of the longtime head of the Communist Party, Erich Honecker. Within hours of a decision by the new communist leadership to end travel restrictions, crowds began pouring through checkpoints into West Berlin. Not long afterward, the physical dismantling of the Wall began. In a period of just six months, all the communist regimes in Eastern Europe lost power, in every case except Romania without bloodshed.

The Bush administration hoped for the integration of Eastern Europe into existing capitalist financial and political arrangements, but the lead came from West German chancellor Helmut Kohl, who soon after the breach of the Berlin Wall laid out a plan for the reunification of Germany. Initially, Soviet and most European leaders opposed joining the two states, fearing the power and potential threat of a united Germany. But the Euro-peans ultimately dropped their objections (the French only after Germany agreed to adopt a common European currency). So did the Soviet Union, as Gorbachev came to see reunification as inevitable and faced increasing problems at home, with republics in his own country pressing for indepen-dence. Gorbachev even agreed to allow a reunified Germany to stay in NATO. On October 3, 1990, West Germany absorbed East Germany.

The end of the Soviet Union itself came not all that long after. An August 1991 coup by communist leaders opposed to Gorbachev's reforms fell apart after three days as a result of popular opposition, including large demonstra-tions led by Boris Yeltsin, who headed the Russian Federation. But Gor-bachev never fully regained power, which quickly devolved to the individual Soviet republics. Accepting the new reality, on December 25, 1991, Gor-bachev issued a decree dissolving the Soviet Union and resigned from office. In many of the former Soviet republics the communists quickly lost power or reorganized themselves under a new banner (and sometimes a new ideology as well). Over the dizzying period of two years, the Cold War, the Soviet Union, and communist hegemony in Eastern Europe all came to an end.

The winding down of the Cold War facilitated the resolution of regional conflicts that had been proxy wars between the Soviet Union and the United States or at least had been shaped by the superpower rivalry. In Africa, the Soviet Union and Cuba pulled their advisers and troops out of Ethiopia, and the United States and the Soviet Union helped work out agreements under which foreign forces (by then largely from Cuba) withdrew from Angola. South Africa, at that point still white-led, accepted the independence of Namibia, an area it had long administered and effectively treated as its own. Profound change soon came to South Africa itself. With the Cold War over, South African defenders of apartheid and their allies in the United States no longer could justify their stance as an anticommunist necessity, easing the way for the victory of the decades-long struggle against the race-caste system and the adoption of genuine democracy. In Asia, the Soviet Union pressured Vietnam to pull its troops out of Cambodia, where they had overthrown the murderous Khmer Rouge regime, leading to the United Nations' creation of a new government. In Central America, James Baker, Bush's secretary of state, reversed course in Nicaragua, abandoning the Contras in return for a pledge from the Sandinista government to hold a free election. A coalition led by independent reformer Violeta Chamorro beat the Sandinistas, who peacefully ceded power (giving the lie to the intellectual justification for Reagan's embrace of nondemocratic anticommunist forces in the third world). In El Salvador, Baker, with cooperation from the Soviet Union, pressured the right-wing government to end its war against the FMLN. Some regional disputes remained intractable, including the Palestinian-Israeli conflict and the tensions between India and Pakistan, but with the world no longer organized around superpower rivalry, many difficult long-standing conflicts came to a rapid resolution.

For four decades, the Cold War had structured economic, political, and military relationships around the world. For the United States, it had been the defining element in its foreign policy, the impetus for two major wars, and the occasion for an unprecedented level of peacetime military mobilization. The Cold War had shaped domestic life in myriad ways, narrowing the spectrum of political debate, justifying the expansion of the government, infusing the culture, and being used as an argument for particular policies in regard to race relations, sexuality, family life, and spending priorities. With the Cold War ending in an unexpected, rapid fashion, the United States faced an unusual moment of national redefinition, as one era of its history ended and another began.

PART IV

The New World Order
(1990–2000)

CHAPTER 17

"I'm Running Out of Demons"

Americans felt a thrill watching television coverage of German crowds tearing down the Berlin Wall. Yet there was something anticlimactic about the end of the Cold War. The four-decades-long contest ended without a decisive battle or a dramatic final engagement. American troops entered no cities as conquerors and took part in no victory parades. Unlike after the Civil War or World War I, when the mass citizen armies raised for battle rapidly dispersed, the United States did not demilitarize after the Cold War. Many Americans felt that their country had won, but they did not have the feeling of triumph that came after the great military engagements of the past. The United States prevailed by staying in place as the Soviet Union transformed itself and then dissolved. The contradictions of the Soviet system, broad changes in the global economy and communications, and the rise of a new generation of communist leaders ended the Cold War, not something the United States did.

Bereft of the satisfactions of martial victory, some Reagan supporters tried to make the case that the United States actively defeated the Soviet Union by forcing it into an arms race it could not afford and bleeding it in Afghanistan. Those drains of funds and lives did contribute to the exhaustion of the Soviet system but did not fundamentally cause the collapse of a regime that had been able to survive far, far worse in the past. In an era of media omnipresence, Americans saw with their own eyes the Berlin Wall come down and the Soviet Union dissolve without any U.S. involvement, making narratives of national triumph difficult to sustain.

Without victory, at least in the usual form, the end of the Cold War left many Americans befuddled about what was to come next. Intellectuals, politicians, government officials, and financiers plunged into discussions about the meaning of the dissolution of the Soviet bloc and what post–Cold War policies the United States should pursue. But most ordinary people seemed to pay little attention, more concerned with their day-to-day lives and, starting in 1990, with the problems they confronted as the country slipped into a recession. While considerable debate took place over specific foreign policies, particularly the decision to go to war in the Persian Gulf, the United States adopted a post–Cold War military and diplomatic stance without thorough national deliberation, as elected and unelected leaders set the trajectory for a new phase of American empire.

"The End of History?"

While it proved hard to argue that the United States had defeated the Soviet Union rather than outlasted it, the claim that Western liberalism had proved itself the best system of social organization won greater traction. The extraordinary attention and praise for a 1989 article by Francis Fukuyama, an obscure State Department official, entitled "The End of History?" provided evidence of its appeal, not only in conservative circles (the article appeared in the conservative journal *The National Interest*), but also more broadly. Fukuyama contended, "What we may be witnessing is not just the end of the Cold War, or the passing of a particular period of postwar history, but the end of history as such: that is, the endpoint of mankind's ideological evolution and the universalization of Western liberal democracy as the final form of human government." With the defeat of fascism and communism as major world forces, Fukuyama argued, the combination of liberal democracy and mass consumerism that characterized the developed Western nations had become the only significant idea and ideal for the organization of society. While other organizing principles continued to exist, like nationalism and religious fundamentalism, they lacked, in Fukuyama's view, the potential for universal appeal. It would take time, he acknowledged, for actual social practices to catch up with ideology, and some strife might continue in the less developed world, but essentially the social evolution of the species had reached its culmination and endpoint with the intellectual triumph of liberal democracy.

Fukuyama's article, like Jeane Kirkpatrick's claims about the relative likelihood of left-wing and right-wing autocracies evolving toward democracy, turned out to be wrong in its view of the future, but its bold assertion, confident air, and message of triumph made it one of the most influential essays of its time. The core idea that Fukuyama put forth already had been gaining ground in the policymaking circles of the major capitalist countries:

that history had proved there was no viable alternative to the free market and parliamentary democracy for a successful society. Seizing the moment, the World Bank, International Monetary Fund, and U.S. government began promoting what came to be called the "Washington Consensus," a version of Cold War triumphalism that argued not only for capitalism as the one best path for social development but for a specific brand of capitalism in which the state would play a minimal role in regulating the economy, distributing wealth, and controlling the flow of capital and goods across borders. "Consensus" backers argued that governments should reduce trade barriers, allow foreign investment and increased imports, privatize state enterprises, maintain fiscal discipline even if it meant imposing austerity measures, end subsidies for favored industries and in general deregulate, and provide strong legal protections for property rights. These policies, promoted as self-evident wisdom, won broad acceptance in the developing world in part because international lending agencies made their offers of loans and refinancing contingent on their adoption. (China and India, the most important rising powers, with the ability to finance their own growth, proved less willing to embrace the favored program of capitalist reform than less powerful nations.)

George H. W. Bush

George H. W. Bush fervently embraced Cold War triumphalism. In his inaugural address, he declared, "We know what works: Freedom works. We know what's right: Freedom is right. We know how to secure a more just and prosperous life for man on earth: through free markets, free speech, free elections and the exercise of free will unhampered by the state. For the first time . . . in perhaps all history—man does not have to invent a system by which to live."

Bush came to the presidency with extensive experience in government, but as vice president he had not been close to Reagan, nor had he exercised much influence on his administration. Until 1980, he had been in the moderate wing of the Republican Party, backing abortion rights, family planning, and the ERA. But by the time he sought the presidency in 1988, he had recast himself as a hard-line conservative, opposing abortion, pledging not to raise taxes (in spite of the huge deficit), supporting constitutional amendments requiring balanced budgets and allowing school prayer, and building ties to conservative Christian groups. Running against Massachusetts governor Michael Dukakis, a bland technocrat whom he initially trailed in the polls, Bush ran an ugly, negative campaign. In a measure of how much liberalism had become delegitimized during the Reagan years, Bush's main charge against Dukakis was simply that he was a liberal. The Republican campaign calculated that being labeled with the "L word," as Bush called it, would have much the same effect that charges of communist sympathy once had. The Bush campaign did not stop there; it implicitly questioned Dukakis's patriotism by harping on his veto of a bill that would have required teachers to lead their classes in the Pledge of Allegiance. It also hammered away at a Massachusetts prison furlough program that had released a murderer, Willie Horton, who then committed a rape, running sensational ads with racialized imagery (Horton was black) to raise white fears of African American violence.

Bush won 54 percent of the popular vote and carried forty states. But the election did not represent a ringing endorsement of Reaganism or even a repudiation of liberalism. In the Democratic primaries, Jesse Jackson proved highly effective in advocating traditional liberal ideas about the need for state intervention to promote economic growth, help those in need, and end discrimination. He won primaries in seven states and caucuses in four before being bested by Dukakis, the most impressive performance in the country's history by an African American candidate. (Among the primaries Jackson won were Louisiana, Alabama, Mississippi, and Georgia, states George Wallace won in the 1968 presidential election and, except for Georgia, Strom Thurmond carried in 1948, a measure of the extraordinary transformation of the South over the course of four decades.) In the general election, Dukakis proved to be a dismal campaigner, creating an opening for Bush's far more professional (if at times sleazy) effort. Bush had no coattails, as the Democrats held on to their 55–45 majority in the Senate and made a net gain of two seats in the House, suggesting that with a stronger candidate the Democrats might have been able to win back the White House.

At times it seemed as if Bush, like Fukuyama, believed that history had ended. Though he very much wanted to be president, having spent a decade in quest of the office, once in power there seemed to be little he wanted to change. The massive deficit he inherited from Reagan and Democratic control of Congress circumscribed his possibilities for new domestic initiatives, but in any case he did not have much of an agenda he hoped to push through. Rather, he saw himself as a steward for the status quo, particularly in domestic affairs. He lacked what he once derisively called "the vision thing."

Bush saw foreign policy rather than domestic affairs as the arena in which he would make his mark. Even there, he initially took a fairly passive stance, instituting a "pause" in Reagan's headlong rush to improve Soviet-American relations. But Bush did share Reagan's desire to relegitimize the use of force and maintain a massive military capacity.

His chance came in Panama. Its leader, Manuel Noriega, had been a paid agent of the United States and assisted the Contra resupply operation. But to cover his bets and enrich himself, Noriega also built ties with Cuba and got heavily involved in arms and drug trafficking. As the Cold War wound down, he became expendable to the United States. In early 1988, the Justice Department indicted him on drug charges but had no way to extradite him. Tensions increased when Noriega nullified an election that would have pushed him out of power at a time when the Bush administration had begun working to replace Latin American dictatorships with democratic regimes. On December 16, 1989, Panamanian soldiers shot and killed an American soldier who had gotten lost, sought help, and then fled a gathering crowd. They also roughed up a Navy officer and his wife who witnessed the shooting. Almost immediately, the Bush administration put into action a plan it already had developed to oust the Panamanian strongman. On December 20, 27,000 American soldiers invaded Panama, supported by massive airpower. They quickly seized control of the country. Noriega evaded them for five days before taking refuge in the Vatican embassy. After a week, he surrendered and eventually was convicted in Florida of drug running, money laundering, and racketeering.

The Panama invasion further eroded post-Vietnam public resistance to the use of force and gave a new sheen to the military, which used the brief war to display its technological prowess, including stealth aircraft and upgraded special forces. The success of the invasion (called "Operation Just Cause" in an apparent reaction to the sense that Vietnam had been seen by many people as anything but) helped reduce resistance to the use of force within the military itself, which had grown reluctant after Vietnam to take on missions with uncertain chances of success and lacking clear support from the public and the political establishment.

Panama eased the way for the Bush administration when it decided to launch a much larger military operation in reaction to Iraq's occupation of Kuwait. Saddam Hussein was Noriega writ large. Over the years, the United States had aided the Iraqi dictator when it served its purposes. During the Iran-Iraq War, the Reagan and Bush administrations had sold arms and provided credit to Iraq and opposed sanctions on Hussein's regime for its repression of the Kurds, seeking to bolster what it saw as a useful check on Iranian power. But when on August 2, 1990, Iraq invaded neighboring Kuwait, the Bush administration moved rapidly to force its withdrawal.

In opposing Iraq, the administration and Bush himself pointed to Saddam's brutality, the dictatorial nature of his regime, and claimed atrocities committed during its occupation of Kuwait (some of which were made up for the purpose). While the United States could rightly criticize the violation of the sovereignty of one nation by another, the wholly undemocratic nature of the Kuwaiti regime made it difficult to moralize the conflict. Oil, not evil, drove the Bush administration response. With its occupation of Kuwait, Iraq had come to control a huge share of world oil production. The Bush administration feared it might next try to take over Saudi Arabia, which would make it by far the most important player in the global oil economy. Following a well-established foreign policy axiom, Bush believed that allowing so much of the Middle Eastern oil reserves to fall into the hands of a regime not allied with the United States represented a threat to national security.

Within days of the occupation of Kuwait, Bush began constructing an international coalition demanding Iraqi withdrawal. He won early support from the Soviet Union and key Arab nations, clearing the way for a UN Security Council resolution calling for sanctions against Iraq if it did not leave Kuwait. Bush also won permission from the Saudi king to allow the United States and its allies to amass troops in his country to protect it from an Iraqi invasion and provide a base for possible military action against Iraq. In the months that followed, as Saddam announced his intention to annex Kuwait, the Bush administration lined up a growing roster of allies in its campaign against the occupation. Ultimately, more than thirty countries contributed military forces (though many were just token units). The United States even got other nations to pay for the military effort, with Kuwait, Saudi Arabia, and the United Arab Emirates together paying nearly two-thirds of the cost and Germany, Japan, and Korea another quarter, making it—for its size—a cheap endeavor for the United States.

In the fall of 1990, with Saddam showing no signs of retreat, the Bush administration moved toward military action. After Vietnam, military leaders had restructured the Army, assigning key functions to Reserve units, to ensure that civilian leaders could not order large-scale combat without a clear national commitment, symbolized by a Reserve call-up. By doing so, they hoped to avoid the kind of stealth escalation, without a clear, public decision-making process, that they believed had been one of the mistakes of Vietnam. Also, led by General Colin Powell, chairman of the Joint Chiefs of Staff, top officers had become committed to the idea that the United States should go into battle only if it had an overwhelming superiority of force that ensured victory with few casualties.

Bush proved willing to go to war on those terms. To bolster the coalition army in Saudi Arabia, he mobilized forty thousand reservists, the first call-up since the Tet offensive. In early November, he announced that he was increasing the U.S. force in Saudi Arabia from an already large 230,000 troops to a half million, roughly the size of the U.S. military in Vietnam at the height of the war. Later that month, he secured a Security Council resolution authorizing the use of force by the U.S.-led coalition if Iraq did not leave Kuwait by January 15. Finally, to forestall the possibility that Congress might exert its authority under the War Powers Act, Bush asked for explicit congressional backing for sending the military into combat. Resolutions opposing war won strong minority support (getting forty-seven votes in the Senate), but after extended debate Bush got the authorization he sought. Determined to unleash the enormous fighting machine that had been assembled in Saudi Arabia, Bush spurned last-minute efforts by other countries, including France and the Soviet Union, to mediate the dispute while rejecting proposals from Iraq to leave Kuwait without accepting other U.S. conditions.

On January 17, 1991, the U.S.-led coalition launched a massive air attack on Iraq. Network television cameras in Baghdad sent images of the nighttime bombardment live to viewers in the United States and around the world. The pummeling from the air of Iraq and Iraqi forces in Kuwait continued for thirty-eight days, as the United States and its allies unleashed just about every nonnuclear aerial weapon they had in their arsenals. Finally, with Iraqi troops still hunkered down in Kuwait, the coalition launched a ground assault. In just one hundred hours it forced the Iraqi army to retreat from Kuwait and all but decimated it in a rout of what had been the largest military in the Middle East. The coalition forces suffered only 240 deaths during the course of the war (including 148 Americans), while tens of thousands of Iraqis died.

The New World Order

The victory in the Gulf War seemed to validate George Bush's assertion that a "new world order" had emerged from the end of the Cold War, in which the United States would take the lead, with the Soviet Union (before its dissolution) as a junior partner, in opposing aggression by any nation, ensuring global stability if need be by military force. In a radio address to U.S. troops at the end of the war, Bush declared, "The first test of the new world order has been passed." "The specter of Vietnam," he exulted, "has been buried forever in the desert sands of the Arabian Peninsula."

Bush proved to be half right. The triumph against Iraq bolstered those who advocated keeping a large, globally deployed military—including leaders of the armed services, the defense industry, and their ideological allies—though they had to struggle to make their case in the absence of an obvious enemy. Soon after the Gulf War, Colin Powell bemoaned, "I'm running out of demons. I'm running out of villains. I'm down to Castro and Kim Il Sung." Yet even in the absence of enemies with anything like the resources of the United States, civilian leaders concurred with the military contention that the country should have the capacity to fight two large conventional wars at the same time. No serious discussion occurred of returning to a pre–World War II policy of maintaining only a small peacetime military or of dismantling the vast global network of American military facilities. The Bush administration did not even consider dissolving NATO once its original purpose of resisting Soviet aggression became meaningless. Military spending did decrease substantially but remained at a level far above pre–Cold War norms.

If the Gulf War chased away the "specter of Vietnam" and helped cement militarism as a central feature of post–Cold War America, the "new world order" that Bush saw being tested in Iraq proved little more than a turn of phrase. The end of the Cold War and the anti-Iraq coalition did not lead to the creation of a set of institutions to sustain a new global system equivalent to those created at the end of World War II, like the UN, the IMF, and the World Bank. Instead, the Gulf War moved the United States toward using its own armed forces, with the cover of enabling UN resolutions and modest military support from some allies, to take on what it decided were rogue states and terrorist movements. Well before Bush left office, the phrase "new world order" had become the subject of derision for its hollow, authoritarian-sounding pomposity (as well as the subject of paranoia among fringe rightists, who thought it signaled a plot to impose world government on the United States).

Unlike Reagan, who at least rhetorically made the spread of freedom a principle objective of American foreign policy, Bush gave higher priority to maintaining stability. The Gulf War aimed at restoring the status quo ante, not spreading democracy to Iraq, or for that matter to Kuwait. When in June 1989 the Chinese government used its army to crush the pro-democracy student protest in Tiananmen Square, resulting in hundreds of deaths and mass imprisonment, the Bush administration took only mild measures in response and privately assured the Chinese leadership that it would not let the repression derail the growing economic and other ties between the countries. Like previous presidents (including Reagan), Bush saw the attractions of economic relations and a tacit anti-Soviet alliance with China as outweighing moral or ideological concerns.

The Gulf War and the supposed new world order did not achieve the stability Bush sought, even in the region where it was fought. Anticipating the political and military problems that would come with an occupation of the country, Bush stuck to his pledge that the military would be used only to force Iraq out of Kuwait, not to conquer Iraq or overthrow Saddam. But the Bush administration expected that either the Iraqi military or a popular uprising would oust Saddam for bringing massive defeat to his country. Instead, Saddam maintained his grip on power and used his remaining military to suppress revolts that broke out by Shiites in the south of the country and Kurds in the north. Iraq remained an irritant to the United States for another decade, leading to a second, full-scale, far more costly war against it.

The end of the Cold War lessened the fear and likelihood of full-scale nuclear war. But it did not bring an end to conflict or a universal acceptance of Western liberalism. While some former communist states adopted Western-style parliamentary democracy and capitalist property relations, in others authoritarian regimes took hold and state control over the economy remained extensive. The breakup of the Soviet bloc accelerated a worldwide trend toward nationalism, ethnic and religious strife, and intolerance. The decades of superpower rivalry left behind enormous stockpiles of arms that flowed into the hands of insurgent movements, criminal enterprises, and terrorists. Rather than a new world order, global disorder became normalized, as even relatively small groups, through low-tech terror tactics and guerrilla warfare, found that they could disrupt less developed and even advanced societies. Some of those groups, like the Islamic fundamentalists the United States had armed and aided in Afghanistan, would eventually make the United States itself their target.

In the years that followed the Cold War, the world seemed as dangerous a place—or more so—for the United States and its citizens as it had when the Soviet-American conflict dominated global affairs. Rather than a sense of security and peace, the end of the Cold War ushered in a period of unsettledness, at home and abroad. The United States had an opportunity to redefine its priorities, its goals, its way of life, but as it turned out it had little interest in doing so.

CHAPTER 18

Triangulation

W hen Bill Clinton became president in 1993, he represented a generational break in national politics. The United States went
from a leadership shaped by the experience of the Depression,
the New Deal, and World War II to one shaped by postwar prosperity, the
civil rights movement, the Vietnam War, counterculture, feminism, and the
backlash against cultural change. Until Clinton, every president after Harry
Truman had served in the military during World War II, with the exception
of Jimmy Carter, who entered the Naval Academy during the war but graduated after it ended. By contrast, Clinton's father, not Clinton himself,
served in the World War II Army, before dying in a car crash while Clinton's
mother was pregnant with Bill.

During the 1960s and 1970s, Clinton, like millions of baby boomers, embraced cultural and political departures from the past, even as he pursued
traditional goals and ambitions. Fascinated by electoral politics from an
early age, he began working in campaigns for liberal Democrats while still
in college, first in his home state of Arkansas and then around the country,
never entertaining the rejection of the electoral process like some of his more
radical peers. But he did come to oppose the Vietnam War, helping organize
a few antiwar demonstrations while a Rhodes Scholar in England. "Sympathetic to the zeitgeist," as he later put it, he grew a beard and long hair and
lived with Hillary Rodham, whom he met at Yale Law School, before they
married. When they had a daughter, they named her Chelsea, having been
enchanted by folksinger Judy Collins's version of the Joni Mitchell song
"Chelsea Morning."

After law school, Clinton served as Arkansas attorney general and six
two-year terms as governor. He had high ambitions for himself and the

Democratic Party. To regain the White House and national dominance, Clinton believed that Democrats had to recapture white middle-class voters who had moved over to the Republicans, especially men in the South and the suburbs who were put off by liberal positions on cultural issues and the increased influence of blacks within the national Democratic Party. Clinton rejected the moral perfectionism that had marbled the New Left. When he met Hillary, he recalled, "She was as tired as I was of our side getting beat and treating defeat as evidence of moral virtue and superiority." Clinton believed in doing what it took to win. In the mid-1980s, he joined with other moderates and conservatives in the Democratic Leadership Council (DLC) to push the party toward the center and provide a counterweight to liberal groups that played a large role in setting party policy, like the National Organization for Women, Jesse Jackson's Rainbow Coalition, and the AFL-CIO. During his 1992 presidential campaign, he flew back to Arkansas to make sure that the execution proceeded of a brain-damaged murderer, Ricky Ray Rector, in an apparent effort to prove that he did not share the alleged Democratic Party softness on crime.

Clinton retained a nostalgic affection for the cultural and political rebellion of the 1960s. At his presidential inaugural concert, held on the steps of the Lincoln Memorial where Martin Luther King Jr. had given his most famous speech, Bob Dylan, who sang at that occasion, returned to sing his 1964 song "Chimes of Freedom." But Clinton also invited two Pentecostal friends to sing at another inaugural event, about whom he said, "Knowing people like them was one reason I got elected President."

The 1992 Election

Before the 1992 campaign began, most observers expected that George Bush would easily win reelection because of his extraordinarily high approval rating in the wake of the Gulf War. With many leading Democrats staying out of what looked like a losing race, Clinton won the Democratic nomination, overcoming revelations about his draft avoidance and extramarital affairs. ("Bimbo eruptions," a campaign aide called them.) He then focused his campaign almost entirely on domestic affairs, especially the economy, unfavorable terrain for the incumbent.

Bush had a thin record of domestic achievement. The major laws of his years in office, the Americans with Disabilities Act and the Clean Air Act Amendments, had not been his initiatives, though he did work with Democrats to win their passage. The Disabilities Act required businesses, public buildings, and transportation facilities to provide access for people with disabilities and outlawed discrimination against them in hiring and job assignments. The Clean Air Act Amendments contained enforcement provisions for urban air standards, regulated sulfur dioxide emissions (which were causing acid rain), lowered permitted levels of industrial and vehicle emissions, and took the first steps toward countering the depletion of the ozone layer, measures that over time led to very significant improvements in the environment. But beyond these laws, for which he could take only partial credit, Bush had little to show. He lost a great deal of support in the conservative base of the Republican Party when in 1990, in negotiations with congressional leaders to deal with the massive deficit, he agreed to a large tax increase, breaking the "Read my lips; no new taxes" pledge he had made two years earlier.

Bush's failure to act when the economy went into a tailspin in 1990 proved costly. By mid-1991, the unemployment rate neared 8 percent. Even as conditions worsened, Bush, fearful that a stimulus program would add to the still large budget deficit and drive up interest rates, did little, even vetoing a measure to improve unemployment benefits. His approval rating plummeted from 84 percent at the end of the Gulf War in February 1991 to just 29 percent in mid-1992.

Complicating the 1992 election, multimillionaire Ross Perot ran as an independent, capitalizing on broad public distaste for politicians of all stripes, evident in the continuing adoption of state term limit laws for elected officials. An opponent of the Gulf War, Perot made the federal deficit and opposition to free trade the centerpieces of his idiosyncratic campaign. For his part, Bush could not overcome the public perception that he was a privileged patrician, disengaged from the problems of ordinary Americans. During one campaign stop, he expressed wonder at a bar code reader at a supermarket checkout (of the type that had been in use for a decade), inadvertently revealing that he simply did not share, and had not done so for a very long time, the common experiences of everyday life that bound people together.

A massive riot in Los Angeles early in the campaign brought home the urgency of addressing domestic affairs. The acquittal by an all-white jury of four California highway patrolmen who had been captured on videotape beating Rodney King, an unresisting black motorist, touched off the worst riot the country had experienced since the Civil War. Looting and arson hit widespread areas of the city. Television pictures of a brutal assault by black assailants on a white truck driver who happened to be passing through South Central Los Angeles contributed to the initial perception that the city was experiencing a race riot. But while there were racial aspects to the carnage—including the heavy targeting of Korean American–owned stores—both the perpetrators and victims of violence came from a wide array of ethnic and racial backgrounds. Over half those arrested and a third of those killed were Hispanic. In its own way a testament to the increasing demographic complexity of the country, the riot, which lasted four days, took more than fifty lives, and resulted in well over two thousand injuries, was more a dark carnival of violence, theft, and desperation by the poor than a racial disturbance of the sort that had occurred during the 1960s. Clinton, by arriving in the city before the president, managed to turn the horrendous event to partisan advantage.

In the end, Clinton won the election by focusing on the economy and adeptly repulsing personal attacks from the Republicans. He succeeded in winning back a sizable number of centrist onetime Democrats, while retaining the support of African Americans, unionists, and liberals, who had nowhere else to go. But it was far from an overwhelming victory. Perot, with little in the way of a campaign organization, managed to win 19 percent of the popular vote, the best showing for a third-party candidate since Teddy Roosevelt's Progressive Party run in 1912, leaving Clinton with a plurality of 43 percent of the vote, to Bush's 38 percent.

Democracy Contained

During his transition and first year as president, Clinton learned hard lessons about where power lay. Confronted by the common wisdom of the financial industry, well-organized business lobbies, and congressional conservatives, he found himself endorsing measures to the right of his centrist campaign platform.

The dynamic became clear as he crafted his first budget. As a candidate, Clinton had linked a commitment to deficit reduction to federal investment in infrastructure, worker training, and job creation, which he believed would stimulate the economy and lay the basis for future growth. But in staffing his administration, he gave key economic posts to Wall Street backers and Democratic centrists who put much greater stress on balancing the budget than on reducing unemployment or providing paths for upward mobility. Goldman Sachs co-head Robert Rubin, whom Clinton appointed director of the National Economic Council and then as secretary of the treasury, emerged as one of the president's closest advisers and a highly effective advocate for policies benefiting the financial sector. Like Federal Reserve chairman Alan Greenspan, Rubin and other "deficit hawks" argued to Clinton that the key to economic recovery would be low interest rates, which meant convincing bond dealers that he would attack the deficit and reduce federal borrowing requirements.

Clinton bought the argument, while verbally lashing out at the ability of capital to undermine the economy. "You mean to tell me," he blurted out at an economic planning meeting shortly before his inauguration, "that the success of the [economic] program and my reelection hinges on the Federal Reserve and a bunch of fucking bond traders?" Clinton dropped his campaign proposal for a middle-class tax cut and most of his proposed stimulus and investment programs. James Carville, who had helped mastermind Clinton's victory, told the *Wall Street Journal,* "I used to think if there was reincarnation, I wanted to come back as the president or the pope or a .400 baseball hitter. But now I want to come back as the bond market. You can intimidate everybody."

The bond market was not the only constraint Clinton faced. In Congress, conservatives in both parties wanted less spending and lower taxes. To get a budget plan through, Clinton removed a proposed broad energy tax, designed as an environmental measure as well as to produce revenue, replacing it with a small hike in the gasoline tax. He did manage to keep small increases in corporate taxes and income taxes for the wealthy and a boost in the Earned Income Tax Credit, a program, first established in 1975, that gave refundable tax credits to low-income working families.

In addition to deficit reduction, Clinton embraced another favored Wall Street policy, free-trade treaties that reduced tariffs on imports and opened up other countries to U.S. investment and agricultural products. Clinton had waffled during the campaign, endorsing the North American Free Trade Agreement (NAFTA) with Canada and Mexico, which Bush was in the process of negotiating, but saying that he would insist that it be accompanied by side agreements protecting labor and environmental standards. Once in office, he broke with the labor movement, which feared NAFTA would lead to job losses and wage reductions, lobbying hard for its passage with toothless environmental and labor supplements. Clinton won the battle, with House Republicans providing more votes than Democrats.

In April 1993, Clinton said with some bitterness to a group of his advisers, "I hope you're all aware we're all Eisenhower Republicans. We're Eisenhower Republicans here, and we are fighting the Reagan Republicans. We stand for lower deficits and free trade and the bond market. . . . At least we'll have health care to give them, if we can't give them anything else." But as things turned out, Clinton could not give his supporters health-care reform either.

The cost of health care had been rising for years, amounting to over 13 percent of GNP by the time Clinton took office, while the percentage of the population under age sixty-five without health insurance had risen to over 17 percent. The thirty-nine million people without health insurance were not the poorest Americans, who by and large received Medicaid, or the elderly, covered by Medicare, but members of working- and middle-class families who could not afford or chose not to buy coverage if they did not receive it through an employer. A surprise victory by Harris Wofford in a 1991 special election for a Pennsylvania Senate seat, after a campaign in which the former Kennedy administration official stressed his support for national health insurance, convinced the political class of the saliency of the issue. Within months, virtually every major politician was putting forth some sort of plan to improve the health insurance system.

Clinton's plan, developed by a task force headed by Hillary Clinton and Ira Magaziner, aimed to provide universal insurance coverage and slow the escalation of health-care costs without greatly increasing government spending, reflecting the president's reluctance to add to the large deficit he had inherited or allow himself to be tagged as a tax-and-spend liberal. His plan proposed expanding the employment-based system of health insurance that had grown up since World War II, rather than moving to a government system that would build on Medicare and Medicaid (what its proponents euphemistically termed a "single-payer" system). All employers would be required to offer their employees health insurance. To contain costs, in most cases they would be compelled to join large regional purchasing groups. With savings from cuts in Medicare and Medicaid and an anticipated slowing of health-care inflation, individuals who could not afford insurance would receive subsidies and Medicare recipients would get prescription drug and long-term-care coverage.

Clinton's complicated plan, unveiled in September 1993, initially won a high level of public support and considerable bipartisan backing. But health-care interest groups—employers, insurance companies, drug companies, and doctors—soon began to resist. Some opposed the basic thrust of the plan or the need for any plan at all, while others objected to particular provisions that would cost them money or impose unwanted regulations. A trade group of small and midsize insurance companies, which believed that the plan would favor their larger rivals, ran memorable television advertisements featuring a fictional middle-class couple, "Harry and Louise," who expressed their fears that the Clinton plan would create a vast new government bureaucracy and deprive them of their right to choose their doctors.

Conservatives and Republicans joined the opposition, seeing an ideological opportunity to win support for less government and a political opportunity to deal the Clinton administration and liberals a blow.

The combination of interest group and partisan opposition proved deadly. Most Americans already had health insurance, and the endless drumbeat of criticism of Clinton's plan convinced many of them that the uncertainty and new regulatory regime that would come with it outweighed its potential benefit. The Clintons proved unable to get even those who generally supported their approach to fight hard for their proposal. After a year of battling, the plan died in Congress without even receiving a formal vote.

Washington at War

The defeat of Clinton's health plan ended the possibility of health-care reform for another generation and energized the Republican right. Clinton's election had not ended partisan combat, which if anything intensified once he entered the White House, as a kind of permanent political war settled into place in Washington. Partisanship had been growing since the early 1980s. Conservatives had achieved power through bold rhetoric and combative tactics, which had shaped a harsh political culture during a period when neither party proved able to win long-lasting, decisive electoral victories. The end of the "Fairness Doctrine" allowed the growth of highly opinionated talk radio, largely on the conservative side of the political spectrum, with Rush Limbaugh and other radio hosts, who depended on rage and intemperance to attract listeners, increasingly driving political discourse. The burgeoning Washington-based class of operatives who made their living off partisan politics—lobbyists, pollsters, media advisers, think tank denizens, and party staffers—gave the parties expanded capacity for extended combat, while constituting an interest group that needed conflict to keep salaries flowing.

The cultural and social divides that began in the 1960s and 1970s contributed to the intensity of the political battling. "To me," said Republican Dick Armey, shortly after he became House majority leader in 1995, "all the problems began in the Sixties." His colleague, conservative Republican Newt Gingrich, identified the "counterculture" as the principal source of the nation's woes, faulting the Democratic Party for indulging a "multicultural nihilistic hedonism that is inherently destructive of a healthy society." Conservatives could not let the 1960s go because, to their fury, in spite of their decades of growing political influence and twelve years of Republican control of the White House, accepted norms of behavior continued to move in a more liberal, permissive direction. While conservatives reshaped national thinking about political economy and the role of government, they failed to recast the national culture in their image or regulate personal behavior, especially in the realm of sexuality.

For many conservatives, the Clintons—Hillary as much as Bill—embodied all that they hated about the 1960s. Bill's political success in spite of his draft avoidance, opposition to the Vietnam War, dabbling in the counterculture, womanizing, and embrace of the language of therapeutic self-help (even though many of his harshest critics, like Gingrich, had avoided the draft themselves and were far from model family men) worked conservatives into a frenzy. So did Hillary's success as a lawyer, failure to adopt Bill's last name until it seemed necessary for reviving his political career after he lost his first reelection bid for governor, assertiveness, and occasional flashes of contempt for housewives ("I suppose I could have stayed home and baked cookies and had teas, but what I decided to do was to fulfill my profession," she said during the 1992 campaign). The religious right would not forgive Clinton for ending its influence on federal policy, even though organized religion played a much larger role in his life than in Bush's or Reagan's. Clinton's failed effort, shortly after he took office, to make good on his campaign promise to end the ban on military service by homosexuals reinforced the belief of many conservatives that, if given his way, the new president would undermine long-established legal and moral codes, threatening the very basis of the Republic.

The centrism of Clinton's economic program and health plan did nothing to bank conservative fires. Attacks on the regulations that would have come with the Clinton health reform plan stoked antigovernment sentiment. To take advantage of it, conservative Republicans, led by Gingrich, created a national antistatist program for their party's congressional candidates in the 1994 election, framed in the language of populist disgust with politicians. The "Contract with America" called for term limits for members of Congress, a constitutional amendment requiring a balanced budget, reform of congressional rules, anticrime measures, and new restrictions on welfare. While local issues dominated many congressional races, the unified Republican effort, attacks on the Clintons, and a strong campaign effort by the National Rifle Association, which bitterly opposed gun control measures passed with the president's support, proved important in some tight races. So did turnout. Gun control and the increase in taxes on the wealthy brought Republicans to the polls in large numbers, while many Democrats, disgusted with Clinton's support of NAFTA and loss of the health-care fight, sat out the election. The result was a very big win for the Republicans, who gained control over both houses of Congress for the first time since Eisenhower's first term, with Gingrich becoming the new Speaker of the House.

The post-election configuration of power in Washington reflected the continuing southernization of American politics. Not only was Clinton, like every successful Democratic presidential candidate since 1964, a southerner, but also the conservative congressional wing of the Republican Party had become increasingly southern-led. Gingrich, chief strategist for the conservative forces, was not a southern native but a northern transplant who adopted many of the South's conservative values without all of its historical baggage. Born in Pennsylvania, the son of an Army officer, he spent part of his childhood in Europe before moving to Georgia, where he graduated from an all-white high school. He later wrote that he found segregation "shocking." After getting degrees from Emory and Tulane, he went to Congress representing the suburbs of Atlanta. As he rose to power in the House, he found common political ground with southern-born conservatives like Dick Armey, Tom DeLay, and William Archer.

Gingrich's suburban base typified the new character of southern political power. The drive for racial equality had hastened the movement of middle-class whites out of southern cities and out of the Democratic Party. In the suburbs where they decamped, they wanted low taxes and little government regulation, while becoming less fixated on the issue of race, in part because residential segregation minimized the flash points for racial conflict, such as school integration. Conservative suburban evangelical churches helped fuse religion and partisan politics. Southern religiosity contributed to a public and media fixation on sin and redemption among political leaders, especially Clinton.

In the end, the 1994 Republican victory did not lead to a rollback of New Deal–Great Society welfare programs and 1970s environmental regulations, as the House Republican leadership and its business allies had hoped. Conservative environmental and government reorganization proposals, which included defunding environmental agencies, dissolving the National Endowments for the Arts and Humanities, and terminating the Departments of Energy, Commerce, and Education and the Council of Economic Advisers, failed when Republican moderates joined with Democrats to oppose them. Clinton and congressional Democrats also blocked efforts by the Republican leadership and business lobbyists to reduce social welfare spending, eliminate the Earned Income Tax Credit, and cut taxes for the wealthy. Gingrich's plan for a major reduction in Medicare spending proved politically disastrous, mobilizing opposition from senior citizen and health-care groups. The Democrats made hay when it came out that the amount of Medicare spending to be eliminated almost exactly matched a proposed tax cut for the rich.

The most dramatic moment in the confrontation between the president and the Republican Congress came during the fall and early winter of 1995–96, when Clinton vetoed a series of appropriations bills, continuing resolutions (to allow government operations to continue without a budget), and measures raising the debt ceiling because they included drastic budget cuts or changes in environmental regulations. With the federal government running out of money and unable to borrow more, Clinton twice shut down all but its most vital operations, leaving most federal offices closed and federal employees without paychecks for twenty-seven days. Finally, congressional leaders gave in, agreeing with Clinton on continuing resolutions that got the government going again.

While the Republican assault largely failed on its own terms, it pushed Clinton significantly toward the right, a process that had begun even before the 1994 election. After the health reform plan failed, Clinton proposed stricter limits on welfare and won a costly new anticrime program that included tougher sentencing guidelines and funding for more prisons and police officers. He also supported the Defense of Marriage Act, which defined marriage as heterosexual and allowed states to refuse to recognize same-sex marriages from other jurisdictions.

Once he saw the efficacy of Gingrich's antistatist rhetoric, Clinton further distanced himself from liberal policies and symbols, betting his political survival on appropriating popular Republican themes and proposals. The strategy paid off for him personally but not for the Democratic Party, which continued to lose power and a distinct identity during the remainder of his presidency. Accepting a basic tenet of the Reagan revolution, in his 1996 State of the Union address Clinton proclaimed, "The era of big government is over." True to his word, though he periodically floated ideas for new liberal programs, he refrained from pressing for any major new federal spending. His restraint, along with an economic upturn, led to a federal budget surplus in 1998, for the first time since 1969. By the time Clinton left the White House, he had become the first president since Truman to reduce the number of civilian federal workers.

Clinton's chastened stance matched the diminished hopes that many Americans had during the 1990s, particularly on the liberal end of the political spectrum. Reformers largely abandoned their belief in grand designs and major breakthroughs, settling, like Clinton, for modest technocratic tinkering in spite of the end of the Cold War, the seeming absence of serious national security threats, and the enormous economic power of the country.

The utopian enthusiasms that had been so common during Clinton's college years had come to seem very distant, except, to a limited extent, on the Republican right, which brought to its counterreformist program millennial dreams. Gingrich, in particular, had a utopian (sometimes apocalyptic) streak almost completely lacking on the other side of the aisle, as he held forth on the fantastic possibilities of space exploration and "the Third Wave Information Age" and the glories that would come with a conservative restoration.

Welfare reform represented the most important manifestation of what Clinton's pollster and adviser Dick Morris called "triangulation," an effort to find politically defensible space between the Republicans and the Democrats. Accounting for only 1 percent of federal spending, "welfare," as the term was usually used—meaning Aid to Families with Dependent Children (AFDC)—was dwarfed by Social Security, Medicare, and Medicaid, which together ate up nearly half of all federal spending. But welfare had disproportionate ideological, cultural, and political importance. Its critics portrayed it as a source of moral decay, replacing self-reliance and self-discipline with government dependency, a view that resonated with broad swaths of the public. With African Americans making up a large segment of the welfare population (37 percent in 1996, down from 46 percent in 1973), racism often lurked behind antiwelfare rhetoric. Because welfare benefited relatively few voters, defending it was difficult, in contrast to Medicare and Social Security, which with their vast pools of beneficiaries were politically untouchable.

The Democratic Leadership Council had viewed welfare as deadweight on its effort to win national power. In 1992, Clinton called for ending "welfare as we know it." He wanted to shift control over the system to the states and force recipients to go to work after receiving aid for two years, if need be having the government help create jobs for them. The Republican-proposed Personal Responsibility Act, part of the Contract with America, echoed some of these ideas, but it did not include the job creation, training, health-care, and daycare programs Clinton wanted to help ease welfare mothers into the labor market. Clinton vetoed two versions of the Republican bill, but after some modifications, in 1996 he signed a bill that terminated AFDC, replacing it with Temporary Assistance for Needy Families. The new program handed control of welfare to the states, limited to two consecutive years and a lifetime total of five years the time recipients could stay on the rolls even if they could not find employment, reduced childcare and nutrition programs for welfare recipients, and made most teenage mothers of illegitimate children ineligible for assistance. The end of the federal commitment to helping mothers of children without other means of support, which had been in place since 1935, was one of the few terminations of a major New Deal program since the end of World War II.

In 1996, Clinton easily beat veteran Republican senator Robert Dole, who ran a weak campaign, to become the first Democratic president since Franklin Roosevelt to win reelection. The 1993 National Voter Registration Act significantly increased the number of citizens registered to vote by re-quiring states to provide voter registration applications with applications for driver's licenses and otherwise increasing outreach efforts. But the number of actual voters did not increase proportionately, as turnout for the election fell to a postwar low of 49 percent. In spite of (or perhaps because of) the intense partisanship in Washington, most Americans did not think it was worth their effort to vote. All the states Dole carried, with the exceptions of Indiana and Alaska, lay in the South or the Great Plains–Rocky Mountain region, while Clinton, benefiting from an economic upturn, dominated ev-erywhere else, confirming the regional divide that had come to characterize national politics. The Republicans maintained control over Congress, deny-ing Clinton the ability to pass any major initiatives even if he wanted to.

Culture War

Social and cultural issues loomed large on the political landscape of the 1990s, as fierce fights raged over efforts to use the power of the state to en-force moral standards. In many of these contests, liberals and conservatives reversed their usual positions: while conservatives generally argued for less government regulation, many of them—libertarians excepted—wanted to use government to control sexual and reproductive behavior and impose moral codes, while liberals, who tended to support more government regula-tion, wanted less of it in the personal realm. Power, not culture per se, lay at the heart of the so-called culture wars of the 1990s.

Some of the most intense battles concerned sexuality and women's con-trol over their bodies. Many conservatives found the continuing liberaliza-tion of attitudes toward sex outside of marriage, homosexuality, and gender roles threatening to their moral beliefs and the strength of American society. Abortion in particular remained deeply divisive. Though the Supreme Court, even as it became more conservative, continued to uphold the basic princi-ples of *Roe v. Wade,* its 1989 ruling in *Webster v. Reproductive Health Services* permitted states to ban the use of public money for abortions and impose some restrictions on abortion rights. Under pressure from antiabortion ac-tivists, over half the states forbade the use of public money for terminating pregnancies. Many also made getting an abortion more difficult through rules such as requiring women to go through a waiting period.

Opponents of abortion engaged in direct action as well as lobbying, blockading abortion clinics, and harassing their clients. A few went further, bombing clinics, setting them on fire, and assaulting abortion providers. In a two-year stretch from 1993 to 1994, two doctors, one clinic escort, and two clinic receptionists were murdered. Between legal restrictions, the elimination of public funding, and harassment and violence, access to abortion services diminished or disappeared in large parts of the country.

Attacks on abortion providers were part of a burgeoning of violence and threats of violence on the far right, including from the so-called militias, secretive armed groups that popped up in some largely rural parts of the country in opposition to federal power, especially gun control. In the late 1960s and early 1970s, a few groups on the fringe of the New Left and Black Power movements had openly advocated violence as a path to social change. Twenty years later, no left-wing groups still held such views (few left-wing groups even existed anymore), while the mantle of transformative violence had been taken up by the far right. Mostly it took the form of preparations, arming, and manifestos, not action. But in 1995, militia sympathizers Timothy McVeigh and Terry Nichols used a truck bomb to blow up the Alfred P. Murrah Federal Building in Oklahoma City, killing 168 people, the worst single incident of domestic terrorism in American history.

Sex education provoked almost as intense battling as abortion. Starting in the 1960s, sex education in schools became more common and more broadly conceived. Its supporters argued that it would reduce teenage pregnancy and the prevalence of sexually transmitted diseases, while encouraging healthier attitudes toward sex. But many conservatives believed that it would have the opposite effect, encouraging immoral acts and leading to more disease and pregnancies among unmarried teenagers. Christian conservatives used sex education as a mobilizing issue, moving from opposition to any sex education to trying to shape its content, with considerable success. Mandates that sex education teach only abstinence as a way to avoid pregnancy and sexually transmitted diseases became increasingly common during the late 1980s and 1990s. When soon after the 1994 election Surgeon General Joycelyn Elders, in response to a question about masturbation, said that it was "part of human sexuality and it's part of something that perhaps should be taught," President Clinton responded to a storm of criticism by firing her.

Implicit in the fights over abortion and sexuality were disagreements over the place of women in society, though the idea that they had equal rights to men had become broadly accepted, at least in the abstract, and rarely challenged frontally. Somewhat similarly, continuing fights over affirmative action spoke to the position of African Americans in the society, without challenging the national consensus supporting equal racial rights that came out of the civil rights movement. Conservatives led the opposition to affirmative action, including a few African Americans like Clarence Thomas, whose antagonism to affirmative action and quota hiring led to widespread opposition to his appointment to the Supreme Court from liberals and civil rights groups.

Much of the fight over affirmative action took place in the courts, which narrowed what constituted illegal discrimination and the circumstances under which group targets for admissions or hiring could be used. In the early 1990s, the Supreme Court ruled that school districts did not have an obligation to continue school busing or other racial integration measures if the resegregation of schools resulted from new patterns of residential segregation not caused by legal restrictions. "When resegregation is a product not of state action but of private choices, it does not have constitutional implications," Justice Anthony Kennedy wrote in a 1992 decision. With just such segregation accompanying the ongoing suburbanization of the nation, the Court in effect gave hundreds of local governments and school boards a free pass from responsibility for integrating schools.

A bitter 1996 battle in California demonstrated the political salience of opposition to affirmative action. Its critics put a measure on the ballot to ban government entities, including the California public university system, from granting preferential treatment in employment, contracting, or education to any individual or group on the basis of race, sex, color, ethnicity, or national origin. The proposal won backing from national Republican leaders and Ward Connerly, an African American member of the University of California Board of Regents, who became the public face of the campaign. Belatedly, key Democrats, including President Clinton, came out against the measure, but it won passage by an eight-point margin. In the first year after the University of California was forced to end its affirmative action programs, the Berkeley law school enrolled only one new African American student and the number of black undergraduates accepted fell by well over half.

Immigration and Immigrant Rights

California also saw sharp battles over immigrant rights. The rapid growth of emigration from Mexico and other parts of Latin America swelled anxiety and resentment where the newcomers settled, especially in California, the destination of nearly two-thirds of Mexican migrants between 1985 and 1990. The recession that hit Southern California with the post–Cold War drop in spending on military equipment—a major regional industry—increased worries about economic competition from immigrants and their downward pressure on wages. Because much of the migration took place outside legal channels, fears grew that the country had lost control of its borders. Many Americans felt threatened or were angered by the spread of foreign ways, foreign languages, and foreign cultures, undermining what they saw as a shared national culture. The late-twentieth-century celebration of diversity, ethnic heritage, and bilingualism stoked doubts that newcomers would assimilate. "The historic idea of a unifying American identity is now in peril," wrote historian and former presidential aide Arthur M. Schlesinger Jr. in 1992, "in our politics, our voluntary organizations, our churches, our language."

In 1986, Congress attempted to address the central contradiction of immigration policy with the Simpson-Rodino Act. On the one hand, business and the daily functioning of the country depended on a steady flow of low-wage workers, which discouraged any serious effort to lessen immigration, legal or illegal. On the other, growing popular opposition to large-scale and illegal immigration pushed politicians toward gestures that at least symbolically asserted the law and raised the bar to illegal entry into the country. Simpson-Rodino required employers, for the first time, to check the immigration status of workers they hired. It also expanded the Border Patrol from a small, low-tech police force into a massive agency deploying over ten thousand uniformed officers. Along with these provisions designed to reduce illegal immigration, the law made it possible for undocumented immigrants who had been in the country since 1982 to achieve legal status. To address fears of a fragmenting culture, the legalization process required applicants to take English and civics courses.

Simpson-Rodino only temporarily slowed illegal immigration. Worksite enforcement proved ineffective, since companies did not have to validate the authenticity of the documents workers presented to prove their eligibility to work and the federal government devoted few resources to inspections. Instead, the Bush and Clinton administrations concentrated on trying to harden the border. But in spite of high fences, motion sensors, and heavy patrolling, immigrants (and drug runners) found ways to get through. Illegal immigrants became such a pervasive presence that in 1996 the AFL-CIO reversed its historic position demanding strict enforcement of immigration laws to become an advocate for the rights of undocumented workers, concluding that only by reaching out to them would it ever succeed in organizing the service sector and other parts of the economy where they were a growing part of the workforce.

The hypocrisy of the immigration system and continued high inflow during periods of economic downturn, like the early 1990s, sparked growing hostility to immigrants themselves. Prior to 1980, five states had laws making English their official language. Over the next two decades, twenty more added such measures. In 1994, California voters by a wide margin backed the anti-immigrant Proposition 187 (the "Save our State" initiative), which Republican governor Pete Wilson, locked in a tight reelection bid, made a centerpiece of his campaign. The measure called for denying illegal immigrants virtually all government benefits, including public schooling. A federal judge immediately blocked the implementation of most of its provisions, declaring them unconstitutional. But the proposition legitimized harsh anti-immigration measures that previously had been unthinkable. The federal welfare reform bill enacted two years later barred illegal immigrants from receiving most government services (though not public schooling) and forbade legal immigrants from receiving a long list of federal benefits during the first five years after their admission to the country, including Medicaid, food stamps, and the new version of welfare.

The anti-immigrant measures of the 1990s had little impact on the fundamental dynamics of immigration. Mexicans seeking better economic opportunities and to escape the hardships that NAFTA brought to some regions and economic sectors of their country continued to travel to the United States in large numbers, with and without visas, while businesses continued to eagerly recruit foreign-born workers, with little concern about their legal status, seeing them as a cheap, hardworking, compliant workforce. As in so many of the social and cultural disputes of the 1990s, conservatives changed public discourse and won a series of fights over specific measures but failed to reverse the basic social trajectory.

Impeachment

Bill Clinton's reelection if anything intensified conservative attacks on him. Not only did he epitomize to many conservatives the things they found distasteful about how the country had changed since the 1960s, but even more importantly his ascent broke what many conservatives had come to see as their rightful control over the reins of power. From the moment he took office, Clinton faced a well-funded conservative effort to weaken or destroy his presidency by uncovering and publicizing his personal transgressions. Sloppy in his financial affairs and personal life, Clinton left enough hints of

irregular, unethical, and possibly illegal behavior in his wake to keep his
adversaries going and allow them to mobilize the institutions of law on their
behalf.

The investigations and lawsuits began with Clinton's behavior while governor of Arkansas. They included allegations of corruption in connection
with his investment in a real estate development scheme called Whitewater;
that he used state troopers to procure women; and that he had sexually ha-
rassed a state clerical worker named Paula Jones, who sued him for damages. While most of these charges ultimately proved untrue, the murky
circumstances surrounding them, the seemingly unlimited resources of
Clinton's opponents, and Clinton's penchant for evasive responses kept the
suggestions of scandal alive. In early 1994, facing renewed questions, he
asked Janet Reno, whom he had nominated as the country's first female attorney general, to appoint a special prosecutor to investigate the Whitewater
land deal. Reno chose an independent-minded Republican, Robert Fiske. A
few months later, a new law changed the procedure for selecting special prosecutors, handing the power over to a special panel of judges appointed by
the chief justice of the United States. William Rehnquist, a conservative
Republican with a history of partisanship before his ascension to the Court,
picked a conservative-dominated panel that replaced Fiske with Kenneth
Starr, who had been solicitor general during the Bush administration.

Starr reported after a prolonged investigation no evidence of wrongdoing
in connection to Whitewater. But he created a constitutional crisis by pursuing another matter. In the fall of 1997, attorneys in the Paula Jones lawsuit
learned that Clinton had had sex with a White House intern, Monica Lewinsky (at age twenty-two, only seven years older than his daughter). Starr soon
expanded his investigation to include her. Before any of this became public,
Clinton was asked in a deposition in the Jones suit if he had had sexual relations with Lewinsky, which he denied. Starr made Clinton's effort to hide his
relationship with Lewinsky the centerpiece of his investigation.

Things quickly got tawdry. Reports of the Lewinsky affair leaked to the
press, leading Clinton to publicly deny having sex with her (lying to his family and lawyers as well). Starr hauled Lewinsky before a grand jury, where
she produced a dress stained with Clinton's semen. Only then did Clinton
confess that he had lied. In September 1998, Starr sent Congress a report
that went into lurid detail about Clinton's relationship with Lewinsky,
charged him with perjury and obstruction of justice, and suggested that his
behavior presented grounds for impeachment. (The Jones lawsuit itself
faded into oblivion, thrown out by a judge for lack of evidence and eventually settled, during Jones's appeal, by a payment from Clinton.)

The House quickly began impeachment inquiries, with Republican leaders thinking that Clinton's personal behavior gave them a powerful political weapon. Events proved them wrong. In the 1998 election, the Republicans lost five seats in the House and did not add to their 55–45 majority in the Senate, a departure from the historical pattern of gains by the nonpresidential party in midterm elections. Facing recriminations, Newt Gingrich resigned as House Speaker, setting off a farce of one Republican politician after another being accused of sexual misconduct, including Robert Livingston, initially chosen by the Republicans to succeed Gingrich, who resigned after the revelation of his marital infidelity. Whatever moral edge the Republicans had claimed lost its credibility.

On December 19, 1998, the House of Representatives voted to impeach Clinton on the grounds of perjury and obstruction of justice, making him only the second president to face trial by the Senate, and the first since Andrew Johnson. Impeachment was mostly a piece of political theater, since the Republicans lacked the two-thirds Senate majority needed to convict. Clinton's continuing popularity helped ensure that congressional Democrats would stay loyal and his presidency would survive. In the end, forty-five senators voted to convict Clinton on one charge and fifty on the other, far short of the number needed to oust him. Through his last years in office, while the Lewinsky affair and impeachment dominated the news, Clinton remained one of the more popular second-term presidents in history. Most of the public disapproved of his personal behavior, but they appreciated the peaceful international relations the United States enjoyed during his years in office and the prosperous economy of his second term.

Ambivalent Imperialism

The Clinton administration acted on a set of assumptions about the relationship between the United States and the rest of the world that did not radically differ from prior administrations and that still owed a great deal to the Cold War. Clinton had the good luck to be president during a period of few major threats to American national security and global hegemony. But in accepting the givens of post–World War II foreign policy, he continued the country down a road of militarism and imperial reach, with profound dangers and unclear rewards.

Like Bush, Clinton endorsed the idea that the United States needed to maintain a large, worldwide military apparatus, even at times of peace and with no nation possessing anything near its war-making capacity. He did make cuts in defense spending on top of those Bush had made. As a percentage of federal outlays, the defense budget fell from 26 percent in 1989 to 21 percent in 1992 and 16 percent in 2000. Several hundred military bases were closed or downsized on the recommendation of specially appointed commissions, used to circumvent the difficulty in getting members of Congress to accept job losses in their districts. But when Clinton left office, the American military empire remained gigantic, with a million and a half men under arms, thousands of bases within the United States, and more than seven hundred abroad. In 2001, the United States accounted for 37 percent of all worldwide military expenditures. Though China had more military personnel, in every other regard the U.S. military operated on a scale unapproached by other nations.

Under Clinton, the United States maintained—and even enlarged—the overseas alliances that had been built to contain the Soviet Union. The Clinton administration pressed NATO to expand eastward, taking into its ranks Poland, Hungary, and the Czech Republic. NATO enlargement caused considerable resentment in Russia, as former Soviet leaders claimed that Secretary of State James Baker had promised that the alliance would not move into Eastern Europe (a misunderstanding, according to the Americans). The United States and its allies had little to fear militarily from Russia. But NATO expansion served other ends besides as an insurance policy against a possible Russian resurgence. For one thing, continuing NATO's role as a major vehicle of European policy sustained U.S. influence on the Continent, which might have been diminished if the European Union or some other strictly continental body became the major security apparatus for the region. For another thing, NATO expansion opened up new markets for U.S. weapons, important to preserving defense industries facing profit pressures with the end of the Cold War and in generating exports at a time of huge trade imbalances.

The American military system had become its own reason for being. The military-industrial complex that Eisenhower had warned about remained an important influence on government policy and spending priorities. Having been in place for a half century or more, the defense industries, intelligence agencies, secret weapons systems, massive army, widespread overseas deployment of military personnel, web of military alliances, and economic burden of maintaining global military superiority were taken for granted by most Americans and rarely the subject of serious debate. The majority of the population had never known a time when the United States was not mobilized for war.

Yet the United States remained a nonmartial society even as it maintained the world's most potent military, with a relatively low cultural and social presence of the armed services outside of the immediate environs of major military facilities. Also, for a country with an archipelago of defense establishments spanning the globe and ever-growing international economic interests, the United States evinced a low level of public curiosity about the rest of the world. Most Americans had little interest in foreign places, cultures, or languages, even as much of the world became obsessed with American popular culture and English became the global lingua franca. The mixture of militarism and civilian culture, empire and cultural isolationism led few politicians or segments of the public to raise fundamental questions about military or foreign policy.

Clinton, perhaps because of his history as a draft avoider and Republican attacks on the Democrats as weak on national defense, proved particularly susceptible to pressure from military leaders. At the start of his administration, he suffered a grievous blow when Colin Powell, as head of the Joint Chiefs of Staff, successfully organized opposition to his plan to end the ban on gays in the military. Pressure from the Pentagon also scuttled another Clinton initiative, his support for ridding the world of land mines. An estimated 100 million land mines remained planted around the world, in many cases the residue of long-ended conflicts, killing or maiming some twenty-five thousand people a year. Clinton's backing helped lead to a 1996 conference that drafted a treaty banning the use of land mines. But the United States became one of the very few countries that refused to sign it after it failed to get an exemption that the military wanted to allow the continued deployment of mines along the divide between North and South Korea.

Clinton centered his foreign policy, especially during his early years in office, on economic issues, specifically promoting a global free-trade regime. He fully embraced the idea that free-market/free-trade capitalism provided the best—and perhaps the only—path toward freedom and prosperity. Clinton believed globalization—the increased integration of national economies through greater flow of goods and capital across borders—was inevitable, irreversible, and beneficial. It also served well the particular economic sectors that had supported his presidential bid and that he saw as key to domestic growth: high-tech and internationally oriented industrial concerns, the entertainment and software industries, and, above all, finance.

The Clinton administration worked to open up foreign markets to American products; gain access for American companies to inexpensive labor, natural resources, and financial markets abroad; protect their intellectual property rights; and remold the economies of other countries along free-market lines. Clinton followed up NAFTA by negotiating additional free-trade agreements and the 1995 creation of the World Trade Organization

(WTO), a new umbrella body for establishing international trade rules. Under Secretary Ron Brown, the Commerce Department became an aggressive promoter of U.S. business abroad. The World Bank and the International Monetary Fund, under heavy U.S. influence, pressured countries in economic trouble to move toward free markets, smaller state sectors, and reduced social benefits, using the lever of their lending capacity to override popular resistance. Opposition by the AFL-CIO to free-trade agreements that did not protect labor standards, along with conflicting interests among American trading partners, slowed the pace of trade liberalization. But only near the end of the Clinton administration, with the large, dramatic, heavily reported protests at the November 1999 meeting of the WTO in Seattle, did free-trade globalization face significant political and ideological opposition questioning the idea that its net benefits were a proven, neutral economic fact.

As globalization triumphed, at least as ideology, the role of military power became murkier. Under Clinton, loans, investments, international treaties, technical expertise, and cultural capital were the main instruments of globalization, not guns and missiles. If once international economic expansion and military power had been closely linked, by the late twentieth century their relationship to one another had become opaque and attenuated.

The vexing issue of humanitarian military interventions displayed the uncertainty in the Clinton administration and elite policy circles about the function of the armed services and their role in maintaining and extending American values and power. International agreements in the late 1940s had enumerated universal human rights and declared genocide to be a crime under international law. Starting in the late 1970s, the idea of defending human rights across national borders became increasingly prominent in the wake of disappointed hopes for radical reform on both sides of the Iron Curtain. Presented as a way of transcending ideology and downsizing utopian visions to concentrate on protecting basic standards of freedom, the notion of human rights meshed well with post–Cold War politics and political economy. The radical movements that had reached their height in the late 1960s had looked toward the transformation of the deep structures of society, both capitalist and communist. By contrast, human rights, as commonly defined in the 1970s and beyond, seemingly could be fully compatible with liberal capitalism.

The United States, as the only remaining superpower, had a greater ability than any other nation or organization to use arms to support humanitarian efforts, stop armed conflicts, protect human rights, and end genocide.

The very existence of its massive military raised the option for American policymakers, international organizations, and human rights groups to turn to it to solve crises. But in a world awash with misery and violence, the Clinton administration proved inconsistent in deciding when to use military force in situations that did not threaten the national security of the United States. In some cases it intervened under UN auspices, in other cases it declined, and in still others, to avoid possible vetoes at the UN, it acted through NATO. In the process, even as he avoided large-scale war, Clinton created precedents for the unilateral use of arms by the United States against foreign nations and forces that had not attacked it.

A chain of events in Somalia, which began during Bush's presidency, influenced the U.S. approach to intervention in the name of humanitarianism and human rights. A 1992 UN effort to deliver relief supplies to Somalia, which was racked by civil war, faltered as rival warlords stole food and other goods. To protect the relief operation, the UN Security Council authorized armed force and eventually asked the United States to take the lead in the humanitarian effort. Bush sent in twenty-five thousand troops, joined by thirteen thousand more from other countries. As the situation seemed to stabilize, Clinton began a withdrawal. But after the forces of Mohamed Farrah Aidid ambushed a UN detachment, the Somali effort increasingly became a conflict between Aidid and the U.S.-led forces. On October 3, 1993, Aidid's group carried out a carefully planned ambush that led to the downing of two U.S. Black Hawk helicopters and a daylong battle in which hundreds of Somalis and eighteen Americans died. Pictures of Somalis dragging the body of a dead American through the streets of Mogadishu outraged the American public, which was unprepared to accept the loss of American lives in a place it knew little about and for a cause that did not directly affect the United States. Clinton cut his losses and within six months withdrew all U.S. forces from Somalia.

Determined to avoid any similar loss of U.S. life, Clinton backed off from a plan to send a small contingent of troops to Haiti, where the military had overthrown President Jean-Bertrand Aristide. But in September 1994, partly out of a desire to stem the flow of refugees to the United States, he did send troops there in accord with a UN Security Council resolution. The Americans landed without resistance, paving the way for Aristide's return to power.

In the case of Rwanda, where no issue like refugees directly impacted the United States, Clinton made the opposite decision, refusing to intervene. When hard-line leaders of the Hutu majority launched a campaign of genocide against the Tutsi minority and Hutu moderates, which resulted in the deaths of over 800,000 people, the Clinton administration did nothing. It even rejected the use of the term "genocide" to describe what was happening in order to minimize pressure to send the military to stop the killing.

Clinton also avoided, at least at first, intervening in the wars and killing that came in the wake of the breakup of Yugoslavia. When ethnic fighting broke out in Bosnia, the United States, first under Bush and then under Clinton, declined to send forces to provide relief or stop the fighting. Only after the July 1995 murder by Serbian forces of over seven thousand un-armed Muslim men and boys at Srebrenica, the worst mass murder in Eu-rope since World War II, did the United States, as part of a NATO force, intervene with aerial attacks. It then brokered the Dayton Accords, ending the fighting, and agreed to send a large U.S. contingent to Bosnia as part of a NATO peacekeeping force.

The United States got involved in the Balkans again in 1999 when NATO—with the United States providing most of the firepower—launched a full-scale air war against Serbia to stop its ethnic cleansing of Albanian Muslims in Kosovo. The Clinton administration believed that it could quickly force the Serbians to cease their campaign using airpower alone, minimizing the risk to American lives. However, the Serbs held fast for eleven weeks, during which time they accelerated their displacement and killing of Albanians. Only after NATO extended its bombing to Serbia proper, including Belgrade, did Serbian leaders finally capitulate. The bomb-ing campaign, conducted in the name of human rights, which resulted in the deaths of hundreds of civilians and hundreds and possibly thousands of Serbian soldiers but no Americans, reinforced the self-appointed global leadership of the United States, as it waged war against a country that had not attacked it, and bolstered the illusion that it could reshape or control faraway parts of the world with little cost in its own blood.

But a series of terrorist attacks gave the lie to any notion that a large, technically sophisticated military deployed around the world could make the country invulnerable. Just days after Clinton became president, Mir Aimal Kasi, a Virginia resident who had grown up in Pakistan near the Afghan border, angry at American support for Israel, drove to the entry road to the CIA headquarters in Langley and opened fire with a locally purchased AK-47 on cars waiting to get onto the property, killing two agency employees before escaping the country. A month later, followers of a radical Egyptian imam living in New York detonated a rental van loaded with homemade explosives in the garage of the World Trade Center, killing six people and causing half a billion dollars' worth of damage.

Clinton authorized a more aggressive antiterrorism program in 1995, as fears grew that terrorists might obtain nuclear, chemical, or biological weapons. By the next year, the CIA had begun to focus on Osama bin Laden, a wealthy Saudi who had been an indirect ally of the United States in funding and helping organize the anti-Soviet war in Afghanistan. Bin Laden turned against the United States after it stationed troops in Saudi Arabia during the buildup to the Gulf War. In August 1998, members of the al Qaeda network, which bin Laden headed, used truck bombs to cause massive damage and loss of life at the U.S. embassies in Kenya and Tanzania, with most of the casualties Africans who just happened to be passing by. In retaliation, Clinton ordered cruise missile strikes against a chemical plant in Sudan and a camp in Afghanistan, which the United States claimed were al Qaeda installations. Unilateral use of force had become so normalized that there was little protest or even comment at home about launching missiles at countries with which the United States was not at war.

The United States tried to stop bin Laden from launching further attacks, as CIA head George Tenet and other officials believed he would, possibly inside the United States. But the reluctance of the military to use force against al Qaeda in Afghanistan, which bin Laden used as his base under the protection of the Taliban government, and the hesitation of the Clinton administration to engage in assassination or kill civilian bystanders, made an inherently difficult task more so. Endlessly, the Clinton administration made plans to kill bin Laden, debated scenarios, vetted possible actions with lawyers, worried about killing women and children, but never had what it considered reliable enough evidence or a good enough chance to kill its target alone to launch an attack. Meanwhile, it privately fretted over what it saw as a much greater threat than bin Laden, the global spread of weapons of mass destruction and missiles to deliver them, as the orderly confrontation of the Cold War was replaced by chaotic multifronted conflicts and crusades, with enormous stockpiles of Cold War weapons and the knowledge about how to make them diffusing around the globe.

Boom Again

From 1991 until March 2001, the United States experienced the longest continual economic expansion in its modern history. Overall, the economy performed better than during the previous two decades, though it did not match its performance during the quarter century after World War II. Recovery started even before Clinton took office. As his stress on fiscal discipline and minimizing inflation kept wages flat, credit readily available, and investment and productivity increasing, the expansion soon accelerated.

Early in the expansion, export-oriented manufacturing helped lead the way, benefiting from a cheap dollar in relation to the yen and the deutsche mark. However, the Clinton administration soon worried that the exchange rates that favored U.S. manufacturing would so weaken Japanese industry that they would throw Japan into a recession, which in turn might lead to a sell-off of Japanese investments in the United States and an international economic crisis. To avert that possibility, in 1995 the United States, Japan, and Germany agreed to increase the value of the dollar relative to the yen and the deutsche mark. Japanese goods became cheaper in the United States, while export-oriented manufacturing in the United States cooled down.

But the U.S. economy continued to grow, now increasingly tied to a huge run-up in stock prices, which far exceeded the rate of growth in corporate profits. The bull market stemmed in part from corporations making enormous share purchases, either as part of mergers and acquisitions or to push up their own stock prices. Also, foreign investors put more and more money into American securities, helping to boost prices. The Federal Reserve and the Clinton administration encouraged the market boom and the increasing dominance of the financial sector, with Congress and the president agreeing on the 1999 repeal of the Glass-Steagall Act, the New Deal law that had forced a separation between investment and commercial banking. As the century drew to a close, the stock market seemed to defy gravity and rationality, as the dot-com bubble in media, telecommunications, and Internet stocks pushed prices far out of line with historic price/earnings ratios, until the market finally tumbled in late 2000 and 2001.

While it lasted, the soaring stock market stimulated spending and economic growth. Corporations and well-off households borrowed huge amounts of money using inflated equities as collateral, which they then spent on investments and consumption. The personal savings rate fell from 8.7 percent in 1992 to −0.12 percent in 2000, as people—especially in the upper income brackets—not only borrowed money but spent down what they had saved in the past. Corporations also raised money by issuing shares at inflated prices, an important mechanism for financing Silicon Valley start-ups as well as more established companies, which in the past had looked to retained earnings and bond sales for capital.

Most Americans did not experience significant benefits from the economic expansion until its later years. During the first half of the 1990s, real wages continued their long stagnation. From 1989 through 1994, median family income actually declined after adjusting for inflation. Though the unemployment rate began to fall in 1993, mass layoffs continued to be common. With nearly two and a half million workers in 1993 and 1994 losing jobs that they had held for at least three years, due to plant closings, relocations, or cuts in production, the chronic job insecurity that had been haunting the country since the 1980s continued.

The weak returns for workers even as the economy improved helped spark a revolt within organized labor. During the late 1980s and early 1990s, reform movements gained strength in a number of unions, most importantly the Teamsters, where an insurgent candidate, Ron Carey, with backing from the rank-and-file Teamsters for a Democratic Union, ousted the candidate of the old guard. The 1994 Republican congressional victories brought dissatisfaction with AFL-CIO president Lane Kirkland to a head. Under pressure from a group of union presidents, Kirkland resigned, succeeded by his secretary-treasurer. But at the AFL-CIO convention in October 1995, dissatisfied union leaders ran their own slate of candidates, with Service Employees International Union president John Sweeney, who had overseen militant action and membership growth in his own organization, capturing the federation presidency in the first contested leadership election since the AFL and CIO merged in 1955.

Sweeney reenergized the AFL-CIO and reached out to liberal, student, and religious groups of the sort with which labor once had strong tries but from which it had become isolated. He won an early victory when his "America Needs a Raise" campaign pressured Congress to boost the minimum wage, the value of which had been deeply eroded by inflation. Labor issues began receiving more attention in the media and on campuses, where students launched campaigns against goods produced under sweatshop conditions. But Sweeney's effort to reverse the decline in union membership failed, as only a few unions took up his call to greatly increase their spending on organizing and as employers continued to be effective in defeating unionization drives. In 2000, fewer than 14 percent of workers belonged to a union, and only 9 percent in the private sector.

With such a small percentage of the workforce unionized, organized labor no longer had much impact on national wage levels. But as unemployment continued to drop in the second half of the 1990s, falling to 3.9 percent in late 2000, the lowest level since 1970, the tight labor market brought substantial increases in real wages. Adjusted for inflation, between 1995 and 1999 the median wage went up 7.3 percent. Low-wage workers made the greatest gains. Black workers did particularly well, as the gap between black and white household incomes diminished. College enrollment and home-ownership rates both moved up, while fewer families lived in poverty. Full

employment—or as close as the country had come to it since the end of the
long postwar boom—proved remarkably effective in raising the overall standard of living and helping the least privileged sectors of society.

But the broad economic gains of the late 1990s did not reverse the basic
dynamic of the economy since the recessions of the 1970s and the corporate
revolution. Income and wealth inequality continued to increase during the
Clinton years, while economic mobility decreased. In 2000, the top 1 percent
of income recipients received more after-tax income than the bottom 40 percent, with the gap between the two groups having doubled over the course
of two decades. The average real hourly wage in private industry was still 5
percent below what it had been in 1979.

The growing gulf between the rich and the ordinary manifested itself
dramatically in the soaring compensation for CEOs. In 1999, they took
home on average 107 times what workers did, up from 56 times in 1989 and
29 times in 1978, far exceeding the ratio in other economically advanced nations.

Even though income inequality reached a level not seen since before the
New Deal, the fortunes made in the last years of the twentieth century did
not carry with them the moral disrepute associated with wealth in earlier
generations. Some CEOs did undergo criticism for cavalier disregard for
their workers, like Al Dunlap, known as "Chainsaw Al" for his massive firing of workers at Scott Paper and Sunbeam. But fortunes gained through
financial maneuvers, speculation, and monopoly were no longer viewed as
parasitic, as they had been through the Great Depression. Wall Street had
managed to remake its image as an arena of mobility, democracy, and social
good, while money made in high-tech industries generally was seen as benign. The lack of social pretension of many of the new billionaires, like Bill
Gates and Warren Buffett, provided a degree of cultural and political armor.
When *Chicago* magazine calculated the all-time richest residents of the city,
in the number two slot stood Ty Warner, who made his money selling the
cute Beanie Babies toys, a personage far less likely to raise populist hackles
than Samuel Insull, Cyrus McCormick, or George Pullman, industrial titans of earlier times, whose once-famed fortunes, even adjusted for inflation,
were no match for later, lesser-known real estate and insurance billionaires.

Deadlock

The robust economy gave the Democrats a strong card going into the 2000
elections. But Vice President Al Gore proved to be a mediocre candidate,
stiff and lecturing. The Republican nominee, George W. Bush, the son of the

former president, was not well known outside of Texas, where he served as governor, but he won strong backing from both conservative activists and the Republican establishment. Though once in office Bush became one of the most conservative presidents in the country's history, on the campaign trail he portrayed himself not as a radical reformer but as a "compassionate conservative," committed not only to reduced taxes and government but also to bipartisanship and maintaining support for people in need. The election generated only modest interest, with voter turnout at 51.3 percent of eligible voters, a bit higher than in 1988 and 1996 but somewhat lower than in 1980, 1984, and 1992.

The electorate split almost down the middle, with Gore beating Bush in the popular vote by half a percentage point (with left-leaning consumer advocate Ralph Nader taking 2.7 percent of the vote and conservative Pat Buchanan .4 percent). The electoral vote was even closer, with the election in several states that could determine the overall outcome too close to call on election night. The regional polarization of presidential politics had become extreme. Bush won the electoral votes from the entire South and all the Plains and Mountain states except New Mexico, where Gore eked out a 366-vote victory. Gore carried all the Northeast, Middle Atlantic, and West Coast states except New Hampshire and Alaska. (In the desert West and upper South, he lost several states that Clinton had carried, including his home state of Tennessee.)

The election came down to who won Florida, where both sides claimed victory. Recounts, legal challenges, and political maneuvering proliferated, as the country went through the strange experience of having the election over but not knowing for five weeks who had won. In the end, it all rested on the political sympathies of the Supreme Court. In fragmented and largely incoherent decisions, a majority of justices in *Bush v. Gore* first stayed a partial recount of Florida ballots that seemed to be eliminating Bush's slim lead and then gave the state's electoral votes and with it the election to Bush because a full recount could not be completed within a time limit specified in Florida law. Using the political and cultural capital the Court had accumulated during the rights revolution, the Republican-nominated majority, with only thin pretense of legal consistency and reasoning, picked the next president.

The 2000 election seemed to confirm the idea of a deeply divided country, with politically and socially conservative "red" states and liberal "blue" states corresponding to two very different ideological and cultural tribes of Americans. The notion had some truth to it. But in many states, the election was quite close, countering the impression of clear regional divisions.

Furthermore, for all the intense partisanship of the election and its aftermath, the candidates, though they sharply disagreed on some issues, like abortion rights and gun control, were not terribly far apart about political economy and the role of government. Bush accepted the idea of at least a limited welfare state, seeking to trim back and partially privatize the New Deal–Great Society system of social benefits but not eliminate it, while Gore came from an administration that had accepted many of the basic tenets of Reaganism, including the deregulation of business and finance and the downsizing of government.

When the dust settled on the disputed election, few Americans viewed the presidency of George W. Bush as illegitimate, while the Supreme Court lost little public respect for its role in determining the outcome. An odd combination of intense partisanship, political apathy, and centrist consensus had come to characterize national politics. Compared to the past, fewer Americans thought much of government, or felt it was worth their while to engage in politics, seeing the private realm and the private market as more important determinants of the quality of their lives. At least intuitively, many Americans recognized the extent to which power had shifted outside the control of the institutions of civic life that had been democratized in the decades after World War II.

CHAPTER 19

Living Large

"Fifty-inch screen, money green leather sofa / Got two rides, a limousine with a chauffeur," intoned rapper Biggie Smalls on his 1994 hit "Juicy." Rap music emerged from the South Bronx in the mid-1970s, amid New York's fiscal crisis, part of a hip-hop culture that included graffiti and break dancing as well. From its home ground, hip-hop quickly spread to downtown clubs and galleries and black neighborhoods across the country. Two decades later, rap had become utterly mainstream, the dominant music not only among young African Americans, who pioneered it, but among suburban white youth too. Thematically multifarious, rap lyrics chronicled ghetto hardships, whipped up party frenzies, hailed "gangsta" life, and boasted of sexual conquest. And over and over, rappers celebrated consumption, extolling luxury cars, designer clothes, expensive jewelry, and top-shelf liquor, often by brand name. Puff Daddy, whose Gatsbyesque rise from Harlem to the Hamptons was chronicled by the celebrity magazines at supermarket checkout lines, even acclaimed money itself as a kind of brand in "It's All About the Benjamins" (alluding to hundred-dollar bills, graced with a picture of Benjamin Franklin). The rap music celebration of things—the more, the more expensive, the more glittery, the better—captured something central to American life a half century after World War II, a testament to the complex fluidity of the United States that artists presenting themselves as representatives of an outlaw underclass became the public face of its dominant values.

At the end of the twentieth century, Americans lived on a scale of consumption and resource usage unprecedented in human history and unmatched elsewhere on the planet. No radical departures brought this about. With the resumption of economic expansion in the 1980s and sustained growth during the 1990s, development along lines already laid out remade the built environment and social landscape. Through incremental change, the United States became a very different society than it had been at the end of World War II, or even at the end of the Vietnam War. The cumulative effect of decisions made in the private sector and the public realm led it to a down-home imperial grandiosity, with implications not just for Americans but for the ecological status of the earth itself.

Immigration

The United States puffed up in part because of population growth. Between the end of the Vietnam War and the end of the century, the country's population increased by over a quarter. The rate of population growth, which slowed after 1950, picked up between 1990 and 2000, when the number of residents swelled from 249 million to 281 million, making the United States the third most populous country after China and India. It lagged behind the world as a whole in its rate of population growth but exceeded by several-fold the rate for most industrialized countries, which typically had very low or even negative growth.

During these years, the birth rate in the United States hovered near historic lows, rising modestly after hitting bottom in the mid-1970s. (It began to fall again during the 1990s.) Among major population groups, only Hispanic women had a fertility rate significantly above the replacement level. Non-Hispanic white women averaged only 1.8 children apiece. Rather than decreased sexual activity, the decline in fertility reflected increased use of contraception and the availability of legal abortion. In the late 1990s, the number of abortions equaled a third the number of live births. By gaining more control over their lives and bodies, women transformed the demography of the country. They married later, had children later, spaced births more widely, and stopped childbearing earlier.

Immigration more than compensated for the low birth rate. From World War II to the end of the century, the number of immigrants coming to the United States through legal channels rose steadily: 1.0 million in the 1940s, 2.5 million in the 1950s, 3.3 million in the 1960s, 4.5 million in the 1970s, 7.3 million in the 1980s, and 9.0 million in the 1990s. In addition, millions more came illegally, with at least seven million undocumented foreign-born residents in the country in 2000. Immigration peaked in 1991, when the 1.8 million arrivals equaled .72 percent of the total population. In absolute terms, never before had so many immigrants entered the country (though the rate of immigration had been higher early in the century). The exceptionally large flow of immigrants accounted, to a large measure, for the exceptionally high rate of population growth in the United States compared to other industrialized nations.

Increased immigration stemmed from broad global changes. Improved health in less developed countries contributed to rapid population growth, exceeding the capacity of local agriculture or urban job markets to absorb the ever larger generations of people seeking work. In many places the spread of market relations and the arrival of international capital disrupted traditional economic arrangements. So did civil wars and civil strife. The growing ubiquity of television, tape recorders, CD players, and other mass media brought knowledge of the wealth, economic opportunities, and culture of the United States to people around the world. With most rich countries imposing far more severe restrictions on immigration, it became the favored destination for emigrants, particularly from countries in its economic, military, and political orbits. According to the United Nations, between 1995 and 2000, more than half the people (net) moving from less developed regions of the world to more developed regions went to the United States.

The 1965 immigration act made possible the growth of immigration and profoundly changed its nature. The elimination of national quotas opened the door for emigrants leaving poor countries around the world. Very quickly, arrivals from Asia and Latin America eclipsed arrivals from Europe, as the immigration stream became much more heterogeneous in national origin, occupation, and class status than ever before. In 1990, immigrants from Europe made up only 3 percent of the total inflow, down from 90 percent in 1900. Mexicans constituted nearly a quarter of immigrants during the 1980s and 1990s, while substantial numbers of Central Americans, Caribbeans, and South Americans arrived too. By the end of the 1990s, more Hispanics lived in the United States than African Americans, a break from the long historical pattern in which white descendants of European immigrants and black descendants of slaves constituted the largest population groups and to a great extent defined, separately and in their interaction, the dynamic of the country. Immigration from Asia trailed that from the Western Hemisphere, but it far exceeded the pre-1965 levels and included national groups that previously had been all but unrepresented: Indians, Pakistanis, Bangladeshis, Iranians, Vietnamese, Laotians, Cambodians, and Thais.

Post-1965 immigrants clustered in a handful of gateway cities, including New York, Los Angeles, San Francisco, Miami, Chicago, Houston, and Washington, D.C. But over time, they also filtered into areas that had not seen substantial numbers of immigrants for generations, if ever. In 1980, Green Bay, Wisconsin, a tidy midwestern town, best known for its professional football team, the Green Bay Packers, had an almost entirely white, native-born population. But then Hispanic immigrants moved to the area to work in the meatpacking plants that gave the football team its name, while Hmong refugees, allies of the United States during the Vietnam War, were resettled in the city. In 2000, one out of ten Green Bay residents was Hispanic, Black, or Asian, a dramatic change from the extreme homogeneity of the past. In many towns and cities in the South—especially in Virginia, North Carolina, and Georgia—a region that historically had very low levels of immigration, substantial communities of Hispanics and other immigrants could be found by the late 1990s, drawn to jobs in meatpacking and food processing plants, textile mills, furniture factories, and other industrial enterprises. In 2000, in twenty-seven states 5 percent or more of the population was foreign born. (Nationally, foreign-born residents and children of foreign-born parents together constituted a fifth of the population.) Though immigrants continued to be heavily concentrated in urban, coastal areas, they had become a presence everywhere except in parts of the Deep South and the Great Plains states.

During the nineteenth and early twentieth centuries, the overwhelming majority of newcomers arrived without skills relevant to an industrial economy. By contrast, the late-twentieth-century immigration surge included a substantial number of well-educated professionals, white-collar workers, and businesspeople, who came with skills and in some cases capital that allowed them to move directly into well-paid jobs and middle-class lives. Still, most immigrants, like their predecessors, did not have the skills, connections, or language facility to escape low-wage work in service, agricultural, or blue-collar jobs. In many cases they filled occupational niches abandoned by native-born workers as pay and conditions deteriorated with deunionization and business pressure to lower costs. In Massachusetts, after a spurt of immigration during the 1990s, foreign-born workers held 45 percent of the semiskilled blue-collar jobs and 27 percent of the service industry jobs. In much of the country, the basic labor of social reproduction, including childcare, eldercare, and cleaning, cooking, and maintenance in homes and hospitals, was largely performed by immigrant workers. In California, immigrants and sojourners, mostly from Latin America, made up more than 90 percent of the agricultural workforce. As business succeeded in downgrading pay and conditions for workers in the lower occupational strata, immigrant labor became utterly crucial to the economy and to sustaining the American way of life.

Big Cities, Empty Plains

As the population of the country increased, so did its density. In 1940, the country had thirty-seven people per square mile; in 2000, nearly eighty. That was well below the global density of 120 people per square mile and far below the density of the major European powers (not counting Russia, whose vast land area brought its density down to just twenty-two people per square mile). Nevertheless, the unequal distribution of population made parts of the country feel downright crowded. In 1990, for the first time, more than half the population resided in metropolitan areas with more than one million people. And in 2000, over half of all Americans lived in just ten states. New Jersey, the most densely populated state, had 1,134 people per square mile.

Regions once thought of as rural became crowded in parts. Between 1980 and 2000, the share of the population living in the West rose from 19 percent to 22 percent and in the South from 33 percent to 36 percent. Most western and southern growth took place in urban and suburban areas, not the thinly populated countryside, leading to extensive sprawl.

Even as traffic jams and crowded schools testified to increased population density, some sections of the interior of the country depopulated, particularly a band running from the Mexican border just east of Big Bend, Texas, north through the Great Plains to the Canadian border. In 2000, over a century after the superintendent of the census declared that the country no longer had a continuous frontier, an area in its center as large as the Louisiana Purchase, nearly 900,000 square miles, met the nineteenth-century federal definition of "frontier," two to six people per square mile. People had been moving out of the dry lands of the Great Plains for seventy years, as cattle raising and irrigated agriculture proved difficult or impossible to sustain. In some areas, large companies bought up and consolidated family operations, so that crop raising continued—aided by federal agricultural subsidies—but population dropped and the small towns that dotted the region became ghosts of what they once were, with stores, banks, churches, restaurants, and schools closing. In other areas, especially in the northern Great Plains, land reverted to prairie.

As whites moved out of the Plains, Indians moved back in. The Native American populations of North and South Dakota, Montana, Nebraska, and Kansas rose between 1990 and 2000 by 12 to 23 percent. Indians returned to reservations from elsewhere in the country, attracted by life in communities of other Indians and jobs at the casinos that provided the main source of economic growth for many of the Great Plains tribes (though their reservations remained among the poorest places in the country). The spread of Indian-owned casinos was an offshoot of the increased militancy and tribal resurgence of the 1960s and 1970s, facilitated by a 1987 Supreme Court ruling that severely limited the power of states to regulate tribal gambling operations.

Indian tribes played an important role in the return of the buffalo, which had been on the verge of extinction at the start of the twentieth century. Tribes built herds and systematically managed them. When the century ended, 300,000 bison roamed the Great Plains, as the movie of history seemed to be running backward. Euro-American dry lands agriculture had not panned out as homesteaders once assumed. Instead, in much of the region it proved to be a brief, unsuccessful interlude.

Crime and punishment were among the few new sources of income in economically hard-pressed rural areas. Over the course of the 1990s, small-scale laboratories producing methamphetamine—a drug of choice for rural whites—popped up in small towns and rural backwaters across the country. With them came more drug use and a wave of rural crime. In some rural counties, the crime rate far exceeded urban norms. While crime brought in some money, so did incarceration. Many small communities found a source of jobs and money in attracting new prisons. Often they were built and operated by private companies and housed convicts from other states that, in an era of soaring incarceration rates, had run out of room in their own institutions.

Suburbia

Even as some parts of the countryside depopulated, others disappeared beneath suburban development. The combination of rising population, decreasing household size, and easy credit stimulated a gigantic residential building boom. Between 1990 and 2000 alone, fourteen million housing units were constructed. Home construction and sales became a major economic driving force, with real estate industry employment jumping from less than a million in 1980 to over a million and a half in 2000. (Women made up more than half the sales force.)

The United States encompassed a wide variety of patterns of life, but by 2000 the suburb had become clearly dominant. That year, exactly one-half of all Americans lived in a suburb. (Thirty percent lived in a central city and the remainder in rural regions.) Jobs as well as people kept migrating to the outer parts of metropolitan regions, often quite far out along radiating highways. Ninety percent of new office space built during the 1990s was suburban, leaving Chicago and New York as the only major metropolitan regions with more office space in their central cities than their surrounding suburbs.

Ever more people grew up taking suburban life for granted, as the only way of life they knew. Suburban sensibilities and physical forms became templates even for social institutions located in other settings, from enclosed central-city malls to sprawling, car-oriented universities.

Culturally, from John Cheever to *Father Knows Best* to *American Beauty* (which won the 1999 Academy Award for Best Picture), suburbia was treated as the land of the white, middle-class nuclear family—paradisaical, dysfunctional, or somewhere in between. But by the end of the twentieth century, the reality was far more complex. In 2000, married couples with children made up only slightly more than a quarter of suburban households. When Levittown, New York, celebrated its fiftieth anniversary in 1997, a quarter of the homes were occupied by either single-parent families or mothers and grown daughters living together.

In 2000, barely half of all households—suburban or otherwise—included a married couple, down from nearly three-quarters in 1960. A third of men and a quarter of women never married (including 42 percent of black women). As in most of Europe, more and more children were born to unmarried mothers, with the proportion of births outside of marriage reaching one-third at the century's end. (African Americans had a much higher percentage of children out of wedlock than other groups, but starting in the early 1990s, unlike whites, they experienced a modest increase in the proportion of children born to married couples.) Even among married families, the *Father Knows Best* household of a male breadwinner, stay-at-home wife, and live-at-home children became the exception.

Most families with children had no stay-at-home parent. Stagnating wages made it difficult for even two-parent families to maintain what was seen as a comfortable way of life without maximizing their time at work, one of the factors that led to an increase in the average number of hours Americans worked each year. From 1,905 hours in 1979, the average work year rose to 1,966 hours in 1998, a boost equivalent to an extra week and a half of work a year, which pushed the country past Japan to have the longest work year among the major industrial powers. Along with a higher percentage of adults in the workforce than in any other advanced industrial country, this kept U.S. per capita income the highest among industrial nations. Americans could afford what by world standards remained on average an exceptionally bountiful way of life by spending less and less time at home and more and more time at work. And getting to work. As metropolitan regions sprawled over ever larger areas, workers faced longer and longer commutes.

Levittown, as it approached its half-century celebration, remained remarkably racially homogeneous; whites made up 97 percent of its residents in

1990. But some nearby Long Island suburbs, like Freeport, had integrated in the wake of the civil rights movement. Nationally, suburbs slowly became somewhat more racially mixed. They also housed a growing number of immigrants who moved directly to suburban areas, bypassing the central cities that in the past had been the main entry points to the country. During the 1990s, more Central Americans lived on Long Island than in New York City.

The vast Inland Empire east of Los Angeles, with well over three million people in 2000, epitomized the diversity that had come to characterize many suburban regions. A center for warehousing and transshipping goods entering the country through the ports of Los Angeles and Long Beach (including the flood of goods from China on their way to Wal-Mart stores across the country), the Inland Empire attracted a racially and ethnically mixed working class looking for local jobs and affordable housing as well as more upscale professionals and white-collar workers, many of whom undertook long commutes to Los Angeles. At least for a while, cheap homes and cheap mortgages made a suburban way of life possible for a broad cross section of the population. (When the subprime mortgage crisis hit in 2007, the Inland Empire was one of its epicenters.)

Still, there remained in the DNA of suburbia an impulse for exclusivity and escape from racial, ethnic, and economic diversity. The most extreme manifestation came in the spread of gated communities, developments physically enclosed by walls or fences with access restricted to residents and their guests. Such developments could be found as far back as the nineteenth century, exclusive communities for wealthy families. In the 1960s, gated communities for the upper middle class began to be built, initially retirement or second-home resort communities, generally in parts of the country with year-round warm weather. Twenty years later, they began to be marketed as primary residences for families with working adults. Easy credit from deregulated savings and loans financed many of the gated developments, which often offered the good life in the form of swimming pools, tennis courts, fitness centers, landscaped or wooded grounds, and golf courses. By 2000, just over four million households (3.4 percent of the total) lived in communities with controlled access, while another three million lived in developments surrounded by walls or fences but without gatehouses or electronic gates.

Fear provided the impetus for gating suburbia. The rate of violent crime was at a postwar high during the 1980s when the construction of gated communities took off. Their popularity continued to grow even after the crime rate began falling in the early 1990s. Generalized apprehension as much as immediate danger pushed people to locate themselves behind barriers. Even when the crime rate was at its height, it remained relatively low in suburban areas, with little evidence that controlled access prevented criminal activity. But by the 1990s, fear of crime and general fearfulness had become free-floating, disassociated from the actualities of crime and threat. A 1995 poll found that nearly 90 percent of the respondents believed (falsely) that crime was getting worse, while a majority worried that they would be the victim of a crime.

Many factors played into the fearfulness of the last decades of the century, including crime rates that remained high compared to earlier eras, drug-related violence, a resurgence of urban youth gangs, growing economic inequality, and the increased flow of immigrants. Many whites had highly racialized perceptions of crime and threats to their person and property, with their fears focused on African Americans and, in some parts of the country, Hispanic immigrants. When in 1984 a white New York subway rider, Bernhard Goetz, pulled out a gun and shot four young black men he believed were about to rob him, he became something of a national hero, a real-life embodiment of the Charles Bronson character in the two *Death Wish* urban vigilante movies that had come out during the previous decade.

Gated communities provided a physical and psychological barrier against what many people saw as a dangerous, unpredictable society and against people different from themselves. Like high-priced outer suburbs in general, they provided a way of escaping the racial and ethnic hodgepodge of urban life, which had spread to many inner suburbs as well. Southern California and Florida, both of which had very high levels of immigration and suffered major urban riots in the 1980s, housed the largest concentrations of gated communities. By contrast, in the Northeast and Midwest, where suburbs were more racially segregated, suburbanites apparently did not feel the same need for physical barriers.

Gated communities promised order and predictability not only by providing security but also by privatizing functions usually performed by the state. Typically, in these communities, as in many nongated subdivisions, homeowners shared ownership of common facilities and even streets and sidewalks (where there were any) through homeowners' associations and had to abide by detailed rules and regulations incorporated as covenants to their deeds. Homeowners bore the cost of amenities, security, and routine maintenance, like road repairs, that elsewhere were government responsibilities.

The creation of what were in effect private suburban governments came as part of a broader privatization of American life during the 1980s and 1990s. Individuals and groups who could afford it increasingly provided themselves, through the private sector, services once performed primarily or exclusively by government. Between the early 1980s and the early 1990s, the number of private security guards soared, so that by the end of the period much more money was being spent on private security than on public law enforcement. Private gyms and health clubs multiplied, serving an increasingly health-conscious (and appearance-conscious) population at a time when many towns and cities were cutting back on their recreation budgets (particularly in areas hard-hit by the antitax movements of the late 1970s). School vouchers gained support, with a number of cities, starting with Milwaukee in 1990, experimenting with them. Many states began what in effect was a partial privatization of public higher education, as they reduced the percentage of state college and university costs covered by tax money, forcing increases in tuition.

None of this was completely new. Private and church-affiliated schools predated public education, the wealthy had long had their country clubs and private athletic facilities, and private guards had been used by companies and rich individuals for over a century. But as the income distribution became more top-heavy, a larger group of Americans had the ability and desire to buy themselves out of the use of public services, which in an era of tax-cutting often had deteriorated. Antistate thinking and the extolling of private enterprise, central to Reaganite ideology, legitimated the transfer of functions once seen as the very essence of state responsibility—like educating children, protecting the citizenry, and incarcerating criminals—into the private sector.

People who paid privately for functions like zoning, security, education, street cleaning, and recreation often resented paying taxes to finance parallel government services that they themselves did not use, creating an ongoing political pressure to keep taxes low. Changing demography reinforced this trend. During the 1950s, nearly 70 percent of adults had a child in school, providing a huge bloc of support for public education. By the early 1990s, largely as a result of smaller families and an aging population, the figure had fallen to 28 percent. In many communities, the annual vote on the school budget turned into an ugly battle, with high school athletes and cheerleaders standing by roadsides urging voters to back budgets funding their programs. Just as the post–World War II system of employment-based health and pension benefits created a two-tiered welfare state, the privatization of government services created two-tiered systems of security, education, and recreation, sparking mutual resentments between those who did and did not depend on state services.

Big

Perhaps the most striking aspect of late-twentieth-century suburban growth was the enormous size of just about everything. More than ever before, the country lived large. The original Levittown houses had 750 square feet of living space. By 1970, the average new single-family home was twice as large. By 2000, it had grown by half again, to 2,200 square feet. Since during these years households were getting smaller, the space per person rose even more quickly, far exceeding international norms. As the twenty-first century began, the typical American house provided 718 square feet of space per resident, compared to 544 square feet in Australia, the runner-up in the size derby, 442 square feet in Canada, 256 in Holland, and 170 in Japan.

If one of the great divides in human history was before and after the indoor toilet, the United States did miraculously well in pushing almost all of its residents across that line into convenience and modernity. In 1940, nearly half of all homes lacked indoor plumbing. In 1960, 17 percent still did. But by 2000, only 671,000 houses remained lacking, less than 1 percent of all dwellings. The United States had gone very far in providing decent, spacious, comfortable homes for its residents, especially outside of some central cities and poor rural regions that still had serious housing problems.

But Americans were not content to stop at decent, spacious, and comfortable. By the millions, they moved into suburban and exurban megahouses, "McMansions" as their critics called them, homes of a size that in the past only the very wealthiest might have built. Whereas in the 1970s an exceptionally large suburban home might have had 4,000 square feet, by the end of the century houses of twice or even three times that size had become common. In 2000, a third of all new homes had four or more bedrooms. Wine cellars, media rooms, home gyms, swimming pools, double-height entry halls, three-car garages, huge walk-in closets, and bathrooms with multiple sinks and multiple toilets and Jacuzzis and steam rooms became common features in the massive houses that sprang up on what had been cornfields and wooded lots beyond the older suburbs of the more prosperous metropolitan regions.

The mushrooming of McMansions reflected the substantial number of families who did very well during the Reagan-Bush-Clinton years. An extraordinary 60 percent of all income growth during the 1980s went to the richest 1 percent of the population, but the rest of the top 20 percent saw their income soar as well. (The income of the bottom 40 percent of earners, adjusted for inflation, fell.) By the end of the century, 17 percent of households earned $100,000 a year or more, constituting what conservative writer David Brooks dubbed "a mass upper class," up from less than 7 percent receiving an equivalent amount twenty years earlier. One in fourteen households had a net worth of more than a million dollars.

Owners of big homes drove a lot, and they liked to drive big vehicles. Since the advent of the automobile, suburban living had involved a lot of driving, and as suburbs spread farther outward, roads weaving together housing developments, office buildings, industrial parks, and shopping centers became ever more crowded. Typically, drivers traversed the roadways alone. In 1990, nearly three out of four workers commuted to their jobs in a vehicle that only they occupied. By 2003, the typical American household had more vehicles than drivers. The wealthier a household was, the more driving it did.

An increasing number of drivers chose to not to purchase cars but sport utility vehicles that were larger, heavier, and more fuel-consuming than traditional automobiles. SUVs made up less than 2 percent of the vehicles sold in 1982, but fifteen years later they had captured over 16 percent of the market. The SUV boom stemmed from an automobile industry effort to evade federal regulation of tailpipe pollution and gasoline consumption. Auto industry lobbying helped convince the Environmental Protection Agency to classify SUVs as light trucks rather than cars, which kept them from being subject to the limits on car pollution under the 1970 Clean Air Act. Similarly, in 1975, Congress allowed the Transportation Department to establish separate fuel efficiency standards for cars and for light trucks, a category that included SUVs. Automobile companies had to achieve fleet-wide average fuel consumption for their cars of 27.5 miles per gallon by 1985 but only 20.5 for light trucks. To meet the car standard, companies began producing small, fuel-efficient vehicles, on which they made little profit, while cutting down on production of large, gas-consuming sedans, traditionally favored family vehicles. Beginning with the Jeep Cherokee in 1983, they also introduced a growing number of SUV models, which they could make as big and powerful as they wanted.

SUVs proved immensely profitable for American automobile makers, more so than minivans, the other new type of vehicle that in effect replaced large sedans. For one thing, they initially faced no foreign competition. In 1964, in the course of a trade dispute with Europe, the United States had placed a 25 percent tariff on light trucks, which effectively kept European and Japanese car manufacturers out of the U.S. market for SUVs and pickup trucks. (Eventually, some foreign companies built plants in the United States—in southern, antiunion regions—to circumvent the tariff.) For another thing, automakers did not have to design SUVs from scratch, instead using engines and chassis already designed for trucks. The Michigan Truck Plant, which made the Ford Expedition and the Lincoln Navigator, proved to be one of the most profitable manufacturing facilities in human history. With a profit margin of $12,000 on the Expedition and even more on the Navigator, in 1998 its workers produced a pretax profit of $3.7 billion.

Some people bought SUVs for their putative safety, though in reality they were not safer than cars and had serious problems with tipping over and braking. But more important, as in the case of gated communities, fear of crime and the desire for security propelled the market. Upper-income families that bought the very large, very plush SUVs that manufacturers began introducing in the mid-1990s wanted vehicles that looked and felt secure, an antidote, they believed, to criminal attacks and other threats. Carmakers played along, designing their upscale mega-vehicles to appear as menacing as possible, four-wheeled monsters that could be used—or so they looked— to mow down whatever marauding herds of ne'er-do-wells their owners might encounter on their way to work or shop.

And shop they did, as an explosion of consumption took place during the last decades of the century. Much of the buying took place in the suburbs, where the proliferation of shopping centers kept going until there were more than forty-three thousand at the beginning of the new millennium, the supply side of the buying bonanza. Institutional investors replaced family firms as the major players in financing shopping centers, malls, and suburban-sited office buildings. Pension funds, banks no longer constrained by government regulation, and real estate investment trusts (a highly liquid means of owning real estate and mortgages, with significant tax advantages, authorized by Congress in the 1960s) poured billions into suburban development. Half the money to build the largest mall in the country, the vast Mall of America outside Minneapolis–St. Paul, which opened in 1992, came from the Teachers Insurance and Annuity Association (TIAA), a pension fund, set up in 1918, for educators (the more tweedy of whom no doubt would have been appalled by this source of money for their golden years).

Earlier, TIAA had helped finance the Woodfield Shopping Center in Schaumburg, Illinois, an outer suburb of Chicago, which epitomized what Joel Garreau called, in a popular 1988 book, an "edge city," a suburban hub that contained not only housing but major shopping centers, hotels, and office complexes as well. In the mid-1990s, Sears, Roebuck and Company moved its world headquarters from the iconic Sears Tower in downtown Chicago, the country's tallest building, to the nondescript Schaumburg area. The innovative financial engineering of the 1980s and 1990s literally remade the landscape of the nation, as a generally characterless and often banal architecture of mini-manses, strip malls, big shopping centers, and low-rise office buildings wrapped in reflective glass became the built environment for a huge share of the population (an environment largely constructed using nonunion labor, since unions by and large failed to expand into the most rapidly growing parts of the country).

Large discount stores and purveyors of luxury goods dominated the new landscape of selling. The segmentation of wealth and the segmentation of consumption did not fully coincide. Well-off families, as well as ones of more modest means, took advantage of the low prices that could be found at "superstores" like Wal-Mart, which stocked everything from food and clothing to appliances and CDs. They also patronized "big box" stores that specialized in particular categories of items, like electronics, books, and home furnishings. The growing size of houses, with more and more storage space, made it possible for many families to shop at so-called buying club stores like Costco, founded in 1983, low-price bulk sellers that straddled the line between wholesale and retail business. At the other end of the scale, the 1980s and 1990s saw an explosion in the market for luxury goods and things represented as such, not only among the rich but among the middle class too, and even to some extent among the poor. Consumer companies, most iconically Nike, learned to use branding to turn ordinary items like sneakers and polo shirts into premium goods, for which they could charge higher prices and earn higher margins. Premium cars and ice creams and clothing served as treats, small or large, that consumers gave to themselves. Luxury clothing and jewelry stores inhabited the same suburban environment as the big-box stores, often in shopping malls just down the road.

The decline in the cost of food facilitated the shopping boom. During the 1930s, about a third of household spending went to food. At the end of the century, urban households devoted less than 10 percent of their spending to food, freeing up money for other kinds of purchases. But not enough. Stagnating wages, at least until the last half of the 1990s, forced Americans to borrow more and more money to make all this buying possible. Total consumer debt rose from $352 billion in January 1980 to $803 billion in January 1990 and $1.552 trillion in January 2000. Nearly half of it came in the form of credit card debt. By the end of the 1990s, households on average spent over 12 percent of their income on debt service (including mortgages). Ballooning debt would be an important element in the economic collapse that came less than a decade into the new millennium.

As houses and vehicles and shopping centers and credit card bills became larger and larger, so did the bodies of Americans. But in this case the relationship to social class was reversed; the less money people had, the larger their bodies tended to be. In the early 1960s, American men between ages twenty and seventy-four weighed on average 166 pounds and women 140 pounds. By the start of the twenty-first century they had bloated up to 191 and 164 pounds, respectively. (Over those decades, the average height of both men and women had gone up an inch, but the increase in weight proportionately exceeded the increase in height.) Three-fifths of the population was overweight, with one-fifth so much so that its life expectancy was reduced as a result of too many pounds. Americans had become, with the exception of some South Sea islanders, the fattest people in the world.

The bulking up of Americans stemmed from basic metabolic calculus; on average they took in more calories than they had in the past, especially if they were poor, and exercised less, at least if they did not have money. Between 1971 and 2000, the caloric intake of men went up by 7 percent and women by 22 percent. The availability of new, cheaper, high-caloric food ingredients put more affordable calories in easy reach. High-fructose corn syrup, introduced in the early 1970s, tasted six times sweeter than cane sugar and could be cheaply produced from the country's bountiful crop of corn (encouraging even more corn production). By the early 1980s, both Coke and Pepsi were entirely sweetened by corn syrup. Palm oil provided a parallel development for fats, a cheap, highly saturated oil, much of which was imported from Malaysia, which had many of the characteristics of lard and became widely used in commercial baked goods, potato chips, baby formula, and for cooking french fries. The low cost of these ingredients meant that food manufacturers could increase the size of offerings while staying within existing price frames.

Where people ate, and where their food was prepared, shifted, another reason for rising caloric intake. Home-cooked family meals became something of an oddity. The growing time pressure on families—more adults working, workers working more hours, and a decline in fixed, daytime work schedules—meant that in more and more homes getting family members together to eat a home-cooked meal became difficult or impossible. (In 1997, only a bare majority of workers had regular, weekday, daytime jobs, as nighttime, weekend, and irregular work became more common.) Instead, people increasingly ate out, often on the run, or ate take-out meals at home, very often not in family groups but individually. In 1995, 29 percent of all meals were eaten away from home, up from 16 percent in 1977.

Fast-food restaurants, which spread from suburban roadsides to city streets and into institutions like colleges and hospitals, provided billions of those meals. And the meals they provided, on average, had ever more calories. In the 1970s and 1980s, fast-food companies discovered that customers would buy more food and drink when offered combinations of items priced at a discount, so-called value meals, and when the size of offerings grew. A single serving of McDonald's french fries went from 200 calories in 1960 to 320 in the late 1970s, 540 in the late 1990s, and 610 in the early 2000s (at a time when the federal government recommended a total daily input of 1,600 calories for women and 2,200 for men). An oceanic proliferation of high-calorie snack foods also put pounds on bodies. The poor snacked more than the middle and upper classes, and snacking increased more among Hispanics and African Americans than whites, contributing to their higher levels of overweight and obesity.

Young Americans got more calories at school, too. Chronically starved of funds, many school districts, particularly in states like California that had passed tax limitation laws or referenda, did not have the money to maintain cafeterias that cooked food from scratch. Instead, they turned to buying food prepared off-site, often by fast-food companies that specialized in high-calorie items. Many California high schools allowed restaurant chains like Pizza Hut to set up their own vending stations on their campuses, which students preferred to cafeteria fare. And all across the country school districts signed so-called pouring contracts with beverage companies, which in return for cash payments and sometimes a share of their receipts gave the companies the exclusive right to advertise and sell soft drinks—a major source of caloric intake—in district schools.

The tax limitation movement and the squeeze on school finances contributed to the other half of the bloating equation, too, the decline in physical exercise, especially among those in the lower economic strata. Many schools dealt with the requirement in Title IX of the 1972 Education Act that they provide equal funding for boys' and girls' athletics by redistributing funds rather than substantially increasing resources, leading to a decline in standards, at least for boys. In 1976, California allowed school districts to entirely exempt high school juniors and seniors from physical education requirements. More generally, the coincidence of the fitness boom of the 1970s and beyond with the era of tax caps and denunciations of the public sector meant that the infrastructure for exercise and sports increasingly grew up in the private sector rather than in schools and public recreation facilities. Poor children, without nearby parks or public gyms or public recreation workers or a stay-at-home parent with the time to shuttle them to the private soccer and other youth sports leagues that burgeoned during this era, had fewer opportunities to engage in sports or exercise than their wealthier peers.

As children spent more time watching television and playing video and computer games, youth fitness suffered. But not all groups suffered equally. Poor, African American, and Mexican American children watched more television than white and well-off children, with associated consequences for weight and health. In many cases, their parents encouraged them to do so because their neighborhoods were so dangerous that the health risks of violence and drugs outside their homes exceeded the risks of physical inactivity within them. The decline in manufacturing also contributed to weight gain, as more workers sat in sedentary jobs. Culture, ethnicity, gender, and race all mattered in body size, but the most important variable in determining the likelihood of obesity was economic class.

In spite of growing bigger, Americans lived longer. Life expectancy at birth rose to just under seventy-seven years in 2000 (seventy-four years for men, seventy-nine and a half for women), from seventy-three in 1975. Blacks had a life expectancy of seventy-two years, whites a bit over seventy-seven, a modest narrowing of the gap over the previous quarter century. By this most basic of health measures, Americans were doing very well.

But some others were doing even better: Australians, Belgians, British, Canadians, Dutch, French, Germans, Greeks, Italians, Japanese, and Spaniards all could expect to live longer. Differences in social structures and health-care delivery systems accounted for most of the gap. Although the United States spent a much larger share of its GNP on health care than other countries, a substantial number of its residents didn't have easy access to medical services due to a lack of health insurance (universal in almost every other advanced industrial nation) or an absence of nearby medical facilities. In part for this reason, the United States had a higher infant mortality rate than most industrialized countries. Other particularities of American life also retarded the country's health standing compared to other industrial nations. Driving more meant a higher death rate from motor vehicle accidents. More firearms meant more firearms deaths, over twice the number per capita than in France and thirty-four times the rate in England and Wales, which had very strict gun control laws. More obesity portended more cardiovascular and coronary heart disease and led to an epidemic of type 2 diabetes, including among children, for whom it rarely had been a problem until the 1990s. One demographic historian concluded that at the start of the twenty-first century, "a large share of the American population," more likely to be poor and nonwhite than the rest, had "health standards more common to less developed countries than to the advanced industrial world."

Global Impact

Living large had planetary effects. In 1997, the United States, with less than 5 percent of the world's population, consumed almost a quarter of the energy used by human society. Per person, the United States used twice the amount of energy as Germany, France, and Great Britain. Globally, it was responsible for nearly a quarter of the emissions from fossil fuel.

The whole suburban system of living, working, and shopping depended on large amounts of low-cost energy. The ever-bigger, single-family houses that Americans bought required large amounts of energy to heat and cool. By the early twenty-first century, almost 90 percent of new homes and virtually all new cars had air-conditioning. Increasingly, people and businesses left air-conditioning running all the time. (The United States used more electricity for air-conditioning than the total amount of electricity used in India, a country with more than three times its population.) Because of the increased popularity of SUVs and pickup trucks, the average fuel economy for new passenger vehicles actually fell during the 1990s, from 22.1 miles per gallon in 1987 to 20.8 miles in 2003.

Even the vast amount of lawn that came with suburbanization—the country had an estimated twenty-five to forty million acres of domesticated grass—pushed up energy usage. To keep lawns green and looking vigorous, Americans applied huge amounts of fertilizer made from natural gas. To cut, trim, clear, and manicure lawns and yards, power lawn mowers, leaf blowers, and other motorized equipment was deployed, usually in the hands of low-paid immigrant workers, as Latinos came to dominate the lawn care workforce. (All that equipment made a racket, so the roar of the small-bore gasoline engine became one of the sensory markers of suburban life.) The EPA estimated that seventeen million gallons of gasoline were spilled each summer in the course of trying to refuel lawn mowers and other garden machinery, nearly twice the estimated amount of petroleum that leaked into Prince William Sound, Alaska, in 1989 from the *Exxon Valdez* in one of the most notorious environmental disasters in the country's history.

What made the consequences of the high-energy, high-pollution way of life in the United States so globally significant was the country's large and growing population. Measured per person, energy use in the United States essentially plateaued from the mid-1970s on, as appliances and industry became more efficient, but with more and more people each year, the total energy consumption of the country kept rising. Eighty percent of the country's energy (in 2000) came from fossil fuels, so rising energy consumption meant increased emission of carbon dioxide, the main greenhouse gas responsible for global warming.

Similarly, per capita water use dropped by 25 percent during the last quarter of the twentieth century as a result of more efficient appliances and local and state conservation efforts, but growing population resulted in a small increase in total water use. (Nearly half the water went to cooling power plants and another third to irrigation.) While in much of the country water resources remained plentiful, in the arid West, with its fast-growing population, getting all the water that agricultural businesses sought along with supplying residential and industrial needs became an increasing problem. In dry years it simply could not be done. The Ogallala Aquifer, the largest single source of groundwater in the country (underlying eight states in the Southwest and Great Plains) dropped an average of a foot a year from the 1970s on, as withdrawals far exceeded natural replenishment.

Without substantial technological or social changes, late-twentieth-century American life was unsustainable on a long-term basis. So many people living so large required such large amounts of energy, water, and other resources and produced so much pollution, including greenhouse gases, that over time inputs inevitably would be depleted and outputs severely damage the environment, locally and globally. Yet the country, by and large, kept doing more of the same, a collective self-destructiveness that could be seen as a kind of social psychosis.

Many people did not believe that pollution or climate warming or resource depletion were serious problems or had faith that they could be addressed by gradual future changes or technological fixes. After all, the country had faced serious problems in the past and overcome them. The lived experience of most Americans was of an improved environment, not its degradation. Largely as a result of legislation passed in the 1960s and 1970s, rivers and drinking water had become cleaner, the air less smoggy, and open dumps of waste less common. Many of the most severe environmental problems of the late twentieth century, like increased greenhouse emissions, did not have easily observable effects. Also, because a disproportionate number of polluting facilities, from petrochemical plants to dumps to sewage treatment plants, were located in neighborhoods of poor, working-class, or nonwhite residents, members of the politically and culturally influential white middle class were less touched by the downside of living large.

Economic interest often overcame ecological concern. It never had been a secret that the world had only a limited amount of oil, which was being used up at a good clip, and that burning gasoline resulted in dangerous emissions. Yet the automobile industry, seeing mandated energy efficiency as a threat to its profits, led long, largely successful campaigns against raising fuel consumption standards and uniformly regulating all passenger vehicles, including SUVs. The auto companies mobilized allies with political clout to support them, most importantly auto dealers and the United Automobile Workers. Though the union supported environmentalism in general, during the George H. W. Bush, Clinton, and George W. Bush administrations it lobbied successfully against efforts to significantly raise fuel efficiency requirements, buying into the industry argument that tougher controls would lead to a loss of jobs.

Population size, which along with per capita resource usage and pollution determined the environmental impact of American society, rarely was addressed during the 1980s and 1990s. Before then, there had been a great deal of discussion of controlling population abroad and, to a lesser extent, in the United States. In the late 1960s, both major parties took for granted the need to limit population in the face of the rapidly growing number of people on the planet. The federal government linked foreign aid to the willingness of recipient countries to establish population control programs. Advocates focused their efforts on poor, nonwhite countries with high rates of population growth, a heritage of the eugenics movement that helped spawn the push to limit population. But some promoters of population control argued for its need in the United States, too. Stanford University entomologist Paul Ehrlich, whose 1968 book *The Population Bomb* sold two million copies by the mid-1970s, suggested that the optimal population of the United States would be about seventy-five million.

The most complete federal statement on population came from a commission appointed by Richard Nixon, headed by John D. Rockefeller Jr., a longtime advocate of population planning. Its 1972 report said that "in the long run, no substantial benefits will result from further growth of the Nation's population." The report identified one aspect of the "population problem" as "the effect on natural resources of increased numbers of people in search of a higher standard of living." Its proposals to achieve a "gradual stabilization of . . . population" included education in the schools about population; sex education "available to all"; state laws "affirming the desirability that all persons have ready and practicable access to contraceptive information, procedures, and supplies"; the elimination of legal restrictions on voluntary sterilization and abortion; more funds for family planning; measures to reduce illegal immigration; freezing the level of legal immigration; and periodically reviewing immigration policy "to reflect demographic conditions and considerations."

The sweeping recommendations of the Rockefeller Commission came out of a political moment that proved short-lived. The many dissenting statements by commission members presaged a shift against population control. Nixon himself, under pressure from the Catholic hierarchy, rejected the recommendations of his commission. In the 1968 encyclical "Humanae Vitae," Pope Paul VI reaffirmed church opposition to any use of abortion, sterilization, or artificial contraception. Around the world, the church took the lead in fighting population control programs with remarkable effectiveness, joined in the United States by conservatives of other faiths, as abortion became an ever more prominent issue. The Reagan administration acceded to the church and other abortion opponents when it instituted a policy of refusing to give money to international family planning programs that provided or funded groups that provided abortion services.

Even many supporters of contraception and abortion mobilized against the population control movement, denouncing it for its historic concentration on the poor and nonwhites while paying little attention to the social and environmental impact of the high-consumption ways of well-off nations and individuals. (The Johnson administration had concentrated its domestic population control efforts on Puerto Rico and other U.S. island possessions, Indian reservations, and inner-city residents.) Also, many population control backers were willing to deny women control over their bodies. Such gender, class, and racial biases became increasingly unacceptable in the wake of the civil rights movement, feminism, and decolonization. Moreover, as Malthusian predictions by population control advocates like Ehrlich that population growth would lead to mass starvation and global chaos proved false, much of the argument justifying the movement disappeared. So by the 1990s, population growth was rarely discussed as a problem within the United States, except as an occasional subsidiary part of arguments against immigration.

Most Americans did not consciously reject the idea that a growing society living large had negative consequences for the national and global environment and might be unsustainable. Rather, they simply did not think about it. People lived large because they could. Living in big houses, driving big cars, going to big malls, even being big, brought physical, psychological, and spiritual satisfactions. Living large created a sense of well-being, of security, of power, a sense of worth and superiority. Just as the aftermath of the Cold War renewed the U.S. sense of limitless power abroad, the unevenly distributed economic bounty of the 1980s and 1990s allowed a large upper stratum of society to have a sense of limitlessness in its lifestyle and consumption. Others liked to live large too, even if it only took the form of consuming a very large serving of fast food washed down by a very large cup of soda. Americans had developed the habit of believing themselves exempt from history and the consequences of their actions. Led by men and women doing very well at the expense of the rest of the society, most Americans had little interest in spurning whatever possibilities lay before them for the comforts of a high-consumption way of life.

America After 9/11

On September 11, 2001, Deputy Secretary of State Richard Armitage declared, "History begins today." He was meeting with the head of the Pakistani intelligence service, who happened to be in Washington when al Qaeda terrorists flew hijacked airplanes into the twin towers of New York's World Trade Center and the Pentagon and hijacked a fourth plane, which crashed in Pennsylvania after passengers tried to seize control. Armitage warned that the United States gave no brief to the history that led Pakistan to support the Taliban government in Afghanistan, which was allowing Osama bin Laden to operate there. But Armitage's assertion had a broader meaning, widely shared in Washington and the nation, that a radical disjuncture had taken place. President George W. Bush said that on September 11 "night fell on a different world."

The 9/11 attacks and the reaction to them seemed to start a new phase of American history. Within less than two years, the United States began two wars, declared it had the right to take preemptive military action against countries it deemed threatening, and hardened its campaign against terrorism to include torturing prisoners captured abroad. At home, the government undertook a sweeping security program that included electronic surveillance without warrants, intrusive searches at airports, and color-coded alerts that raised and lowered national anxiety. In the process, Washington accrued new powers, often with little public debate or even public knowledge. The enhanced powers of the state were not restricted to security; in 2008, when the economy nosedived, the government lent hundreds of billions of dollars to banks and financial firms with much secrecy and little oversight.

The United States felt different in 2011 than it had ten years earlier. But much that seemed novel after 9/11 had roots in the previous fifty-six years, in the country's quest for international power and stability, in struggles over the meaning of democracy, in debate over the proper role of government, in the push to expand mass consumption, in the shift from industry to finance, and in changing ideas of national greatness. The troubled first decade of the twenty-first century represented the legacy of postwar America as much as a break from it.

September 11, the War on Terrorism, and the Costs of Empire

The 9/11 attacks came out of history, not from outside it. For over a half century, the United States had pursued an expansive international political, economic, military, and cultural presence. Across the world it figured large, directly and indirectly, in the lives of billions of people, just as life within the United States depended more than ever on what happened outside it. Before World War II, it would have been difficult to imagine that developments in so distant a place as Afghanistan mattered to many Americans, but a half century of imperial reach brought echoes of events halfway around the world back home, sometimes with deadly effect.

September 11 stunned America. There had not been a foreign-launched attack on the United States proper since 1814. The scale of death and suffering in New York, Washington, and Pennsylvania exceeded the toll of any accident or violent incident since World War II. The experience millions of Americans had watching the 110-story World Trade Center towers collapse, live on television, had no precedent, as the solidity of their society seemed to disintegrate before their eyes.

During the years after World War II, most Americans had believed their country to be benign in its global activities, helping others as much as promoting its own interests, leaving the country ill-prepared for the murderous hostility it faced on 9/11. In his justifications for terrorism, bin Laden, while denouncing "Crusaders," Jews, and Western involvement in the Middle East, pointed to specific historical events and political grievances, including the establishment of U.S. military bases in Saudi Arabia prior to the first Gulf War, Western control of Middle Eastern resources, and American backing for Israel and corrupt Arab regimes. Washington spurned any effort to review the events, circumstances, and policies that led to 9/11, as if that would somehow excuse the attacks or shift blame away from the perpetrators. The attacks, the president repeatedly said, were an act of evil, the work of "evildoers," positioning them as a form of moral and spiritual pathology rather than an outgrowth of political and military conflict. Bush's rhetoric echoed the Manichean formulations used during World War II and the Cold War that counterposed free and slave worlds, good and evil, rights and repression. Like Harry Truman before him, Bush described a battle not over national interests or geostrategy but over a "way of life."

Though the huge military-security apparatus that the United States had built up since the outbreak of World War II had failed to protect it on 9/11, seven decades of militarism conditioned American leaders to see the problem of terrorism in martial terms. The Bush administration responded to the attacks by launching a "war on terror" directed at "every terrorist of global reach" and "any nation that continues to harbor or support terrorism." Just hours after the attacks, Secretary of Defense Donald Rumsfeld, according to the notes of one of his aides, said the United States had to "go massive— sweep it all up—things related and not" to bin Laden.

Many senior figures in the Bush administration had held government posts during the latter part of the Cold War and had sought to build up military strength to counter the Soviet bloc. Once the Soviet Union collapsed, the major restraint on the use of military power disappeared. Easy victories against overmatched opponents like Grenada, Panama, Serbia, and Iraq (the first time) fueled overconfidence in the ability of the United States to reshape other nations and bred a recklessness that American leaders had generally avoided during the Cold War.

At first it seemed that the United States would be able to leverage its technological and economic superiority to project military power and impose order on its own terms. Right after 9/11, the United States demanded that the Afghan government turn over al Qaeda leaders and close the group's training camps. When the Taliban government refused, the United States launched a military offensive against it, using a combination of airpower, special forces, and intelligence operatives and massive cash outlays to buy the cooperation of warlords and dissident political factions. Within two months, the Taliban regime collapsed.

But the victory turned out to be far from complete. The new Afghan government, headed by exiled anti-Taliban leader Hamid Karzai, proved limited in its ability to exert its authority, allowing for the eventual resurgence of the Taliban. Renewed violence took an increasing toll on American forces, with 1,446 deaths as of the end of 2010. And while the United States succeeded in shutting down al Qaeda operations in Afghanistan and killing many members of the group, bin Laden managed to escape into Pakistan when American armed forces failed to mobilize sufficient troops to surround him during a fierce battle in the Tora Bora mountains in late 2001.

Even as the World Trade Center and Pentagon smoldered, Rumsfeld, his deputy, Paul Wolfowitz, and other Bush administration leaders pressed for a response that encompassed more than going after terrorists. September 11, they believed, presented the opportunity for a broader reordering of the world, especially the Middle East, along lines congenial to American interests and values. Getting rid of Iraqi leader Saddam Hussein, they argued, would be a start toward reconstructing the Middle East and a demonstration to terrorists and hostile states of the reach of American power and its willingness to use it.

The Bush administration put forth two reasons for invading Iraq. Most importantly, it claimed that Iraq had defied UN resolutions demanding it shut down its programs to develop chemical, biological, and nuclear weapons of mass destruction [WMD]. Bush and Vice President Dick Cheney also claimed that Saddam had ties to al Qaeda and promoted terrorism. Both assertions were false. In July 2002, the head of British foreign intelligence reported after meetings in Washington, "Bush wanted to remove Saddam, through military action, justified by the conjunction of terrorism and WMD. But the intelligence and facts were being fixed around the policy." That summer a senior Bush adviser told a reporter, "We're an empire now, and when we act, we create our own reality."

During the Bush administration, the United States behaved more frankly as an imperial power than at any time since the early twentieth century. In a June 2002 speech at West Point, Bush said the Cold War strategies of deterrence and containment did not suffice against new kinds of threats. In the face of terrorism and "unbalanced dictators with weapons," the United States needed "to be ready for preemptive action."

The Iraq War implemented the doctrine. The United States attacked Iraq because it seemed like it could, at relatively low cost; supply-side war. Kenneth Adelman, a onetime aide to Rumsfeld and Jeane Kirkpatrick, captured the mood of conservatives when he wrote in the *Washington Post* that "liberating Iraq would be a cakewalk."

Post-9/11 fear, patriotism, and deference to authority facilitated the drive to war. The media swallowed whole-hog false administration claims, with liberal newspapers like the *New York Times* and the *Washington Post* beating the drums of war. Large demonstrations against an invasion of Iraq, at home and around the world, had no impact on the actions of the United States and its allies. Some Republicans and Democrats opposed invading Iraq, but the president easily won congressional authorization for military action.

Within three weeks of the initial attack on Iraq in mid-March 2003, American forces captured Baghdad and the Iraqi army melted away. The war, though, had just begun.

Bush administration leaders thought that removing Saddam and his circle would be all that was needed to create a new, democratic, free-market Iraq, given what they believed was a sophisticated society, with oil reserves that could pay for reconstruction, and a population they assumed would be grateful to the United States for ridding it of a brutal dictator. They pointed to post–World War II Germany and Japan as examples of how democratic societies could emerge under U.S. tutelage once autocratic regimes had been decapitated.

Nothing could have been more wrong. In Germany and Japan, not a single U.S. soldier was killed during their occupations. Over four thousand Americans died during the occupation of Iraq. Bush and his closest advisers paid little attention to postwar planning, having rejected before taking office the idea that the United States should get itself involved in "nation building." Instead, they assumed that the Iraqi military and police would maintain postwar order, while a new political leadership would quickly emerge and the economy would blossom with privatization and increased oil production.

None of this happened. Instead, as soon as U.S. troops reached Baghdad, looting began. It continued for weeks, as American soldiers stood by, too few, as a result of Rumsfeld's lean war plan, to impose order. By the time the looting ended, innumerable industrial facilities and almost every government building, from the national museum to ministry headquarters to ammunition dumps, had been stripped of everything of value, making it impossible to quickly restore any semblance of normality and putting tons of arms and explosives into circulation. Within months, serious military resistance to the occupation ramped up from Saddam loyalists, anti-occupation nationalists and Shiite groups, and foreign terrorists who flocked to Iraq, eager to take on the Americans. Sectarian violence, primarily between Shia and Sunni, took a ghastly toll.

As the Bush administration belatedly realized it would have to actually administer Iraq, it assembled an occupation bureaucracy stunning in its incomprehension and incompetence. Since World War II, the United States had developed far-reaching global interests while remaining parochial in its domestic culture, leaving it ill-equipped for old-fashioned, on-the-ground imperialism. The head of the Coalition Provisional Authority (CPA), L. Paul Bremer, a longtime diplomat and associate of Henry Kissinger's, styling himself an imperial consul like MacArthur in Japan, quickly made a series of disastrous decisions, including banning every member of Saddam's Baath Party from government service and dissolving the Iraqi army, leaving tens of thousands of armed men without pay, many of whom joined the anti-occupation insurgency.

The CPA staff had little expertise or experience in postwar reconstruction or the Middle East. As in Vietnam, the United States tried to run another country from a small island of America, the "Green Zone" in the heart of Baghdad, complete with swimming pool, sports bars, American food, a fleet of SUVs, and almost no Americans who could speak Arabic. Recent college graduates with connections to the Republican Party or conservative think tanks were given huge authority over a country they knew nothing about. As what started as a brief conventional war morphed into a long, brutal counterinsurgency struggle, more and more Iraqis turned against the American-led coalition.

After years of fighting and a "surge" of U.S. troops sent to Iraq in 2007, violence in the country diminished and the government set up after national elections took increasing responsibility for basic state functions. But Iraq remained violent, unstable, and underdeveloped. Five years after the invasion, electricity production only modestly exceeded the preinvasion level, which had been depressed by years of international sanctions, making infrastructure development and maintenance difficult. Oil production remained below what it had been under Saddam.

The cost of the war was horrendous. For the United States, it was the bloodiest conflict since Vietnam. An estimated 100,000 Iraqi civilians died.

A vast expansion of the national security apparatus accompanied the war on terror. One of the great changes in American life after World War II had been the development of a national security state, which in the name of fighting communism and other dangers engaged in a wide range of often secret activities. The end of the Cold War brought a modest cutback in covert surveillance and policing, but 9/11 reversed that trend, as the security sector grew larger, more intrusive, and more willing to push legal and constitutional limits.

The shock, fear, and national unity after 9/11 enabled the Bush administration to accrue extraordinary powers. In late October 2001, Congress, with massive majorities, passed the USA Patriot Act, which expanded authority for domestic wiretapping, allowed the government to track Internet and financial activity, and eased the requirements for search warrants. Congress appropriated $40 billion for domestic security and the fight against al Qaeda, followed by over $80 billion more over the course of the next two years. Bush established the Office of Homeland Security, later made a cabinet department, which took over border security and immigration control and included the Transportation Security Administration, set up to replace the private contractors providing air travel security. By the end of the decade, the counterterrorism apparatus had grown staggeringly large, according to the *Washington Post* involving over a thousand government agencies and nearly two thousand private companies working at ten thousand locations, with an estimated 854,000 people holding top-secret security clearances.

Some steps the Bush administration took secretly, without congressional approval, including setting up a program of warrantless electronic domestic surveillance. Bush directives denied captured foreign terror suspects access to any court, allowed them to be held indefinitely without charges, and permitted the use of "enhanced interrogation techniques" that in some cases amounted to torture. In February 2002, Bush announced that the United States would not consider the Geneva Conventions on the treatment of prisoners of war, to which it was party, applicable to fighters captured in the war on terror.

In choosing to conduct the antiterror campaign as it did, the Bush administration was promoting an agenda that predated 9/11. Many of its top members bemoaned what they saw as a weakening of the executive branch, especially the presidency, in the wake of Vietnam and Watergate. Reversing a historical pattern in which liberals had been the main backers of a strong presidency, conservatives embraced the idea of a potent executive branch. Dick Cheney—more powerful than any previous vice president— aggressively promoted far-reaching presidential action unrestrained by congressional or court oversight, international agreements, or public disclosure.

The U.S. government used all the power it gave itself, and then some, to try to extract information from captives accused of terrorism. Some suspects were handed over to allies that the United States knew would use rough treatment or torture to extract information, so-called rendition. Others were whisked off to secret CIA prisons set up around the world, where they were subjected to isolation, violence, and torture (often conducted by contractors, part of a general policy of hiring civilian companies to do work once done by military, intelligence, and police organizations). For less important captives, the United States erected a large prison complex, with open-air cages, at its Guantánamo Bay base in Cuba.

Though such post-9/11 practices shocked many Americans when they eventually were revealed, seen as departures from long-standing notions of law, morality, and national values, they had historical roots. The most notorious torture technique used after 9/11, waterboarding, the simulated drowning of prisoners, was a variation of a torture method used by the U.S. Army on Filipino independence fighters early in the twentieth century. During the Cold War, the federal government had been explicit in saying that it would do whatever was necessary to defend the United States, and it did many unsavory things, from attempting assassinations to supporting death squads to using mind-altering drugs and other coercive techniques in interrogations. But the revelations of torture at CIA detention centers, the leaking of photographs of American soldiers abusing Iraqi prisoners at the Abu Ghraib prison, and the shooting of Iraqi civilians by contractors working for the American government undermined the claims by the United States of moral superiority, on which the justification for its wars partly rested, and presented a disturbing image of what kind of society it had become.

Americans selectively looked to the past to guide themselves forward. In his diary, Bush called 9/11 "the Pearl Harbor of the 21st Century" and took to calling himself a "war president," putting himself in the same category as Lincoln and FDR. The media called the site of the collapsed World Trade Center "ground zero," an adoption of the World War II term for the point directly below the nuclear bombs exploded at the Trinity test site and in Japan. In his 2002 State of the Union address, Bush used the phrase "axis of evil" to describe Iraq, Iran, and North Korea, recalling Germany, Japan, and Italy, the Axis powers of the Second World War. Later, in announcing the end of major combat in Iraq on the aircraft carrier USS *Abraham Lincoln*, the White House drew on the dramaturgy of the Japanese surrender aboard the USS *Missouri* in Tokyo Bay, with a speechwriter consulting General MacArthur's address in preparing Bush's remarks. (Bush also looked to World War II in rejecting anything like the internment of Japanese Americans and seeking to minimize public and government discrimination against Muslims.) But analogies to the past obscured the changes that had taken place in the United States and its circumstances. Al Qaeda, a small if deadly organization, never represented the existential threat to the United States once posed by Germany and Japan and later by the Soviet Union, while North Korea, Iraq, and Iran had far fewer resources and much more modest records of aggression than the original Axis powers.

To the extent that global military power had once served Americans well, its worth became less clear as its cost in lives, dollars, and international standing mounted. The Bush administration wars, especially Iraq, dissipated the worldwide goodwill toward the United States evident after 9/11. The United States proved itself to be a can't-do imperial power, an incompetent, blustering, sometimes brutal nation, whose hubris and carelessness caused enormous harm to its allies, those it claimed to be helping, and itself. Yet empire had become so interwoven in the fabric of American life that even as public support for the Iraq and Afghanistan wars diminished, issues of war and peace and foreign policy remained subsidiary notes in national politics and discussion.

Reaganism Redux

During the dark days after 9/11, few Americans anticipated the kinds of hardship their country would go through when the economy plunged into a severe recession in 2008. The quarter century after World War II had been a period of exceptionally robust growth and shared benefits, laying the basis for a democratic revolution in politics and culture. The next quarter century saw slower growth, stagnant income for most Americans, growing inequality, and a shift of power to the private sector. But only on the fringes of political discourse did suggestions arise that the American system of political economy might not be sustainable. The free fall after 2008 changed that, making it painfully obvious that the economy no longer served most Americans as well as it once had.

In domestic policy, the Bush administration in many respects amounted to a rerun of the Reagan years. Like Reagan, Bush believed the country would prosper if the government reduced its role in the economy, giving free rein to market forces. Like Reagan, he gave top priority to tax-cutting, especially for the well-off, and loosening of government regulations. Though the bitter partisan battling that characterized the Clinton years continued and fights over so-called social issues like abortion rights, embryonic stem cell research, and gay marriage raged, few significant changes in public policy occurred. Instead, the major transformations in daily life largely resulted from developments in the economy, especially the financial sector, continuing the pattern since the 1970s that increasingly put the power to shape society in private hands.

When Bush took office, the federal government was well on its way toward paying off the entire national debt for the first time since 1835, having run budget surpluses for four consecutive years. Bush wanted to distribute excess federal funds through tax cuts, arguing, "The surplus is not the government's money; the surplus is the people's money," a Reaganite formulation that did not see government, as Abraham Lincoln did, "of the people, by the people, for the people," but in opposition to them. The recession that began in March 2001, following the collapse of the stock market bubble, led the newly inaugurated president to shift his argument for lower taxes to the need for an economic stimulus. Congress gave him most of what he wanted, a $1.3 trillion tax cut that reduced both the top and bottom income tax rates and increased the amount exempt from estate taxes ("death taxes," Bush called them).

The 9/11 attacks hurt an economy already in trouble, leading to a 20 percent drop in stock prices and a jump in unemployment. Bush sought to boost the weak economy with another tax cut, heavily skewed to the rich. With the federal government already having gone from running a surplus to running a deficit and the cost of the war on terror soaring, the second round of tax cuts faced more opposition than the first. But with the vice president casting the deciding vote in a deadlocked Senate, in May 2003 Congress accelerated the implementation of the previous tax cuts, lowered the top rate for capital gains and dividend taxes, and increased depreciation allowances for small businesses. Most taxpayers ended up with only slightly smaller tax bills, but wealthy payers got very substantial reductions.

The Bush administration seemed at ease with the rising tide of red ink created by its tax policy. Cheney reportedly said, "Reagan proved deficits don't matter." Bush took no steps to increase revenue even as the national debt ballooned over the course of his presidency from $3.3 trillion, representing 33 percent of GDP, to $5.8 trillion, 41 percent of GDP.

While the United States had gone through periods of high deficits in the past without lasting damage, Bush broke all precedent in not seeking new taxes to finance the wars the country was fighting. Afghanistan and Iraq had immediate fiscal consequences, accounting for about a third of the deficits run up between 2004 and 2006. Their long-run cumulative costs (including expenses that would continue for decades, such as medical care for injured soldiers) were staggering, by one estimate reaching roughly $2 trillion by 2011, $17,000 for every household in the country. One of the president's few successful domestic initiatives, a prescription drug plan for senior citizens approved by Congress in 2003, also proved costly.

The drug plan and the 2001 education law, No Child Left Behind, reflected Bush's willingness to support some expansion of the welfare state, especially if market mechanisms were employed. But more broadly, especially in economic regulation, the Bush administration displayed hostility to government action. Like Reagan, Bush used funding cuts, administrative action, and staffing decisions to undermine or diminish regulatory standards and enforcement. Though as a candidate he had acknowledged the problem of global warming and pledged to address it, once in office he reversed course, refusing to ratify the UN Kyoto Protocol on global warming and challenging the scientific consensus that human activity was altering atmospheric conditions.

Bush administration skepticism of government and expertise—a well-established conservative outlook—contributed to its catastrophic bungling of rescue and relief efforts during Hurricane Katrina in 2005 (much as it did to the failed occupation of Iraq). Bush's first head of the Federal Emergency

Management Agency (FEMA), his longtime aide Joe M. Allbaugh, told Congress that the agency had become "an oversized entitlement program." Bush put political allies with no expertise in handling emergencies into top agency posts. Placed within the Department of Homeland Security in 2003, FEMA saw resources and attention diverted to counterterrorism.

When Hurricane Katrina bore down on New Orleans, top FEMA officials received up-to-the-minute reports on the horrendous damage it was wreaking. But as levees gave way, flooding much of the city, FEMA did little to help overwhelmed local and state agencies, having failed to pre-position necessary supplies or mobilize federal assets. While television networks broadcast images of people stranded on roofs, floating on mattresses, and clinging to trees, as conditions at a domed football stadium being used as a mass shelter became hellish and looting broke out across the city, the federal government remained inert and oblivious, with the president congratulating FEMA director Michael Brown for a job well done, when in reality the agency had barely swung into action.

An estimated eleven hundred people died in New Orleans as a result of Katrina. It is impossible to say how many could have been saved if the full resources of the U.S. government had been mobilized in a timely, effective manner, but surely the death toll would have been lower and the suffering less. Live television coverage of a major American city being essentially abandoned to its terrible fate shocked the nation and the rest of the world. Driven by an ideological aversion to government, cronyism, and a view of national security narrowly focused on terrorism, the Bush administration failed to protect the lives and safety of Americans when a predictable and predicted crisis arrived, a damning measure of how inept the world's only superpower had become.

Bubble and Bust

Borrowed money fueled the economy during the Bush years, inflating an unprecedented bubble in housing prices. For a while, housing-driven growth masked fundamental economic problems, including stagnant income, growing inequality, declining manufacturing, and huge trade imbalances. When the housing bubble burst in 2007 and 2008, it brought down the financial sector, which had profited enormously from selling dubious mortgage-related securities, plunging the United States into its worst economic crisis since the Great Depression.

Government policy helped create the debt-based post-9/11 bubble economy. The Federal Reserve responded to the 2001 recession by lowering interest rates to historically low levels and keeping them there, even after the economy began to recover. In 2003 and 2004, the Fed set interest rates below the rate of inflation, an extraordinary inducement to private borrowing.

Over time, borrowing had become ever more important to keeping the economy going because of the stagnation of earnings, except for the wealthy, since the 1970s and the decline in personal savings. Consumer spending and the stimulus it provided to the economy depended on borrowed money. Federal deficit spending provided further stimulus.

The Bush-era borrowing spree was possible because foreigners were willing to lend massive amounts of money to the government and consumers. By 2008, nearly a third of mortgage debt was owed to foreigners, as was two-thirds of federal borrowing. Some money flowed in from abroad because investors believed they could make good profits, for example by buying securitized mortgages. But with interest rates low, money came for other reasons as well. Foreign governments, institutions, and individuals saw Treasury bonds as extremely safe investments, a good place to park money even if the return would be negligible. Countries that exported goods to the United States, most importantly China, bought its debt to keep the dollar strong, which made it cheap for Americans to buy foreign-produced goods.

For a while it seemed like sheer magic, a system in which everyone won: the U.S. government could cut taxes even as it fought expensive wars; consumers could borrow vast amounts of money at low interest rates to buy houses, cars, and other goods; foreign governments could keep their money safe and their factories humming; and the financial sector could profit handsomely from all the lending and borrowing, with its share of GDP rising to 8.3 percent in 2007, from 7.0 percent in 1998. But the growing mountain of debt eventually toppled, because real economic growth occurred at too slow a rate to support it.

Even before the collapse, between 2000 and 2007 the United States lost three and a half million manufacturing jobs. Though some economic sectors shielded from international competition did well, including construction (which benefited from the housing boom), retail (which had lots of cheap imported goods to sell), and hospitality, overall economic growth was anemic. The GDP rose an average of 2.3 percent a year between 2000 and 2007, well below the rate in the previous decade, the decade before that, and the decade before that. The mighty economic engine, once based on making, growing, and processing things, which had propelled the United States to world greatness and transformed life at home, was slowly winding down.

The housing boom accounted for much of the growth that did occur. Housing prices had begun to rise faster than inflation during the late 1990s and kept rising as the Federal Reserve drove down interest rates and new lending practices expanded the pool of buyers. Because median family income remained flat, even after the economy recovered from the recession of the early 2000s, the number of families eligible for mortgages did not rise. So financial institutions, with the backing of the government, lowered the qualifications and documentation needed for loans. The policy reflected the financial sector's quest for robust profits in a slow-growing economy and the long-standing national belief in homeownership as a social good. Subprime mortgages that did not require borrowers to meet traditional criteria accounted for a quarter of all home loans by 2006 and helped push up the homeownership rate to a historic peak. In 2004, 69 percent of American families owned their own home.

Mortgage lenders were willing to make riskier loans because increasingly they only briefly retained them, selling them to other financial institutions, which bundled them into large pools—supposedly to lower the risk—and then selling securities backed by the income stream from those mortgage packages. To further reduce the risk, many buyers of such securitized instruments also bought credit default swaps, a lightly regulated form of insurance.

Home prices rose on average 51 percent between 2000 and 2005. In some areas, especially in the South and Southwest, the increases were staggering. The average price of a home in Los Angeles went from $161,000 in 1995 to $228,000 in 2000 and $585,000 in 2006. Such valuations led to a wave of speculation—in 2004 nearly a quarter of homes were bought as investments, not for owner occupation—further fueling price hikes. Soaring home prices allowed millions of Americans to get cash for other purchases by remortgaging their homes or taking out home equity loans. As long as house prices kept increasing, homeowners remained confident that they could pay back their growing debt when they eventually sold their houses.

It all worked as long as house prices kept rising, but at some point, as occurs with all bubbles, prices began to fall, at first slowly, beginning in mid-2006, then at a stomach-wrenching rate, down 10 percent during the second half of 2007 and 20 percent in 2008. As prices dropped, owners were unable to keep pulling money out of their homes, pushing down the increase in personal consumer spending to near zero in 2008. By the start of 2009, a sixth of houses with mortgages were worth less than their owners had borrowed, leading many families to simply walk away from their loans. More than one-fifth of homes being sold were in foreclosure, further driving down prices and effectively shutting down new construction.

The housing crisis spread to the financial sector as mortgage defaults began leading to defaults on mortgage-backed securities, or the fear of default, which caused their value to plummet. Hedge funds holding such securities began to totter as investors tried to withdraw their money, forcing large asset sales, depressing prices even more. Banks facing huge potential losses became reluctant to lend money for any purpose at all.

By the second half of 2007, the economy was sinking toward recession, with the Federal Reserve trying, unsuccessfully, to shore up the financial system. In March 2008, the giant brokerage firm Bear Stearns had to be bailed out. When in September 2008 Lehman Brothers went bankrupt, leading to something close to a worldwide credit halt, it seemed possible that the entire financial system would melt down. Federal Reserve chairman Ben Bernanke told congressional leaders and Bush administration policymakers, "We are headed for the worst financial crisis in the nation's history. . . . We're talking about a matter of days."

As the Bush administration drew to a close, Congress, scared into action, allocated $700 billion for a financial rescue program to be shaped by the Treasury, with few guidelines and little oversight. By pumping massive streams of taxpayer money into the banks whose poor judgment and lack of due diligence had driven the country to the edge of catastrophe, the federal government managed to keep the financial system afloat. But with the collapse of the housing market and the credit crunch, the country slipped into the most serious recession in over three-quarters of a century.

The 2008 crisis had been a long time in the making. In its immediate aftermath, journalists, politicians, and pundits found plenty of proximate causes: Alan Greenspan's refusal in the early 2000s to recognize that a housing bubble was developing from his low-interest policies; the fraudulent practices that riddled the mortgage industry; the hubris of the titans of finance, wielding ever more arcane mathematical models to claim to have created a risk-free world of pure profit; the incestuous ties between regulators and those they regulated. But the collapse had deep roots in the very nature of the political economy that had developed since the 1970s. The decline of manufacturing, deregulation, the financialization of the economy (the financial sector accounted for more than 30 percent of all corporate profits in 2004), globalization, and the grab of an ever greater proportion of national income by those already rich (by 2005 income inequality was at the level of the 1920s) had hollowed out the U.S. economy.

Though differences in economic policy had existed between administrations since the 1970s, there had been a broad continuity of vision. The Reagan administration had encouraged the corporate revolution that restructured the economy. The Clinton administration had been at least as aggressive in promoting free trade and the growth and deregulation of the financial sector. Even after the financial plunge and the election of Barack Obama, the basic contours of public policy continued along lines established in the 1980s and 1990s.

Obama's election was a measure of how much the United States had changed since World War II. It was literally unimaginable to most Americans in 1945 or 1965 or even 1985 that an African American would be elected president of the United States. But his ascension also made clear—in spite of his campaign theme of "change"—the stubborn persistence of old ideas and old forces. In the decades after World War II, politics had become more formally democratic, but the political influence of business had so grown since the 1970s that meaningful democracy had become stunted. Deregulation, free rein for the financial sector, free-trade globalization, promotion of private homeownership, and the use of federal money to maintain an empire while physical and social infrastructure deteriorated were policies supported for a quarter century or more by both parties. The considered responses to the 2008 economic crisis all centered on preserving existing hierarchies of wealth and power. Obama signaled his restorationist economic agenda when he picked as secretary of the treasury Timothy Geithner, who as head of the Federal Reserve Bank of New York had been deeply involved in bailing out the banks, and as his chief economic adviser Larry Summers, who in the Clinton administration had helped spearhead the financial deregulation that made possible the massive economic problems of the decade that followed.

As the first decade of the twenty-first century ended, the American empire was on the decline. Wars being fought after years of sacrifice, without clear purpose or victory, had sapped the country's finances and global standing. The economy no longer provided enough jobs or opportunities to maintain the living standards that had once been widely shared. In manufacturing, infrastructure, and education, the United States no longer led other industrial and industrializing countries, and in some respects lagged way behind. A small-minded, fractious political system proved unable to seize the moment or chart the future. The challenge of reinvention once again faced the nation.

Acknowledgments

I am grateful to Eric Foner for asking me to write this volume. Though there were times when I wondered what I was thinking when I agreed to take it on, among the pleasures it provided was the opportunity to work with him again. I benefited enormously from his support, advice, and remarkable knowledge of American history. I also valued the opportunity to work again, after a very long interlude, with Wendy Wolf. She and Kevin Doughten were terrific editors. Thanks, too, to Brittney Ross, Roland Ottewell, and the whole staff at Viking Penguin.

Steve Fraser and David Nasaw generously agreed to read the full manuscript of this long volume, for which I am greatly appreciative. Their comments and suggestions proved invaluable and helped shape the final form of the book. Steve and I have collaborated on so many projects and discussed history (and everything else) so many times since our first day as graduate students that his ideas and ways of thinking have become deeply intertwined with my own.

Betsy Blackmar, Jack Metzgar, Kim Phillips-Fein, and Gilda Zwerman read substantial portions of the manuscript and provided extremely valuable criticism and suggestions, for which I am grateful. So did members of my family, Deborah Bell, Julia Bell, and Lena Bell, whose sage advice and remarkable tolerance were a great gift, in this project as in everything else. Mark Levinson and Mark Naison steered me to sources I otherwise would not have known.

Over the years I worked on this book I had valuable research assistance from doctoral students at the CUNY Graduate Center. I want to thank Matthew Cotter, Edwin Tucker, Amy Van Natter, Paul Naish, Chad Turner, Vanessa Weller, John Blanton, and Katherine Uva for all their help.

I have the privilege of working for a public university that takes seriously its mission to educate "the children of the whole people." It has given me the opportunity to teach at every level, from night classes for working people returning to school after many years to doctoral courses for gifted students from around the world. For the faculty at the City University of New York, chronic underfunding means that their working lives are often overburdened and their time for research and writing constrained. I thank the colleagues and administrators who made it possible for me to complete this book, especially William P. Kelly, president of the Graduate Center; James L. Muyskens, president of Queens College; Frank Warren, chairman of the Queens College History Department; and Gregory Mantsios, director of the Joseph S. Murphy Institute for Worker Education and Labor Studies.

As a synthetic study, *American Empire* rests on the work of hundreds of other scholars and writers. While the interpretations are my own, the information and ideas that inform this book are the product of a collective endeavor, across time and discipline, to understand the American past. Without the work of the authors cited in the bibliography, this book could not exist. To them I owe the greatest acknowledgment.

Bibliography

American Empire rests on the work of scholars, journalists, writers, and public figures, as listed below. In the interest of space, books and articles generally are cited only in connection with the chapter for which they were most important. With some exceptions, statistical sources and individual newspaper articles are not listed, again because of the constraint of space. Primary sources that proved exceptionally valuable include various editions of the *Statistical Abstract of the United States* and *Historical Statistics of the United States*; the online databases maintained by the Board of Governors of the Federal Reserve System, the Bureau of Labor Statistics, and the U.S. Census Bureau; and the *Public Papers of the Presidents of the United States.* Also valuable were articles in the *Boston Globe, BusinessWeek, New York Times, Time, Wall Street Journal,* and *Washington Post.*

Introduction

For the idea of empire and its application to the United States, see William Appleman Williams, *Empire as a Way of Life: An Essay on the Causes and Character of America's Present Predicament Along with a Few Thoughts About an Alternative* (New York: Oxford University Press, 1980); Charles S. Maier, *Among Empires: American Ascendancy and Its Predecessors* (Cambridge, MA: Harvard University Press, 2006); William K. Tabb, "Imperialism: In Tribute to Harry Magdoff," *Monthly Review* 58 (March 2007): 26–37.

Prologue: E Pluribus Unum

For surveys of the physical, social, and political landscape, see George R. Stewart, *U.S. 40: Cross Section of the United States of America* (Boston: Houghton Mifflin, 1953); Henry G. Alsberg, ed., *The American Guide* (New York: Hastings House, 1949); John Gunther, *Inside U.S.A.* (New York: Harper & Brothers, 1947); Samuel Lubell, *The Future of American Politics,* 2nd ed., revised (Garden City, NY: Doubleday, 1956); Alfred J. Wright, *United States and Canada: An Economic Geography* (New York: Appleton-Century-Crofts, 1948); David L. Rigby, "Urban and Regional Restructuring in the Second Half of the Twentieth Century," in *American Place/American Space: Geographies of the Contemporary United States,* ed. John A. Agnew and Jonathan M. Smith (New York: Routledge, 2002); Carol E. Heim, "Structural Changes: Regional and Urban," in *The*

Cambridge Economic History of the United States, vol. 3, The Twentieth Century, ed. Stanley L. Engerman and Robert E. Gallman (Cambridge: Cambridge University Press, 2000).

For the population makeup, see Donald J. Bogue, *The Population of the United States* (Glencoe, IL: Free Press, 1959); Frank Hobbs and Nicole Stoops, *Demographic Trends in the 20th Century: Census 2000 Special Reports* (Washington, D.C.: U.S. Government Printing Office, 2002); Herbert S. Klein, *A Population History of the United States* (Cambridge: Cambridge University Press, 2004).

For the impact of the New Deal and World War II, see William E. Leuchenburg, *Franklin D. Roosevelt and the New Deal, 1932–1940* (New York: Harper & Row, 1963); Richard Polenberg, *War and Society: The United States, 1941–1945* (Philadelphia: Lippincott, 1972).

For the Midwest, see James H. Madison, ed., *Heartland: Comparative Histories of the Midwestern States* (Bloomington: Indiana University Press, 1988); Federal Writers' Project, *North Dakota: A Guide to the Northern Prairie State,* 2nd ed. (New York: Oxford University Press, 1950); Jon C. Teaford, *Cities of the Heartland: The Rise and Fall of the Industrial Midwest* (Bloomington: Indiana University Press, 1993); Meridel Le Sueur, *North Star Country* (New York: Duell, Sloan & Pearce, 1945); Eric Thane, *High Border Country* (New York: Duell, Sloan & Pearce, 1942); James R. Grossman, Ann Durkin Keating, and Janice L. Reiff, eds., *The Encyclopedia of Chicago* (Chicago: University of Chicago Press, 2004); Studs Terkel, *Working* (New York: Pantheon, 1974); Alan L. Olmstead and Paul W. Rhode, "The Transformation of Northern Agriculture, 1910–1990," in *Cambridge Economic History of the United States, vol. 3,* ed. Engerman and Gallman.

For Fordism and the automobile industry, see David A. Hounshell, *From the American System to Mass Production, 1800–1932: The Development of Manufacturing Technology in the United States* (Baltimore: Johns Hopkins University Press, 1984); Works Projects Administration, *Michigan: A Guide to the Wolverine State* (New York: Oxford University Press, 1941); Keith Sward, *The Legend of Henry Ford* (New York: Rinehart & Company, 1948); Robert Asher and Ronald Edsforth, eds., *Autowork* (Albany: State University of New York Press, 1995); Steve Jeffreys, *Management and Managed: Fifty Years of Crisis at Chrysler* (Cambridge: Cambridge University Press, 1986); Ronald Edsforth, *Class Conflict and Cultural Consensus: The Making of a Mass Consumer Society in Flint, Michigan* (New Brunswick, NJ: Rutgers University Press, 1987); Steve Babson, *Working Detroit: The Making of a Union Town* (New York: Adama Books, 1984).

For the midwestern population and racial and ethnic tensions, see Chad Berry, *Southern Migrants, Northern Exiles* (Urbana: University of Illinois Press, 2000); Thomas J. Sugrue, *The Origins of the Urban Crisis: Race and Inequality in Postwar Detroit* (Princeton, NJ: Princeton University Press, 1996); Arnold R. Hirsch, *Making the Second Ghetto: Race and Housing in Chicago, 1940–1960* (Cambridge: Cambridge University Press, 1983); Dionicio Nodín Valdés, *Barrios Norteños: St. Paul and Midwestern Mexican Communities in the Twentieth Century* (Austin: University of Texas Press, 2000).

For the Northeast and its forms of industrialization, see Joshua B. Freeman, *Working-Class New York: Life and Labor Since World War II* (New York: New Press, 2000); Andrew Hurley, *Diners, Bowling Alleys and Trailer Parks: Chasing the American Dream in the Postwar Consumer Culture* (New York: Basic Books, 2001); George W. Long, "Rhode Island, Modern City-State," *National Geographic Magazine* 94 (August 1948): 137–70; Philip Scranton, "Diversity in Diversity: Flexible Production and American Industrialization, 1880–1930," *Business History Review* 65 (Spring 1991): 27–90; Russell F. Weigley, ed., *Philadelphia: A 300-Year History* (New York: Norton, 1982); Philip Scranton and Walter Licht, *Work Sights: Industrial Philadelphia, 1890–1950* (Philadelphia: Temple University Press, 1986); Ronald W. Schatz, *The Electrical Workers: A History of*

Labor at General Electric and Westinghouse, 1923–60 (Urbana: University of Illinois Press, 1983).

For the financial industry, see David Rockefeller, *Memoirs* (New York: Random House, 2002); Sidney M. Robbins and Nestor E. Terleckyj with the collaboration of Ira O. Scott Jr., *Money Metropolis: A Locational Study of Financial Activities in the New York Region* (Cambridge, MA: Harvard University Press, 1960); William Greider, *Secrets of the Temple: How the Federal Reserve Runs the Country* (New York: Simon & Schuster, 1989); Steve Fraser, *Every Man a Speculator: A History of Wall Street in American Life* (New York: HarperCollins, 2005); Eugene N. White, "Banking and Finance in the Twentieth Century," in *Cambridge Economic History of the United States, vol. 3*, ed. Engerman and Gallman.

For race, ethnicity, and discrimination in the Northeast, see Cheryl Lynn Greenberg, *"Or Does It Explode?": Black Harlem in the Great Depression* (New York: Oxford University Press, 1991); Merl E. Reed, *Seedtime for the Modern Civil Rights Movement: The President's Committee on Fair Employment Practice, 1941–1946* (Baton Rouge: Louisiana State University Press, 1991); Norman Podhoretz, *Making It* (New York: Random House, 1967); Alfred Kazin, *A Walker in the City* (New York: Harcourt, Brace, 1951); Deborah Dash Moore, *G.I. Jews: How World War II Changed a Generation* (Cambridge, MA: Harvard University Press, 2004).

For the South, see Numan V. Bartley, *The New South, 1945–1980* (Baton Rouge: Louisiana State University Press, 1995); James C. Cobb, *The Most Southern Place on Earth: The Mississippi Delta and the Roots of Regional Identity* (New York: Oxford University Press, 1992); Frederick Simpich, "Arkansas Rolls Up Its Sleeves," *National Geographic Magazine* 90 (September 1946): 273–312; Robert Palmer, *Deep Blues* (New York: Viking, 1981); Douglas Flamming, *Creating the Modern South: Millhands and Managers in Dalton, Georgia, 1884–1984* (Chapel Hill: University of North Carolina Press, 1992); Pete Daniel, *Lost Revolutions: The South in the 1950s* (Chapel Hill: University of North Carolina Press, 2000).

For race relations in the South, see William H. Chafe, Raymond Gavins, and Robert Korstad, eds., *Remembering Jim Crow: African Americans Tell About Life in the Segregated South* (New York: New Press, 2001); Timothy B. Tyson, *Blood Done Sign My Name: A True Story* (New York: Crown, 2004); Neil R. McMillen, *Dark Journey: Black Mississippians in the Age of Jim Crow* (Urbana: University of Illinois Press, 1990); Eric Arnesen, *Brotherhoods of Color: Black Railroad Workers and the Struggle for Equality* (Cambridge, MA: Harvard University Press, 2001); John Egerton, *Speak Now Against the Day: The Generation Before the Civil Rights Movement in the South* (New York: Knopf, 1994).

For race relations nationally, see Stetson Kennedy, *Jim Crow Guide to the U.S.A.* (London: Lawrence & Wishart, 1959); J. Robert Moskin, *The U.S. Marine Corps Story* (New York: McGraw-Hill, 1977); Peter Wallenstein, *Tell the Court I Love My Wife: Race, Marriage, and the Law—an American History* (New York: Palgrave Macmillan, 2002).

For the impact of World War II on the South, see Charles M. Payne, *I've Got the Light of Freedom: The Organizing Tradition and the Mississippi Freedom Struggle* (Berkeley: University of California Press, 1995); Lee E. Williams II, *Post-War Riots in America, 1919 and 1946: How the Pressure of War Exacerbated American Urban Tensions to the Breaking Point* (Lewiston, NY: Edwin Mellen Press, 1991); Neil R. McMillen, ed., *Remaking Dixie: The Impact of World War II on the American South* (Jackson: University Press of Mississippi, 1997).

For energy use and the oil industry, see [U.S.] Energy Information Administration, *Annual Energy Review 2001* (Washington, DC: Department of Energy, 2001); Daniel Yergin, *The Prize: The Epic Quest for Oil, Money, and Power* (New York: Simon & Schuster, 1991).

For the Southwest, see Marc Reisner, *Cadillac Desert: The American West and Its Disappearing Water,* revised ed. (New York: Penguin, 1993); Donald Worster, *Dust Bowl: The Southern Plains in the 1930s* (New York: Oxford University Press, 1979); James N. Gregory, *American Exodus: The Dust Bowl Migration and Okie Culture in California* (New York: Oxford University Press, 1989); Randolph B. Campbell, *Gone to Texas: A History of the Lone Star State* (New York: Oxford University Press, 2003); Frederick Simpich, "Louisiana Trades with the World," *National Geographic Magazine* 92 (December 1947): 705–38; Rick Perlstein, *Before the Storm: Barry Goldwater and the Unmaking of the American Consensus* (New York: Hill & Wang, 2001).

For the West, see Richard White, *"It's Your Misfortune and None of My Own": A History of the American West* (Norman: University of Oklahoma Press, 1991); Kevin Starr, *Embattled Dreams: California in War and Peace, 1940–1950* (New York: Oxford University Press, 2002); Stephen Haycox, *Alaska: An American Colony* (Seattle: University of Washington Press, 2002); Fern Chandonnet, ed., *Alaska at War, 1941–1945: The Forgotten War Remembered* (Anchorage: Alaska at War Committee, 1995); Russell Thornton, *American Indian Holocaust and Survival: A Population History Since 1492* (Norman: University of Oklahoma Press, 1987); Patricia Limerick, *The Legacy of Conquest: The Unbroken Past of the American West* (New York: Norton, 1987); T. M. Sell, *Wings of Power: Boeing and the Politics of Growth in the Northwest* (Seattle: University of Washington Press, 2001); Marilynn S. Johnson, *The Second Gold Rush: Oakland and the East Bay in World War II* (Berkeley: University of California Press, 1993); Katherine Archibald, *Wartime Shipyard: A Study in Social Disunity* (Berkeley: University of California Press, 1947); Leo A. Borah, "Oregon Finds New Riches," *National Geographic Magazine* 90 (December 1946): 681–720; W. Robert Moore, "Nevada, Desert Treasure House," *National Geographic Magazine* 90 (January 1946): 1–38; Frederick Simpich, "More Water for California's Great Central Valley," *National Geographic Magazine* 90 (November 1946): 645–63.

Chapter 1: Power and Politics

For Harry Truman, see Alonzo L. Hamby, *Man of the People: A Life of Harry S. Truman* (New York: Oxford University Press, 1995); Robert J. Donovan, *Conflict and Crisis: The Presidency of Harry S Truman, 1945–1948* (New York: Norton, 1977); Harry S. Truman, *Memoirs, vol. 1, Year of Decisions* (Garden City, NY: Doubleday, 1955); Bert Cochran, *Harry Truman and the Crisis Presidency* (New York: Funk & Wagnalls, 1973); Donald R. McCoy, *The Presidency of Harry S. Truman* (Lawrence: University Press of Kansas, 1984); David McCullough, *Truman* (New York: Simon & Schuster, 1992).

For the impact of the New Deal and World War II, see Richard Lingeman, *Small Town America: A Narrative History, 1620–the Present* (Boston: Houghton Mifflin, 1980); Michael Edelstein, "War and the American Economy in the Twentieth Century," in *The Cambridge Economic History of the United States, vol. 3, The Twentieth Century,* ed. Stanley L. Engerman and Robert E. Gallman (Cambridge: Cambridge University Press, 2000); Nelson Lichtenstein, *Labor's War at Home: The CIO in World War II* (Cambridge: Cambridge University Press, 1982); U.S. Bureau of the Census, Current Population Reports, Population Characteristics, series P-20, no. 14, *Internal Migration in the United States: April 1940 to April 1947* (Washington, DC: Bureau of the Census, 1948).

For the way the wartime experience changed thinking about the state, see Alan Brinkley, *The End of Reform: New Deal Liberalism in Recession and War* (New York: Knopf, 1995); Alan Brinkley, *Liberalism and Its Discontents* (Cambridge, MA: Harvard University Press, 1998); Robert M. Collins, *More: The Politics of Economic Growth in Postwar America* (New York: Oxford University Press, 2000); Gabriel Kolko, *Main Currents in Modern American History* (New York: Harper & Row, 1976).

For plans to expand the New Deal, see Frank Freidel, *Franklin D. Roosevelt: A Rendezvous with Destiny* (Boston: Little, Brown, 1990); Norman D. Markowitz, *The Rise and Fall of the People's Century: Henry A. Wallace and American Liberalism, 1941–1948* (New York: Free Press, 1973); Steven Fraser, *Labor Will Rule: Sidney Hillman and the Rise of American Labor* (New York: Free Press, 1991).

For opposition to New Deal expansion, see Wendy L. Wall, *Inventing the "American Way": The Politics of Consensus from the New Deal Through the Civil Rights Movement* (New York: Oxford University Press, 2008); Kim Phillips-Fein, *Invisible Hands: The Making of the Conservative Movement from the New Deal to Reagan* (New York: Norton, 2009); Ira Katznelson, Kim Geiger, and Daniel Kryder, "Limiting Liberalism: The Southern Veto in Congress, 1933–1950," *Political Science Quarterly* 108 (Summer 1993): 283–306; Louis Galambos, "The U.S. Corporate Economy in the Twentieth Century," in *Cambridge Economic History of the United States, vol. 3,* ed. Engerman and Gallman.

For the GI Bill, see Michael J. Bennet, *When Dreams Came True: The GI Bill and the Making of Modern America* (Washington, DC: Brassey's, 1996); Suzanne Mettle, *Soldiers to Citizens: The G.I. Bill and the Making of the Greatest Generation* (New York: Oxford University Press, 2005); Glenn C. Altschuler and Stuart M. Blumin, *The GI Bill: A New Deal for Veterans* (New York: Oxford University Press, 2009); Margot Canaday, "Building a Straight State: Sexuality and Social Citizenship Under the 1944 G.I. Bill," *Journal of American History* 90 (December 2003): 935–57.

For voting rights, citizenship, and changing meanings of freedom, see Alexander Keyssar, *The Right to Vote: The Contested History of Democracy in the United States* (New York: Basic Books, 2000); Ronald Takaki, *Strangers from a Different Shore: A History of Asian Americans,* updated and revised ed. (Boston: Little, Brown, 1998); Eric Foner, *The Story of American Freedom* (New York: Norton, 1998).

For congressional representation and rules, see James Patterson, *Grand Expectations: The United States, 1945–1974* (New York: Oxford University Press, 1997); Robert A. Caro, *The Years of Lyndon Johnson: Master of the Senate* (New York: Knopf, 2002).

For trials and juries, see Michael J. Klarman, "Is the Supreme Court Sometimes Irrelevant? Race and the Southern Criminal Justice System in the 1940s," *Journal of American History* 89 (June 2002): 119–53; Linda K. Kerber, *No Constitutional Right to Be Ladies: Women and the Obligations of Citizenship* (New York: Hill & Wang, 1998); Verna Hildebrand, "A Historical Note on Jury Service for Women," *Humanist* 40 (July–August 1980): 38–39; Joanna Grossman, "Women's Jury Service: Right of Citizenship or Privilege of Difference?," *Stanford Law Review* 46 (May 1994): 1115–60; M. Catherine Miller, "Finding 'the More Satisfactory Type of Jurymen': Class and the Construction of Federal Juries, 1926–1954," *Journal of American History* 88 (December 2001): 979–1005.

For postwar strikes, see George Lipsitz, *Rainbow at Midnight: Labor and Culture in the 1940s* (Urbana: University of Illinois Press, 1994); Art Preis, *Labor's Giant Step: Twenty Years of the CIO* (New York: Pathfinder Press, 1972); Robert H. Zieger, *The CIO, 1935–1955* (Chapel Hill: University of North Carolina Press, 1995); Nelson Lichtenstein, *The Most Dangerous Man in Detroit: Walter Reuther and the Fate of American Labor* (New York: Basic Books, 1995); Irving Richter, *Labor's Struggles, 1945–1950: A Participant's View* (Cambridge: Cambridge University Press, 1994); Joshua B. Freeman, *Working-Class New York: Life and Labor Since World War II* (New York: New Press, 2000); Stan Weir, "American Labor on the Defensive: A 1940's Odyssey," *Radical America* 9 (July–August 1975): 163–85; Mark McColloch, "Consolidating Industrial Citizenship: The USWA at War and Peace, 1939–1946," in *Forging a Union of Steel: Philip Murray, SWOC, and the United Steelworkers,* ed. Paul F. Clark, Peter Gottlieb, and Donald Kennedy (Ithaca, NY: ILR Press, 1987); Jack Metzgar, "The 1945–1946 Strike Wave," in *The Encyclopedia of Strikes in American History,* ed. Aaron Brenner, Benjamin Day, and Immanuel Ness (Armonk, NY: M. E. Sharpe, 2009).

For postwar working-class living standards, see CIO Wage Research Committee, "American Living Standards Endangered," October 23, 1945; Peter Guralnick, *Last Train to Memphis: The Rise of Elvis Presley* (Boston: Little, Brown, 1994); Judith Stein, *Running Steel, Running America: Race, Economic Policy, and the Decline of Liberalism* (Chapel Hill: University of North Carolina Press, 1998); Jack Metzgar, *Striking Steel: Solidarity Remembered* (Philadelphia: Temple University Press, 2000); Robert Bruno, *Steelworker Alley: How Class Works in Youngstown* (Ithaca, NY: Cornell University Press, 1999).

For blue-collar and female employment, see Claudia Goldin, "Labor Markets in the Twentieth Century," in *Cambridge Economic History of the United States, vol. 3,* ed. Engerman and Gallman; Susan M. Hartmann, *The Home Front and Beyond: American Women in the 1940s* (Boston: Tawyne, 1995).

For union political influence, see John Barnard, *American Vanguard: The United Auto Workers During the Reuther Years, 1935–1970* (Detroit: Wayne State University Press, 2004); Dudley W. Buffa, *Union Power and American Democracy: The UAW and the Democratic Party, 1935–72* (Ann Arbor: University of Michigan Press, 1984); Milton Derber, *Labor in Illinois: The Affluent Years, 1945–1980* (Urbana: University of Illinois Press, 1989).

For business anti-unionism, see Sanford M. Jacoby, *Modern Manors: Welfare Capitalism Since the New Deal* (Princeton, NJ: Princeton University Press, 1997); Elizabeth A. Fones-Wolf, *Selling Free Enterprise: The Business Assault on Labor and Liberalism, 1945–60* (Urbana: University of Illinois Press, 1994).

For price controls and consumer activism, see Meg Jacobs, "'How About Some Meat?': The Office of Price Administration, Consumption Politics, and State Building from the Bottom Up, 1941–1946," *Journal of American History* 84 (December 1997): 910–41; Anne Stein, "Post-War Consumer Boycotts," *Radical America* 9 (July–August 1975): 156–61; Lizabeth Cohen, *A Consumers' Republic: The Politics of Mass Consumption in Postwar America* (New York: Knopf, 2003); Annelise Orleck, *Common Sense and a Little Fire: Working Women and Working-Class Politics in the United States, 1900–1965* (Chapel Hill: University of North Carolina Press, 1995).

For the pattern of postwar collective bargaining, see David Brody, *Workers in Industrial America: Essays on the 20th Century Struggle,* 2nd ed. (New York: Oxford University Press, 1993); Daniel Bell, "Labor's Coming of Middle Age," *Fortune* 44 (October 1951): 114–15, 137–50.

For Taft-Hartley and its effects, see Christopher L. Tomlins, *The State and the Unions: Labor Relations, Law, and the Organized Labor Movement in America, 1880–1960* (Cambridge: Cambridge University Press, 1985); Howell John Harris, *The Right to Manage: Industrial Relations Policies of American Business in the 1940s* (Madison: University of Wisconsin Press, 1982); Melvyn Dubofsky, *The State and Labor in Modern America* (Chapel Hill: University of North Carolina Press, 1994); James A. Gross, *Broken Promise: The Subversion of U.S. Labor Relations Policy, 1947–1994* (Philadelphia: Temple University Press, 1994); Nelson Lichtenstein, "'The Man in the Middle': A Social History of Automobile Industry Foremen," in *On the Line: Essays on the History of Autowork,* ed. Nelson Lichtenstein and Stephen Meyer (Urbana: University of Illinois Press, 1989).

For southern union organizing efforts, see Barbara S. Griffith, *The Crisis of American Labor: Operation Dixie and the Defeat of the CIO* (Philadelphia: Temple University Press, 1988); Michael K. Honey, "Operation Dixie, the Red Scare, and the Defeat of Southern Labor Organizing," in *American Labor and the Cold War: Grassroots Politics and Postwar Political Culture,* ed. Robert W. Cherny, William Issel, and Kieran Walsh Taylor (New Brunswick, NJ: Rutgers University Press, 2004); Numan V. Bartley, *The New South, 1945–1980* (Baton Rouge: Louisiana State University Press, 1995); Timothy J. Minchin,

What Do We Need a Union For?: The TWUA in the South, 1945–1955 (Chapel Hill: University of North Carolina Press, 1997).

Chapter 2: Cold War

For broad frameworks for understanding the relationship between the United States and the world, see William Appleman Williams, *The Tragedy of American Diplomacy* (Cleveland: World Publishing Co., 1959); Gabriel Kolko, *Main Currents in Modern American History* (New York: Harper & Row, 1976); John Lewis Gaddis, *Strategies of Containment: A Critical Appraisal of Postwar American National Security Policy* (New York: Oxford University Press, 1982); Eric Hobsbawm, *The Age of Extremes: A History of the World, 1914–1991* (New York: Vintage, 1996); Roger Latham, *The Liberal Moment: Modernity, Security, and the Making of the Postwar International Order* (New York: Columbia University Press, 1997).

For the U.S. economic position in the world, see Paul Kennedy, *The Rise and Fall of the Great Powers: Economic Change and Military Conflict from 1500 to 2000* (New York: Random House, 1987); Harry Magdoff, *The Age of Imperialism: The Economics of U.S. Foreign Policy* (New York: Monthly Review Press, 1969); Henry C. Dethloff, *The United States and the Global Economy Since 1945* (Fort Worth, TX: Harcourt Brace College Publishers, 1997).

For the postwar military and demobilization, see R. Alton Lee, "The Army 'Mutiny' of 1946," *Journal of American History* 53 (December 1966): 555–71; Lori Lyn Bogle, *The Pentagon's Battle for the American Mind: The Early Cold War* (College Station: Texas A&M University Press, 2004).

For Luce and the "American Century," see Henry R. Luce, *The American Century* (New York: Farrar & Rinehart, 1941); Neil Smith, *American Empire: Roosevelt's Geographer and the Prelude to Globalization* (Berkeley: University of California Press, 2003).

For perceptions of insecurity, see John Lewis Gaddis, "The Insecurities of Victory: The United States and Perception of the Soviet Threat After World War II," in *The Truman Presidency,* ed. Michael J. Lacey (Cambridge: Cambridge University Press, 1989); Melvyn Leffler, *A Preponderance of Power: National Security, the Truman Administration, and the Cold War* (Stanford, CA: Stanford University Press, 1992).

For globalism and its conservative critics, see Ernest Jackh, *The War for Man's Soul* (New York: Farrar & Rinehart, 1943); Ronald Radosh, *Prophets on the Right: Profiles of Conservative Critics of American Globalism* (New York: Simon & Schuster, 1975); John Fousek, *To Lead the Free World: American Nationalism and the Cultural Roots of the Cold War* (Chapel Hill: University of North Carolina Press, 2000).

For the foreign policy establishment, see Godfrey Hodgson, *The Colonel: The Life and Wars of Henry Stimson, 1867–1950* (New York: Knopf, 1990); C. Wright Mills, *The Power Elite* (New York: Oxford University Press, 1956); Thomas J. McCormick, *America's Half-Century: United States Foreign Policy in the Cold War,* 2nd ed. (Baltimore: Johns Hopkins University Press, 1995); George F. Kennan, *Memoirs 1925–1950* (Boston: Atlantic–Little, Brown, 1967); Dean Acheson, *Present at the Creation: My Years in the State Department* (New York: Norton, 1969).

For efforts by mass organizations to influence foreign policy, see Penny M. Von Eschen, *Race Against Empire: Black Americans and Anticolonialism, 1937–1957* (Ithaca, NY: Cornell University Press, 1997); Thomas Borstelmann, *The Cold War and the Color Line: American Race Relations in the Global Arena* (Cambridge, MA: Harvard University Press, 2001); CIO Political Action Committee, *The People's Program for 1946* (New York: CIO-PAC, 1946); Victor Silverman, *Imagining Internationalism in American and British Labor, 1939–1949* (Urbana: University of Illinois Press, 2000).

For the United Nations and international economic institutions, see Stephen C. Schlesinger, *Act of Creation: The Founding of the United Nations* (Boulder, CO: Westview

Press, 2003); Mary Ann Glendon, *A World Made New: Eleanor Roosevelt and the Universal Declaration of Human Rights* (New York: Random House, 2001); Richard N. Gardner, *Sterling-Dollar Diplomacy in Current Perspective: The Origins and Prospects of Our International Economic Order* (New York: Columbia University Press, 1980); Charles S. Maier, "The Politics of Productivity: Foundations of American International Economic Policy After World War II," *International Organization* 31 (September 1977): 607–33; Mark Levinson, "Trade Places: Globalization from the Bottom Up," *New Labor Forum* 11 (Fall–Winter 2002): 20–28.

For U.S.-Soviet relations, see Frank Freidel, *Franklin D. Roosevelt: A Rendezvous with Destiny* (Boston: Little, Brown, 1990); Arnold A. Offner, *Another Such Victory: President Truman and the Cold War, 1945–1953* (Stanford, CA: Stanford University Press, 2002); Walter LaFeber, *America, Russia and the Cold War, 1945–2002,* updated 9th ed. (Boston: McGraw-Hill, 2004); Stephen E. Ambrose and Douglas G. Brinkley, *Rise to Globalism: American Foreign Policy Since 1938,* 8th revised ed. (New York: Penguin, 1997); Vladislav Zubok and Constantine Pleshakov, *Inside the Kremlin's Cold War: From Stalin to Khrushchev* (Cambridge, MA: Harvard University Press, 1996); Ralph B. Levering, Vladimir O. Pechatnov, Verena Botzenhart-Viehe, and C. Earl Edmondson, *Debating the Origins of the Cold War: American and Russian Perspectives* (Lanham, MD: Rowman & Littlefield, 2002); Melvyn P. Leffler, "The Cold War: What Do 'We Now Know'?" *American Historical Review* 104 (April 1999): 501–24.

For oil and Middle East policy, see Daniel Yergin, *The Prize: The Epic Quest for Oil, Money and Power* (New York: Simon & Schuster, 1991); Bruce R. Kunihom, "U.S. Policy in the Near East: The Triumphs and Tribulations of the Truman Administration," in *Truman Presidency,* ed. Lacey.

For the origins of the Truman Doctrine and the Greek civil war, see Charles S. Maier, "Alliance and Autonomy: European Identity and U.S. Foreign Policy Objectives in the Truman Years," in *Truman Presidency,* ed. Lacey; Gabriel and Joyce Kolko, *The Limits of Power: The World and United States Foreign Policy, 1945–54* (New York: Harper & Row, 1972); Carolyn Eisenberg, "The Cold War in Europe," in *A Companion to Post-1945 America,* ed. Jean-Christophe Agnew and Roy Rosenzweig (Malden, MA: Blackwell, 2006); Lawrence S. Wittner, *American Intervention in Greece, 1943–1949* (New York: Columbia University Press, 1982); Richard M. Freeland, *The Truman Doctrine and the Origins of McCarthyism: Foreign Policy, Domestic Politics, and Internal Security, 1946–1948* (New York: New York University Press, 1985); Milovan Djilas, *Conversations with Stalin* (New York: Harcourt, Brace & World, 1962).

For the creation of the national security apparatus, see Michael J. Hogan, *A Cross of Iron: Harry S. Truman and the Origins of the National Security State, 1945–1954* (Cambridge: Cambridge University Press, 1998).

Chapter 3: Stalemate in Washington

For divisions in liberal groups, see J. Angus Johnston, "Questions of Communism and Anticommunism in Twentieth-Century American Student Activism," *Peace & Change* 26 (July 2001): 301–15; Ronald Schatz, "Philip Murray and the Subordination of Industrial Unions to the United States Government," in *Labor Leaders in America,* ed. Melvyn Dubofsky and Warren Van Tine (Urbana: University of Illinois Press, 1987); Bert Cochran, *Labor and Communism: The Conflict That Shaped American Unions* (Princeton, NJ: Princeton University Press, 1977); Philip Taft, *The A.F. of L. from the Death of Gompers to the Merger* (New York: Harper & Brothers, 1959).

For civil rights and the 1948 election, see Jack M. Bloom, *Class, Race, and the Civil Rights Movement: The Changing Political Economy of Southern Racism* (Bloomington:

Indiana University Press, 1987); Michael R. Gardner, *Harry Truman and Civil Rights: Moral Courage and Political Risks* (Carbondale: Southern Illinois University Press, 2002); Steven F. Lawson, *Running for Freedom: Civil Rights and Black Politics in America Since 1941* (New York: McGraw-Hill, 1991); Harry S. Truman, *Memoirs, vol. 2, Years of Trial and Hope* (Garden City, NY: Doubleday, 1956); Jennifer A. Delton, *Making Minnesota Liberal: Civil Rights and the Transformation of the Democratic Party* (Minneapolis: University of Minnesota Press, 2002); Robert A. Caro, *The Years of Lyndon Johnson: Master of the Senate* (New York: Knopf, 2002).

For the campaign and its outcome, see James T. Patterson, *Mr. Republican: A Biography of Robert A. Taft* (Boston: Houghton Mifflin, 1972); Harold I. Gullan, *The Upset That Wasn't: Harry S. Truman and the Crucial Election of 1948* (Chicago: Ivan R. Dee, 1998); David Plotke, *Building a Democratic Political Order: Reshaping American Liberalism in the 1930s and 1940s* (Cambridge: Cambridge University Press, 1996).

For Fair Deal legislation, see Paul Starr, *The Social Transformation of American Medicine* (New York: Basic Books, 1982); Colin Gordon, *Dead on Arrival: The Politics of Health Care in Twentieth-Century America* (Princeton, NJ: Princeton University Press, 2003); Robert Griffith, "Forging America's Postwar Order: Domestic Politics and Political Economy in the Age of Truman," in *The Truman Presidency,* ed. Michael J. Lacey (Cambridge: Cambridge University Press, 1989); Richard O. Davies, *Housing Reform During the Truman Administration* (Columbia: University of Missouri Press, 1966).

Chapter 4: National Security State

For the Korean War, see Steven Hugh Lee, *The Korean War* (Harlow, UK: Longman, 2001); William W. Stueck, *The Korean War: An International History* (Princeton, NJ: Princeton University Press, 1995); Rudy Tomedi, *No Bugles, No Drums: An Oral History of the Korean War* (New York: John Wiley & Sons, 1993); Donald Knox, *The Korean War: Pusan to Chosin; An Oral History* (San Diego: Harcourt Brace Jovanovich, 1985); Donald Knox, with additional text by Alfred Coppel, *The Korean War: Uncertain Victory; An Oral History* (San Diego: Harcourt Brace Jovanovich, 1988); Conrad C. Crane, *American Airpower Strategy in Korea, 1950–1953* (Lawrence: University Press of Kansas, 2000); Ron Robin, "Behavioral Codes and Truce Talks: Images of the Enemy and Expert Knowledge in the Korean Armistice Negotiations," *Diplomatic History* 25 (Fall 2001): 625–46.

For decolonization and the beginning of the Cold War in Asia, see Eric Hobsbawm, *The Age of Extremes: A History of the World, 1914–1991* (New York: Vintage, 1996); James I. Matray, "The United States and East Asia in the Postwar Era," in *A Companion to Post-1945 America,* ed. Jean-Christophe Agnew and Roy Rosenzweig (Malden, MA: Blackwell Publishing, 2002); Robert J. McMahon, "Toward a Post-Colonial Order: Truman Administration Policies Toward South and Southeast Asia," in *The Truman Presidency,* ed. Michael J. Lacey (Cambridge: Cambridge University Press, 1989).

For the militarization of American foreign policy, see Robert A. Pollard, "The National Security State Reconsidered: Truman and Economic Containment, 1945–1950," and John W. Dower, "Occupied Japan and the Cold War in Asia," in *Truman Presidency,* ed. Lacey; Ernest R. May, *American Cold War Strategy: Interpreting NSC 68* (Boston: Bedford/St. Martin's, 1993); John W. Dower, *Embracing Defeat: Japan in the Wake of World War II* (New York: Norton/New Press, 1999).

For atomic weapons and research, see Paul Boyer, *By the Bomb's Early Light: American Thought and Culture at the Dawn of the Atomic Age* (New York: Pantheon Books, 1985); McGeorge Bundy, *Danger and Survival: Choices About the Bomb in the First Fifty Years* (New York: Random House, 1988); Gregg Herken, *The Winning Weapon: The Atomic Bomb in the Cold War, 1945–1950* (Princeton, NJ: Princeton University Press,

1981); Kai Bird and Martin J. Sherwin, *American Prometheus: The Triumph and Tragedy of J. Robert Oppenheimer* (New York: Knopf, 2005); Rebecca Solnit, *Savage Dreams: A Journey into the Landscape Wars of the American West* (San Francisco: Sierra Club Books, 1994); Valerie L. Kuletz, *The Tainted Desert: Environmental Ruin in the American West* (New York: Routledge, 1998); Eileen Welsome, *The Plutonium Files: America's Secret Medical Experiments in the Cold War* (New York: Dial, 1999).

For the influence of the military and intelligence agencies, see C. Wright Mills, *The Power Elite* (New York: Oxford University Press, 1956); Samuel P. Huntington, *The Soldier and the State: The Theory and Politics of Civil-Military Relations* (Cambridge, MA: Harvard University Press, 1967); Frances Stoner Saunders, *The Cultural Cold War: The CIA and the World of Arts and Letters* (New York: New Press, 2000).

For the federal role in postwar research and development, see David Mowery and Nathan Rosenberg, "Twentieth-Century Technological Change," in *The Cambridge Economic History of the United States, vol. 3, The Twentieth Century,* ed. Stanley L. Engerman and Robert E. Gallman (Cambridge: Cambridge University Press, 2000); Walter A. MacDougall, *The Heavens and the Earth: A Political History of the Space Age* (New York: Basic Books, 1985); D. Graham Burnett, "A Mind in the Water: The Dolphin as Our Beast of Burden," *Orion* (May–June 2010): 38–51.

For defense spending, see Michael Edelstein, "War and the American Economy in the Twentieth Century," in *The Cambridge Economic History of the United States, vol. 3,* ed. Engerman and Gallman; Michael J. Hogan, *A Cross of Iron: Harry S. Truman and the Origins of the National Security State, 1945–1954* (Cambridge: Cambridge University Press, 1998).

For postwar anticommunism, see Ellen Schrecker, *Many Are the Crimes: McCarthyism in America* (Boston: Little, Brown, 1998); Robert Griffith and Athan G. Theoharis, eds., *The Specter: Original Essays on the Cold War and the Origins of McCarthyism* (New York: New Viewpoints, 1974); Richard M. Fried, *Nightmare in Red: The McCarthy Era in Perspective* (New York: Oxford University Press, 1990); David Caute, *The Great Fear: The Anti-Communist Purge Under Truman and Eisenhower* (New York: Simon & Schuster, 1978); Joel Kovel, *Red Hunting in the Promised Land: Anticommunism and the Making of America* (New York: Basic Books, 1994); Donald F. Crosby, S.J., *God, Church, and Flag: Senator Joseph R. McCarthy and the Catholic Church, 1950–1957* (Chapel Hill: University of North Carolina Press, 1978); Corey Robin, *Fear: The History of a Political Idea* (New York: Oxford University Press, 2004); Herbert S. Parmet, *Richard Nixon and His America* (Boston: Little, Brown, 1990); David Oshinsky, *A Conspiracy So Immense: The World of Joe McCarthy* (New York: Free Press, 1983); Jeff Woods, *Black Struggle, Red Scare: Segregation and Anti-Communism in the South, 1948–1968* (Baton Rouge: Louisiana State University Press, 2004); Michael J. Ybarra, *Washington Gone Crazy: Senator Pat McCarran and the Great American Communist Hunt* (Hanover, NH: Steerforth Press, 2004); Daniel Bell, ed., *The Radical Right: The New American Right* (Garden City, NY: Anchor, 1964); Steve Fraser, *Labor Will Rule: Sidney Hillman and the Rise of American Labor* (New York: Free Press, 1991); David Nasaw, *The Chief: The Life of William Randolph Hearst* (Boston: Houghton Mifflin, 2000).

For the language of anticommunism, see Eric Foner, *The Story of Freedom* (New York: Norton, 1998); Les Adler and Thomas G. Paterson, "Red Fascism: The Merger of Nazi Germany and Soviet Russia in the American Image of Totalitarianism, 1930's–1950's," *American Historical Review* 74 (April 1970): 1046–64; Jim Tuck, *McCarthyism and New York's Hearst Press: A Study in Roles in the Witch Hunt* (Lanham, MD: University Press of America, 1995).

For government investigations of communism and homosexuality, see Eric Bentley, ed., *Thirty Years of Treason: Excerpts from Hearings Before the House Committee on Un-American Activities, 1938–1968* (New York: Viking, 1971); David K. Johnson, *The*

Lavender Scare: The Cold War Persecution of Gays and Lesbians in the Federal Government (Chicago: University of Chicago Press, 2004); Robert D. Dean, *Imperial Brotherhood: Gender and the Making of Cold War Foreign Policy* (Amherst: University of Massachusetts Press, 2001); Richard M. Freeland, *The Truman Doctrine and the Origins of McCarthyism: Foreign Policy, Domestic Politics, and Internal Security, 1946–1948* (New York: New York University Press, 1985); Richard Nixon, *Six Crises* (Garden City, NY: Doubleday, 1962); John Earl Haynes and Harvey Klehr, *Venona: Decoding Soviet Espionage in America* (New Haven, CT: Yale University Press, 1999).

For McCarthy and housing, see Rosalyn Baxandall and Elizabeth Ewen, *Picture Windows: How the Suburbs Happened* (New York: Basic Books, 2000); Neil J. Sullivan, *The Dodgers Move West* (New York: Oxford University Press, 1987).

For anticommunism and labor, see Steve Rosswurm, ed., *The CIO's Left-Led Unions* (New Brunswick, NJ: Rutgers University Press, 1992); Harvey A. Levenstein, *Communism, Anti-Communism, and the CIO* (Westport, CT: Greenwood Press, 1981); Robert W. Cherny, William Issel, and Kiernan Walsh Taylor, eds., *American Labor and the Cold War: Grassroots Politics and Postwar Political Culture* (New Brunswick, NJ: Rutgers University Press, 2004).

For the left-wing influence on mass culture and the blacklist, see Michael Denning, *The Cultural Front: The Laboring of American Culture in the Twentieth Century* (London: Verso, 1996); Paul Buhle and David Wagner, *Blacklisted: The Film Lover's Guide to the Hollywood Blacklist* (New York: Palgrave Macmillan, 2003); Victor S. Navasky, *Naming Names* (New York: Viking, 1980).

For religion and the Cold War, see Patrick Allitt, *American Religion Since 1945: A History* (New York: Columbia University Press, 2003); Andrew J. Rotter, "Christians, Muslims, and Hindus: Religion and U.S.–South Asian Relations, 1947–1954," *Diplomatic History* 24 (Fall 2000): 593–613; Thomas A. Kselman and Steven Avella, "Marian Piety and the Cold War in the United States," *Catholic Historical Review* 72 (July 1986): 403–24.

For the 1952 election and Eisenhower, see Barton J. Bernstein, "Election of 1952," in *History of American Presidential Elections, 1789–2001,* vol. 8, ed. Arthur M. Schlesinger Jr. (Philadelphia: Chelsea House, 2002); Gary W. Reichard, *Politics as Unusual: The Age of Truman and Eisenhower* (Arlington Heights, IL: Harlan Davidson, 1988); Stephen E. Ambrose, *Eisenhower, vol. 2, The President* (New York: Simon & Schuster, 1984); Robert Griffith, "Dwight D. Eisenhower and the Corporate Commonwealth," *American Historical Review* 87 (February 1982): 87–122; Arthur Larson, *A Republican Looks at His Party* (New York: Harper, 1956).

For militarism, see Alex Roland, *The Military-Industrial Complex* (Washington, DC: Society for the History of Technology and the American Historical Association, 2001); Laura McEnaney, *Civil Defense Begins at Home: Militarization Meets Everyday Life in the Fifties* (Princeton, NJ: Princeton University Press, 2000).

For McCarthy's downfall and the continuation of anticommunism, see A. M. Sperber, *Murrow: His Life and Times* (New York: Freundlich Books, 1986); Natalie Robins, *Alien Ink: The FBI's War on Freedom of Expression* (New York: William Morrow, 1992); Ellen Schrecker, *The Age of McCarthyism: A Brief History with Documents* (Boston: Bedford, 1994).

Chapter 5: Suburban Nation

For Florence Thompson, see Rebecca Markel, "Migrant Madonna," *Smithsonian* 32 (March 2002): 21–22; Bill Ganzel, *Dust Bowl Descent* (Lincoln: University of Nebraska Press, 1984).

For general histories of postwar living, see James T. Patterson, *Grand Expectations: The United States, 1945–1974* (New York: Oxford University Press, 1997); Douglas T.

Miller and Marion Nowak, *The Fifties: The Way We Really Were* (New York: Doubleday, 1977); David Halberstram, *The Fifties* (New York: Villard Books, 1993); John Patrick Diggins, *The Proud Decades: America in War and Peace, 1941–1960* (New York: Norton, 1988).

For suburban living as the image of the United States, see Kevin Starr, *Embattled Dreams: California in War and Peace, 1940–1950* (New York: Oxford University Press, 2002); Lynn Spiegel, *Make Room for TV: Television and the Family Ideal in Postwar America* (Chicago: University of Chicago Press, 1992); George Lipsitz, *Time Passages: Collective Memory and American Popular Culture* (Minneapolis: University of Minnesota Press, 1989); Victoria de Grazia, *Irresistible Empire: America's Advance Through Twentieth-Century Europe* (Cambridge, MA: Harvard University Press, 2005).

For precursors of postwar society, see Ellis W. Hawley, *The Great War and the Search for a Modern Order: A History of the American People and Their Institutions, 1917–1933* (New York: St. Martin's Press, 1979).

For postwar manufacturing, see David M. Gordon, Richard Edwards, and Michael Reich, *Segmented Work, Divided Workers: The Historical Transformation of Labor in the United States* (Cambridge: Cambridge University Press, 1982).

For federal infrastructure projects, see Marc Reisner, *Cadillac Desert: The American West and Its Disappearing Water,* revised and updated ed. (New York: Penguin, 1993); T. L. Hills, *The St. Lawrence Seaway* (London: Methuen, 1959); William R. Willoughby, *The St. Lawrence Waterway: A Study in Politics and Diplomacy* (Madison: University of Wisconsin Press, 1961); Arnold R. Hirsch, "New Orleans: Sunbelt in the Swamp," in *Sunbelt Cities: Politics and Growth Since World War II,* ed. Richard M. Bernard and Bradley R. Rice (Austin: University of Texas Press, 1983); Mark H. Rose, *Interstate: Express Highway Politics, 1941–1956* (Lawrence: Regents Press of Kansas, 1979); Tom Lewis, *Divided Highways: Building the Interstate Highways, Transforming American Life* (New York: Viking Penguin, 1997).

For demography, life expectancy, and diet, see Centers for Disease Control and Prevention, *National Vital Statistics Reports* 51 (December 19, 2002); Roger Horowitz, *Putting Meat on the American Table: Taste, Technology, Transformation* (Baltimore: Johns Hopkins University Press, 2006); Richard A. Easterlin, "Twentieth-Century American Population Growth," in *The Cambridge Economic History of the United States, vol. 3, The Twentieth Century,* ed. Stanley L. Engerman and Robert E. Gallman (Cambridge: Cambridge University Press, 2000); Stephen Lassonde, "Family and Demography in Postwar America: A Hazard of New Fortunes?," in *A Companion to Post-1945 America,* ed. Jean-Cristophe Agnew and Roy Rosenzweig (Malden, MA: Blackwell, 2002); Stephanie Coontz, *The Way We Never Were: American Families and the Nostalgia Trap* (New York: Basic Books, 1992).

On unions, social benefits, and the transformation of working-class life, see Joshua B. Freeman, "Labor During the American Century: Work, Workers, and Unions Since 1945," in *A Companion to Post-1945 America,* ed. Agnew and Rosenzweig; Judith Stein, *Running Steel, Running America: Race, Economic Policy, and the Decline of Liberalism* (Chapel Hill: University of North Carolina Press, 1998); Joshua B. Freeman, *Working-Class New York: Life and Labor Since World War II* (New York: New Press, 2000); Nelson Lichtenstein, "From Corporatism to Collective Bargaining: Organized Labor and the Eclipse of Social Democracy in the Postwar Era," in *The Rise and Fall of the New Deal Order, 1930–1980,* ed. Steve Fraser and Gary Gerstle (Princeton, NJ: Princeton University Press, 1989); Melvyn Dubofsky and Warren Van Tine, *John L. Lewis: A Biography* (New York: Quadrangle/New York Times Book Co., 1977); Robert H. Zieger, *John L. Lewis: Labor Leader* (Boston: Twayne, 1988); David L. Stebenne, *Arthur J. Goldberg: New Deal Liberal* (New York: Oxford University Press, 1996); Jennifer Klein, *For All These Rights: Business, Labor, and the Shaping of America's Public-Private Welfare State*

(Princeton, NJ: Princeton University Press, 2003); Jack Metzgar, *Striking Steel: Solidarity Remembered* (Philadelphia: Temple University Press, 2000); Seth Wigderson, "How the CIO Saved Social Security," *Labor History* 44 (November 2003): 483–507; Richard B. Freeman and James L. Medoff, *What Do Unions Do?* (New York: Basic Books, 1984).

For the anti-union offensive, see Nelson Lichtenstein, *State of the Union: A Century of American Labor* (Princeton, NJ: Princeton University Press, 2002); Arthur Schlesinger Jr., *Robert Kennedy and His Times* (Boston: Houghton Mifflin, 1978); Thaddeus Russell, *Out of the Jungle: Jimmy Hoffa and the Remaking of the American Working Class* (New York: Knopf, 2001); Kim Phillips-Fein, " 'If Business and the Country Will Be Run Right': The Business Challenge to the Liberal Consensus, 1945–1964," *International Labor and Working-Class History* 72 (2007): 192–215; Melvyn Dubofsky, *The State and Labor in Modern America* (Chapel Hill: University of North Carolina Press, 1994); Mike Davis, *Prisoners of the American Dream* (New York: Verso, 1986).

For consumer credit, see Louis Hyman, *Debtor Nation: The History of America in Red Ink* (Princeton, NJ: Princeton University Press, 2011); Roger Lowenstein, "Tax Break: Who Needs the Mortgage-Interest Deduction?," *New York Times Magazine,* March 5, 2006; David S. Evans and Richard Schmalensee, *Paying with Plastic: The Digital Revolution in Buying and Borrowing,* 2nd ed. (Cambridge, MA: MIT Press, 2005).

For discount stores, see Sandra S. Vance and Roy V. Scott, "Sam Walton and Wal-Mart Stores, Inc.: A Study in Modern Southern Entrepreneurship," *Journal of Southern History* 58 (May 1992): 231–52; Susan Strasser, "Woolworth to Wal-Mart: Mass Merchandising and the Changing Culture of Consumption," in *Wal-Mart: The Face of Twenty-First-Century Capitalism,* ed. Nelson Lichtenstein (New York: New Press, 2006).

For media and advertising, see Susan J. Douglas, "Mass Media: From 1945 to Present," in *A Companion to Post-1945 America,* ed. Agnew and Rosenzweig.

For suburbanization, see Gwendolyn Wright, *Building the Dream: A Social History of Housing in America* (New York: Pantheon, 1981); Kenneth T. Jackson, *Crabgrass Frontier: The Suburbanization of the United States* (New York: Oxford University Press, 1985); Rosalyn Baxandall and Elizabeth Ewen, *Picture Windows: How the Suburbs Happened* (New York: Basic Books, 2000); Richard Polenberg, *One Nation Divisible: Class, Race, and Ethnicity in the United States Since 1938* (New York: Penguin, 1980); Richard M. Bernard and Bradley R. Rice, eds., *Sunbelt Cities: Politics and Growth Since World War II* (Austin: University of Texas Press, 1983); Joan Didion, *Where I Was From* (New York: Knopf, 2003); D. J. Waldie, *Holy Land: A Suburban Memoir* (New York: Norton, 1996); *The Lakewood Story: History, Tradition, Values* (Lakewood, CA: City of Lakewood, 2004); Herbert J. Gans, *The Levittowners: Ways of Life and Politics in a New Suburban Community* (New York: Vintage, 1967); David Beers, *Blue Sky Dream: A Memoir of America's Fall from Grace* (New York: Doubleday, 1996); Andrew Wiese, *Places of Their Own: African American Suburbanization in the Twentieth Century* (Chicago: University of Chicago Press, 2004).

For residential segregation and resistance to integration, see Douglas S. Massey and Nancy A. Denton, *American Apartheid: Segregation and the Making of the Underclass* (Cambridge, MA: Harvard University Press, 1993); Thomas J. Sugrue, *The Origins of the Urban Crisis: Race and Inequality in Postwar Detroit* (Princeton, NJ: Princeton University Press, 1996); Arnold R. Hirsch, *Making the Second Ghetto: Race and Housing in Chicago, 1940–1960* (New York Cambridge University Press, 1983); David Kushner, *Levittown: Two Families, One Tycoon, and the Fight for Civil Rights in America's Legendary Suburb* (New York: Walker & Company, 2009); James Wolfinger, *Philadelphia Divided: Race and Politics in the City of Brotherly Love* (Chapel Hill: University of North Carolina Press, 2007); John T. McGreevy, *Parish Boundaries: The Catholic Encounter with Race in the Twentieth-Century North* (Chicago: University of Chicago Press, 1996).

For the decline in rural work, see Richard Lingeman, *Small Town America: A Narrative History, 1620–the Present* (Boston: Houghton Mifflin, 1980); Jacqueline Jones, *American Work: Four Centuries of Black and White Labor* (New York: Norton, 1998).

For migration of people and jobs, see Chad Berry, *Southern Migrants, Northern Exiles* (Urbana: University of Illinois Press, 2000); Jacqueline Jones, *The Dispossessed: America's Underclass from the Civil War to the Present* (New York: Basic Books, 1992); Pete Daniel, *Lost Revolutions: The South in the 1950s* (Chapel Hill: University of North Carolina Press, 1950); Nan Elizabeth Woodruff, "Mississippi Delta Planters and Debates over Mechanization, Labor, and Civil Rights in the 1940s," *Journal of Southern History* 60 (May 1994): 263–84; James N. Gregory, *American Exodus: The Dust Bowl Migration and Okie Culture in California* (New York: Oxford University Press, 1989); Gail Cooper, *Air-Conditioning America: Engineers and the Controlled Environment, 1900–1960* (Baltimore: Johns Hopkins University Press, 1998); Jefferson Cowie, *Capital Moves: RCA's 70-Year Quest for Cheap Labor* (Ithaca, NY: Cornell University Press, 1999).

For immigration, see Ronald Takaki, *Strangers from a Different Shore: A History of Asian Americans,* updated and revised ed. (Boston: Little, Brown, 1998); Reed Ueda, *Postwar Immigrant America: A Social History* (Boston: Bedford, 1994); Mae M. Ngai, *Impossible Subjects: Illegal Aliens and the Making of Modern America* (Princeton, NJ: Princeton University Press, 2004).

For shopping centers, see Dell Upton, *Architecture in the United States* (Oxford: Oxford University Press, 1998); Thomas W. Hanchett, "U.S. Tax Policy and the Shopping-Center Boom of the 1950s and 1960s," *American Historical Review* 101 (October 1996): 1082–1110; Lizabeth Cohen, *A Consumers' Republic: The Politics of Mass Consumption in Postwar America* (New York: Knopf, 2003).

For suburban religion, see Elaine Tyler May, "Cold War—Warm Hearth: Politics and the Family in Postwar America," in *The Rise and Fall of the New Deal Order, 1930–1980,* ed. Steve Fraser and Gary Gerstle (Princeton, NJ: Princeton University Press, 1989); James T. Fisher, "American Religion Since 1945," in *A Companion to Post-1945 America,* ed. Agnew and Rosenzweig.

For suburban energy use and environmental impact, see Adam Rome, *The Bulldozer in the Countryside: Suburban Sprawl and the Rise of American Environmentalism* (Cambridge: Cambridge University Press, 2001).

For postwar sexuality and gender roles, see Marcia M. Gallo, *Different Daughters: A History of the Daughters of Bilitis and the Rise of the Lesbian Rights Movement* (New York: Carroll & Graf, 2006); Brett Harvey, *The Fifties: A Women's Oral History* (New York: HarperCollins, 1993); Elaine Tyler May, *Homeward Bound: American Families in the Cold War Era* (New York: Basic Books, 1988); Leila J. Rupp and Verta Taylor, *Survival in the Doldrums: The American Women's Rights Movement, 1945 to the 1960s* (Columbus: Ohio State University Press, 1990); Rosalind Rosenberg, *Divided Lives: American Women in the Twentieth Century* (New York: Hill & Wang, 1992).

For female labor force participation, see Alice Kessler-Harris, *Out to Work: A History of Wage-Earning Women in the United States* (Oxford: Oxford University Press, 1982); Ruth Milkman, *Gender at Work: The Dynamics of Job Segregation by Sex During World War II* (Urbana: University of Illinois Press, 1987); Nancy F. Gabin, *Feminism in the Labor Movement: Women and the United Auto Workers, 1935–1975* (Ithaca, NY: Cornell University Press, 1990); Paddy Quick, "Rosie the Riveter: Myths and Realities," *Radical America* 9 (July–October 1975): 115–31.

For housewives and housework, see Juliet B. Schor, *The Overworked American: The Unexpected Decline of Leisure* (New York: Basic Books, 1991); Betty Friedan, *The Feminine Mystique* (New York: Norton, 1963); Selma James, "A Woman's Place," in Mariarosa Dalla Costa and Selma James, *The Power of Women and the Subversion of the Community* (Bristol, UK: Falling Wall Press, 1972).

Chapter 6: "We the Union Army"

For the effect of World War II on the struggle for African American rights, see Robert Korstad and Nelson Lichtenstein, "Opportunities Found and Lost: Labor, Radicals, and the Early Civil Rights Movement," *Journal of American History* 75 (December 1988): 786–811.

For state and local antidiscrimination laws, see Paul D. Moreno, *From Direct Action to Affirmative Action: Fair Employment Law and Policy in America, 1933–1972* (Baton Rouge: Louisiana State University Press, 1997); Martha Biondi, *To Stand and Fight: The Struggle for Civil Rights in Postwar New York City* (Cambridge, MA: Harvard University Press, 2003); Duane Lockard, *Toward Equal Opportunity: A Study of State and Local Antidiscrimination Laws* (New York: Macmillan, 1968).

For Supreme Court rulings, see Michael J. Klarman, *From Jim Crow to Civil Rights: The Supreme Court and the Struggle for Racial Equality* (New York: Oxford University Press, 2004); Eric Arnesen, *Brotherhoods of Color: Black Railroad Workers and the Struggle for Equality* (Cambridge, MA: Harvard University Press, 2001).

For black voting and officeholding, see Charles M. Payne, *I've Got the Light of Freedom: The Organizing Tradition and the Mississippi Freedom Struggle* (Berkeley: University of California Press, 1995); Timothy B. Tyson, *Radio Free Dixie: Robert F. Williams and the Roots of Black Power* (Chapel Hill: University of North Carolina Press, 1999); William H. Chafe, *Civilities and Civil Rights: Greensboro, North Carolina, and the Black Struggle for Freedom* (New York: Oxford University Press, 1980).

For broadened notions of democracy, see Nicholas Lemann, *Out of the Forties* (New York: Simon & Schuster, 1985); Alexander Keyssar, *The Right to Vote: The Contested History of Democracy in the United States* (New York, Basic Books, 2000); Linda K. Kerber, *No Constitutional Right to Be Ladies: Women and the Obligations of Citizenship* (New York: Hill & Wang, 1998).

For the desegregation of sports, see Jules Tygiel, *Baseball's Great Experiment: Jackie Robinson and His Legacy* (New York: Oxford University Press, 1983).

For liberal views of race relations and civil rights, see Gunnar Myrdal, *An American Dilemma: The Negro Problem and Modern Democracy* (New York: Harper & Brothers, 1944); Martin Bauml Duberman, *Paul Robeson: A Biography* (New York: Knopf, 1989); David L. Chappell, *A Stone of Hope: Prophetic Religion and the Death of Jim Crow* (Chapel Hill: University of North Carolina Press, 2004).

For *Brown,* see Richard Kluger, *Simple Justice: The History of Brown v. Board of Education and Black America's Struggle for Equality* (New York: Knopf, 1976); James T. Patterson, *Brown v. Board of Education: A Civil Rights Milestone and Its Troubled Legacy* (New York: Oxford University Press, 2001); "Roundtable: *Brown v. Board of Education,* Fifty Years After," *Journal of American History* 91 (June 2004): 19–118.

For Emmett Till, see Stephen J. Whitfield, *A Death in the Delta: The Story of Emmett Till* (Baltimore: Johns Hopkins University Press, 1991); Ann Moody, *Coming of Age in Mississippi* (New York: Dial, 1968).

For the Baton Rouge and Montgomery bus boycotts, see Aldon D. Morris, *The Origins of the Civil Rights Movement: Black Communities Organizing for Change* (New York: Free Press, 1984); David J. Garrow, *Bearing the Cross: Martin Luther King, Jr., and the Southern Christian Leadership Conference* (New York: Random House, 1986); Taylor Branch, *Parting the Waters: America in the King Years, 1954–1963* (New York: Simon & Schuster, 1988); Rosa Parks with Jim Haskins, *Rosa Parks: My Story* (New York: Dial Books, 1992); Jo Ann Gibson Robinson, *The Montgomery Bus Boycott and the Women Who Started It: The Memoir of Jo Ann Gibson Robinson* (Knoxville: University of Tennessee Press, 1996); Stephen B. Oates, *Let the Trumpet Sound: A Life of Martin Luther King, Jr.* (New York: Harper & Row, 1982).

For concern about the international impact of southern racism, see Mary L. Dudziak, *Cold War Civil Rights: Race and the Image of American Democracy* (Princeton, NJ: Princeton University Press, 2000); Penny M. Von Eschen, *Satchmo Blows Up the World: Jazz Ambassadors Play the Cold War* (Cambridge, MA: Harvard University Press, 2004).

For Eisenhower and civil rights, see Steven F. Lawson, *Running for Freedom: Civil Rights and Black Politics in America Since 1941* (New York: McGraw-Hill, 1991); Herbert S. Parmet, *Eisenhower and the American Crusades* (New York: Macmillan, 1972).

For Alaska and Hawaii statehood, see Stephen Haycox, *Alaska: An American Colony* (Seattle: University of Washington Press, 2002); Benjamin F. Shearer, ed., *The United States: The Story of Statehood for the Fifty United States* (Westport, CT: Greenwood Press, 2004).

For civil rights activity in the late 1950s and early 1960s, see Harvard Sitkoff, *The Struggle for Black Equality, 1954–1992* (New York: Hill & Wang, 1993); Robert J. Norrell, *Reaping the Whirlwind: The Civil Rights Movement in Tuskegee* (New York: Knopf, 1985); Barbara Ransby, *Ella Baker and the Black Freedom Movement: A Radical Democratic Vision* (Chapel Hill: University of North Carolina Press, 2003); Clarence Taylor, *Knocking at Our Own Door: Milton A. Galamison and the Struggle to Integrate New York City Schools* (New York: Columbia University Press, 1997); James Forman, *The Making of Black Revolutionaries* (New York: Macmillan, 1972).

Chapter 7: "Hour of Maximum Danger"

For Kennedy, see Robert Dallek, *An Unfinished Life: John F. Kennedy, 1917–1963* (Boston: Little, Brown, 2003); Herbert S. Parmet, *JFK: The Presidency of John F. Kennedy* (New York: Dial, 1983); Garry Wills, *The Kennedy Imprisonment: A Meditation on Power* (Boston: Little, Brown, 1982); James N. Giglio, *The Presidency of John F. Kennedy* (Lawrence: University Press of Kansas, 1991).

For Eisenhower's foreign policy, see Blanche Wiesen Cook, *The Declassified Eisenhower: A Divided Legacy of Peace and Political Warfare* (New York: Doubleday, 1981); Stephen E. Ambrose, *Eisenhower, vol. 2, The President* (New York: Simon & Schuster, 1984); Richard M. Nixon, *RN: The Memoirs of Richard Nixon* (New York: Grosset & Dunlap, 1978); Zachary Karabell, *Architects of Intervention: The United States, the Third World, and the Cold War, 1946–1962* (Baton Rouge: Louisiana State University Press, 1999).

For the CIA, see John Ranelagh, *The Agency: The Rise and Decline of the CIA* (New York: Simon & Schuster, 1986); William Colby, *Honorable Men: My Life in the CIA* (New York: Simon & Schuster, 1978); Philip Agree, *Inside the Company: CIA Diary* (New York: Stonehill, 1975).

For the Soviet side of the Cold War, see Vladislav Zubok and Constantine Pleshakov, *Inside the Kremlin's Cold War: From Stalin to Khrushchev* (Cambridge, MA: Harvard University Press, 1996); William Taubman, *Khrushchev: The Man and His Era* (New York: Norton, 2003).

For Latin America, see Deborah Levenson-Estrada, *Trade Unionists Against Terror: Guatemala City, 1954–1985* (Chapel Hill: University of North Carolina Press, 1994); Greg Gandin, *The Last Colonial Massacre: Latin America in the Cold War* (Chicago: University of Chicago Press, 2004); Walter LeFeber, *Inevitable Revolutions: The United States in Central America* (New York: Norton, 1993); Greg Gandin, "Off the Beach: The United States, Latin America, and the Cold War," in *A Companion to Post-1945 America,* ed. Jean-Christophe Agnew and Roy Rosenzweig (Malden, MA: Blackwell, 2006); Richard M. Nixon, *Six Crises* (Garden City, NY: Doubleday, 1962); Aleksandr Furesenko and

Timothy Naftali, *"One Hell of a Gamble": Khrushchev, Castro, and Kennedy, 1958–1964* (New York: Norton, 1997).

For Kennedy-era masculinity, see Barbara Ehrenreich, *The Hearts of Men: American Dreams and the Flight from Commitment* (Garden City, NY: Anchor/Doubleday, 1983).

For Rostow and modernization theory, see W. W. Rostow, *The Stages of Economic Growth: A Non-Communist Manifesto* (Cambridge: Cambridge University Press, 1960); W. W. Rostow, *The Diffusion of Power: An Essay in Recent History* (New York: Macmillan, 1972).

For debates over economic growth, see John Kenneth Galbraith, *A Life in Our Times* (Boston: Houghton Mifflin, 1981); Robert M. Collins, *More: The Politics of Economic Growth in Postwar America* (New York: Oxford University Press, 2000); David L. Stebenne, *Arthur J. Goldberg: New Deal Liberal* (New York: Oxford University Press, 1996).

For Kennedy and the civil rights movement, see Raymond Arsenault, *Freedom Riders: 1961 and the Struggle for Racial Justice* (New York: Oxford University Press, 2006); Maurice Isserman, *If I Had a Hammer: The Death of the Old Left and the Birth of the New Left* (New York: Basic Books, 1987); Clayborne Carson, *In Struggle: SNCC and the Black Awakening of the 1960s* (Cambridge, MA: Harvard University Press, 1981); Diane McWhorter, *Carry Me Home: Birmingham, Alabama, the Climactic Battle of the Civil Rights Revolution* (New York: Simon & Schuster, 2001); Robert Weisbrot, *Freedom Bound: A History of America's Civil Rights Movement* (New York: Plume, 1990).

For voting rights, see Gene Graham, *One Man, One Vote: Baker v. Carr and the American Levellers* (Boston: Little, Brown, 1972); Michael Schudson, *The Good Citizen: A History of American Civil Life* (New York: Free Press, 1998); Lucas A. Powe Jr., *The Warren Court and American Politics* (Cambridge, MA: Belknap Press, 2000).

For civil rights activity in the North, see Joshua B. Freeman, *Working-Class New York: Life and Labor Since World War II* (New York: New Press, 2000); Clarence Taylor, *The Black Churches of Brooklyn* (New York: Columbia University Press, 1994).

For the Kennedy assassination, see Arthur M. Schlesinger Jr., *A Thousand Days: John F. Kennedy in the White House* (Boston: Houghton Mifflin, 1965); Michael R. Beschloss, ed., *Taking Charge: The Johnson White House Tapes, 1963–1964* (New York: Simon & Schuster, 1997).

Chapter 8: The Democratic Revolution

For overviews of the 1960s, see Stephen Macedo, ed., *Reassessing the Sixties: Debating the Political and Cultural Legacy* (New York: Norton, 1997); Maurice Isserman and Michael Kazin, *America Divided: The Civil War of the 1960s* (New York: Oxford University Press, 2008).

For higher education, see Jodi Vandenberg-Davies, "'There's Got to Be More Out There': White Working-Class Women, College and the 'Better Life,' 1950–1985," *International Labor and Working-Class History* 62 (Fall 2002): 99–120; Helen Lefkowitz Horowitz, *Campus Life: Undergraduate Cultures from the End of the Eighteenth Century to the Present* (New York: Knopf, 1987); Nicholas Lemann, *The Big Test: The Secret History of the American Meritocracy* (New York: Farrar, Straus & Giroux, 1999); Perdita Buchan, "Cliffe Notes," *Harvard Magazine* 104 (May–June 2002): 16–18.

For intellectual and cultural dissent, see Howard Brick, *Age of Contradiction: American Thought and Culture in the 1960s* (New York: Twayne, 1998); Godfrey Hodgson, *America in Our Time* (Garden City, NY: Doubleday, 1976); Thomas Frank, *The Conquest of Cool: Business Culture, Counterculture, and the Rise of Hip Consumerism* (Chicago: University of Chicago Press, 1997).

For youth culture, see Joan Didion, *The White Album* (New York: Simon & Schuster, 1979); William Graebner, *Coming of Age in Buffalo: Youth and Authority in the Postwar Era* (Philadelphia: Temple University Press, 1990); Thomas Hine, *The Rise and Fall of the American Teenager* (New York: Bard, 1999); Bradford W. Wright, *Comic Book Nation: The Transformation of Youth Culture in America* (Baltimore: Johns Hopkins University Press, 2001).

For rock and roll, see Joel Whitburn, *The Billboard Book of Top 40 Hits* (New York: Billboard Publications, 1987); Peter Guralnick, *Last Train to Memphis: The Rise of Elvis Presley* (Boston: Little, Brown, 1994); Peter Guralnick, *Dream Boogie: The Triumph of Sam Cooke* (New York: Little Brown, 2005).

For student protest, see W. J. Rorabaugh, *Berkeley at War: The 1960s* (New York: Oxford University Press, 1989); Kirkpatrick Sale, *SDS* (New York: Random House, 1973); James Miller, *"Democracy Is in the Streets": From Port Huron to the Siege of Chicago* (New York: Simon & Schuster, 1987); David Harris, *Dreams Die Hard: Three Men's Journey Through the Sixties* (New York: St. Martin's/Marek, 1982); Todd Gitlin, *The Sixties: Years of Hope, Days of Rage* (New York: Bantam, 1987); Terry H. Anderson, *The Movement and the Sixties* (New York: Oxford University Press, 1995).

For activist groups, see Amy Swerdlow, *Women Strike for Peace: Traditional Motherhood and Radical Politics in the 1960s* (Chicago: University of Chicago Press, 1993); Van Gosse, *Where the Boys Are: Cuba, Cold War America, and the Making of the New Left* (London: Verso, 1993); Daniel Horowitz, *Betty Friedan and the Making of the Feminine Mystique: The American Left, the Cold War, and Modern Feminism* (Amherst: University of Massachusetts Press, 1998).

For southern civil rights struggles, see Doug McAdam, *Freedom Summer* (New York: Oxford University Press, 1988); Timothy B. Tyson, *Blood Done Sign My Name: A True Story* (New York: Crown, 2004).

For Goldwater and the New Right, see Rick Perlstein, *Before the Storm: Barry Goldwater and the Unmaking of the American Consensus* (New York: Hill & Wang, 2001); Barry Goldwater, *The Conscience of a Conservative* (Shepherdsville, KY: Bottom of the Hill Publishing, 1960); Michael Miles, *The Odyssey of the American Right* (New York: Oxford University Press, 1980); John A. Andrew III, *The Other Side of the Sixties: Young Americans for Freedom and the Rise of Conservative Politics* (New Brunswick, NJ: Rutgers University Press, 1997); Lisa McGirr, *Suburban Warriors: The Origins of the New American Right* (Princeton, NJ: Princeton University Press, 2001).

For *Engel v. Vital*, see Lucas A. Powe Jr., *The Warren Court and American Politics* (Cambridge, MA: Belknap Press, 2000); Patrick Allitt, *Religion in America Since 1945* (New York: Columbia University Press, 2003).

For Lyndon Johnson, see Robert A. Caro, *The Years of Lyndon Johnson: The Path to Power* (New York: Knopf, 1982); Robert A. Caro, *The Years of Lyndon Johnson: Means of Ascent* (New York: Knopf, 1990); Robert A. Caro, *The Years of Lyndon Johnson: Master of the Senate* (New York: Knopf, 2002); Robert Dalleck, *Flawed Giant: Lyndon Johnson and His Times, 1961–1973* (New York: Oxford University Press, 1998); Doris Kearns, *Lyndon Johnson and the American Dream* (New York: St. Martin's Press, 1976); Michael Beschloss, ed., *Taking Charge: The Johnson White House Tapes, 1963–1964* (New York: Simon & Schuster, 1997); Irving Bernstein, *Guns or Butter: The Presidency of Lyndon Johnson* (New York: Oxford University Press, 1996); Sidney M. Milkis, "Lyndon Johnson, the Great Society, and the 'Twilight' of the Modern Presidency," in *The Great Society and the High Tide of Liberalism,* ed. Sidney M. Milkis and Jerome M. Mileur (Amherst: University of Massachusetts Press, 2005).

For civil rights and women's rights legislation, see Charles and Barbara Whalen, *The Longest Debate: A Legislative History of the 1964 Civil Rights Act* (Cabin John, MD:

Seven Locks Press, 1985); Dorothy Sue Cobble, *The Other Women's Movement: Workplace Justice and Social Rights in Modern America* (Princeton, NJ: Princeton University Press, 2004); Nancy Woloch, *Women and the American Experience,* 2nd ed. (New York: McGraw-Hill, 1984).

For the antipoverty program, see James T. Patterson, *America's Struggle Against Poverty, 1900–1985* (Cambridge, MA: Harvard University Press, 1986); Frances Fox Piven and Richard A. Cloward, *Regulating the Poor: The Functions of Public Welfare* (New York: Pantheon, 1971); Allen J. Matusow, *The Unraveling of America: A History of Liberalism in the 1960s* (New York: Harper & Row, 1984).

For the 1964 election, see Theodore H. White, *The Making of the President, 1964* (New York: HarperCollins, 1969): Steven F. Lawson, *Black Ballots; Voting Rights in the South, 1944–1969* (New York: Lexington Books, 1976); Dan T. Carter, *The Politics of Rage: George Wallace, the Origins of the New Conservatism, and the Transformation of American Politics* (New York: Simon & Schuster, 1995).

For Medicare-Medicaid, see Jennifer Klein, *For All These Rights: Business, Labor, and the Shaping of America's Public-Private Welfare State* (Princeton, NJ: Princeton University Press, 2003); Edward Berkowitz, "Medicare: The Great Society's Enduring National Health Insurance Program," in *The Great Society and the High Tide of Liberalism,* ed. Milkis and Mileur.

For immigration reform, see Hugh Davis Graham, *Collision Course: The Strange Convergence of Affirmative Action and Immigration Policy in America* (New York: Oxford University Press, 2002); Mae M. Ngai, *Impossible Subjects: Illegal Aliens and the Making of Modern America* (Princeton, NJ: Princeton University Press, 2004); Kitty Calavita, *Inside the State: The Bracero Program, Immigration, and the INS* (New York: Routledge, 1992).

For the environmental movement and legislation, see Ian Tyrrell, "Modern Environmentalism," in *A Companion to Post-1945 America,* ed. Jean-Christophe Agnew and Roy Rosenzweig (Malden, MA: Blackwell, 2006); J. R. McNeill, *Something New Under the Sun: An Environmental History of the Twentieth-Century World* (New York: Norton, 2000); Samuel P. Hays, in collaboration with Barbara D. Hays, *Beauty, Health, and Permanence: Environmental Politics in the United States, 1955–1985* (Cambridge: Cambridge University Press, 1987); Rachel Carson, *Silent Spring* (Boston: Houghton Mifflin, 1962); Andrew Hurley, *Environmental Inequalities: Class, Race, and Industrial Pollution in Gary, Indiana, 1945–1980* (Chapel Hill: University of North Carolina Press, 1995); Adam Rome, *The Bulldozer in the Countryside: Suburban Sprawl and the Rise of American Environmentalism* (Cambridge: Cambridge University Press, 2001).

For Watts, see Robert Conot, *Rivers of Blood, Years of Darkness* (New York: Bantam, 1967); Gerald Horne, *Fire This Time: The Watts Uprising and the 1960s* (Charlottesville: University Press of Virginia, 1995).

For labor and the Great Society, see Kevin Boyle, *The UAW and the Heyday of American Liberalism, 1945–1968* (Ithaca, NY: Cornell University Press, 1995); David Brody, *Workers in Industrial America: Essays on the Twentieth-Century Struggle,* 2nd ed. (New York: Oxford University Press, 1993).

For the politics of race in northern cities, see John T. McGreevy, *Parish Boundaries: The Catholic Encounter with Race in the Twentieth-Century North* (Chicago: University of Chicago Press, 1996); Kenneth D. Durr, *Behind the Backlash: White Working-Class Politics in Baltimore, 1940–1980* (Chapel Hill: University of North Carolina Press, 2003); Frances Fox Piven and Richard A. Cloward, "The Politics of the Great Society," in *The Great Society and the High Tide of Liberalism,* ed. Milkis and Mileur.

For the 1966 election, see John Patrick Diggins, *Ronald Reagan: Fate, Freedom, and the Making of History* (New York, Norton, 2007); Alan Draper, "Labor and the 1966 Elections," *Labor History* 30 (Winter 1989): 76–92.

Chapter 9: Apocalypse Now

For the events surrounding the dedication of the Vietnam Veterans Memorial, see contemporary coverage in the *Washington Post;* United Press International; Associated Press; Facts on File World News Digest.

For the Vietnam War in general, see U.S. Department of Defense, *The Pentagon Papers: The Defense Department History of United States Decisionmaking on Vietnam,* Senator Gravel Edition, vols. 1–5 (Boston: Beacon Press, 1971–72); George C. Herring, *America's Longest War: The United States and Vietnam, 1950–1975,* 4th ed. (Boston: McGraw-Hill, 2002); James Pickney Harrison, *The Endless War: Fifty Years of Struggle in Vietnam* (New York: Free Press, 1982); Gabriel Kolko, *Anatomy of a War: Vietnam, the United States, and the Modern Historical Experience* (New York: Pantheon, 1985); Loren Baritz, *Backfire: A History of How American Culture Led Us into Vietnam and Made Us Fight the Way We Did* (New York: William Morrow, 1985); James William Gibson, *The Perfect War: Technowar in Vietnam* (Boston: Atlantic Monthly Press, 1986); Neil Sheehan, *A Bright Shining Lie: John Paul Vann and America in Vietnam* (New York: Random House, 1988); Tom Mangold and John Penycate, *The Tunnels of Cu Chi* (New York: Random House, 1985); Michael Herr, *Dispatches* (New York: Knopf, 1977); David Harris, *Our War: What We Did in Vietnam and What It Did to Us* (New York: Crown, 1996); Robert S. McNamara, James G. Blight, and Robert K. Brigham, *Argument Without End: In Search of Answers to the Vietnam Tragedy* (New York: PublicAffairs, 1999); Daniel Ellsberg, *Secrets: A Memoir of Vietnam and the Pentagon Papers* (New York: Viking, 2002); U.S. Department of State, Office of the Historian, *Foreign Relations of the United States, 1964–1968, vol. 27, Mainland Southeast Asia; Regional Affairs* (Washington, DC: U.S. Government Printing Office, 2000).

For shipping to Vietnam, see Marc Levinson, *The Box: How the Shipping Container Made the World Smaller and the World Economy Bigger* (Princeton, NJ: Princeton University Press, 2006).

For the makeup of the American armed services in Vietnam, see Lawrence M. Baskir and William A. Strauss, *Chance and Circumstance: The Draft, the War, and the Vietnam Generation* (New York: Knopf, 1978); Christian G. Appy, *Working-Class War: American Combat Soldiers and Vietnam* (Chapel Hill: University of North Carolina Press, 1993).

For the press and Vietnam, see David Halberstam, *The Making of a Quagmire* (New York: Random House, 1965); William Prochnau, *Once Upon a Distant War* (New York: Times Books, 1995).

For the Supreme Court and Vietnam, see Michal R. Belknap, "The Warren Court and the Vietnam War: The Limits of Legal Liberalism," *Georgia Law Review* 33 (Fall 1998): 65–154.

For the antiwar movement, see Thomas Powers, *Vietnam: The War at Home; Vietnam and the American People, 1964–1968* (New York: Grossman, 1973); Melvin Small, *Johnson, Nixon, and the Doves* (New Brunswick, NJ: Rutgers University Press, 1988); Melvin Small, *Antiwarriors: The Vietnam War and the Battle for America's Hearts and Minds* (Wilmington, DE: SR Books, 2002); Michael S. Foley, *Confronting the War Machine: Draft Resistance During the Vietnam War* (Chapel Hill: University of North Carolina Press, 2003); Richard Lee Howell, "Harvard University and the Indochina War: From the Takeover of University Hall in the Spring of 1969 Through the Aftermath of the Invasion of Cambodia and the Kent State Killings in the Spring of 1970" (PhD dissertation, Michigan State University, 1987).

For CIA and FBI involvement with domestic political groups, see Frances Stoner Saunders, *The Cultural Cold War: The CIA and the World of Arts and Letters* (New York: New Press, 2000); J. Angus Johnston, "The United States National Student Association: Democracy, Activism, and the Idea of the Student, 1947–1978" (PhD dissertation, City

University of New York, 2009); David Cunningham, *There's Something Happening Here: The New Left, the Klan, and FBI Counterintelligence* (Berkeley: University of California Press, 2004).

For the Supreme Court, see Lucas A. Powe Jr., *The Warren Court and American Politics* (Cambridge: Harvard University Press, 2000); Peter Wallenstein, *Tell the Court I Love My Wife: Race, Marriage, and the Law—an American History* (New York: Palgrave Macmillan, 2002).

For crime, riots, and law and order, see Bruce J. Cohen, ed., *Crime in America: Perspectives on Criminal and Delinquent Behavior* (Itasca, IL: F. E. Peacock, 1970); President's Commission on Law Enforcement and Administration of Justice, *The Challenge of Crime in a Free Society: A Report* (Washington, DC: U.S. Government Printing Office, 1967); Michael W. Flamm, "The Politics of 'Law and Order,'" in *The Conservative Sixties,* ed. David Farber and Jeff Roche (New York: Peter Lang, 2003); National Advisory Commission on Civil Disorders, *Report of the National Advisory Commission on Civil Disorders* (New York: Bantam, 1968).

For the economic impact of the Vietnam War, see Michael Edelstein, "War and the American Economy in the Twentieth Century," in *The Cambridge Economic History of the United States, vol. 3, The Twentieth Century,* ed. Stanley L. Engerman and Robert E. Gallman (Cambridge: Cambridge University Press, 2000); Robert M. Collins, "The Economic Crisis of 1968 and the Waning of the 'American Century,'" *American Historical Review* 101 (April 1996): 396–422; Julian E. Zelizer, *Taxing America: Wilbur D. Mills, Congress, and the State, 1945–1975* (Cambridge: Cambridge University Press, 1998).

For the Dump Johnson movement, see William H. Chafe, *Never Stop Running: Allard Lowenstein and the Struggle to Save American Liberalism* (New York: Basic Books, 1993); Penetration Research Inc., "A Survey of the Political Climate in Wisconsin–March 1, 1968" (Larry Berman Collection, Vietnam Archive, Texas Tech University).

For Black Power, see Stokely Carmichael and Charles Hamilton, *Black Power: The Politics of Liberation in America* (New York: Random House, 1967); Peniel E. Joseph, *Waiting 'Til the Midnight Hour: A Narrative History of Black Power in America* (New York: Henry Holt, 2006).

For riots after King's death, see Irving Bernstein, *Guns or Butter: The Presidency of Lyndon Johnson* (New York: Oxford University Press, 1996); Adam Cohen and Elizabeth Taylor, *American Pharaoh: Mayor Richard J. Daley: His Battle for Chicago and the Nation* (Boston: Little, Brown, 2000); Theo Lippman Jr., *Spiro Agnew's America* (New York: Norton, 1972).

For student protest internationally, see Ronald Fraser, ed., *1968: A Student Generation in Revolt* (New York: Pantheon, 1988); Mark Kurlansky, *1968: The Year That Rocked the World* (New York: Ballantine, 2004); George Katsiaficas, *The Imagination of the New Left: A Global Analysis of 1968* (Boston: South End Press, 1987).

For the ideological underpinnings of the 1968 election, see Garry Wills, *Nixon Agonistes: The Crisis of the Self-Made Man* (Boston: Houghton Mifflin, 1970); Dan T. Carter, *The Politics of Rage: George Wallace, the Origins of the New Conservatism, and the Transformation of American Politics* (New York: Simon & Schuster, 1995); William H. Chafe, *The Unfinished Journey: America Since World War II,* 5th ed. (New York: Oxford University Press, 2002).

Chapter 10: Sixties to Seventies, Dreams to Nightmares

For civil rights struggles after 1968, see Cass R. Sunstein, "What the Civil Rights Movement Was and Wasn't," and Anita Lafrance Allen, "The Half-Life of Integration," in *Reassessing the Sixties: Debating the Political and Cultural Legacy,* ed. Stephen Macedo (New York: Norton, 1997); James T. Patterson, *Brown v. Board of Education: A Civil*

Rights Milestone and Its Troubled Legacy (New York: Oxford University Press, 2001); Dean J. Kotlowski, *Nixon's Civil Rights: Politics, Principle, and Policy* (Cambridge, MA: Harvard University Press, 2001); Jerome C. Hafter and Peter M. Hoffman, "Segregation Academies and State Action," *Yale Law Journal* 82 (June 1973): 1436–61; J. Anthony Lukas, *Common Ground: A Turbulent Decade in the Lives of Three American Families* (New York: Knopf, 1985); Ronald P. Formisano, *Boston Against Busing: Race, Class, and Ethnicity in the 1960s and 1970s* (Chapel Hill: University of North Carolina Press, 1991); Jerald E. Podair, *The Strike That Changed New York: Blacks, Whites, and the Ocean Hill–Brownsville Crisis* (New Haven, CT: Yale University Press, 2002).

For Black Power movements, see Peniel E. Joseph, *Waiting 'Til the Midnight Hour: A Narrative History of Black Power in America* (New York: Henry Holt, 2006); Jeanne Theoharis and Komozi Woodard, eds., *Freedom North: Black Freedom Struggles Outside the South, 1940–1980* (New York: Palgrave Macmillan, 2003); Bobby Seale, *Seize the Time: The Story of the Black Panther Party and Huey P. Newton* (New York: Random House, 1970); Elaine Brown, *A Taste of Power: A Black Woman's Story* (New York: Pantheon, 1992).

For African American officeholding, see David R. Colburn and Jeffrey S. Adler, eds., *African-American Mayors: Race, Politics, and the American City* (Urbana: University of Illinois Press, 2001); Clyde Woods, *Development Arrested: The Blues and Plantation Power in the Mississippi Delta* (London: Verso, 1998); Adolph Reed Jr., *Stirrings in the Jug: Black Politics in the Post-Segregation Era* (Minneapolis: University of Minnesota Press, 1999).

For Mexican American activism, see Cletus E. Daniel, "Cesar Chavez and the Unionization of California Farm Workers," in *Labor Leaders in America,* ed. Melvyn Dubofsky and Warren Van Tine (Urbana: University of Illinois Press, 1987); Lorena Oropeza, *¡Raza Sí! ¡Guerra No!: Chicano Protest and Patriotism During the Viet Nam War Era* (Berkeley: University of California Press, 2005).

For the Young Lords, see Johanna L. del C. Fernandez, "Radicals in the Late 1960s: A History of the Young Lords Party in New York City, 1969–1974" (PhD dissertation, Columbia University, 2004); Miguel Melendez, *We Took the Streets: Fighting for Latino Rights with the Young Lords* (New York: St. Martin's Press, 2003).

For the women's movement, see Jo Freeman, *The Politics of Women's Liberation: A Case Study of an Emerging Social Movement and Its Relation to the Policy Process* (New York: McKay, 1975); Sara Evans, *Personal Politics: The Roots of Women's Liberation in the Civil Rights Movement and the New Left* (New York: Knopf, 1979); Alice Echols, *Daring to be Bad: Radical Feminism in America, 1967–1975* (Minneapolis: University of Minnesota Press, 1989); Ruth Rosen, *The World Split Open: How the Modern Women's Movement Changed America* (New York: Viking, 2000); Kathleen M. Barry, *Femininity in Flight: A History of Flight Attendants* (Durham, NC: Duke University Press, 2007); Carol Giardina, *Freedom for Women: Forging the Women's Liberation Movement, 1953–1970* (Gainesville: University Press of Florida, 2010); Robin Morgan, ed., *Sisterhood Is Powerful: An Anthology of Writings from the Women's Liberation Movement* (New York: Random House, 1970); Rosalyn Baxandall and Linda Gordon, eds., *Dear Sisters: Dispatches from the Women's Liberation Movement* (New York: Basic Books, 2000); Rosalind Rosenberg, *Divided Lives: American Women in the Twentieth Century* (New York: Hill & Wang, 1992).

For the gay movement, see Martin Duberman, *Stonewall* (New York: Plume, 1993); Marcia Gallo, *Different Daughters: A History of the Daughters of Bilitis and the Rise of the Lesbian Rights Movement* (New York: Carroll & Graf, 2006); Jeff Kisseloff, *Generation on Fire: Voices of Protest from the 1960s: An Oral History* (Lexington: University Press of Kentucky, 2007).

For rights consciousness, see Michael Schudson, *The Good Citizen: A History of American Civil Life* (New York: Free Press, 1998); Martha Minow, "Whatever Happened to Children's Rights?," in *Reassessing the Sixties,* ed. Macedo; *Kevin M. Krause, White Flight: Atlanta and the Making of Modern Conservatism* (Princeton, NJ: Princeton University Press, 2005); Eric Foner, *The Story of American Freedom* (New York: Norton, 1998).

For welfare reform, see James T. Patterson, *America's Struggle Against Poverty, 1900–1985* (Cambridge, MA: Harvard University Press, 1986); Premilla Nadasen, *Welfare Warriors: The Welfare Rights Movement in the United States* (New York: Routledge, 2005).

For OSHA, see Thomas O. McGarity and Sidney A. Shapiro, *Workers at Risk: The Failed Promise of the Occupational Safety and Health Administration* (Westport, CT: Praeger, 1993); Les Leopold, *The Man Who Hated Work and Loved Labor: The Life and Times of Tony Mazzocchi* (White River Junction, VT: Chelsea Green, 2007); Nelson Lichtenstein, *State of the Union: A Century of American Labor* (Princeton, NJ: Princeton University Press, 2002).

For workplace discrimination, see Nancy MacLean, *Freedom Is Not Enough: The Opening of the American Workplace* (Cambridge, MA: Harvard University Press, 2006); Judith Stein, *Running Steel, Running America: Race, Economic Policy, and the Decline of Liberalism* (Chapel Hill: University of North Carolina Press, 1998); David H. Golland, *Constructing Affirmative Action: The Struggle for Equal Employment Opportunity* (Lexington: University Press of Kentucky, 2011).

For bilingual education, see Gareth Davies, "The Great Society After Johnson: The Case of Bilingual Education," *Journal of American History* 88 (March 2002): 1405–29.

For international economic issues, see Judith Stein, *Pivotal Decade: How the United States Traded Factories for Finance in the Seventies* (New Haven, CT: Yale University Press, 2010); Allen J. Matusow, *Nixon's Economy: Booms, Busts, Dollars, and Votes* (Lawrence: University of Kansas Press, 1998).

For Nixon's foreign policy, see Joan Hoff, *Nixon Reconsidered* (New York: Basic Books, 1994); Jeremi Suri, *Henry Kissinger and the American Century* (Cambridge, MA: Harvard University Press, 2007); Jeffrey Kimball, *Nixon's Vietnam War* (Lawrence: University of Kansas Press, 1998); Larry Berman, *No Peace, No Honor: Nixon, Kissinger, and Betrayal in Vietnam* (New York: Free Press, 2001).

For antiwar protest, see George Katsiaficas, *The Imagination of the New Left: A Global Analysis of 1968* (Boston: South End, 1987); Rick Perlstein, *Nixonland: The Rise of a President and the Fracturing of America* (New York: Scribner, 2008); Rusty L. Monhollon, *"This Is America?": The Sixties in Lawrence, Kansas* (New York: Palgrave Macmilla, 2002).

For labor, see Kim Moody, *An Injury to All: The Decline of American Unionism* (London: Verso, 1988); *Work in America: Report of a Special Task Force to the Secretary of Health, Education, and Welfare* (Cambridge, MA: MIT Press, 1973); Edmund F. Wehrle, *Between a River and a Mountain: The AFL-CIO and the Vietnam War* (Ann Arbor: University of Michigan Press, 2005).

Chapter 11: The End of the American Century

For Watergate, see Stanley I. Kutler, *The Wars of Watergate: The Last Crisis of Richard Nixon* (New York: Knopf, 1990); John W. Dean, *Blind Ambition: The White House Years* (New York: Simon & Schuster, 1976); Jeb Stuart Magruder, *An American Life: One Man's Road to Watergate* (New York: Atheneum, 1974); H. R. Haldeman, *The Haldeman Diaries: Inside the Nixon White House* (New York: G. P. Putnam's Sons, 1994); Katharine Graham, *Personal History* (New York: Knopf, 1997); Bob Woodward, *The Secret Man: The Story of Watergate's Deep Throat* (New York: Simon & Schuster, 2005); Richard M. Nixon, *In the Arena: A Memoir of Victory, Defeat, and Renewal* (New York: Simon & Schuster, 1990).

For the FBI harassment of Martin Luther King Jr., see David J. Garrow, *The FBI and Martin Luther King, Jr.: From "Solo" to Memphis* (New York: Norton, 1981).

For postwar Vietnam, see Gabriel Kolko, *Vietnam: Anatomy of a Peace* (London: Routledge, 1997).

Chapter 12: The Landscape of Decline

For the landscape, see Thomas R. Vale and Geraldine R. Vale, *U.S. 40 Today: Thirty Years of Landscape Change in America* (Madison: University of Wisconsin Press, 1983); U.S. Department of Agriculture Forest Service, *U.S. Forest Facts and Historical Trends* (Washington, DC: U.S. Department of Agriculture Forest Service, 2001).

For the Rust Belt, see Joel Garreau, *The Nine Nations of North America* (Boston: Houghton Mifflin, 1981); Joshua B. Freeman, "Seeing It Through: New York in the 1970s," in *New York 400,* ed. John Thorn (Philadelphia: Running Press, 2009); Alfred Kazin, *Alfred Kazin's Journals,* selected and edited by Richard M. Cook (New Haven, CT: Yale University Press, 2011); John T. Cumbler, *A Social History of Economic Decline: Business, Politics, and Work in Trenton* (New Brunswick, NJ: Rutgers University Press, 1989); Russell F. Weigley, ed., *Philadelphia: A 300-Year History* (New York: Norton, 1982); Jon C. Teaford, *Cities of the Heartland: The Rise and Fall of the Industrial Midwest* (Bloomington: Indiana University Press, 1994); Margaret Pugh O'Mara, "Uncovering the City in the Suburb: Cold War Politics, Scientific Elites, and High-Tech Spaces," in *The New Suburban History,* ed. Kevin M. Kruse and Thomas J. Sugrue (Chicago: University of Chicago Press, 2006); Paul R. Josephson, *Motorized Obsessions: Life, Liberty, and the Small-Bore Engine* (Baltimore: Johns Hopkins University Press, 2007).

For the Sun Belt, see Bruce Schulman, *The Seventies: The Great Shift in American Culture, Society, and Politics* (Cambridge, MA: Da Capo, 2001); Kirkpatrick Sale, *Power Shift: The Rise of the Southern Rim and Its Challenge to the Eastern Establishment* (New York: Random House, 1975); Richard M. Bernard and Bradley R. Rice, eds., *Sunbelt Cities: Politics and Growth Since World War II* (Austin: University of Texas Press, 1983); Barry Bluestone and Bennett Harrison, *The Deindustrialization of America: Plant Closing, Community Abandonment, and the Dismantling of Basic Industry* (New York: Basic Books, 1982); Chad Berry, *Southern Migrants, Northern Exiles* (Urbana: University of Illinois Press, 2000).

For cultural developments, see Craig Werner, *A Change Is Gonna Come: Music, Race, and the Soul of America* (New York: Penguin, 1999); Edward Berkowitz, *Something Happened: A Political and Cultural Overview of the Seventies* (New York: Columbia University Press, 2006); Philip Jenkins, *Decade of Nightmares: The End of the Sixties and the Making of Eighties America* (New York: Oxford University Press, 2006); George Leonard and Robert Leonard, "Sha Na Na and the Woodstock Generation," *Columbia College Today* (Spring–Summer 1989): 28–31; Tom Wolfe, *Mauve Gloves and Madmen, Clutter and Vine* (New York: Macmillan, 1976); David Harvey, *The Condition of Postmodernity* (Cambridge, MA: Wiley-Blackwell, 1990); Lester C. Thurow, *The Zero-Sum Society: Distribution and the Possibilities for Economic Change* (New York: Penguin, 1980).

For college life, see Helen Lefkowitz Horowitz, *Campus Life: Undergraduate Cultures from the End of the Eighteenth Century to the Present* (New York: Knopf, 1987); Bethany E. Moreton, "Make Payroll, Not War: Business Culture as Youth Culture," in *Rightward Bound: Making America Conservative in the 1970s,* ed. Bruce J. Schulman and Julian E. Zelizer (Cambridge, MA: Harvard University Press, 2008).

For physical fitness, see the President's Council on Physical Fitness and Sports, "History of the President's Council on Physical Fitness and Sports (1956–2006)," http://www.fitness.gov/50thanniversary/toolkit-firstfiftyyears.htm.

For religion and spirituality, see Mark Oppenheimer, *Knocking on Heaven's Door: American Religion in the Age of Counterculture* (New Haven, CT: Yale University Press, 2003); Leo Calvin Rosten, ed., *Religions of America: Ferment and Faith in an Age of Crisis; A New Guide and Almanac* (New York: Simon & Schuster, 1975); Paul Boyer, "The Evangelical Resurgence in 1970s American Protestantism," in *Rightward Bound,* ed. Schulman and Zelizer; Mark Oppenheimer, "The Sixties' Surprising Legacy: Changing Our Notions of the Possible," *Chronicle of Higher Education* 50 (October 3, 2003): B11–B12.

For the ethnic revival, see Matthew Frye Jacobson, "Hyphen Nation: Ethnicity in American Intellectual and Political Life," in *A Companion to Post-1945 America,* ed. Jean-Christophe Agnew and Roy Rosenzweig (Malden, MA: Blackwell, 2002); Kenneth D. Durr, *Behind the Backlash: White Working-Class Politics in Baltimore, 1940–1980* (Chapel Hill: University of North Carolina Press, 2003); Donna R. Gabaccia, *We Are What We Eat: Ethnic Food and the Making of Americans* (Cambridge, MA: Harvard University Press, 1998).

Chapter 13: The Politics of Stagnation

For changes in Congress and partisan politics, see Julian E. Zelizer, *Taxing America: Wilbur D. Mills, Congress, and the State, 1945–1975* (Cambridge: Cambridge University Press, 1998); Edward Berkowitz, *Something Happened: A Political and Cultural Overview of the Seventies* (New York: Columbia University Press, 2006); Benjamin Ginsberg and Martin Shefter, *Politics by Other Means: The Declining Importance of Elections in America* (New York: Basic Books, 1990); H. W. Brands, *The Strange Death of American Liberalism* (New Haven, CT: Yale University Press, 2001).

For Gerald Ford and the Ford administration, see Yanek Mieczkowski, *Gerald Ford and the Challenges of the 1970s* (Lexington: University Press of Kentucky, 2005).

For CETA, see Grace A. Franklin and Randall B. Ripley, *CETA: Politics and Policy, 1973–1982* (Knoxville: University of Tennessee Press, 1984); William Mirengoff, Lester Rindler et al., *CETA: Accomplishments, Problems, Solutions: A Report by the Bureau of Social Science Research, Inc.* (Kalamazoo, MI: W. E. Upjohn Institute for Employment Research, 1982).

For the demise of détente, see James Mann, *The Rise of the Vulcans: The History of Bush's War Cabinet* (New York: Viking, 2004); Robert D. Schulzinger, "The Decline of Détente," in *Gerald R. Ford and the Politics of Post-Watergate America,* ed. Bernard J. Fireston and Alexej Ugrinsky (Westport, CT: Greenwood, 1993).

On neoconservatives and foreign policy, see John Ehrman, *The Rise of Neoconservatism: Intellectuals and Foreign Affairs, 1945–1994* (New Haven, CT: Yale University Press, 1995); Andrew J. Bacevich, *The New American Militarism: How Americans Are Seduced by War* (New York: Oxford University Press, 2005).

For Carter's economic policy, see Anthony S. Campagna, *Economic Policy in the Carter Administration* (Westport, CT: Greenwood, 1995); W. Carl Biven, *Jimmy Carter's Economy: Policy in an Age of Limits* (Chapel Hill: University of North Carolina Press, 2002); Melvyn Dubofsky, "Jimmy Carter and the End of the Politics of Productivity," in *The Carter Presidency: Policy Choices in the Post–New Deal Era,* ed. Gary M. Fink and Hugh Davis Graham (Lawrence: University Press of Kansas, 1998); Judith Stein, *Pivotal Decade: How the United States Traded Factories for Finance in the Seventies* (New Haven, CT: Yale University Press, 2010); William Greider, *Secrets of the Temple: How the Federal Reserve Runs the Country* (New York: Simon & Schuster, 1989).

For energy policy, see John C. Barrow, "An Age of Limits: Jimmy Carter and the Quest for a National Energy Policy," in *Carter Presidency,* ed. Fink and Graham; Daniel

Yergin, *The Prize: The Epic Quest for Oil, Money, and Power* (New York: Simon & Schuster, 1991).

For Carter's foreign policy, see William Stueck, "Placing Jimmy Carter's Foreign Policy," in *Carter Presidency,* ed. Fink and Graham; Stephen E. Ambrose and Douglas G. Brinkley, *Rise to Globalism: American Foreign Policy Since 1938,* 8th revised ed. (New York: Penguin, 1997).

For the urban fiscal crisis, see Joshua B. Freeman, *Working-Class New York: Life and Labor Since World War II* (New York: New Press, 2000); William E. Simon, *A Time for Truth* (New York: Berkley, 1978); Todd Swanstrom, *The Crisis of Growth Politics: Cleveland, Kucinich, and the Challenge of Urban Populism* (Philadelphia: Temple University Press, 1985).

For Proposition 13 and the tax revolt, see Clarence Y. H. Lo, *Small Property Versus Big Government: Social Origins of the Property Tax Revolt* (Berkeley: University of California Press, 1990); Paul Peretz, "There Was No Tax Revolt!," *Politics and Society* 11 (June 1982): 231–49; Mike Davis, *City of Quartz: Excavating the Future in Los Angeles* (London: Verso, 1990); Robert O. Self, "Prelude to the Tax Revolt: The Politics of the 'Tax Dollar' in Postwar California," in *The New Suburban History,* ed. Kevin M. Kruse and Thomas J. Sugrue (Chicago: University of Chicago Press, 2006); Daniel A. Smith, "Howard Jarvis, Populist Entrepreneur: Reevaluating the Causes of Proposition 13," *Social Science History* 23 (Summer 1999): 173–210; David Lowery, "After the Tax Revolt: Some Positive, If Unintended, Consequences," *Social Science Quarterly* 67 (December 1986): 736–50.

For crime and punishment, see David Levinson, ed., *Encyclopedia of Crime and Punishment* (Thousand Oaks, CA: Sage, 2002); Marie Gottschalk, *The Prison and the Gallows: The Politics of Mass Incarceration in America* (New York: Cambridge University Press, 2006); Sasha Abramsky, *American Furies: Crime, Punishment, and Vengeance in the Age of Mass Imprisonment* (Boston: Beacon, 2007); David Garland, "Capital Punishment and American Culture," *Punishment & Society* 7 (October 2005): 347–76.

For ERA, abortion, and gay rights, see Philip Jenkins, *Decade of Nightmares: The End of the Sixties and the Making of Eighties America* (New York: Oxford University Press, 2006); Matthew D. Lassiter, "Inventing Family Values," in *Rightward Bound: Making America Conservative in the 1970s,* ed. Bruce J. Schulman and Julian E. Zelizer (Cambridge, MA: Harvard University Press, 2008); Kristin Luker, *Abortion and the Politics of Motherhood* (Berkeley: University of California Press, 1984); Fred Fejes, *Gay Rights and Moral Panic: The Origins of America's Debate on Homosexuality* (New York: Palgrave Macmillan, 2008).

Chapter 14: The Corporate Revolution

For economic decline in general, see Robert Brenner, *The Boom and the Bubble* (London: Verso, 2002); Michael A. Bernstein and David E. Adler, eds., *Understanding American Economic Decline* (Cambridge: Cambridge University Press, 1994).

For the steel industry, see David Bensman and Roberta Lynch, *Rusted Dreams: Hard Times in a Steel Community* (New York: McGraw-Hill, 1987); Mark Reutter, *Making Steel: Sparrows Point and the Rise and Ruin of American Industrial Might* (New York, Simon & Schuster, 1988); William Serrin, *Homestead: The Glory and Tragedy of an American Steel Town* (New York: Times Books, 1992); Milton Rogovin and Michael Frisch, *Portraits in Steel* (Ithaca, NY: Cornell University Press, 1993).

For the automobile industry, see Steve Babson, *Working Detroit: The Making of a Union Town* (Detroit: Wayne State University Press, 1984); Ruth Milkman, *Farewell to the Factory: Auto Workers in the Late Twentieth Century* (Berkeley: University of California Press, 1997); Dana Frank, *Buy American: The Untold Story of Economic Nationalism* (Boston: Beacon, 1999).

For the impact of factory closings, see Jon C. Teaford, *Cities of the Heartland: The Rise and Fall of the Industrial Midwest* (Bloomington: Indiana University Press, 1993); Becky Nicolaides, *My Blue Heaven: Life and Politics in the Working-Class Suburbs of Los Angeles, 1920–1965* (Chicago: University of Chicago Press, 2007); Michael K. Honey, *Going Down Jericho Road: The Memphis Strike, Martin Luther King's Last Campaign* (New York: Norton, 2007).

For the decline of union power, wages, and benefits, see Kim Moody, *An Injury to All: The Decline of American Unionism* (London: Verso, 1988); Lawrence Mishel, Jared Bernstein, and John Schmitt, *The State of Working America, 2000/2001* (Ithaca, NY: Cornell University Press, 2001).

For the reorganization of production, see Steve Babson, ed., *Lean Work: Empowerment and Exploitation in the Global Auto Industry* (Detroit: Wayne State University Press, 1995); Richard Feldman and Michael Betzold, eds., *End of the Line: Autoworkers and the American Dream; An Oral History* (New York: Illini Books, 1988).

For corporate reorganization and financialization, see David M. Gordon, *Fat and Mean: The Corporate Squeeze of Working Americans and the Myth of Managerial "Downsizing"* (New York: Free Press, 1996); Alfred D. Chandler Jr., "Corporate Strategy and Structure: Some Current Considerations," *Society* 28 (March–April 1991): 35–38; Mary Zey and Brande Camp, "The Transformation from Multidivisional Form to Corporate Groups of Subsidiaries in the 1980s," *Sociological Quarterly* 37 (Spring 1996): 327–51; Mary Zey and Tami Swenson, "The Transformation and Survival of Fortune 500 Industrial Corporations Through Mergers and Acquisitions, 1981–1995," *Sociological Quarterly* 42 (Summer 2001): 461–86; Steve Fraser, *Every Man a Speculator: A History of Wall Street in American Life* (New York: HarperCollins, 2005).

For the political mobilization of business, see David Vogel, *Fluctuating Fortunes: The Political Power of Business in America* (New York: Beard Books, 1989); John Judis, *The Paradox of American Democracy: Elites, Special Interests, and the Betrayal of Public Trust* (New York: Pantheon, 2000).

For labor law reform efforts, see Joseph A. McCartin, "Turnabout Years: Public Sector Unionism and the Fiscal Crisis," in *Rightward Bound: Making America Conservative in the 1970s*, ed. Bruce J. Schulman and Julian E. Zelizer (Cambridge, MA: Harvard University Press, 2008); Marc Linder, *Wars of Attrition: Vietnam, the Business Roundtable, and the Decline of Construction Unions* (Iowa City: Fanpihua Press, 1999).

For diminished regulation, see Thomas O. McGarity and Sidney A. Shapiro, *Workers at Risk: The Failed Promise of the Occupational Safety and Health Administration* (Westort, CT: Praeger, 1993); Eugene N. White, "Banking and Finance in the Twentieth Century," and Richard H. K. Vietor, "Government Regulation of Business," in *The Cambridge Economic History of the United States, vol. 3, The Twentieth Century*, ed. Stanley L. Engerman and Robert E. Gallman (Cambridge: Cambridge University Press, 2000).

For meatpacking, see Wilson J. Warren, *Tied to the Great Packing Machine: The Midwest and Meatpacking* (Iowa City: University of Iowa Press, 2007); Charles R. Perry and Delwyn H. Kegley, *Disintegration and Change: Labor Relations in the Meat Packing Industry* (Philadelphia: Industrial Research Unit, Wharton School, University of Pennsylvania, 1989); Deborah Fink, *Cutting into the Meatpacking Line: Workers and Change in the Rural Midwest* (Chapel Hill: University of North Carolina Press, 1998); Roger Horowitz, *"Negro and White United and Fight!": A Social History of Industrial Unionism in Meatpacking, 1930–90* (Urbana: University of Illinois Press, 1997); Peter Rachleff, *Hard-Pressed in the Heartland: The Hormel Strike and the Future of the Labor Movement* (Boston: South End Press, 1993).

For the computer industry, see Paul E. Ceruzzi, *A History of Modern Computing,* 2nd ed. (Cambridge, MA: MIT Press, 2003); Steven Levy, *Hackers: Heroes of the Computer Revolution* (Garden City, NY: Anchor/Doubleday, 1984); John Markoff, *What the Dormouse Said: How the Sixties Counterculture Shaped the Personal Computer Industry* (New York: Viking, 2005); Sanford M. Jacoby, *Modern Manors: Welfare Capitalism Since the New Deal* (Princeton, NJ: Princeton University Press, 1997); Eden Medina, "Computers," in *Encyclopedia of U.S. Labor and Working-Class History, vol. 1,* ed. Eric Arnesen (New York: Routledge/Taylor & Francis, 2007).

For the retail industry, see Nelson Lichtenstein, ed., *Wal-Mart: The Face of Twenty-First-Century Capitalism* (New York: New Press, 2006); Sandra S. Vance and Roy V. Scott, *Wal-Mart: A History of Sam Walton's Retail Phenomenon* (New York: Twayne, 1994); Charles Fishman, *The Wal-Mart Effect: How the World's Most Powerful Company Really Works—and How It's Transforming the American Economy* (New York: Penguin Press, 2006).

Chapter 15: The Reagan Revolution

For Reagan's political and personal outlook, see John Patrick Diggins, *Ronald Reagan: Fate, Freedom, and the Making of History* (New York: Norton, 2007); Randall Balmer, *God in the White House: A History; How Faith Shaped the Presidency from John F. Kennedy to George W. Bush* (New York: HarperCollins, 2008); Lou Cannon, *President Reagan: The Role of a Lifetime* (New York: PublicAffairs, 2000); Thomas W. Evans, *The Education of Ronald Reagan: The General Electric Years and the Untold Story of His Conversion to Conservatism* (New York: Columbia University Press, 2006).

For the intellectual and cultural tone of Reaganism, see Haynes Johnson, *Sleepwalking Through History: America in the Reagan Years* (New York: Norton, 1991); Nicolaus Mills, ed., *Culture in an Age of Money: The Legacy of the 1980s in America* (Chicago: Ivan R. Dee, 1990); William A. Henry III, *Visions of America: How We Saw the 1984 Election* (Boston: Atlantic Monthly Press, 1985).

For economic policy, tax cuts, and the budget, see David M. Gordon, Thomas E. Weisskopf, and Samuel Bowles, "Right-Wing Economics in the 1980s: The Anatomy of a Failure," in *Understanding American Economic Decline,* ed. Michael A. Bernstein and David E. Adler (Cambridge: Cambridge University Press, 1994); David Alan Stockman, *The Triumph of Politics: How the Reagan Revolution Failed* (New York: Harper & Row, 1986); Iwan W. Morgan, *Deficit Government: Taxing and Spending in Modern America* (Chicago: Ivan R. Dee, 1995).

For military spending, see Benjamin Ginsberg and Martin Shefter, *Politics by Other Means: The Declining Importance of Elections in America* (New York: Basic Books, 1990); Michael Edelstein, "War and the American Economy in the Twentieth Century," in *The Cambridge Economic History of the United States, vol. 3, The Twentieth Century,* ed. Stanley L. Engerman and Robert E. Gallman (Cambridge: Cambridge University Press, 2000).

For environmental policy, see Philip Shabecoff, *A Fierce Green Fire: The American Environmental Movement,* revised ed. (Washington, DC: Island Press, 2003); J. R. McNeill, *Something New Under the Sun: An Environmental History of the Twentieth-Century World* (New York: Norton, 2000).

For labor, see Steve Babson, *The Unfinished Struggle: Turning Points in American Labor, 1877–Present* (Lanham, MD: Rowman & Littlefield, 1999); Jonathan D. Rosenblum, *Copper Crucible: How the Arizona Miners' Strike of 1983 Recast Labor-Management Relations in America* (Ithaca, NY: ILR Press, 1995); John Logan, "Permanent Replacements and the End of Labor's 'Only True Weapon,'" *International Labor and Working-Class History* 74 (2008): 171–92.

For financial industry corruption and its cultural effect, see Robert M. Collins, *Transforming America: Politics and Culture in the Reagan Years* (New York: Columbia University Press, 2007); Steve Fraser, *Every Man a Speculator: A History of Wall Street in American Life* (New York: HarperCollins, 2005).

For income inequality, see Thomas Byrne Edsall, with Mary D. Edsall, *Chain Reaction: The Impact of Race, Rights, and Taxes on American Politics* (New York: Norton, 1991); Kevin Phillips, *The Politics of Rich and Poor: Wealth and the American Electorate in the Reagan Aftermath* (New York: Random House, 1990).

For AIDS policy, see Randy Shilts, *And the Band Played On: Politics, People, and the AIDS Epidemic* (New York: St. Martin's Press, 1987); Jennifer Brier, *Infectious Ideas: U. S. Political Responses to the AIDS Crisis* (Chapel Hill: University of North Carolina Press, 2009).

Chapter 16: Cold War Redux

For Afghanistan, see Zbigniew Brzezinski, *Power and Principle: Memoirs of the National Security Adviser, 1977–1981* (New York: Farrar, Straus & Giroux, 1983); Steve Coll, *Ghost Wars: The Secret History of the CIA, Afghanistan, and bin Laden from the Soviet Invasion to September 10, 2001* (New York: Penguin, 2004).

For Reagan and the Soviet Union, see David S. Painter and Thomas S. Blanton, "The End of the Cold War," in *A Companion to Post-1945 America,* ed. Jean-Christophe Agnew and Roy Rosenzweig (Malden, MA: Blackwell, 2006); Richard Reeves, *President Reagan: The Triumph of Imagination* (New York: Simon & Schuster, 2005); James Mann, *The Rebellion of Ronald Reagan: A History of the End of the Cold War* (New York: Viking, 2009): Melvyn Leffler, *For the Soul of Mankind: The United States, the Soviet Union, and the Cold War* (New York: Hill & Wang, 2007).

For Central America policy, see Greg Grandin, *Empire's Workshop: Latin America, the United States, and the Rise of the New Imperialism* (New York: Metropolitan Books, 2006); Jeane Kirkpatrick, "Dictatorships and Double Standards," *Commentary* 68 (February 1979): 34–45.

For Lebanon and Grenada, see Peter Huchthausen, *America's Splendid Little Wars: A Short History of U.S. Engagement from the Fall of Saigon to Baghdad* (New York: Penguin, 2003); Mike Davis, *Buda's Wagon: A Brief History of the Car Bomb* (London: Verso, 2007).

For Iran-Contra, see Jane Mayer and Doyle McManus, *Landslide: The Unmaking of the President, 1984–1988* (Boston: Houghton Mifflin, 1988).

For the end of the Cold War in Europe, see Tony Judt, *Postwar: A History of Europe Since 1945* (New York: Penguin, 2005).

Chapter 17: "I'm Running Out of Demons"

For the cultural and ideological aftermath of the Cold War, see Tom Engelhardt, *The End of Victory Culture: Cold War America and the Disillusioning of a Generation* (New York: Basic Books, 1995); Francis Fukuyama, "The End of History?," *National Interest* 16 (Summer 1989): 3–18; John Williamson, "A Short History of the Washington Consensus," in *The Washington Consensus Reconsidered: Toward a New Global Governance,* ed. Narcis Serra and Joseph E. Stiglitz (New York: Oxford University Press, 2008).

For Bush's election and administration, see Michael Duffy and Dan Goodgame, *Marching in Place: The Status Quo Presidency of George Bush* (New York: Simon & Schuster, 1992); Michael Schaller, *Right Turn: American Life in the Reagan-Bush Era, 1980–1992* (New York: Oxford University Press, 2007); Steve Fraser and Gary Gerstle, epilogue to *The Rise and Fall of the New Deal Order, 1930–1980* (Princeton, NJ: Princeton

University Press, 1989); John Robert Greene, *The Presidency of George Bush* (Lawrence: University Press of Kansas, 2000).

For the Gulf War and renewed militarism, see Andew J. Bacevich, *The New American Militarism: How Americans Are Seduced by War* (New York: Oxford University Press, 2005); Thomas M. Magstadt, *An Empire If You Can Keep It: Power and Principle in American Foreign Policy* (Washington, DC: CQ Press, 2004); James Mann, *The Rise of the Vulcans: The History of Bush's War Cabinet* (New York: Viking, 2004).

Chapter 18: Triangulation

For Bill Clinton and the Clinton administration, see Bill Clinton, *My Life* (New York: Random House, 2004); James T. Patterson, *Restless Giant: The United States from Watergate to Bush v. Gore* (New York: Oxford University Press, 2005); Peter B. Levy, *Encyclopedia of the Clinton Presidency* (Westport, CT: Greenwood, 2002); Bob Woodward, *The Agenda: Inside the Clinton White House* (New York: Simon & Schuster, 1994); Christopher Hitchens, *No One Left to Lie To: The Triangulations of William Jefferson Clinton* (London: Verso, 1999).

For health-care reform, see Theda Skocpol, *Boomerang: Health Care Reform and the Turn Against Government* (New York: Norton, 1996); Colin Gordon, *Dead on Arrival: The Politics of Health Care in Twentieth-Century America* (Princeton, NJ: Princeton University Press, 2003).

For Newt Gingrich and other conservative opponents of Clinton, see Todd Gitlin, afterword to *Reassessing the Sixties: Debating the Political and Cultural Legacy,* ed. Stephen Macedo (New York: Norton, 1997); David Remnick, "Lost in Space," *New Yorker* 70 (December 5, 1994): 79–86; Newt Gingrich, *To Renew America* (New York: HarperCollins, 1995).

For welfare reform, see Jill Quadagno, "Social Security Policy and the Entitlement Debate: The New American Exceptionalism," Frances Fox Piven, "Welfare and the Transformation of Electoral Politics," and Ronald Walters, "The Democratic Party and the Politics of Welfare Reform," in *Social Policy and the Conservative Agenda,* ed. Clarence Y. H. Lo and Michael Schwartz (Malden, MA: Blackwell, 1998); James MacGregor Burns and Georgia J. Sorenson, *Dead Center: Clinton-Gore Leadership and the Perils of Moderation* (New York: Lisa Drew/Scribner, 1999).

For sex education, see Janice M. Irvine, *Talk About Sex: The Battles over Sex Education in the United States* (Berkeley: University of California Press, 2002).

For immigration and immigrant rights, see Douglas S. Massey, Jorge Durand, and Nolan J. Malone, *Beyond Smoke and Mirrors: Mexican Immigration in an Era of Economic Integration* (New York: Russell Sage Foundation, 2002); Otis L. Graham Jr., *Unguarded Gates: A History of America's Immigration Crisis* (Lanham, MD: Rowman & Littlefield, 2004); Arthur M. Schlesinger Jr., *The Disuniting of America: Reflections on a Multicultural Society* (New York: Norton, 1992).

For military spending and bases, see David E. Lockwood and George Siehl, *Military Base Closures: A Historical Review from 1988 to 1995* (Washington, DC: Congressional Research Service, 2004); Chalmers Johnson, *The Sorrows of Empire: Militarism, Secrecy, and the End of the Republic* (New York: Henry Holt, 2004); Chalmers Johnson, *Blowback: The Costs and Consequences of American Empire* (New York: Henry Holt, 2000); William Greider, *Fortress America: The American Military and the Consequences of Peace* (New York: PublicAffairs, 1998).

For NATO expansion, see Peter Gowan, *The Global Gamble: Washington's Faustian Bid for World Dominance* (London: Verso, 1999); Warren I. Cohen, *America's Failing Empire: U.S. Foreign Relations Since the Cold War* (Malden, MA: Blackwell, 2005).

For Clinton international economic policy, see Greg Grandin, *Empire's Workshop: Latin America, the United States, and the Rise of the New Imperialism* (New York: Metropolitan Books, 2006); Michael Lind, "Conservative Elites and the Counterrevolution Against the New Deal," in *Ruling America: A History of Wealth and Power in America,* ed. Steve Fraser and Gary Gerstle (Cambridge, MA: Harvard University Press, 2005).

For humanitarian interventions and human rights, see Samuel Moyn, *The Last Utopia: Human Rights in History* (Cambridge, MA: Harvard University Press, 2010); David Rieff, *At the Point of a Gun: Democratic Dreams and Armed Intervention* (New York: Simon & Schuster, 2005); Samantha Power, *"A Problem from Hell": America and the Age of Genocide* (New York: HarperCollins, 2002).

For the economy, see Robert Brenner, *The Boom and the Bubble* (London: Verso, 2002); Steven Hipple, "Worker Displacement in an Expanding Economy," *Monthly Labor Review* 120 (December 1997): 26–39; Louis Uchitelle, *The Disposable American: Layoffs and Their Consequences* (New York: Random House, 2006); Dennis Rodkin, "The Richest Chicagoans of All Time," *Chicago* 55 (April 2006): 81–83.

For the union movement, see Kim Moody, *U.S. Labor in Trouble and Transition: The Failure of Reform from Above, the Promise of Revival from Below* (London: Verso, 2007); John J. Sweeney, *America Needs a Raise: Fighting for Economic Security and Social Justice* (Boston: Replica Books, 1996).

Chapter 19: Living Large

For population and immigration, see Herbert S. Klein, *A Population History of the United States* (Cambridge: Cambridge University Press, 2004); United Nations, Department of Economic and Social Affairs, Population Division, *International Migration 2002* (New York: United Nations, 2002); Reed Ueda, *Postwar Immigrant America: A Social History* (Boston: St. Martin's, 1994); Ruth Milkman, *L.A. Story: Immigrant Workers and the Future of the U.S. Labor Movement* (New York: Russell Sage Foundation, 2006); Marc J. Perry and Paul J. Mackun, *Population Change and Distribution, 1990 to 2000* (Washington, DC: U.S. Census Bureau, 2001).

For suburban growth, see Joel Garreau, *Edge City: Life on the New Frontier* (New York: Anchor, 1991); David Brooks, *On Paradise Drive: How We Live Now (and Always Have) in the Future Tense* (New York: Simon & Schuster, 2004); Rosalyn Baxandall and Elizabeth Ewen, *Picture Windows: How the Suburbs Happened* (New York: Basic Books, 2000); Richard D. Alba et al., "Immigrant Groups in the Suburbs: A Reexamination of Suburbanization and Spatial Assimilation," *American Sociological Review* 64 (June 1999): 446–60; Mike Davis, "The Inland Empire," *Nation* 276 (April 7, 2003): 15–18; Elizabeth Blackmar, "Of REITS and Rights: Absentee Ownership in the Periphery," in *City, Country, Empire: Landscapes in Environmental History,* ed. Jeffry M. Diefendorf and Kurk Dorsey (Pittsburgh: University of Pittsburgh Press, 2005).

For gated communities, see Setha Low, *Behind the Gates: Life, Security and the Pursuit of Happiness in Fortress America* (New York: Routledge, 2003); Edward J. Blakely and Mary Gail Snyder, *Fortress America: Gated Communities in the United States* (Washington, DC: Brookings Institution Press, 1997); Elena Vesselinov, "Members Only: Gated Communities and Residential Segregation in the Metropolitan United States," *Sociological Forum* 23 (September 2008): 536–55.

For education spending, see State Higher Education Executive Officers, *State Higher Education Finance, FY 2006* (Boulder, CO: State Higher Education Executive Officers, 2007).

For car usage and SUVs, see Tom Lewis, *Divided Highways: Building the Interstate Highways, Transforming American Life* (New York: Viking Penguin, 1997); Keith

Bradsher, *High and Mighty: SUVs—the World's Most Dangerous Vehicles and How They Got That Way* (New York: PublicAffairs, 2002).

For retailing, see James B. Twitchell, *Living It Up: Our Love Affair with Luxury* (New York: Simon & Schuster, 2002); Naomi Klein, *No Logo: Taking Aim at the Brand Bullies* (New York: Picador, 1999).

For body size and diet, see Cynthia L. Ogden, Cheryl D. Fryar, Margaret D. Carroll, and Katherine M. Flegal, "Mean Body Weight, Height, and Body Mass Index, United States 1960–2002," *Advance Data from Vital and Health Statistics No. 347* (Hyattsville, MD: National Center for Health Statistics, 2004); Greg Critser, *Fat Land: How Americans Became the Fattest People in the World* (Boston: First Mariner Books, 2003); Harriet B. Pesser, "Toward a 24-Hour Economy," *Science* 284 (June 11, 1999): 1778–79.

For the environmental impact of living large, see Ted Steinberg, "Lawn and Landscape in World Context, 1945–2000," *OAH Magazine of History* 19 (November 2005): 62–68; Victoria D. Markham, with Nadia Steinzor, *U.S. National Report on Population and the Environment* (New Canaan, CT: Center for Environment and Population, 2006).

For population control, see Matthew Connelly, *Fatal Misconception: The Struggle to Control World Population* (Cambridge, MA: Harvard University Press, 2008); Paul R. and Anne H. Ehrlich, "The Most Overpopulated Nation," in Lindsey Grant, ed., *Elephants in the Volkswagen: Facing Tough Questions About Our Overcrowded Country* (New York: W. H. Freeman, 1992); United States Commission on Population Growth and the American Future, *Population and the American Future* (Washington, DC: U.S. Government Printing Office, 1972).

Epilogue: America After 9/11

For al Qaeda, the 9/11 attacks, and their aftermath, see National Commission on Terrorist Attacks Upon the United States, *The 9/11 Commission Report: Final Report of the National Commission on Terrorist Attacks upon the United States* (Washington, DC: U.S. Government Printing Office, 2004); John W. Dower, *Cultures of War: Pearl Harbor/Hiroshima/9-11/Iraq* (New York: Norton/New Press, 2010); Peter L. Bergen, *The Longest War: The Enduring Conflict Between America and al-Qaeda* (New York: Free Press, 2011); Christian Parenti, *The Soft Cage: Surveillance in America from Slave Passes to the War on Terror* (New York: Basic Books, 2003).

For the Iraq War, see Bob Woodward, *Plan of Attack* (New York: Simon & Schuster, 2004); George Packer, *The Assassin's Gate: America in Iraq* (New York: Farrar, Straus & Giroux, 2005); Craig Unger, *The Fall of the House of Bush* (New York: Scribner, 2007); Seymour M. Hersh, *Chain of Command: The Road from 9/11 to Abu Ghraib* (New York: HarperCollins, 2004); Rajiv Chandrasekaran, *Imperial Life in the Emerald City: Inside Iraq's Green Zone* (New York: Knopf, 2007); Michael R. Gordon and Bernard E. Trainor, *Cobra II: The Inside Story of the Invasion and Occupation of Iraq* (New York: Pantheon, 2006); Special Inspector General, Iraq Reconstruction, *Hard Lessons: The Iraq Reconstruction Experience* (Washington, D.C.: U.S. Government Printing Office, 2009).

For the Bush administration, see James Mann, *The Rise of the Vulcans: The History of Bush's War Cabinet* (New York: Viking, 2004); Barton Gellman, *Angler: The Cheney Vice Presidency* (New York: Penguin, 2008); Julian E. Zelizer, ed., *The Presidency of George W. Bush: A First Historical Assessment* (Princeton, NJ: Princeton University Press, 2010); Robert Draper, *Dead Certain: The Presidency of George W. Bush* (New York: Free Press, 2007); Frank Rich, *The Greatest Story Ever Sold: The Decline and Fall of Truth from 9/11 to Katrina* (New York: Penguin, 2006); Jed Horne, *Breach of Faith: Hurricane Katrina and the Near Death of a Great American City* (New York: Random House, 2006).

For the economy, see Dean Baker, *Plunder and Blunder: The Rise and Fall of the Bubble Economy* (Sausalito, CA: PoliPoint Press, 2009); Robert Brenner, "What Is Good for Goldman Sachs Is Good for America: The Origins of the Current Crisis," Center for Social Theory and Comparative History, UCLA, April 18, 2009; Menzie D. Chinn and Jeffry A. Frieden, *Lost Decades: The Making of America's Debt Crisis and the Long Recovery* (New York: Norton, 2011).

Index

Abdul-Jabbar, Kareem, 125–26
abortion, 139, 238, 264, 340, 341, 368–70,
    409, 427–28, 446, 464–65, 474
Abu Ghraib, 473
academic life, 89–90
Acheson, Dean, 52, 63, 66, 81, 87, 94,
    100, 101, 246
Adelman, Kenneth, 469
Afghanistan, 415, 439, 466–68, 473, 475
  Soviet invasion of, 332, 333, 390–92, 396,
    402, 407, 439
AFL, 39, 47–48, 55, 73, 441
AFL-CIO, 213, 217–18, 270, 285, 417, 430–31,
    436, 441
Africa, 171, 226, 325, 391–92, 404
African Americans, 6, 14–18, 23, 31, 33–35,
    37, 38, 48, 54, 152, 159, 316
  Black Power movement and, 247–48, 250,
    258–59, 273, 316
  employment and, 133, 135, 140–41, 145–
    46, 184, 271–73, 348, 349, 441
  GI Bill and, 33–34
  housing and, 15, 23, 34, 98, 129–30, 133,
    145–46, 198, 214–16, 272, 369
  incarceration and, 339
  migration to North, 6, 38, 133, 144, 152
  military and, 15–16, 18, 35, 74, 75
  political officeholders, 259
  residential segregation and, 135, 257
  slavery and, 12, 14
  in South, 14–18
  at universities, 256, 258
  voting by, 14, 35, 37, 38, 77, 145, 152, 156,
    161, 180, 204, 206, 207, 209, 326
  welfare and, 426

  see also civil rights
Agnew, Spiro, 250, 252, 279, 289, 290, 293
agriculture, 22, 77, 78, 116, 117, 131–32, 134,
    295–96, 375, 449
  cotton, 12–13, 15, 20, 131–32
  in Midwest, 3–4, 7
  in Northeast, 11
  in South, 12–13
  in Southwest, 19–20
  in West, 23–24
AIDS, 388–89
airlines, 262–63, 360
air traffic controllers, 377, 382, 387
Alaska, 21, 22, 74, 157–58
Ali, Muhammad, 327
Alinscough, Horace, 120
Allbaugh, Joe M., 476
Allen, Anita Lafrance, 257–58
Allen, Paul, 362
Allende, Salvador, 281
Allison, John, 84
al Qaeda, 439, 466, 468, 469, 471, 473
Americans for Democratic Action, 72
American Veterans Committee, 72–73
Anderson, John, 320, 372
Anderson, Marian, 162
Angola, 325–26
Apple, 362–63
Arbenz, Jacobo, 170, 171
Archibald, Katherine, 24
Armey, Dick, 422, 424
Armitage, Richard, 466
arts, 213
Asian Americans, 22–23, 35, 145, 157
Attlee, Clement, 60, 84

automobile industry, 5–6, 115, 116, 133,
　　347–49, 351, 360, 463–64
automobiles, 136–39, 211–12, 378
　large, 455–57, 462, 463, 465

Baker, Charles, 181
Baker, James, 404, 434
Baker, Ella, 160
Bakker, Jim, 315, 384
Baldwin, James, 265
Balkans, 438
Baltimore, Md., 305
banks, 8–9, 10, 357–58, 380, 384, 479, 480
Baraka, Amiri, 259
Barnett, Ross, 182
Bartley, Robert L., 371
Baruch, Bernard, 56, 63–64
Bates, Daisy, 159
Baum, L. Frank, 4
Beats, 189–90, 235
Beck, Dave, 122
Bentley, Elizabeth, 94–95
Bernanke, Ben, 479
Bernstein, Carl, 288
Berry, Chuck, 191
bin Laden, Osama, 439, 466–68
birth control, 236, 237–38, 263, 446, 464–65
birth rate, 119, 446
Bishop, Maurice, 397–98
Boesky, Ivan, 383
Bork, Robert, 401
Bosnia, 438
Boulware, Lemuel, 368
Bowles, Chester, 322
Bozell, L. Brent, 196
Bradley, Tom, 259
Bremer, L. Paul, 470
Brewster, Kingman, 313
Brezhnev, Leonid, 280–82, 392, 402
Bricker, John, 76, 91, 104–5
Bricker Amendment, 104–5, 107
Brinkley, David, 252
Britain, 49–51, 54, 56, 58, 62, 65–67, 69–70,
　　80, 84, 168–69, 302, 333
　Iran and, 60–61, 167
Brooks, David, 455
Brown, Edmund, 187
Brown, Linda, 149
Brown, Michael, 476
Brown, Norman O., 189
Brown, Oliver, 149
Brown, Pat, 217
Brown, Ron, 436
Brownell, Herbert, 156
Bryant, Anita, 341–42

Brzezinski, Zbigniew, 390
Buchanan, Pat, 443
Buckley, William F., 197
buffalo, 450
Bundy, Harvey, 54
Bundy, McGeorge, 54
Bundy, William, 54
Burford (Gorsuch), Anne, 376, 380–81
Burger, Warren E., 257
Burke, Edmund, 368
Bush, George H. W., 11, 371, 409–15
　Gulf War and, 411–15, 418
　in 1992 election, 417–19
　Soviet Union and, 402–3
Bush, George W., 11
　counterterrorism and, 471–72, 475
　economy and, 474–79
　in election of 2000, 442–44
　financial crisis and, 476–79
　Hurricane Katrina and, 475–76
　Iraq War and, 469–73
　9/11 and, 466–69, 471–75
Bush, Prescott, 11
businesses, 343–66
　downsizing by, 344–49, 352
　federal regulation of, 357, 358
　financialization of capital and, 352–54
　Japanese, 351
　labor costs and, 344–45, 349–52
　management in, 351–52
　new models in, 358–66
　politics and, 354–58
Byrnes, James F., 59, 63, 64, 67

Caldwell, Erskine, 2
California, 21, 22, 336–38, 429–31, 452, 453
Cambodia, 222, 223, 229, 276–79, 286,
　　292–95, 404
Camus, Albert, 197
capitalism, 52, 54, 113–14, 119, 312–13, 343,
　　384, 408–9, 415, 435, 436
　Iron Curtain and, 62–70
capital punishment, 339
Carey, Ron, 441
Carmichael, Stokely, 247, 248
Carson, Rachel, 192, 210–11
Carter, Jimmy, 285, 319–21, 324, 326–31, 334,
　　356, 367, 382, 416
　coal strike and, 350
　economy and, 328–31, 371–73, 376
　energy and, 330–31
　foreign affairs and, 331–34, 371, 374,
　　390–92, 396, 398
　hostage crisis and, 333, 371, 398
　religious faith of, 315, 326–27, 370

Carville, James, 420
Casey, William, 396, 399, 400
Castro, Fidel, 171–73, 175, 186, 332, 414
censorship, 237
Central America, 393–94, 398, 404
Chambers, Whittaker, 94–95
Chaney, James, 193
Chávez, César, 260
Cheney, Dick, 324, 469, 472, 475
Chicano movement, 260–61
children's rights, 266, 341–42
Chile, 281, 332
China, x, 51, 58, 79, 82, 86–87, 96, 167, 168,
    222, 225, 231, 275, 409
    Korea and, 84, 85, 105–6
    Nixon and, 275, 280–82
    repression in, 414
    Soviet Union and, 87, 105, 275
    Vietnam and, 228, 277, 281
Churchill, Winston, 58, 60, 63, 65, 66
CIA, 69, 90, 108, 164, 168, 170–73, 186, 226,
    232, 234, 235, 281, 288, 291–92, 311, 318,
    321, 396, 398, 399, 438, 439, 472–73
CIO, 30, 32, 39, 47–48, 54–55, 73, 98,
    121, 198, 441
cities, 126, 129, 131, 134, 135, 215, 306,
    311, 449
civil rights, xi, xii, 73–78, 143–61, 185–86,
    187, 192–93, 198, 204, 207–9, 214–16,
    235, 241, 247, 250, 255–59, 283, 316, 424
    affirmative action and, 272, 273, 388, 429
    anticommunism and, 98, 147
    buses and, 144, 147–48, 153–55, 178–79
    Civil Rights Act, 200–202, 204, 205, 207,
        208, 247, 262, 271, 272
    Democratic Party and, 75–76, 146, 156,
        160, 204, 216
    Freedom Rides and, 178–80, 183, 192
    Freedom Summer and, 193, 194, 204
    influence on other movements, 192–93,
        262, 263, 266
    Johnson and, 156, 157, 158, 199–202, 208
    Kennedy and, 160–61, 162, 178–85, 198, 200
    King and, see King, Martin Luther, Jr.
    March on Washington and, 184–85
    militant activism and, 144, 185, 216,
        247–48, 250, 258–59
    Nixon and, 156, 160, 161, 255–57
    opposition to integration, 266, 369
    Reagan and, 388
    school desegregation and, 98, 148–52,
        155–57, 181–84, 200, 215–16, 256–58,
        266, 337, 369, 388, 429
    sit-ins and, 158–60, 192
    in South, 143, 152–56, 160, 178–80

    Truman and, 74–76
    World War II and, 143–45
Civil War, x, 143
Clark, Kenneth B., 241
Clay, Lucius, 64
Clayton, William, 56, 66
Cleveland, Ohio, 335–36
Clifford, Clark, 243, 245
Clinton, Bill, 416–42
    affairs of, 417, 423, 431–33
    economy and, 419–20, 423, 439–42, 479–80
    election of, 417–19
    foreign policy and, 433–39
    health care and, 420–22, 423, 425
    impeachment of, 431–33
    reelection of, 427
    taxes and, 420, 423
    Whitewater and, 432
Clinton, Hillary Rodham, 416, 417, 421, 423
Cold War, xi, xiii, 69, 85, 87, 89, 95–96, 104,
    106–9, 167–69, 186, 205, 206, 237,
    291–92, 390–404, 436, 439
    Eisenhower and, 163–67
    end of, 401–4, 407–9, 411, 413–15, 425
    Kennedy and, 163, 171–77, 196
    patriotism and, 90–92, 101, 189
    Reagan and, 374
    religion and, 101–3
    see also communism and anticommunism
Coleman, Thomas J., 100
colleges and universities, 134, 313, 441
    anticommunism and, 100
    black students at, 256, 258
    military and, 89, 90
    student activism at, 187, 188, 190–95,
        233–34, 249–50, 263, 277–78, 313
colonialism, 50, 54, 57, 80, 167
comic books, 190–91
communism and anticommunism, 31, 72–73,
    77, 78, 195–97, 199, 291, 408, 436
    civil rights movement and, 98, 147
    Communist Control Act, 109
    domestic, 72, 80, 90–94, 96–101
    espionage and, 94–96
    HUAC and, 92–95, 99, 192
    Iron Curtain and, 62–70
    labor unions and, 47, 73, 90–91, 98
    McCarthyism and, 96–101, 108–9
    religion and, 101–3
    Taft-Hartley Act and, 47
    see also Cold War
computer industry, 358, 361–64
congressional representation, 36–37, 180–81
Congress of Racial Equality (CORE), 144,
    160, 178–79, 185, 194, 247

Connally, Tom, 75
Connerly, Ward, 429
Connor, Eugene "Bull," 182–83
conservatism, xi, xii–xiii, 31, 78, 188, 195,
    422–24, 427
  neoconservatism, 325, 332
  New Right, 195–99
  Reagan and, 367, 369–72, 386–88
  World War II and, 31
Constitution, 2, 83, 236, 237
  First Amendment, 198, 237
  Fourteenth Amendment, 17, 148, 181,
    209, 238, 257, 264
  Fifteenth Amendment, 209
  Twenty-Second Amendment, 46
  Twenty-Third Amendment, 180
  Twenty-Fifth Amendment, 290
construction workers, 272–73, 278–79, 356
consumers, 6, 27, 114, 118–19, 124–25, 357, 358
  stores and shopping areas, 124–25, 136–
    37, 358, 364–66, 457–58, 465
contraception, 236, 237–38, 263, 446, 464–65
Coors, Joseph, 355, 376
Coplon, Judith, 95
Coppola, Francis Ford, 310, 316
corporate headquarters, 9, 307, 457
cotton, 12–13, 15, 20, 131–32
counterculture, 235–36, 293, 422
Counterintelligence Program
    (COINTELPRO), 109, 258
Cox, Archibald, 181, 289, 290
credit cards, 124, 357, 383, 458
crime, 238–39, 241, 320, 338–39, 417, 425,
    450, 452–54
criminal procedures, 237, 238–39, 338–39, 450
  trials, 37, 238
Cronkite, Walter, 245
Cuba, 171–75, 186, 224, 225, 332, 391–92,
    394, 404, 411
Cuyahoga River, 306
Czechoslovakia, 68, 168, 250

Daddy, Puff, 445
Daley, Richard J., 215–16, 251
dam building, 117
Dean, John, 288, 289
death penalty, 339
Decter, Midge, 325
Defense Department, 69, 232
democracy, xii, 35, 74, 143, 145, 167, 187–88,
    194, 255, 318–19, 394–95, 408, 415, 467, 480
Democratic Party, 28, 29, 31, 45–46, 72, 73,
    77, 157, 177, 193, 205–6, 217, 279, 324–25,
    372, 422, 425
  civil rights and, 75–76, 146, 156, 160, 204, 216

communism and, 97, 104
  National Convention of 1968, 251–52
  unions and, 40–41, 45
Depression, Great, 3, 9, 24, 28, 29, 49, 50, 52,
    113, 119, 343, 384
Dewey, Thomas E., 45, 74, 76, 77, 103, 195
Dominick, Peter H., 11
DeVoto, Bernard, 10
Didion, Joan, 190, 251
Diem, Ngo Dinh, 176, 223–25, 228, 232
Dingell, John, 31
Disabilities Act, 417–18
Dixiecrats, 76, 146
Dole, Robert, 427
dolphins, 89–90
Dominican Republic, 226
Donovan, Raymond, 385
Doolittle, James, 169–70
Dos Passos, John, 6
Douglas, Helen Gahagan, 97
Douglas, Paul, 218
Douglas, William O., 109
drugs, 450
DuBois, W. E. B., 147
Dukakis, Michael, 409–10
Dulles, Allen, 173
Dulles, John Foster, 94, 101, 166, 168, 173
Dunlap, Al, 442
Dunlop, John T., 356
Durr, Clifford and Virginia, 153
Dylan, Bob, 417

Eagleton, Thomas, 284–85
Eastland, James, 75, 179
economy, xi, 27, 31, 32, 49–51, 107, 161, 177–78,
    206, 243, 274–75, 287, 310, 313, 317, 322
  Carter and, 328–31, 371–73, 376
  Clinton and, 419–20, 423, 439–42, 479–80
  deregulation and, 328, 375–76, 378, 379
  financial crisis of 2008, 476–80
  Ford and, 322–23, 326, 328, 376
  growth of, xi–xii, 113–14, 118–19, 132, 177,
    439–42, 445–46, 474
  international trade, 52, 56–57, 328–29
  Nixon and, 282–84, 295, 297
  prices and inflation in, 6, 42–44, 48, 78,
    178, 282–84, 295–97, 322, 323, 372, 378
  Reagan and, 371–76, 378–81, 383, 386, 387,
    474, 475, 479
  recessions in, 113, 118, 121, 122, 161, 282,
    287, 295, 297, 310, 346, 347, 378–80, 474
  stagflation in, 322, 327, 345
  supply-side economics and, 370–71, 375
  Vietnam War and, 243–44
  World War II and, 30, 32

Edelman, Marian Wright, 266
education, 78, 123–24, 133, 166, 188, 191,
    198, 212–13, 322, 454, 475
  bilingual, 273–74
  minority groups and curricula in, 257–58
  privatization of, 454
  school desegregation, 98, 148–52, 155–57,
    181–84, 200, 215–16, 256–58, 266, 337,
    369, 388, 429
  religion and, 198, 204, 369–70, 386, 409, 454
  school lunches, 375, 460
  sex, 428
  sexual discrimination in, 264
  standardized testing in, 188–89
Egypt, 168–69, 295, 396
Ehrlich, Paul, 464
Ehrlichman, John, 289
Eisenhower, Dwight, 72, 94, 97, 102–8, 123,
    150, 169, 174, 177, 195, 196, 272, 291
  Alaska and, 157–58
  civil rights and, 151, 156–57
  Cold War and, 163–67
  highways and, 118
  Indochina and, 223
  Kennedy and, 162–63, 171
  Korean War and, 103–6, 163
  Latin America and, 170–71
  military and, 107–8
  Suez crisis and, 168–69
elderly, 267–68
Elders, Joycelyn, 428
elections:
  of 1946, 45, 48, 66
  of 1948, 71, 72, 76–77
  of 1952, 103–4, 147
  of 1960, 160–61, 254
  of 1964, 204–6
  of 1966, 217–18
  of 1968, 245, 248–49, 251–54
  of 1972, 282–85, 287, 293, 297
  of 1980, 371–72
  of 1984, 380–82
  of 1988, 409–10
  of 1992, 417–19
  of 1996, 427
  of 2000, 442–44
  voter participation in, 319, 371
Ellender, Allen J., 31
Ellsberg, Daniel, 292
El Salvador, 394, 395, 404
employment, 38–42, 52, 74, 119, 198, 441–42
  African Americans and, 133, 135, 140–41,
    145–46, 184, 271–73, 348, 349, 441
  anticommunist loyalty programs and,
    92–94, 100, 237

benefit programs and, 120–21, 132, 134,
    337, 350
  Comprehensive Employment and Train-
    ing Act and, 323, 327–28
  Equal Employment Opportunity Com-
    mission and, 262–63, 271
  Fair Employment Practices Committee
    and, 10, 37, 74, 144, 184, 200
  Fair Labor Standards Act and, 28, 33, 213
  Full Employment Act and, 32, 48, 323
  number of hours worked, 350–51, 451, 459
  unemployment, 121, 184, 282, 297, 322,
    323, 372, 378, 475
  unions and, see labor unions
  wages and, 38–39, 42–44, 78, 119, 123–24,
    132, 177, 178, 184, 201, 283–84, 295, 350,
    351, 360, 441, 442
  women and, 140–41, 201, 262–63, 351
  workplace safety and, 270–71
energy, 139, 296, 323–24, 330–31, 380, 461–64
  see also oil
environment, 192, 210–12, 268–69, 357,
    358, 461–64
  Clean Air Act, 417–18, 456
  forests, 11, 302
  global warming, 462, 463, 475
  pollution and, 128–29, 192, 211, 306, 462, 463
  Reagan and, 376, 379–81
  suburbanization and, 139, 302
  water use, 462–63
Ervin, Sam, 288
Europe, 275
  Eastern, 57–60, 65, 68, 96, 164, 204, 281,
    326, 332, 393, 403, 404, 434
  economic growth in, 113–14
  immigrants from, 6, 77, 134, 315–16
  Marshall Plan and, 67–70, 73, 98
Evers, Medgar, 184, 186, 249
Exxon Valdez, 462

Fair Deal, 78, 97, 177, 193, 199
Falwell, Jerry, 368, 384–85
family, 114, 139–42, 172, 340, 368, 409, 451, 459
Faubus, Orval, 157
FBI, 93–95, 97, 109, 179, 186, 193, 197, 205,
    235, 258, 289–93, 321
Federal Reserve, 329–30, 345, 346, 373, 378,
    380, 419, 420, 440, 476–79
Federal Writers' Project, 2, 3
Felt, Mark, 293, 321
Ferraro, Geraldine, 381
financial crisis of 2008, 476–80
financial industry, 8–9
  banks, 8–9, 10, 357–58, 380, 384, 479, 480
Fonda, Jane, 264, 314

Fiske, Robert, 432
food, 458, 459
    fast, 137, 459–60
    meat, 44, 114, 296
    school lunches, 375, 460
Ford, Betty, 320
Ford, Gerald R., 267, 290, 291, 293, 294, 319,
        320–24, 327, 334, 335, 356, 367, 382, 392
    economy and, 322–23, 326, 328, 376
    energy and, 323–24
    Nixon pardoned by, 320–21, 326
    Soviet Union and, 324–26
Ford, Henry, 5
Ford Motor Company, 5–6, 116, 120, 121, 347
foreign policy, xiii, 49
    business and, 115–16
    imperialism and, ix–x, 50, 52, 53,
        433–49, 469
    internationalism and, 52–57, 436
    lobbying and, 54–55
    religion and, 101
    role of U.S. in world, 49–55, 287, 294–97,
        310, 332
forests, 11, 302
Forrestal, James, 54, 61, 66
France, x, 50, 51, 56, 57, 58, 64, 67, 69–70,
        250, 297, 302
    Suez crisis and, 168–69
    Vietnam and, 222–24
Frank, Robert, 115
Free Speech Movement, 194–95
Friedan, Betty, 140–42, 201, 262
Friedman, Milton, 268, 329
Fuchs, Klaus, 95
Fukuyama, Francis, 408, 410

Galbraith, John Kenneth, 177–78, 203
Gans, Herbert, 142
Ganzel, Bill, 113
Gardner, John, 211
Garrity, W. Arthur, Jr., 257
Gates, Bill, 362, 366, 442
Geithner, Timothy, 480
General Electric (GE), 133, 305, 351–52,
        353, 368, 387
General Motors (GM), 6, 7, 39, 42–43,
        120, 283, 305, 347, 366
Germany, x, 49, 87, 274, 440
    Berlin, 166, 174, 176, 224, 402, 403, 407
    East, 164, 166, 174, 403
    post-World War II, 57, 58, 60, 64, 66–68, 470
    reunification of, 403
    West, 69–70, 166, 174, 274, 297
    GI Bill, 32–35, 48, 127, 188
    GI Rights, 266

Gibson, Kenneth, 259
Gilder, George, 370
Gilmore, Gary, 339
Gingrich, Newt, 422–26, 433
Ginsberg, Allen, 189, 190, 265
Ginsburg, Ruth Bader, 264
Giuliani, Rudolph, 383
Glazer, Nathan, 325
Goetz, Bernhard, 453
Gold, Harry, 95
Goldwater, Barry, 195–96, 198–99, 205, 206,
        217, 239, 285
Goodman, Andrew, 193
Goodman, Paul, 189
Goodwin, Richard, 204
Gorbachev, Mikhail, 401–3
Gore, Al, 442–44
Gorsuch (Burford), Anne, 376, 380–81
government:
    agencies of, 23, 28, 137–38
    reforms of, 318–19
    size and role of, xii–xiii,
        27–35, 45, 48, 334–38, 375,
        378, 386, 425, 467
    spending by, 116–18, 119, 134
Graham, Billy, 102, 150, 315
Gramm, Phil, 371
Gratton, Charles, 18
Griffiths, Martha, 201–2
Greece, 59, 65–68, 81, 222
Greenspan, Alan, 419, 479
Grenada, 397–98, 468
Gruening, Ernest, 227
Guantánamo Bay, 472
Guatemala, 169–70, 226
Gulf War, 411–15, 418, 439, 467, 468
gun control, 338, 423, 428, 461
Gunther, John, 2, 10, 11, 17, 104–5
Guthrie, Woody, 19, 113, 117

Haber, Al, 194
Haig, Alexander, 281
Haiti, 437
Halberstam, David, 234
Haldeman, H. R., 289, 291
Haley, Alex, 316
Harriman, Averell, 59
Harrison, George, 54
Hatcher, Richard, 259
Hawaii, 74, 157
Hawkins, Augustus F., 323
Hayden, Tom, 204
Hayes, Ira, 35
Hayes, Wayne, 320
Haynes, Katherine, 3

health:
    life expectancy, 461
    physical fitness, 313–14, 454, 460–61
    weight, 458–61, 465
health care, 31, 78, 120, 337, 454, 461
    Clinton and, 420–22, 423, 425
    Medicare and Medicaid, 206–7, 268, 322,
        337, 341, 374, 421, 424–26, 431
Hearst, William Randolph, 92
Herling, John, 270
Hickel, Walter, 269
highways, 117–18, 128, 134, 269–70, 306
Hispanics, 259–61, 274, 448, 453
    Mexican Americans, 17, 23, 135, 209, 250,
        260–61, 274, 429–31, 447
Hiss, Alger, 94–95
Ho Chi Minh, 223, 286
Hodgson, Godfrey, 54
Hoffa, Jimmy, 122, 186
Hollywood, 92, 99, 109
homosexuality, 34, 93–94, 139, 265–66,
        341–42, 368, 370, 387, 388, 425, 427,
        435, 474
Hoover, J. Edgar, 197, 293
Horton, Willie, 410
hotels and motels, 137
housing, 31, 44–45, 78, 125–26, 135, 177, 193,
        297, 322, 337
    air-conditioning in, 134, 308, 462
    anticommunism and, 98
    discrimination and, 15, 23, 34, 98, 129–30,
        133, 145–46, 198, 214–16, 272, 369
    financial crisis and, 476–79
    homeownership, 123, 126–28, 306, 441
    home size, 450, 454–55, 458, 462, 465
    indoor plumbing in, 455
    public, 129
    suburban, see suburbs
Houston, Tex., 308
HUD, 385
human rights, 55, 74, 332, 436
Humphrey, Hubert H., 75, 212, 248–49,
        252–54, 267, 323
Hunt, E. Howard, 288, 289
Hurricane Katrina, 117, 475–76

IBM, 361, 363, 377
immigrants, x, 6, 77, 119, 134–35, 209–10,
        429–31, 446–48, 453
    ethnic revival and, 315–17
imperialism, ix–x, 50, 52, 53, 433–49, 469
International Monetary Fund (IMF), 56, 62,
        409, 414, 436
international organizations, 55–57
International Trade Organization, 57

Iran, 60–62, 81, 167–69, 329, 330, 333, 371,
        391, 395, 398, 411
Iran-Contra affair, 385, 398–401
Iraq, 169, 415
    Gulf War, 411–15, 418, 439, 467, 468
    Iraq War, 89, 469–73, 475
Iron Curtain, 62–70
Israel, 54, 77, 168–69, 295, 325, 396–98,
        404, 467

Jackh, Ernest, 53
Jackson, Henry, 325
Jackson, Jesse, 381–82, 410, 417
Jackson, Maynard, 259
Japan, 60, 81, 87, 274, 275, 302, 351, 440, 451
    occupation of, 87, 470
Japanese Americans, 22–23, 74
Jarvis, Howard, 336
Jemison, T. J., 148
Jenner, William, 100, 104
Jews, 10, 54, 77, 198, 209, 314, 315, 325
Jobs, Steve, 362–63
John Birch Society, 196
Johns, Barbara, 149
Johns, Vernon, 149
Johnson, Lyndon B., 101, 105, 173, 186,
        199–207, 213, 215–17, 236, 240, 241, 266,
        272, 291–92, 367, 465
    civil rights and, 156, 157, 158,
        199–202, 208
    education and, 212–13
    environment and, 210–12
    Great Society of, 203–4, 206, 212–16, 231,
        240, 244, 267, 268, 322, 334
    in 1964 election, 204–5
    1968 election and, 245
    poverty and, 202–3
    Vietnam War and, 205, 225–28, 231–32,
        234, 235, 241, 243–47, 253, 276, 277
Jones, Paula, 432
jury service, 37, 145, 318

Kahn, Alfred, 328
Kaiser, Henry J., 21, 127
Kaltenborn, H. V., 53
Kansas City, 7
Karzai, Hamid, 468
Kazin, Alfred, 10, 304
Keats, John, 141
Kefauver, Estes, 103
Kelly, Walt, 270
Kemp, Jack, 371
Kennan, George, 54, 62–63, 66, 86, 170, 275
Kennedy, Anthony, 429
Kennedy, Edward "Ted," 328

Kennedy, John F., 101, 173, 199–203, 205, 206, 210–11, 213, 226, 227, 252, 254, 272, 293, 314, 367
   assassination of, 185–86, 199, 249
   Bay of Pigs and, 172–73, 224
   civil rights and, 160–61, 162, 178–85, 198, 200
   Cold War and, 163, 171–77, 196
   Eisenhower and, 162–63, 171
   inaugural address of, 162–63, 204
   New Frontier of, 177–78, 193
   Vietnam and, 224–25, 231, 234, 277
Kennedy, Robert F., 121, 160–61, 173, 179, 245, 248–49
Kent State University, 277, 278, 283
Kerner, Otto, 240
Kerner Commission, 240–41
Kerouac, Jack, 115, 189, 190
Keynes, John Maynard, 56
Keyserling, Leon, 86
Khomeini, Ayatollah Ruhollah, 333
Khrushchev, Nikita, 164–67, 169, 173–76, 224
Kim Il Sung, 81, 84, 414
King, Martin Luther, Jr., 154–55, 159–61, 179, 182, 183, 185, 208, 215–16, 247–48, 252, 266, 291–92, 417
   assassination of, 247–49
King, Rodney, 418
Kirkland, Lane, 441
Kirkpatrick, Jeane, 394–95, 408, 469
Kissinger, Henry, 275, 276, 280–82, 292, 293, 324, 325, 333, 402
Kleindienst, Richard, 289
Knowland, William, 156, 217
Koop, C. Everett, 389
Korea, 80–81
Korean War, 79–85, 95–97, 103–6, 108, 109, 163, 190, 222, 243
   militarism and, 80, 85–90
Kristol, Irving, 325
Kucinich, Dennis, 335–36
Ku Klux Klan, 149, 152, 159, 178–79, 183, 185, 193, 208
Kuwait, 61, 399, 411–15

labor costs, 344–45, 349–52
labor unions, 6, 29, 45, 48, 77, 78, 119–24, 132, 213, 217–18, 253, 282–84, 313, 328, 343, 349–51, 355–58, 360, 441
   communism and, 47, 73, 90–91, 98
   Democratic Party and, 40–41, 45
   Ford Motor Company and, 5
   National Labor Relations Act (Wagner Act) and, 28, 33, 46, 47, 356
   National Labor Relations Board and, 47, 120, 377, 387
   picket lines and, 356
   prices and, 42–44, 282–84
   Reagan and, 368–69, 377, 382, 387
   in South, 47–48
   strikes and, 38–43, 45–48, 122–23, 159, 283, 343, 350, 377–78, 382, 387
   Taft-Hartley Act and, 46–48, 72, 73, 78, 199, 213, 350, 356
Laffer, Arthur, 370, 371, 374
LaGuardia, Fiorello, 31
Laird, Melvin, 276
land mines, 89, 435
Lange, Dorothea, 113
Laos, 174, 222, 223, 229, 246, 276, 277, 279, 280
Latin America, 170–71, 174, 226, 281, 332, 391–92, 411
Lawson, James, 159
Leahy, William, 54
Lebanon, 396–98
LeMay, Curtis, 253
Le Sueur, Meridel, 2, 3
Levitt, Alfred, 127
Levitt, William, 126–27, 130
Levittown, N.Y., 126–27, 130, 136, 138, 451–52, 455
Lewinsky, Monica, 432, 433
Lewis, John, 179
Lewis, Oscar, 203
libel, 237
liberalism, xiii, 66, 71–78, 97, 142, 187–88, 192–94, 200, 204–18, 409–10, 415, 422–23, 425, 427
life expectancy, 461
Lilienthal, David E., 63
Lilly, John Cunningham, 89–90
Lindsay, John, 239
Lippmann, Walter, 67, 69
Livingston, Robert, 433
Loeb, Philip, 100
Los Angeles, Calif., 22, 98, 308, 311, 418–19, 452
Lovett, Robert, 53, 54
Lubell, Samuel, 4
Lucas, George, 311
Luce, Henry R., 49, 52, 55, 391
Lucy, Autherine, 155–56

MacArthur, Douglas, 82, 84–85
Magaziner, Ira, 421
Malcolm X, 185, 247, 249
Malenkov, Georgy, 105
manufacturing, 4–8, 20, 297, 303, 383, 387
   mass production in, 5, 6, 114–16
Marcantonio, Vito, 97
Marcus, Herbert, 189

market and business, xii
marriage, 16, 46, 119, 139–41, 236, 237, 262, 263, 340, 387, 425, 427, 451, 474
Marshall, Garry, 311
Marshall, George, 54, 67–68, 100
Mayaguez, 295
McCarran, Pat, 96
McCarthy, Eugene, 245, 248–49, 252
McCarthy, Joseph, 80, 96–98, 100–101, 104, 108, 195
McCarthyism, 96–101, 108–9
McClellan, John, 121
McCloy, John, 54
McCord, James, 288
McFarlane, Robert, 399
McGovern, George, 284–85, 293
McIntyre, James Francis, 102
McKinney, Doris, 349
McNamara, Robert S., 228, 232, 233, 243
McNaughton, John, 228
McVeigh, Timothy, 428
meat consumption, 44, 114, 296
meatpacking industry, 44, 358–61, 366
Meese, Edwin, 400
Menjou, Adolphe, 99
Meredith, James, 182, 247
Metzgar, Jack, 123
Mexican Americans, 17, 23, 135, 209, 250, 260–61, 274, 429–31, 447
Microsoft, 362, 363, 366
Middle East, 167–69, 226, 295, 325, 398, 467, 469
Midwest, 2–7, 302, 303, 305–6
militarism, xiii, 80, 85–90, 106–8, 127, 468
military, xiii, 50, 51, 106–7, 430, 434–37
    academic life and, 89–90
    blacks in, 15–16, 18, 35, 74, 75
    demobilization after World War II, 51, 52, 83
    dolphins used in, 89
    draft in, 69, 74, 106, 230, 249, 276
    Eisenhower and, 107–8
    peacetime preparedness, 69, 80, 85
    Reagan and, 374
    religion and, 102–3
    spending on, 86, 90, 106–8, 116, 118, 119, 134, 164, 274–75, 374, 380
    U.S. global presence, 51, 53, 80, 87, 107, 227, 243, 433–35
Milk, Harvey, 342
Milken, Michael, 353–54, 383
Mills, C. Wright, 108
Mills, Wilbur, 207, 244, 320
miners, mining, 7, 12, 13, 19–21, 120, 131, 283, 350

missiles, 164, 165, 280, 392, 393, 401, 402
    Cuban Missile Crisis, 174–75
Mississippi Freedom Democratic Party, 204–5
Mississippi River, 13, 117
Mitchell, John, 289, 385
Molotov, Vyacheslav, 59
Mondale, Walter, 381–82
money, paper and coins, 102
Montgomery Improvement Association, 154, 155
Moore, Amzie, 18
Morris, Dick, 426
Morse, Wayne, 227
Moscone, George, 342
Mossaddegh, Mohammad, 167–68
movies, 310–11, 316, 384
Moynihan, Daniel Patrick, 325
Mumford, Lewis, 141
Murray, James E., 31
Murray, Philip, 73
Murrow, Edward R., 108
music, 191, 235, 236, 309–11, 445
Myrdal, Gunnar, 38, 147
Myers, Daisy and Bill, 130

Nader, Ralph, 270, 328, 357, 443
NASA, 165, 361, 375
Nash, Diane, 179
Nasser, Gamal Abdel, 168, 169
National Association for the Advancement of Colored People (NAACP), 18, 55, 74, 129, 144–46, 148–53, 155, 158–60, 184, 266
National Geographic Magazine, 2, 24
National Security Act, 69
National Security Council, 69, 86, 163, 281, 398
National Student Association, 73
Native Americans, 22, 23, 88, 261, 449–50
    voting and, 35, 37, 145
Neustadt, Richard, 171–72
Newark, N.J., 304
New Deal, 2–4, 9, 13, 27–38, 40, 42, 45–46, 52, 53, 71–73, 76–78, 90–91, 94, 97, 104, 118, 119, 142, 143–45, 187, 195, 196, 198, 200, 228, 267, 317, 322, 323, 328, 334, 338, 368, 387
New Left, 194, 195, 234, 283, 284, 312, 321, 325
New Right, 195–99
New York, N.Y., 7–9, 303–4, 311, 334
    fiscal crisis in, 334–35, 337
New York Times, 234, 246, 292, 469
Nicaragua, 332, 385, 392–94, 399, 404
Nichols, J. C., 136
Nichols, Terry, 428
9/11 attacks, x, xiii, 466–69, 471–75

Nitze, Paul, 86
Nixon, E. D., 144, 153, 154
Nixon, Richard, 91, 97, 103, 123, 162, 166,
    167, 171, 196, 217, 254, 255, 264, 296, 318,
    320, 322, 323, 327, 343, 367, 377, 402, 464
  China and, 275, 280–82
  civil rights and, 156, 160, 161, 255–57
  economy and, 282–84, 295, 297
  elected president, 252–54
  Ford's pardon of, 320–21, 326
  in 1972 election, 282–85, 287, 293, 297
  reforms and, 266–74
  resignation of, 291, 318
  Soviet Union and, 280–82, 324, 325
  Vietnam War and, 253, 275–83, 285–86,
    287, 292
  Watergate and, 287, 288–93, 310, 318,
    320–22, 326, 400
Noriega, Manuel, 411
North, Oliver, 396, 399–400
North American Free Trade Agreement
    (NAFTA), 420, 423, 431, 435
North Atlantic Treaty Organization (NATO),
    70, 166, 174, 205, 414, 434, 437, 438
Northeast, 7–11, 302–6
North Korea, 244, 435
  see also Korean War
nuclear weapons, 57, 60, 63–64, 82, 84, 87–
    88, 95, 108, 116, 163, 164, 167, 174, 176,
    205, 332, 402
  in Soviet Union, 63–64, 82, 86, 88, 164,
    174, 275, 401, 402
  tests of, 82, 88–89, 210

Obama, Barack, 480
O'Connor, Sandra Day, 386
Occupational Safety and Health
    Administration (OSHA),
    270–71, 357, 376
Oklahoma City bombing, 428
oil, 19, 61, 139, 167–69, 171, 295, 296, 308,
    323, 330, 334, 412, 462, 463, 470
  price of, 139, 296, 310, 329, 330–31, 347,
    376, 391
Oppenheimer, J. Robert, 88
Ortega, Daniel, 395
Oswald, Lee Harvey, 186

Paine, Tom, 368, 389
Pakistan, 404, 466, 468
Palestine, 54, 325, 396–97, 404
Panama, 326, 332, 394, 411, 468
Parks, Rosa, 144, 153
Patterson, Robert, 54
Paul VI, Pope, 464

Peace Corps, 174
Pendergast, Tom, 60
Pentagon Papers, 292
Pepper, Claude, 97
Perkins, Merwin, 83
Perot, Ross, 418, 419
Peterson, Esther, 201
Philadelphia, Pa., 11, 304–5
Philippines, 80, 82, 107
Phillips, Howard, 370
Pledge of Allegiance, 102, 410
Podhoretz, Norman, 9, 10, 325
Poindexter, John, 400
Poland, 58–60, 393, 403
Polanski, Roman, 311
political action committees, 355
population, 302
  control of, 464–65
  growth of, x, 119, 126, 446–47, 450, 464
  shifts and migrations, 6, 7, 19, 24, 38,
    131–35, 302, 310, 449, 450
Portman, John, 309
postal workers, 283
poverty, 53, 177, 193, 202–3, 217,
    268, 375, 441
  in South, 12–14, 18, 307
Powell, Adam Clayton, Jr., 36, 156
Powell, Colin, 412, 414, 435
Powell, Lewis, 343–44
Presley, Elvis, 39, 191
Progressive Citizens of America, 72
Pueblo, USS, 244
Puerto Rico, 135, 145, 261, 465

railways, 10, 303
Rand, Ayn, 92, 197
Randolph, A. Philip, 160, 184
Rankin, Jeanette, 249
Rankin, John, 34
Ray, James Earl, 248
Reagan, Nancy, 372
Reagan, Ronald, 217, 218, 319–20, 324, 326,
    333, 367–89, 409
  AIDS epidemic and, 388–89
  civil rights and, 388
  conservatism and, 367, 369–72, 386–88
  economy and, 371–76, 378–81, 383, 386,
    387, 474, 475, 479
  elected president, 372
  environment and, 376, 379–81
  federal budget cuts of, 375, 378
  foreign involvements and, 393–401, 414
  Iran-Contra and, 385, 398–401
  judiciary and, 386
  labor and, 368–69, 377, 382, 387

military and, 374
in 1984 election, 380–82
religion and, 367–68, 370, 384, 465
scandals and, 383–85
Soviet Union and, 367, 381, 390, 392–93,
    401–2, 407, 410
taxes and, 373–75, 379–83, 387
regions, 1–2, 24, 301–2, 317
    Midwest, 2–7, 302, 303, 305–6
    Northeast, 7–11, 302–6
    South, 12–18, 302, 307–9
    Southwest, 18–20, 302, 307–9
    West, 20–24, 302
Rehnquist, William, 432
Reid, Charles S., 14
religion, 6, 90, 132, 138, 312, 314–15, 423
    anticommunism and, 101–3
    Baptists, 132, 315, 370
    Catholics, 10, 45, 54, 97, 102, 103, 158, 198,
        208, 209, 216, 237, 285, 314, 337, 341
    civil rights and, 150, 155, 158, 159, 208, 216
    Cold War and, 101–3
    Jews, 10, 54, 77, 198, 209, 314
    Protestants, 9–10, 101–3, 132, 198, 314,
        315, 316, 341, 368, 369
    Reagan and, 367–68, 370, 384, 465
    scandals and, 384–85
    schools and, 198, 204, 369–70, 386,
        409, 454
    sexuality and gender norms and, 339–40
Republican Party, 29, 41, 45–46, 48, 53, 66,
    73, 75–78, 157, 195, 196, 198, 205, 217,
    279, 372, 422
    civil rights and, 146–47, 156
restaurants, fast-food, 137, 459–60
retail industry, 124–25, 136–37, 358, 364–66,
    457–58, 465
Reuther, Walter, 42–43
Rhee, Syngman, 81, 105–6
Ribicoff, Abraham, 211, 251–52
Richardson, Elliot, 289, 290
rights, xii, 27, 35–38, 48, 255, 265–66, 283,
    318, 338
    human, 55, 74, 332, 436
    see also civil rights
riots, 214, 215, 239–41, 247,
    248, 293, 418–19
Roberts, Ed, 362
Robeson, Paul, 147
Robinson, Jackie, 146
Robinson, Joanne, 153
Rockefeller, John D., 354
Rockefeller, John D., Jr., 464
Rockefeller, Nelson, 160, 196, 199
Romney, George, 272

Roosevelt, Eleanor, 55, 201
Roosevelt, Franklin Delano, 12, 27–30, 33,
    35, 45, 46, 53–55, 58–61, 72, 74, 78, 91,
    94, 104, 117, 145, 162, 185, 199, 200, 202,
    205, 206, 369
Rosenberg, Ethel and Julius, 95
Rostow, Walt W., 173, 226
Roth, Philip, 127
Roth, William, 371
Rubin, Robert, 419
Ruby, Jack, 186
Rumsfeld, Donald, 324, 468, 468–70
Rusk, Dean, 84, 101
Russell, Richard B., 75, 231
Russia, x, 434
Rust Belt, 302, 303–6
Rustin, Bayard, 159, 184
Rwanda, 437–38

Saddam Hussein, 411, 412, 415, 469–71
Sadlowski, Edward, 348–49
St. Lawrence Seaway, 117
Salazar, Rubén, 261
Saudi Arabia, 61, 167, 169, 226, 295, 392, 396,
    412–13, 439, 467
savings and loan scandal, 384
Savio, Mario, 187, 194, 195
Scaife, Richard Mellon, 355
Schlafly, Phyllis, 340
Schlesinger, Arthur, Jr., 178, 186, 203, 430
Schlesinger, James, 324
schools, see education
Schwerner, Michael, 193
scientific research, 89, 134
Secord, Richard, 399
Seigenthaler, John, 179
September 11 attacks, x, xiii, 466–69, 471–75
Serbia, 438, 468
sexuality, xiii, 93, 139–40, 172, 189, 235, 236,
    339–42, 387, 389, 423, 427
    education on, 428
    homosexuality, 34, 93–94, 139, 265–66,
        341–42, 368, 370, 387, 388, 425, 427,
        435, 474
Sha Na Na, 311
Shehan, Cardinal Lawrence, 216
Shlakman, Vera, 100
Shuttlesworth, Fred, 155, 182
Simon, William, 335, 343, 344
Sinclair, Upton, 358
Sirica, John J., 288, 290
slavery, 12, 14
Sly and the Family Stone, 310
Smalls, Biggie, 445
Smathers, George, 97

Smiley, Glenn, 159
Smith, Howard, 200–202
Snow Belt, 302, 305
Social Security, 15, 28, 31, 33, 46, 78, 120, 121,
    134, 177, 205, 207, 267, 337, 374–75, 426
Somalia, 437
Somoza Debayle, Anastasio, 332, 394–95
South, 12–18, 302, 307–9
Southern Christian Leadership Conference
    (SCLC), 155, 159, 160, 182, 183, 207–8, 215
Southern Conference for Human Welfare, 73
South Korea, 320, 393, 435
    see also Korean War
Southwest, 18–20, 302, 307–9
Soviet Union, 45, 51, 54, 72–74, 80, 85–86,
    156, 163–67, 171, 176, 196, 225, 274, 275,
    296, 412
    Afghanistan and, 332, 333, 390–92, 396,
        402, 407, 439
    alliance with U.S., 49, 57–62, 64, 70
    Carter and, 332
    China and, 87, 105, 275
    in Cold War, see Cold War
    collapse of, 407–8, 415, 468
    containment policy toward, 86
    Cuba and, 174–75, 391–92
    détente with U.S., 176, 280, 324–26, 392
    Eastern Europe and, 57–60, 65, 68, 96,
        164, 204, 281, 326, 332, 393, 403, 404
    espionage and, 95–96
    Greece and, 66
    Iran and, 60–61, 167–68
    Iron Curtain and, 62–70
    Korea and, 79, 81, 84, 85
    Nixon and, 280–82, 324, 325
    nuclear weapons of, 63–64, 82, 86, 88, 164,
        174, 275, 401, 402
    Reagan and, 367, 381, 390, 392–93, 401–2,
        407, 410
    religion and, 102, 103
    SALT treaties with, 280, 332
    South Korean jet (KAL 007) and, 393
    space race between U.S. and, 164–65, 171
    Suez crisis and, 169
    Turkey and, 61–62
    Vietnam and, 277, 281
space, 164–65, 171, 174
Spain, 87
Sparkman, John, 147
Spellman, Francis Cardinal, 102
spying, 94–96, 291, 393
    U-2 planes, 165, 167, 175
sports teams, 133, 146
Stalin, Joseph, 58–60, 63, 64, 66, 84, 97, 105,
    163, 167

Starr, Kenneth, 432
State Department, 94, 108
States' Rights Party (Dixiecrats), 76, 146
steel industry, 39–43, 120, 122–23, 283,
    345–49, 360, 366
Steinbeck, John, 113, 115
Stettinius, Edward, 55, 59
Stevenson, Adlai, 102–4, 147, 151, 173
Stewart, George R., 1, 2, 11, 301, 317
Stimson, Henry, 54
Stockman, David, 371, 373–74, 375
stock market, 9, 297, 353, 440, 474–75
Stokes, Carl, 259
stores and shopping areas, 124–25, 136–37,
    358, 364–66, 457–58, 465
student activism, 187, 188, 190–95, 233–34,
    249–50, 263, 277–78, 313
Student Nonviolent Coordinating
    Committee (SNCC), 160, 179, 185, 193,
    204, 216, 247
Students for a Democratic Society (SDS),
    193, 194, 195, 204, 233, 234, 250, 278
suburbs, 114, 125–30, 131, 136–39, 141–42, 212,
    272, 302, 306, 308, 424, 449, 450–57, 462
    gated communities in, 452–53
    lawns in, 462
Suez crisis, 168–69
Summers, Larry, 480
Sun Belt, 302, 307–9
Supreme Court, 16–18, 37, 98, 129–30, 145,
    148–53, 155, 178–82, 187, 204, 236–39,
    241, 256, 257, 264, 273, 274, 290–92, 318,
    339, 343, 357, 369, 386, 388, 401, 427,
    429, 450
    Baker v. Carr, 180–81, 206, 318
    Brown v. Board of Education, 98, 148–53,
        200, 256
    Bush v. Gore, 443, 444
    Colgrove v. Green, 180
    Engel v. Vitale, 198
    Gideon v. Wainwright, 237
    Griggs v. Duke Power Co., 273
    Griswold v. Connecticut, 237
    Loving v. Virginia, 237
    Miranda v. Arizona, 238
    Milliken v. Bradley, 257
    Plessy v. Ferguson, 148
    Shelley v. Kraemer, 130
    Smith v. Allwright, 18
    Times v. Sullivan, 237
    Webster v. Reproductive Health
        Services, 427
    Roe v. Wade, 238, 264, 341, 386, 427
Sweeney, John, 441
Syria, 295, 396–97

Taft, Robert, 31, 53, 68, 76–78, 83, 85, 97, 103, 107, 195
Taft-Hartley Act, 46–48, 72, 73, 78, 199, 213, 350, 356
Taliban, 439, 466, 468
taxes, 136, 177, 178, 200, 283, 337–38, 409, 424, 474–75
    in California, 336–38
    Clinton and, 420, 423
    income, 29, 46, 124, 232, 244, 336, 337, 383
    Reagan and, 373–75, 379–83, 387
Teamsters, 121–22, 441
television, 125, 311, 376–77, 460
Tenet, George, 439
Tennessee Valley Authority (TVA), 28, 31, 78, 117, 205, 228
Terkel, Studs, 3
terrorist attacks, 438–39
    counterterrorism and, 471–72, 475
    9/11, x, xiii, 466–69, 471–75
textile and garment industry, 8, 11, 13, 14, 16, 39, 48, 271, 305, 360
Thane, Eric, 4
Thieu, Nguyen Van, 282, 286, 294
think tanks, 355
Thomas, Clarence, 429
Thompson, Florence, 113, 134
Thurmond, Strom, 76, 77, 264, 320, 410
Thurow, Lester, 313
Tijerina, Reies López, 260
Till, Emmett, 152–53
torture, 472–73
transportation, 129, 269
    discrimination and, 144, 145, 147–48, 153–55, 178–79
    highways, 117–18, 128, 134, 269–70, 306
    railways, 10, 303
Trenton, N.J., 304
Truman, Harry S., 27, 31, 32, 38, 39, 42–46, 48, 51, 53, 55, 59–68, 70, 71–78, 82–83, 86, 87, 91, 94, 96, 98, 104, 107, 117, 145, 157, 164, 185, 201, 202, 207, 222–23, 468
    anticommunism and, 96–97
    civil rights and, 74–76
    Fair Deal of, 78, 97, 177, 193, 199
    Korean War and, 79, 81–85, 103, 104
    loyalty program of, 92–94
Truman Doctrine, 66–67, 73
Turkey, 60–62, 66–68, 222

U-2 planes, 165, 167, 175
Unions, see labor unions
United Auto Workers (UAW), 40–42, 120, 121, 146, 195, 218, 262, 347, 349, 463–64
United Farm Workers, 260

United Nations (UN), 55–57, 66, 74, 79, 82–85, 94, 104, 105, 169, 325, 412, 414, 437, 447, 469
United Steelworkers of America, 40–43, 120, 122–23, 346
universities, see colleges and universities

Vale, Thomas and Geraldine, 301, 302, 317
Vandenberg, Arthur, 63
Van Hoof, Mary Ann, 102
Vietnam, 174–76, 222–24, 228, 294, 404
Vietnam War, ix, 217, 218, 219–36, 248, 251, 253, 263, 275, 287, 317, 321, 327, 392, 400
    antiwar movement and, 232–35, 249, 261, 263, 277–79, 416
    China and, 228, 277, 281
    cost of, 231–32, 241, 243–44, 274, 282
    dolphins used in, 89
    end of, 276–78, 282, 285–86, 287, 293–94, 310, 313, 324
    escalation of, 225–28, 233
    fall of Saigon, 293–94, 324
    films about, 310–11
    Gulf of Tonkin incident in, 226–27, 231, 279
    invasion of Cambodia, 277–79
    Johnson and, 205, 225–28, 231–32, 234, 235, 241, 243–47, 253, 276, 277
    Kennedy and, 224–25, 231, 234, 277
    misleading information given about, 231–32, 234
    Nixon and, 253, 275–83, 285–86, 287, 292
    Soviet Union and, 277, 281
    strategies in, 228–30
    Tet offensive in, 241–46, 247, 276
    troops in, 230–31
    Veterans Memorial, 219
Viguerie, Richard, 370
Vinson, Fred, 150
Voinovich, George, 336
Volcker, Paul, 329, 373, 378
von Hayek, Friedrich, 31
voting, 35–37, 74, 144, 145, 208, 318, 427
    by blacks, 14, 35, 37, 38, 77, 145, 152, 156, 161, 180, 204, 206, 207, 209, 326
    participation in, 77, 319, 371
    unequal representation and, 180–81
    Voting Rights Act, 208–9, 214, 247, 272, 326

Wagner, Robert F., 31, 76
Walker, Wyatt Tee, 182
Wallace, George, 184, 204, 252–54, 284, 370, 410
Wallace, Henry A., 31, 52, 53, 64–65, 68, 72, 73, 75, 77, 239, 320

Wall Street Journal, 370, 371, 395, 420
Wall Street scandals, 383–84
Wal-Mart, 125, 364–66, 458
Walton, Sam, 125, 364, 366
Wanniski, Jude, 370
Warner, Ty, 442
Warren, Earl, 31, 76, 134, 150, 151, 181, 186, 236–38, 257
Washington, D.C., 74, 78, 157, 158, 180, 215, 305
Washington, Walter, 259
Washington Post, 96, 288, 293, 320, 321, 469, 471–72
Watergate scandal, 287, 288–93, 310, 318, 320–22, 326, 400
water use, 462–63
Watt, James, 376, 379, 381, 385
Weaver, Robert, 215
Welch, Jack, 351–52, 353
Welch, Robert, 196
welfare, 268, 425–26, 431
welfare state, 28, 78, 104, 205, 206, 334, 335, 370, 444, 454, 475
West, 20–24, 302
Westmoreland, William C., 219, 241
Weyrich, Paul, 370
Wheeler, Earle C., 243
White, Dan, 342
White, Harry Dexter, 56, 95
Wilkins, Roy, 160
Williams, G. Mennen, 41, 218
Williams, Robert, 159
Willkie, Wendell, 76
Wilson, Sloan, 141–42
Wilson, Woodrow, 53, 199
wiretapping, 241, 292, 471
Wofford, Harris, 421
Wolfe, Tom, 312, 314, 384
Wolfowitz, Paul, 469

women:
  abortion and, 139, 238, 264, 340, 341, 368–70, 409, 427–28, 446, 464–65, 474
  contraception and, 236, 237–38, 263, 446, 464–65
  Equal Rights Amendment and, 201, 264, 340–41, 342, 370, 409
  gender roles and, xi, xiii, 139–42, 339–40, 387, 427–29
  jury service and, 37, 318
  liberal activism and, 192
  women's movement, 201–2, 262–65, 339, 342
  working, 140–41, 201, 262–63, 351
Woodward, Bob, 288, 293
Woodward, Isaac, 17
work, *see* employment
World Bank, 56, 62, 409, 414, 436
World Trade Center, 438, 466–68, 473
World Trade Organization, 435–36
World War I, 249
World War II, ix, x, xii, 1, 24, 31, 35, 53, 61, 80–81, 104, 230, 243, 317
  agriculture and, 3–4
  breakdown of alliances in, 49, 57–62
  civil rights and, 143–45
  economy and, 30, 32
  effect on U.S. foreign policy, 49, 50, 53
  government and, 29–30
  industry and, 5, 20, 40, 50–51, 114
  9/11 and, 473
  West Coast operations, 20–22
Wozniak, Steve, 138, 362, 363
Wright, Moses, 153

Yarborough, Ralph, 273–74
Yeltsin, Boris, 403
Young, Coleman, 259
Young Americans for Freedom, 197
youth culture, 188–91, 235–36
Yugoslavia, 68, 167, 250, 438